THE HANDBOOK OF
EQUIPMENT LEASING

THE HANDBOOK OF
EQUIPMENT LEASING

TERRY A. ISOM

SHAWN D. HALLADAY

SUDHIR P. AMEMBAL

R. DOUGLAS LEININGER

JONATHAN M. RUGA

AMEMBAL & ISOM
LEASE EDUCATION AND CONSULTING

Managing Editor: Shawn D. Halladay
Project Editor: Christine Pickett
Design: Bailey-Montague & Associates, Salt Lake City, Utah
Typesetting: Type Center, Salt Lake City, Utah
Printing: Publishers Press, Salt Lake City, Utah

Library of Congress Catalog Card Number: 88-70510

ISBN 0-945988-00-1

Printed in the United States of America

Address orders to:

Amembal & Isom
1406 South 1100 East
Salt Lake City, UT 84105
(801) 484-8555

Amembal & Isom
Lease Education and Consulting

To those who, through their knowledge, experience and, at times, sheer determination, have made equipment leasing the vibrant and healthy industry it is today.

ABOUT AMEMBAL & ISOM

During the past decade, Amembal & Isom has become the undisputed authority in the field of equipment and vehicle lease education — worldwide. Over 14,000 professionals have participated and benefited from the knowledge and insight obtained through attendance at a broad range of leasing seminars and conferences throughout the United States and Canada, as well as in Europe, Asia, Africa and Australia. As such, Amembal & Isom has played a critical role in the growth and advancement of the leasing industry. Their contribution of knowledge and ideas has established and fostered numerous practices and techniques currently used within the equipment leasing industry.

No other firm in the world has responded to the educational needs of the leasing industry in as timely or comprehensive a manner as Amembal & Isom. Their immediate response to the implications and potential impact of the 1986 tax reform, via their series of one-day conferences, 'Tax Reform and the Future of Leasing,' is one illustration of their continuing commitment to helping industry players master the complexities of a dynamic environment.

Amembal & Isom prides itself on being in the forefront of lease education, continually striving to initiate change and advancement at all levels of experience and responsibility throughout the industry. In keeping with this tradition, the following full complement of products and services is provided to the industry:

- A broad range of public leasing seminars, which include:

  Leasing: The Creative Financing Alternative
  Accounting For Leases
  Leasing: The Lessee Acquisition Process
  Leasing: Tax Considerations & Analysis
  Leasing: Advanced Structuring & Analysis
  Fundamentals of Finance, Accounting &
    Taxation for the Lease Professional

  Leasing: Captive & Vendor Strategies &
    Techniques
  Leasing: Marketing Skills Development
  Leasing: Credit Analysis & Risk
    Assessment
  Leasing: The Legal Intricacies
  The Dynamics of Vehicle Leasing
  Leasing: Coping with the Alternative
    Minimum Tax

- Highly specialized conferences and symposiums that address current issues affecting the industry
- A video training program for the leasing novice, entitled *An Orientation to Leasing*, that has become the number one selling lease training video in the nation
- Six leasing publications that address the various levels of lease sophistication and are geared toward increasing the knowledge and, thus, profitability of the industry. The most recent of these publications is, of course, *The Handbook of Equipment Leasing*
- A bimonthly newsletter entitled *The Leasing Forum*, which apprises its readership of recent developments that impact the industry
- In-house seminars, available at any location, which are tailored to meet the unique training needs of individual corporate environments
- Consulting that covers a wide range of leasing issues

- Instructors/consultants who are available to speak at association conferences and sales conventions.

Amembal & Isom will undoubtedly continue to contribute new ideas, products and services to the industry in the future, as well as promote the advancement of leasing. These actions are based upon the firm belief that continued growth in the industry is a direct function of the increased recognition of opportunities that knowledge provides.

FOR FURTHER INFORMATION, MAIL THE ENCLOSED POSTCARD OR CALL 801-484-8555.

PREFACE

It is with great pleasure that I introduce you to *The Handbook of Equipment Leasing*. I am proud to say that this book is the most comprehensive treatment of equipment leasing available today. It represents the culmination of thousands of hours of research, years of experience in the leasing industry and significant effort on the part of the authors. Four of the authors — Terry A. Isom, myself, Shawn D. Halladay and R. Douglas Leininger — are associated with Amembal & Isom.[1] The other author, Jonathan M. Ruga, is the Chief Operating Officer of Sentry Financial Corporation of Salt Lake City, Utah.

Amembal & Isom has been, and continues to be, proud to serve the industry. Over the last decade, leasing has mushroomed from $22.3 billion per year to the $108 billion per year industry it is today, as more and more companies recognize the numerous benefits leasing offers. As part of that growth, we have seen implementation of many of our ideas and thoughts; some have even developed into industry practices — a tribute that has been, to say the least, psychologically very rewarding. Our contribution has been more than the dispensing of information, however. By increasing the level of leasing knowledge and the awareness of lessees and lessors around the country, we also have been responsible for a meaningful dollar increase in leasing volume.

Many of you have asked if this latest work is a rewrite of the old book. Definitely not! Amembal & Isom has come a long way since we wrote the old book on leasing. We have learned more, become more sophisticated in our courses, have explored new frontiers in leasing and expanded our role in the industry. All of these factors, I am pleased to say, have been incorporated in *The Handbook of Equipment Leasing*, which is completely new and totally eclipses the old one in terms of content and current matter.

The Handbook of Equipment Leasing is intended to be a statement on the leasing industry, and our position in it. I believe it is, for the book contains information on all aspects of leasing

---

[1] For more information regarding our firm, please refer to the section, "About Amembal & Isom," preceding this preface.

— current theories; existing tax, judicial and accounting guidelines; and a large portion of the most important ingredient, practical experience. It is also broad in its applications. We have chosen to provide an even balance between all sectors and aspects of the leasing industry in *The Handbook of Equipment Leasing*, so as to provide value to all who read it. Additionally, we have attempted to provide relevance to the various concepts by discussing the impact of each on your daily operations.

Of course, in such a constantly changing and dynamic industry, it is virtually impossible to keep totally current, and this book is no exception; however, as a service to you, the reader, we will provide updates to any changes in the tax laws, if you so desire. Simply send in the enclosed postage-paid postcard and we will send your one-time tax update to you.

The book itself is organized by discipline, so as to provide a logical progression of topics. It is intended for use by all segments of the industry; lessors, lessees and the professionals that serve both groups. We recognize that, within the industry, there are various ticket sizes, differing practices and many levels of experience; therefore, terminology and experience may vary slightly among readers. Even given this diverse readership, however, *The Handbook of Equipment Leasing* will stand out, for it is cohesive, cogent and of lasting value. I am pleased to offer this product to you, and know it will prove to be of immeasurable value. Enjoy it and thank you for your past and continuing support.

Sudhir P. Amembal
President & Chief Executive Officer
April 15, 1988

ACKNOWLEDGEMENTS

The authors wish to gratefully acknowledge the many parties who aided in making this book possible. Special thanks are due to:

Robert D. Apgood, Ph.D., who coauthored the chapter on credit. Dr. Apgood is a Senior Lease Consultant with Amembal & Isom. He has taught accounting at San Francisco State University and gained his public accounting experience with a national firm in Los Angeles. He is active in teaching and consulting, having consulted with both lessees and lessors.

Steven C. Gilyeart, who authored the chapter on legal issues in leasing. Mr. Gilyeart is an attorney with the law firm of Dempcy, Braley, Gilyeart & Vane, P.S., 414 Olive Way, Suite 400, Seattle, Washington 98101, and an Amembal & Isom instructor. He is a prominent member of a number of leasing industry associations and a frequent speaker and author on leasing topics. Questions concerning the subject matter of Mr. Gilyeart's chapter may be addressed to him at the above address or at (206) 464-1975.

Mark Isom, who contributed to the chapter on operating lease accounting. Mr. Isom has provided services to Amembal & Isom in the past and is currently a manager at Matrix Computer Funding Corporation.

Scott Young, who authored the chapter on lease documentation and is also Amembal & Isom's corporate counsel. Mr. Young is an attorney with the law firm of Davis, Graham & Stubbs, 1600 Eagle Gate Tower, 60 East South Temple, Salt Lake City, Utah 84111. Questions concerning the subject matter of Mr. Young's chapter may be addressed to him at the above address or at (801) 328-6000.

GE Capital Corporation, which so graciously gave of its vast knowledge and skills by contributing 'Methods of Servicing Vendor Lessors by Third-Party Lessors' to the chapter on captives and vendor leasing.

The Financial Accounting Standards Board for allowing us to quote portions of their literature. This literature is copyrighted by the Financial Accounting Standards Board, High Ridge Park, Stamford, Connecticut, 06905, U.S.A., and is reprinted with permission. Copies of the complete documents are available from the Financial Accounting Standards Board.

In addition we would like to extend our appreciation to Christine Pickett for her editing skills and insights. Our greatest thanks go to those at Amembal & Isom who, as always, put forth their best efforts; specifically David C. Aanenson, Lynn Leary-Meyers and Hal G. Halladay, for their countless hours of research and review; and the word processing staff for their perseverance in preparing the multitudinous drafts and changes necessary to complete this book.

CONTENTS

PART 1
INTRODUCTION

CHAPTER ONE
OVERVIEW OF THE INDUSTRY

Leasing is, without doubt, the creative financing alternative of today. The demand for leasing has created an industry of imposing scope and size, and even greater potential, as more and more of the world's equipment needs are met through this unique form of financing. What is the genesis of this complex, yet exciting, industry? Why has it caught the imagination and attention of the press, business world and consuming public?

The benefits that leasing offers to the parties are many — low payments and off balance sheet financing to the lessee, and financing income to the lessor, to name but a few. The range of equipment being leased is incredible, from basic copier leases to extremely large and complex leveraged leases involving nuclear facilities. Leasing truly has something to offer everyone.

The breadth of its appeal also contributes to its complexity, however. Leasing is a multidisciplinary industry, with taxes, accounting and finance all playing an integral role in virtually every transaction. Combine these with other factors, such as legal, credit and asset management concerns, and the need for adequate knowledge and understanding becomes evident. In order to provide perspective on this fascinating industry, and a basis for the remaining portions of this book, this chapter addresses the following topics:

- Evolution of Leasing
- Equipment Leasing Today
- Elements of a Lease.

EVOLUTION OF LEASING

Equipment leasing has a rich and lengthy history. While the complexities involved in today's leases may be a far cry from the leases of old, there are many similarities between the two; a common thread based upon the utility and, hence, demand for the leasing mechanism. In gaining an understanding of the lease process it is important to have perspective into where leasing came from, and why it has become what it is today.

Early History

Although the exact date of the first leasing transaction is unknown, the earliest records of leasing are those of transactions occurring sometime before 2000 B.C., in the ancient Sumerian city of Ur. Sumerian lease documents, which were produced in damp clay, recorded transactions ranging from leases for agricultural tools, land and water rights, to oxen and other animals. These clay tablets, some of which were found as recently as 1984, indicate the priests of the temples (lessors) leased to the local farmers (lessees). These early documents, however, do not preclude the possibility that leasing may have existed elsewhere in the world at an earlier date; it is just that no documentation of such leases has been preserved.

Many early legal systems make mention of the financial tool called leasing. The most noteworthy record of leasing laws dates to roughly 1700 B.C., when the famous Babylonian king, Hammurabi, incorporated ancient Sumerian and Achaian mores concerning leasing into his extensive collection of laws.

Just southeast of Babylon, in the ancient city of Nippur, the Murashu family began what was to become a well-known bank and leasing house in approximately 400 to 450 B.C. The Murashus were adept at providing financial services that reflected the current economic and social conditions of the Persian Empire. They specialized in land leasing, but also considered oxen and agricultural equipment, as well as the "lending" of seed.

Other ancient civilizations, including the Greeks, Romans and Egyptians, found leasing to be an attractive, affordable, and, at times, the only viable method of financing equipment, land and livestock. The ancient Phoenicians, long known for their expertise in shipping and trade, were involved with ship charters, which resembled a very pure form of an equipment lease. Many short-term charters provided for use of the crew as well as the ship. Longer-term charters also were written for periods covering the estimated economic life of the ships and required the lessee to assume most of the benefits and obligations of ownership. Many of the same kind of negotiating issues that today's lessors and lessees face were addressed in these ancient ship charters.

As can be seen, leasing in earlier times was not limited to the leasing of only one or two types of property, as many assume. In fact, historical evidence provides illustrations of the leasing of various types of agricultural and industrial equipment, as well as equipment used in militaristic endeavors. As an example, in 1066 A.D., two large invasion fleets sailed towards England within a 2-week period (one Norwegian and one Norman), both of which were great undertakings for their time. Neither the Norwegian King nor Norman Duke possessed the economic resources to finance such large projects and, hence, utilized forms of lease financing to secure the necessary ships, crews and equipment.

In medieval times, lease-related activities were limited primarily to horses and farming implements, although unique opportunities to utilize leasing occasionally presented themselves. Many knights of old were known to have leased their armor. For instance, in 1248 one Bonfils Manganella of Gaeta leased a suit of armor for the Seventh Crusade, paying a lease rental of close to 25% of its original value.

For centuries, the leasing of personal property was not recognized under English common law. The long-term leasing of real property was allowed, however, and was, in many cases, the only means available to acquire the use of land, due to a very rigid system of land laws. Eventually, with the writing of the Statute of Wales in 1284, the leasing of personal property became permissible. There were people, however, who used leasing as a means to secretly transfer property, with the intention of defrauding creditors who had based credit decisions on the strength of the apparent ownership of the property. An act was passed in 1571 that prohibited such fraudulent practices, but that still allowed legitimate leases entered into for reasonable consideration.

The early 1800s saw a great increase in the amount and types of equipment being leased in the United Kingdom. The development of the agricultural, manufacturing and transportation industries brought about new types of equipment, many of which were suitable for lease financing. The concomitant expansion of the railroads also brought about major advances in the development and use of leasing. Most early railroad companies were able to supply only the track, and charged tolls for the use of their lines. This left open the opportunity for many entrepreneurs to separately provide the railroad companies and independent shippers with locomotives and railcars.

Development of a US Leasing Industry

As the demand for lease financing of all kinds and types of equipment continued to grow in the United Kingdom, so too did the need for a similarly creative form of finance in the United States. The first recorded leases of personal property in the US were in the 1700s, and provided for the leasing of horses, buggies and wagons by liverymen. As the types of, and need for, equipment increased, so too did the use and development of leasing. The real growth in US leasing, however, was caused by the railroad industry.

HISTORIC FACTORS

Railroad companies in the US faced many of the same problems their counterparts in the United Kingdom were experiencing. Because expansion was called for, yet conventional financing was hard to come by, the railroad companies searched for ways to either obtain use of the railcars, or to have the cars provided directly to the private shippers.

This need created opportunities for investors to earn a profitable return by providing financing for locomotives and railcars through equipment trusts. Banks or trust companies set up and administered these trusts, and equipment trust certificates, representing the right to receive a return of principal and interest on invested funds, were sold to the investors. The trust's administrator would pay the manufacturer for the equipment and then collect rentals from the end-user during the term of the trust. The rentals would, of course, cover the obligation of the equipment trust certificates issued to the investors.

There were many variations of the equipment trust that came into being. The most widely recognized type of railroad financing was the Philadelphia Plan, which allowed for the transfer of ownership to the end-user upon completion of an initial term. The Philadelphia Plan became the forerunner of today's conditional sales contracts and money-over-money leases.

In the early 1900s, many railroad leasing companies recognized that a growing number of shippers did not want the long-term control, or ownership, of railcars inherent in the equipment trust, but, instead, wanted only their short-term use. These leasing companies began offering shorter-term contracts, at the expiration of which the railcar was to be returned to the leasing company, who continued to retain title. These types of leases marked the beginning of the true, or operating, leases that are offered so commonly today.

In other areas of leasing growth, a developing economy, as well as the desire of manufacturers to provide financing for their products, caused a surge of installment credit in the US during the early 1900s. Manufacturers, or vendors, felt they would be able to sell more products if they were able to offer an affordable payment plan along with the desired equipment; hence, the beginning of lease financing provided by vendors. Apparently those early manufacturers were right, as vendor leasing is continuing as a significant force in the equipment leasing industry today.

Certain manufacturers, however, were looking for something more. Although definitely interested in the profits that could be made by offering financial services, manufacturers were equally interested in protecting the proprietary technology they had developed and built into their new machinery. Many viewed the leasing (versus selling) of equipment as a way to protect the ownership of such technology, thereby creating a monopoly of sorts.

As early as 1877, the Bell Telephone Company made it a policy to provide equipment in a customer's home or office only on a rental basis. Similarly, the Hughes Tool Company kept strict control over the amount paid for its specialized 166-edged drill bit by providing it to wellhead operators on a lease basis only. Other examples followed, most notably U.S. Shoe Machinery, which manufactured boot and shoe making equipment and also employed clauses tying customers to its products exclusively. Eventually, however, the enforcement of federal antitrust legislation required manufacturers to offer their equipment for sale.

World War II and the US government's use of cost-plus contracts provided another important impetus to the development of the leasing industry. In most contracts, government contractors were allowed to earn only a certain amount above and beyond their costs. These contractors realized that many of their goods or services were needed by the government only during wartime, and that the government would not, in all likelihood, renew those contracts once the war was over. A company that purchased machinery for a specific governmental project could be exposed to a high degree of risk if the contract was not renewed, for the contractor may have not yet recovered its equipment purchase costs. Furthermore, if the equipment was specialized, it may have had little market value. Government contractors recognized that the leasing, as opposed to buying, of production equipment during a specific contract period minimized their exposure to contract nonrenewals. In some cases, where large specialized machinery and tools were required, the government had to act as the lessor to the contractors.

During this same time period, the vehicle leasing industry was beginning to develop on a large scale. While the first car rental business dates back to 1918, Zollie Frank, a Chicago car dealer who offered long-term fleet leasing of automobiles in the early 1940s, is credited as the originator of the vehicle leasing industry. Today, the vehicle leasing industry has annual lease revenues in excess of $50 billion.

As was previously mentioned, many manufacturers recognized the value of providing financing for their products throughout the development of the US leasing industry. Some manufacturers even went so far as to set up their own finance organizations. The manufacturers that chose not to, or who were unable to provide financing, were left with two options: to let the customer independently seek financing, as before, or to work with an independent financial concern to set up some type of vendor financing arrangement or program. Independent, or third-party, leasing companies were formed to provide this specific product financing for manufacturers and dealers. Eventually independent leasing companies also began providing leasing services directly to the lessee for other, unrelated equipment.

MODERN-DAY LEASING

The tax attributes of equipment ownership, which have become a major force in the leasing industry, did not become so until the advent of accelerated depreciation and the Investment Tax Credit (ITC) during the 1950s and 1960s. These tax benefits, inuring to the owners of equipment, had little value to companies that could not fully utilize them. Lessors and lessees soon realized that the lessor in a tax-oriented lease could claim the tax benefits of ownership and pass them back to the lessee in the form of reduced rentals, which were often much lower than the payment on a corresponding equipment loan. This type of lease created a potentially twofold benefit: (1) lower lease payments and (2) a pass-through of tax benefits to lessees who otherwise could not use them.

In order to realize the expected tax benefits of ownership in a tax-oriented lease, however, lessors had to be very careful to make certain their agreement with the lessee was, in fact, a lease in the eyes of the Internal Revenue Service (IRS). In 1955, the IRS issued Revenue Ruling 55-540, which gave guidance as to what characteristics should (or should not) be included in a tax lease.

The technology revolution of the 1960s had a major impact upon the growth of modern-day equipment lease financing, as firms recognized the competitive advantages of using equipment, such as computers and communication systems, that incorporated the most advanced technology. Although these firms needed this new equipment, they were often wary of its future economic value. They found leasing to be a flexible way to hedge against potential technological obsolescence. Additionally, the cost of acquiring this new technology was, at times, prohibitive. Many firms that could not afford the down payment required by the bank, let alone the full purchase price, found leasing to be an affordable means of acquiring the necessary equipment. The significant amount of computers and other office equipment leased during the 1960s was very critical to the growth of the leasing industry, as those leases represented many firms' introduction to equipment leasing.

Independent and manufacturer-related leasing companies have continued to grow in size and number over the years, as can be seen from the previous discussions. This growth, however, has not been to the exclusion of financial institution lessors such as banks, savings and loans and insurance companies. Banks were given the go-ahead to lease equipment in 1963, when the US Comptroller of the Currency issued a ruling that permitted national banks to own and lease personal property. The involvement of banks in equipment leasing was further legitimized in 1970 through an amendment to the Bank Holding Company Act, allowing banks to form holding companies, under which they could engage in a number of nontraditional financing activities, such as equipment leasing.

Although officially in the leasing business, banks at first were allowed (due to regulatory constraints) to offer only leases that, in form, resembled long-term financing. Many of the legislative barriers for bank-related leasing companies are coming down, however. The Competitive Equality Banking Act of 1987, for instance, removed the maximum residual value limit for a portion of bank lessors' business, thus allowing them to competitively enter the operating lease marketplace.

TAX AND ACCOUNTING FACTORS

During the late 1960s and early 1970s, the modern leveraged lease structure came of age. An investor, or equity participant, in a leveraged lease was entitled to 100% of the available tax benefits of ownership, while paying out only a portion of the leased equipment's cost. The rest was borrowed from a nonrecourse funding source. Investors in this type of lease were concerned over the availability of tax benefits in a specific transaction, as these benefits represented a major portion of the investor's return in the lease. Due to this concern, the entities putting these complex transactions together would often apply for an advance ruling from the IRS as to the actual tax status of a proposed lease transaction. By 1975, the IRS was so completely inundated with such requests that they issued a set of guidelines that must be adhered to for an advanced ruling (Revenue Procedure (Rev. Proc.) 75-21). While initially intended as a mechanism for the handling of advance rulings, the impact of Rev. Proc. 75-21 has been felt across the board for all tax leases, as it further clarifies what a lease should be from an IRS viewpoint.

The tides of tax law changes definitely have had a significant impact on the growth, as well as the direction, of the equipment leasing industry. ITC, which fueled many tax-oriented leases, has changed in amount over the years, and has been made available and taken away three different times since its introduction in 1962. As can be expected, a major force in the tax-oriented lease market is absent whenever ITC is unavailable.

The value of accelerated depreciation in lease structures has also been impacted by tax law change. The Economic Recovery Tax Act of 1981 (ERTA '81) did away with the use of the Asset Depreciation Range for depreciation purposes and replaced it with the Accelerated Cost Recovery System (ACRS). ACRS has since been modified by both the Tax Equity and Fiscal Responsibility Act of 1982 (TEFRA '82), and more recently, the Tax Reform Act of 1986 (TRA '86).

The constantly changing tax laws of the 1980s have altered not only the tax benefits of equipment ownership, and, hence, the economics of tax-oriented leasing, but also the specific definitions of what constitutes a lease in the eyes of the IRS. Safe harbor leases, including tax benefit transfer leases, were introduced by ERTA '81, but were repealed shortly thereafter by TEFRA '82. TEFRA '82 also introduced the finance lease, which later was modified by the Tax Reform Act of 1984.

The financial reporting attributes of a lease have faced no less of a dynamic history. The rapid growth of tax-oriented leases in the 1960s and early 1970s brought about many questions as to the appropriate financial reporting treatment for such transactions. Attempts were made to formulate accounting guidelines; however, it was not until 1976, prompted by pressure on the accounting profession from the Securities and Exchange Commission, that the newly formed Financial Accounting Standards Board (FASB) issued FASB Statement No. 13 (FASB 13), which set forth comprehensive guidelines for both lessor and lessee lease accounting. FASB 13 has given much greater uniformity to the financial reporting of equipment leases, although since 1976 many other statements, interpretations and technical bulletins have been issued by the FASB in an attempt to further clarify FASB 13.

SUMMARY

The leasing industry has evolved from, and been impacted by, various significant events. Many of these important events, such as the technology boom, the proliferation of sales-aid financing and tax and accounting guidelines, have occurred in the past 20 to 30 years. In spite of all the changes, however, the core leasing concepts of over 4,000 years ago are still a part of today's industry. Because of this, it should be evident, to both outsider and insider alike, that the leasing industry is very dynamic. The strength of the industry as a whole is characterized by its resiliency, and its ability to adapt to (and make the most of) a changing environment.

EQUIPMENT LEASING TODAY

Today, the equipment leasing industry is enjoying tremendous growth. Whether due to the benefits of obsolescence avoidance, off balance sheet financing, income tax factors, 100% financing or flexibility, leasing remains the single most widely-used method of external finance in the US today. The Department of Commerce has estimated that, for 1987, the leasing industry will reach a level of $107.9 billion in new lease volume and will provide one-quarter of the external financing for investment in capital equipment. This amount reflects a 6.6% growth over 1986 estimates, which is identical to the expected increase in the rate of business investment in equipment.

Market Segments

Now more than ever before, all types of equipment are leased. Automobiles, aircraft, personal computers, mainframes, laboratory equipment, nuclear magnetic imagers, adding machines, satellites, trucks and ships are all commonly leased. The differing types of equipment and respective price ranges help to divide the overall leasing industry into three core segments: the small ticket, middle and large ticket market. Each market is characterized by the range of its transaction sizes, the key decision factors influencing lessees and the most common types of lease products available.

The small ticket market is that portion of the overall marketplace that concentrates on leasing lower-priced equipment, such as copiers, personal computers and word processors. The cut-off point between the small ticket and middle markets ranges from $25,000 to $100,000, depending upon individual firms' interpretations. The lessee in this market is more concerned with the convenience of acquisition, maintenance and disposal than it is with cost. While tax-oriented leases can be written in the small ticket market, money-over-money leases and conditional sales contracts are more common.

The large ticket market, on the other hand, is very price sensitive, as it focuses on higher-priced equipment, such as aircraft, mainframe computers, ships and telecommunications equipment. The large ticket market is typically defined as equipment having a cost of $1,000,000 or more, and is quite competitive due to the number of interested parties vying for these transactions. This market, for the most part, consists of large, tax-oriented leveraged leases. Documentation tends to be more involved than in the small ticket market due to the size, as well as the complexity, of each individual transaction.

The middle market, by definition, fills the very wide gap, both in size and complexity, between the small and large ticket markets. This market is influenced by a number of different, and, at times, conflicting factors. Price and convenience are both common issues surfacing in the negotiation process. Lessors focusing on the middle market will often offer both tax and money-over-money leases, depending upon the specific needs of an individual lessee.

Today's Lessors

Industry estimates approximate the number of active equipment lessors at roughly 3,000 to 4,000 companies. Few accurate statistics exist concerning the proportion of the leasing industry that any individual lessor group represents. Nevertheless, all leasing companies can be classified into one of three groups: independent leasing companies, captive finance organizations and lease brokers, or packagers.

Independent leasing companies represent a large part of the leasing industry. These companies are independent of any one manufacturer. They purchase equipment from various manufacturers, and then lease the equipment to the end-user or lessee. Independent leasing companies are often referred to as third-party lessors. The three parties are the lessor, the unrelated manufacturer and, of course, the lessee (see Figure 1). Financial institutions involved in leasing, such as banks, thrift institutions and insurance companies, are also considered independent lessors. Many of these financial institution lessors not only provide lease financing to lessees, but funding to other leasing companies as well. Independent lessors may also provide lease financing (sometimes called vendor programs) to equipment manufacturers.

The second type of lessor is a captive lessor. Such a lessor is created when a manufacturer (or equipment dealer) decides to set up its own leasing company to finance its products. The manufacturer realizes that, by providing lease financing, it can increase the sales of its products over the level of sales utilizing traditional financing alone. The captive lessor is also referred to as a two-party lessor. One party consists of the consolidated parent and captive leasing subsidiary, and the other party is the lessee (or actual user) of the equipment (see Figure 2).

The final type of leasing company is the lease broker, or packager. The lease broker may find the interested lessee, arrange for the equipment with the manufacturer, secure debt financing for the lessor to use in purchasing the leased equipment and locate the ultimate lessor in the lease transaction (see Figure 3). The lease broker typically does not own the equipment or retain the lease transaction for its own account. The broker provides one or more various services, depending upon what is needed in a given lease transaction.

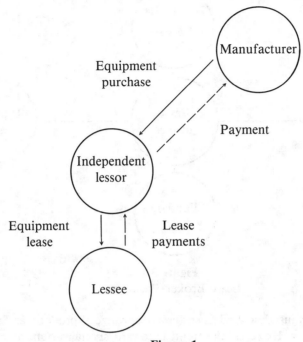

Figure 1
Independent
(third-party lessor)

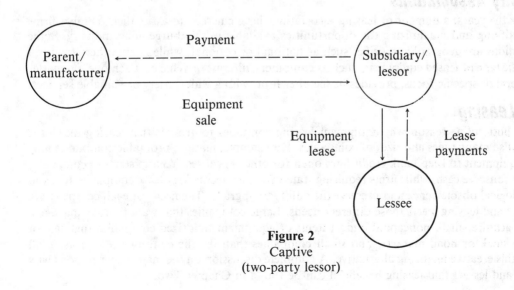

Figure 2
Captive
(two-party lessor)

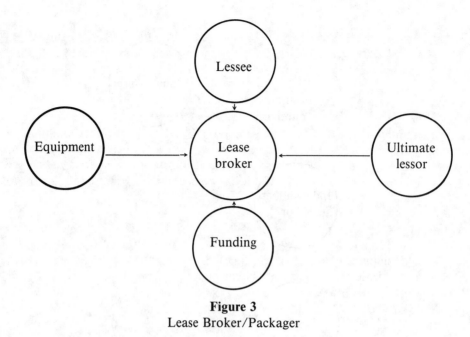

Figure 3
Lease Broker/Packager

The leasing companies just described can offer a wide range of products and services to many different market segments. However, the trend is toward specialization, as many lessors are finding substantial market niches by providing tailored lease financing for just one type of equipment and/or customer.

Industry Associations

Over the years, a number of leasing associations have emerged to assist their member firms in identifying and maximizing the opportunities available in this burgeoning industry. Some associations are geographic-specific, such as national or regional, while many others focus on a specific type of leased equipment, such as computers, aircraft or vehicles. Each one, no matter its general or specific focus, provides its member firms with a wide variety of valuable services.

Why Leasing

The bottomline reason why equipment leasing continues to grow is that leasing meets the needs of so many types and sizes of companies. For example, mature, profitable companies may lease equipment to keep bank credit lines open for other purposes. Young, start-up companies lease to conserve cash, while firms requiring state-of-the-art technology lease equipment to avoid technological obsolescence and preserve the ability to upgrade. The needs of each company are different and leasing meets those different needs. Large companies that want to leave managers free to acquire small, noncapital budget items of equipment; midsized companies that cannot tap the stock or bond markets; and small companies that like the convenience of leasing all utilize this creative financing alternative. A complete discussion on the many other reasons why lessors and lessees find leasing beneficial can be found in Chapter Two.

Now that an appreciation for the development, or evolution, of the equipment leasing industry in the financial products marketplace has been gained, it is appropriate to discuss the fundamental concepts and components of a lease.

ELEMENTS OF A LEASE

Leasing is a multidisciplinary industry, embodying tax, finance and accounting concepts, among others. The fact that the lease transaction itself consists of many elements compounds this complexity. Because each of these elements directly impacts the character and nature of the transaction, the basic elements of a typical lease transaction are discussed in this section.

Parties to a Lease

Fundamentally, an equipment lease is an usage agreement between an equipment owner (a lessor) and a user of the property (a lessee). The lessee remits to the lessor a periodic rental fee as compensation for the usage of the property. An example of a basic lease is illustrated in Figure 4.

Lease agreements generally take the form of written contracts, and specifically set forth the various terms and conditions of the lease transaction. Such terms and conditions include the number of periods the equipment is to be used, the amount and timing of the lease payments, the specifications of the equipment leased and any end-of-term conditions.

Lessors are the providers of the equipment to be leased and may supply services and add value as well. They purchase, manage and remarket equipment as part of the lease process, and also tailor the financing to fit the individual, sometimes highly complex, needs of each equipment user. Typically, the lessor is viewed as the owner of the equipment. It must not be assumed, however, that such a view implies ownership from an IRS perspective. If the lease agreement does not meet various tax lease criteria, the lessor may be unable to claim the normal tax benefits of equipment ownership. Instead, the lessee would be considered the tax owner and, therefore, entitled to the tax benefits.

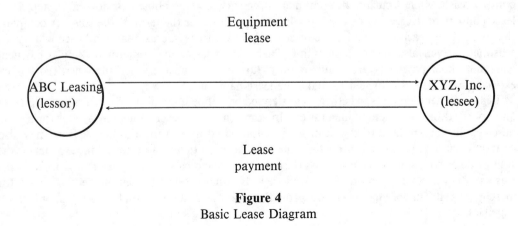

Figure 4
Basic Lease Diagram

The lessee is the user of the equipment. The lessee, at this point, has gone through the preliminary steps necessary to acquire the equipment, and has made the decision to use lease financing. The lessee's equipment, servicing and financing needs, of course, are critical in the development of an appropriate lease product and overall transaction.

Lease Payments and Residual Value

Lessees are required to pay a periodic rental fee or charge to the lessor over the prescribed term of the lease for the use of the leased equipment. The rental payment compensates the lessor for numerous investment costs and operating expenses incurred to provide the leased services, including:

1. Depreciation of the equipment (physical wear and tear as well as technological obsolescence)
2. Interest expense on debt used to fund the lease
3. General and administrative expenses supporting the operations of the lease company
4. Initial direct costs, such as sales commissions, attorneys' fees, credit check fees, etc., incurred at the inception of a lease
5. Costs of bundled services, such as maintenance, warranties, supplies, reagents, etc.
6. Reasonable profit on the outstanding investment over its economic life.

PAYMENTS

Lease payments are generally structured on a monthly basis, although quarterly, semiannual and annual repayment schedules are also used. (Leasing is a very flexible financing tool due to the wide range of possible lease payment schedules.) Payments are commonly structured in advance, where the payment is due at the beginning of each period, but they can also be structured in arrears, where the payment is due at the end of each period. Most leases call for equal or even payments over the term of the lease; however, to match the cash flow of the lessee, payments can be varied in amount and/or timing, as in step leases or skip leases.

A step-up lease consists of increasingly larger lease payments during the lease term. Frequently, a start-up company may be interested in step-up payments, which enable it to conserve cash, while securing the equipment necessary to get the business moving. A step-down lease consists of decreasing or declining lease payments over the term of the lease. A company that is currently cash heavy might request a step-down lease. Occasionally, a lessee will have a seasonal or cyclical cash flow constraint. This type of lessee may opt for a skipped payment lease, in which payments are required only during those business periods when the lessee's expected cash flow is sufficient to make the lease payments.

Lease payment amounts, whether even, stepped or skipped, are normally determined up front and specified in the lease documentation. In some cases, however, a lease may call for a fixed base rental plus an additional contingency rental based upon future usage. A lease may also contain a variable (as opposed to fixed) rate that has been tied to an external index, such as the prime rate or consumer price index. As the external rate increases or decreases, so, too, does the lease payment. Such indexed contingent rentals usually serve to reimburse the lessor for increases in its underlying costs of providing the lease services (debt costs, maintenance expenses, etc.).

RESIDUAL

No matter what method is used to arrive at the rental payment, the future expected residual value of the equipment is taken into consideration in the pricing of most types of leases. Residual value and lease payments both represent potential cash inflow to the lessor. The higher the assumed residual value, the less the lessor needs to charge in the form of lease payments. As an example, if the lessor expects to sell the equipment at the end of the lease for 10% of its original cost, it needs to recover only 90% of the equipment cost through the lease payments (see Figure 5). It is plain to see that the higher the expected residual value, the lower the lease payment will be to the lessee.

If a lessor recovers, through the lease payments, all costs incurred in the lease plus an acceptable rate of return, without any reliance on a future residual value, it is referred to as a full-payout lease. In an operating lease (not to be confused with an operating lease for financial reporting purposes), however, the lessor does rely on the residual for payment (takes a residual position). In the operating lease, the lessor must receive a certain value for the equipment at the end of the term in order to earn its rate of return.

End-of-Term Options

At the termination of a lease, lessors allow lessees to select one of three alternatives:
1. Return the equipment without further obligation except for, perhaps, deinstallation and shipping costs
2. Purchase the equipment at an exercise price determined by appraisal at the lease termination (fair market value purchase option), or by agreement at the lease inception (fixed purchase option)
3. Renew the lease at a renewal rate determined by appraisal or by earlier agreement.

Some lessors do not provide purchase or renewal rights to the lessee. Such leases are referred to as closed-end leases since renewal or purchase rights are closed off to the lessee.

Certain leases require that the lessor receive a predetermined value (termed a guaranteed residual value) upon return of the equipment to the lessor. If the equipment is appraised or salvaged for an amount less than this value, the deficiency is paid by the lessee guarantor. Lessees, equipment vendors and/or manufacturers, insurance companies, etc., can all guarantee lessor residual values. It should be noted, however, that the inclusion of certain end-of-term options or obligations in a lease contract, such as bargain purchase options or lessee guaranteed residual values, can affect the specific tax and financial reporting attributes of the lease.

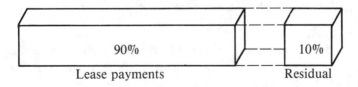

Figure 5
Impact of Residual Amounts

Bundled Services

A lease for the use of equipment can include other services, such as maintenance, product warranties, supplies, software, consulting time, swaps (replacement equipment to be used while waiting for a major repair on the leased property), etc. The equipment portion of a service package may be minimal depending upon how many other products and services have been bundled. Such bundled service packages are referred to as full-service leases. Net leases, on the other hand, have few, if any, services included in the lease, which implies the lessee must arrange for the services apart from the lease agreement. Service bundling is very natural in leasing, especially when a lease is viewed as a service (temporary equipment usage for a rental fee) as opposed to an equipment purchase.

Funding Aspects

Lessors fund their leased equipment in a number of different ways. In a single-investor lease, the cash paid for the equipment represents the lessor's own equity as well as pooled funds that have been borrowed from a variety of sources, normally on a recourse basis. In a recourse borrowing the lessor is fully at-risk for any borrowed funds (see Figure 6).

In a leveraged lease, the lessor borrows a significant amount of nonrecourse money by assigning, or discounting, the lease payment stream to the lender, in return for up-front cash. This cash amount represents the amount of the loan and is equal to the present value of the future lease payments discounted at the lessor's borrowing rate (see Figure 7). The assignment or discounting of lease payments represents a funding technique used by a large segment of the leasing industry for both single investor and leveraged leases.

In nonrecourse borrowing, the lender looks to the creditworthiness of the lessee and the value of the equipment for payment, not to the lessor. In fact, the lessee will generally make lease payments directly to the lender in a leveraged lease. The lessor will have to put equity (cash and/or recourse borrowings) into the transaction in the amount of the difference between the cost of the equipment and the debt. In an assignment, the debt is equal to the present value of the assigned lease payments.

Tax and Accounting Lease Attributes

From an industry standpoint, a lease is a contract that has been labeled a lease, and contains many of the other elements mentioned earlier. Aside from this somewhat generic definition of a lease, each contract also has certain tax and accounting attributes. These various attributes help delineate the tax status and financial reporting treatment of the lease.

TAX ATTRIBUTES

As mentioned earlier, federal tax law, as interpreted by the IRS, dictates the classification of a lease from a tax perspective. The determination as to whether the IRS views a lease transaction as a lease is outlined in several IRS pronouncements, offering both general and specific insights. Particularly, the issue of at-risk is the major criterion for determining whether a lease is a tax lease or a nontax lease. If the lease is to be a tax lease, the issue of whether the lessor is at-risk

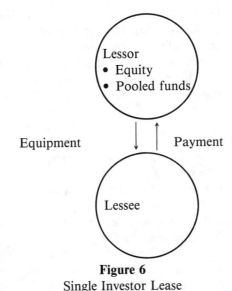

Figure 6
Single Investor Lease

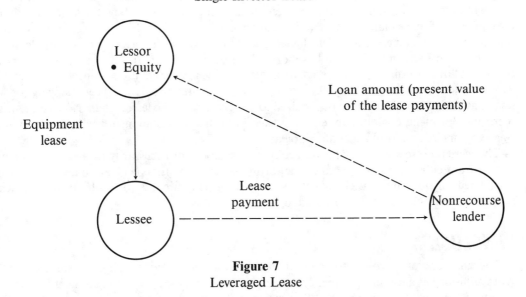

Figure 7
Leveraged Lease

determines whether or not the lessor will receive the tax benefits of ownership and the lessee will be entitled to deduct the lease payments as a business expense.

In those cases where the lease conditions fail to meet the IRS criteria for a tax lease the transaction is determined not to be a tax lease, and is referred to as a money-over-money lease. This transaction is nothing more than an installment sale contract in the guise of a lease. A money-over-money lease is the opposite of a tax lease. The lessee is bearing the risks of ownership and will be entitled to the tax benefits, such as depreciation, but will not be entitled to deduct the entire lease payments as it does in a tax lease.

If the lessor is to claim the tax benefits of ownership, risk of ownership must be evident. For instance, a tax lease should not contain a bargain purchase option or specify a lessee guaranteed residual value. Either of these two events removes the residual risk from the lessor. If the lessor bears the risks of ownership, the lease will be termed a tax lease. If the lessee bears those risks, the lease will be termed a money-over-money lease.

ACCOUNTING ATTRIBUTES

The financial reporting treatment of a lease is a completely separate matter from its tax treatment. Rather than being concerned with the tax characteristics of a lease, the various financial reporting criteria, as determined by the FASB (not the IRS), determine how a lease should be reported in a firm's financial statements.

Since in-depth treatments of lessor and lessee lease accounting are accomplished in subsequent chapters, suffice it to say that the focus of the financial reporting criteria is to determine whether a specific lease transaction resembles a purchase agreement or a usage agreement. If a lease contains the characteristics of a purchase agreement, such as 1) an automatic transfer of ownership from lessor to lessee, 2) a purchase option that is considerably less than expected fair market value or 3) terms and conditions that allow the lessee control of the equipment for the major portion of its economic life, or require the lessee to pay for a major portion of the equipment cost, then the lease agreement will be classified as a capital lease.

If, on the other hand, the lease has more of the characteristics of a usage agreement, as in the concept of a true fixed-period rental arrangement, the agreement is classified as an operating lease. The term operating lease has become synonymous with off balance sheet financing for the lessee, as the lease obligation is not required to be reflected on the lessee's balance sheet. Due to reporting treatment, the latter appears as a lease in the financial statements, whereas the capital lease appears as an installment sale/purchase.

The mere representation or appearance of a lease does not necessarily mean a lease is truly a lease from either a tax or a financial reporting standpoint. Independent guidelines must be considered for both areas of classification. The major determinants for both tax and financial reporting purposes, however, are risk and intent.

CONCLUSION

The simplicity of its concept has given leasing a timeless value. Leasing has survived 4,000 years of history as a useful equipment financing tool. Today, the need for equipment leasing has only increased, with the many benefits it has to offer contributing to its huge popularity. The affordability and desirability of leasing, particularly as portrayed in the press, have heightened businesses' awareness of the value of the equipment lease as a means for acquiring equipment. Leasing is a dynamic and creative (albeit complex) industry, and is still undergoing significant changes, changes that will result in an industry of tomorrow that is even more flexible in meeting the financial needs of lessees.

CHAPTER TWO
DYNAMICS OF THE INDUSTRY

The demand for leasing continues to grow at a tremendous rate, as evidenced by the increased amount of equipment being leased each year. Leasing currently accounts for approximately one-quarter of all capital expenditures in the United States, as corporations and individuals are becoming more and more aware of the many different advantages, benefits, options and flexibility offered by this creative form of financing. All types of assets are being leased and several thousand leasing companies, varying in size, type and market focus, have emerged to meet the diverse financial needs of lessees.

This chapter reviews the many benefits of leasing, and the underlying force shaping today's leasing industry, in the context of how these benefits apply to the two principal parties to the lease transaction. This review will consist of the following sections:

- Lessee Reasons to Lease
- Lessor Motivations to Provide Leasing Services.

LESSEE REASONS TO LEASE

There are between 35 to 40 reasons for the acquirers of equipment to utilize leasing. Some of them may lease for only one reason, others for a variety of reasons. Some of the more common and popular reasons for leasing are presented in this section.

Technological Considerations

Several of the technological reasons for leasing are presented in this subsection.

A NATURAL OBSOLESCENCE HEDGE

Perhaps one of the strongest reasons for acquiring the use of equipment through leasing, as opposed to purchasing, is that leasing helps lessees avoid many of the risks of ownership. One of the key risks of ownership is that of equipment obsolescence. Much of today's equipment is based upon technology that is rapidly changing, making the equipment subject to technological obsolescence. For example, a computer that may have been expected to be worth 20% of its original value at the end of 5 years could easily be worthless in 3 years, given the advances in technology that are constantly occurring. The inherent risk of owning technologically-sensitive equipment is that the equipment may become economically useless for the company owning it much earlier than expected, and long before the obligations to acquire the equipment have been satisfied.

Leasing can help lessees avoid the risk of owning equipment that is no longer technologically useful by initially transferring that risk to a lessor. When entering into a short-term lease, a leasing company assumes the technological risk to the extent that it has built an assumed residual value into the lease pricing. If a piece of leased equipment, in which a residual position has been taken, is completely worthless at the end of the lease term, the lessor will not recover all its costs or earn its pretargeted return. The lessee, on the other hand, has benefited by not having to pay 100% of the cost of a piece of equipment that is now technologically useless to it.

Obviously, lessors cannot take unjustifiable residual positions and remain viable for very long. Lessors, however, long ago perceived two very important market realities that enable them to take upon themselves the risk of technological obsolescence. First, a piece of obsolete equipment may be of little value to one lessee at the end of the initial lease term, but could still have considerable value to another firm not requiring state-of-the-art technology, for what is obsolete to one user is not necessarily obsolete to another.

Second, a lessor's equipment knowledge, combined with its greater access to secondary equipment markets, may cause the equipment to be of greater value in the hands of the lessor than in those of the lessee. In many cases, the lessor can sell the equipment for a higher price than if the lessee had purchased the equipment outright and then salvaged it on its own. Because of these factors, lessors are able to take residual positions in the equipment, thus helping to transfer the risk of obsolescence from the lessee to the lessor.

TAKEOUTS, ROLLOVERS AND UPGRADES

Short-term leases in which the lessor has assumed a residual position certainly help the lessee to avoid the risk of obsolescence at the end of the lease term. Two common lease options, takeouts and rollovers, however, also give the lessee flexibility during the lease term should the leased equipment become obsolete prior to the termination of the lease.

A takeout occurs when a lessor replaces obsolete equipment with updated equipment. The lessee is "taken out" of the outmoded equipment and then leased equipment incorporating the newer technology. Sometimes a lessee may need only an upgrade of its current equipment as opposed to complete replacement. Many contracts today are written with upgrade provisions that allow additional equipment to be added to the existing system (through leasing) to increase either its efficiency or capability.

As can be seen, the transfer of the technological obsolescence risk from the lessee to the lessor throughout the lease term is made quite easy due to the many flexible options that can be built into a lease agreement. Purchasing equipment, on the other hand, forces the equipment owner to assume all of the risks of ownership, including the risk of obsolescence.

Financial Reporting Reasons

Financial reporting reasons play an important role in many equipment acquisition decisions. Several of these reasons are presented in this subsection.

OFF BALANCE SHEET FINANCING

When a company purchases equipment it must capitalize the equipment on its balance sheet by showing it as an asset, along with a corresponding liability for any loans used to finance the equipment's purchase. Since the cost of the capitalized equipment must be amortized over its economic life, depreciation expense will appear on the company's income statement. Depreciation expense, along with the interest expense on the loan, represent the financial statement cost of purchasing the equipment and financing it with a loan. Capital leases, while not true purchases of equipment, are treated much the same way per Financial Accounting Standards Board Statement No. 13 (FASB 13).

If a lease is classified as an operating lease for the lessee's financial reporting purposes, however, it is not required to be capitalized in the financial statements. (Neither an asset nor a liability would appear on the lessee's balance sheet, although certain information is required to be included in a footnote, hence, the term off balance sheet financing.) Furthermore, the only expense appearing on the lessee's income statement that is attributable to the lease would be the lease rental expense.

Off balance sheet financing is sought for many different reasons. The use of operating leases helps a firm to "window dress" its financial statements. Many, if not all, of the firm's financial ratios and measurements are improved, at least initially, such that the firm appears to be stronger, more liquid and more profitable. As the operating lease does not create a liability on the balance sheet, the firm also appears to be less leveraged. If lenders are not fully on top of the situation, they may be more willing to lend additional funds to such a seemingly less indebted company. Keep in mind, however, that the actual cash flow of the lease is not affected by whether it is treated as a capital or operating lease, but, rather, only how it appears on the lessee's financial statements.

IMPROVED REPORTED EARNINGS

Similarly, the operating lease tends to have a more favorable impact on a lessee's income statement in the early years of the lease. Initially, the operating lease expense is less than the depreciation and interest expense for the loan or capital lease, thus boosting the lessee's overall reported earnings.

INCREASED RETURN ON ASSETS

Due to its effects of lowering a lessee's asset base, as well as increasing the lessee's reported earnings, an operating lease helps a lessee to report a higher return on assets (ROA). Many managers are sensitive to the level of the reported ROA, as oftentimes bonus arrangements are tied to the ROA attained by the division or company.

Companies are constantly striving to have their financial statements look as strong and healthy as possible to shareholders and lenders. Operating lease treatment, which is discussed in further detail in Chapter Fourteen, can help lessees to accomplish this goal.

LOWER-LEVEL DECISION MAKER

Managers of all levels who wish to acquire the use of equipment, but who do not have the appropriate authority to expend the necessary level of funds, find leasing to be a convenient method of acquiring the equipment's use. Through the use of a lease they are able to pay monthly lease rentals out of the department's or division's operating budget, as the amount of the monthly lease payment oftentimes falls within their spending authority guidelines.

Cash Management Considerations

Some of the cash management considerations are discussed in this subsection.

AFFORDABILITY TO LESSEES

The acquisition of assets through leasing, as opposed to purchasing, becomes even more desirable as the cost of equipment rises. As new and more sophisticated equipment is available in the marketplace, often with expensive price tags, many companies will, out of necessity, choose to acquire the use of the equipment through leasing as opposed to purchasing for affordability reasons. This is true for several reasons.

First, as a general rule, leasing companies require lower down payments than other financial institutions. For example, the typical lease requires one, or possibly two, lease rental payments paid in advance (representing roughly 2 to 4% down), whereas many banks require a 10 to 20% down payment. Second, other incidental costs of acquiring the asset, such as sales tax and installation charges, can be included as part of the lease payment itself, rather than being paid in advance with a large down payment as is the case in most purchase situations. Obviously, in a credit-tight economy, not tying up cash in large down payments and other incidental costs allows a company to employ cash savings for other more profitable working capital requirements. Frequently, the opportunity cost of tying up cash in equipment acquisitions almost necessitates leasing as an alternative, especially for rapidly growing companies whose available cash is invested in highly profitable inventory and receivables.

Firms oftentimes mistakenly use funds earmarked for short-term working capital needs to purchase long-lived assets, thereby hindering the firm's day-to-day operations, as well as its ability to meet short-term credit obligations. Leasing, of course, helps a firm to conserve working capital for its intended purpose.

A lease alternative also may be more affordable to a company than conventional loan financing due to the potentially lower monthly payment in a lease versus a loan. The amount of the lease payment can be impacted by a number of variables, such as the value of the tax benefits received by the lessor in a tax lease, the residual position taken by a lessor that is built into the lease pricing and the longer lease terms available in the marketplace.

Any financing alternative with affordable repayment options is greatly sought after in today's financial products marketplace. Certainly leasing offers an affordable alternative method of acquiring equipment due to its low, if any, up-front costs and resulting conservation of working capital, its general ability to finance soft costs (delivery, installation, etc.) and lower periodic lease payments.

IMPROVED CASH FORECASTING

In a lease agreement, the lessee is permitted to use the leased equipment for a specific period of time and, in return, must pay a periodic usage or rental charge. The fixed contractual nature of the lease obligation eliminates any uncertainties regarding the future cost of the equipment. This fact enables companies to prepare more accurate cash forecasts and plans. In addition, a company knows that a decision must be made at the end of the base lease term, as to whether the equipment should be purchased, returned to the lessor or the lease renewed. Once the decision has been made, the cost of the chosen end-of-term option can be determined and integrated into the planning and forecasting process, thereby facilitating the accurate preparation of the overall company budget.

CIRCUMVENTING CAPITAL BUDGET CONSTRAINTS

Many large and profitable firms choose to lease for one very real reason — to circumvent various capital budget constraints. A division or department of a large firm may have sufficient funds to purchase a new piece of equipment outright. However, if the division or department has already fully utilized its budgeted amount for capital expenditures, it most likely will be precluded from purchasing the equipment. Such a department or division could request additional capital expenditure funds, of course, but that process is all too often unsuccessful. Even if successful, the steps required to acquire equipment beyond the capital budget are onerous and time-consuming and, therefore, unpopular. On the other hand, the department or division could lease the necessary equipment and pay for the lease rentals out of its operating budget instead of the capital budget. (As previously mentioned, a lease structured as an operating lease for financial reporting purposes appears as a periodic expense on the lessee's income statement, is not reflected on the lessee's balance sheet and is paid for out of its operating budget.) By utilizing leasing, the department obtains the equipment it needs and avoids the capital budget scrutiny that may not have worked in its favor.

Along the same lines, many state and local governments are required to have special capital appropriations made by the legislature or decision-making bodies to acquire equipment through purchasing. These capital appropriations are generally made once a year, thus, perhaps, prohibiting midyear acquisition of equipment required for unanticipated needs or emergencies. In these cases leasing can solve the problem, as lease payments can be paid out of operating budgets rather than the already depleted capital acquisition appropriation. Operating expenses generally require only days or weeks for approval as compared to the annual capital appropriations approval.

REIMBURSEMENT POLICIES

Companies operating in certain regulated industries, as well as private contractors for the federal government, are reimbursed in various ways for the expenses they have incurred, depending upon the nature of the expense. Oftentimes, lease expense can be recovered more quickly than depreciation and interest expense incurred in purchasing an asset. In many cases lease expense is viewed as an expense tied to a certain project or time period, whereas interest expense or depreciation for a long-lived asset may not be accepted as a project expense and, therefore, may not be immediately reimbursable.

Income Tax Motivations

The tax laws impact all aspects of leasing, and the acquisition of equipment by the lessee is no exception. Income tax motivations are presented in this subsection.

RECIPROCITY OF TAX BENEFITS

When leases are structured such that they qualify as tax leases per Internal Revenue Service (IRS) criteria, the lessor will be considered the tax owner of the equipment and, as such, receive certain tax benefits in the transaction, most notably accelerated depreciation. As a result of these benefits, lessors in a higher tax bracket experience meaningful tax savings that they in turn may fully or partially pass on to the lessee in the form of a reduced lease rental. Consequently, the lessee can indirectly share in the lessor's tax benefits. This reciprocity, or exchange of tax benefits for a lower lease rate, is particularly important for a company that is currently in a nontaxpaying position, and, therefore, cannot utilize the tax benefits of ownership directly. If the same company were to obtain conventional bank financing in purchasing the equipment, not only would its payments be higher than the tax lease payments, but it would not be able to benefit from the tax benefits currently available, such as accelerated depreciation.

Equipment leasing will continue to be used, and increasingly so, by nonprofit organizations (the federal government, churches, organizations such as the Boy Scouts of America, nonprofit hospitals, etc.) who cannot take advantage of the tax benefits resulting from equipment ownership. Although tax advantages are not available to these nonprofit organizations, they can still receive indirect benefit if any tax benefits retained by the lessor in a tax lease are partially or fully passed on to the nonprofit groups in the form of lower lease rental payments.

In certain leases (municipal leases) to state, local or county governments, there are no tax benefits of ownership, such as accelerated depreciation, available to the lessor. The municipal lease resembles a conditional sales contract in form, usually having a nominal purchase option ($1), stated interest rate, etc. However, the implicit interest to the lessor in this otherwise conditional sales contract is exempt from federal income taxes. The lessor can pass part of this tax saving on to the municipal lessee by charging a lower payment to the lessee than it would normally need to charge a taxable organization.

LOWER LEVERAGED LEASE RATES

Other benefits can be obtained from the use of financial leverage in addition to the tax savings derived by the lessor in a tax lease. In a leveraged lease the lessor of the equipment provides roughly 10 to 20% of the necessary capital to acquire the equipment. The remainder of the capital is borrowed from a funding source on a nonrecourse basis. The nonrecourse loan is secured by an assignment of the lease payments, an assignment of the lease and a collateral lien on the equipment itself. The advantage to the lessor in the leveraged lease is that all tax benefits incidental to ownership of the equipment pass through to the lessor even though its equity interest in the lease is only 10 to 20%. This financial leverage creates greater than proportionate tax savings to the lessor. For example, first year depreciation benefits alone can come close to offsetting a lessor's 10% equity investment. This leveraging of tax benefits normally will result in a lower leveraged lease payment being charged to the lessee.

Leveraged lease rates are also impacted by the size of the specific transaction. Generally, leveraged leases are written for very large dollar amounts; therefore, lessors attempt to fine-tune their bids in order to be competitive, which results in a lowering of leveraged lease rates to the lessee.

DEDUCTIBILITY OF RENTALS

Lease payments in a tax lease are fully deductible for federal income tax purposes. While the lessee, as user, not owner, will not receive any accelerated depreciation benefits, the deductibility of the payments provides a clear tax benefit for the lessee. In regard to this deductibility of lease payments, short-term leases provide an even greater tax incentive to lease.

When leases are written for noncancellable terms shorter than the equipment's Modified Accelerated Cost Recovery (MACRS) classlife, an incremental tax advantage is created to the degree that the deductible lease payments exceed the expenses plus MACRS deductions that would have been available to the user had the equipment been purchased. For example, if an equipment user were to purchase office equipment, the taxpayer would have to depreciate the 7-year MACRS equipment over 8 years, due to the half-year convention, as shown in Figure 1. However, if the equipment user were to lease the equipment through a 4-year full-payout lease, the lessee would be able to write off 100% of the equipment cost in 4 years, as shown in Figure 2. Had the lessee purchased the equipment instead, the equipment-user would have received only cost recovery (depreciation) benefits equal to roughly 69% of the equipment cost over the same 4-year period.

NEGATIVE IMPACT OF ADDITIONAL PURCHASES

Recent tax law changes have placed many companies in the position of being penalized, from a tax standpoint, when purchasing additional equipment. While the impact of federal income tax law on leasing is discussed in Chapter Four, it is important to mention here that companies either facing or approaching the alternative minimum tax (AMT) or the midquarter depreciation convention will be penalized when purchasing new equipment by having to pay more taxes, due to the loss or reduction in value of certain tax benefits.

For a company that is in or approaching an AMT position it makes more sense for the company to lease, as opposed to purchase, any necessary equipment because a purchase may cause the company to pay additional taxes under AMT due to accelerated depreciation, whereas a lease will not.

In addition, a company that is in need of new equipment in the fourth quarter of its fiscal year may fall subject to the midquarter depreciation convention through purchasing the equipment. This aspect of tax law lessens the overall first year depreciation benefits for all personal property placed in service that year. A company with equipment acquisition needs in its fourth quarter that is also facing the possibility of triggering the midquarter convention should choose to lease, as leasing and leased assets have no bearing or effect on the rules governing the application of this depreciation convention.

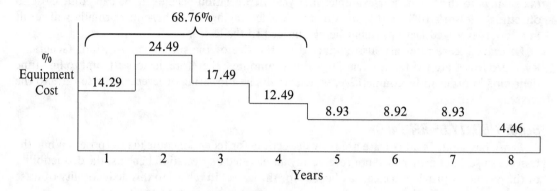

Figure 1
Purchase: MACRS Deductions

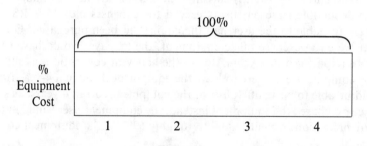

Figure 2
Lease: Payment Deductions

Ownership Aspects

The reasons for lessees to lease relating to ownership aspects are covered in this subsection.

USE VERSUS OWNERSHIP

For years, enlightened businesspeople have realized the use of a piece of equipment is far more important to the production of income than a piece of paper conveying title to the equipment, as it is the use of equipment that produces profit, not ownership. In fact, if equipment can be used for most of its economic life without the user having the full legal responsibilities, risks and burdens of ownership, then little value exists in the actual ownership of the equipment.

While psychologically many people are unwilling or unable to separate the concept of asset use from asset ownership, a growing number of individuals and firms are finding that ownership of equipment is not nearly as important as other aspects of equipment acquisition. For example, ownership of the equipment may not be as important to a firm as acquiring the use only of the equipment at the lowest possible cost, or with the least expense. Obtaining the use of equipment through leasing may result in lower acquisition costs, which in turn implies greater profitability for a firm.

OWNERSHIP NOT AVAILABLE OR FEASIBLE

In certain cases, the only realistic means of acquiring an asset's use is through leasing. Ownership may be unavailable or impractical. For instance, a company may need the use of a satellite to transmit data on a regular basis from its headquarters to regional offices in various parts of the world. The cost of the entire satellite may be prohibitive, especially when the company may need but a fraction of the satellite's power and capabilities. Through leasing, however, the company could obtain the use of a portion of the satellite's power in exchange for affordable, periodic rental payments.

AVOIDING STRANDED ASSETS

For financial reporting purposes, a piece of equipment that has been capitalized on a firm's balance sheet is depreciated over its estimated economic life. Occasionally estimates are missed, or changes in technology make original estimates of economic life inaccurate. If equipment is deemed obsolete before the end of its depreciable life for whatever reasons, the company would then own a worthless piece of equipment that is not fully depreciated on its books. If the company is able to sell the equipment, it will be sold at a loss, thus having a negative impact on reported earnings. Such a piece of equipment is deemed a stranded asset when the firm decides to hold on to the equipment until it is fully depreciated, simply to avoid the negative impact of a current loss on the sale of equipment for reported earnings. To avoid the risk of a stranded asset on its financial statements, a firm should choose to lease, as opposed to purchase, the equipment, and should specifically select a short-term lease that specifies reasonable renewal terms for additional periods of use.

LESSEE'S POTENTIAL FOR OWNERSHIP

Another important aspect of leasing that has influenced its popularity is that the lessee generally has the ability to purchase the equipment at the end of the lease term and, thus, eventually become the owner of the equipment. Some purchase options are set at prestated amounts while many leases, for a number of reasons, state the purchase option amount is to be equal to the equipment's established fair market value at the end of the lease term — not at a fixed or predetermined amount. Fixed purchase option amounts can vary from the equipment's actual value at the end of the term, so this practice may appear risky for the lessee intending to purchase the leased equipment upon lease termination. The exercise of purchase options at fair market value, however, is certainly acceptable to those lessees that expect to use the equipment for many more years beyond the initial lease term.

Flexibility and Convenience

Leasing is a very flexible and convenient method of acquiring the use of equipment. Since the leasing industry is relatively young and unregulated and thus tends to be more aggressive, leasing companies are often in a position to adapt to the specific needs of lessees. This adaptability, of course, translates directly into convenience and flexibility for the lessee.

CONVENIENCE TO THE LESSEE

Leasing offers many convenience advantages over conventional forms of financing. Acquiring the use of an asset through a lease can involve less red tape and time than conventional financing. Furthermore, many, if not all, of the headaches of ownership are transferred to the lessor in a lease. As an example, the lessee can simply return the equipment to the lessor upon termination of the lease without further obligation. The lessor must bear the burden and risk of disposing of the equipment for an adequate price.

Leasing also provides for very convenient "one-stop shopping." When acquiring a piece of equipment, a company has many product and model options, several financing options (including leasing) and can obtain any given financing option from several sources. A lessor takes some of the legwork out of this process by providing product variety and knowledge, the product itself, financing, maintenance, insurance and many flexible options, all under one roof. Documentation can be standardized such that the necessary paperwork is ready for the lessor and lessee to immediately consummate a transaction.

Additional convenience and cost savings are obtained with operating leases. These leases require much less bookkeeping than outright purchases. Purchased assets must be capitalized and depreciated on a firm's financial statements, and loan payments must be separated into principal and interest. All of this requires additional time and effort.

Cash flow projections, as mentioned earlier, are made easy through leasing since most leases have fixed equal periodic payments. Commercial loan financing of equipment, on the other hand, may require payments that fluctuate with the prime rate. Furthermore, financing with internal funds is subject to the vagaries of changing costs of capital. Similarly to this thought, prior to purchasing equipment most firms require a rigorous capital budgeting analysis. Oftentimes, these same companies do not require the same lengthy analysis for leasing a piece of equipment, possibly due to the perceived shorter-term nature of a lease. Government agencies frequently can acquire assets through leasing rather than waiting for time-consuming appropriations for purchases.

A few of the many reasons to lease have been reviewed from a convenience standpoint. Each of the remaining reasons builds and expounds upon the overall concept of the flexibility and convenience inherent in leasing as opposed to purchasing equipment.

FLEXIBILITY IN LEASE STRUCTURING

Leases are a flexible tool in meeting the various needs of lessees. A brief description of several unique types of leases best illustrates the flexibility of leasing.

1. Step leases: A lease agreement that allows the lessee's payments to either increase (step-up lease) or decrease (step-down lease) over the term of the lease to better meet the lessee's cash flow constraints (see Figure 3)

2. Skipped payment leases: A lease agreement requiring the lessee to make payment only during certain months or periods each year. Skipped payment leases are structured to meet the seasonal or other cash flow constraints of a specific lessee (see Figure 3). For example, a farmer may prefer a lease with payments required only in late summer and

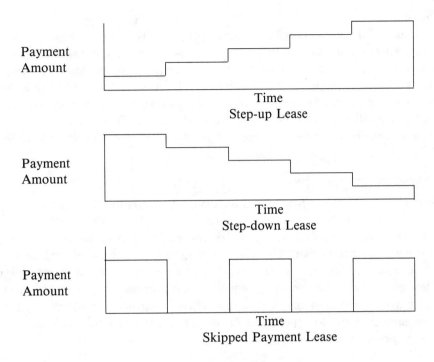

Figure 3
Flexible Lease Structures

fall, when the cash flow from the sale of harvested crops is available to service the lease obligation

3. Swap lease: A swap lease allows the lessee to temporarily exchange equipment in need of major repair with properly working replacement equipment to avoid costly maintenance and repair delays. Of course, lessors who carry inventory of equipment would be the most able to provide such services

4. Upgrade lease: This flexible option allows additions to existing leased equipment to improve its capacity or efficiency; or an exchange during the lease of outmoded equipment with newer model upgraded equipment

5. Master lease: This is a lease line of credit that allows a lessee to add equipment to a lease (up to a maximum amount for a certain period of time), under the same basic terms and conditions, without having to renegotiate a new lease contract. The lease rate generally is set for each piece of equipment as it is placed in service and put on lease

6. Short-term or experimental lease: Sometimes leases are written for short periods or to provide trial use periods. During this time the lessee decides whether the equipment will accomplish the required task and, more importantly, generate revenue. This removes a good deal of the speculative risk from the lessee's acquisition of an asset.

BUNDLED SERVICES

Usually, the subject of a lease is tangible personal property. However, other products or services can be bundled with the lease to offer a full-service package that is either less expensive than if the lessee were to separately purchase the same services, or is simply more convenient. Products or services that are commonly bundled into a full-service or bundled lease include maintenance, insurance and property taxes. As more manufacturing companies utilize leasing as a marketing tool, they will eventually offer more full-service leases, as they can typically offer bundled services more readily and profitably than independent leasing companies, due to their in-depth knowledge of the product and customer needs.

PLANNED REPLACEMENT OF EQUIPMENT

Many managers prefer to lease equipment because leasing facilitates the planned replacement of existing equipment with new technology. A lease contract is written for a specific period of time, after which the lessee must purchase the equipment, return it or renew the lease. High technology equipment more than likely will be returned to the lessor at the end of the lease term, because newer and better technology is then available; therefore, new equipment will be acquired upon lease termination. If the equipment had been purchased, however, no outside forces (i.e., a lease agreement) exist that would compel the company to replace its existing equipment. A manager's intent to replace equipment at a certain point easily could be side-tracked by a temporary corporate freeze on capital expenditures.

EXCESSIVE USE OF LEASED EQUIPMENT

Many lessees prefer leasing when they expect to overburden the equipment, which generally results in little, if any, residual value at the end of the lease term. They would rather lease, not own, a rapidly depreciating asset. This perceived benefit of leasing may be a misconception, however. The leasing company, no doubt, realizes that the lessee will excessively use the equipment and will price the excess wear and tear on the equipment into the lease structure accordingly.

PRIORITY DELIVERY

When a company realizes an immediate need for new equipment, delivery delays might cost it a great deal in terms of lost sales, customer goodwill and incremental profits. From time to time, a certain piece of equipment may be in such high demand that a long lead time is required between order and delivery of the equipment. Companies with a dire need will consider every conceivable means of shortening this market-established lead time. If the company has little clout with the manufacturer, it would be wise to contact a large leasing company, or one that specializes in that type of equipment and purchases regularly from the manufacturer. The leasing company may then be able to obtain a priority delivery of equipment by virtue of its relationship with the manufacturer. Leasing, therefore, may be the company's answer to a speedier delivery of equipment, thereby preserving potentially lost sales, profits and goodwill.

CONTROL OVER LESSOR-MANUFACTURER

A lessee may lease from the vendor leasing company of an equipment manufacturer so that if, for any reason, the equipment does not perform as it should, the lessee can withhold lease payments to the vendor lessor until the equipment is in working order. In other words, it feels that a vendor leasing company provides implicit warranties for the equipment being leased. This notion, from a legal perspective, is typically false. Even though the leasing company is related to the manufacturing parent, the parent normally provides, and is at-risk for, all warranty claims. Therefore, regardless of outstanding warranty claims, the lessee must still make regular lease payments to the vendor leasing company according to the lease agreement.

To the extent that a lessee ignores its legal responsibility to continue paying lease rentals during a warranty dispute with the manufacturer, the lessor generally will approach the manufacturing parent and try to resolve the dispute before aggressively seeking payment from the lessee. In this case, the lessee has de facto, but not necessarily de jure, control over the lessor. This de facto control causes the lessor to act as an arbitrator in settling warranty claims once lease payments have been withheld.

Economic Reasons

Many of the economic reasons for lessees to lease are discussed in this subsection.

DIVERSIFICATION OF FINANCING SOURCES

The US economy has seen several swings in the availability of conventional bank financing. Many businesses are acutely aware of the dangers of depending solely upon conventional sources of equipment financing. Diversification of financing sources makes good business sense whether credit is in short supply or not. It is important to note that federally chartered banks have, by regulatory law, built-in limits on the availability of loanable funds to any single customer.

ADDITIONAL SOURCE OF DEBT FINANCING

Adding to the rapid growth in the volume of leasing since the 1960s have been the continued capital needs for business expansion and modernization, combined with a limited availability of capital funds from the usual channels of equity issues and bond financings. Many economic factors have led to the drying up of conventional capital financing sources. Notable among them are (1) the use of loanable funds for government spending and consumer credit and (2) the shifting of equity investors away from the stock market to higher yielding investments in the money market, real estate, etc.

This dearth of conventional capital forced many companies to seek installment loans from banks for equipment financing. Yet banks, and other similar financial institutions, had been suffering from their own capital shortages during the same period and could not totally or effectively solve the problem. In order to sell their products, many manufacturing companies turned to leasing to make financing for their equipment available to those customers who otherwise could not obtain the use of the equipment. Thus, during periods of capital shortages stemming from numerous underlying economic factors, leasing's popularity was enhanced by its capacity to provide an additional source of funds not otherwise available.

During periods when bank financing is generally available, it is conceivable a business, due to credit concerns, etc., simply may fall out of favor with its primary, or only, bank, and not be able to borrow additional funds. Fortunately, leasing provides an additional source of financing that may be available to a specific company when conventional financing is not obtainable. Due to a lessor's knowledge of asset values, and access to secondary equipment markets, lessors are generally more willing than conventional lenders to take the value of the leased equipment into consideration when granting credit approval for a specific transaction.

LESS RESTRICTIVE FORM OF FINANCING

When lending to a company, a banker typically builds restrictive loan covenants into the loan agreement. The covenants are used by the bank to help minimize, or at least bring to its attention, any potential default on the loan by the borrower. Restrictive covenants typically include current ratio and debt-to-equity ratio limits, a minimum times-interest-earned ratio level and certain other minimum measures of profitability. The violation of any of the covenants flags potential default risk for the lender, who then has the option to demand repayment of the loan obligation.

Loan covenants, while attempting to minimize the lender's risk, oftentimes can be very restrictive. A company subject to numerous restrictive covenants is greatly reduced in its decision-making autonomy or independence. Some covenants state the company cannot incur any additional debt without the bank's prior approval.

Lease agreements rarely contain restrictive covenants. The lessor builds its perceived risk into the pricing of the lease by adjusting yield requirements, the amount of refundable security deposits, up-front fees or the number of advance rentals. Of course, the leasing company also considers the value of its collateral in the lease (the leased equipment), along with the viability of its repossession if the need should arise. Leasing can offer greater freedom or flexibility than a loan, as it does not tie up a company's future financing options through restrictive covenants.

ECONOMIES OF SCALE IN LESSOR PURCHASING AND SERVICING

Certain lease companies, due to their large size, can generate savings in the form of quantity discounts received from volume purchasing. Such savings might be partially passed on to the lessee. Additional savings from economies of scale might be obtained through the full-service lease, where the cost of maintaining the leased equipment is included as part of each rental payment. In this case, if the leasing company is able to procure low-cost maintenance because of its large size, savings can be passed on to the lessee. However, it does not always follow that large size and reduced cost go hand-in-hand. Therefore, savings must be ascertained by comparison with lease rates charged by competing companies.

In addition, large leasing companies have greater access to secondary markets in which returned equipment may be resold. A lessor's ability to quickly sell returned equipment for a high resale amount allows it to take a higher residual position for lease pricing purposes. This greater reliance on residual value permits the lessor to charge a lower lease payment to the lessee. Though large scale operations do not guarantee savings to lessees, at least they present the possibility of savings. With proper negotiation the lessee should be able to receive some of the savings of economies of scale in cases where the lessor is receiving such efficiency benefits.

LOWER COST

Not only does leasing provide the many advantages discussed so far, but, at times, it can be the less expensive method of acquiring the use of equipment. Typically, financial alternatives such as a lease versus a loan are compared on a present value, after-tax basis. The alternative with the lower cost, adjusted for the impact of taxes and the time value of money, would be selected. For a variety of reasons, leasing can be the less expensive form of financing in such a comparison. In order to properly make a determination as to whether a lease will cost less than an outright purchase of equipment, however, a formal analysis should be performed. The techniques used in the lease versus buy decision are the subject of Chapter Six.

The reasons for leasing's popularity — why 8 out of 10 companies lease today — have been presented in the preceding pages. From this, it can be seen that lessees lease for a variety of reasons. At times, a lessee leases to avoid the risks of technological obsolescence, to benefit from off balance sheet operating leases or to take advantage of the many flexible structuring options available in a lease.

The benefits of leasing to the lessee are numerous. Some of the reasons mentioned can be a single source of motivation for a company to lease. Other reasons may not single-handedly sway a corporation's financing decision toward leasing, but, when combined with the other technological considerations, financial reporting reasons, cash management considerations, income tax motivations, ownership aspects, flexibility and convenience factors and economic reasons, they can overwhelmingly support the case for leasing versus purchasing equipment.

LESSOR MOTIVATIONS TO PROVIDE LEASING SERVICES

Naturally, there are at lease two parties to any lease. Just as there are many reasons for lessees to lease, so also are there reasons for lessors to be in the leasing business. Understanding these reasons can be beneficial for all parties to the lease transaction.

Lessor Earnings and Profitability

Lessors provide leasing products and services to meet the various market-driven needs of the lessee. In so doing, the lessors' main objective is to assure reasonable profitability in each lease transaction they enter into.

A lessor realizes that each lease transaction is not without its associated risks. The lessor requires little, if any, up-front payments and typically charges lower lease payments throughout the lease term, based upon the expected realization of either tax benefits or residual value, or both. Due to these many risks a lessor's earnings and profitability are based upon a number of complex components. These many components and related opportunities, including income tax benefits, residual value and so forth, are discussed in the remainder of this chapter.

Income Tax Benefits

When leases have been structured in conformity with the various IRS criteria defining tax lease status, the lessor will be considered the tax owner of the leased equipment. As such, the lessor will be entitled to the numerous tax benefits of ownership. The primary benefits are: (1) depreciation, (2) refundable security deposits, (3) gross profit tax deferral, when the lessor is also a dealer in, or a manufacturer of the leased equipment, (4) Investment Tax Credits (ITC), which were generally eliminated by the Tax Reform Act of 1986, and (5) tax-exempt interest earnings in municipal leases to qualifying state, county and city governments.

Accelerated depreciation provides the lessor with a write-off of its equipment acquisition costs according to the MACRS guidelines. For example, the first and second year deductions for 5-year classlife equipment (computers, buses, certain manufacturing equipment) are 20% and 32%, respectively, of the equipment cost. Therefore, the lessor can write off over 50% of its equipment acquisition costs over a short 2-year period.

Refundable security deposits retained by a lessor do not enter the lessor's taxable income unless the deposits are nonrefundable, or if they are forfeited due to nonperformance on the lease obligation. Therefore, the lessor has the entire amount of the refundable security deposit available to use in generating additional income during the term of the lease.

Gross profit tax deferral provides manufacturer-lessors or dealer-lessors with a valuable tax benefit. Any gross profit in the overall transaction is deferred, and recognized over time. Since the taxes on the deferred gross profit in a tax lease will be recognized and paid over the MACRS classlife of the leased asset, there is a distinct tax saving, on a present value basis, to the parent manufacturer.

ITC has had significant value to lessors who have had sufficient tax appetite to utilize it. Tax credits, unlike tax deductions, represent dollar for dollar reductions in a lessor's tax liability. As an example, for a 34% tax bracketed lessor, a 10% ITC is worth the same as a 15.15% deduction (as a percent of the leased equipment's cost). However, the Tax Reform Act of 1986 eliminated ITC, subject to some complex transitional rules.

Tax-exempt interest earnings are available to lessors leasing to qualifying state, local and county governments. The lease agreement resembles a conditional sales contract in that it states an interest rate and provides for a nominal purchase option at lease termination. The lessor would not qualify for any tax benefits of ownership, such as depreciation, but would receive earnings that would be exempt from federal income taxes.

Financial Leverage Considerations

One of the more significant economic aspects of leasing is financial leverage. Contractually fixed lease rentals permit lessors to finance the acquisition cost of their leased equipment with large proportions of debt relative to equity. To the degree the debt costs less than the interest rate charged in the lease, the lessor can earn substantial returns on its equity. Use of significant amounts of financial leverage is commonplace in leasing due to the fixed, contractual nature of lease revenue, the availability of tax benefits, as well as the additional expectation of residual value.

Debt acquired by the lessor for use in purchasing the equipment to be leased can often be obtained on either a recourse or a nonrecourse basis. If a lessor borrows funds on a recourse basis, it must honor this obligation to the bank or lending institution whether or not the lessee defaults on the underlying lease. If the lessor borrows funds on a nonrecourse basis, however, and the lessee subsequently defaults on the lease, the lending institution cannot demand repayment from the lessor, but must seek recovery of any losses from the lessee or from the salvage of the leased equipment (collateral).

Lessors in large leveraged lease transactions generally are able to offer very favorable lease pricing to lessees. A lessor typically will borrow from 80 to 90% of the equipment cost, thus paying for only a fraction of the cost from its own funds, or equity. The lessor can afford to offer lower tax lease rates since it is receiving 100% of the tax benefits available to the lessor in the lease in exchange for payment upfront of a fraction (10 to 20%) of the equipment's cost.

Residual Speculation Motivations

The residual value of leased equipment can represent an important cash inflow to the lessor, and may be a significant part of the lessor's overall return in the lease. At the end of the lease term, assuming no purchase or renewal option has been exercised, the lessee returns the leased equipment to the lessor. The lessor then will re-lease or sell it for the highest possible amount. In order to offer competitive lease pricing, the lessor must factor some of this expected future value into the lease rates. For instance, if the lessor is confident the equipment will be worth at least 10% of its original value at lease termination, the lessor can price the lease payments so that it recovers 90% of the equipment cost. It is hoped the remaining 10% will be realized once the equipment is returned and subsequently salvaged or re-leased. Keep in mind that the amount of the residual used in the lessor's pricing is not the exact amount the lessor expects to receive at the end of the term, but, rather, the amount the lessor is willing to be at-risk for in the lease. The lessor must receive the at-risk residual amount in order to recover all of its costs and earn a pretargeted return.

Leasing companies are also motivated by the opportunity to earn higher than expected returns from the realization of residual values that exceed the values used in pricing their leases. Of course, the downside risk to leasing companies is that the residual value in a lease will be less than the amount assumed in the lease pricing. Lessors, however, are generally conservative in the residual value used in pricing, so that they are confident of earning at least the required residual value, if not more.

In a leveraged lease, the lessor's return comes from two primary sources, the tax benefits (as previously discussed) and the residual value of the equipment. Since the lease transaction is highly leveraged with nonrecourse borrowings, the lease payments will most likely go to the lending institution to cover the lessor's loan obligations. Therefore, the lessor's other sources of income — the residual value at lease termination and the tax benefits throughout the lease term — become even more crucial to its overall return in the leveraged lease transaction.

Vendor Leasing Issues

Since the inception of the US leasing industry, manufacturers of equipment have recognized that providing lease financing for their customers has helped them to realize many of their firms' objectives. Vendor leasing, whether provided by the manufacturer's captive finance company or by an independent lessor, is increasing in importance and value today.

Providing lease financing is a successful way for manufacturers to distinguish their product from their competitors'. Providing the equipment, as well as the financing, may entice a potential customer to choose a certain manufacturer's product due to the convenience offered.

The vendor not only has provided the customer with one-stop shopping, but also has been able to exert a form of market control — locking in the sale with financing so it will not be lost to a competitor as the customer searches for financing.

One aspect of market control for a vendor lessor that can result from providing one-stop shopping for its customers has already been mentioned. Another type of market control exists that is of equal importance. Since the vendor lessor is providing leasing services for the manufacturer, the manufacturer knows when its customer, the lessee, will be in need of a new piece of equipment (i.e., at the termination of the existing lease term). Therefore, the manufacturer can begin marketing a new piece of equipment to its current leasing customer, long before a competitor is aware a potential transaction exists.

Increased revenue and profitability can also accompany a vendor leasing program. Incremental sales of equipment may be made, as leasing can make equipment acquisition affordable for customers who could not purchase the equipment outright. Along the same lines, customers may be able, and willing, to lease more expensive models or additional accessories now that leasing has put these extras within their reach.

Manufacturers can also greatly benefit from the marketing synergy, as well as profitability, which exists in providing bundled services as a part of a full-service lease contract. The vendor lessor can further the concept of one-stop shopping by providing maintenance, insurance and paying property taxes for the lessee. The vendor lessor is at a real, or at least highly perceived, advantage in providing these services, since it is in some form related to the equipment manufacturer. The vendor lessor may be able to provide these services at a cost below what the lessee could separately procure them for, and, as a result, profit from these additional revenues.

Integration Opportunities

Integration refers to ways in which a company can expand operations. Vertical integration refers to acquisition of the means of producing a product from the raw material sources, through production and transportation, to the final wholesale and retail outlets. Horizontal integration refers to expansion into the sales and production of related products (like wax production for an oil company). Conglomerate integration is where a company enters into a wholly unrelated business venture.

Manufacturing firms, as discussed, use leasing as an additional way to sell goods. Establishing a vendor leasing program to further promote sales is an important step in vertically integrating a company. An additional advantage of such integration is that the leasing company can better serve the client due to its extensive knowledge of the product. For example, knowledge of the product permits the lessor to predict with greater accuracy residual values, which removes some risk from leasing. This enhanced knowledge of residual values may enable the vendor leasing company to fine tune the lease payment amount charged the lessee. Control over residuals also allows the vendor lessor to sell new equipment at the termination of the lease to a somewhat captive clientele.

Some vendor lease companies find leasing so profitable that they begin leasing equipment other than that manufactured by the parent company. This expansion into new, unrelated product leasing is a form of horizontal integration that is becoming popular among manufacturer-lessors.

Some other companies enter into the leasing business as a totally unrelated business opportunity in relation to their normal operations. New business ventures involved with leasing would represent a form of conglomerate integration. A utility acquiring a lease company would be an example of conglomerate integration. However, a bank acquiring a leasing company would be a form of horizontal integration since the leasing service is closely related to the bank's loan service.

Thus, the natural path of expansion from a vertically integrated manufacturing company beginning to lease others' products (horizontal integration), to other companies acquiring lease companies as new investment opportunities (conglomeration) has led to an increase in leasing's popularity.

International Leasing

Overseas leasing is expected to expand significantly in order to serve large multinational companies abroad as well as foreign companies who are also seeking new forms of asset financing. Although equipment leasing abroad by US companies started only 20 years ago, the amount of equipment on lease in Western Europe and other parts of the world has grown significantly. One of the reasons for the growing popularity of leasing as a form of financing new equipment abroad is that many foreign banks generally offer loans for about 3 years and equipment buyers are, therefore, required to negotiate two or three loans during the life of a particular piece of equipment.

As in the United States, all types of equipment are being leased abroad: tankers, railroad cars, computers, machine tools, printing presses, aircraft, restaurant equipment, mining equipment and drilling rigs. Since foreign tax laws differ from US tax laws, many international leases do not offer the same benefits of depreciation or the possibility of residual value gains.

Despite restrictive foreign government regulations concerning percent local ownership requirements, varying tax laws, foreign exchange fluctuations and export laws, many equipment leasing companies are still interested in the expanding leasing markets abroad. Many US based multinationals use leasing to promote foreign sales. In addition, there are numerous tax, import and investment tax credit benefits available to the experienced international lessor. In essence, the same reasons that led to an expansion of leasing in this country have also stimulated leasing abroad. Thus, international markets have created another factor leading to the popularity of leasing.

Tax Shelter Attributes

In years past, one important reason to lease for a segment of lessors was for tax shelter purposes. Notwithstanding the severe curtailment of such tax shelter practices by the Tax Reform Act of 1986, a market still exists for such tax shelter lease investments. (The tax shelter attributes of leasing will be further addressed in Chapter Four.) Lessors have always been quick to understand the equipment financing needs of lessees, and will continue to adapt their products and services to address those changing needs.

CONCLUSION

The dynamics of the leasing industry is not a topic to quickly dismiss as too elementary or straightforward. There are many important reasons or motivations to lease that exist for the two primary parties to the lease transaction. A full understanding of the dynamic forces that drive this multibillion dollar industry, therefore, is absolutely necessary for success today. Lessors who understand lessee needs are better positioned to offer lease products that will be acceptable to the lessee marketplace. In fact, it certainly would not be unreasonable to suggest that those lessors who more clearly understand lessee needs will sell more leases. Successful lessors will also continue to satisfy their main goal, that of greater earnings and profitability, through careful consideration of the many components of a lessor's return in a lease. By the same token, all involved in the industry (lessors, lessees, professionals, etc.) will be more effective in their future roles in this exciting industry if they have a solid feel for its dynamics.

Part 2
TAXATION

CHAPTER THREE
IRS QUALIFICATIONS OF A LEASE

Although there are many legal and tax risks and uncertainties encountered in the field of equipment leasing, no other issue is as controversial, or has as pervasive an effect as whether the transaction, even though characterized as a lease, is really a lease or whether it is in substance a sale. Since leasing made its dramatic appearance after World War II as an increasingly important component of our nation's economy, the Internal Revenue Service (IRS), the courts and even Congress have attempted, from time to time, to develop guidelines to be used by lessors and lessees in structuring their transactions to avoid this continuing controversy. Unfortunately, the guidelines have, in most cases, merely served to complicate the situation even more.

To a person not generally familiar with the ins and outs of this subset of academia's finance discipline, it is, of course, unclear why all of this concern occurs over what superficially appears to be such a simple and unimportant question. Hence, this chapter has a threefold focus:

- Definitions of a Lease
- Lease or Sale: Issues of Concern
- True Lease or Sale: Factors, Guidelines and Tests.

As discussed later, the federal income tax consequences to the parties are very significant. Therefore, the aforementioned focus will be primarily on the federal income tax law.

This chapter is not intended to be, and is not, a legal or tax treatise on the controversy of lease versus sale. Consequently, it is not a substitute for independent tax or legal advice. It is, however, an extensive overview of this multifaceted issue, which can and should be used by those persons involved directly, or peripherally, with initiating and structuring equipment leasing transactions.

DEFINITIONS OF A LEASE

In its simplest legal terms, a lease has four attributes. It is first an agreement between the owner of an asset (the lessor) and the prospective or current user of that asset (the lessee). Second, pursuant to the agreement, the lessor transfers the use (but not the ownership) of the asset to the lessee. Third, the lessee compensates the lessor for the use of the asset, usually in the form of rent. Finally, after the predetermined period of use (the lease term), which is less than the asset's economic life, the lessee returns the asset to the lessor.

From a different vantage point, a lease is (under current tax law) a tax advantaged installment loan with either a guaranteed or unguaranteed residual. Both this definition and the one from the paragraph above are correct and both contain a common element essential to the existence of a lease, i.e., residual value. As will be discussed later, an agreement whereby the lessor transfers to the lessee the use of an asset for its entire economic life is nothing more than a disguised sale.

To help determine exactly what a lease is, it is important to understand what a transaction, characterized as a lease, is if it is not a lease. In today's legal environment, an owner of an asset can transfer some or all of the benefits of that asset to another party in only three different ways — a lease, a sale or a service arrangement. A lease, for tax purposes commonly referred to as a true lease or a tax lease, is an agreement whereby the lessor (who is the owner of an asset) transfers the use (but not the ownership) of the asset to the lessee for consideration for a predetermined period and, whereby, for federal income tax purposes, the lessor is treated as the owner of the asset. The federal income tax criteria, of course, are the primary focus of this chapter and, therefore, will be discussed later in great detail. At this juncture, however, suffice it to say that a true lease is a lease meeting those criteria and encompasses several other types of leases, including a guideline lease, a tax-exempt lease and a terminal rental adjustment clause (TRAC) lease, all of which will also be discussed later in the chapter.

A sale, in its truest form, involves the transfer for consideration by the owner of an asset (the seller) to another party (the buyer) of all rights to the asset, including ownership and use. A seller generally has no continuing interest in or right to the asset. Three types of sales are common in today's marketplace. In a conditional sales contract (CSC), the seller sells the asset and transfers possession to the purchaser, but retains title to the asset until the purchaser has fully paid for it. A secured sale occurs when the seller transfers title to the asset to the purchaser at the point of sale, but where the purchaser grants to the seller a security interest in the asset to secure payment by the purchaser of the purchase price. Upon full payment by the purchaser, the seller releases the security interest. Finally, in an absolute sale, the seller transfers title to the asset to the purchaser and does not take back a security interest in the asset, irrespective of whether the purchase price is paid in full. In an absolute sale, if all of the purchase price is not paid at the time title is transferred, the seller relies solely on the purchaser's general financial ability to pay the purchase price.

The third legal method to transfer some or all of an asset's benefits to another party involves a service contract. A service contract exists where the service provider provides a service to the service recipient and where providing the service, e.g., copies or computer time, requires the use of a type of asset, but not any particular asset. This arrangement differs from a lease because, among other things, it is not dependent on the use of any particular asset. Similarly, a service arrangement differs from a sale for many reasons, one of them being that title to the asset necessary to provide the service is retained by the service provider. The only benefit transferred to the service recipient is the service, e.g., copies or computer time.

From the preceding discussion, one can immediately recognize that the essence of the relationship between two parties characterizing their transaction as a lease may be questionable. The agreement may in fact be a sale, or it could be a service contract. Unfortunately, there is no simple test that can be employed in every case to determine the substance of the agreement. In many instances the distinctions become blurred and uncertain. It is important, therefore, at the very least, to be able to ascertain if the issue of lease or sale arises and whether, in that particular case, it is important enough to resolve it.

LEASE OR SALE: ISSUES OF CONCERN

Simply stated, there are four very important reasons — each with myriad subsets — that the parties to a lease transaction should be concerned with, whether their transaction is a lease or whether it is, in reality, a sale: federal income tax consequences, financial reporting requirements, Uniform Commercial Code (UCC) ramifications and bankruptcy effects. Although this chapter deals primarily with the first reason, all of the reasons play an important role and, therefore, are mentioned. The financial reporting aspects, however, are covered in depth in Chapters Thirteen through Sixteen. The effects of the UCC and the Bankruptcy Reform Act are considered in much greater detail in Chapter Twenty.

Federal Income Tax Consequences

While it is true that the legal and tax infrastructure within which business transactions must be conducted has a pervasive influence on these transactions, business people are very adaptable creatures. They can learn to operate within any reasonable set of requirements and constraints if there is some modicum of predictability associated with the major components of the infrastructure. Unfortunately, that is not currently the case and has not been since the Reagan Administration has endeavored to adjust the economy by way of the tax laws on an almost annual basis. US federal income tax laws have a deep and far-reaching effect on every facet of the economy, as the laws traditionally have been used to accomplish innumerable and complex social and fiscal objectives. However, in the long run, the almost continuous change in those social and fiscal objectives (and therefore in the tax law enacted to achieve them) can only have a deleterious effective on business, and thus on the economy as a whole.

If, for federal income tax purposes, a transaction cast in the form of a lease is a true lease or a tax lease, the lessor is entitled not only to all tax benefits associated with the purchase and ownership of property, e.g., the Investment Tax Credit (ITC) and depreciation deductions, but also must recognize lease payments as income. Conversely, if the transaction is in reality a sale, the lessor recognizes income (generally ordinary) to the extent of the excess of the sales price over its basis in the leased property. The lease payments received from the lessee are classified as return of basis, interest income and gain. Because the property has been sold to the lessee, the lessor is not entitled to any tax benefits attendant to ownership.

If the transaction is a true lease, the lessee is entitled to deduct the full amount of the lease payments as ordinary and necessary business expenses. If, on the other hand, the transaction is a sale of the asset to the lessee, the lessee becomes the owner of the asset and, therefore, is entitled to any tax benefits attendant to ownership. In the event of sale status, the lease payments paid by the lessee are treated as payments on the purchase price and are classified as principal and interest.

The classification of the agreement is, therefore, very important because of the significance of the tax treatment on the yields associated with the transactions. Over the years, the lease market has become somewhat efficient in transferring the tax benefits of ownership to the parties most able to use them, thus enabling lessors to transfer some portion of the tax benefits to the lessees in the form of lower lease payments. This, of course, results in a lower effective cost of equipment to lessees, further resulting in greater profits and the ability to expand, thereby fueling the growth of the economy. If a lessor cannot be reasonably certain of its entitlement to the ownership tax benefits (whatever they are at the time), the cost of equipment to lessees is certain to rise. The importance of tax benefits to an equipment leasing transaction does not mean they are essential to the viability of the leasing industry, however. Obviously, the market mechanism of sharing tax benefits can exist only if tax benefits exist. Leasing is important to lessors and lessees for a number of additional reasons, as discussed in Chapter Two.

Financial Reporting Requirements

It is essential for all persons involved in leasing to recognize that the classification of a lease as a lease or as a sale also has important ramifications with respect to the way the transaction is reflected on the financial statements of the parties to the transaction. The criteria used to make that decision for tax purposes, however, are different (although conceptually similar) from those used for financial reporting purposes. Even the concomitant terminology is different.

As discussed in detail in Chapter Thirteen, a lease that is truly a lease is called an operating lease for accounting purposes. If the lease is an operating lease, the lessor's financial statements would reflect its ownership of the asset, showing a corresponding expense for depreciation and interest, if any. That treatment is similar to true lease treatment by the lessor under the tax law. In the case of an operating lease, the only direct effect on the lessee's financial statements is a periodic expense on the income statement for lease payments.

On the other hand, a lease that is really a sale is referred to as a capital lease. A capital lease must be capitalized by the lessee, i.e., it must be shown as an asset on the balance sheet of the lessee. In the case of a capital lease to the lessee, the lessee is treated for accounting purposes as the owner of the asset. Where the lease is a capital lease to the lessor, the lessor's books indicate that it has sold the asset. Therefore, this asset will not be found on the lessor's balance sheet but the sale will be reflected as a receivable. The lessor would report any gain or loss, if any, on the sale and would classify the lease payments as return of capital, interest and gain.

A very interesting yet confusing element of the accounting rules is that a lease will not necessarily be classified the same for both the lessor and lessee. In other words, it is distinctly possible (and in fact very likely) that a lessor will classify a lease as a capital lease and the lessee, in that very transaction, will properly treat the lease as an operating lease.

Uniform Commercial Code Ramifications

Forty-nine states (all except Louisiana) have adopted a set of laws governing a variety of business transactions including, among others, the sale of goods (personal, not real, property) and secured transactions. This set of laws is referred to as the UCC. Chapter Twenty delves into this area more fully. Suffice it to say at this point, however, that the rules developed under the UCC for determining whether a lease is in fact a lease or a sale are different (even though conceptually similar) from those existing under either the tax law or accounting standards.

Bankruptcy Effects

An unfortunate, but fairly common, occurrence in the equipment leasing environment is lessee bankruptcy. If that happens, what are the lessor's rights? The answer to that question depends, to a large extent, on whether the lease is really a lease or whether it is a sale. The standards used to decide the lease versus sale controversy in the context of bankruptcy are essentially the same as those developed under the UCC. The complexities of leasing and bankruptcy are discussed in Chapter Twenty in more detail.

TRUE LEASE OR SALE: FACTORS, GUIDELINES AND TESTS

The following discussion provides insight into the many factors considered in determining whether a transaction is a lease or a sale.

Statutory Basis

As is true with most questions arising under federal income tax law, the starting point for resolution of the issues is the Internal Revenue Code (IRC). The true lease versus sale controversy is no different. The IRC, which was enacted, and is frequently changed, by Congress contains two sections that together form the basis for the definition of a lease from a federal income tax viewpoint. IRC §167, which sets forth the first half of the standard, from the lessor's perspective, provides that:

> There shall be allowed as a depreciation deduction a reasonable allowance for the exhaustion and wear and tear (including a reasonable allowance for obsolescence) of property used in a trade or business or held for the production of income [IRC §167(a)].

Although IRC §167 does not explicitly define who is entitled to the depreciation deduction, court decisions over many years make it clear that only the "owner in substance" is so entitled, i.e., the person who has made a capital investment in the property and who is in a position to suffer an economic loss by reason of the wear and tear, decay, exhaustion or obsolescence of the property.

IRC §162, on the other hand, enumerates the second half of the standard, from the perspective of the lessee:

> There shall be allowed as a deduction all the ordinary and necessary expenses paid or incurred for the taxable year in carrying on any trade or business including . . . (3) rentals and other payments required to be made as a condition to the continued use or possession, for purposes of the trade or business, of property to which the taxpayer has not taken or is not taking title or in which he has no equity [IRC §162(a)].

IRC §162 and §167 establish the statutory basis for the true lease versus sale determination. Both the courts and the IRS have struggled over the years to elaborate on and expand that foundation in an effort to provide some meaningful guidance to taxpayers. Consequently, a series of general rules has been established. Unfortunately, however, the general rules have many exceptions, and, as might be expected, do not adequately address all of the intricacies of equipment leasing, many of which are the inherent result of the flexibility and change in this complex subset of finance.

Judicial Tests and Criteria

There are myriad cases that have addressed the issue of whether a transaction is a lease or a sale. Nonetheless (and in fact a result of the sheer number of such cases), the case law developing therefrom is by no means a paragon of clarity. However, broad concepts have been established within which most factual settings fall. Therefore, although some inconsistency exists when analyzing specific criteria — much of which is due in large part to the changes over time in the economic realities of and business practices found in the equipment leasing environment — the general principles are really quite clear and set forth a sufficient basis for resolving most cases. It should be emphasized at this point that the objective of analyzing what courts have done in the past, and why they have decided a particular way, is to provide a general knowledge base that can be utilized by leasing professionals to avoid encountering a true lease versus conditional sale problem. That can be accomplished, of course, only if the transaction is in the planning or structuring phase. The focus of this chapter, therefore, is on how to structure equipment leasing transactions to avoid, or at least mitigate, the true lease versus sale controversy.

BASIC JUDICIAL TESTS

Using the IRC as the basis for answering the true lease versus sale question, the courts have developed two broad tests to be applied to a specific factual setting. The first test arises in the context of a lessor's entitlement to depreciation of an asset. In that case, the basic test is whether the substance of the transaction is such that the lessor no longer has a sufficient connection with the property to constitute a depreciable interest therein. In other words, by virtue of the agreement characterized as a lease, has the lessor retained sufficient indicia of ownership such that the lessor is still in a position to suffer an economic loss by reason of the wear and tear, decay, exhaustion or obsolescence of the property? If not, the lessor has no right to depreciate the property because the lessor stands to lose nothing even if the property is lost or destroyed.

The second test ordinarily applies in the context of a lessee's entitlement to a deduction for lease payments made pursuant to what is ostensibly a lease transaction. In that case, the basic test is whether the substance of the transaction is such that the lessee will receive an equity in, or take title to, the property through the making of the payments denominated by the parties as rent. If either of those events occurs, the lease payment deduction generally will be denied because the lessee will be treated as having purchased the property.

JUDICIALLY ESTABLISHED CRITERIA

Because of the many cases that have been decided in this area of tax law, most of which have divergent factual scenarios, the courts have considered innumerable factors in their decision making processes. Many of those factors have precedential value, i.e., they may be used in subsequent cases of a similar nature. Many factors considered in a particular case, however, because of special facts peculiar to that case, have no general applicability. In addition, some of the factors deemed insignificant by courts change over time as business and economic conditions and practices evolve and develop. Typically, however, courts are reluctant to diverge from rules established in prior cases. Consequently, there is often a time lag between the changing practices and conditions of business and the courts' adaptation thereto.

The following criteria outlined here have been gleaned from several cases that have been decided over the past three decades. They by no means comprise a comprehensive list of the criteria that courts have deemed relevant in the true lease versus conditional sale analysis. However, they are certainly representative of the types of concerns addressed by courts in this context. It should be noted that, although there are times that one criterion will be conclusive in and of itself, more often than not all criteria taken together influence the courts' decisions one way or another. Later in this chapter, the relevance and significance of these criteria are ranked in order of relative importance to facilitate understanding. The judicially established true lease versus conditional sale criteria (in no particular order) are as follows:

1. Intent of the parties at the time of execution of the agreement
2. Whether title to the property automatically passes to the lessee upon its payment of the lease rentals
3. Whether the agreement provides that title will not pass to the lessee
4. Whether the lessor retains title during the lease term
5. Whether the lease is a net lease
6. Frequency that equipment is returned to the lessor at lease termination
7. Extent of the lessor's remarketing capabilities
8. Lease term compared to the useful life of the equipment
9. Industry practices
10. Nature of the lessor's business
11. Nature of the lessee's business
12. The extent to which the lessor keeps track of the leased equipment
13. Amount of minimum lease payments compared with original purchase price plus financing charges
14. Amount of the lease payments compared with the fair rental value of the equipment
15. Whether the lease payments are constant, increasing or decreasing
16. Existence of tax avoidance motives
17. Existence of dealer guarantees or repurchase agreements
18. Existence of a purchase option; analysis of the exercise price
    a. Side agreements: letters, oral understandings

    b.   Exercise price compared with the original purchase price of the equipment

    c.   Exercise price compared with total rents

    d.   Exercise price compared with the equipment's fair market value at the end of the lease term

    e.   Whether the lessee is economically compelled to exercise the purchase option

        1)   Lessee improvements to the property

        2)   Disruption of the lessee's business

    f.   Whether the lessee is able to exercise the purchase option

    g.   Whether some portion or all of the rent payments is credited toward the purchase option price

19. Whether the lease agreement contains an automatic renewal provision
20. Type of property that is the subject of the lease
21. Existence of lessor put or similar options
22. Extent, if any, of the lessor's equity investment
23. Whether the lease transaction is match funded
24. Whether the lease transaction has economic substance
25. Whether the taxpayer accounted for the transaction as a lease in its books and records.

The criteria are many and diverse. Each criterion is examined by a court before a decision is reached. A few of these criteria no longer are considered important by the courts by virtue of the changed practices in the equipment leasing industry, together with a better understanding by the courts of the economic realities of the leasing industry. Most of the criteria have current and general applicability. Some criteria have extreme significance and should be closely scrutinized in the planning stages of every transaction. Several of these are illustrated in the following discussion of landmark decisions.

LANDMARK DECISIONS

Although literally hundreds of cases have addressed the lease versus sale issue, there are five cases that clearly enunciate some of the most important principles discussed in the preceding sections. These cases, in chronological order, are summarized below.

In *Helvering vs. F & R Lazarus & Co.*, 308 U.S. 252 (1939), the Supreme Court held that the lessor's retention of title was not an absolute prerequisite to the lessor's entitlement to depreciation deductions. In that case, Lazarus & Co. entered into a loan arrangement with a bank where the form of the transaction was a sale by and leaseback to Lazarus. The Supreme Court analyzed the transaction from the perspective of a lessor, and determined that Lazarus was the party who stood to gain or lose from the exhaustion and wear and tear of the equipment, and who otherwise maintained the attributes and indicia of ownership. This case is important because it requires a court, when questioning the entitlement to depreciation deductions, to look beyond the form of the transaction. Consequently, from the perspective of entitlement to depreciation, who holds the title to the property is only a factor, and not necessarily a conclusive one, in the determination of who the owner is for federal income tax purposes.

Lockhart Leasing Co. vs. Commissioner, 446 F.2d 269 (1971), *aff'g* 54 T.C. 301 (1970), involved the disallowance by the IRS of investment credits taken by Lockhart that were generated in connection with Lockhart's equipment leasing activities. The IRS contended, among other things, that Lockhart was in the financing business, not the leasing business, and that the agreements between Lockhart and its customers, although cast in the form of leases, were in reality loans secured by the underlying equipment. The tax court held (which was affirmed on appeal) that Lockhart was the owner of the equipment for federal income tax purposes and, therefore, it was entitled to the depreciation deductions and investment credits. This case is important for two reasons. First, it recognizes that finance leasing is an alternative method of financing the acquisition of equipment, and is not the equivalent of a sale or a loan. Second, it confirms that the mere existence of a purchase option in a lease does not render that lease a sale for income tax purposes, nor does the fact that some transactions in a lessor's portfolio are sales taint the validity as true leases of the balance of the portfolio.

In *The LTV Corp. vs. Commissioner*, 63 T.C. 39 (1974), the IRS contested the validity of a lease transaction from the perspective of the lessee, and asserted that LTV, the lessee, was not entitled to deduct the lease payments made pursuant to a lease of IBM computer equipment entered into between LTV and an independent leasing company. The lease term was 5 years, was a standard net lease, provided step-down payments and contained a 10% purchase option. The court held the lease was a true lease for federal income tax purposes, and LTV was thus entitled to deduct the lease payments. The existence of the 10% purchase option, the reasonable estimate of the fair market value of the equipment at the expiration of the term of the lease, the fact that the lease was a standard net lease and the step-down payment structure did not result in LTV taking title to, or acquiring an equity in, the computer equipment.

Frank Lyon Co. vs. United States, 435 U.S. 561 (1978), involved the issue of entitlement to depreciation where Lyon entered into a complex sale-leaseback of a building with Worthen Bank. Worthen, which was prohibited by federal and state banking regulations from utilizing conventional financing methods regarding the construction of its new building, sold the building to Lyon for approximately $7,500,000 and then leased it back for 25 years. Lyon made a down payment of $500,000 and obtained the balance of the purchase price from a third-party lender. Worthen negotiated for a series of repurchase options that, if exercised, would have provided Lyon with a return of its down payment together with interest at the rate of 6%. The transaction was match funded, i.e, the lease payments exactly matched the loan payments, and the lease was a net lease. The IRS disallowed Lyon's depreciation deductions, contending that Lyon was not really the tax owner of the building.

The Supreme Court ruled in favor of Lyon, holding that the form of the transaction should be respected so long as the lessor retains significant and genuine attributes of a traditional lessor, and provided the transaction was motivated by a business purpose and could be supported by economic substance. This case is especially important because it almost establishes a presumption in favor of the taxpayers, as long as they can support the form of the transaction with a legitimate business purpose and if the transaction would be viable on its own without tax benefits.

Finally, in *Rice's Toyota World, Inc. vs. Commissioner*, 752 F.2d 89 (4th Cir. 1985), *aff'g* 81 T.C. 184 (1983), the IRS disallowed the depreciation deductions taken by Rice's Toyota in connection with a complex computer leasing transaction referred to as a wrap lease. The facts in that case were extremely unfavorable to Rice's Toyota (see Chapter Five for a detailed discussion of wrap leases). It was clear from even a cursory review of the economics of the transaction that Rice's Toyota had entered into the transaction solely for tax benefits. With even very optimistic assumptions regarding the value of the computer equipment at the expiration of the wrap lease, the transaction would not have been viable without tax benefits.

The Rice's Toyota case is important because it applies the business purpose/economic substance tests mandated by the Supreme Court in the Frank Lyon case to the area of computer leasing. It also emphasizes the need for passive investors in tax shelter transactions to conduct a reasonable amount of due diligence with respect to the economics of the transaction.

There have been a number of other cases since the Rice's Toyota case, many of which have been decided in favor of the taxpayer. In those cases, however, although tax benefits played a material role in the taxpayers' decisions to enter into the leasing transactions, they were not the only reason.

IRS Tests and Criteria

Our democratic form of government operates under a system of checks and balances. The most significant check and balance occurs as a result of the respective duties of the three branches of our government. The legislative branch (Congress) enacts the laws; the executive branch (the President and administrative agencies) implements and enforces the laws; and the judicial branch (the courts) interprets the laws. In the context of federal income taxation, the IRS is the administrative agency that enforces the tax law.

As part of its enforcement and implementation process, the IRS issues primarily four different types of guidance to help taxpayers comply with the law, i.e., regulations, revenue rulings, revenue procedures and letter rulings. Although it is the primary domain of the courts to interpret the laws enacted by Congress, because Congress is generally unable to consider every aspect of the tax laws it enacts, the IRS is burdened with the responsibility of completing the myriad details left either untouched or ambiguous by Congress. In that regard, the IRS issues regulations, which explain and expound upon the law, and which are binding on both the taxpayer and the IRS unless they are determined by a court to be contrary to the Congressional intent existing at the time the law was enacted.

The IRS issues revenue rulings in response to specific taxpayer requests. A revenue ruling sets forth the position of the IRS with respect to a particular set of actual facts submitted to it by a taxpayer. The taxpayer to whom the revenue ruling is issued can rely on it in consummating and reporting the applicable transaction. In other words, once the IRS has issued the ruling, so long as the transaction occurs the way it was represented by the taxpayer, the IRS cannot reverse its position as stated to the taxpayer in the revenue ruling. In addition, unlike private letter rulings discussed below, revenue rulings generally have precedential value, i.e., taxpayers in general can rely on the position taken by the IRS in the ruling.

Private letter rulings, on the other hand, although they set forth the position of the IRS with respect to a particular set of actual facts submitted to it by the taxpayer, have no precedential value, i.e., they may be relied on only by the taxpayers to whom they are issued.

A revenue procedure is an IRS pronouncement of the way in which taxpayers are to interact with the IRS. In other words, revenue procedures establish the steps that must be taken by a taxpayer with respect to a particular matter in order for the IRS to respond to the taxpayer. For example, Revenue Procedure (Rev. Proc.) 75-21, 1975-1 C.B. 715, enunciates the requirements with which taxpayers must comply in order to obtain from the IRS an advance ruling on the issue of whether a prospective transaction constitutes a lease for federal income tax purposes.

REVENUE PROCEDURE 75-21, 1975-1 C.B. 715

Although leveraged leasing has been a method of financing the acquisition of capital for several decades, its utilization began increasing at a geometric rate in the late sixties and early seventies. Not a mere coincidence, this increase was in part the result of the tremendous technological advancements that were occurring in the computer field, among others. The flourishing use of that financing method was also tied to the availability of significant tax benefits, e.g., ITC and accelerated depreciation to the tax owner of the asset. The combination of the increasing popularity of leveraged leasing and the significance of the tax benefits attendant to that structure prompted the IRS to issue Rev. Proc. 75-21. In order to obtain an advance ruling from the IRS as to whether the IRS considers a lease in a leveraged lease transaction to be a true lease for federal income tax purposes, the lease must comply with the requirements of that revenue procedure. For purposes of the revenue procedure, a leveraged lease is generally a lease (a) involving three parties: the lessor, the lessee and the lender; (b) in which the responsibilities of maintenance, insurance and taxes (not including the lessor's income taxes) rest with the lessee, i.e., a net lease; (c) the term of which covers a substantial part of the property's useful life; and (d) with respect to which the lease payments are sufficient to discharge the lessor's nonrecourse loan payments to the lender.

It is important at this juncture to recognize the scanty definition of a leveraged lease set forth in Rev. Proc. 75-21 is not the same definition of a leveraged lease used for financial reporting purposes. Please refer to Chapter Sixteen for the Financial Accounting Standards Board Statement No. 13 (FASB 13) definition of a leveraged lease. In addition, what the leasing industry considers to be a leveraged lease may or may not be a leveraged lease for purposes of Rev. Proc. 75-21. From an industry perspective, a leveraged lease is simply one in which the lease payments due by the lessee fully amortize the nonrecourse loan obtained by the lessor from a third-party lender. It is not necessary that the lease term cover "a substantial part of the property's useful life," as suggested in the revenue procedure, although most leveraged leases in the marketplace do so.

The revenue procedure contains six requirements with which a taxpayer must comply before the IRS will issue an advance ruling. Compliance with these requirements does not absolutely ensure true lease status but, as a practical matter, compliance (even without a ruling request) provides virtually complete protection against an IRS argument on the issue. Both the courts and the marketplace in general, however, do not suggest that compliance with these requirements is necessary to have a true lease for tax purposes. In fact, the Rev. Proc. 75-21 guidelines are much more restrictive than the standards and criteria established by the courts. In addition, the revenue procedure itself states the guidelines are not intended to be used by revenue agents for audit purposes, implying the advance ruling requirements are more conservative than what the tax law requires.

The Requirements

To obtain the advance ruling, the following six requirements must be complied with:

1. The lessor must have a 20% minimum at-risk investment in the property at the inception, during and at the end of the lease term
2. The exercise price of any lessee purchase option must not be less than fair market value
3. The lessee may not make an investment in the lease, nor can it lend to the lessor any purchase money or guarantee any lessor loans
4. The value of the property at the end of the lease term must be equal to at least 20% of the property's original cost, and the useful life of the property at the end of the lease term must be at least equal to the greater of (a) one year or (b) 20% of the originally estimated useful life
5. The lessor must have positive cash flow and a profit from the transaction independent of tax benefits
6. A lease with step-up or step-down payments must fall within certain guidelines.

The 20% minimum unconditional at-risk investment. As indicated, the lessor must have made a "minimum unconditional 'at-risk' investment in the property (the 'Minimum Investment') when the lease begins, must maintain such Minimum Investment throughout the entire lease term, and such Minimum Investment must remain at the end of the lease term" [Rev. Proc. 75-21, Sec. 4 (1)]. The purpose of this requirement appears to be to ensure the lessor has and maintains a significant depreciable interest in the property. The revenue procedure further provides:

> The Minimum Investment must be an equity investment (the 'Equity Investment') which, for purposes of this Revenue Procedure, includes only consideration paid and personal liability incurred by the lessor to purchase the property. The net worth of the lessor must be sufficient to satisfy any such personal liability [Rev. Proc. 75-21, Sec. 4.(1)].

The greater the level of Equity Investment, the more of an interest the lessor has in the property.

The revenue procedure analyzes the Minimum Investment at three different times: at the inception of the lease (the Initial Minimum Investment), during the term of the lease (the Maintenance of the Minimum Investment) and at the end of the lease term (the Residual Investment).

To satisfy the Initial Minimum Investment requirement, the Minimum Investment must be equal to at least 20% of the cost of the property when the property is first placed in service or use by the lessee [Ibid. at (1)(A)]. Although it is not directly prohibited by that language, it certainly appears that the placed-in-service requirement precludes a sale-leaseback.

In addition, the Minimum Investment must be unconditional. In other words, after the property is first placed in service or use by the lessee, the lessor cannot be entitled to a return of any portion of the Minimum Investment through any arrangement with the lessee, any shareholder of the lessee or any party related to the lessee (collectively, the Lessee Group). Compensation to the lessor from other than the Lessee Group, however, is permissible if the property fails to satisfy written specifications for the supply, construction or manufacture of the property [Ibid.].

In order to comply with the Maintenance of the Minimum Investment requirements, the Minimum Investment must remain equal to at least 20% of the cost of the property at all times throughout the entire lease term. In other words, the net cash flow to the lessor during the lease term cannot result in a return to the lessor that has the effect of reducing the Initial Minimum Investment below 20%. To ensure that the Minimum Investment is maintained, the revenue procedure contains the following textual formula:

> . . . the excess of the cumulative payments required to have been paid by the lessee to or for the lessor over the cumulative disbursements required to have been paid by or for the lessor in connection with the ownership of the property must never exceed the sum of (i) any excess of the lessor's initial Equity Investment over 20 percent of the cost of the property plus (ii) the cumulative pro rata portion of the projected profit from the transaction (exclusive of tax benefits) [Rev. Proc. 75-21, Sec. 4.(1)(B)].

The projected profit from the transaction is determined in accordance with a similar textual formula:

> . . . the aggregate amount required to be paid by the lessee to or for the lessor over the lease term plus the value of the residual investment . . . exceed an amount equal to the sum of the aggregate disbursements required to be paid by or for the lessor in connection with the ownership of the property and the lessor's Equity Investment in the property, including any direct costs to finance the Equity Investment . . . [Ibid. at Sec. 4.(6)].

To illustrate, assume that a lessor agreed to lease to a lessee for 5 years equipment constituting 5-year recovery property. Assume further that the lease was a net lease and that the required lease payments were $23,261 annually in advance for 5 years. The lessor's cost was $100,000 and the residual value at the end of the lease term was reasonably estimated to be $20,000. The lessor purchased the equipment from the manufacturer using $25,000 of its own funds and obtaining a nonrecourse loan in the principal amount of $75,000, with an interest rate of 12.5%, payable in five equal annual installments in advance. To determine whether the lessor maintained at least a 20% Minimum Investment in the equipment, the lessor must apply the above stated formula. That formula, restated in a simplified fashion, is as follows:

[a] Cumulative cash inflow from lessee minus [b] cumulative cash outflow of lessor, must be less than or equal to [c] initial equity over 20% plus [d] cumulative pro rata profit.

The profit formula, similarly restated in a simplified form, is as follows:

$$\text{Profit} = (\text{lease payments} + \text{value of residual})$$
$$\text{less}$$
$$(\text{loan payments} + \text{equity investment}).$$

Application of the Maintenance of Minimum Investment test, which is applied on a cumulative basis, is set forth in Table 1.

With respect to the Residual Investment, the lessor must comply with two requirements. First, it must show that an amount equal to 20% of the original cost of the property is a reasonable estimate of what the fair market value of the property will be at the end of the lease term. In that regard, fair market value must be determined (i) without including in such value any increase or decrease for inflation or deflation during the lease term, and (ii) after subtracting from such value any cost to the lessor for removal and delivery of possession of the property to the lessor at the end of the lease term. Second, it must show that a remaining useful life of (i) the

Table 1

Illustration of Maintaining 20% Minimum
Unconditional At-Risk Investment

Cash Flow Item	Years				
	1	2	3	4	5
Equity investment	($25,000)	$ 0	$ 0	$ 0	$ 0
Loan payments	(18,724)	(18,724)	(18,724)	(18,724)	(18,724)
Lease payments	23,361	23,361	23,361	23,361	23,361
Residual	0	0	0	0	20,000
Net cash flow	($20,363)	$ 4,637	$ 4,637	$ 4,637	$24,637

Year 1 Test: $a - b \leq c + d$
$$\$23,361 - \$18,724 \leq \$5,000 + \$3,637$$
$$\$4,637 \leq \$8,637 \text{ (test satisfied)}$$

Year 2 Test: $a - b \leq c + d$
$$\$46,722 - \$37,448 \leq \$5,000 + \$7,274$$
$$\$9,274 \leq \$12,274 \text{ (test satisfied)}$$

Year 3 Test: $a - b \leq c + d$
$$\$70,083 - \$56,172 \leq \$5,000 + \$10,911$$
$$\$13,911 \leq \$15,911 \text{ (test satisfied)}$$

Year 4 Test: $a - b \leq c + d$
$$\$93,444 - \$74,896 \leq \$5,000 + \$14,548$$
$$\$18,548 \leq \$19,548 \text{ (test satisfied)}$$

Year 5 Test: $a - b \leq c + d$
$$\$116,805 - \$93,620 \leq \$5,000 + \$18,185$$
$$\$23,185 \leq \$23,185 \text{ (test satisfied)}$$

longer of 1 year, or (ii) 20% of the originally estimated useful life of the property is a reasonable estimate of what the remaining useful life of the property will be at the end of the lease term.

Lessee purchase options. In order to ensure that the lessee is not obtaining an equity interest in the property, and that the lessor is retaining a significant depreciable interest in the property, Section 4.(3) of the revenue procedure establishes a dual requirement. First, no member of the Lessee Group may have a contractual right to purchase the property from the lessor at a price less than fair market value at the time the right is exercised. Although the fair market value standard is clearly established, it is not unequivocally clear when fair market value must be determined, whether it can be reasonably estimated at the inception of the lease or whether it must be determined at the expiration of the lease term. The language seems to support the latter, although the general non-Rev. Proc. 75-21 position is that reasonable estimates of fair market value at lease inception are permissible.

Second, when the property is first placed in service by the lessee, the lessor must not have a contractual right, or have the intention to acquire such a right, to cause any party to purchase the property (except that a manufacturer or vendor repurchase agreement triggered in the event of the property's failure to meet written specifications for the supply, construction or manufacture of the property is apparently permitted). A lessor right of abandonment is tantamount to a contractual right to require a party to purchase the property.

No investment by the lessee. In general, no part of the cost of the property or of improvements, modifications or additions to the property (improvements) may be furnished by any member of the Lessee Group. This "no lessee investment" requirement is intended to ensure that the lessee is not taking, or has not taken, title to the property, and is not acquiring an equity in the property. For purposes of this rule, where the lease agreement requires the lessee to maintain and repair the property during the lease term, ordinary repairs and maintenance by a member of the Lessee Group will not constitute an improvement.

A lessee, however, generally may furnish some portion or all of the cost of a severable improvement, i.e., an improvement that is readily removable without causing material damage to the leased property, and that is not required to render the leased property complete for its intended use by the lessee. In addition, if certain conditions are met, a lessee may furnish the cost of a nonseverable improvement, i.e., an improvement that is not readily removable without causing material damage to the leased property [Rev. Proc. 75-21 Sec. 4(4).03].

No lessee loans or guarantees. To ensure that the lessee has not even a semblance of an ownership interest in the leased property, no member of the Lessee Group may lend to the lessor any of the funds necessary to acquire the property, or guarantee any indebtedness created in connection with the acquisition of the property by the lessor. This requirement would seem to eliminate sale-leaseback transactions (which include wrap leases) from the transactions with respect to which the IRS will issue an advance ruling on the true lease question.

Fortunately, however, a guarantee by any member of the Lessee Group of the lessee's obligations under the lease (including the obligation to pay rent) does not constitute the guarantee of the indebtedness of the lessor [Ibid. at Sec. 4.(5)]. Similarly, the assignment to a lender in return for a nonrecourse loan from the lender to the lessor, secured by the lease and the leased property, apparently does not violate the "no lessee loans or guarantees" requirement.

Although that position is somewhat inconsistent with the concept of the requirement, it validates the way leveraged leases are typically structured.

Profit and cash flow requirement. As stated in the discussion regarding Maintenance of Minimum Investment, the lessor must represent and demonstrate that it expects to receive a profit from the transaction, completely independent of tax benefits. This is a widely accepted standard generally employed by the IRS and the courts to invalidate business transactions entered into solely for tax avoidance motives. In the leasing context, this test is generally referred to as the economic substance test.

In addition to the profit requirement, although only articulated in the textual profit formula, the lessor must also show that it expects to receive a positive cash flow from the transaction during the lease term (thereby excluding the positive cash inflow effect of the realization of the residual value of the equipment at the end of the lease term). Although many of the revenue procedure's requirements are stringent and conservative, the cash flow test is the one most inconsistent with industry practice. As explained above, most leveraged lease are match funded, i.e., the loan is fully amortized by the lease payments, such that the periodic (generally monthly) loan payments are exactly equal to the periodic lease payments. The cash flow aspect of the formula is as follows:

> . . . the aggregate amounts required to be paid to or for the lessor over the lease term exceed by a reasonable amount the aggregate disbursements required to be paid by or for the lessor (excluding the lessor's initial Equity Investment, but including any direct costs incurred by the lessor to finance the Equity Investment) in connection with the ownership of the leased property [Rev. Proc. 75-21 Sec. 4.(6)].

The uneven rent test. If the lease provides for other than equal payments over the lease term, the issue of prepaid or deferred rent arises. In the case of uneven rent, if such payments do not fall within either of two guidelines, the lessor must request a ruling as to whether any portion of the uneven rent constitutes prepaid or deferred rent. The IRS concern is the timing of (i) the lessor's recognition of lease revenue for tax purposes, irrespective of receipt, and (ii) the lessee's deductibility of lease payments, irrespective of payment. At the time Rev. Proc. 75-21 was pronounced, it was a relatively simple and commonplace endeavor to structure lease transactions to reduce the overall payment of income taxes, by, for example, providing for step-down lease payments (higher payments in the first part of the term and lower payments thereafter) where the lessee was a high tax bracket cash basis taxpayer and the lessor was a lower bracket accrual basis taxpayer. Under current tax law, as the result of the uneven rent limitations imposed by IRC §467, enacted under the Tax Reform Act of 1984, as well as other tax deferral limitations recently enacted, the prepaid/deferred rent game is much less common.

The uneven rent guidelines of the revenue procedure are as follows:

1. The annual rent for any year cannot be more than 10% above or below the amount calculated by dividing the total rent payable over the lease term by the number of years in such term; or

2. The annual rent for any year during the first two-thirds of the lease term is not more than

10% above or below the amount calculated by dividing the total rent payable over such initial portion of the lease term by the number of years in such initial portion of the lease term, and the annual rent for any year during the remainder of the lease term is no greater than the highest annual rent for any year during the initial portion of the lease term and no less than one-half of the average annual rent during such initial portion of the lease term.

To recap, uneven rent payments that may result in prepaid or deferred rent ordinarily will not be questioned by the IRS if the annual rent for any year (i) is not more than 10% above or below the average annual rent, i.e., total rent payable over the lease term divided by the number of years in such term, or (ii) during at least the first two-thirds of the lease term, is not more than 10% above or below the average annual rent payments during the first two-thirds and the annual rent for any year during the remainder of the lease term is no greater than the highest annual rent for any year during the first two-thirds of the lease term and no less than one-half of the average annual rent during the first two-thirds. Application of the two guidelines can be illustrated by the following example:

Taxpayer leases equipment according to the following payment schedule:

Months	Payment	Total Payment
1-18	$1,800	$ 32,400
19-42	2,000	48,000
43-60	2,200	39,600
		$ 120,000

This payment schedule will not result in an uneven rent determination by the IRS because the payments in any one year are not more than 10% above or below the average annual rental, as shown in Table 2.

Limited use property. At the time of issuance by the IRS of Rev. Proc. 75-21, the IRS had not yet decided whether it would issue advance rulings involving limited use property, i.e., property expected not to be useful or usable by the lessor at the end of the lease term except for purposes of continued leasing to the lessee or transfer to any member of the Lessee Group. In Rev. Proc. 76-30, 1976-2 C.B. 647, the IRS announced that it would not issue an advance ruling under Rev. Proc. 75-21 where the leased property was limited use property. The later revenue procedure stated that:

> . . . in the case of limited use property, at the end of the lease term[,] there will probably be no potential lessees or buyers other than members of the Lessee Group. As a result, the lessor of limited use property will probably sell or rent the property to a member of the Lessee Group, thus enabling the Lessee Group to enjoy the benefits of the use or ownership of the property for substantially its entire useful life [Rev. Proc. 76-30, Sec. 3].

Although the leasing of limited use property, in and of itself, does not result in the transaction being recharacterized as a sale under federal income tax law, the IRS position in Rev. Proc. 76-30 is consistent with the balance of the conservatism contained in Rev. Proc. 75-21.

Table 2
Uneven Rent Test

| Average Annual Rental | | $24,000 ($120,000 ÷ 5) | |
Year	Annual Rent	+ 10%	− 10%
1	$21,600	$26,400	$21,600
2	22,800	26,400	21,600
3	24,000	26,400	21,600
4	25,200	26,400	21,600
5	26,400	26,400	21,600

REVENUE RULING 55-540, 1955-C.B.

Leasing began to take hold in the United States after World War II, although leveraged leasing did not begin to flourish until the mid-sixties. Because leasing did start to become popular after the war, however, the IRS was often faced with the task of analyzing whether a particular transaction, although denominated by the parties as a lease, was in fact a lease for tax purposes. In response to the increasing use of leasing to finance equipment, the IRS set forth some general guidelines to distinguish a lease from a sale in Revenue Ruling 55-540 (Rev. Rul. 55-540). Although far from definitive, the guidance contained in that ruling did provide some insight into the IRS approach to the issue, and contained a fair recap of prior case law on the issue. For 20 years (from 1955 to 1975, when Rev. Proc. 75-21 was issued), Rev. Rul. 55-540 was the most significant and comprehensive statement from the IRS that addressed the lease/sale question.

The revenue ruling approached the analysis from the viewpoint of the lessee, i.e., whether the lessee was entitled to a deduction for rent payments. Tracking the language of IRC §162, the ruling initially stated that "it is necessary to determine whether by virtue of the agreement the lessee has acquired or will acquire title to or an equity in the property."

After repeating the rhetoric contained in many cases about the relevance of the intent of the parties, and that no general rule could be laid down, the IRS stated that:

> . . . in the absence of compelling persuasive factors of contrary implication, an interest warranting treatment of a transaction for tax purposes as a purchase and sale rather than as a lease or rental agreement may in general be said to exist if, for example, one or more of the following conditions are present:
>
> (a) Portions of the periodic payments are made specifically applicable to an equity to be acquired by the lessee.
>
> (b) The lessee will acquire title upon the payment of a stated amount of rentals which under the contract he is required to make.
>
> (c) The total amount which the lessee is required to pay for a relatively short period of use constitutes an inordinately large proportion of the total sum required to be paid to secure the transfer of the title.

(d) The agreed rental payments materially exceed the current fair rental value. This may be indicative that the payments include an element other than compensation for the use of property.

(e) The property may be acquired under a purchase option at a price which is nominal in relation to the value of the property at the time when the option may be exercised, as determined at the time of entering into the original agreement, or which is a relatively small amount when compared with the total payments which are required to be made.

(f) Some portion of the periodic payments is specifically designated as interest or is otherwise readily recognizable as the equivalent of interest [Rev. Rul. 55-540 Sec. 4.].

The standards set forth in subsections (a) and (b) are derived directly from IRC §162, which proscribes the lessee's acquisition of title to or an equity in the property. The standards enumerated in subsections (d) and (e) are attempts to preclude the building of equity by the lessee during the lease term. Subsection (f) is an attempt to properly characterize a transaction that truly is, and was in all likelihood intended by the parties to be, a loan. Subsection (c) sets forth a total consideration test: if the lease payments are substantially equal to the payments that would have been required had the lessee purchased the equipment, then the transaction should be characterized as a purchase. Although the ruling provides a reasonably concise summary of the standards established by the case law, it did not add anything new and, in fact, perpetuated some of the erroneous tests and criteria established by the courts.

Application of the Judicial and Administrative Factors

From a quick review of the case law and the IRS pronouncements, it becomes clear there are only a few hard and fast rules applicable in the true lease versus sale controversy. Those rules are derived from the statutes: §162 (from the lessee's perspective) and §167 (from the lessor's viewpoint). In fact, upon very close scrutiny, it becomes evident that only §162 contains an ostensibly black and white test: did the lessee acquire title to, or is it acquiring title to, or an equity in the property through the payments denominated as rent? Even that test occasionally can have some definite shades of gray. The depreciable interest test of §167 merely begs the question.

Of all the factors considered by the courts and the IRS, there are four, upon examination, that appear to be of utmost importance. They rise to that level of importance either because they determine the essence of a leasing transaction, or because they have been elevated by Congress or the Supreme Court to that level. Those factors are as follows:

1. Whether title to the property has passed or will pass to the lessee for no consideration beyond the required lease payments

2. Whether the agreement contains bargain purchase and/or renewal options

3. Whether the lease term is substantially equivalent to the useful life of the asset

4. Whether the transaction has economic substance.

The reason for the first factor is obvious. IRC §162 prohibits passage of title upon the payment of the lease payments. If title does pass, with no additional consideration from the lessee, Congress has concluded that the lessee cannot deduct the lease payments. Therefore, the transaction is not a lease for federal income tax purposes. If the lessee does not have a leasehold interest, it would seem to have an ownership interest for federal income tax purposes.

The second factor also derives its relevance from IRC §162 and it is critical to the tax and theoretical ownership of, and thus the extent of the lessor's depreciable interest in, the property. IRC §162 provides, among other things, that lease payments are nondeductible if the lessee acquires title to or an equity in the asset upon the payment of the rentals. If the lessee is able to purchase the asset or use it at less than its fair market or fair rental value, then arguably the lessee has acquired an equity in the property during the original lease term.

From a theoretical and nontax perspective, the lease versus sale test (has the lessor retained a significant residual interest in the leased asset?) has two prongs: first, at the end of the lease term, does the property have any significant value? Second, if it does, does that value inure, at least primarily, to the benefit of the lessor? If the answer to the first prong of the test is no, then the transaction is not a lease, because the lessor has retained nothing — all of the value of the asset has been transferred to and used by the lessee, even though legal title may have been retained by the lessor. If, however, the first prong of the test is answered in the affirmative, the second prong must be addressed. If the value at the end of the lease term, although significant, does not inure to the benefit of the lessor, then again the lessor has not retained the residual interest in the asset. In many instances, the vehicle used by parties to a lease agreement to transfer the residual value from the lessor to the lessee is either a fair market value purchase option or a fair rental value renewal option, thereby establishing the relevance from a theoretical perspective of the second of the four factors.

The third factor also has its roots in the essence of a lease analysis. If the lease term is substantially equivalent to the asset's useful (economic) life, then the lessor has not retained a significant residual interest in the asset. Where, pursuant to the initial lease term, the lessee has used the asset for substantially its economic life, the lessee should be treated as having purchased the asset.

Conversely, the fourth factor is entirely tax related. The Supreme Court (and several lower courts) has consistently held that a transaction cannot be entered into solely for tax avoidance motives; there must be a legitimate business purpose. Therefore, if the lessor cannot reasonably expect to realize a profit in the transaction completely independent of tax benefits, the form of the transaction will be collapsed. In other words, the lessor will not be treated as the owner of the asset for federal income tax purposes and, consequently, will not be entitled to the tax benefits that normally attend ownership, e.g., depreciation and credits. Now, although it does not necessarily follow that simply because the lessor may have entered into the transaction solely for tax avoidance motives, and thus is not treated as the owner of the asset for tax purposes, the lessee should be treated as the asset's owner; that result is much greater than a remote possibility. It is logical to suggest that someone must be the owner of the asset. If it is not the lessor, then it must be the lessee. This, however, may not always be the case. Because the economic substance test is entirely tax related, to achieve certain social objectives a business purpose must exist in all transactions. If not, the normal tax benefits (to the party who entered into the lease without a proper purpose) can simply be denied, without having any effect whatsoever on the other party to the transaction.

Although, as previously mentioned, there are only four factors that rise to the superior level of utmost importance, there are two other factors that are close behind, not because they are analytically sound but, rather, because they have their roots in the two applicable IRC sections, and are used to help determine whether the statute is being violated or complied with. The fifth factor is the relationship between fair rental value and the lease payment. The more the lease payment exceeds fair rental value, the more it looks as if the lessee is building equity in the property. Otherwise, why would the lessee be paying more than required in the marketplace? The theoretical and practical problem with that factor is that, in and of itself, the payment of an amount in excess of fair rental value cannot create an equity in the asset for the lessee. Any equity can be realized only by the lessee through below market purchase or renewal options. Therefore, unless excess lease payments are coupled with a transfer of title (which itself violates §162) or bargain purchase and/or renewal options, the only effect is that the lessee, by definition, paid too much for the use of the equipment, and the lessor made a disproportionate amount of profit! Nevertheless, the courts and the IRS continually focus on this factor.

Finally, because of the desire to ensure that the lessor has a depreciable interest in the asset, i.e, that the lessor retains the residual risk (and benefit), the IRS (and the courts to a lesser degree) focuses on the amount the lessor has at-risk in the transaction. The at-risk analysis in this context has nothing to do with loss deductibility or eligibility for the investment credit. The at-risk requirement in the true lease/conditional sale controversy approaches the "retention of a significant residual interest" test from the opposite direction. Rather than looking at the end of the lease term, the at-risk requirement attempts to ensure that the lessor truly has something to lose if the residual value is not realized by imposing a lease inception equity investment on the lessor. As the result largely of the 20% test of Rev. Proc. 75-21 previously discussed, even otherwise knowledgeable practitioners and commentators seem to believe that, in order to maintain true lease status for federal income tax purposes, it is essential to comply with the revenue procedure's 20% at-risk test. That is simply not true. The dynamics of the marketplace together with the lessor's residual value expectations dictate the amount of equity insertion that a lessor is willing to put into lease transactions — not a conservative IRS pronouncement issued well over 10 years ago. In defense of those practitioners and commentators espousing the 20% requirement, however, there is little question that a lessor can expect to fare more favorably under IRS audit the closer it complies with the requirements of Rev. Proc. 75-21, albeit a very conservative approach.

The TRAC Lease: An Anomaly

Notwithstanding the preceding discussion about the essential elements of a lease, if a transaction meets the requirements enumerated by Congress in IRC §7701(h), the parties to the transaction are permitted to treat it as a lease — even though it would not meet the criteria for a true lease set forth in the prior sections of this chapter.

In general, any lease that contains a TRAC shifts the risk of depreciation to the lessee. A TRAC is a provision in a lease agreement that requires a rental adjustment at the end of the lease term depending on the actual value of the vehicle as compared with the originally estimated value of the vehicle upon which the lease payments were based. If the actual value is less than the estimated value, the lessee is required to pay the deficiency to the lessor as the final rental. If, on the other hand, the actual value is greater than the estimated value, the lessor pays to the lessee the surplus, which payment essentially reduces the amount of the lease payments theretofore paid by the lessee.

But for the Qualified Motor Vehicle Operating Agreement provisions originally enacted as part of the Tax Equity and Fiscal Responsibility Act of 1982, TRAC leases would be treated as sales by the lessors to the lessees. See *Swift Dodge v. Commissioner*, 692 F. 2d 651 (9th Cir. 1982). In the case of lease agreements falling within the parameters of the TRAC provisions, however, the existence of a terminal rental adjustment clause will not invalidate the characterization of an agreement as a lease, provided the lease would otherwise be treated as a lease for federal income tax purposes.

To comply with the TRAC provisions, the lease must be a qualified motor vehicle operating agreement, which is an agreement with respect to a motor vehicle (including a trailer) that meets the following three requirements. First, the sum of (i) the amount the lessor is personally liable to repay, and (ii) the net fair market value of the lessor's interest in any property pledged as security for property subject to the agreement, equals or exceeds all amounts borrowed to finance the acquisition of property subject to the agreement [IRC §7701(h)(2)(B)]. In other words, all debt used to finance the leased property must be recourse.

Second, the lessee must sign a separate written statement (i) in which the lessee certifies, under penalty of perjury, that it intends that more than 50% of the use of the leased property is to be in a trade or business of the lessee, and (ii) which clearly and legibly states that the lessee has been advised that it will not be treated as the owner of the lease property for federal income tax purposes [IRC §7701(h)(2)(C)]. Third, the lessor must not know that the lessee's certification described above is false [IRC §7701(c)(2)(D)].

In light of the significance of compliance with the TRAC provisions of the IRC, those lessors involved with automobile and tractor and trailer leasing should periodically review both their lease agreements and their practices and procedures to ensure compliance.

CONCLUSION

It is very important to understand that this chapter is not intended to be an exhaustive analysis of the complex and continually changing standards employed by the various authorities with respect to the true lease issue. However, it is intended to provide a basic understanding of the issues, factors and structuring approaches encountered in this area. Nevertheless, it is always important to obtain the opinion of tax counsel with regard to the true lease versus conditional sale issue when tax benefits constitute a material portion of the yield on a lease transaction.

CHAPTER FOUR
INCOME TAX CONSIDERATIONS

Members of Congress are currently contemplating different ways to modify the Internal Revenue Code (IRC) in an effort to address the myriad goals of the nation. As in the past, some of these changes will have little or no direct effect on the leasing industry. The most likely changes, such as those involving tax rates, depreciation rules, acquisition incentives and the alternative minimum tax (AMT), will have a pervasive effect on all aspects of equipment leasing, just as they have in the past.

Some of the more recent modifications have presented substantial obstacles to many in the leasing industry while at the same time providing specialized opportunities for those nimble enough to take advantage of them. Irrespective of the overall nature of the changes, each time the industry has adjusted and has, in fact, continued to grow and contribute much to the country's economic strength.

This adaptability may be attributed to a simple, but very meaningful, common thread inherent throughout the industry: creativity. Once provided with the rules, the leasing industry accomplishes its goals in ways traditional financing sources cannot, either because of internal or regulatory constraints. In order to adapt and succeed, however, it is important to know the rules. Presenting those rules, from an income tax perspective, is the primary focus of this chapter. Although the elements of federal income tax law change, the basic concepts have, at least so far, remained basically the same.

For ease of categorization, this chapter is presented in two separate but closely related parts:

- Tax Benefits
- Tax Limitations.

TAX BENEFITS

The various tax benefits available to owners of equipment, as they relate to equipment leasing, are discussed in this section. Although these benefits are, for the most part, provisions of general tax law, they are presented in a leasing application. (This chapter focuses on the consequences of ownership, not the determination thereof. Issues regarding true leases versus conditional sales contracts are discussed in Chapter Three).

Accelerated Cost Recovery System

The Accelerated Cost Recovery System (ACRS) was enacted in 1981 as part of the Economic Recovery Tax Act (ERTA). The federal income tax approach to depreciation changed markedly as the focus was shifted from depreciating an asset over its useful life to recovering its cost over Congressionally-mandated time periods (called recovery periods) that are generally shorter than the projected useful lives.

Since the ACRS was originally enacted in 1981, it has been amended several times. Each time, some of the original benefits have been eliminated or restricted. The latest and most significant amendments were enacted as part of the Tax Reform Act of 1986 (TRA '86). For ease of reference, the cost recovery system incorporating the 1986 amendments is referred to as the Modified Accelerated Cost Recovery System (MACRS). MACRS generally applies to property placed in service on or after January 1, 1987.

Under ACRS, as compared to pre-ERTA depreciation law, the cost of capital investments is recovered over predetermined recovery periods generally shorter than the useful lives of the applicable property. The rates of depreciation are generally based on the 150% declining balance method of depreciation, and there is no distinction between new and used property. All property, new or used, falling within a particular recovery class is depreciated at the same rate. In calculating the deduction under ACRS, salvage value is ignored. Recovery property includes all tangible property (real and personal) subject to the allowance for depreciation that is used in a trade or business or held for the production of income. ACRS generally applies to property placed in service on or after January 1, 1981 but before January 1, 1987.

There are four primary differences between ACRS and MACRS. First, as mentioned above, cost recovery under ACRS is based on the 150% declining balance method. Under MACRS, cost recovery is, for the most part, based on the 200% declining balance method. Second, under ACRS, the cost of recovery property is completely recovered over the applicable recovery period. Under MACRS, on the other hand, full recovery does not occur until 1 year beyond the stated recovery period, as the result of different application of the half-year convention. Third, certain property has been reclassified into longer recovery periods. Fourth, to avoid year-end depreciation shopping, a midquarter convention (as opposed to the standard half-year convention) applies, depending on the percentage of property placed in service by a taxpayer in the last quarter of its fiscal year. The preceding facets of MACRS, along with others, are addressed in detail in this section.

RECOVERY CLASSES

Property under MACRS has been classified into eight categories, six of which deal with personal property and two of which deal with real property. With respect to personal property, cost recovery for the 3-, 5-, 7- and 10-year classes is based on the 200% declining balance method with a maximizing switch to straight-line. Cost recovery for the 15- and 20-year classes, however, is based on the 150% declining balance method with a maximizing switch to straight-line.

To determine into which recovery class property falls, reference is made to the Asset Depreciation Range (ADR) midpoint lives, together with certain changes enacted by TRA '86. The ADR tables consist of descriptions of the many different asset types compiled and introduced in 1970 by the Internal Revenue Service (IRS) to provide guidance to taxpayers with respect to pre-ERTA depreciable lives. Although the MACRS recovery periods are generally shorter than the midpoint lives set forth in the ADR tables, the tables provide the reference point for recovery period classifications.

For example, property having an ADR midpoint life of 4 years or less, except automobiles and light trucks, constitutes 3-year MACRS property. Property with an ADR midpoint life of more than 4 years and less than 10 years (which is the majority of leased property), together with automobiles, light trucks, qualified technological equipment, research and experimentation property, as well as other property, falls in the 5-year class. Property with an ADR midpoint of at least 10 years, but less than 16 years, together with single purpose agricultural or horticultural structures and property without an ADR midpoint life not classified elsewhere, is termed 7-year property.

COST RECOVERY METHODOLOGY

The cost of depreciable property is generally depreciated over the applicable MACRS recovery period. For 3-year class property, that period is 4 years (as the result of the required application of the half-year convention). Similarly, the recovery period is 6 years for 5-year property, 8 years for 7-year property and so on.

For the first four recovery classes (3-, 5-, 7- and 10-year property), the double declining balance method with the optimal straight-line switch (the year in which the straight-line deduction exceeds the declining balance deduction) is utilized to calculate the cost recovery deductions. To determine the cost recovery percentages for 5-year property, the following steps must be taken. First, the straight-line rate is computed:

$100\% \div 5 \text{ years} = 20\% \text{ per year}$

Second, the double declining percentage is calculated:

$2 \times 20\% = 40\%$

Therefore, without applying the half-year convention, 40% of the remaining balance of the cost of the asset would be recovered each year, including the first year.

Third, the half-year convention must be applied. This convention suggests that any property placed in service (or disposed of) in a year is entitled to only one-half year's deduction in the year of acquisition and in the year of disposition. Therefore, the first year's deduction for 5-year property is 20% (40% ÷ 2).

Fourth, the declining balance method must be applied to each of the succeeding years until the straight-line method (for prospective years) would result in a greater deduction, at which time the straight-line amount is used. Table 1 sets forth this process and its results. Therefore, the MACRS cost recovery percentages for 5-year property are 20%, 32%, 19.2%, 11.52%, 11.52% and 5.76%, respectively, for each of the 6 years, including the year of acquisition. Table 2 contains the cost recovery percentages for each of the six personal property MACRS recovery classes.

MIDQUARTER CONVENTION

As discussed above, cost recovery percentages are generally calculated using the half-year convention. However, if more than 40% of all personal property placed in service during the year is placed in service in the last 3 months of the taxable year, all MACRS recovery property placed in service during the entire year is subject to the midquarter convention. This convention can be a trap for even the most sophisticated companies.

The midquarter convention treats all MACRS recovery property placed in service during a quarter as having been placed in service at the midpoint of such quarter. This has the effect of providing greater first year cost recovery deductions for property placed in service during the first and second quarters, but lower first year deductions for property placed in service during the third and fourth quarters. This occurs because, unlike the half-year convention that treats all property as having been placed in service for 6 months, the midquarter convention treats MACRS recovery property placed in service in the first, second, third and fourth quarters of the fiscal year as having been placed in service for 10.5, 7.5, 4.5 and 1.5 months, respectively.

Table 1

Derivation of MACRS Percentages

Year	Undepreciated Basis	200% Declining Balance	Prospective Straight-line Deductions	MACRS Depreciation
1	1.0000	**.2000** (40% × ½)	.1000 (20% × ½)	.2000
2	.8000	**.3200** (40% ×.8)	.1778 (.8 ÷ 4½)	.3200
3	.4800	**.1920** (40% ×.48)	.1371 (.48 ÷ 3½)	.1920
4	.2880	**.1152** (40% ×.288)	.1152 (.288 ÷ 2½)	.1152
		Crossover to Straight-line		
5	.1728	.0691 (40% ×.1728)	**.1152** (.1728 ÷ 1½)	.1152
6	.0576		**.0576** (.1152 × ½)	.0576
				1.0000

Table 2
MACRS Classlife Percentages

Recovery Year	3-Year Class (200%)	5-Year Class (200%)	7-Year Class (200%)	10-Year Class (200%)	15-Year Class (150%)	20-Year Class (150%)
1	33.33	20.00	14.29	10.00	5.00	3.75
2	44.45	32.00	24.49	18.00	9.50	7.22
3	14.81	19.20	17.49	14.40	8.55	6.68
4	7.41	11.52[1]	12.49	11.52	7.70	6.18
5		11.52	8.93[1]	9.22	6.93	5.71
6		5.76	8.92	7.37	6.23	5.29
7			8.93	6.55[1]	5.90[1]	4.89
8			4.46	6.55	5.90	4.52
9				6.56	5.91	4.46[1]
10				6.55	5.90	4.46
11				3.28	5.91	4.46
12					5.90	4.46
13					5.91	4.46
14					5.90	4.46
15					5.91	4.46
16					2.95	4.46
17						4.46
18						4.46
19						4.46
20						4.46
21						2.23

Therefore, this convention could multiply the number of depreciation schedules applicable to a taxpayer during any one year by as much as four.[1]

Calculation of the deductions under the midquarter convention is as follows (assuming 5-year property). Multiply the amount of property placed in service in a given quarter by a fraction, the numerator of which is the number of months the property is deemed to have been placed in service, i.e., 10.5, 7.5, 4.5 and 1.5, and the denominator of which is 12. That fraction is then multiplied by the declining balance percentage, which is 40% in the case of 5-year property.

---

[1] Year of switch to straight-line to maximize the depreciation deduction.

Based on this methodology, the cost recovery percentage in the first year is 35% for property placed in service in the first quarter. On the other side of the spectrum, the cost recovery percentage for property placed in service in the last quarter is only 5%. Where the midquarter convention is not applicable (i.e., the half-year convention applies), the recovery percentage is 20%. For the remaining years, the process is identical to that set forth in Table 1. The 5-year property midquarter percentages are reproduced in Table 3.

EFFECTIVE DATES AND ANTICHURNING

ACRS generally applies to property placed in service on or after January 1, 1981 and before January 1, 1987. For property placed in service prior to January 1, 1981, depreciation is governed by the pre-ERTA law, i.e., the taxpayer elects to depreciate its property under either the facts and circumstances method or in accordance with the ADR guidelines. For property placed in service on or after January 1, 1987, MACRS generally applies. MACRS does not apply to transition property, property for which the taxpayer elects ACRS (5-month window property) or property falling within the antichurning rules.

Transition Property

Transition property consists of property that is constructed, reconstructed or acquired by the taxpayer pursuant to a written contract that was binding on March 1, 1986 (or property constructed or reconstructed by the taxpayer under certain conditions), and which is placed in service by the following dates:

ADR Midpoint	Required Date
At least 7 but less than 20 years	January 1, 1989
No ADR midpoint	January 1, 1989
20 years or more	January 1, 1991

Property with an ADR midpoint of less than 7 years does not qualify as transition property. The cost of transition property is recovered under ACRS (not MACRS).

Table 3
Midquarter Recovery Percentages

Quarter	Year					
	1	2	3	4	5	6
1st	.35	.26	.156	.1101	.1101	.0138
2nd	.25	.30	.180	.1137	.1137	.0426
3rd	.15	.34	.204	.1224	.1130	.0706
4th	.05	.38	.228	.1368	.1094	.0958

Window Property

Five-month window property consists of property placed in service after July 31, 1986 and before January 1, 1987 (excluding transition property). At the taxpayer's election, and on an asset-by-asset basis, the taxpayer can recover the cost of such property under either ACRS or MACRS.

Antichurning Rules

The antichurning rules were designed to prevent a taxpayer from converting pre-ERTA property (in the case of ACRS) and ACRS property (in the case of MACRS) to the newer, and generally more favorable, cost recovery system. ACRS must be used regarding certain pre-1987 property involved in post-1986 churning transactions entered into to obtain the benefits of MACRS (even if the taxpayer acquired the property after the effective date, January 1, 1987) where:

1. Such property was owned or used at any time during 1986 by the taxpayer or a related person
2. Such property is acquired from a person who owned such property at any time during 1986 and, as part of the transaction, the user of the property does not change
3. Such property is leased by the taxpayer to a person (or a person related to such person) who owned or used such property at any time during 1986
4. Such property is acquired in a transaction in which the user of such property does not qualify for MACRS in the hands of the person from whom the property is so acquired due to 2 or 3 above.

If, however, application of the antichurning rules would result in a more favorable deduction than if the rules did not apply (assuming utilization of the half-year convention), the antichurning rules will not apply. This may occur where property has been reclassified under MACRS into a longer recovery period.

Examples. The following examples illustrate the application of the antichurning rules.

1. DC Corporation leased computer equipment from AC Company in 1986 for a 3-year term. In 1989, DC exercised its fair market value purchase option and acquired the equipment formerly leased from AC. DC must use ACRS because it used the equipment during 1986

2a. DC, the owner of a computer system, entered into a sale-leaseback in 1987 with AC, whereby DC sold the equipment to AC and leased it back from AC for a 5-year term. AC must use ACRS because it acquired the equipment from DC (who owned it in 1986), and the user of the property (DC) did not change

2b. AC entered into a lease of computer equipment in 1986 with DC. In 1987, AC sold the equipment subject to the lease and assigned the lease to Equity Source. Equity Source is required to use ACRS because it acquired the equipment from AC, which owned the equipment during 1986, and the user (DC) did not change

3. AC entered into a lease of computer equipment in 1986 with DC. In 1987, AC sold the equipment subject to the lease and assigned the lease to First Equity Source. First Equity Source then sold the equipment subject to the lease and assigned the lease to Second

Equity Source. Second Equity Source must use ACRS because the equipment is leased, by assignment, by Second Equity Source to DC, a user of the property during 1986.

ALTERNATIVE DEPRECIATION SYSTEM

As of January 1, 1987, three broad methods of depreciation (or cost recovery) apply. First, a taxpayer may recover the cost of its property under the normal MACRS, as discussed above. Second, a taxpayer may recover the cost on a straight-line basis over the MACRS recovery period, with the half-year convention generally applicable. The available MACRS cost recovery percentages for 5-year property would be as shown in Table 4.

Third, a taxpayer can recover the cost of its property in accordance with the Alternative Depreciation System (ADS), which generally requires the use of the straight-line method over the ADR midpoint life. Although the ADS is usually an election of the taxpayer, there are certain instances where it is mandated. It is required, for example, where property is used predominantly outside the United States, or where the property is tax-exempt use property, both of which are addressed next.[2] In addition, the ADS must be used to compute cost recovery deductions in the computation of the AMT, although a somewhat more favorable taxpayer method is permitted.

Predominantly Outside the US

If property is physically located (whether by the owner-user or the user-lessee) outside the US for more than 50% of the taxable year, it is generally considered used predominantly outside the

Table 4
MACRS Versus Straight-line

Year	MACRS	Straight-line	Difference
1	20	10	10
2	32	20	12
3	19.2	20	(.8)
4	11.52	20	(8.48)
5	11.52	20	(8.48)
6	5.76	10	(4.24)

---

[2] There are other situations requiring the use of the ADS, including the computation of earnings and profits of a domestic corporation, when the property is financed with tax-exempt bonds, and in the case of certain imported property, per IRC § §168(g)(1)(c),(d); 168(g)(5),(6).

US, and thus must be depreciated under the ADS. There are some complex exceptions to the 50% test in the cases of aircraft, rolling stock and vessels.[3]

If recovery property ceases to be used predominantly outside the US, but continues to be used by the taxpayer as recovery property, at the option of the taxpayer the recovery allowance for the taxable year of cessation (and subsequent taxable years) is determined as though the property were placed in service in the year of the cessation. Alternatively, the taxpayer can continue to depreciate the property as though the cessation had not occurred.

For example, for 3 years a taxpayer has leased 7-year ACRS property with a 12-year classlife to a firm outside the US. At the end of the third year the lease expires, so the taxpayer takes back the equipment and re-leases it to a firm located in the US. Assuming that the equipment originally cost $100,000, and its basis net of depreciation is $75,000, in the current and subsequent years the taxpayer can continue using 12-year straight-line for the remaining 9 years, i.e.,

$$\frac{\$100,000}{12} = \$8,333 \text{ depreciation each year,}$$

or apply the 5-year MACRS rate to the remaining basis over the MACRS life, i.e., 20% × $75,000 = $15,000 depreciation in the first year.

Tax-Exempt Use Property

In general, tax-exempt use property means that portion of any tangible property (other than nonresidential real property) leased to a tax-exempt entity. A tax-exempt entity includes (1) the US, any state or political subdivision thereof, and US possessions, or any agency or instrumentality of any of the foregoing,[4] (2) most charitable organizations[5] and (3) any foreign person or entity.[6]

The general ADS rule mentioned above (i.e., straight-line over the ADR midpoint life) is modified slightly in the case of property leased to a tax-exempt entity. In general, a lessor must compute cost recovery deductions on a straight-line basis over a recovery period equal to the ADR midpoint life or 125% of the lease term, whichever is greater. For example, a lease of property with a 5-year lease term and 6-year ADR midpoint would be depreciated over 6.25 years (5 × 1.25 > 6).

There are two exceptions to the general rule applicable to tax-exempt use property. First, property leased to a tax-exempt entity under a short-term lease is not considered to be tax-exempt use property. In general, a short-term lease is a lease with a term of less than (1) 3 years and (2) the greater of 1 year or 30% of the property's present classlife. As an example, a taxpayer leases equipment to a governmental entity on an 18-month lease. The equipment has

---

[3] IRC §168(g)(4) and §48(a)(2)(B)(i),(ii)(I) & (II), (iii).
[4] IRC §168(h)(2)(A)(i).
[5] IRC §168(h)(2)(A)(ii).
[6] IRC §168(h)(2)(A)(iii).

a 6-year ADR classlife. The lease qualifies as a short-term lease because the lease term of 18 months is less than (1) 3 years and (2) the greater of 1 year or 30% of the property's present classlife of 6 years (22 months).

The second exception to the general tax-exempt use property rule involves qualified technological equipment, which is tangible personal property that is any:

1. Computer or peripheral equipment (which does not include typewriters, calculators, adding machines or copiers)

2. High technology telephone station equipment installed on the customer's premises, e.g., teletypewriters, telephones, private exchanges, but only if such equipment has a high technology content making it reasonably likely that it will become obsolete prior to the expiration of its physical useful life

3. High technology medical equipment, e.g., electronic, electromechanical or computer-based high technology equipment used in screening, monitoring, observing, diagnosing or treating patients in a laboratory, medical or hospital environment. Some specifically mentioned items are CAT scanners, nuclear magnetic resource equipment, clinical chemical analyzers, drug monitors, diagnostic ultrasound scanners, nuclear cameras, radiographic and fluoroscopic systems, Holter monitors and bedside monitors. Such property qualifies even if it is used for research. As with the telephone station equipment, it must be reasonably likely that the medical equipment will become obsolete before the expiration of its useful physical life.

Where the lease term, with respect to qualified technological equipment, is less than or equal to 5 years, the lessor can use standard MACRS. If the lease term is more than 5 years, however, the cost is recovered using the straight-line method with the half-year convention over the MACRS recovery period.

SHORT TAXABLE YEAR

For any recovery year in which there are less than 12 months, the cost recovery deduction is determined by multiplying the deduction that would have been available in a full year by:

$$\frac{\text{number of months and part months in the short year}}{12}$$

This rule generally prevents a taxpayer not previously in business from starting a business toward year end, placing depreciable property in service and then claiming a full year's deduction. The rule is usually applied by the IRS in the case of noncorporate taxpayers entering into year-end tax shelters.

Recovery allowances in years subsequent to a short taxable year are determined without regard to the short taxable year. In other words, the second year's deduction is the same irrespective of whether the first year was a short year. To illustrate, in the case of 5-year property placed in service in a short taxable year of only 2 months, the MACRS deductions are as follows:

Year	Allowance
1	3.33% (2/12 × 20%)
2	32.00
3	19.20
4	11.56
5	11.56
6	22.35

In the tax year following the last year in the recovery period, the deduction is equal to the remaining unrecovered cost.

The tax year of the taxpayer placing property in service does not include any month before the month in which the taxpayer begins engaging in a trade or business or holding recovery or depreciable property for the production of income. It is generally not possible to circumvent application of the short year rule by placing a relatively small amount of property in service early in the year (just to attempt to comply in form with the rule) and then later in the year placing a significant amount in service. The proposed regulations provide that, in such a case, the taxable year would begin in the month in which the significant amount of property was placed in service, not earlier in the year.

Investment Tax Credit

The Investment Tax Credit (ITC), as the name implies, is a credit (dollar for dollar reduction) against income taxes. The ITC has had a very tumultuous history. ITC was originally enacted during the Kennedy Administration, at the 7% level, to stimulate investment in new assets to be used in a trade or business or held for the production of income. In 1969 it was repealed, but was restored in 1971 and then increased to 10% in 1975. It was repealed again by TRA '86 for years beginning after 1985. There are some transitional rules, however, that permit the credit to continue beyond 1985 in isolated instances. Those rules are the subject matter of this subsection.

AMOUNT OF TRANSITIONAL ITC

For transitional property, the regular percentage, which under the old law is 10%, is reduced by 35% for taxable years beginning after June 30, 1987. For taxable years beginning after 1986 but before July 1, 1987, the 35% reduction is phased in on a pro rata basis. This reduction is tied to the TRA '86 phase-in of lower tax rates. Because ITC is a credit against income taxes, if taxes are lower, a reduction of the credit is required to maintain some semblance of proportionality between the tax liability and the amount of the credit. Table 5 includes the scheduled corporate tax rate reductions juxtaposed with the ITC reduction. For tax years beginning after 1985, the amount of ITC that can be used to reduce tax liability is equal to $25,000 plus 75% of the tax liability in excess of $25,000. Under the old law, the percentage was 85%.

ITC CARRYOVERS

The carryover and carryback rules relative to transitional ITC are very similar to the old law. For example, ITC is still required to be applied on a first-in, first-out basis, i.e., first use the

Table 5
Transitional Percentages

Fiscal Years	ITC Reduction	Tax Rates
07/01/86 to 06/30/87	0.0000%	46%
08/01/86 to 07/31/87	2.9166	45
09/01/86 to 08/31/87	5.8330	44
10/01/86 to 09/30/87	8.7500	43
11/01/86 to 10/31/87	11.6600	42
12/01/86 to 11/30/87	14.5833	41
01/01/87 to 12/31/87	17.5000	40
02/01/87 to 01/31/88	20.4166	39
03/01/87 to 02/28/88	23.3300	38
04/01/87 to 03/31/88	26.2500	37
05/01/87 to 04/30/88	29.1660	36
06/01/87 to 05/31/88	32.0833	35
07/01/87 to 06/30/88	35.0000	34

amounts carried forward to the current year, then use the amount generated in the current year and finally use the amounts carried back to the current year. If the amount of carryovers to the current taxable year, together with the amount generated in the current year, exceed the tax reduction limitation (addressed below), the excess attributable to the amount currently generated is first carried back to each of the three immediately preceding tax years in the order of the oldest year first, and second, carried forward to each of the 15 succeeding tax years in the order of the closest year first.

It is important to note, however, that the amount of ITC allowable for carryovers (not carrybacks) is also subject to the phase-in of the 35% reduction discussed above. The following example illustrates the interrelationship among carryovers, currently generated ITC and the phase-in rules. Assume the corporate taxpayer had a fiscal year end of January 31, 1988, and that it purchased 5-year, transitional ITC property for $100,000. In addition, assume that the taxpayer had an ITC carryforward of $118,848, and that $15,000 of the carryforward of $118,848 (after taking into account the amount of the applicable reduction) was utilized. The amount of ITC available to be used in future years is $71,500, as calculated in Table 6. The applicable reduction percentage in this example is 20.4166 (from Table 5). Therefore, if $15,000 of ITC could be used, in light of the taxpayer's tax reduction limitations, it would take $18,848 [($18,848 × (1 −.204166)] of prereduction carryforwards to generate a $15,000 credit.

Table 6
ITC Reduction

Status	Available	Used	Remaining	Reduction	Balance
Current	$ 10,000	$ 0	$ 10,000	35%	$ 6,500
Carryforward	$ 118,848	$ 18,848	$ 100,000	35%	65,000
Total					$ 71,500

FULL BASIS REDUCTION

As an additional method of generating taxes, Congress enacted a provision requiring taxpayers taking transitional ITC to reduce the depreciable basis of such property by an amount equal to 100% of the transitional ITC taken (after giving effect to the 35% reduction). Under pre-TRA '86 law, the basis reduction was only 50% and taxpayers had the choice of either taking the reduction to basis, or reducing the amount of ITC by two percentage points, e.g., from 10% to 8%. Under the new law, taxpayers no longer have an option to reduce ITC as the full basis reduction is now required.

Under the old law, if ITC were required to be recaptured (as when the asset was sold prior to the full vesting of the ITC), the basis of the asset was increased by 50% of the amount of ITC recaptured. This had the effect of reducing the taxpayer's gain (or increasing its loss). The intent of this provision was to ensure that, if the taxpayer did not realize the full benefit of the ITC, it would not be penalized by the full amount of the basis reduction. Under the new law, however, even though the amount of the basis reduction has been increased to 100% of the transitional ITC taken, upon recapture the depreciable basis is increased by only 50% of the recaptured amount. Although this appears to be simply a Congressional oversight, it has the effect of a double penalty to a taxpayer who is required to recapture transitional ITC.

TRANSITIONAL ITC PROPERTY

Certain property placed in service after the effective date of the repeal of ITC (December 31, 1985) is still eligible for transitional ITC. Such property is referred to as transitional ITC property. Because, for the most part, it is treated under pre-TRA '86 law, it must be depreciated using the pre-TRA '86 depreciation system, i.e., ACRS (not MACRS). In general, transitional ITC property consists of property constructed, reconstructed or acquired pursuant to a written contract that was binding as of December 31, 1985, and that is placed in service as indicated in Table 7.[7]

---

[7] Other transitional property includes certain mass commuting vehicles, a qualified lessee's automotive manufacturing property and a qualified lessee's farm property, per TRA '86 §204(a)(4).

Table 7
Transition Property Dates

Property with an	Placed in Service On or Before
ADR midpoint of less than 5 years	July 1, 1986
ADR midpoint of at least 5 but less than 7 years	January 1, 1987
Computer-based telephone central office switching equipment	January 1, 1987
ADR midpoint of at least 7 but less than 20 years	January 1, 1989
Property with no ADR midpoint	January 1, 1989
ADR midpoint of 20 years or more	January 1, 1991

For purposes of the binding contract rules, a contract is binding only if it (1) is enforceable under state law against the taxpayer, and damages are not limited to a specified amount (a limitation of damages equal to at least 5% of the total contract price is permissible) and (2) cannot be substantially modified after December 31, 1985. There has been controversy regarding whether volume purchase agreements constitute binding contracts and what kinds of changes are substantial. An option to acquire property is not considered a binding contract. Similarly, where supply agreements with manufacturers fail to specify the amount or design specifications of property to be purchased, they are not treated as binding contracts until purchase orders are actually placed. Therefore, most volume purchase agreements do not constitute binding contacts for purposes of the transitional ITC rules, even though the purchaser could suffer significant penalties if the required quantities were not purchased.

Changes to contract terms that permit improved technical or economic efficiencies are not considered substantial modifications, provided that such changes result in only an insignificant increase in the original price. Those changes generally consist of design changes made for reasons of technological or economic efficiencies of operation. If, however, a binding contract exists to purchase an aircraft engine, a subsequent contract to purchase the entire aircraft will not fall within the binding contract rule. The binding contract rule nevertheless will continue to apply to the engine.

Foreign Tax Credit

The foreign tax credit (FTC) was instituted by Congress in 1918 and provides US taxpayers with a dollar-for-dollar reduction in US tax liability on foreign earned income, for certain qualified income taxes paid to foreign countries, and subject to certain limitations.[8] The purpose of the credit is to eliminate double taxation on the foreign earned income of domestic corporations.

Fundamental to understanding and applying the FTC is the concept of limitation. In 1921, Congress limited the amount of the credit to the US tax amount imposed on a corporation's foreign earned taxable income. Therefore, the credit is limited to the lesser of (1) the amount of foreign taxes paid or (2) the US tax on foreign source taxable income for the year. It is interesting to note that the recent drop in the maximum US tax rate also will effectively reduce the allowable FTC limitation of many corporations with foreign operations, thereby placing them in an excess FTC position. This occurs when foreign taxes paid exceed the limitation amount and generally will be the case when the foreign tax rate exceeds the applicable US tax rate.

The formula for calculating the maximum credit allowed is as follows:

$$\text{FTC limitation}[9] = \frac{\text{Foreign source taxable income}}{\text{Worldwide income}} \times \frac{\text{Total US tax liability}}{\text{on worldwide income}}$$

However, corporations are required to classify income (from both foreign and domestic sources) by type into separate categories or baskets as defined by the law.[10] Therefore, separate FTC limitation calculations must be made for each type or basket of income. The sum of these separately calculated amounts equals the total allowable credit. The purpose of separating income into various categories is to segregate income that is subject to highly disparate tax rates. This segregation of income effectively eliminates the opportunity to average tax rates. Without this provision, corporations could eliminate an excess credit position by combining their income taxed at higher rates with income subject to low tax rates, thereby effectively subsidizing the excess amount.

Currently, there are 10 separate baskets or income categories defined by the law, four of which potentially apply to various types of rental or lease income. These four baskets of income include: passive income, financial services income, shipping income and overall or active income. As an example, the lease income of a leasing company, wholly owned by a financial institution, generally is classified as financial services income. However, the lease income of an independent leasing company generally is classified as active income (if certain conditions are met), unless the leased property is an aircraft or vessel, in which case the lease income is included in the shipping income basket.

As shown in the equation, the FTC limitation for each basket of income depends upon the amount of a taxpayer's income that is treated as foreign source income. Therefore, it is critical to understand what constitutes foreign income and expense versus domestic income and expense. The following points outline the applicable sourcing, or classification, rules for various leasing-related income and expense items:

---

[8] IRC §§862(a),(b); 901(b); 904(a).
[9] Regulation (Reg.) §1.904-1.
[10] IRC §904(d)(1).

1. Rental income is sourced (considered foreign or domestic income) based upon the location of the leased property[11]
2. Depreciation deductions are allocated to the location of the income generated by the asset[12]
3. Rental expense is directly allocated against the income generated by the activity to which it relates[13]
4. Interest expense of each member of an affiliated group is allocated as if all members of the group were a single corporation, and must be allocated and apportioned among various groupings of income on the basis of a taxpayer's assets in each group[14]
5. Nonrecourse debt interest expense may be directly allocated to the class of gross income generated by the property that was acquired from the proceeds of the nonrecourse loan, which is an important exception to the general rule stated in 4.[15]

Perhaps the most critical of the new sourcing rules with respect to its impact on leasing is the new mandatory method of allocating interest expense to foreign source income on the basis of assets. The changes in this provision alone may cause many corporations to lease rather than to purchase future assets with borrowed funds in an attempt to maximize the corporation's FTC limitation. Refer to Chapter Six for a more detailed discussion of the lease versus buy implications.

For corporations subject to AMT, the FTC is calculated in the same manner as previously discussed, with the exception of the following items:

1. AMT income (AMTI) replaces taxable income and the tentative minimum tax liability replaces the regular US tax liability in the FTC limitation formula[16]
2. The credit is applied against the tentative minimum tax liability
3. AMTI will retain the same proportion of foreign to worldwide source income after a pretax book income adjustment as prior to the adjustment (prior to 1990)
4. Apportionment of interest expense must be done based upon the AMT asset basis (150% declining balance). Thus, interest expense will be apportioned differently for a corporation subject to the AMT
5. A corporation can offset a maximum of 90% of AMT liability with the AMT FTC. This exception attempts to ensure that US multinationals with predominantly foreign source income pay a minimum US tax.

The changes in the interest expense allocation methodology, coupled with the recent reduction in the US maximum tax rate, will place many US corporations with foreign operations in an excess FTC position, thereby making them unable to apply all current foreign taxes paid against their US tax liability on foreign income.[17] The ultimate result of this will be

---

[11] IRC §861(a)(4); Reg. § §1.861-5; 1.862-1(a)(iv).
[12] Reg. §1.861-8(b)(2).
[13] Id.
[14] Reg. § §1.861-9(c); 1.861-8(e)(2)(vii).
[15] Reg. §1.861-8(e)(2)(iv).
[16] IRC §59(a).
[17] IRC §904(c).

an increase in the US tax liability of many multinational corporations in the current taxable year.

Deferred Intercompany Transactions

When two members of the same consolidated group of corporations transact business, nothing has really happened from a federal income tax perspective; therefore, there is no tax consequence. (An oversimplified analogy is the taking of money out of the right pocket and putting it into the left.) However, once the money is transferred to someone else outside of the consolidated group, a taxable event has occurred. In a deferred intercompany transaction during a consolidated return year, the difference between the price charged in connection with the sale of property by one member to another and the cost of the property to the selling member is generally deferred and later restored in accordance with the deferred intercompany transaction rules.

REQUIREMENTS

In order to have a deferred intercompany transaction, the transaction must occur between members of an affiliated group during a consolidated return year. An affiliated group exists where at least 80% of each corporation (except the common parent) is owned directly by one or more of the other corporations, and the common parent owns directly at least 80% of at least one of the other corporations. A consolidated return year is any taxable year in which all corporations, which at any time during the taxable year have been members of the affiliated group, file a consolidated return.

To determine the amount of gross profit generated in connection with a deferred intercompany transaction that is deferred and later restored, reference must be made to the cost to the selling member (manufacturer's cost). In general, manufacturer's cost is the sum of direct and indirect production costs computed under the uniform capitalization rules enacted as part of TRA '86. Under the uniform capitalization rules, production costs, which must be either deducted currently or capitalized, are allocated to goods produced during the taxable year, whether sold during the taxable year or remaining in inventory at the close of the taxable year.

Since 1973, the full-absorption regulations have dictated the costs that must be included in inventory for manufacturers. All direct materials and labor must be capitalized, as well as certain indirect costs. Indirect costs were divided into three categories of fixed and variable costs:

1. Category One: costs required to be capitalized to inventory (i.e., repairs, maintenance, utilities and rent)
2. Category Two: costs not capitalized to inventory (i.e., marketing, advertising, interest, research and development and general and administrative expenses)
3. Category Three: costs capitalized to inventory or deducted consistent with the financial reporting treatment (i.e., employee benefits, insurance costs, direct rework, labor, scrap and spoilage and taxes under §164).

The uniform capitalization rules now require all Category Three costs to be capitalized to inventory irrespective of the taxpayer's financial reporting treatment. In addition, certain

Category Two costs must also be included in inventory. All direct materials and labor and Category One costs continue to be capitalized under the new rules.

APPLICATION TO LEASING

In the typical case in which gross profit from an intercompany transaction arises, the parent (manufacturer) sells the asset it has manufactured to the subsidiary (captive), which subsequently enters into a transaction with a customer (not a member of the consolidated group). In the leasing environment, the transaction with the customer generally takes one of four forms: it can be a true lease, a conditional sales contract, a money-over-money lease (a sale that is denominated by the parties as a lease, but that is in reality a sale) or an outright cash sale. The gross profit of the parent will be deferred and restored differently, depending on which of the four structures is utilized by the captive in its transaction with the customer.

Assume, for example, that the parent manufactures a computer that, under the appropriate application of the uniform capitalization rules, costs the parent $550,000 to manufacture. Further assume that the captive purchases the computer from the parent for $1,000,000, which is its fair market value. The gross profit on the sale to the captive is $450,000, which is deferred and will be restored based upon the type of financial instrument the captive writes on the subsequent disposition of the computer.

True Lease

If the captive leases the property to its customer, the parent will restore the gain as the captive depreciates the property. The rule states that if the property is depreciable, amortizable or depletable in the hands of the purchaser, the seller (parent) restores the gain as the cost recovery, depletion or amortization deductions are taken by the purchaser (captive). The annual amount of deferred gain recognized by the parent is equal to the product of the total amount of the deferred gain and a fraction, where the numerator is that year's cost recovery, depletion or amortization deduction for the asset, and the denominator is the purchaser's basis immediately following the purchase.

Assuming that equipment under a tax lease is 5-year MACRS property, the captive lessor's cost recovery deductions would be 20%, 32%, 19.2%, 11.52%, 11.52% and 5.76%, for years 1 through 6, respectively. In year 1, therefore, the parent would recognize income equal to 20% (the MACRS deduction of the captive) times the gross profit on the sale. If the asset is not transferred outside of the consolidated group, the same process would be applied for years 2 through 6.

By deferring income, and thus tax liability, over the period that the asset is depreciated by the captive, the consolidated group realizes a present value tax savings when compared to a cash sale, which is the benefit of gross profit tax deferral. An illustration is presented to quantify that benefit as a percentage of equipment cost (fair market value, as opposed to manufacturer's cost). Assume the cost of the 5-year MACRS property to the parent is $550,000, and the sales price to the captive (and the fair market value) is $1,000,000. In addition, assume a 5-year lease and a discount rate of 12%. Due to the deferral of the taxes on the gross profit, the consolidated group realizes an after-tax present value benefit of 2.59%, calculated as follows.

The tax due in the year of sale if the asset were sold for $1,000,000 without gross profit tax deferral is $153,000.

$$\$1,000,000 - \$550,000 = \$450,000$$
$$\$450,000 \times .34 = \$153,000$$

The taxes due over the recovery period, if the asset were sold to the captive with gross profit tax deferral, are shown in Table 8. The present value of the tax liability over the recovery period is $127,080, as compared to the liability of $153,000 if the taxes were payable in the year of sale. The difference is $25,920, which is approximately 2.59% of the cost (fair market value) of the equipment. It should be noted that a change in the gross profit percentage will have a direct effect on the value of gross profit deferral; the greater the amount of gross profit, the greater the amount of the benefit. Similarly, changes in the tax and discount rates also will affect the magnitude of the benefit.

Conditional Sale

Even if the agreement between the captive and the customer is called by those parties a lease, the transaction will not be treated as a lease if it is a sale and specifies an interest rate charged by the captive to the customer. Instead, the parent will recognize gross profit on the sale to the captive as payments of principal are received by the captive from the customer.

If property acquired in a deferred intercompany transaction is disposed of outside the consolidated group, and the purchasing member (captive) reports income on the installment method, the selling member (parent) restores the deferred gain on a year-to-year basis in the same ratio that the principal payments received during the year from the outsider (customer) bear to the total principal portion of the contract price. The principal payments are determined in accordance with the actuarial method of principal amortization. In the example, assuming that the captive-customer agreement calls for 60 payments in advance, each in the amount of

Table 8
Tax Deferral Schedule

Year	Gross Profit Restored	Tax Liability
1	$ 90,000	$ 30,600
2	144,000	48,960
3	86,400	29,376
4	51,840	17,626
5	77,760	26,438
Total	$ 450,000	$ 153,000

$22,024.21 beginning on January 1, 1988, with a specified interest rate of 12%, the gross profit would be restored as shown in Table 9.

Money-over-Money Lease

A money-over-money lease is a transaction characterized by the parties as a lease, but which is, in reality, a sale. This could occur, for example, where the customer (lessee) has the option to acquire title to the asset at the end of the lease for no additional consideration, or for $1. In a transaction that is a sale for federal income tax purposes in which no interest rate is stated, the IRC first requires an interest rate to be imputed, and, second, requires the total interest to be paid by the customer to be included by the purchasing member (captive) on an actuarial basis (prior to 1984, a straight-line basis was mandated). Although the formula for gross profit restoration is the same in the case of money-over-money leases as it is for conditional sales contracts, the gross profit recognition may be different from that occurring under the conditional sale approach because the imputed interest rate may be different from the implicit rate.[18]

Cash Sale

If the captive sells the property outright to the customer, all deferred gain is then recognized. The rules provide that all remaining gain or loss is restored on the earlier of (1) the date the property is disposed of outside of the group (except via a lease or conditional sales agreement as previously discussed); (2) the date the installment obligation (the conditional sales agreement or the money-over-money lease) is written off, satisfied, discharged or disposed of outside of the group, or the date the subject property is repossessed; or (3) the date the selling member (parent) or owner member (captive) ceases to be part of the group.

Table 9
Restoration of Gross Profit

Year	Principal Received	Gross Profit Restored
1988	$ 163,653.77	$ 73,644[18]
1989	173,252.47	77,964
1990	195,225.23	87,851
1991	219,984.31	98,993
1992	247,884.22	111,548
Total	$ 1,000,000.00	$ 450,000

[18] $\dfrac{\$\ 163,653.77}{\$1,000,000.00} \quad \times \quad \$450,000$

Effect of ACRS to MACRS

Where transactions with third parties are structured as true leases, the change in the cost recovery percentages (from ACRS to MACRS) will alter the value of gross profit tax deferral. The more accelerated the depreciation, the more quickly the deferred gross profit is recognized. Similarly, where the depreciation under MACRS is not as favorable as it would have been under ACRS (such as when an asset has been reclassified into a longer recovery class or where the midquarter convention is applicable), the disadvantage is somewhat mitigated by a slower recognition by the parent of the deferred gain.

Corporate Tax Rates

The current corporate tax rates as enacted by TRA '86 are as follows:

Taxable Income	Tax Rate
Not more than $50,000	15%
More than $50,000, but not more than $75,000	25%
More than $75,000	34%

These rates are effective for taxable years beginning on or after July 1, 1987, with a 12-month phase-in period preceding the fully effective date. The tax rate phase-in is presented in Table 10.

Table 10
Tax Rate Phase-In

Fiscal Years	Tax Rates
07/01/86 to 06/30/87	46%
08/01/86 to 07/31/87	45
09/01/86 to 08/31/87	44
10/01/86 to 09/30/87	43
11/01/86 to 10/31/87	42
12/01/86 to 11/30/87	41
01/01/87 to 12/31/87	40
02/01/87 to 01/31/88	39
03/01/87 to 02/28/88	38
04/01/87 to 03/31/88	37
05/01/87 to 04/30/88	36
06/01/87 to 05/31/88	35
07/01/87 to 06/30/88	34

TRA '86 phases out the benefit of the graduated rates more rapidly than under prior law, and, after a company reaches $335,000 of taxable income, they are fully phased out. To accomplish this phase-out, there is an additional tax (a surtax) equal to 5% of taxable income levied on taxable income between $100,000 and $335,000. Therefore, taxable income of $335,000 and above is taxed at an effective rate of 34%.

TRA '86 also modified the rules governing corporate capital gains. Under prior law, the maximum tax rate for corporate capital gains was 28%. The act eliminated the distinction between ordinary income and capital gains income, so the tax rate is the same for both types of corporate income, which (after the phase-in) is 34%. There is no change, however, in the provisions regarding the deductibility of capital losses.[19]

TIMING

Tax benefits are realized, and tax costs are incurred, when the corporation is actually required to pay its federal income taxes. A corporation with a reasonably estimated taxable income of $40 or more is required to remit 25% of its projected tax liability for the current year on the 15th day of months 4, 6, 9 and 12 of its current fiscal year. However, the underpayment penalty provisions do not call for a penalty if 90% of the required installment is made on or before the respective due date. Therefore, in the case of a calendar year corporation, estimated tax payments may be made in accordance with Table 11 without incurring underpayment penalties.

Even if the 90% requirement is not met, no underpayment penalty will be imposed if the total of the corporation's estimated tax payments made on or before the respective due dates would have been sufficient if the estimated tax for the current taxable year equalled the lesser of:

1. The amount of tax shown on the corporation's original return (or an amended return filed on or before the due date of the original return) for the preceding year, as long as

Table 11
Due Dates and Amounts

Due Dates	Percentage of Actual Tax
April 15	22.5%
June 15	22.5%
September 15	22.5%
December 15	22.5%
March 15	10.0%

---

[19] In the case of corporations, losses from sales or exchanges of capital assets shall be allowed only to the extent of gains from such sales or exchanges [IRC §1211(a)].

the preceding year covered 12 months and a tax liability was incurred for that year. In other words, the 90% test can be applied to last year's income to determine this year's estimated tax payments. This route, however, is not available for large corporations[20]

2. The amount equal to the tax calculated at the current year's rates, but otherwise on the basis of the original return (or an amended return filed on or before the due date of the original return) for the preceding year. In other words, if the current year's tax rates are different from last year's rates, the 90% test can be applied to last year's income, with the tax being calculated using this year's rates. This exception, too, is not available for large corporations

3. The amount equal to 90% of the tax for the current year, calculated by annualizing taxable income for the months preceding an installment date. In other words, a corporation can take its taxable income for part of the current year and then, on that basis, extrapolate to determine the taxable income for the year, and thereafter apply the 90% test to the projected taxable income

4. The amount equal to 90% of the tax for the current year calculated under the seasonal method, which applies to corporations with recurring seasonal income.

Although certain corporations fall within one of the exceptions enumerated above, most companies pay their estimated taxes in accordance with Table 11. When a corporation does pay its taxes in accordance with Table 11, it must consider the applicable dates of the savings or payments in a present value analysis in order to determine the actual value of the tax benefits (or, conversely, the actual cost of the tax payments). In addition, whether the transaction is budgeted or incremental must be factored into the analysis.

A budgeted transaction is one that is part of the company's overall plan for the taxable year. Although the specifics of the particular transaction would not be known at the time the plan was formulated (generally sometime the year before), many companies are able to predict with a fair degree of certainty the timing and amount of transactions that will be consummated during the year. In that case, the tax savings and costs from those budgeted transactions are reflected at each estimated tax payment date, even though the subject transaction may not occur for several months. For example, if a calendar year corporation consummates a lease on December 31, 1988 as part of its budgeted transactions, the value of the 1988 MACRS deduction attributable to that transaction would be 104.15%, as calculated in Table 12 (assuming a cost of capital of 12%).

It should be noted that the analysis of Table 12 applies to the overall tax posture arising from the transaction, not just to the deduction side of the equation. The amount of lease revenue includable for the year, together with any interest expense and other expenses associated with that particular transaction, must be considered also to determine the overall tax effect of the transaction in each year in which the lease generates any tax attributes.

An incremental transaction, on the other hand, is one that was not part of the planned transactions for the year. An analysis of its tax savings and cost features looks only forward to future estimated tax payment dates. Therefore, using the same example, the value of the MACRS deduction taken in 1988 would be only 97.54% of its face value, because the benefit

---

[20] The term large corporation means any corporation that had taxable income of $1,000,000 or more for any taxable year during the three taxable years immediately preceding the taxable year involved [IRC §6655 (i)(2)].

Table 12
Present Value of Tax Benefits

Estimated Tax Dates	Estimated Tax Percentages	Number of Months to Future Value (FV) or Present Value (PV) Taxes	Future Value or Present Value
4-15-88	22.5	8.5 (FV)	.2449
6-15-88	22.5	6.5 (FV)	.2400
9-15-88	22.5	3.5 (FV)	.2330
12-15-88	22.5	.5 (FV)	.2261
3-15-89	10.0	2.5 (PV)	.0975
Total			1.0415

of the deduction would not be realized until March 15, 1989, the next estimated tax payment date. By their very nature, incremental transactions always cause the attendant tax benefits or costs to have a present value of less than the face value. Budgeted transactions, on the other hand, and depending on the consummation date, cause the tax benefits or costs to be greater or less than the face value of the actual payment or savings.

TAX LIMITATIONS

Just as there are tax benefits applicable to leasing, there are also tax limitations. These limitations are also part of general tax law. How the limitations apply to leasing are discussed in this section.

Corporate Alternative Minimum Tax

The AMT has been a part of the system of taxation for almost two decades. Although in a form much different from its current composition, the AMT was originally enacted under the Tax Reform Act of 1969 to curb Congressionally perceived abuses of tax preference items. The items of tax preference have changed (generally expanded) since then and, for corporate taxpayers, the methodology was substantially revised with the enactment of TRA '86.

The AMT provisions are now among the most complex found in the IRC, and impose a heavy administrative burden on taxpayers. The AMT is conceptually simple. To the extent that tax preference items, such as certain accelerated depreciation and tax-exempt interest, are utilized by a corporation in excess of prescribed levels, a tax is levied on such excess. Unfortunately, however, the application of the AMT is many times more complex than this.

As will be illustrated, a thorough understanding, which is required in order to comply with the law, of the web of rules relating to deferral and exclusion preferences, the minimum tax credit, tax preference items and credit limitations, to name but a few, is difficult to come by. Help, in the form of either a full-time staff of tax professionals, or outside educational resources, will become a necessity in order to continue to do business.

GENERAL PROVISIONS

The framework for the AMT, which is effective for tax years beginning after December 31, 1986, diverges sharply from the pre-TRA '86 law. Instead of imposing the tax based on the add-on concept,[21] the AMT is now based on an entirely supplemental tax recording system. A taxpayer must now maintain a separate set of tax books side-by-side with the existing regular tax system. The items of income and deductions that apply for regular tax purposes do not, in many cases, apply in the AMT environment. There is a much stronger relationship now between a corporation's books used for financial reporting purposes and its tax books. At the very minimum (and ignoring the idiosyncrasies of state and local tax laws), three sets of books will be maintained by US companies: financial reporting books, regular tax books and AMT books.

Tax preference items have been expanded to include, among others, accelerated depreciation on personal property, tax-exempt interest on certain private activity bonds, one-half of the excess of pretax book income over other AMTI and gain from the disposition of certain assets treated under the installment method. Each of these leasing specific tax preference items will be addressed in more detail.

To exempt small corporations from the taxpaying requirements of the AMT (but not necessarily the bookkeeping requirements), there is a $40,000 exemption used to reduce AMTI before the tax rate of 20% is applied to determine the AMT. That exemption, however, is phased out by 25 cents for every $1 of AMTI over $150,000. Therefore, if a corporate taxpayer's AMTI is $310,000 or more, there is no benefit from the exemption.

DETERMINING THE TAX LIABILITY

Both the regular tax for the taxable year and the tentative minimum tax for the taxable year are computed and the greater of the two becomes the tax due. The tentative minimum tax is equal to 20% of the difference between the AMTI for the taxable year, and the exemption amount, reduced by the AMT FTC for the taxable year. The AMTI is the corporation's taxable income calculated in accordance with the AMT provisions of the IRC, and basically consists of regular taxable income plus or minus preference items.

TAX PREFERENCE ITEMS

In computing AMTI, using the regular tax calculations as the starting point, a corporation is required to redetermine taxable income by supplanting certain items of income and deductions with those required under the AMT provisions. Those items of income and deductions affected are referred to generically as tax preference items. Generally, the AMT methodology results in greater income and lower deductions than under the regular tax system.

---

[21] Prior to TRA '86, the alternative minimum tax was calculated by adding all of the corporate tax preferences together, subtracting $10,000, and multiplying the difference by 15%. If the resulting amount exceeded the corporation's regular tax liability for the year, the alternative tax was payable.

The following tax preference items are those most commonly encountered in an equipment leasing context.

Accelerated Depreciation on Personal Property

For equipment placed in service before 1987, and for transitional property, the pre-TRA '86 law applies. This preference (under pre-TRA '86 law) does not apply to taxpayers in general; it applies only to leased personal property owned by an individual or a personal holding company.[22] Where applicable, the amount of the preference is the excess of the accelerated depreciation taken by the taxpayer for regular tax purposes over depreciation calculated under the straight-line method, using the same useful lives.

For property placed in service after 1986, and for property placed in service after July 31, 1986 and before January 1, 1987, for which MACRS was elected, the depreciation deduction for AMT purposes is calculated using the 150% declining balance method with a maximizing switch to straight-line over the ADS life, i.e., the ADR midpoint life. MACRS property placed in service during the August 1 to December 31 window period will enter into the AMT calculation in 1987.

Notwithstanding the preceding, however, the personal property preference does not apply to property where the taxpayer elects or is required to use the straight-line method of depreciation for regular tax purposes. Table 13 recaps the interrelationship between the regular tax depreciation methods and the methods required under the AMT provisions. The depreciation amounts applicable to $100,000 of 5-year MACRS property for regular tax and AMT purposes are shown in Table 14. Although the total is, of course, the same as under MACRS, the AMT deductions are less accelerated, resulting in less of a deduction.

The AMT depreciation preference has widespread impact in both pricing and lease versus buy decisions. Many lessors and lessees are of the opinion that using straight-line depreciation will be economically more beneficial. Although it certainly does not create preferences, use of the straight-line method does result in economic loss, because the amount of the taxes saved on the preference amount is much less than the tax savings associated with the foregone MACRS.

Tax-Exempt Interest

Although tax-exempt interest is not includable in gross income for regular tax purposes, tax-exempt interest on private activity bonds (other than qualified Sec. 501 (c)(3) bonds) issued generally on or after August 15, 1986 is fully includable in income for AMT purposes. TRA '86 replaces the concept of industrial development bonds with that of private activity bonds. Therefore, under TRA '86, federal income tax is imposed on the interest of a state or local bond if it constitutes a private activity bond that is not a qualified bond.

A private activity bond is any bond that meets the private business use test, such that greater than 10% of the bond issue proceeds are used for a private business, and also meets the private payment test such that the payment of principal or interest on more than 10% of the proceeds

---

[22] A personal holding company is a corporation where at least 60% of the income is from passive sources, and where at any time during the last half of the taxable year more than 50% in value of the outstanding stock is owned, directly or indirectly, by or for not more than five individuals. See IRC §542.

Table 13
Depreciation Methods

Regular Tax Method	AMT Method	Preference
MACRS	150% declining balance over ADR	Yes
Straight-line over MACRS	Straight-line over ADR	Yes, if ADR life > MACRS life
Straight-line over ADR	Straight-line over ADR	No

Table 14
Depreciation Comparison

Year	MACRS	150% Declining Balance	Straight-line MACRS	Straight-line ADR
1	$ 20,000	$ 15,000	$ 10,000	$ 10,000
2	32,000	25,500	20,000	20,000
3	19,200	17,850	20,000	20,000
4	11,520	16,660	20,000	20,000
5	11,520	16,660	20,000	20,000
6	5,760	8,330	10,000	10,000
Total	$ 100,000	$ 100,000	$ 100,000	$ 100,000

is secured by an interest in property used for private business. A bond will also qualify as a private activity bond if greater than 5% of the proceeds, or $5,000,000, is used to finance loans to entities other than governmental units.

A qualified Section 501(c)(3) bond is any bond where all property provided by the bond issue proceeds is owned by a 501(c)(3) organization or governmental unit[23] and the face amount of the issue is less than $150 million. A 501(c)(3) organization is defined as any nonprofit corporation, foundation or fund organized and operated exclusively for religious, charitable, scientific, literary or educational purposes, etc., that does not participate in any political activities.

---

[23] The term governmental unit does not include the US or any of its agencies or instrumentalities, per IRC §150(a)(2).

Installment Method of Accounting

As was discussed earlier, the installment method generally permits a taxpayer to recognize income as cash is received. Where a transaction is subject to the proportionate disallowance rules enacted as part of TRA '86, however, the installment method is not permitted to be used by the taxpayer to calculate its AMT. Instead, the entire amount of the profit must be recognized for AMT purposes in the year of sale.

Untaxed but Reported Business Profits

This preference will undoubtedly have the most pervasive effect on the business community (beyond merely the leasing industry) for two reasons. First, those corporations with a significant disparity between the results of operations reported to shareholders and the results as reported for federal income tax purposes will be directly disadvantaged economically, i.e., the income tax payable will be increased. Second, it will be administratively costly for corporations to properly keep track of this preference. As might be surmised, the purpose of this preference is to partially bridge the gap between a corporation's financial reporting books and its tax books. Congress is attempting to reduce what is frequently a huge disparity, and to impose income taxes on a base that more closely approximates economic income.

Through 1989, the amount of the preference is 50% of the excess of pretax book income over the AMTI before this preference, often referred to as other AMTI. Pretax book income is the income reported by the corporation for financial reporting purposes (excluding any impact of foreign or federal income taxes), and other AMTI is the AMTI before taking into consideration this preference. For example, assuming pretax book income of $50,000 and other AMTI of $32,000, the preference would be calculated as $9,000.

Pretax book income	$ 50,000
Other AMTI	32,000
Difference	$ 18,000
	× .50
Preference	$ 9,000

Congress has established a hierarchy of financial statements to be used in determining the pretax book income amount: financial statements required to be filed with the Securities and Exchange Commission; audited financial statements; financial statements required to be provided to the US, a state or any agency or political subdivision thereof and unaudited financials used for credit purposes, reports to shareholders or any other substantial nontax purpose. If a corporation does not have one of the foregoing, it must use its earnings and profits[24] for the taxable year as its book income. The rules for determining pretax book income are very complex in the cases of consolidated tax returns, foreign subsidiaries' income reported by the US parent and any required restatement of prior years' financial statements.

For tax years beginning after 1989, the amount of the preference is 75% of the difference between adjusted current earnings and preadjustment AMTI before this preference. Adjusted

---

[24] Earnings and profits is a concept used in the IRC to approximate economic income. See IRC §312(n).

current earnings is a new tax concept designed to better approximate the true economic income of the corporation. The percentage will increase from its present level of 50% to 75%, thereby further reducing the spread between income for federal income tax purposes and economic income.

CREDITS AND LOSSES

The AMT may not be reduced by the targeted jobs credit, the credit for producing fuel from a nonconventional source, the credit for qualified clinical testing expenses and (except as noted) the general business credit. These credits are generally referred to as incentive tax credits. A corporation's ITC, however, may be used to offset the greater of (1) either the regular tax liability for the taxable year, or the excess of its regular tax liability over 75% of its AMT, whichever is less, or (2) 25% of its tentative minimum tax. For example, if the corporation's regular tax liability for the year was $600,000 and its tentative minimum tax liability was $1.5 million, the corporation could use available investment credits to offset its AMT liability by $375,000. If, on the other hand, the corporation's regular tax liability was $1.5 million and its AMT liability was $600,000, the corporation could use up to $1,050,000 of ITC to reduce its regular tax liability to $450,000. Except as set forth in the preceding formula, ITC cannot reduce the regular tax below the AMT.

FTCs are also allowed against the AMT. They cannot, however, offset more than 90% of the AMT (determined prior to application of FTCs and net operating losses (NOLs)). Assuming AMT of $5,000,000 and AMT FTCs of the same amount, AMT of $500,000 would still be paid, as follows:

AMT	$ 5,000,000
Limitation	× 90%
Amount available	$ 4,500,000

$5,000,000 – $4,500,000 = $500,000

NOLs cannot offset more than 90% of AMTI; any unutilized losses, however, may be carried forward. As an example, a company's AMTI (before NOLs) is $7,500,000 and it has minimum tax NOLs of $8,250,000. The maximum amount of minimum tax NOLs that can be offset against AMTI is $6,750,000.

AMTI	$ 7,500,000
Limitation	× 90%
	$ 6,750,000

The taxpayer's AMTI would be reduced to $750,000 ($7,500,000 – $6,750,000), resulting in a tentative AMT of $150,000. $1,500,000 ($8,250,000 – $6,750,000) of minimum tax NOLs would be carried forward.

An illustration combining the various limitations previously discussed is appropriate at this time, in order to present the interaction (and overall view) of the limitations. Assume the following:

AMTI (pre-NOL): $10,000,000
AMT NOL: $8,000,000
AMT FTC: $350,000

The floor to which the tax can be reduced is $200,000.

($10,000,000 × .20 × .10)

Utilization of the available credits would occur as follows:

AMTI (pre-NOL)	$ 10,000,000
AMT NOL	(8,000,000)
AMTI	$ 2,000,000
	× .20
AMT	$ 400,000
AMT FTC	(200,000)[25]
Tentative minimum tax	$ 200,000

MINIMUM TAX CREDIT

There are two broad types of preferences arising under the AMT system: exclusion preferences and deferral preferences. An exclusion preference connotes a permanent difference between the regular tax system and the AMT system. A deferral preference, on the other hand, is only a timing difference between the two systems. Interest on certain private activity bonds that is tax-exempt for regular tax purposes, but taxable for AMT purposes, is an example of a permanent or exclusion preference.

Depreciation is the classic example of a timing or deferral preference. Over the entire depreciable period, the same amount of depreciation will be taken, irrespective of whether the deductions are calculated under MACRS (for regular tax purposes) or using the 150% declining balance method (for AMT purposes). The sole difference between the two methods is the timing of the deductions, as illustrated in Table 14.

Under MACRS, deductions are greater in the early years; therefore, taxes are deferred to later years. Under AMT depreciation, however, the depreciation deductions are less than the MACRS deductions in the early years and greater in the later years; therefore, taxes would be paid sooner under AMT depreciation. Assuming that the tax base and rates were the same, and that there was no change in the tax rates during the depreciable period, the same amount of tax would be paid, in the aggregate, under both the regular tax and AMT systems; only the timing of the payments would be different.

As exemplified using the differences in depreciation, timing differences will result in a lower regular taxable income in the early years (thereby activating the AMT) and a lower AMTI in the later years (thereby activating the regular tax). If that were the case, not only would the taxpayer pay taxes sooner (because the timing benefits of MACRS would be reduced), but it would be

---

[25] NOLs and foreign tax credits, in combination, cannot reduce AMT below 2% (20% rate × 10% limitation); therefore, only $200,000 of the available FTC can be utilized. The remaining $150,000 is carried forward.

taxed twice, as those timing benefits reversed. The mechanism enacted by Congress to avoid this inequitable result is the minimum tax credit. The minimum tax credit is a credit against regular tax liability in years after AMT has been paid as the result of timing differences between the two systems.

The minimum tax credit is equal to the excess, if any, of (1) the AMT for all prior taxable years beginning after 1986, over (2) the regular tax liability for such years. The amount of the credit is reduced by the AMT credits already taken. In addition, each year it is limited to the amount by which the regular tax for the taxable year exceeds the AMT for that taxable year. Because its purpose is to avoid the potential double tax inequity caused by the timing differences between the two systems, the amount of the credit does not include any amount attributable to exclusion items. Therefore, to calculate the credit, the AMT must be recomputed including only the exclusion preference items. The difference between that number and the AMT yields the AMT attributable only to deferral preferences.

For example, assume that ABC Company does not have regular taxable income in 1989, but does have deferral preferences and exclusion preferences of $400,000 and $100,000, respectively. The AMT credit generated (but not utilized) in 1989 would be $88,000, as calculated in Table 15. As can be seen from Table 15, the exemption amount is applied at the exclusion calculation level.

Large corporations will not be concerned with the exemption because it is totally phased out by the time AMTI reaches $310,000. Including the exemption calculation at the exclusion level is the more beneficial approach (from the taxpayer's perspective), since the difference between total AMT and exclusion AMT is increased. The $88,000 credit can be used to offset future regular tax liability, but never below the AMT liability for the year of offset. The minimum tax credit can be carried forward indefinitely (but cannot be carried back), and is calculated before application of any investment credits.

Table 15
Minimum Tax Credit Computation

	Total AMT	Exclusion AMT	Minimum Tax Credit
Regular	$ 0	$ 0	
Preferences	500,000	100,000	
Exemption	0	(40,000)	
AMTI	$ 500,000	$ 60,000	
Tax rate	× 20%	× 20%	
AMT	$ 100,000	$ 12,000	$ 88,000

Proportionate Disallowance

The proportionate disallowance rules of TRA '86 have the effect of deeming payments under installment sales contracts to have been received, even though they have not yet actually been received. As a general rule, gain or loss from a sale of property is required to be recognized for federal income tax purposes in the taxable year of the sale, which is consistent with one of the basic principles of tax law: wherewithal to pay. The law generally assumes that a taxpayer has the ability to pay the tax arising from the gain on sale of property in the year in which the property is sold. Hence, the tax should be paid.

Under the installment method, however, the gain from certain sales of property where the seller-taxpayer receives deferred payments is required to be recognized as the payments are received, unless the taxpayer elects otherwise. The installment method is also consistent with the wherewithal to pay philosophy: if the seller receives the money over time, then it has the ability to pay over time, not all today. Each year, the seller would recognize gain based on the gross profit percentage, as follows:

$$\text{Principal portion of payments received} \quad \times \quad \frac{\text{Gross profit}}{\text{Total principal portion of contract price}}$$

APPLICATION

The proportionate disallowance rules, as the name implies, disallow the installment method with respect to a portion of a company's installment receivables, determined by reference to the debt facet of the seller's capitalization. (Although the proportionate disallowance rules affect installment sales, they do not apply to true lease transactions.) In other words, a portion of all installment receivables is treated as having been paid to the seller-taxpayer, even though it has not yet actually been paid by the seller-taxpayer's customer. The amount treated as a payment, which is referred to as the allocable installment indebtedness (AII), depends on the seller's ratio of debt to total assets. The larger the ratio, the more of a payment is deemed to have been received, resulting in an accelerated remittance of the applicable income taxes.

To fully understand the application of the rules, certain definitions are required. Applicable installment obligations (AIO) are defined as any installment receivables arising from a post-February 28, 1986 sale of:

1. Personal property on the installment plan by one who regularly sells personal property
2. Real property held by a taxpayer for sale to customers in the ordinary course of a trade or business
3. Real property used in a taxpayer's trade or business or held for the production of rental income if the sales price exceeds $150,000, if the receivables are held by the seller (or by another member of its affiliated group).

Average quarterly indebtedness is defined as the total indebtedness of the seller-taxpayer at the end of each quarter (including accounts payable and accrued expenses) divided by four.

The amount of the deemed payment, the AII, is calculated in accordance with the following formula:

$$\text{AII} = \left(\frac{a}{b+c} \times d\right) - \text{AII (p), where}$$

a = the face amount of AIOs outstanding at year end

b = the face amount of all installment obligations (applicable and non-applicable) outstanding at year end

c = the adjusted basis of all other taxpayer assets (straight-line depreciation may be elected for determining adjusted basis)

d = average quarterly debt and

AII (p) = AII from prior years' AIOs less any payments received relating to the AIOs.

To illustrate the computation of AII for only 1 year, assume the following facts:

AIOs: $100,000
All installment obligations: $200,000
Other assets' adjusted basis: $300,000
Average quarterly indebtedness: $200,000
AII (p): 0

$$\text{AII} = \left(\frac{\$100,000}{\$200,000 + \$300,000} \times \$200,000\right) - 0$$

$$= \$40,000$$

Therefore, even though the seller may not have actually received any money from its customers on its AIOs, the seller is required to treat $40,000 as having been received under the proportionate disallowance rules. The rationale is simple and, basically, assumes a pledging of AIOs. As the result of the amount of debt the seller has incurred, the seller is deemed to have already received cash. Therefore, under the wherewithal to pay principle, the seller is required to pay tax in the current year.

In subsequent years, as actual payments are received from customers, the seller is not required to recognize gain attributable to prior year's AIOs to the extent those actual payments do not exceed AII. Such payments reduce the AII attributable to that year's installment receivables. Therefore, it is only the deferral aspect that is affected; no double tax is imposed.

EFFECT ON GROSS PROFIT TAX DEFERRAL

As previously discussed, in a sale by a manufacturer-parent to its captive subsidiary, and a subsequent sale or lease by the captive to its customer, the gross profit on the sale by the parent to the captive is recognized as the captive depreciates the equipment (where the captive leases the equipment to the customer), or as the captive receives principal payments (where the captive sells the equipment to the customer via a money-over-money transaction or a conditional sales agreement). It is in the latter two instances that the proportionate disallowance rules are applicable.

As discussed above, the proportionate disallowance rules affect the timing of the receipt of payments made under the installment method. In essence, the rules accelerate the receipt of payments by the captive by deeming them to be received based on the proportion of the consolidated group's debt to its total capitalization. Because payments are deemed to be received earlier by the captive, the parent's gross profit will also be recognized sooner, thus reducing the benefit of gross profit tax deferral.

Uneven Rent Limitations

Prior to the enactment, in 1984, of the uneven rent limitation codified in IRC §467, it was very common for an accrual basis lessor and a cash basis lessee (or vice versa) to enter into a stepped payment lease, where the payments either increased or decreased over the lease term. Such arrangements created substantial timing differences in the payment of taxes. For example, in a stepped-up payment lease (where the payments increase), a cash basis lessor could defer recognition of income by including only the lower payments now, while, in the same transaction, an accrual basis lessee could take current deductions based on a straight-line lease payment approach.

The uneven rent limitation, in an effort to restrict the scope for taxpayers to play these types of deferral games, consists of a series of rules placing lessors and lessees on an accrual basis regarding most leases, and requiring the use of present value principles for those lease transactions affected. With certain transitional exceptions, the uneven rent limitation rules apply to lease agreements entered into after June 8, 1984, although leases actually falling under the purview of §467 are not common.

APPLICABLE LEASES

It first should be noted that even if a lease agreement meets the definition set forth below, it will not be subject to the uneven rent limitation if the value of all consideration (including rental payments) received by the lessor for the use of the property does not exceed $250,000. The §467 limitation applies to what are termed §467 rental agreements, i.e., any rental agreement for the use of tangible property where:

1. At least one payment allocable to the use of property during a calendar year is to be paid after the close of the calendar year following the calendar year in which such use occurs; or

2. There are increases or decreases in the amount to be paid as rent under the agreement.

Criterion 2 addresses stepped payment leases. Criterion 1, on the other hand, addresses a more blatant attempt to defer inclusion of rent. Assume, for example, that AC Corporation leases a computer to DC Company in September 1988 for a 36-month term. The lease agreement requires lease payments to be paid for the months of September and October of 1988, although they are not required to be paid by DC until August of 1990. Because the September and October payments are not required to be paid until after 1989, which is the calendar year following the calendar year of use, the lease is a §467 rental agreement.

APPLICATION OF THE RULES

Irrespective of receipt, the lessor must include two items in income each year (for which the lessee obtains a corresponding deduction):

1. Accrued rent; and
2. Interest on previously accrued rent that remains unpaid (calculated at 110% of the applicable federal rate, compounded semiannually).

Except as provided below, accrued rent consists of the amount allocated under the lease to the taxable year, plus the present value of any consideration to be paid after the end of the lease period to which it relates. Interest on previously accrued rent that remains unpaid imposes an additional penalty on the lessor and applies present value principles to the accrued rent concept.

For example, assume that a lessor and lessee have entered into a 5-year lease that is deemed to be a §467 rental agreement. The lease calls for annual payments, in advance, of $40,000, $50,000, $60,000, $70,000 and $80,000, respectively, and a $50,000 payment at lease termination. If the present value of the $50,000 payment due at lease termination is $28,000 (using as the discount rate the applicable federal rate under §1274(d)), the lessor will have to include $45,600 as lease revenue for year 1 [$40,000 + ($28,000 ÷ 5)], that is, the amount allocated under the lease to year 1 ($40,000), together with the pro rata portion of the present value of the $50,000 lease termination payment ($5,600). If the additional $5,600 is not paid by the end of year 2, the lessor must include $692.16 of interest income for year 2 (assuming that the applicable federal rate is 11%), and, in addition, will have $55,600 of rent income [$50,000 + ($28,000 ÷ 5)] due in that year.

Rent Leveling

Accrued rent can have a different and more restrictive meaning in certain cases. Accrued rent will equal a pro rata share of the present value of the total lease consideration in two circumstances: (1) where tax avoidance is a principal purpose of the structure of the transaction, and (2) where either (a) the lease agreement does not allocate the payments, e.g., the agreement simply provides for a lump sum payment at some point during the term of the lease, or (b) the lease is a disqualified leaseback or a long-term agreement. Accrued rent as defined in this fashion results in what is referred to as rent leveling.

A disqualified leaseback is a lease to any person who had an interest in the property at any time within 2 years prior to the lease. Therefore, all traditional sale-leaseback transactions constitute disqualified leasebacks. A long-term lease is a lease with a term in excess of 75% of the MACRS recovery period, i.e., for 3-year property the lease term must be greater than 27 months; for 5-year property the lease term must be greater than 45 months, etc. Therefore, a large percentage of leases in the marketplace constitute long-term leases as defined under the uneven rent rules.

Consequently, the key ingredient is the definition of a tax avoidance purpose, a concept that Congress left vague and ambiguous. The Committee Reports do indicate, however, two situations in which a tax avoidance purpose is most likely: first, where one of the parties to the lease is a high bracket taxpayer and the other is a low bracket taxpayer; and second, where a tax-exempt entity is sandwiched between the lessor and the lessee. Both of these situations give rise to the potential for tax deferral abuse and will be closely scrutinized by the IRS.

Congress instructed the IRS to issue regulations defining with more specificity the meaning of tax avoidance purpose in this context. In addition, the IRS was instructed to incorporate certain specified allowances such as changes in lease payments that are tied to the Consumer Price Index, lease payments based on the lessee's receipts or similar amounts, reasonable rent holidays (not to exceed 12 months generally, and in no event more than 24 months) and changes in lease payments based on changes in amounts paid to unrelated parties. Those situations essentially constitute exceptions to the meaning of tax avoidance purpose.

Recapture

Where the lease is a disqualified leaseback or a long-term lease, but where there is no tax avoidance purpose (so that rent leveling is not required), the lessor is subject to recapture upon its disposition of the property. The purpose of this recapture provision is to prevent the recharacterization of what should be ordinary income into capital gain income.[26]

The recapture amount, which constitutes ordinary income, is the difference between the amount that would have been accrued under rent leveling, and the amount that was actually accrued. The recapture amount is limited to gain realized on the disposition, which is reduced by the recapture required under § §1245 and 1250.

Assume, for example, that a computer is leased for 4 years, and the annual payments, in advance, are $30,000, $60,000, $90,000 and $120,000, respectively. If the present value of the total lease payments is $240,730, under rent leveling the lessor would have to recognize $60,182.50 of rental income in year 1, even though it actually received only $30,000. If no tax avoidance purpose existed, however, and if the lessor sold the computer at the end of year 3 for $15,000 when its adjusted basis was $12,600, the amount of the §467 recapture would be 0, calculated as follows.

First, the difference between the rent leveling inclusion and the actual inclusion must be determined. Under rent leveling, the inclusion in the first 3 years of the lease would have been $180,547.50. The lessor actually included $180,000. The difference, therefore, is $547.50. Consequently, the maximum recapture under §467 is $547.50.

Second, §467 recapture is limited to the gain realized on the sale, which gain is reduced by any recapture required under §1245 or §1250. The gain realized on the sale is $2,400 ($15,000 – $12,600), all of which must be recaptured under §1245. Therefore, there is no recapture required under §467.

At-Risk and Loss Deductibility

Originally enacted with the Tax Reform Act of 1976, the at-risk rules of §465 are designed to limit the deductibility of losses arising from the activities of certain taxpayers to the amount the taxpayer has at-risk in the activity (i.e., the amount the taxpayer may actually lose by virtue of participating in the activity). These rules have been expanded over the years to apply to

---

[26] This provision has little effect on a taxpayer when there is no distinction between capital gains tax rates and ordinary income tax rates, as is the case in taxable years beginning on July 1, 1987.

virtually all activities, to apply to the availability of ITC and, most recently, to apply to real estate. The original abuse sought to be curbed by Congress, however, was the common taxpayer practice of purchasing equipment with little or no down payment and a nonrecourse loan, and then depreciating and deducting other expenses relating to the asset based on its full purchase price.

AFFECTED TAXPAYERS

A limitation on certain taxpayers with regard to the deductibility of losses arising in connection with trade or business or income producing activities is imposed by §465. The rules apply to individuals, partnerships, S corporations and closely-held C corporations (i.e., a corporation where more than 50% of the value of the outstanding stock of the corporation is owned, directly or indirectly at any time during the last half of the taxable year, by or for not more than five individuals). Those taxpayers were the greatest abusers in this area, as perceived by Congress.

Notwithstanding the general applicability of the at-risk rules to closely-held corporations, those actively engaged in equipment leasing are excluded from the purview of §465. Both the terms actively engaged and equipment leasing, however, have very specific meanings. For purposes of the exclusion from the at-risk rules, equipment leasing is defined as the leasing of §1245 property and the purchasing, servicing and selling of such equipment. It does not include leasing master sound recordings and other similar contractual arrangements relating to assets associated with literary, artistic or musical properties. In general, a corporation is actively engaged in equipment leasing, for purposes of the §465 exclusion, if at least 50% of the corporation's gross receipts for the taxable year is attributable to equipment leasing.

The component members of a controlled group of corporations are generally treated as a single corporation for purposes of the actively engaged in equipment leasing test. It is often impossible, therefore, for a controlled group to meet the 50% test. To address that problem, if there are members of the controlled group that constitute a qualified leasing group, the rules required to be met to fall within the exception are applied at that level, although the rules are more restrictive than the general 50% test.

A qualified leasing group is a controlled group of corporations that, for the current taxable year and each of the two immediately preceding taxable years, satisfies the following requirements:

1. During the entire year the group had at least three full-time employees, substantially all of whose services were directly related to the equipment leasing activity of the qualified leasing members
2. During the year, the qualified leasing members (in the aggregate) entered into at least five separate equipment leasing transactions.

A qualified leasing member refers to a component member of the controlled group that, for each of the three taxable years referred to above, derives at least 80% of its gross receipts from equipment leasing activities.

In summary, for a controlled group of closely-held corporations to qualify for the equipment leasing exception to the application of §465, the gross receipts test is increased to 80% and the group must have at least three full-time employees and have entered into at least five separate lease transactions for the current taxable year as well as the two preceding taxable years.

LIMITATIONS

The following are the limitations that apply to affected taxpayers under §465.

Loss

As provided in §465, losses are deductible for a taxable year only to the extent of the taxpayer's amount at-risk at the close of the taxable year. The definition of a loss is straightforward and what one would naturally expect: the excess of allowable deductions for the taxable year over the income received or accrued by the taxpayer during the taxable year. In the typical equipment leasing transaction, therefore, the loss would be the excess of MACRS and interest deductions over lease revenue. Nondeductible losses may be carried forward indefinitely and deducted when the amount at-risk increases sufficiently.

Amounts At-Risk

For the most part, what constitutes an amount at-risk is intuitive: the amount of money and the adjusted basis of other property (not to exceed its fair market value net of encumbrances) contributed by the taxpayer to the activity; and amounts borrowed for use in the activity for which the taxpayer is personally liable for repayment or has pledged property, other than property used in such activity, as security for repayment (where such pledged property has a fair market value net of encumbrances at least equal to the loan amount). In general, therefore, equity and recourse debt constitute amounts at-risk.

Any amounts borrowed from a person who has an interest in the activity, or from a person related to a person (other than the taxpayer) having such an interest, are not considered at-risk. Borrowing from a partner in the activity, therefore, even if on a full recourse basis, will not provide at-risk basis.

Borrowing from a person who has an interest in the activity solely as a creditor, however, does not jeopardize the at-risk status of the loan. A corporation that borrows from one of its shareholders, for example, does not tarnish the at-risk status. A lender is considered a person with an interest other than as a creditor only if the lender has either a capital or net profits interest in the activity. A capital interest is an interest in the assets of the activity that is distributable to the owner of the capital interest upon the liquidation of the activity. Partners of a partnership and shareholders of a corporation, for example, have capital interests.

The definition of an interest in net profits is a little more elusive. It is not necessary for a person to have any incidents of ownership in the activity (such as a capital interest) to have an interest in net profits. An employee or independent contractor, any part of whose compensation is determined with reference to the net profits of the activity, is considered to have an interest in the net profits of the activity.

The proposed regulations to §465 contain some helpful examples. A, the owner of a cattle herd, sold the herd to Partnership B. The Partnership paid A $10,000 in cash and executed a full recourse note for $30,000. The Partnership-purchaser then entered into an agreement with A-seller obligating A to take care of the cattle in return for 6% of the Partnership's net profits from the activity. A has an interest in the Partnership's net profits. Therefore, the recourse note does not increase the partners' amount at-risk in the activity. If, however, A's compensation was based on 1% of the Partnership's gross receipts, A would not have an interest other than as a creditor. Therefore, the Partnership's recourse note to A would add to the partners' at-risk basis.

The at-risk rules can be very tricky in lease transactions, particularly in the case of wrap leases (discussed in Chapter Five). Where at-risk considerations are important to the tax benefits of the owner-lessor in a simple sale-assignment structure, if the lease originator lends any money to the owner-lessor and, as part of the transaction, requires the owner-lessor to execute a remarketing agreement, the compensation to the lease originator as the owner's remarketing agent generally should be based on gross (not net) remarketing proceeds.

APPLICABLE ACTIVITIES

When §465 was first enacted as part of the Tax Reform Act of 1976, it was directed primarily at motion films and videotapes, farming, oil, gas and geothermal exploration and equipment leasing. Since that time, it has been expanded to include each activity engaged in by a taxpayer in carrying on a trade or business or for the production of income, including the holding of real property. To make things even more complex, §465 is generally applied separately to each film or videotape, each farm, each oil and gas property, each geothermal property, each equipment lease, etc. Therefore, except as noted below, the at-risk rules are applied separately to each equipment lease transaction.

Fortunately, though, all activities with respect to §1245 properties leased or held for lease by a partnership or S corporation, and placed in service in any taxable year of the partnership or corporation, are treated as a single activity. In addition, if the applicable activities constitute a trade or business, the taxpayer actively participates in the management of the trade or business or the trade or business is carried on by a partnership or S corporation and at least 65% of the losses for the taxable year is allocable to persons who actively participate in the management of the trade or business, the trade or business shall be treated as one activity and §465 shall be applied to the entire activity.

Passive Loss Limitations

Although the focus of this chapter is on the federal income taxation of equipment leasing as it applies to corporations, the passive loss limitation rules have such a pervasive effect and create such dramatic pitfalls and opportunities in the industry's equity marketplace, it is important to become at least familiar with their application. These rules limit the ability of taxpayers to utilize tax benefits arising from certain activities to reduce their salary and portfolio income. Since 1976 and the enactment of the at-risk rules, there has been a systematic curtailment of available tax deferral loopholes. This curtailment is the result of an emerging policy position within the government that tax benefits can add to the attractiveness of an investment; however, they should not be the primary incentive to enter into the transaction. The passive loss rules shift the emphasis (at least for the taxpayers affected) of an investment from the tax benefits to the economic merits.

AFFECTED TAXPAYERS

The passive loss limitation rules, codified as §469 of the IRC, apply generally to individuals, estates, trusts and personal service corporations. For purposes of these rules, a personal service corporation is one in which the principal activity is the performance of personal services substantially performed by owner-employees, i.e., any employee who owns any of the outstanding stock of the corporation. In addition, to a more limited extent as discussed below, the passive loss rules apply to closely-held corporations, i.e., corporations with respect to which at least 50% of the outstanding stock is owned at any time during the last half of the taxable year by, or for, not more than five individuals.

APPLICATION OF THE RULES

For affected taxpayers, the passive loss rules establish three different types of income and losses: active or trade or business income, portfolio income and passive income. The first category consists generally of salary, wages and income from general business pursuits where the taxpayer materially participates in the income earning activity. It is the catch-all category, i.e., if it is not portfolio income or passive income, it is active or trade or business income, and as such, is the broadest of the three categories.

Portfolio income, as the name implies, consists of interest, dividends, royalties, annuities and gain or loss from the sale or exchange of portfolio assets. Portfolio income retains its character, even if it is generated in connection with a passive activity.

The third category, passive income, is any activity that involves the conduct of a trade or business, and in which the taxpayer does not materially participate, and any rental activity where payments are primarily for the use of tangible property,[27] which conclusively includes equipment leasing. Material participation is defined as involvement by the taxpayer in the activity on a regular, continuous and substantial basis. Although there is certainly some gray area in this definition, the most commonly encountered investment vehicle where the law conclusively presumes material participation not to exist is a limited partnership. Therefore, all losses generated in connection with limited partnership interests are passive losses.

Limitation

It is, of course, the third category that is the primary focus of this section, and that has provided both consternation and challenge for taxpayers and sellers of investments alike. For all affected taxpayers other than closely-held corporations, and subject to the transition rules, losses from passive activities cannot be used to offset income generated in either the active or portfolio categories. Instead, passive activity losses can be used only to offset income from passive activities. The rule is not applied on an activity-by-activity basis; passive activities are viewed in the aggregate. Therefore, a passive activity loss is the amount by which the aggregate losses from all passive activities for the taxable year exceed the aggregate income from all passive activities for such year.

---

[27] Working interests in oil or gas properties where the taxpayer's liability is not limited are specifically exempted from the application of the passive loss rules.

For closely-held corporations, passive activity losses can be used to offset passive income as well as trade or business income. The only restriction is that passive losses of a closely-held corporation cannot be used to offset portfolio income. Disallowed passive losses are not lost; they are carried forward indefinitely until usable.[28] Upon disposition by the taxpayer of its entire interest in a passive activity, allowance of all theretofore suspended passive losses attributable to that activity is triggered.[29] To the extent that any loss recognized on the disposition is from the sale or exchange of a capital asset, the capital loss limitation is applied before the passive loss allowance, i.e., the suspended passive loss is limited to the amount of gains from the sales or exchanges of capital assets plus $3,000.

The intended and general effect of the passive loss rules is, once again, to mitigate the ability of taxpayers to defer income taxes through the use of investments generating tax losses in their early years. However, as will always be the case where the tax rates are anything above insignificant, taxpayers (and those relying, to at least some extent, on the taxpayers' general aversion to paying taxes) will attempt to find methods to utilize restrictions and limitations to their benefit.

With respect to the passive loss rules, one such approach involves the purchase by a taxpayer (who has passive investments generating nondeductible losses) of investments that generate passive gains, so as to maximize the benefit of the otherwise suspended passive losses. Conversely, taxpayers whose passive investments are now in the phantom income stage can purchase passive investments that generate losses. These losses can offset income that would otherwise create current tax liability. Therefore, there is still some scope for tax deferral. However, the hurdles presented to taxpayers by the web of limitations created over the past several years by Congress (of which the passive loss rules are the capstone) make it too complex or burdensome for many taxpayers.

Rental Real Estate Exception

To provide some relief for the middle income taxpayer, Congress saw fit to create a small exception to the blanket application of the passive loss rules: up to $25,000 of losses and credits arising from the ownership and rental of real property can be used to offset the nonpassive income of the taxpayer. To take advantage of this exception, the taxpayer must actively participate in the management of the rental activity, and its ownership interest in the activity must be at least 10%. Active participation is a lesser standard than material participation and generally connotes some supervisory role with respect to the business decisions attendant to the activity.

The taxpayer must net its income and losses from all of its rental real estate activities in which it actively participates. If there is a net loss, it must first offset it against any passive income. Any remainder up to $25,000 can then offset income from nonpassive activities. The $25,000

---

[28] Interest deductions arising in connection with passive activities are subject to the passive loss rules, and are not also subject to the investment interest limitation under IRC §163(d).

[29] Suspended losses will not be permitted to be recognized, however, if the disposition of the interest in the passive activity is to a related party.

allowance is phased out between $100,000 and $150,000 of the taxpayer's adjusted gross income (calculated without regard to Individual Retirement Account contributions, if any, and taxable social security benefits).

Phase-In Rules

For interests in passive activities held by a taxpayer on October 22, 1986 (the date of enactment of TRA '86), the passive loss limitation rules are phased in over 5 years as shown in Table 16. If a taxpayer acquired an interest in a passive activity after the date of enactment (but on or before the last day of 1986), the limitations are inapplicable for any 1986 loss, but are applicable to the losses of any subsequent year (i.e., no phase-in is available for passive investments purchased after October 22, 1986 and on or before December 31, 1986).

As with almost all transitional rules, a binding contract exception exists in the case of the passive loss rules. Any interest acquired after October 22, 1986 pursuant to a written binding contract in effect on October 22, 1986 and at all times thereafter, is treated as held on the date of enactment.

CONCLUSION

The preceding material addresses many of the issues encountered daily in the leasing industry. Although the material contained in this chapter is believed to be correct in all respects as of the time it was written, it should be clear to all by now that if Congress is not currently in the process of changing the tax law, then at least the Treasury Department and/or the courts are interpreting it. In any event, additional and needed clarification undoubtedly will be forthcoming. In the meantime, it is suggested that taxpayers rely on their own independent tax counsel to resolve the specific and myriad issues that arise in this fascinating and challenging business.

Table 16
Phase-in Percentages

Year	% of Loss That Is Nondeductible
1987	35%
1988	60
1989	80
1990	90
1991 and thereafter	100

CHAPTER FIVE
WRAP LEASES

Wrap lease transactions became fairly widespread among high tax bracket taxpayers in the mid-1970s. Since the maximum federal income tax bracket was 70% prior to the Economic Recovery Tax Act of 1981, and thereafter (through 1986) was 50%, the typical wrap structure provided significant tax deferral potential for maximum bracket taxpayers. In some instances, however, whether a wrap lease transaction had any economic merit, aside from the tax benefits, was suspect, to say the least. Consequently, the Internal Revenue Service (IRS) began scrutinizing wrap leases in the late '70s and early '80s and, in many instances, denied the claimed tax benefits on the basis, among other things, of a lack of economic substance (i.e., but for the tax benefits, the transaction would not have resulted in a profit to the taxpayer). Upon review by the courts, the IRS position with respect to many of the early transactions was upheld. However, as the wrap lease marketplace assimilated some of the standards enunciated by the courts, the IRS success ratio declined considerably. Today, although wrap leases can still provide some tax deferral benefits, they are often consummated for the economic benefits to both the wrap lessor and the wrap lessee. This chapter examines the following aspects of wrap leases:

- Basic Structure
- Variations and Complexities
- Investor Tax Concerns
- Future of the Wrap Lease
- Example and Analysis.

BASIC STRUCTURE

Although there have been myriad esoteric and very complex versions of the wrap lease, the basic structure is not unduly complex, depending, of course, on such things as the availability of tax credits, whether the wrap lessor was subject to the at-risk rules and whether the wrap lessee had sufficient tax benefits from other transactions to absorb the often significant phantom income resulting during the term of the user lease.

Standard Leveraged Lease

To begin with, a standard leveraged lease transaction is structured, as illustrated in Figure 1. For example, the lessor (or lease originator) enters into a 5-year lease of computer equipment with the lessee (or user-lessee). Assume that the cost of the equipment from the manufacturer is $1 million and the 60 monthly lease payments are due in advance, each in the amount of $18,337.00. The lease originator thereafter assigns its right to receive the lease payments to a lender in return for a nonrecourse, purchase money loan made by the lender to the lease originator. The amount of the loan is equal to the present value of the lease payments, discounted at the interest rate agreed to by the lender and the lease originator, determined by reference to such things as the term of the lease, the prevailing interest rates, the credit rating of the user-lessee and the lender's cost of funds. As part of the loan transaction, the lease originator grants the lender a security interest in the equipment and, of course, assigns the lease to the lender.

Assuming the interest rate charged by the lender in this example was 9%, the amount of the loan would be $889,980.19. Therefore, to pay the manufacturer for the equipment, the lease originator would combine the proceeds of the loan with $110,019.81 of its internal funds, or raw equity. If nothing more were done, the foregoing would constitute a leveraged lease, where the lease payments would be paid directly to the lender to fully amortize the loan. At the end of the lease, the lease originator would remarket the equipment by either re-leasing it or selling it to the user-lessee, or by selling or leasing it to another user.

At this point, the lease originator determines whether it will maintain the lease in its own portfolio or sell the equipment to an investor, or equity source. In the latter case, the lease originator can accomplish its objective essentially two different ways: via a straight sale-assignment or via a wrap lease.

In a straight sale-assignment, the lease originator sells the equipment to the equity source, subject to the lease and to the loan. The purchase price would be equal to the sum of the outstanding balance of the loan, the raw equity and a transaction fee, which generally ranges from ½ to 3% of the cost of the equipment. In a sale-assignment, the equity source assumes the rights of the lease originator in the equipment and the lease, and typically assumes the lease originator's obligations under the nonrecourse loan. Therefore, from a federal income tax perspective, and during the initial lease term, the equity source includes in its income the lease revenue paid by the user-lessee, and deducts the interest expense on the loan, as well as the Modified Accelerated Cost Recovery System (MACRS) depreciation deductions.

From a cash flow perspective, the equity source pays the raw equity and fee, obtains the tax benefits and/or pays the tax liability, as the case may be, and receives the residual value of the equipment at the end of the lease. Depending on the level of sophistication of the equity source, the lease originator may be employed as the remarketing agent, at which time it would use its best efforts to re-lease, lease or sell the equipment in return for a remarketing fee, generally ranging from 5 to 20% of the remarketing proceeds.

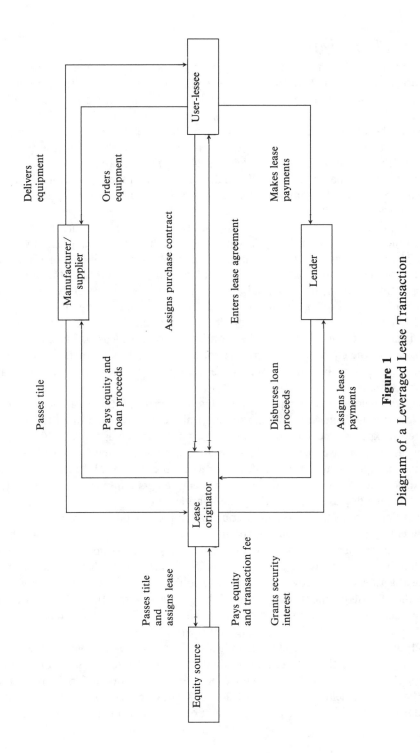

Figure 1

Diagram of a Leveraged Lease Transaction

Wrap Lease Alternative

The lease originator also may sell the equipment to the equity source via the wrap lease vehicle, as illustrated in Figure 2. In this case, the equity source purchases the equipment from the lease originator, and then leases it back to the lease originator for a term generally 1 to 3 years longer than the term of the user lease. The lease payments due by the lease originator (who has now become the wrap lessee) during the term of the wrap lease typically have the same present value as the lease payments due by the user-lessee during the user lease term. In this example, assume that the term of the wrap lease is 84 months, and that the discount rate used to discount the wrap lease payments is 9.5% (slightly higher than the 9% charged by the lender in the user lease because of the somewhat longer term). The 84 monthly wrap lease payments, therefore, would each be in the amount of $14,431.57.

The purchase price of the equipment paid by the equity source (who has now become the wrap lessor) to the lease originator/wrap lessee is equal to the sum of the present value of the wrap lease payments, the raw equity and the fee — in other words, the cost of the equipment plus the fee. The raw equity and fee are typically paid in cash. The balance of the purchase price is paid via a promissory note, the principal amount of which is the present value of the lease payments due during the wrap lease term. In this example, the interest rate on the note is 9.5%. Therefore, although the equity source/wrap lessor owes the lease originator/wrap lessee $14,431.57 per month, for 84 months, on the promissory note, the lease originator/wrap lessee is obligated to pay to the equity source/wrap lessor the same amount, for the same period, as a lease payment due under the wrap lease. Consequently, neither pays the other that amount during the wrap lease term.

From a federal income tax perspective, during the term of the wrap lease the equity source/wrap lessor must include in income the monthly lease payments of $14,431.57. It will deduct the interest expense incurred on the promissory note, as well as the MACRS deductions. After the expiration of the user lease, the lease originator/wrap lessee will use its best efforts to re-lease or lease the equipment to the user-lessee or to another lessee. The amount of such lease payments to which the equity source/wrap lessor is entitled generally ranges from 50 to 75%, and must also be included as income during the wrap lease term.

From a cash flow perspective, the equity source/wrap lessor pays, as part of the purchase price, the raw equity and the fee. During the first several years of the wrap lease, the equity source/wrap lessor will benefit from the tax savings resulting from deductions exceeding income. Tax liabilities are generated during the last few years, although the re-lease revenue is intended to be at least enough to cover the taxes. The equity source/wrap lessor begins to receive its portion of the re-lease payments at the end of the user lease term. In addition, at the end of the wrap lease term, the equity source/wrap lessor is entitled to the residual value proceeds (less any remarketing fee charged by the lease originator/wrap lessee).

As the analysis at the end of this chapter indicates, in a wrap lease structure (depending on the applicable tax rates and the re-lease and residual value assumptions) the pretax yield can be somewhat less than the risk-free rate, while, because of the tax deferral aspects of the transaction, the after-tax yield can be quite attractive. That, of course, is why the wrap lease has been so popular with high bracket taxpayers. In light of the decreasing tax rates, the desirability

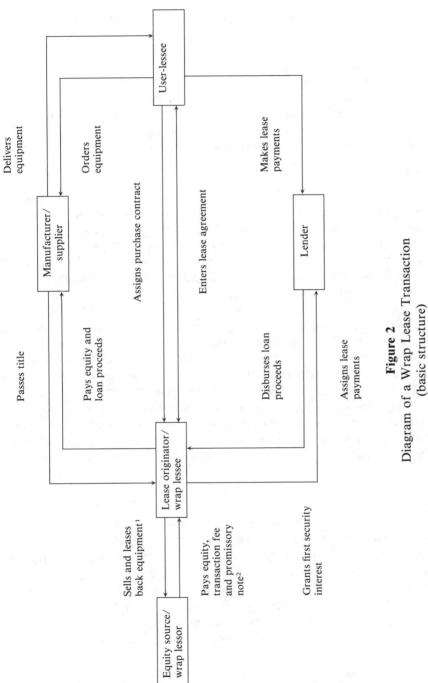

Figure 2
Diagram of a Wrap Lease Transaction
(basic structure)

[1] The wrap lease term is generally 1 to 3 years longer than the user lease term.
[2] The payments due under the note generally equal the wrap lease payments; therefore, actual cash payments are not made by either party.

of the wrap lease from a tax deferral perspective has diminished. There are, on the other hand, significant economic reasons for the continued viability of wrap leases.

VARIATIONS AND COMPLEXITIES

The preceding discussion provided an overview of the basics of wrap leases. While this section is not intended to comprehensively analyze the variety of intricate structures wrap leases can take, or the reasons for them, it is important to understand some of the complexities of wrap leases and how the leases can be structured to overcome such complexities.

Phantom Income

In the basic structure set forth earlier, the wrap lessee is required to absorb a significant amount of phantom income during the term of the wrap lease. In the example, the lease originator/wrap lessee is obligated to pay a monthly lease payment under the wrap lease of $14,431.57. During the term of the user lease, however, the lease originator/wrap lessee is required to include in income as lease revenue the amount of $18,337.00. This results in phantom income of almost $47,000 per year and, assuming a 34% federal income tax rate, a tax liability of almost $16,000 per year. There is no cash generated from the transaction that inures to the benefit of the lease originator/wrap lessee from which to pay that tax liability.[3]

To avoid this problem, which, depending on the size of the transaction, can be quite substantial, the lease originator will first sell the equipment to a company in a net operating loss (NOL) position, that will, in turn, sell the equipment to, and lease it back from, the equity source/wrap lessor. The NOL company then becomes the wrap lessee and absorbs the phantom income, which will not result in tax liability because the phantom income arising from the wrap lease transaction is offset by the NOL carryforwards. The NOL company generally is paid some nominal amount to act as the wrap lessee. To ensure its entitlement to the re-lease revenue during the period after the expiration of the user lease, through the expiration of the wrap lease (or shirttail period), the lease originator may enter into a remarketing agreement with the wrap lessee.

Other Factors

First, if the wrap lessor is subject to the at-risk rules, the promissory note executed by it in favor of the wrap lessee should be recourse and any sharing of revenue by the wrap lessee should be structured as a percentage of gross (not net) proceeds. Such a structure should comply with the proposed regulations defining an interest other than as a creditor.

Second, Revenue Procedure (Rev. Proc.) 75-21 provides that a lessor cannot borrow any money for the purchase of the leased equipment from the lessee. It is clear that violation of that rule, in and of itself, will not result in the invalidation of the lease transaction. However, because wrap leases are suspect to begin with, some commentators and practitioners advise that

---

[3] During this period, the lease originator/wrap lessee also will be recognizing interest income on the promissory note, and interest expense on the nonrecourse borrowing.

the lease originator sell the equipment to the wrap lessor, who, in turn, leases it to an unrelated, third-party company. This, of course, heightens the complexity of the documentation, but may overcome a legitimate concern.

Third, the wrap transaction can take the form of one leveraged lease superimposed on another. In other words, the wrap portion of the transaction can involve an independent third-party lender to which the lease payments from the wrap lessee are assigned in return for a second loan. The second loan is used by the wrap lessor to pay off the balance of the purchase price, rather than by executing a note in favor of the wrap lessee. This approach also solves the Rev. Proc. 75-21 concern indicated in the preceding paragraph.

There are several additional variations that have been used from time to time, primarily to avoid particular tax problems. As one might imagine, many of those variations were created where the wrap lessee attempted to retain the Investment Tax Credit or it was taken for the account of a closely-held wrap lessor.

INVESTOR TAX CONCERNS

As previously indicated, the critical inquiry of the IRS with respect to a wrap lease transaction, particularly involving an individual taxpayer, is whether the transaction has economic substance, i.e., whether, apart from tax benefits, there is a reasonable expectation of profit from the transaction. That determination generally is made based on an analysis of pretax cash flow. In a wrap lease, pretax cash flow consists of equity invested (outflow) together with the equity source/wrap lessor's share of re-rentals and residual (inflow). Because the expectation of profit determination is made as of the inception of the transaction, it is important for the equity source/wrap lessor to have legitimate residual value projections prepared by independent third-party experts. In many recent tax cases, whether the taxpayer or the IRS prevailed depended almost entirely on the credibility of the third-party expert.

Because the wrap lease is a lease, the taxpayer should structure the transaction so that it meets the requirements of a true lease, as discussed in Chapter Three. In many instances, it is more difficult to meet the Rev. Proc. 75-21 advance ruling requirements in a wrap transaction. Recall, though, that a true lease can exist even if those requirements are not met in their entirety.

Depending on the type of taxpayer, there may be some at-risk and investment interest limitations, as well as passive loss limitations, as discussed in Chapter Four. The at-risk and investment interest rules have become less important with the enactment of the passive loss rules. Nevertheless, both must be considered. Another tax limitation is the amount of MACRS available in the first year if the taxpayer is a noncorporate taxpayer and has not owned any substantial amounts of depreciable property in the past. Application of the short taxable year rules can severely curtail the tax savings in the first year, which will have a similar effect on the transaction's after-tax yield.

As with all transactions involving depreciable property, the alternative minimum tax implications must be addressed. Wrap leases can become complex and, therefore, require extensive tax, legal and accounting expertise in their structuring. As discussed next, however, wrap leases do have a continuing role in the tax-oriented investment community.

FUTURE OF THE WRAP LEASE

The wrap lease will continue to be a viable method of marketing lease transactions to equity investors, but probably for different reasons than in the past. There are presently four categories of reasons for the continued use of wrap leases.

First, many taxpayers (not subject to the passive loss limitations) will continue to enter into wrap leases for the tax deferral benefits arising therefrom. These benefits are exaggerated in a wrap lease because of the 5-year depreciation expense being deducted from a 7-year revenue stream. Of course, most taxpayers will require the transaction to have some modicum of economic merit; however, for some taxpayers, the economic justification will continue to be only secondary to the tax benefits. In this first category are also taxpayers who are subject to the passive loss rules and who currently have passive investments in the phantom income stage. By investing in properly structured wrap leases, such taxpayers can (temporarily) solve their phantom income problems.

Second, as a direct result of the decrease in tax rates and the enactment of the passive loss limitation rules, the market for primarily tax motivated wrap leases is contracting and will continue to do so. However, if the transaction is properly structured with reputable parties, the wrap lease can be economically advantageous to the wrap lessor. Therefore, equity investors who are looking primarily for investment potential, but who can utilize the tax benefits, will continue to invest in wrap transactions as a part of their total investment strategy.

Third, wrap leases will be promoted by lease originators desiring to mitigate their residual risk. The trend in wraps is for a lease originator to enter into a shorter term lease, e.g., 36 months, with a user-lessee, whereby the equity insertion is around 20 points. The lease originator will then enter into a wrap lease with an equity source/wrap lessor whereby the term of the wrap lease will be 60 months. Because the equity source/wrap lessor has purchased a 60-month transaction, its equity insertion will be around 8 points. Therefore, the lease originator/wrap lessee's exposure in the transaction is 12 points. The lease originator/wrap lessee will take the re-lease income generated during the shirttail period to recover its remaining equity exposure plus a profit. At the end of the wrap lease, the equity investor/wrap lessor is entitled to the residual value of the equipment (less any remarketing fee). By this approach, the lease originator/wrap lessee has effectively reduced its residual risk immediately by 8 points, and the equity investor/wrap lessor has purchased a transaction with a blend of tax and economic benefits.

Fourth, wrap leases are used more and more frequently by larger, creditworthy lessors as a vehicle to upgrade the credit standing of smaller lessees. For example, when a large financial institution enters into a large lease transaction with a regional credit, often the credit standing of the bank lessor is greater than that of the user-lessee. It is, therefore, easier to obtain a loan based on the financial strength of the bank lessor. Consequently, in the event that the transaction is sold to an equity investor, the investor will have a greater comfort level, as will the lender discounting the lease payment stream, with an assignment of the wrap lease (where the lessee is the bank lessor).

EXAMPLE AND ANALYSIS

The structure and characteristics of a wrap lease have been presented, along with a general description of each aspect of the wrap lease. In order to understand the economics of a transaction, an example using numbers and facts must be used. The example in this chapter presents the wrap lease from the equity source/wrap lessor perspective, and is based on the assumptions in Table 1. The assumptions have been categorized by user lease and wrap lease characteristics for clarity of understanding.

The equity source/wrap lessor's annualized, monthly pretax return in this lease is 2.84%, and is based on the equity insertion of $135,019.81 required to gain annual re-lease rentals of $27,708.61 per year plus a net residual of $108,000 at the end of the lease term. The after-tax internal rate of return in this example would be based upon the comparison of monthly cash flows to the net outflow of $63,064.81 at the lease inception. Table 2 represents the annual summary of the monthly cash flows in this example. Note how the wrap lease payment from the lease originator/wrap lessee to the equity source/wrap lessor exactly equals the amount of the payment on the promissory note from the equity source/wrap lessor to the lease originator/wrap lessee. The tax attributes, which are a very important aspect of wrap leasing, are shown in Table 3.

Table 1
Assumptions

Description	User Lease	Wrap Lease
Equipment	Computer equipment	Computer equipment
Total list price	$1,000,000	N/A
Total sale price	N/A	$1,025,000
Initial lease term	60 months	84 months
Rent commencement date	January 1, 1989	January 1, 1989
Basic rent amount, in advance	$18,337.00	$14,431.57
Tax rate (includes 5% state taxes)	N/A	39%
Required equity	$110,019.81	$135,019.81
Assumed debt rate	9.0000%	9.5000%
Loan amount	$889,980.19	$889,980.19
Residual value to equity source/ wrap lessor (net of remarketing)	N/A	$108,000
Lessor's fiscal year-end	N/A	December 31
Equipment in-service date	N/A	December 16, 1988
Closing date (date of investor/equity payment)	N/A	December 31, 1988
Re-rental payments	N/A	$27,708.61

Table 2
Annual Cash Flow Summary
(as of December 31)

	1988	1989	1990	1991	1992	1993	1994	1995	1996
Investment/residual	($135,019.81)	$ 0.00	$ 0.00	$ 0.00	$ 0.00	$ 0.00	$ 0.00	$ 0.00	$108,000.00
Rental income	0.00	173,178.84	173,178.84	173,178.84	173,178.84	173,178.84	173,178.84	173,178.84	0.00
Debt service	0.00	(173,178.84)	(173,178.84)	(173,178.84)	(173,178.84)	(173,178.84)	(173,178.84)	(173,178.84)	0.00
Re-rental income	0.00	0.00	0.00	0.00	0.00	0.00	27,708.61	27,708.61	0.00
Tax savings (cost)[4]	71,955.00	87,925.55	41,964.38	5,556.13	(1,837.69)	(27,313.59)	(65,289.48)	(74,415.77)	(49,619.53)
Net cash flow	($ 63,064.81)	$ 87,925.55	$ 41,964.38	$ 5,556.13	($ 1,837.69)	($ 27,313.59)	($ 37,580.86)	($ 46,707.16)	$ 58,380.47
Cumulative cash flow	($ 63,064.81)	$ 24,860.74	$ 66,825.12	$ 72,381.25	$ 70,543.56	$ 43,229.97	$ 5,649.11	($ 41,058.05)	$ 17,322.42

Table 3
Annual Tax Computation Summary
(as of December 31)

	1988	1989	1990	1991	1992	1993	1994	1995	1996
Rental income	$ 0.00	$173,178.84	$173,178.84	$173,178.84	$173,178.84	$173,178.84	$173,178.84	$173,178.84	$ 0.00
Re-rental income	0.00	0.00	0.00	0.00	0.00	0.00	27,708.61	27,708.61	0.00
Residual less book value	0.00	0.00	0.00	0.00	0.00	0.00	0.00	0.00	$108,000.00
Depreciation	(205,000.00)	(328,000.00)	(196,800.00)	(118,080.00)	(118,080.00)	(59,040.00)	0.00	0.00	0.00
Loan interest	0.00	(72,901.20)	(70,633.00)	(60,455.57)	(49,268.06)	(36,970.22)	(23,451.84)	(8,591.80)	0.00
Taxable income (loss)	($205,000.00)	($227,722.36)	($ 94,254.16)	($ 5,356.73)	$ 5,830.78	$ 77,168.62	$177,435.62	$192,295.66	$108,000.00
Tax savings (cost)	$71,955.00	$87,925.55	$ 41,964.38	$ 5,556.13	($ 1,837.69)	($ 27,313.59)	($ 65,289.48)	($ 74,415.77)	($ 49,619.53)

[4] Refer to Table 3.

CONCLUSION

Wrap leasing is one of the most complex areas of leasing. The wrap lease structure may range from basic to exotic, and the motivations for this form of leveraged lease are just as diverse as the many ways it can be structured. Although the heyday of wrap leasing is apparently past, due to the many limitations of tax benefits, the wrap lease still remains a viable financing instrument. This viability is a result of the shift in emphasis from primarily tax-oriented, to economic and cash flow factors such as residuals and re-lease income.

PART 3
FINANCE

CHAPTER SIX
LEASE VERSUS BUY

Is it preferable to lease equipment rather than purchase it? Although a seemingly simple question, the lease versus buy decision is one of great complexity, whose solution is commonly oversimplified and, consequently, arrived at incorrectly. This chapter investigates the following aspects of the lease versus buy decision:

- Decision Process
- Decision Input Premises
- Decision Logic and Methodology
- Perspective and Qualitative Ramifications
- Decision Feedback
- Alternative Minimum Tax Impact
- Foreign Tax Credit Impact
- Lease Versus Buy (Loan) Cases.

DECISION PROCESS

Leasing is a viable alternative to conventional forms of equipment financing, and frequently offers substantial cost savings to the lessee. Expense reductions, however, represent only part of the numerous reasons why leasing might be preferable to conventional financing methods. For example, a properly structured lease with a low down payment might alleviate liquidity problems experienced by a growing company whose cash is tied up in the working capital necessary to meet growing market demands. Additionally, a lease might be preferable to the purchase alternative because of certain flexibilities in the lease, such as the privilege of cancelling early, upgrading or swapping. Although the value of flexible lease terms is difficult to quantify, such flexibilities nevertheless influence the lease versus buy decision.

Since lower cost represents only one of the many reasons why leasing might be preferable to purchasing, it follows that the lease versus buy decision process must, to the extent possible, incorporate the numerous variables influencing the overall decision. Typically, a quality decision leading to the right equipment financing choice has four essential elements:

1. Premises represent the data and information that form the input assumptions for any logical conclusions
2. Logic implies cogent reasoning is applied to the premises. Logic must be applied regardless of the complexity of the problem. This process may require interrelating the numerous variables impacting the decision
3. Perspective requires that qualitative factors be considered also, as part of the overall decision. Common sense, feasibility, a holistic approach and other aspects are part of the notion of perspective
4. Feedback confirms the past and assists in adjusting any decision to the dynamics of future change.

The four elements of the decision process are interrelated in that all four must occur at the same time. The lack of any one element may be sufficient to cause an erroneous conclusion concerning the lease versus buy decision. The balance of this chapter is devoted to examining how each of these important decision elements impacts the lease versus buy decision.

DECISION INPUT PREMISES

Premises represent the primary data and information inputs upon which a decision will be based. Input premises must have four characteristics to be considered reliable: (1) validity, (2) completeness, (3) verifiability and (4) objectivity.

Validity

This characteristic implies that all input premises, such as residual disposal assumptions, timeline issues and loan terms, etc., represent faithfully the anticipated borrowing or leasing scenario. Faithful representation is the essence of validity. Premises must represent what they purport to be, otherwise they become invalid and unreliable.

For example, a serious validity problem often arises in the lease versus buy decision where the expected economic life of a piece of equipment exceeds the term of the lease being considered to finance the equipment's acquisition. Some equipment may be expected to last 7 years, considering physical as well as technological obsolescence, while, at the same time, a 5-year lease is contemplated. To compare 7 years of ownership expenses with only 5 years of lease expenses would be an inappropriate mismatching of holding periods. To be valid, the two cost totals must represent the same holding period.

Such equating of the buy to the lease term can be accomplished many ways. The method most indicative of the actual expected holding pattern should be chosen, however. Table 1 depicts numerous holding pattern alternatives used to equate buying with leasing. The anticipated disposition of a purchased asset is described in the first column and the corresponding disposition of the asset (necessary to equate the terms) had it been leased is described in the second column. Table 1 assumes that the economic life of the asset is 7 years, which exceeds the

Table 1
Equating Loan and Lease Holding Patterns

Purchased Equipment Disposition	Leased Equipment Disposition
Salvage the equipment at the end of 5 years	Return the equipment to the lessor at the end of the 5-year base term
Retain the equipment and continue its use until the end of its economic life	Purchase the equipment and retain its use until the end of its economic life
Retain the equipment and continue its use until the end of its economic life	Renew the lease after 5 years and continue to use the equipment until the end of its economic life
Salvage the equipment at the end of 5 years	Purchase the equipment after 5 years and immediately sell it to others (assumes a bargain purchase option exists)
Lease the equipment to others at the end of 5 years	Purchase the equipment after 5 years and immediately lease it to others
Lease the equipment to others at the end of 5 years	Renew the lease after 5 years and immediately sublease the equipment to others
Lease the equipment to others at the end of 5 years	Return the equipment to the lessor at the end of the 5-year lease term
Sell the equipment on an installment basis to others at the end of 5 years	Return the equipment to the lessor at the end of the 5-year lease term
Buy, in succession, five more pieces of equipment totalling 35 years (5 × 7 years). Equating of the total buy holding term to the leasing term obviates any need for residual assumptions	Lease, in succession, seven more similar assets subject to 5-year leases, totalling 35 years (7 × 5 years)
Trade in the existing equipment on new equipment at the end of 5 years	Purchase the equipment and trade it in on new equipment at the end of 5 years

5-year lease term, as it is very common in the leasing industry for the economic life of a particular piece of equipment to exceed its respective lease term.

In the situation where the decision maker is not absolutely certain which disposition alternative will occur, several can be chosen and a weighted average conclusion determined. The percentage weights would be assigned on the basis of the probability of occurrence of one alternative versus the others. (Just a note on the 35-year alternative in Table 1. Although seemingly absurd to forecast so far in the future, this method prevents residual assumptions from influencing the decision, since no salvage is assumed under either the purchase or lease alternatives.)

Another important validity issue relates to the assumed length of the loan used to fund the equipment's purchase (note that a cash acquisition without borrowing also can be assumed). Generally, in the absence of actual quotes from lending institutions to the contrary, the terms of the loan should match those of the lease. Terms to be matched include the down payment amount, the number of months in the loan term and a balloon payment equal to the lease purchase option that is expected to be exercised. Skip, step-up and step-down payments should be the same. Loan origination fees, refundable security deposits and compensating bank balances should not be assumed to exist unless they really do. When these fees do exist, they should be evaluated as they are, without being made to conform to any corresponding cash flows of the lease.

Actual, verifiable, legitimate loan quotes that faithfully represent the best installment borrowing terms available should be used. The assumed borrowing interest rate also should be indicative of rates charged on similar term borrowings. When the appropriate present value discount rate (the lessee's after-tax cost of debt) is applied to the debt costs, loan terms are not very important; however, use of rates higher than the cost of debt (discussed below) makes loan assumptions material in their impact on the lease versus buy decision.

Completeness

This characteristic implies that the required data and information inputs are sufficient to solve the problem without omissions or without the burden of excess, irrelevant or overlapping data. All pertinent costs should be included. Such relevant costs represent differential expenses that occur under each alternative, but that vary in amount (e.g., sales tax), or those costs that impact only one alternative (e.g., interim rent in a lease). Costs that are exactly the same in either the lease or buy alternative can be excluded or included without impacting the final decision. Maintenance costs, for example, frequently cost the same whether one leases or buys equipment.

Typical revenues, benefits, costs and expenses that must be included before a lease versus buy analysis is complete are:

1. Sales tax and/or use tax
2. Property tax
3. Closing, documentation, origination fees, etc.
4. Installation costs
5. Shipping costs — freight in and out
6. Deinstallation — removal costs, etc.

7. Maintenance and any other bundled services included in a full-service lease
8. Security deposits and compensating bank balances
9. Tax benefits derived from tax impacted items such as Modified Accelerated Cost Recovery System (MACRS) and lease rentals
10. Alternative minimum tax (AMT) impact
11. Foreign tax credit (FTC) impact on interest deductibility
12. Insurance (product liability and casualty, etc.).

Verifiability

This characteristic implies that the input premises are bona fide, authentic and based on factual, existing, truthful supporting documents. Lease bids or quotes must be enforceable (able to be acted upon) before being considered verifiable. Residual appraisals must not be delusive (or "made as instructed"). Furthermore, the methodology used to estimate costs, etc., must be subject to reasonable duplication by independent third parties having access to the same facts and assumptions; otherwise, human judgments and estimates might not be considered verifiable.

Objectivity

This characteristic implies a lack of bias. The input premises must not be designed to result in a particular outcome decided beforehand. The decision maker's prejudices and predilections should not impact the decision. If a data processing manager wants to lease a new computer, not because doing so would represent the best financial decision, but because the lease rentals can be hidden as part of departmental operating costs, there is a good chance that the financial inputs will have a bias towards leasing. Typically, such bias would be introduced through an undervaluing of residual values in the purchase alternative so the cost of leasing appears more favorable. As a result of these prejudices, any cost or revenue subject to human judgment must be scrutinized for lack of objectivity.

Without adequate validity, completeness, verifiability and objectivity, input premises might be unreliable. Any resulting logical conclusion might be suspect, not because of faulty reasoning, but because of faulty input premises.

DECISION LOGIC AND METHODOLOGY

In general, the logic of lease versus buy is simply one of cost minimization. The basic decision criterion is that of choosing the alternative with the lowest total cost. The time value of money, however, must impact the cost minimization decision since a dollar of expense incurred today is more costly than a dollar of expense incurred 5 years from today. Therefore, when the time value of money becomes part of the logic process, the decision criterion becomes choosing that financing alternative, lease or buy, with the lowest present value of costs. Costs, of course, must be converted to an after-tax basis before present value discounting since tax benefits play such an important part in the decision.

Beyond present value analysis, other time value of money approaches may be used, such as future value analysis, also known as terminal value analysis (TVA), or internal rate of return (IRR). IRR analysis is difficult since there are no revenues to relate to expenses; hence, the computation becomes theoretically problematic although the IRR of the cash flow differences could be computed. Revenues generally are not considered a part of the lease versus buy decision since the capital budgeting decision that relates revenues to expenses is assumed to already have been made. In other words, once the decision to acquire a piece of equipment has been determined, how it is to be financed (leasing or buying) then follows. If the method of financing an investment in equipment could make the difference between whether it should be acquired in the first place, the acquisition decision would probably be rejected as too marginal.

Capital Budgeting and Lease Versus Buy

Actually, the lease versus buy decision is a subset of the capital budgeting decision, which includes other financial issues to be discussed later in this section. Figure 1 describes five basic financial decisions of equipment acquisition and funding, of which lease versus buy is only one element. As shown in Figure 1, the five basic decisions are capital budgeting, capital structure optimization, liquidity preference versus financial decision, loan versus lease and on or off balance sheet financing.

Decision Complexity

Determination of the overall cost of leasing is a complex process since leasing costs include four separate financial elements, each of which must be separately valued. Futhermore, three of the elements normally appear as part of the capital budgeting process; only the remaining element is considered a true lease versus buy cost. The first three of the following costs are generally considered capital budgeting elements and the fourth is a true lease versus buy financing cost.

1. Obsolescence avoidance
2. Tax benefits (MACRS, etc.)
3. Indirect variable costs
4. Equivalent loan costs.

It is essential to an understanding of lease versus buy to see how these costs interrelate; therefore, each is discussed, followed by an illustrative example using numbers.

OBSOLESCENCE AVOIDANCE

A portion of the total loan or lease payments represents the principal portion of the loan or lease paid to the creditor or lessor. In the case of a lease, if the lessor relies upon 10% future residual proceeds in structuring the lease, the lease rentals amortize only 90% of the equipment's cost. To the degree a lessee anticipates the equipment's future value to be below 10% of the equipment's cost, it has hedged against obsolescence through leasing. However, were the equipment to be worth more than 10% of cost, the lessee would have been in a better economic position through borrowing.

If the equipment user anticipates buying the equipment, then each of the total acquisition costs would be compared as in Figure 2. To the degree the purchase option exercise price is below 10%, the lessee again would have had a lower total net cost through leasing at this juncture. However, purchase option costs in excess of 10% would favor buying.

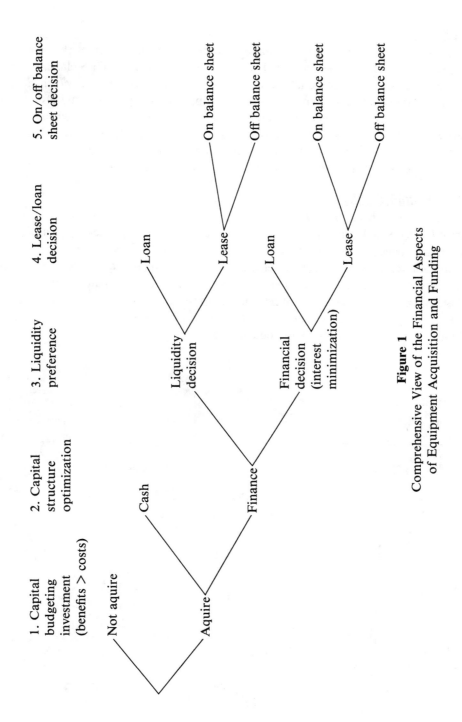

Figure 1

Comprehensive View of the Financial Aspects
of Equipment Acquisition and Funding

TAX BENEFITS

The owner of equipment can take depreciation deductions on 100% of the equipment cost over 6 tax years, in the manner indicated in Figure 3, for 5-year MACRS classlife equipment. The lessee of the equipment could take as a deduction the lease's cost recovery (principal portion of lease rentals) over the lease term of 90% of equipment cost, which would also include any additional time required for the depreciation of purchase options (at 10%) when exercised. To the degree MACRS tax deductions are received faster than the principal or cost recovery portion of the tax lease, buying would be favored. However, when tax leases are written over terms shorter than the MACRS classlife, leasing would be favored.

INDIRECT VARIABLE COSTS

Indirect costs such as sales tax influence the lease versus buy decision based upon their present value costs. Sales tax on leases, for instance, is paid over the lease term as a percentage of each lease payment. The detriment of greater sales tax being paid when leasing (sales tax is paid on both lease principal and interest) might be overcome when the future costs are discounted and compared to the present value of the sales tax paid at time zero (when purchasing). In addition, tax law requires sales tax to be capitalized as part of the tax basis when purchasing equipment; thus the sales tax deduction will be spread over the MACRS classlife in proportion to the annual depreciation deductions.

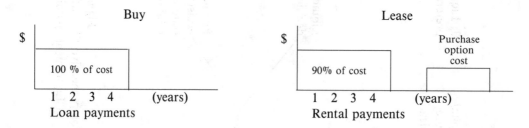

Figure 2
Obsolescence Avoidance

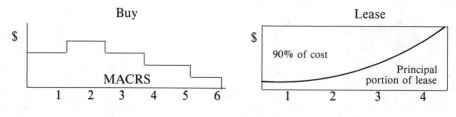

Figure 3
Tax Benefits

EQUIVALENT LOAN COSTS

Just as loan payments can be separated into principal and interest, so, too, can lease rentals be split in the same manner. Usually, interest is imputed in the lease payments at the equipment user's pretax debt cost, in essence assigning the loan cost to the lease alternative; hence, the term equivalent loan cost. To arrive at the amount of interest in the lease payments, the payments are amortized (split into principal and interest) using the pretax debt cost. Use of the equivalent loan costs method provides uniformity of comparison between the two alternatives.

Methodologies

It can be seen that the lease versus buy decision embodies typical capital budgeting costs and benefits such as obsolescence avoidance, salvage values, indirect costs and tax benefits, while at the same time it includes financial costs such as loan interest expense. The real problem is not so much that four basic cost categories complicate the decision, but that two different discount rates should be used in the present value discounting process due to the nature of those categories. Cash flows that are normally part of the capital budgeting process are discounted at the equipment user's cost of capital. However, equivalent loan costs normally will be discounted at an after-tax cost of debt. Use of two different discount rates is called the dual rate discounting method and is discussed later along with an example that uses numbers to describe the dual rate method. Before the more complex, but, perhaps, more accurate dual rate method is described, the more commonplace, but less accurate, single discount rate method will be explained. The single rate discount approach is the most widely used lease versus buy technique today, notwithstanding its theoretical limitations.

SINGLE RATE METHOD

The single rate discount method is described through an example using the following assumptions:

Equipment assumptions
Equipment cost: $1,000
MACRS classlife: 5 years
Sales tax: 6%, on both the initial purchase and the purchase option
Acquisition date: January 1 of the current year.

Equipment user information
Income tax bracket: 34%, calendar year taxpayer
After-tax cost of debt: 6.6%
After-tax, weighted average cost of capital: 12%
After-tax cost of equity: 18.6% (the company is capitalized with 55% debt and 45% equity).

Lease information
Lease rentals: $372 each, payable in three annual payments in arrears
Purchase option: $100, expected to be exercised at the end of the third year.

Loan information

Loan amount: $1,000

Pretax interest: 10%

Loan payments: $402.11 each, payable in three annual payments in arrears.

Present Value Analysis

An analysis of the lease versus loan decision, using cost of debt as the discount rate applied to all after-tax cash flows, appears in Tables 2 and 3. Use of the single discount rate method does not require that lease payments be separated into their principal and interest components since all costs, whether equivalent loan costs or indirect costs, etc., are discounted at the same rate. The example in Tables 2 and 3 demonstrates that the present value of leasing costs of $748.09 is $9.20 less than the present value of the loan alternative whose cost is $757.29.

Table 2
Present Value of Loan Costs
(single rate method)

	0	1	2	3	4	5	6
Loan payments	$ 0.00	($402.11)	($402.11)	($402.11)	$ 0.00	$ 0.00	$ 0.00
Sales tax	(60.00)	0.00	0.00	0.00	0.00	0.00	0.00
Interest benefits[1]	0.00	34.00	23.73	12.43	0.00	0.00	0.00
MACRS benefits[2]	0.00	68.00	108.80	65.28	39.17	39.17	19.58
Sales tax benefits[3]	0.00	4.08	6.53	3.92	2.35	2.35	1.17
Net cash flow	($ 60.00)	($296.03)	($263.05)	($320.48)	$ 41.52	$ 41.52	$ 20.75

Present value of costs discounted at 6.6%: $757.29

---

[1]
Year	
1	$100.00 × .34 = $34.00
2	$ 69.79 × .34 = $23.73
3	$ 36.56 × .34 = $12.43

[2]
Year	
1	$200.00 × .34 = $ 68.00
2	$320.00 × .34 = $108.80
3	$192.00 × .34 = $ 65.28
4	$115.20 × .34 = $ 39.17
5	$115.20 × .34 = $ 39.17
6	$ 57.60 × .34 = $ 19.58

[3] The sales tax of $60 is amortized over the MACRS life. Each year's amortization amount times 34% represents the tax benefit.

Table 3
Present Value of Lease Costs
(single rate method)

	0	1	2	3	4	5	6
Lease rentals	$ 0.00	($ 372.00)	($372.00)	($ 372.00)	$ 0.00	$ 0.00	$ 0.00
Purchase option	0.00	0.00	0.00	(100.00)	0.00	0.00	0.00
Sales tax	0.00	(22.32)	(22.32)	(28.32)	0.00	0.00	0.00
Subtotal	$ 0.00	($ 394.32)	($394.32)	($ 500.32)	$ 0.00	$ 0.00	$ 0.00
Tax impact	0.00	(134.07)	(134.07)	(141.28)[4]	11.53[5]	6.92	10.38[6]
Net cash flow	$ 0.00	($ 260.25)	($260.25)	($ 358.52)	$ 11.53	$ 6.92	$ 10.38

Present value of costs discounted at 6.6%: $748.09

An equally valid method of evaluating the choice between borrowing and leasing is TVA, which is nothing more than the future value of the same cash flows. This technique always gives the same answer as present value, but perhaps gives a better answer in that the true magnitude of the difference between the alternatives is known. This future value amount represents the actual income statement (profit and loss) difference between the two alternatives that would appear over the life of the lease or buy alternative. Present value analysis understates the income statement magnitude even though the right choice is determined by this method. In this example the future value difference between the two methods is $13.50.

Another technique used in lease versus buy analysis is the IRR of the cash flow differences between the two alternatives as shown in Table 4. This particular decision method differs from present value or TVA analysis in that a discount rate is not applied to the cash flows. Instead, the implicit cost of the lease cash flows over the loan cash flows is computed. In this case, the cost of cash flow savings is 3.7373% after-tax. Since this rate is less than the cost of borrowing, the lease alternative is selected as the better choice. Had the cost of cash savings been equal or greater than the cost of debt, the loan alternative would have been preferable. However, if liquidity preference (as explained later in this section) is an issue, any IRR of the cash flow differential that is less than the cost of capital favors leasing. Rates equal to or greater than the cost of capital favor buying, but only when liquidity preference is an issue.

---

[4] $394.32 × .34 = $134.07 (year 3 rent expense)
$100.00 × .20 × .34 = 6.80 (MACRS on the purchased asset)
$ 6.00 × .20 × .34 = .41 (sales tax)
$141.28

[5] ($100 + $6) × .320 × .34 = $11.53 (purchase option + sales tax) x MACRS % x tax rate.
[6] ($100 + $6) × .288 × .34 = $10.38 (purchase option + sales tax) x remaining tax basis % x tax rate.

Table 4
Cash Flow Differential

Year	After-tax Loan Cash Flow	After-tax Lease Cash Flow	Cash Flow Difference
0	($ 60.00)	$ 0.00	($ 60.00)
1	(296.03)	(260.25)	(35.78)
2	(263.05)	(260.25)	(2.80)
3	(320.48)	(358.52)	38.04
4	41.52	11.53	29.99
5	41.52	6.92	34.60
6	20.75	10.38	10.37

The IRR of the cash flow differential is calculated as follows:

60.00	CHS	g	CF_o	
35.78	CHS	g	CF_j	
2.80	CHS	g	CF_j	
38.04		g	CF_j	
29.99		g	CF_j	
34.60		g	CF_j	
10.37		g	CF_j	
		f	IRR	3.7373

Comparison of discount rates:

IRR cash flow differential	3.7%
After-tax cost of debt	6.6%
After-tax cost of capital	12.0%

Were the previous example an actual lease versus loan analysis, the following refinements would be made:

1. Generally lease and loan cash flows would be analyzed on a month-by-month basis, a process that would be too cumbersome and lengthy to be shown here

2. Tax benefits or liabilities would be spread over the five estimated quarterly tax payment dates for each tax year

3. Other termination options, explained earlier, might also be assumed

4. Other pertinent cash flows such as maintenance that might impact the decision could also be included

5. Were the lessee in a net operating loss (NOL) or Investment Tax Credit (ITC) carryforward position, additional adjustments would be required. The same is true if the lessee expected to enter or exit an AMT position during the lease.

The dual rate method (explained next) can be used in lieu of the single rate method. The basic difference between the two methods is that cash flows are categorized according to their nature, i.e., equivalent loan costs, obsolescence avoidance, tax benefits and indirect costs. Under the dual discount rate method, equivalent loan costs are discounted at the after-tax cost of debt; all other costs are discounted at the cost of capital. Additionally, the lease payments are separated into their principal and interest components so that the equivalent loan costs, as well as cost recovery, can be discounted at the appropriate rates.

DUAL RATE METHOD

The following is an analysis of the dual rate method using the same example as the single rate method. The present value analysis for the loan and lease costs is presented in Tables 5 and 6, respectively. The present value of leasing costs of $774.46 under the dual rate method is $19.52 less than the present value of the loan alternative. The equivalent loan costs are identical because the lease was structured with the same pretax 10% interest rate as the loan. Thus, the decision to lease was based primarily on the more accelerated cost recovery found in the 3-year lease. The lease provided a 90% cost write-off after 3 years, whereas only 71.2% of the equipment had been depreciated under MACRS (20% + 32% + 19.2%). The additional write-off in the lease generates an important tax savings.

Were the lease structured with an interest rate higher than 10%, the equivalent loan cost would be higher and might cause the decision to shift towards buying. This difference of $7.83 ($793.98 - $801.81) is shown in Table 7. Notice that the extra interest included in the lease payments was sufficient to overcome the tax benefits of the lease, so the overall decision shifted in favor of buying. Attention also should be directed towards the use of two different discount rates: the after-tax cost of debt for the equivalent loan costs and the cost of capital for all others.

DUAL RATE THEORY

In the preceding example, the equivalent loan costs were discounted at the lessee's cost of debt. The MACRS cost recovery benefits and the indirect costs were discounted at the lessee's cost of capital since such tax deductible expenses are considered to be typical capital budgeting costs. In capital budgeting, revenue from an investment is adjusted for direct variable expenses as well as tax deductible expenses, which include tax depreciation. The adjusted, after-tax cash flow is then compared to the net investment on a net present value (NPV) or IRR basis to establish whether the investment is sufficiently profitable.

The key point here is that MACRS and indirect costs were included in the process of establishing the investment's after-tax net cash flow. The cash flow was then discounted at the cost of capital to determine an NPV, or the IRR was compared to the cost of capital. This is because the cost of capital is the appropriate discount rate to use with capital budgeting elements. Debt-related elements, such as loan payments and interest tax benefits, are typically discounted at the cost of debt.

This dual rate method of evaluating purchase and lease costs is theoretically correct, although not yet commonplace in the industry. Most analysts still use one discount rate (the cost of debt or of capital) for all cash flows. When this technique is used, the process is simplified since the leasing costs do not need to be separated into component parts. Tables 3 and 4 represent the loan

Table 5
Present Value of Loan Costs
(dual rate method)

	Present Value	0	1	2	3	4	5	6
Equivalent loan costs:								
Loan payments		$ 0.00	($402.11)	($402.11)	($402.11)	$ 0.00	$ 0.00	$ 0.00
Interest tax benefits		0.00	34.00	23.73	12.43	0.00	0.00	0.00
After-tax costs	($1,000.00)[7]	$ 0.00	($ 368.11)	($ 378.38)	($ 389.68)	$ 0.00	$ 0.00	$ 0.00
Tax benefits:								
MACRS deductions × .34	$ 250.95[8]	$ 0.00	$ 68.00	$ 108.80	$ 65.28	$ 39.17	$ 39.17	$ 19.58
Indirect costs:								
Sales tax	($ 60.00)	($ 60.00)	$ 0.00	$ 0.00	$ 0.00	$ 0.00	$ 0.00	$ 0.00
Sales tax benefits	$ 15.07[8]	$ 0.00	$ 4.08	$ 6.53	$ 3.92	$ 2.35	$ 2.35	$ 1.17
Net cost of buying	($ 793.98)							

[7] Discounted at 6.6%.
[8] Discounted at 12%.

Table 6
Present Value of Lease Costs
(dual rate method)

	Present Value	0	1	2	3	4	5	6
Equivalent loan costs:								
Lease payments		$ 0.00	($ 372.00)	($ 372.00)	($ 372.00)	$ 0.00	$ 0.00	$ 0.00
Purchase option		0.00	0.00	(100.00)	0.00	0.00	0.00	0.00
Interest tax benefits		0.00	34.00	24.75	14.58	0.00	0.00	0.00
After-tax costs	($1,000.00)[7]	0.00	($ 338.00)	($ 347.25)	($ 457.42)	$ 0.00	$ 0.00	$ 0.00
Tax benefits:								
Cost recovery in the lease rentals		$ 0.00	$ 272.00	$ 299.20	$ 329.12	$ 0.00	$ 0.00	$ 0.00
MACRS on the purchase option		0.00	0.00	0.00	20.00	32.00	19.20	28.80
Tax benefit (×.34)	$ 263.74[8]	$ 0.00	$ 92.48	$ 101.73	$ 118.70	$ 10.88	$ 6.53	$ 9.79
Indirect costs:								
Sales tax (×.66)	($ 38.20)[8]	$ 0.00	($ 14.73)	($ 14.73)	($ 18.69)	$ 0.00	$ 0.00	$ 0.00
Net cost of leasing	($ 774.46)							

Table 7
Present Value of Lease Costs
(with increased rental payments of $387)

	Present Value	0	1	2	3	4	5	6
Equivalent loan costs:								
Lease payments		$0.00	($ 387.00)	($387.00)	($ 387.00)	$ 0.00	$ 0.00	$ 0.00
Purchase option		0.00	0.00	0.00	(100.00)	0.00	0.00	0.00
Interest tax benefits		0.00	34.00	24.24	13.51	0.00	0.00	0.00
Unamortized balance × .34		0.00	0.00	0.00	16.99	0.00	0.00	0.00
After-tax costs	($1,027.23)[7]	$0.00	($ 353.00)	($362.76)	($ 456.50)	$ 0.00	$ 0.00	$ 0.00
Tax benefits:								
Cost recovery in the lease rentals		$0.00	$ 287.00	$ 315.70	$ 297.30[9]	$ 0.00	$ 0.00	$ 0.00
MACRS on the purchase option		0.00	0.00	0.00	20.00	32.00	19.20	28.80
Tax benefit (× .34)	$ 265.06[8]	$0.00	$ 97.58	$ 107.34	$ 107.88	$ 10.88	$ 6.53	$ 9.79
Indirect costs:								
Sales tax (× .66)	($ 39.64)[8]	$0.00	($ 15.33)	($ 15.33)	($ 19.29)	$ 0.00	$ 0.00	$ 0.00
Net cost of leasing	($ 801.81)							

[9]Third year principal of $397.30 less $100 (purchase option).

and lease analysis, respectively, for the single rate example, and all cash flows are discounted at the lessee's debt cost of 6.6%.

The difference between purchase and lease is $9.20 in favor of leasing using the single rate method versus $19.52 in favor of leasing using the dual rate method. In this example, the common method of performing a lease versus buy analysis created a bias in favor of buying. The dual rate method eliminates bias and demonstrates that leasing, in this case, is much more favorable, having increased the leasing benefit by 112.2%.

The dual rate method discounts each element of the lease versus loan decision at an appropriate rate: cost of debt for loan equivalent costs and cost of capital for capital budgeting components. Some financial analysts argue that the tax benefits associated with either the lease or loan decision are an integral part of the cost of borrowing and should, therefore, be discounted at a single rate — the cost of debt after-tax. However, the tax benefits associated with the choice of financing are separate issues even though their occurrence is simultaneous. It could be argued that the real choice in lease versus loan is one of maximizing tax benefits and the financing is ancillary, thus requiring all cash flows to be discounted at the cost of capital. Neither of these single rate arguments is cogent, since the decision is much more complex; two decisions are being made simultaneously — one requiring the cost of debt as a discount rate and the other the cost of capital.

Another argument in favor of the dual rate method is illustrated in the case in which a company that has no debt is attempting to determine whether or not to purchase with cash or to lease. Clearly, the MACRS depreciation would be the only tax benefit available on the buy side of the decision since there are no debt components. MACRS tax benefits would have to be discounted at the cost of capital since cost of debt would be irrelevant due to the nonexistence of debt. On the lease side, the cost recovery portion would be discounted at the cost of capital in order to be consistent in discounting. The debt components (principal and interest) of the lease would be discounted at the cost of debt in the same fashion as the preceding examples.

The single rate method of discounting is an oversimplification of the complex nature of lease versus buy. This oversimplification appears to favor buying to the exclusion of leasing. It does not matter whether a company leases or buys — the concern of the decision maker should be centered primarily on whether the logic of the decision is reasonable. The complexity of the decision is more than a simple comparison of one financing alternative versus another. Rather, the decision embodies a purchase financing decision plus an obsolescence avoidance decision, in addition to tax benefits and indirect costs. These facets of the decision are compared to similar costs on the leasing side.

The comparison would be more obvious if the decision were between a loan and a money-over-money lease (the previous examples have pitted a loan against a tax lease). The money-over-money lease is a nontax lease that is accounted for on the tax books of the lessee as a loan, resulting in lease payments separated into principal and interest and MACRS deductions accruing to the benefit of the lessee. The point is that leases do have two components: debt and cost recovery. Each component has to be evaluated on its own merits without assuming one is a function of the other. In fact, they are coexistent, not cause and effect related.

Appropriate Discount Rates

Within the context of the discussions regarding the single versus dual rate method of discounting, there are certain rules that govern the appropriateness of a particular discount rate. Generally, when liquidity preference is not a consideration, the following discount rates should be used:

1. Single rate method   - after-tax cost of debt
2. Dual rate method
    (a) Equivalent loan costs   - after-tax cost of debt
    (b) Obsolescence avoidance   - after-tax cost of capital
    (c) Tax benefits   - after-tax cost of capital
    (d) Indirect costs   - after-tax cost of capital

When liquidity preference is an issue, the after-tax cost of equity should be used on all costs.

LIQUIDITY PREFERENCE

What is liquidity preference and why does it require use of the cost of equity as a discount rate in the lease versus buy situation? Liquidity preference represents the favoring in the decision process of the extra cash flow generated by a lease, even though a higher intrinsic interest rate than the loan alternative perhaps is paid. For example, even though a particular lease may cost more than a loan from an equivalent loan present value viewpoint, due to the higher interest rate built into the rental factor, the equipment user might still lease.

The user's argument from a liquidity preference viewpoint probably would be that the extra cash flow savings from the lease in its early years (low down payment compared to the loan, etc.), when reinvested in working capital, will more than compensate for any extra interest in the lease. These higher priced funding alternatives are deemed acceptable as long as they generate cash flow savings in the early years that can be reinvested at a sufficiently high enough rate to compensate fully for any extra interest expense in the lease.

Leases typically do create cash savings in their early years because of their low down payments (one or two rentals in advance ranging from 1.8 to 4.5% of cost); whereas installment and commercial lenders frequently require 10 to 20% down payments, which, when coupled with sales tax, could total almost a 30% down payment. Of course, there are many other reasons why a lease might have preferable cash flow savings, e.g., the lessee is in an AMT position and tax lease payments do not create tax preferences.

Actually, the liquidity preference argument is more complex than cited above. For example, excess cash flow in a lease is created primarily from the additional financial leverage created by low down payments, long terms and residual emphasis. To create cash flow simply from borrowing creates several theoretical capital structure hurdles that must be overcome before the liquidity preference approach can be fully justified. Several implicit assumptions must be made when the liquidity preference approach is being taken. The more financial leverage the better, as long as:

1. The company does not care about maintaining a constant debt-to-equity ratio. Indifference to capital structure could occur where a company has not yet reached its targeted optimum debt-to-equity ratio and is in need of more debt. The company would probably

be nonpublic and privately-held and most likely would not be financially rated by Moodys or Standard and Poors. The company, therefore, would not be too concerned about maintaining a constant debt-to-equity ratio

2. Debt at a lower cost (and of equal terms) is not available to the company. Obviously, if one seeks financial leverage to enhance cash flows it should be done at the lowest cost. Frequently, lending institutions will match the terms of any lease, including low down payments and balloon payments, etc. Therefore, leasing should not be preferred based on the assumption that it alone can produce cash flow savings, because other financing alternatives might also be able to produce the same effect. However, in the absence of equally structured financing alternatives leasing might still produce the best cash flows

3. Extra cash flow resulting from the additional borrowings (financial leverage) can be reinvested at a rate greater than the internal rate of return of the cash flow differential between the lease and buy alternatives. Reinvestment rates available to the lessee that are lower than the IRR of the differential cash flow would favor buying. The IRR of the differential cash flow gives the implied borrowing cost of the cash flow savings. If these cash flow savings cannot be invested at a rate high enough to cover the incremental cost of the savings, they are not worth having

4. The borrower can withstand the extra risk caused by increased leverage. Extra debt relative to equity increases the overall economic risk of the firm should a recession occur. Additionally, the more a firm leverages, the more its additional borrowings will cost; therefore, the borrower must be willing to assume such increased risk

5. The proposed debt is self-liquidating and as much financial leverage as possible is to be maintained. For example, an investment in an apartment house that is subject to a fixed-rate, fixed-term mortgage represents a self-liquidating type investment debt. As rentals are received, and the mortgage paid, the investment's debt-to-equity ratio is constantly lowered (unless the project is refinanced at a later date). To minimize the lowering of this ratio, the debt term could be stretched out. This particular reason, along with the next three, helps to further justify the liquidity preference approach

6. Future rates are expected to increase. More financial leverage allows one to lock in a fixed interest cost

7. The lease is classified from an accounting point of view as operating and such operating leases do not exceed 5 to 7% of the company's total assets, so the off balance sheet financial leverage can be obtained without altering bond and commercial paper ratings. Operating leases beyond this range might cause rating agencies to act as though the debt is on balance sheet from their analytical viewpoint and could result in a lowering of the bond ratings

8. Leasing is viewed as an additional source of capital not otherwise available, thereby leaving working capital credit lines intact. Working capital credit lines are typically restricted in amount for small to intermediate size companies. Because expansion of credit lines to accommodate equipment acquisition is restricted, leasing becomes the only viable alternative borrowing source for these smaller companies.

When liquidity preference is not considered an issue, the equipment user is said to be making an interest minimization or equivalent loan decision, which does not place any emphasis on the impact of financial leverage. The following are the basic assumptions justifying the interest minimization approach:

1. Debt is readily available (other than timing) and, therefore, cash flow from financial leverage is always available and should be obtained at the lowest cost

2. The lessee attempts to maintain a constant debt-to-equity ratio and, therefore, debt funding comparisons should not include the impact of various degrees of leverage since this would be contradictory to the assumption of debt-to-equity constancy

3. The company is attempting to lower its financial leverage so that no preference should be placed on higher amounts of debt

4. Costs of debt are dropping over the investment horizon; thus, higher leverage should be avoided since higher borrowing rates would be mistakenly locked in

5. The lease is capital and, therefore, on balance sheet. If a constant debt-to-equity relationship is desired, an equally leveraged debt alternative must be compared to the lease or else undue preference will be given to financial leverage

6. The lease is operating and, therefore, off balance sheet (and within 5 to 7% of total assets). In this case, numbers 1, 3 and 4 might nevertheless still be deemed important enough that off balance sheet leveraged debt should be sought, but only at the lowest interest cost, which means the lease's implicit interest rate should be very close to the cost of borrowing.

COST OF EQUITY

The interest minimization approach requires the after-tax cost of debt as a discount rate, while the liquidity preference approach requires the after-tax cost of equity as a discount rate. This difference in usage between discount rates is because, when comparing two funding alternatives, the difference in their cash flows over the equipment holding period represents return on equity cash flows, and, therefore, should be discounted at the cost of equity. In other words, savings derived from using one method of financing over another inure solely to the benefit of the equity holders. Therefore, the larger total cash flow return on equity (ROE) is the better financing alternative as long as the time value of money has been considered. The time value of equity returns is the required ROE that the company normally expects, which is greater than the firm's cost of debt or cost of capital.

The primary problem with the ROE discount rate approach is not so much the use of a high ROE discount rate as it is the use of a constant ROE discount rate over the equipment's economic life. General financial theory requires the use of higher ROE discount rates for higher degrees of financial leverage.

A second problem with ROE rate discounting is interpretation of the final answer. For example, assume, after having discounted the lease and the loan cash flows at a 16% ROE, a present value of $10,000 results in favor of leasing. Compare this to another lease with lower up-front costs (resulting in more leverage) that has a present value total of $15,000. In reality, if the second alternative were chosen it would be implied that more financial leverage is better than less (given the company can assume the risk of more financial leverage). Certainly, a lease versus buy analysis need not be performed to ascertain this basic financial truth. However, when particular lease versus buy alternatives represent two mutually exclusive and totally exhaustive ways of funding an equipment acquisition, use of the ROE discount rate will give the proper financial answer.

INTEREST MINIMIZATION

Discounting lease or loan costs with the after-tax cost of debt does not consider the impact of financial leverage; therefore, this rate is used in the interest minimization approach. A debt cost discount rate values only the interest in the funding alternative. For example, the after-tax present value of an installment loan's payments over 48 months would be the same as that of a commercial loan in which the total principal plus interest is due in a lump sum in 48 months. Use of a higher discount rate would begin favoring the present value of the commercial loan, not because it has less implicit interest expense, but because of the additional financial leverage it provided (100% debt for 4 years versus the installment loan, where debt was being paid down each month).

Cost of capital is used in nonliquidity preference situations, but is applied only to cash flows that normally would have been discounted at the cost of capital were the analysis solely that of capital budgeting; for example, MACRS depreciation is normally offset against revenues in capital budgeting to determine tax benefits or expenses. The resulting after-tax cash flows are then discounted at the cost of capital. Therefore, MACRS tax benefits in a lease versus buy decision still will be valued at the cost of capital.

Equally important as the appropriateness of discount rate is the standardization of discount periods. The general rule is that all cash flows, whether occurring monthly, quarterly or semiannually, should be discounted at the same periodic discount rate. Thus, if 1% per month is the appropriate monthly discount rate, then an annual cash flow should be discounted over 12 months at 1%, which is different from discounting the event at 12% over 1 year. The basic difference is that a single 12% annual nominal rate does not have the monthly compound interest effect built in. Had the event been discounted at 12.682503% per year (the annual effective rate of 12% with monthly compounding built in), the answer would have been the same as discounting the event at 1% per month for 12 months. Inconsistent discounting could erroneously favor one alternative over another.

PERSPECTIVE AND QUALITATIVE RAMIFICATIONS

Proper perspective is an essential component of the decision process that concentrates on the qualitative aspects of decision making as well as the relevance of the final decision. There are several factors generally considered as rendering perspective in decision making. First, qualitative issues and other interrelationships must be integrated into the overall decision. Variables impacting the decision must be prioritized and critical junctures in the flow of events, and assumptions upon which the decision is based, must be identified. Common sense and intuition should also be considered as part of the decision process. Additionally, all factors, qualitative and quantitative, significant and insignificant, must be viewed as a whole in making the decision (holistic/gestalt viewpoint). Relevant questions must be asked and the problem must be solved. Certainly, however, the problem itself must be significant enough to warrant concern (materiality) and the cost of determining a solution must be less than the benefits derived therefrom (feasibility). Finally, the input premises must be adequately adjusted for risk and uncertainty.

Qualitative Issues

Proper integration of all factors and variables, quantitative as well as qualitative, impacting the decision is essential to a reliable and relevant conclusion. Numerous qualitative factors influence the lease versus buy decision. To the degree possible, some quantitative dollar value should be placed on these qualitative issues; however, in many cases this is virtually impossible. Nevertheless, unquantified or not, these quality attributes of the decision still need to be integrated into the decision process because of their significant impact on the overall conclusion. The following is a list of many of the qualitative factors that typically favor the leasing, instead of buying, of equipment:

1. Off balance sheet financing: when the lease qualifies as operating from an accounting viewpoint, neither the leased asset nor the corresponding lease liability will appear on the face of the lessee's balance sheet. Operating leases favorably impact profitability ratios such as return on assets (ROA), as well as financial ratios (current ratio, etc.)

2. Down payment affordability: relative to typical bank financing for equipment, that requires down payments of 10 to 20%, a lease with only one advance payment (1.8 to 2.2% of equipment cost) is quite affordable

3. Excessive use of leased asset: when excessive wear and tear of the asset is anticipated certain lessees are more apt to lease. If the lease document does not require reimbursement to the lessor for such excess usage, then, to that degree, the lessee has gained economically

4. Ability to hold vendor lessors accountable: when the lessor is also the manufacturer of the equipment, the lessee might feel more confident about lessor service regarding warranties and maintenance because of the lessee's perceived ability to withhold lease payments until the equipment is properly working or adequately serviced

5. Payment for the lease out of an operating budget: when an equipment user's capital acquisition budget has been spent, the only remaining means of obtaining the use of additional equipment is through leasing, because the rentals will be paid out of an operating expense budget as opposed to a capital acquisition budget

6. Working capital credit lines kept intact: if credit lines will be unduly consumed through equipment acquisition, the result might be a serious impairment of the company's growth due to an inability to obtain working capital. Leases might represent an additional source of funding not otherwise practically available

7. Flexible structuring options: swaps, skipped payments and upgrades commonly available in leasing are not as readily found in commercial lending

8. On-the-spot financing: when offered by vendor or manufacturer lessors, product financing saves the lessee time as it obviates the need to shop for funding

9. Avoidance of salvage problems: disposal of purchased equipment can be fraught with uncertainty, risk and hassle, all of which can be avoided through leasing

10. Greater credit leniency: frequently, vendor lessors, who are sales driven, are willing to take greater credit risks in order to make a sale.

Prioritization of Variables

Common sense and intuition represent important inputs to overall decision making. However, these paralogical methods are not always acceptable and are difficult to document. They, nevertheless, serve as cross-checks on the otherwise formal logical and quantitative approaches described. For example, common sense would probably dictate that long-lived assets should be purchased (especially when the lease term exceeds the MACRS classlife of the asset). However, if the long-lived asset also holds its value quite well, then leasing might be feasible in the situation where cash flow is a great concern.

Holistic/Gestalt Viewpoint

All factors, qualitative and quantitative, significant as well as insignificant, must be viewed as a composite whole for decision making purposes. Five seemingly insignificant issues, when viewed in the aggregate, might become material. Holistic thinking is closely allied with common sense. All too often, decisions are made without full contemplation of all the variables influencing the decision. For example, to view lease versus buy solely as an interest minimization problem is to have too narrow a focus, for cash flow considerations, optimal financial structure, etc., are also important to the decision.

Relevance

To be relevant, the conclusion must truly address the appropriate question; otherwise the solution might be moot. Is liquidity preference really at issue? If not, the discount rate must change from an ROE rate to cost of capital and cost of debt rates. Then, too, if off balance sheet financing is required, or affordability is an issue, a lease versus buy need not even be performed if the lease in question is capital, or if the down payment required on the proposed loan is beyond the equipment user's means.

Materiality and Feasibility

The lease versus buy decision must concern equipment whose cost is sufficiently expensive to justify the effort involved; otherwise the cost of analysis will outweigh any benefit derived therefrom. However, such feasibility considerations are often abused, since many a personal computer costing $3,000 has been leased with implicit interest rates above 20%, at a time when the company could borrow at prime plus 1%, with a fixed term of 60 months.

Risk Adjustment

The lease versus buy decision is heavily dependent upon residual assumptions. If the lessee returns the equipment at the end of the noncancellable term, a salvage value must be assumed on the buy side in order to equate the term (explained earlier in the chapter). Furthermore, should the lessee decide to exercise a purchase option or renew the lease, the option exercise price or the renewal rate must be predicted. Predictions necessarily involve risk and uncertainty that must be dealt with. As always, the decision is only as good as the guessing that affects this critical juncture in the lease versus buy decision.

Although there are many ways of addressing risk (such as use of a higher discount rate applied to residual assumptions), one of the best is the expected value approach, which makes use of decision tree and probability analysis. In order to illustrate this concept, an example of a five step process that might be followed in ascertaining the expected cost of exercising a fair market value purchase option in a lease is presented.

Assume a lessee has compiled the following information concerning the possible exercise prices that might be paid in order to purchase equipment at the end of a noncancellable lease term:

Commercial appraisal of the estimated future value	$ 1,000
Lessor's verbal estimate	$ 800
Best possible exercise price	$ 1,200
Worst possible exercise price	$ 600
Lessee's best point estimate	$ 900

STEP ONE

Determine the alternative outcomes (given above), along with their probability of occurrence, using decision tree analysis. At least three alternative outcomes should be used, along with their probabilities of occurrence; however, if there are no clear probabilities of occurrence, the following probabilities can be used:

Best outcome	.16
Average expected outcome	.68
Worst outcome	.16

Since in this case there are five possible outcomes, the probability of their occurrence is assessed, as in Table 8.

STEP TWO

Compute the expected value of the option (EVO) exercise price, assuming perfect information, by multiplying the probability of the event (or joint probabilities when there are additional branches in the decision tree, which is not the case here) times the dollar outcome of the event. Then total the resulting products. This step is summarized in Table 9.

STEP THREE

Calculate the standard deviation of the EVO, which indicates the degree of risk or variability in the EVO caused by the breadth of the range ($1200 to $600) of options and the relative certainty of events (5 to 45%), both of which are subjective guesses. Although guesswork cannot be eliminated from predictions, at least the variability of the guess can be scientifically dealt with in this and the next two steps.

Table 8
Assessment of Outcome

Event	Outcome	Dollar Value	Probability
1	Best exercise price feasible	$ 1,200	.10
2	Commercially appraised value	1,000	.25
3	Lessee's best point estimate	900	.45
4	Lessor's verbal estimate	800	.15
5	Worst exercise price realistically feasible	600	.05

Table 9
EVO Computation

Event	Outcome		Probability		Product
1	$ 1,200	×	.10	=	$ 120
2	1,000	×	.25	=	250
3	900	×	.45	=	405
4	800	×	.15	=	120
5	600	×	.05	=	30
EVO					$ 925

$$\text{EVO standard deviation} = {}_{i=1}\sqrt{\epsilon(O_1 - EVO)^2 P_1}$$

where:

P1	=	probability of the first through the last outcome
O1	=	outcomes 1 through 5
EVO	=	expected value of the option cost (Step Three)

$($1,200 - $925)^2$ = $ 76,625 × .10 = $ 7,662.50
$($1,000 - $925)^2$ = $ 5,625 × .25 = 1,406.25
$($ 900 - $925)^2$ = $ 625 × .45 = 281.25
$($ 800 - $925)^2$ = $ 15,625 × .15 = 2,343.75
$($ 600 - $925)^2$ = $105,625 × .05 = 5,281.25
Total = $16,975.00

$$\text{Standard deviation of EVO} = \sqrt{\$16,975} = \$ \; 130.29$$

STEP FOUR

Compute the EVO cost given a required level of confidence that the exercise price will be equal or less than a certain amount. This requires use of the following equation:

$$EVO_{Expected} = [EVO_{Step\ Two} + (EVO_{Std\ Deviation} \times C)],$$

where C is a confidence coefficient taken from the following table of probabilities of an event being less than or equal to a certain amount:

98%	=	2.06
95	=	1.65
90	=	1.28
85	=	1.04
80	=	.84
75	=	.67
70	=	.52
65	=	.38
60	=	.26

Using a required probability of occurrence of 90% (determined by the degree of the lessee's risk averseness), the expected value of the option cost, given a 90% confidence requirement, would be calculated as follows:

$$EVO_{Expected} = [(EVO_{Step\ Two} + (EVO_{Std\ Dev} \times C)]$$

$$EVO_{Expected} = \$925 + (\$130.29 \times 1.28) = \$1,091.77$$

STEP FIVE

It is concluded, therefore, that the unknown purchase option exercise price will be equal to or less than $1,091.77, given a 90% degree of certainty (and also the degree of guesswork, the range and the outcomes resulting in a $130.29 standard deviation). This amount then could be used as one of the lease versus buy assumptions (lease alternative). The expected value would have been smaller had the range or magnitude of the outcomes been smaller or had some of the outcomes been more likely; however, since the guess was so broad, a higher than expected option price would be anticipated.

DECISION FEEDBACK

Feedback is a process that attempts to confirm past assumptions and expectations as well as determine the changes that might be needed in decision making to adapt to economic change. Business decisions are dynamic, not static, and feedback is the mechanism that seeks adjustment to change or to past error.

In terms of the lease versus buy decision, feedback is needed primarily in two areas — tax assumptions and residual assumptions. If the original lease versus buy decision was made assuming no lessee AMT problem when, in fact, the lessee has gone into an AMT position, feedback would require future decisions to include the impact of AMT. Regarding residual assumptions, if the original lease versus buy decision assumed the leased equipment would be returned at lease termination, but was instead purchased, the original decision might have been in error due to the changed scenario.

Decision feedback is generally assumed to be post facto, but can be approximated in advance through sensitivity analysis. For example, various residual assumptions (described earlier) can be used to determine alternative results. The degree of sensitivity to slight changes in residual values can be used to determine breakeven situations. Better still, a weighted average expected value can combine all residual scenarios. As has often been said, those who do not understand history are destined to repeat it. Feedback is the history lesson that allows one to better predict the future, or to make changes in decision input premises that better reflect economic reality, as confirmed by the feedback of past lease versus buy decisions.

ALTERNATIVE MINIMUM TAX IMPACT

When an equipment user is in an AMT position, there is a direct impact on the lease versus buy decision. The MACRS depreciation creates a tax preference on the buy side, whereas the tax lease payment on the lease side generally does not create any tax preferences. Since tax preferences are taxed at 20%, there is a slight penalty attached to equipment ownership. Thus, to avoid an AMT situation, or to mitigate an existing AMT problem, tax leasing should be considered as an even more viable funding alternative.

The existence of an AMT problem requires certain adjustments to the lease versus buy decision. Assuming a lessee is in an AMT position, with or without a particular transaction's existence, the basic lease versus buy methodology is the same as described in "Decision Logic and Methodology," except a 20% tax rate would be used. However, the difference between a 34% regular tax rate and the 20% AMT rate becomes a tax benefit or liability in the AMT reversal year. In performing a lease versus buy analysis under AMT it is important to recognize that any tax preference items create additional tax liabilities equal to 20% of their total each tax year. These tax liabilities in most situations reverse automatically over time. The following are tax preference issues that occur in the lease versus buy decision when the lessee is in an AMT situation.

1. Purchasing equipment creates a depreciation tax preference equal to the difference between MACRS deductions and 150% declining balance depreciation over the asset's Asset Depreciation Range (ADR) midpoint life
2. Purchasing also creates a pretax book income preference equal to one-half the difference between 150% declining balance depreciation and whatever accounting book depreciation is being used (generally straight-line with some assumed salvage value)
3. Leasing might create pretax book income preferences equal to one-half the difference between tax lease rental deductions and accounting reported operating lease rental expenses or capital lease interest and depreciation expenses. Capital lease accounting could cause negative tax preferences, which might favor leasing even more if the negative preference can be utilized

4. Leasing eventually might create the same tax preferences as in 1 and 2 above if the equipment is ultimately purchased during the lease term
5. Tax lease rentals themselves do not generate depreciation tax preferences, although they might create pretax book income preferences as described in 3 above (which might be beneficial preferences).

AMT Example

Tables 10 and 11 depict a lease and a purchase analysis, respectively, whose tax benefits have been adjusted for AMT considerations. (This is the same lease example from Tables 5 and 6, except the lease is assumed to be an operating lease from an accounting viewpoint.) The lessee is assumed to be in an AMT position for 6 full tax years. In the seventh tax year the lessee exits its AMT position, which means that any AMT credits will be fully utilized in this reversal year.

What is the impact of the equipment user being in an AMT position under either the lease or loan scenario? The answer is found by comparing the present values of the net changes in tax benefits between the two alternatives. Note that an AMT taxpayer's cost of capital and after-tax cost of debt increase during an AMT position since the normal tax benefits associated with the deductibility of interest expense (based upon a 34% tax rate) are reduced to a 20% tax rate basis. Ultimately the difference between a 34% and a 20% tax rate becomes a tax benefit in the year of AMT reversal. In the previous case the taxpayer's cost of debt increased from 6.6% to 7.024%. The cause of this increase is described in Table 12. The IRR represents the after-tax interest costs and is computed as follows:

1,000		g	CF_o
382.11	CHS	g	CF_j
388.15	CHS	g	CF_j
394.80	CHS	g	CF_j
0		g	CF_j
3		g	N_j
28.89		g	CF_j
		f	IRR 7.024

Using the AMT adjusted discount rate of 7.024%, the net changes in tax benefits between leasing and buying result in the present value totals shown in Table 13. The present value of these differences, discounted at the cost of debt and the cost of capital, can be summarized as follows:

	Cost of Debt (7.024%)	Cost of Capital (12%)
Leasing present value	$ 43.88	$ 42.03
Loan present value	44.74	42.84
Difference (favoring leasing)	$ .86	$ .81

It appears in this example, therefore, that leasing benefitted from the taxpayer's AMT position. Research has shown this to be the general conclusion that can be drawn regarding the impact of AMT. However, there are other variables that impact this conclusion: (1) the AMT

Table 10

AMT Adjustments to Lease Costs

	1	2	3	4	5	6	Reversal
Regular tax benefit calculation:							
Lease rentals	($ 372.00)	($ 372.00)	$ 0.00	$ 0.00	$ 0.00	$ 0.00	
MACRS - option	0.00	0.00	(20.00)	(32.00)	(19.20)	(28.80)	
Sales tax	(22.32)	(22.32)	(23.52)	(1.92)	(1.15)	(1.73)	
Taxable loss	($ 394.32)	($ 394.32)	($ 415.52)	($ 33.92)	($ 20.35)	($ 30.53)	
Tax rate	× .34	× .34	× .34	× .34	× .34	× .34	
Tax benefit	$ 134.07	$ 134.07	$ 141.28	$ 11.53	$ 6.92	$ 10.38	
AMT tax benefit calculation:							
Taxable loss	($ 394.32)	($ 394.32)	($ 415.52)	($ 33.92)	($ 20.35)	($ 30.53)	
Depreciation preference[10]	0.00	0.00	5.00	6.50	1.35	12.85	
Book income preference[10]	0.00	0.00	(.85)	4.40	.50	(4.13)	
AMT loss	($ 394.32)	($ 394.32)	($ 411.37)	($ 23.02)	($ 18.42)	($ 47.51)	
AMT rate	× .20	× .20	× .20	× .20	× .20	× .20	
AMT benefit	$ 78.86	$ 78.86	$ 82.27	$ 4.60	$ 3.68	$ 9.50	
Net change in tax benefits	($ 55.21)	($ 55.21)	($ 59.01)	($ 6.93)	($ 3.24)	($ .88)	$ 180.48

[10] These amounts are the same as the tax preferences generated on the purchase example (Table 11) except they are one-tenth of the applicable amounts since the purchase option of $100 was one-tenth of the original $1,000 acquisition cost.

Table 11
AMT Adjustments to Loan Costs

	1	2	3	4	5	6	Reversal
Regular tax benefit calculation:							
Interest	($100.00)	($69.79)	($36.56)	$0.00	$0.00	$0.00	
MACRS - option	(200.00)	(320.00)	(192.00)	(115.20)	(115.20)	(57.60)	
Sales tax	(12.00)	(19.20)	(11.52)	(6.91)	(6.91)	(3.46)	
Taxable loss	($312.00)	($408.99)	($240.08)	($122.11)	($122.11)	($61.06)	
Tax rate	× .34	× .34	× .34	× .34	× .34	× .34	
Tax benefit	$106.08	$139.06	$81.63	$41.52	$41.52	$20.75	
AMT tax benefit calculation:							
Taxable loss	($312.00)	($408.99)	($240.08)	($122.11)	($122.11)	($61.06)	
Depreciation preference[11]	50.00	65.00	13.50	(51.40)	(51.40)	(25.70)	
Book income preference[12]	(8.50)	44.00	5.75	(.20)	(.20)	(40.85)	
AMT loss	($270.50)	($299.99)	($220.83)	($173.71)	($173.71)	($127.61)	
AMT rate	× .20	× .20	× .20	× .20	× .20	× .20	
AMT benefit	$54.10	$60.00	$44.17	$34.74	$34.74	$25.52	
Net change in tax benefits	($51.98)	($79.06)	($37.46)	($6.78)	($6.78)	$4.77	$186.83

[11] Computation of the depreciation preference

	1	2	3	4	5	6
MACRS	$200.00	$320.00	$192.00	$115.20	$115.20	$57.60
150 declining balance depreciation	(150.00)	(255.00)	(178.50)	(166.60)	(166.60)	(83.30)
Preference	$50.00	$65.00	$13.50	($51.40)	($51.40)	($25.70)

[12] Computation of the pretax book income preference

	1	2	3	4	5	6
Book depreciation	$167.00	$167.00	$167.00	$167.00	$167.00	$165.00
150 declining balance depreciation	(150.00)	(255.00)	(178.50)	(166.60)	(166.60)	(83.30)
Difference	$17.00	($88.00)	($11.50)	$.40	$.40	$81.70
Preference (÷ 20)	($8.50)	$44.00	$5.75	($.20)	($.20)	($40.85)

Table 12
AMT Adjusted Discount Rate

	0	1	2	3	4	5	6	7
Loan proceeds	$1,000.00	$ 0.00	$ 0.00	$ 0.00	$ 0.00	$ 0.00	$ 0.00	$ 0.00
Loan payments	0.00	(402.11)	(402.11)	(402.11)	0.00	0.00	0.00	0.00
Tax benefits at 20%	0.00	20.00	13.96	7.31	0.00	0.00	0.00	0.00
AMT reversal (34% – 20%)	0.00	0.00	0.00	0.00	0.00	0.00	0.00	28.89
Net cash cost	$1,000.00	($382.11)	($388.15)	($394.80)	$ 0.00	$ 0.00	$ 0.00	$28.89

Table 13
AMT Impact on Tax Benefits

	1	2	3	4	5	6	7
Net change in leasing tax benefits[13]	($55.21)	($55.21)	($59.01)	($6.93)	($3.24)	($.88)	$180.48
Net change in loan tax benefits[14]	($51.98)	($79.06)	($37.46)	($6.78)	($6.78)	$4.77	$177.29

entry and exit date, (2) whether the lease is accounted for as capital or operating (capital leases generate favorable negative pretax book income preferences), (3) whether MACRS or another depreciation method is used by the taxpayer and (4) the length of the lease relative to the MACRS classlife of the asset. Furthermore, use of a higher AMT adjusted discount rate will affect the other nontax cash flows that were not considered above, as higher discount rates generally favor leasing.

The marketing implication of these facts for lessors should be apparent. First, lessees in an AMT position might favor leasing even if they have never previously tried it. Second, capital leases have a greater AMT advantage than operating leases due to the negative pretax book income preference created by the capital lease, since capital leases generate depreciation and interest expense that exceed the lease rental expense on the tax return. Finally, leasing can help prevent a lessee from ever going into an AMT position.

---

[13] From Table 10.
[14] From Table 11.

FOREIGN TAX CREDIT IMPACT

The FTC was instituted by Congress as a means of eliminating double taxation on the foreign earned income of domestic corporations. As a credit, it provides US taxpayers with a dollar-for-dollar reduction in their US tax liability on worldwide income for certain income taxes paid to foreign countries, subject to certain limitations. (Refer to Chapter Four for a detailed discussion of the FTC provisions, as this section primarily addresses the lease versus buy implications.)

The general formula for calculating the maximum credit allowed is as follows:

$$\text{FTC limitation}^{15} \quad = \quad \frac{\text{Foreign source taxable income}}{\text{Worldwide taxable income}} \quad \times \quad \frac{\text{Total US tax liability}}{\text{on worldwide income}}$$

As this equation readily illustrates, by increasing foreign source taxable income relative to worldwide taxable income, a corporation can increase the amount of the FTC limitation. This, in turn, increases the amount of foreign taxes paid that can be utilized as credits against the US tax liability. As a result of this relationship, taxpayers, over the years, have devised several methods for converting the source of income from US to foreign in an attempt to increase the FTC limitation.

Recognizing the potential for manipulation, Congress, in the 1986 tax act, tightened the sourcing rules in an attempt to eliminate this practice. Perhaps the most critical of these sourcing rules, with respect to its impact on leasing, is the new mandatory method of allocating interest expense to foreign source income. The changes in this specific methodology alone may cause many corporations to lease rather than to purchase future assets with borrowed funds.

Under prior law, interest expense could be allocated on a separate company basis. This allowed corporations to manage the amount of interest expense allocated to foreign income by arranging borrowings within an affiliated group of corporations, such that the interest expense was incurred by a company within the group that had only US income and assets. In doing so, interest expense would be allocated entirely to US source income, thus maximizing the FTC limitation by leaving foreign source income intact.

The new law requires interest expense to be allocated as if all members of an affiliated group are branches of a single corporation. This treatment of interest expense is based upon the principle that money is fungible, such that interest is considered properly attributable to all of a corporation's business activities and properties, regardless of the specific purpose for which the debt was incurred.

The new law also requires the allocation to be made on the basis of assets. Congress reasoned that interest expense should be allocated between US and foreign income based on the proportion of US to foreign asset values, as interest expense is more closely related to the amount of capital utilized in an activity than to the subsequent gross income generated. This

---

[15] Corporations are required to classify income from both foreign and domestic sources by type into various categories or baskets as defined in the law. Therefore, corporations must calculate separate FTC limitations for each basket of income using the above formula. The sum of these amounts is equal to the total allowable FTC. Currently there are 10 separate baskets or income categories.

change in methodology ultimately results in more interest expense being allocated to foreign source income than would otherwise be the case. The result of this decrease in the FTC limitation reduces the amount of foreign taxes paid that can be credited against the US tax liability, thus increasing US taxes payable.

For corporations with foreign income, therefore, there is now a tax penalty associated with incurring additional recourse debt. Given that this penalty is the direct result of interest expense, US corporations with foreign operations will need to modify their lease versus purchase (loan) analysis to reflect this penalty on interest. The lease rentals in a tax lease are not subject to foreign allocation although the rentals contain, in theory, an element of interest. The following lease versus purchase (loan) analysis illustrates this concept:

General assumptions
Equipment: computer system
Cost: $100,000
Inception date: January 1, 1988
Discount rate (after-tax cost of debt): 5.445%
Tax rate: 34%
Foreign tax rate: assumed to be equal to or greater than the US rate.

Lease information
Payments: five annual payments of $23,361, in arrears
Sales tax: 4% of each lease payment ($24,295 total payment)
Purchase option: fair market value, not exercised
Accounting treatment: operating lease.

Buy information
Loan structure: five annual payments of $25,211, in arrears, at 8.25%
Sales tax: 4% of cost ($4,000)
MACRS: 5-year classlife
Estimated salvage value: $15,000.

Given these assumptions, the following present value comparison illustrates the base case lease versus purchase (loan) decision without taking the loss of FTC (due to interest allocation) into account. The present value of the cash flows (net cash cost) is:

Buy	$ 65,543
Lease	(68,577)
Advantage to leasing	($ 3,034)
Decision	Buy

Purchasing, in this example, has approximately a 5% ($3,034 ÷ $65,543) advantage over leasing on a present value basis. However, if the loss of FTC due to interest allocation is taken into account, this advantage is reversed in favor of leasing, as illustrated in the present value comparison of Table 14. (This example assumes the ratio of US to foreign assets is 60/40).

Table 14
FTC Comparison

	1	2	3	4	5
Lease alternative					
Lease payments	$ 24,295	$ 24,295	$ 24,295	$ 24,295	$ 24,295
× tax rate (.34)	(8,260)	(8,260)	(8,260)	(8,260)	(8,260)
Net cash cost	$ 16,035	$ 16,035	$ 16,035	$ 16,035	$ 16,035
Buy alternative					
Down payment	$ 0	$ 0	$ 0	$ 0	$ 0
Sales tax	4,000	0	0	0	0
Sales tax benefit	(272)	(435)	(261)	(157)	(78)
Loan payments	25,211	25,211	25,211	25,211	25,211
Interest tax benefit	(2,805)	(2,329)	(1,814)	(1,257)	(653)
MACRS tax benefit	(6,800)	(10,880)	(6,528)	(3,917)	(1,958)
Loss of FTC due to					
interest allocation[16]	**1,122**	**932**	**726**	**503**	**261**
Salvage value	0	0	0	0	(13,974)
Net cash cost	$ 20,456	$ 12,499	$ 17,334	$ 20,383	$ 8,809

	Without FTC	With FTC
Buy	$ 65,543	$ 68,672
Lease	(68,577)	(68,577)
Advantage to leasing	($ 3,034)	$ 95
Decision	Buy	Lease

Thus, the penalty associated with incurring additional interest expense reverses the lease versus purchase (loan) decision in this example. It is important to note that this penalty increases as the percentage of a corporation's foreign assets relative to total assets increases. Due to the adverse impact of interest expense allocation on the FTC limitation, it becomes critical for corporations with foreign operations to actively manage and carefully analyze the impact of any

---

[16] The after-tax loss of FTC is computed as follows:

Year	Interest	Tax Rate	Percentage of Foreign Assets		Loss of FTC
1	$8,250	× .34	× .40	=	$1,122
2	6,851	× .34	× .40	=	932
3	5,336	× .34	× .40	=	726
4	3,696	× .34	× .40	=	503
5	1,921	× .34	× .40	=	261

additional leverage incurred, as well as to reconsider the impact of existing debt and the associated interest expense. Management techniques such as leasing, in lieu of purchasing, using nonrecourse debt to fund assets (as the interest is not subject to allocation[17]) and the use of sale-leaseback transactions for assets currently encumbered with recourse debt (as a means of converting previously incurred interest expense to lease expense) are methods of managing (i.e., minimizing) interest expense, thereby maximizing the FTC limitation.

LEASE VERSUS BUY (LOAN) CASES

This section consists of a base case (Case 1) that assumes the lessee is an interest minimizer (liquidity preference is not applicable) that uses the dual rate method of evaluation. Case 1 demonstrates the 13 procedural steps required to complete a lease versus buy analysis. Following Case 1, the liquidity preference and single rate evaluation methods are shown in Case 2. Case 3 is the same as the base case except a purchase option is assumed to be exercised rather than the asset being returned to the lessor, as in Case 1. Case 4 is also identical to the base case except the asset is re-leased at the end of the first lease term. The last, Case 5, is a cash versus lease example rather than loan versus lease.

Case Assumptions

The following assumptions are utilized in the base case (Case 1), and also throughout the variation cases presented. Additional assumptions will be added as appropriate.

Equipment assumptions

Equipment cost: $100,000, payable April 1, 1988

MACRS classlife: 5-year

Expected pretax salvage value: $7,500 at the end of 60 months

Sales tax: 6%, paid at inception, but capitalized and amortized in proportion to MACRS for tax purposes.

Equipment user information

Federal income tax rate: 34%, for a calendar year taxpayer

AMT problem: none

Capital costs (all stated after-tax):

	Annual Nominal	Monthly Nominal	Annual Effective
Cost of debt	5.6628%	.4719%	5.8121%
Cost of capital	10.4400%	.8700%	10.9543%
Cost of equity	16.2789%	1.3566%	17.5505%

Capital structure: 45% debt, 55% equity

---

[17] Regulation §1.861-8(e)(2)(iv).

Liquidity preference: not an issue

Accounting treatment: capital lease status is acceptable.

Lease information

Payments: 60 monthly payments of $1,875, in advance

Refundable security deposit: $1,000

Purchase option: lessee expects to return the equipment to the lessor at the end of the 60th month and, thereby, incur deinstallation and shipping expenses of $800

Sales tax: 6% of lease payments.

Loan information

Down payment: $10,000

Loan: $90,000, with interest at 8.58% per annum, requiring 60 payments in arrears at $1,850 per month beginning May 1, 1988

Closing fee: $625 (nonrefundable)

Compensating bank balance: $1,200, which is refundable at the end of the loan term

General issues: considered to be the best financing alternative available; no one else will lend with a lower down payment.

Lease Versus Buy (Loan) Procedures

There are nine procedures required to complete a lease versus buy analysis. Each procedure is explained and discussed in detail as it is applied to each case. The procedures for completing a lease versus buy analysis are as follows:

1. Preparation of a lease versus buy summary format
2. Liquidity preference decision
3. Computation of the intraperiod present value factors (IPVFs) for the various discount rates used
4. Amortization of both the lease and the loan
5. Equalization of the lease and the buy term
6. Determination of all pertinent after-tax costs per the lease versus buy format
7. Adjustments for AMT when deemed appropriate
8. Sensitivity analysis
9. Consideration of other qualitative issues.

Case 1: Original Assumptions

The nine procedures for completing the lease versus buy analysis are explained in detail in Case 1, in order to convey the full scope of the process. Thereafter, in subsequent cases, the procedures are presented in a more abbreviated format, as applicable.

PREPARATION OF SUMMARY FORMAT

The lease versus buy summary format is used to summarize the present value costs of both leasing and buying in a side by side presentation for comparative purposes. The summary is divided into four categories, which indicate the major sources of costs and benefits impacting the decision. The four major categories are: (1) equivalent loan costs, (2) obsolescence avoidance, (3) tax benefits and (4) indirect costs.

Since the format is a listing of the present value totals of various costs it is important to remember that when liquidity preference is deemed applicable, all costs and benefits should be discounted at the cost of equity; and when interest minimization (equivalent loan method) is deemed applicable and the single rate method is being used, all cash flows should be discounted at the after-tax cost of debt. However, if the dual rate method is being used, all equivalent loan costs should be discounted at the after-tax cost of debt, whereas all other costs and tax benefits should be discounted at the cost of capital. Figure 4 illustrates the format to be used in summarizing the lease versus buy cash flows. The numbering of each line item in Figure 4 provides a mechanism for identifying and explaining each aspect of the summary.

LIQUIDITY PREFERENCE DECISION

In this particular case, liquidity preference is not an issue. However, the same case is shown later (Case 2), with liquidity preference considered. When liquidity preference is not an issue, the after-tax cost of debt is used for all costs and benefits when the single rate method of discounting is employed; otherwise, when the dual rate discount method is used the after-tax cost of debt is applied to equivalent loan costs and the cost of capital is applied to all other costs and benefits.

IPVF COMPUTATION

IPVF describes the present value of a tax year's five quarterly estimated tax payment percentages. The IPVFs in Table 15 need to be computed as a preliminary step prior to any further lease versus buy calculations. These IPVFs will be used to save time in present valuing cash flows derived from tax expenses or tax benefits. Refer to Chapter Four for a more complete explanation of an IPVF.

AMORTIZATION OF LOAN AND LEASE

The loan and the lease payments need to be separated into principal and interest in order to determine the tax benefit associated with the interest expense included in the payments. Furthermore, the principal portion of the lease represents the cost recovery that also is needed to evaluate the related tax benefits. The HP-12C readily provides a complete amortization of the two alternatives, although the lease will seldom fully amortize to zero, which has important ramifications. The loan amortization is set up as follows, and the amortization schedule, by tax year, is shown in Table 16.

		g	END
90,000	CHS		PV
1,850			PMT
0			n
8.58		g	12 ÷

The lease amortization is set up as follows, and the amortization schedule, by tax year, is shown in Table 17.

CATEGORY	PRESENT VALUE AMOUNTS	
	Lease	Loan

Equivalent loan cost
1. Advance/down payment
2. Subsequent payments
3. Unamortized principal balance
4. Purchase option exercise price
5. Lease renewals
6. Refundable deposits/compensating balance
7. Closing, origination fees, etc.
8. Interest deduction tax benefits

     Total equivalent loan costs

Obsolescence avoidance
9. Residual salvage value

     Subtotal

Tax benefits
10. Cost recovery
11. AMT
12. Tax credits
13. _____

     Total tax benefits

     Subtotal

Indirect costs
14. Sales tax
15. Installation
16. Maintenance
17. Deinstallation
18. _____
19. _____
20. _____

     Total indirect costs

     Total costs

Figure 4
Lease Versus Buy Summary

Table 15
IPVF Computations

	Quarterly Estimated Tax %	Months from Inception	Cost of Debt .4719/month	Cost of Capital .87/month	Cost of Equity 1.3566/month
April 1	.000	0.0			
April 15	.225	0.5	.22447	.22403	.22348
June 15	.225	2.5	.22237	.22018	.21754
September 15	.225	5.5	.21925	.21453	.20892
December 15	.225	8.5	.21617	.20903	.20065
March 15	.100	11.5	.09473	.09052	.08564
Total IPVFs			.97699	.95829	.93624

Table 16
Loan Amortization Schedule

Months		Interest		Principal		Balance	
8	f	AMORT	4,903	X ≥ Y	9,897	RCL PV	80,103
12	f	AMORT	6,255	X ≥ Y	15,945	RCL PV	64,158
12	f	AMORT	4,832	X ≥ Y	17,368	RCL PV	46,791
12	f	AMORT	3,282	X ≥ Y	18,918	RCL PV	27,873
12	f	AMORT	1,595	X ≥ Y	20,606	RCL PV	7,267
4	f	AMORT	133	X ≥ Y	7,267	RCL PV	0
		Total	21,000		90,000		

Table 17
Lease Amortization Schedule

Months		Interest		Principal		Balance	
9	f	AMORT	5,374	X ≥ Y	11,501	RCL PV	88,499
12	f	AMORT	6,993	X ≥ Y	15,507	RCL PV	72,992
12	f	AMORT	5,609	X ≥ Y	16,891	RCL PV	56,101
12	f	AMORT	4,101	X ≥ Y	18,399	RCL PV	37,702
12	f	AMORT	2,459	X ≥ Y	20,041	RCL PV	17,661
3	f	AMORT	341	X ≥ Y	5,284	RCL PV	12,377
		Total	24,877		87,623		

		g	BEG
100,000	CHS		PV
1,875			PMT
0			n
8.58		g	12 ÷

Note that the lease in this case does not fully amortize. The unamortized balance represents the implied residual position taken by the lessor, which will be considered in Steps Three and Nine of the decision format. The unamortized balance must be the equivalent of the lessor's residual position, since $12,377 of the $100,000 equipment cost can be avoided by the lessee simply by not purchasing the equipment or by renewing the lease at the end of the original lease term.

EQUALIZATION OF LEASE AND BUY TERMS

The term of the purchase alternative must match that of the lease. Table 1 indicates the various options available that will equate the terms. In this particular case, the asset was assumed returned to the lessor at the end of the lease term, at which time the lessor salvaged the equipment. Various other options are shown in Cases 3 and 4.

DETERMINATION OF ALL PERTINENT COSTS

Pertinent costs are those that vary under the loan versus the lease alternative or that occur only in one or the other cases. The pertinent costs beyond the basic lease and loan payments in this case are refundable deposits and compensating bank balances, various residual salvage values, various cost recoveries, sales tax and deinstallation. In fact, most lease versus buy decisions probably will have even fewer variables than this particular case.

The lease versus buy format of Figure 5 has been completed with the present value amounts for the various pertinent lease versus buy costs, and shows that the difference of $522 favors leasing. Following the format is a line by line explanation of 20 costs usually encountered in a lease versus buy situation.

Present Value Explanations

Refer to the following note explanations for the sources of the present value data shown in Figure 5.
1. Advance/down payments
    Per the assumptions
2. Subsequent payments
    a. Lease payments

CATEGORY	PRESENT VALUE AMOUNTS	
	Lease	**Loan**
Equivalent loan cost		
1. Advance/down payment	$ 1,875	$ 10,000
2. Subsequent payments	96,363	96,473
3. Unamortized principal balance	9,331	0
4. Purchase option exercise price	0	0
5. Lease renewals	0	0
6. Refundable deposits/compensating balance	246	295
7. Closing, origination fees, etc.	0	0
8. Interest deduction tax benefits	(7,531)	(6,402)
Total equivalent loan costs	$ 100,284	$ 100,783
Obsolescence avoidance		
9. Residual salvage value	($ 7,360)	($ 5,545)
Subtotal	$ 92,924	$ 95,238
Tax benefits		
10. Cost recovery	($ 22,492)	($ 24,797)
11. AMT	0	0
12. Tax credits	0	0
13. _____	0	0
Total tax benefits	($ 22,492)	($ 24,797)
Subtotal	$ 70,432	$ 70,441
Indirect costs		
14. Sales tax	$ 3,526	$ 4,360
15. Installation	0	0
16. Maintenance	0	0
17. Deinstallation	321	0
18. _____	0	0
19. _____	0	0
20. _____	0	0
Total indirect costs	$ 3,847	$ 4,360
Total costs	$ 74,279	$ 74,801

Figure 5
Lease Versus Buy Summary

.4719			i	
1,875			PMT	
59			n	
		g	END	
			PV	96,362.86 ($96,363 rounded)

b. Loan payments

.4719			i	
1,850			PMT	
60			n	
		g	END	
			PV	96,472.77 ($96,473 rounded)

3. Unamortized principal balance
   a. Lease

.4719		i	
12,377	CHS	FV	(unamortized principal balance in the lease)
60		n	
		PV	9,331.22 ($9,331 rounded)

Typically, a lease, when amortized at a pretax cost of debt (8.58%), will have an unamortized principal balance remaining. This represents the theoretical loan principal that would have been due the lessor had the lessee not returned the equipment at the end of the lease in exchange for forgiveness of this debt. The present value of this amount is temporarily included in the analysis to arrive at the total implied costs of debt before any residual value has been deducted from the debt cost

4 & 5. The purchase option exercise price and lease renewals represent costs that would be incurred if the lessee were desirous of retaining the equipment beyond the original noncancellable lease term, which is not the case here

6. Refundable security deposit/compensating balances
   a. Refundable security deposit

.4719			i	
1,000		g	CF_o (payment of deposit)	
0		g	CF_j	
59		g	N_j	
1,000	CHS	g	CF_j (return of deposit)	
		f	NPV	246.08 ($246 rounded)

   b. Compensating balance

.4719			i
1,200		g	CF_o (payment of compensating balance)
0		g	CF_j
59		g	N_j
1,200	CHS	g	CF_j (return of compensating balance)
		f	NPV 295.30 ($295 rounded)

7. Loan closing fee

   Fee $\times$ [1 – (tax rate $\times$ IPVF)]

   $625 $\times$ [1 – (.34 $\times$ .97699)] = $417.39 ($417 rounded)

8. Interest deduction tax benefits (taken from the amortizations of the loan and lease in Tables 16 and 17, respectively)

   a. Loan interest benefits

5.8121		i
4,903	g	CF_o (current year interest tax deduction)
6,255	g	CF_j (subsequent year interest tax deduction)
4,832	g	CF_j
3,282	g	CF_j
1,594	g	CF_j
133	g	CF_j
	f	NPV 19,272.37
.34	$\times$	6,552.61
.97699	$\times$	6,401.83 ($6,402 rounded)

   b. Lease interest benefits

5.8121		i
5,374	g	CF_o (implied lease interest tax deduction)
6,993	g	CF_j
5,609	g	CF_j
4,101	g	CF_j
2,459	g	CF_j
341	g	CF_j
	f	NPV 22,672.99
.34	$\times$	7,708.82
.97699	$\times$	7,531.44 ($7,531 rounded)

9. Residual salvage value

   a. Lease residual value: the $12,377 unamortized principal balance from the lease amortization in Table 17 is the assumed residual position taken by the lessor. There are no tax consequences associated with this value

```
      .87                    i
   12,377   CHS             FV
       60                    n
                            PV      7,360.28 ($7,360 rounded)
```

b. Loan residual value

1) Net residual cash flow (without the remaining unamortized MACRS tax benefits)

Estimated pretax residual value	$ 7,500.00
Taxes at 34%	$ 2,550
IPVF	× .95829
	2,443.64
Net residual cash flow	$ 5,056.36

2) Present value of the net residual

```
      .87                    i
   5,056.36  CHS            FV
       60                    n
                            PV      3,006.88 ($3,007 rounded)
```

3) Present value of the remaining tax basis in the fifth and sixth tax year (the amount necessary to equate the cost recovery of the lease to the buy, $12,377)

```
   10.9543                  i
        0          g       CF_j
        3          g       N_j
    6,617          g       CF_j  ($12,377 – $5,760)
    5,760          g       CF_j  (6th year's MACRS)

                   f        NPV     7,791.33
      .34                    ×      2,649.05
    .95829                   ×      2,538.56
```

4) Net after-tax residual value

Present value of the net residual	$ 3,006.88
Present value of the tax basis	2,538.56
	$ 5,545.44 ($5,545 rounded)

10. Cost recovery

a. Lease cost recovery per the amortization schedule of Table 17 ($87,623 of cost recovery taken; the $12,377 balance was considered above)

10.9543		i		
11,501	g	CF_o		
15,507	g	CF_j		
16,891	g	CF_j		
18,399	g	CF_j		
20,041	g	CF_j		
5,284	g	CF_j		
	f	NPV	69,032.91	
.34	×		23,471.19	
.95829	×		22,492.20 ($22,492 rounded)	

b. Loan cost recovery ($87,623 of MACRS cost recovery taken; the $12,377 balance was considered above)

10.9543		i	
20,000	g	CF_o	
32,000	g	CF_j	
19,200	g	CF_j	
11,520	g	CF_j	
4,903	g	CF_j ($11,520 – $6,617)[18]	
	f	NPV	76,105.51
.34	×		25,875.87
.95829	×		24,796.59 ($24,797 rounded)

11. AMT: none

12. Tax credits: none

13. Miscellaneous: none

14. Sales tax

   a. Lease sales tax
   .06 × $1,875 = $112.50

.87		i	
112.50	g	CF_o	
112.50	g	CF_j	
59	g	N_j	
	f	NPV	5,286.88

---

[18] The $6,617 represents the amount of cost recovery in the fifth tax year that had already been taken as a deduction in Step 9. See "buy residual value."

Tax benefits on the sales tax

Tax Year	Payments	Sales Tax Per Tax Year
1	9 × $112.50	$ 1,012.50
2	12 × 112.50	1,350.00
3	12 × 112.50	1,350.00
4	12 × 112.50	1,350.00
5	12 × 112.50	1,350.00
6	3 × 112.50	337.50

10.9543		i	
1,012.50	g	CF_o	
1,350	g	CF_j	
4	g	N_j	
337.50	g	CF_j	
	f	NPV	5,405.59
.34	×		1,837.90
.95829	×		1,761.24

$$\$5,286.88 - \$1,761.24 =$$

$3,525.63 is the cost of the sales tax, net of tax benefits ($3,526 rounded)

b. Loan sales tax

$$.06 \times \$100,000 = \$6,000 \text{ expense}$$

Tax benefits on the sales tax

$$\$6,000 \times .2000 \times .34 = \$408.00$$
$$6,000 \times .3200 \times .34 = 652.80$$
$$6,000 \times .1020 \times .34 = 391.68$$
$$6,000 \times .1152 \times .34 = 235.01$$
$$6,000 \times .1152 \times .34 = 235.01$$
$$6,000 \times .0576 \times .34 = 117.50$$

10.9543		i	
408.00	g	CF_o	
652.80	g	CF_j	
391.68	g	CF_j	
235.01	g	CF_j	
2	g	N_j	
117.50	g	CF_j	
	f	NPV	1,711.50
.95829	×		1,640.11
6,000	−		4,359.84 ($4,360 rounded)

15. Installation: none
16. Maintenance: none
17. Deinstallation: shipping expense
    $800 \times [1 - (.34 \times .95829)] = \$539.35$

539.35	CHS	FV
60		n
.87		i
		PV	320.73 ($321 rounded)

18, 19 & 20. Miscellaneous: none

ADJUSTMENTS FOR AMT

An example showing the impact of the AMT adjustments on the lease versus buy decision was presented earlier in this chapter. None of the cases incorporates AMT.

SENSITIVITY ANALYSIS

Sensitivity analysis consists of studying the impact of changes in assumptions on the final lease versus buy cost difference. For example, what if the lease were renewed or the equipment purchased at the end of the lease term (see Cases 3 and 4)? What if liquidity preference were an issue (see Case 2)? What is the terminal (future value) value of the difference between leasing and buying? The answer to questions such as these is typically gained through the process of sensitivity analysis.

As an example, terminal value analysis involves finding the future value of the present value difference between leasing and buying, appreciating at the lessee's cost of capital.

.87		i
522	CHS	PV [$74,801 (buy) – $74,279 (lease)]
60		n
		FV	877.79

The total difference is $877.79 in favor of leasing. This difference represents the actual income statement impact over the lease term of having selected leasing over borrowing, as compared to the $522 present value difference in favor of leasing.

CONSIDERATION OF QUALITATIVE ISSUES

Typical qualitative issues that might have impacted this case were discussed earlier. Note, however, that the lease in question in this case is capital, as shown below:

Compute the FASB 13 comparison base

Fair market value	$ 100,000
	× .90
FASB 13 comparison base	$ 90,000

Compute the present value of the minimum lease payments

8.58	g	12 ÷
2,500	g	CF_o (closing fee of $625 plus the $1,875 advance rental)
1,875	g	CF_j
59	g	N_j
	f	NPV 92,495.40

The lease is capital, since $92,495.40 is greater than $90,000.

Case 2: Liquidity Preference

All cash flows are present valued at the 16.2789% cost of equity using the single rate method. All computations are completed in the same manner as the base case just presented, with the sole difference the higher discount rate applied to all present value calculations. The summary of cash flows is shown in Figure 6. The difference of $1,954 in favor of leasing using the lessee's cost of equity as a discount rate affirms that leasing is definitely favored in this case when liquidity preference is an issue. When liquidity preference was not an issue, leasing was favored by only $522.

Case 3: Exercise of Purchase Option

At the end of the lease term the equipment will be purchased for $7,500, plus sales tax of 6%, and the equipment will be retained for 2 more years, at which time it will be worthless. To avoid bias, the assumed exercise price should be at or near the same price assumed as the salvage value under the buy option in the case just completed. The summary of cash flows is shown in Figure 7. Surprisingly, this one change in assumptions causes numbers 3, 4, 8, 9, 10, 14 and 17 on the lease versus buy format to change. In this case, the difference is $846, also in favor of leasing.

3. The unamortized lease balance is not applicable in this case since the amortization schedule is adjusted in a manner that causes the unamortized balance to become zero. For example, the last year of the amortization schedule before the $7,500 purchase option exercise appears in Table 18. The rationale for the adjustment is that if a loan balance of $12,377 can be paid off with a check of $7,500, then in effect a savings of $4,877 has been realized, which is shown in Table 18 as negative interest.

However, had the residual value been estimated to be $14,000, the adjustment would have been $1,623.

	Interest	Principal	Balance
Year 6 (3 months)	$ 341	$ 5,284	$ 12,377
$14,000 payment	1,623	12,377	(12,377)
Year 6 summary	$ 1,964	$ 17,661	$ 0

In summary, when the lease payments plus the residual are insufficient to amortize the lease using the cost of debt as the discount rate, the unamortized balance is considered to be interest savings, whereas excess payments are treated as interest expense. Excess interest savings or interest expense could be spread over the life of the lease simply by finding the actual pretax IRR of the lease and using this rate in the amortization process.

CATEGORY	PRESENT VALUE AMOUNTS	
Equivalent loan cost	**Lease**	**Loan**
1. Advance/down payment	$ 1,875	$ 10,000
2. Subsequent payments	75,800	75,613
3. Unamortized principal balance	5,514	0
4. Purchase option exercise price	0	0
5. Lease renewals	0	0
6. Refundable deposits/compensating balance	554	665
7. Closing, origination fees, etc.	0	426
8. Interest deduction tax benefits	(6,158)	(5,295)
Total equivalent loan costs	$ 77,585	$ 81,409
Obsolescence avoidance		
9. Residual salvage value	($ 5,514)	($ 4,198)
Subtotal	$ 72,071	$ 77,211
Tax benefits		
10. Cost recovery	($ 19,447)	($ 22,530)
11. AMT	0	0
12. Tax credits	0	0
13.		
Total tax benefits	($ 19,447)	($ 22,530)
Subtotal	$ 52,624	$ 54,681
Indirect costs		
14. Sales tax	3,124	4,408
15. Installation	0	0
16. Maintenance	0	0
17. Deinstallation	545	0
18.		
19.		
20.		
Total indirect costs	$ 3,669	$ 4,408
Total costs	$ 48,955	$ 50,909

Figure 6
Lease Versus Buy Summary
(liquidity preference)

CATEGORY	PRESENT VALUE AMOUNTS	
	Lease	Loan
Equivalent loan cost		
1. Advance/down payment	$ 1,875	$ 10,000
2. Subsequent payments	96,363	96,473
3. Unamortized principal balance	0	0
4. Purchase option exercise price	5,654	0
5. Lease renewals	0	0
6. Refundable deposits/compensating balance	246	295
7. Closing, origination fees, etc.	0	417
8. Interest deduction tax benefits	(6,310)	(6,402)
Total equivalent loan costs	$ 97,828	$ 100,783
Obsolescence avoidance		
9. Residual salvage value	0	0
Subtotal	$ 97,828	$ 100,783
Tax benefits		
10. Cost recovery	($ 24,713)	($ 27,335)
11. AMT	0	0
12. Tax credits	0	0
13.	0	0
Total tax benefits	($ 24,713)	($ 27,355)
Subtotal	$ 73,115	$ 73,448
Indirect costs		
14. Sales tax	$ 3,847	$ 4,360
15. Installation	0	0
16. Maintenance	0	0
17. Deinstallation	0	0
18.	0	0
19.	0	0
20.	0	0
Total indirect costs	$ 3,847	$ 4,360
Total costs	$ 76,962	$ 77,808

Figure 7
Lease Versus Buy Summary
(purchase option exercised)

Table 18
Lease Amortization Schedule

Year	Months		Interest		Principal		Balance	
1	9	f	AMORT	5,374	X ≥ Y	11,501	RCL PV	88,499
2	12	f	AMORT	6,993	X ≥ Y	15,507	RCL PV	72,992
3	12	f	AMORT	5,609	X ≥ Y	16,891	RCL PV	56,101
4	12	f	AMORT	4,101	X ≥ Y	18,399	RCL PV	37,702
5	12	f	AMORT	2,459	X ≥ Y	20,041	RCL PV	17,661
6	3	f	AMORT	341	X ≥ Y	5,284	RCL PV	12,377
Adjustment: 7,500 residual				(4,877)		12,377		
Total				20,000		100,000		

This method has not been chosen, since it is primarily the residual assumption that is creating the interest savings or expense. The residual assumption is subject to uncertainty and risk and, therefore, any interest adjustments should occur at the same time as the event that caused them.

4. Purchase option exercise price

4.719		i
7,500	CHS	FV
60		n
	PV	5,654.37 ($5,654 rounded)

8. Interest deduction tax benefits for the lease based on the adjusted lease amortization (Table 18)

5.8121			i
5,374		g	CF_o
6,993		g	CF_j
5,609		g	CF_j
4,101		g	CF_j
2,459		g	CF_j
4,536	CHS	g	CF_j (interest savings adjustment $4,877 – $341)
		f	NPV 18,996.14
.34		×	6,458.69
.97699		×	6,310.07 ($6,310 rounded)

9. Residual salvage value: none, since the equipment was retained instead of being salvaged

10. Cost recovery
   a. Lease cost recovery based on the adjusted lease amortization of Table 18

10.9543		i	
11,501	g	CF$_o$	
15,507	g	CF$_j$	
16,891	g	CF$_j$	
18,399	g	CF$_j$	
20,041	g	CF$_j$	
11,661	g	CF$_j$ [$17,661 - $7,500 + .2($7,500)]	
2,400	g	CF$_j$ (.32 × $7,500)	
3,600	g	CF$_j$ (balance of MACRS = .48 × $7,500)	
	f	NPV	75,850.43
.34		×	25,789.15
.95829		×	24,713.48 ($24,713 rounded)

   b. Loan cost recovery

10.9543		i	
20,000	g	CF$_o$	
32,000	g	CF$_j$	
19,200	g	CF$_j$	
11,520	g	CF$_j$	
2	g	N$_j$	
5,760	g	CF$_j$	
	f	NPV	83,896.85
.34		×	28,524.93
.95829		×	27,335.15 ($27,335 rounded)

14. Sales tax on the lease
   a. An incremental $450 of sales tax would be owed (6% of the $7,500 purchase option) less the present value of the tax benefit received in proportion to MACRS
   b. Present value the tax benefits associated with the sales tax

   $450 × .20 × .34 = $30.60
   450 × .32 × .34 = 48.96
   450 × .48 × .34 = 73.44

10.9543		i	
30.60	g	CF$_o$	
48.96	g	CF$_j$	
73.44	g	CF$_j$	
	f	NPV	134.38
.95829		×	128.78 ($129 rounded)

Pretax sales tax	$ 450
Present value of the tax benefits	(129)
Net after-tax cost	$ 321
Plus sales tax on the rentals	3,526
	$ 3,847

17. Deinstallation: none, since the equipment was purchased instead of being shipped back to the lessor.

Case 4: Exercise of Renewal Option

At the end of the lease term, the lease will be renewed for 24 payments of $600, beginning May 1. At the end of the renewal the equipment is considered worthless. The summary of cash flows is shown in Figure 8, and indicates that the difference of $2,036 is in favor of the loan. Using the initial case as a starting point the following line items require adjustment: 3, 5, 8, 9, 10, 14 and 17.

3. The unamortized lease principal balance is not applicable in this case since the amortization schedule is adjusted in a manner that causes the unamortized balance to become zero. For example the last year (sixth) before the renewal appears as in Table 19. The $961 adjustment required to cause the principal balance to be fully paid represents extra interest paid by the lessee.

5. Lease renewals

.4719		i
0	g	CF_o
0	g	CF_j
60	g	N_j
600	g	CF_j
24	g	N_j
	f	NPV 10,241.38 ($10,241 rounded)

8. Lease interest deduction tax benefits

5.8121		i
5,374	g	CF_o
6,993	g	CF_j
5,609	g	CF_j
4,101	g	CF_j
2,459	g	CF_j
945	g	CF_j ($341 + $604)
440	g	CF_j
979	g	CF_j ($18 + $961)
	f	NPV 24,101.09
.34	×	8,194.37
.97699	×	8,005.82 ($8,006 rounded)

CATEGORY	PRESENT VALUE AMOUNTS	
Equivalent loan cost	**Lease**	**Loan**
1. Advance/down payment	$ 1,875	$ 10,000
2. Subsequent payments	96,363	96,473
3. Unamortized principal balance	0	0
4. Purchase option exercise price	0	0
5. Lease renewals	10,241	0
6. Refundable deposits/compensating balance	246	295
7. Closing, origination fees, etc.	0	417
8. Interest deduction tax benefits	(8,006)	(6,402)
Total equivalent loan costs	$ 100,719	$ 100,783
Obsolescence avoidance		
9. Residual salvage value	0	0
Subtotal	$ 100,719	$ 100,783
Tax benefits		
10. Cost recovery	(24,709)	(27,335)
11. AMT	0	0
12. Tax credits	0	0
13.	0	0
Total tax benefits	($ 24,709)	($ 27,335)
Subtotal	$ 76,010	$ 73,448
Indirect costs		
14. Sales tax	$ 3,834	$ 4,360
15. Installation	0	0
16. Maintenance	0	0
17. Deinstallation	0	0
18.	0	0
19.	0	0
20.	0	0
Total indirect costs	$ 3,834	$ 4,360
Total costs	$ 79,844	$ 77,808

Figure 8
Lease Versus Buy Summary
(renewal option exercised)

Table 19
Unamortized Lease Principal

Months			Interest	Principal			Balance	
9	f	AMORT	5,374	X ≥ Y	11,501	RCL PV	88,499
12	f	AMORT	6,993	X ≥ Y	15,507	RCL PV	72,992
12	f	AMORT	5,609	X ≥ Y	16,891	RCL PV	56,101
12	f	AMORT	4,101	X ≥ Y	18,399	RCL PV	37,702
12	f	AMORT	2,459	X ≥ Y	20,041	RCL PV	17,661
3	f	AMORT	341	X ≥ Y	5,284	RCL PV	12,377
8 rentals ($4,800)			604		4,196		8,181
12 rentals ($7,200)			440		6,760		1,421
4 rentals ($2,400)			18		2,382		(961)
Adjustment			961		(961)		0
Total			26,900		100,000		

9. Residual salvage value: none, since the equipment was retained instead of being salvaged
10. Cost recovery
    a. Lease cost recovery

10.9543		i
11,501	g	CF_o
15,507	g	CF_j
16,891	g	CF_j
18,399	g	CF_j
20,041	g	CF_j
9,480	g	CF_j ($5,284 + $4,196)
6,760	g	CF_j
1,421	g	CF_j ($2,382 − $961)
	f	NPV 75,837.69
.34	×	25,784.81
.95829	×	24,709.33 ($24,709 rounded)

b. Loan cost recovery

10.9543		i
20,000	g	CF_o
32,000	g	CF_j
19,200	g	CF_j
11,520	g	CF_j
2	g	N_j
5,760	g	CF_j
	f	NPV	83,896.85
.34	×	28,524.93
.95829	×	27,335.15 ($27,335 rounded)

14. Sales tax on the lease
   a. An incremental $36 of sales tax (6% of $600) would be due on each of the additional 24 renewal payments of $600
   b. Present value the pretax sales tax expenses

.87		i
0	g	CF_o
0	g	CF_j
60	g	N_j
36	g	CF_j
24	g	N_j
	f	NPV	461.90 ($462 rounded)

   c. Present value the tax benefits associated with the sales tax

8 × $36	=	$288	6th tax year
12 × 36	=	432	7th tax year
4 × 36	=	144	8th tax year

10.9543		i
0	g	CF_o
0	g	CF_j
4	g	N_j
288	g	CF_j
432	g	CF_j
144	g	CF_j
	f	NPV	472.36
.34	×	160.60
.95829	×	153.90 ($154 rounded)

Present value of the pretax cost	$ 462
Present value of the tax benefits	(154)
Net after-tax cost	$ 308
Plus sales tax on the rentals	3,526
	$ 3,834

Case 5: Cash Versus Lease

Assume the lessee pays 100% cash for the equipment on the buy side, thus alleviating the need to borrow. The cash flow summary for this case is shown in Figure 9, and indicates that the $261 difference is in favor of the loan. This one change in assumptions causes numbers 1, 2, 6, 7 and 8 on the buy side of the lease versus buy format to change as follows:

1. Down payment
   $100,000 per the assumptions, which is the same as a 100% cash purchase
2. Subsequent payments
   Not applicable as the loan is not obtained
6. Compensating balance
   Not applicable as the loan is not obtained
7. Origination fee
   Not applicable as the loan is not obtained
8. Interest reduction tax benefit
   Not applicable as the loan is not obtained.

Summary of Cases

A summarization of the five cases is shown in Table 20. Ignoring Cases 2 and 5, which case best describes whether the lessee should lease or buy? Since each of these cases represents a viable solution to the lease versus buy case, the answer would be the one best describing the anticipated residual position (exercise purchase option or not, etc.). However, if none of the three situations is highly probable, then a weighted average approach should be used similar to the one in Table 21. Assume that the most likely event to occur will be exercise of the purchase option, to which a 50% probability is ascribed. Renewal is considered remote at a 15% probability, and the likelihood of the purchase option not being exercised is assumed to be 35%. The letter F in Table 21 indicates the results favor leasing, and the letter U indicates the results favor buying. The asset should, under the assumptions made, be leased, given the assessment of the various probabilities of occurrence, since the weighted average expected present value difference in expenses favors leasing by $305.30.

CATEGORY	PRESENT VALUE AMOUNTS	
Equivalent loan cost	**Lease**	**Loan** (cash)
1. Advance/down payment	$ 1,875	$ 100,000
2. Subsequent payments	96,363	0
3. Unamortized principal balance	9,331	0
4. Purchase option exercise price	0	0
5. Lease renewals	0	0
6. Refundable deposits/compensating balance	246	0
7. Closing, origination fees, etc.	0	0
8. Interest deduction tax benefits	(7,531)	0
Total equivalent loan costs	$ 100,284	$ 100,000
Obsolescence avoidance		
9. Residual salvage value	($ 7,360)	($ 5,545)
Subtotal	$ 92,924	$ 94,455
Tax benefits		
10. Cost recovery	($ 22,492)	($ 24,797)
11. AMT	0	0
12. Tax credits	0	0
13.	0	0
Total tax benefits	($ 22,492)	($ 24,797)
Subtotal	$ 70,432	$ 69,658
Indirect costs		
14. Sales tax	$ 3,526	$ 4,360
15. Installation	0	0
16. Maintenance	0	0
17. Deinstallation	321	0
18.	0	0
19.	0	0
20.	0	0
Total indirect costs	$ 3,847	$ 4,360
Total costs	$ 74,279	$ 74,018

Figure 9
Lease Versus Cash Summary
(cash versus lease)

Table 20
Lease Versus Buy Case Summary

Explanation	Lease	Buy	Difference	In Favor Of
Case 1: Original assumptions	$ 74,279	$ 74,801	$ 522	Lease
Case 2: Liquidity preference	48,955	50,909	1,954	Lease
Case 3: Exercise of purchase option	76,962	77,808	846	Lease
Case 4: Exercise of renewal option	79,844	77,808	(2,036)	Buy
Case 5: Cash versus lease	74,279	74,018	(261)	Buy

Table 21
Probability Analysis

Action	Results		Probability		Total	
Purchase option not exercised	$ 522	[F]	.35	=	$ 187.70	
Purchase option exercised	$ 846	[F]	.50	=	423.00	
Renewal exercised	($ 2,036)	[U]	.15	=	(305.40)	
					$ 305.30	[F]

CONCLUSION

Lease versus buy is a decision that encompasses far more than its debt surrogate nature. Obsolescence avoidance, tax benefits and numerous other quantitative as well as qualitative costs impact the decision. The right lease versus buy conclusion will contain appropriate input premises, reasonable logic, adequate perspective and dynamic feedback. The AMT position of a lessee tends to favor leasing, especially if the lease is accounted for as a capital lease.

The logic of the lease versus buy decision also requires an understanding of the appropriate discount rate, as well as whether the single rate or dual rate method should be used. Pulling together all the many factors presented in this chapter will require skills and knowledge, as the lease versus buy decision is not only strategically important, but also very complex.

CHAPTER SEVEN
LEASE ANALYSIS

This chapter is devoted to examining existing analytical methods used in determining whether a given lease (or portfolio of leases) is sufficiently profitable to justify an investment or continued interest therein. The very meaning of profitability is examined in the context of the numerous analytical methods used in the industry to determine it: cash flow, yields, accounting reported earnings, present value, payback, etc. Each analytical method is presented along with case studies that require use of a Hewlett Packard 12C or 18C (HP-12C or HP-18C) hand-held financial calculator. Hands-on experience is utilized as the most efficient method of learning and understanding how leases are analyzed. The chapter itself is subdivided into seven sections:

- Analytical Methodologies
- Preliminary Case Assumptions
- Yield Analysis
- Present and Future Value Analysis
- Managerial-oriented Indices
- Marketing-related Techniques
- Maximization Versus Optimization.

ANALYTICAL METHODOLOGIES

Analytical methods tend to gravitate towards the particular financial objective and experiential bias of the decision maker; accountants tend towards maximization of reported book earnings, financial analysts towards yield and net present value (NPV) approaches, managers towards cash flow analysis, while sales personnel are attracted to a host of methods that may or may not have any economic validity, but which have efficacy in marketing. One of the objectives of this section is to interrelate, prioritize and validate the various analytical methods being used in the leasing industry today. Most methods fall under one of the five broad categories discussed in this section.

Yield-oriented Methods

Yield-oriented analytical methods consist of internal rate of return (IRR) and external rate of return (ERR) analysis. (ERR analysis is also known as dual rate of return, adjusted or modified IRR and includes the various types of ERRs that are discussed later in this chapter.) Yield-oriented approaches attempt to determine the interest rate inherent in a lease on a basis that is either pretax or after-tax. This interest rate in a lease is analogous to the annual percentage rate (APR) that a bank would quote a borrower on a loan. The interest rate represents a constant periodic earnings percentage that is applied to a declining principal balance throughout a lease's term. Yields are nothing more than IRRs, which are unique discount rates that cause the present value of the investment's returns (cash inflows) to be equal to the investment's cost.

Unfortunately, the yield, or IRR, might not be necessarily the best method to evaluate a lease, especially when reinvestment opportunities for cash returns on the original investment differ significantly from the investment's IRR. In this situation, the ERR method may be superior, depending upon the reinvestment assumptions. The existence of negative cash flows subsequent to a lease's inception also might require ERR analysis.

Present and Future Value Methods

Present value and future value approaches impose hurdle rates or required rates of return on investments, and include NPV, terminal value analysis (TVA) or future value analysis, modified payback and dual rate present value. In these methods, cash flows are either (1) present valued at a required discount rate to ascertain whether their present value equals or exceeds the cost of the original investment (NPV method), (2) future valued at a designated appreciation rate to ascertain whether their future value equals or exceeds the future value of the original investment (TVA or future value analysis method) or (3) present valued until their present value equals the original investment (modified payback method).

Present value techniques remove interest from cash flows — the remainder is principal; therefore, the present value of the discounted principal must be equal to or greater than the original investment. Future value methods add reinvestment earnings to cash flows, the total future value of which must equal or exceed the future value of the investment assumed to have grown at the required investment return rate.

Present and future value methods are not affected by situations in which reinvestment opportunities differ significantly from the investment's own particular IRR, since both these techniques impose their own reinvestment assumptions on the analytical method. IRR, on the other hand, assumes that all cash flows are reinvested at the IRR of the investment, which may be unrealistically high or low, depending upon the circumstances. Notwithstanding NPV's and TVA's imposition of assumed reinvestment rates, they do not always give the best answer when negative cash flows subsequent to the original investment occur, e.g., in leveraged leasing. Negative cash flows result in what are known as disinvestment, abnormal or credit investment balances and require application of ERR methods or dual-rate present value discounting (explained later in this chapter).

Managerial-oriented Indices

The analytical methods used for managerial purposes are broad and varied, as they must serve many purposes. Common managerial-oriented indices include accounting rates of return (implicit rate and multiple investment sinking fund (MISF) rates, etc.), cash flow rules of thumb, accounting return on average investment, return on risked assets, payback, interest spread analysis, interest accretion and accounting returns on the net investment in the lease.

Managerial-related techniques are not necessarily accurate from a pure financial theory or economic return viewpoint, but they are, nevertheless, quite important. For example, the amount of cash flow a lease generates is important apart from its IRR or NPV. In fact, two leases with identical IRRs and NPVs can have very different undiscounted net cash flows. Beyond cash flow, the amount of accounting reported earnings is extremely important for earnings per share impact. Earnings per share is frequently evaluated independent of the yield or NPV. Other techniques, such as payback, emphasize time at-risk, rather than profitability, and are used in risk assessment.

Many lessors evaluate leases by adding yield increments to their cost of borrowed funds, in order to cover operating costs such as general and administrative (G & A) expense, initial direct costs (commissions, etc.) and a reasonable profit. Other lessors achieve the same objective by building upon an assumed debt payment, which includes both principal and interest, rather than adding costs to yield only.

Marketing-related Techniques

There are several analytical methods that are used for marketing purposes, such as street, running or stream rates, return on equity (ROE), lessee effective or apparent rates, loan equivalent rates of return and various pretax yield approximations. Marketing-related techniques are heavily influenced by marketing expediency, or "tell the potential lessee what it wants to hear." Consequently, the quoting of street, stream or running rates is commonplace. Interestingly enough, it is not that potential lessees are unsuspecting of this type of rate; indeed, they seem to prefer to have these incomplete lease rates quoted to them. Tradition is difficult to change, even though such market rates, from a purely economic standpoint, are incomplete since they frequently ignore such important rate ingredients as tax benefits, residual value, number of advance payments, interim rent, contingent rentals, etc. Market-oriented rates are, nevertheless, useful because the relative cost of one lease versus another can be determined so long as all other variables are the same. Some forms of rate quotes, such as add-on or discount interest in a lease so understate the actual interest cost, however, that they become misleading to the lessee.

Another common problem in marketing is semantics. Lessors frequently quote street rates as implicit rates. Street rates generally do not consider the impact of expected residual values and nonrefundable fees, whereas an implicit rate, as defined by Financial Accounting Standards Board Statement No. 13 (FASB 13), does require their inclusion.

Integrated Approaches

Various analytical methods also can be combined in order to maximize or optimize returns. Debt optimized IRR, MISF and cash flow, ERR with optimized cash flow and accounting earnings, and NPV with optimized cash flow and accounting earnings, are examples of integrated methods.

Integrated approaches attempt to optimize profitability by taking a holistic approach. Yield should be maximized simultaneously with the accounting return, cash flow and risk. Integrated approaches deal with the trade-offs that usually occur between these variables, since all cannot be maximized at the same time. It should be apparent there is no quintessential method of evaluating a lease's profitability. However, there are certain integrated approaches that give, perhaps, a better overall answer than any particular method used in isolation.

Analytical methods of whatever type must deal with two distinct aspects of profitability analysis: quality and quantity. Quality of yield (NPV, etc.) implies that:

1. Cash flows subject to uncertainty have been risk adjusted. For example, lease cash flows such as tax benefits, residual values and contingent rentals are not normally contractually agreed to, as are the lease payments, and, therefore, might be subject to risk

2. Other risks such as general lessee credit risk (allowance for doubtful accounts) have been identified and quantified. The tax consequences of default under a leveraged lease, whereby any nonrecourse debt in excess of the lessor's tax basis at the time of lessee default and foreclosure would be taxed as ordinary income to the lessor, are an example of other risk

3. The appropriate decision method has been used in light of the reinvestment opportunities available to the lessor. Figure 1 describes the appropriate decision methodologies given various reinvestment alternatives

4. The required return has been reached or exceeded.

Beyond the quality of earnings, the quantity of earnings implies that sufficient amounts of cash flow and accounting reported earnings have been generated.

PRELIMINARY CASE ASSUMPTIONS

Before proceeding to a more in-depth discussion of the various analytical methods described above, certain preliminary assumptions for a case study are presented, followed by selected definitions of analytical terminology unique to leasing.

Case Study

The following case study is referred to throughout the remainder of this chapter as the various analytical methods are reviewed. The case is based on a lease with 16 quarterly lease payments. Normally, leases are written on a monthly basis, but, since this payment pattern would result in excessive data to analyze and present, quarterly payments are used. The case assumptions are followed by a summary of the lease cash flows (Table 1) and explanations of the various computations used in arriving at the cash flows.

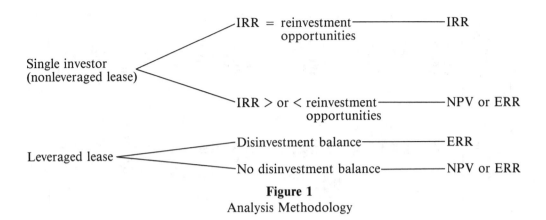

Figure 1
Analysis Methodology

ASSUMPTIONS

The following assumptions are used in this case study:

Equipment cost: $100,000, paid November 15, which is also the lease inception date

Tax depreciation: 5-year Modified Accelerated Cost Recovery System (MACRS) classlife

Payments: 16 quarterly payments of $6,600 due March 15, June 15, September 15 and December 15 of each year. Payments are in advance with the first due at the November 15 lease inception

Interim rent: $2,000, due December 15 of the first tax year

Refundable security deposit: $4,000

Corporate tax rate: 34% (state income taxes ignored). Also see Table 2

Tax status: alternative minimum tax (AMT) problems are ignored. This tax lease is an incremental lease for estimated tax purposes, and the lessor is a cash basis taxpayer

Residual value: $20,000, at the end of the 49th month in the lease (December 15)
The residual sale is viewed as an incremental event for estimated tax purposes

Initial direct costs: $2,500, considered entirely tax deductible in the first tax year

Quarterly G & A costs: $125, except December 15 of the first year when $40 of partial G & A cost is incurred.

Lease Analytical Terminology

The concepts and terms of lease analysis are based upon general financial theory. However, due to the uniqueness of leasing, there are some differences in terminology. The terms used in lease analysis will be explained in this section.

GROSS VERSUS NET

Whether computing yields, NPVs or paybacks, etc., the lease analyst can use gross data or more refined net data. Gross yield analysis takes into consideration pretax lease payments and, possibly, the pretax anticipated residual value. Typically, gross analysis would ignore any or all of the following:

Table 1
Cash Flow Analysis

Payment Period	Date	1 Rentals/ Residual	2 Initial Direct Costs/G & A	3 MACRS	4 Taxable Income	5 Tax (Expense) Benefit[1]	6 Net After-tax Cash Flow (1-2±5)
0	11-15	$ 6,600	($2,500)	($ 20,000)			($91,900)[2]
Tax payment	12-15	2,000	(40)	0		$ 4,266[3]	6,226
Total		$ 8,600	($2,540)	($ 20,000)	($13,940)		
1	3-15	$ 6,600	$ 125	($ 32,000)		474[3]	6,949
Tax payment	4-15	0	0			467	467
2	6-15	6,600	(125)			467	6,942
3	9-15	6,600	(125)			467	6,942
4	12-15	6,600	(125)			467	6,942
Total		$ 26,400	($ 500)	($ 32,000)	(6,100)		
5	3-15	$ 6,600	$ 125	($ 19,200)		206	6,681
Tax payment	4-15	0	0			(513)	(513)
6	6-15	6,600	(125)			(513)	5,962
7	9-15	6,600	(125)			(513)	5,962
8	12-15	6,600	(125)			(513)	5,962
Total		$ 26,400	($ 500)	($ 19,200)	6,700		
9	3-15	$ 6,600	$ 125	($ 11,520)		(226)	6,249
Tax payment	4-15	0	0			(1,100)	(1,100)
10	6-15	6,600	(125)			(1,100)	5,375
11	9-15	6,600	(125)			(1,100)	5,375
12	12-15	6,600	(125)			(1,100)	5,375
Total		$ 26,400	($ 500)	($ 11,520)	14,380		
13	3-15	$ 6,600	$ 125	($ 11,520)		(489)	5,986
Tax payment	4-15	0	0			(595)	(595)
14	6-15	6,600	(125)			(595)	5,880
15	9-15	6,600	(125)			(595)	5,880
16	12-15	20,000	(125)	(5,760)		(595)	10,922[4]
Total		$ 39,800	($ 500)	($ 17,280)	22,020	(4,953)	
Tax payment	3-15	0	0	0	0	(749)	(749)
Total		$ 0	$ 0	$ 0		(749)	
Lease total		$127,600	($4,540)	($100,000)	$23,060	($7,840)	$15,220

[1] From Table 2

[2] Net inception cash flow

Equipment cost	($ 100,000)
Advance rental	6,600
Initial direct costs	(2,500)
Deposit	4,000
	($ 91,900)

[3]

Taxable loss	$ 13,940
Tax rate	× .34
Tax benefit	$ 4,740

Tax remittance dates and amounts (inception year)

12-15	.9 × $4,740	=	$4,266
3-15	.1 × $4,740	=	$ 474

[4] Lease termination cash flow

Residual	$ 20,000
G & A	(125)
Tax expense	(4,953)
Deposit refund	(4,000)
Total	$ 10,922

Table 2

Quarterly Tax Payments

Remittance Date	Percentage	Year 2	Year 3	Year 4	Year 5[5]
4-15	.225	$ 467	($ 513)	($ 1,100)	($ 595)
6-15	.225	467	(513)	(1,100)	(595)
8-15	.225	467	(513)	(1,100)	(595)
12-15	.225	467	(513)	(1,100)	(4,953)
3-15	.100	206	(226)	(489)	(749)
Total benefit (liability)		$ 2,074	($ 2,278)	($ 4,889)	($ 7,487)

1. Initial direct costs such as commissions, credit checking costs, etc.
2. G & A and other overhead costs
3. Interest expense on debt used to fund the lease
4. Tax benefits
5. Origination fees
6. Interim rent
7. Allowance for doubtful accounts.

Net analysis, on the other hand, would include most or all of the above expenses that impact cash flow. Frequently, net analysis does not include any G & A or interest expense; however, capital budgeting would require their inclusion (see Chapter Ten). Gross analysis is used more in competitive analysis with other lease companies where the omitted items are seldom known anyway. Net analysis, in which all related cash flows are incorporated, is used more by the lessor to perform the cost accounting analysis necessary in ascertaining the actual level of profitability of a lease.

---

[5] Fifth year taxable income

	Budgeted	Incremental	Total
Three payments	$ 19,800	$ 0	$ 19,800
Residual	0	0	20,000
MACRS	(11,520)	0	(5,760)
Remaining basis	0	(5,760)	(11,520)
G & A	(500)	0	(500)
Taxable income	$ 7,780	$ 14,240	$ 22,020
Tax rate	× .34	× .34	× .34
Tax expense	$ 2,645	$ 4,842	$ 7,487

Fifth year tax remittance dates and amounts

4-15	.225 × $2,645	$ 595
6-15	.225 × 2,645	595
9-15	.225 × 2,645	595
12-15	(.225 × $2,645) + (.9 × $4,842)	4,953
3-15	(.100 × $2,645) + (.1 × $4,842)	749

INITIAL DIRECT COSTS

Initial direct costs[6] are defined by the FASB as follows:

> . . . Only those costs incurred by the lessor that are (a) costs to originate a lease incurred in transactions with independent third parties that (i) result directly from and are essential to acquire that lease and (ii) would not have been incurred had that leasing transaction not occurred and (b) certain costs directly related to specified activities performed by the lessor for that lease. Those activities are: evaluating the prospective lessee's financial condition; evaluating and recording guarantees, collateral and other security arrangements; negotiating lease terms; preparing and processing lease documents; and closing the transaction. The costs directly related to those activities shall include only that portion of the employees' total compensation and payroll-related fringe benefits directly related to time spent performing those activities for that lease and other costs related to those activities that would not have been incurred but for that lease. Initial direct costs shall not include costs related to activities performed by the lessor for advertising, soliciting potential lessees, servicing existing leases and other ancillary activities related to establishing and monitoring credit policies, supervision and administration. Initial direct costs shall not include administrative costs, rent, depreciation, and other occupancy and equipment costs and employees' compensation and fringe benefits related to activities described in the previous sentence, unsuccessful origination efforts and idle time [FASB 91, paragraph 24].[7]

PRETAX VERSUS AFTER-TAX ANALYSIS

In after-tax analysis, all tax benefits and expenses are considered, such as MACRS depreciation, gross profit tax deferral (when appropriate), taxes on residual disposition, AMT problems, etc. Pretax analysis deals with tax benefits by either (1) ignoring their existence, (2) converting tax benefits, etc., to their pretax equivalent by simply dividing a lease's after-tax IRR by one minus the income tax rate or (3) converting the tax benefits, etc., to their pretax equivalent through a more complex gross-up method that takes tax timing into consideration. The second method assumes the tax benefits occur simultaneously with other cash flows, which, of course, is not the case. The issue of tax timing is examined later in the chapter.

ROI, ROA AND ROE

Return on investment (ROI), return on assets (ROA) and return on equity (ROE) are commonly used measurements of return. Unfortunately, ROI is ambiguous since it is not known if the implied investment is the total asset investment or the equity investment. ROE differs from

---

[6] Initial direct costs shall be offset by nonrefundable fees that are yield adjustments as prescribed in FASB Statement No. 91 (FASB 91), 'Accounting for Nonrefundable Fees and Costs associated with Originating or Acquiring Loans and Initial Direct Costs of Leases.'

[7] The reprinted material quoted from FASB publications does not include the appendices to those documents. These appendices are an integral part of the quoted document.

ROA in that ROE refers to a return on investment (equity in this case) after debt has first received its return. ROAs do not consider the amount or the cost of financial leverage, whereas ROEs consider both. For example, using the income statement and balance sheet information in Figure 2, the ROA and ROE would be computed as follows:

$$\text{ROA} = \frac{\text{EBI}}{\text{Assets}} = \frac{\$1,500}{\$20,000} = 7.5\%$$

$$\text{ROE} = \frac{\text{Net income}}{\text{Equity}} = \frac{\$1,100}{\$10,000} = 11.0\%$$

$$\text{ROI} = 7.5\% \text{ or } 11.0\%, \text{ whichever is implied.}$$

LEVERAGED VERSUS SINGLE INVESTOR

From an industry viewpoint, leveraged leases are those that have been funded at their inception, or subsequently, with any amount of nonrecourse debt to the lessor. By contrast, single investor leases have been funded with recourse debt. Upon default, the recourse lessor would be obliged to pay the creditor. The term single investor is a misnomer, since there could be multiple investors in a recourse debt lease; generally, however, there is only one. The leveraged lease, on the other hand, frequently has multiple investors. The term single investor lease generally means nothing more than a nonleveraged lease. The definition of leveraged leases is more restrictive from an accounting viewpoint (see Chapter Sixteen).

YIELD ANALYSIS

In order to operate a leasing company successfully, the lessor must be able to structure a lease with a yield sufficient to cover not only all operating expenses and initial direct costs, but interest expense and profit as well. Therefore, it is essential to an understanding of leasing to be able to calculate the yield of a lease. Yields may be calculated on several different levels, or in accordance with certain characteristics. These levels and/or characteristics include the four

Income Statement

After-tax income before interest (EBI)	$1,500
After-tax interest expense	(400)
Net income	$1,100

Balance Sheet

Assets		$20,000
Debt costing 4% (after-tax)	$10,000	
Equity	10,000	
Total debt and equity		$20,000

Figure 2
ROA/ROE Calculation Assumptions

previously discussed characteristics: gross or net, pretax or after-tax, ROA or ROE or IRR or ERR level analysis. To begin with, a gross, pretax yield is illustrated. After that, IRR yields are computed on a net, after-tax basis at the ROA level and then on a net after-tax basis at the ROE level (both constant debt-to-equity and match funded). Once the yields have been explained, and also why and how ERR differs from IRR, the conversion of after-tax yields to their pretax equivalents is presented.

Gross, Pretax Yield (IRR)

Gross, pretax yields are those yields that analyze the most basic pretax cash flows of a lease (lease payments, advance payments, initial direct costs and residual expectations). As mentioned earlier, these yields are often referred to in the industry as street rates, running rates, stream rates, lessee effective rates, etc. Variations of the gross, pretax yield of a lease may be derived by including additional or fewer cash flow components in the analysis. Three variations of pretax yields are examined in this subsection. These include a street rate, a street rate with advance payments and an all-inclusive gross, pretax yield. The following three examples, based on the assumptions of the case study, present the computation and relationships of these gross, pretax yields.

STREET RATE

The street rate is the most commonly and frequently used yield when a quick and simplified analysis is required, or when quoting rates to lessees. It is characterized by the paucity of cash flows considered. Advance payments, deposits and purchase options are not included, and depreciation and tax timing also are ignored.

As in any form of financial analysis, identification of the cash flows is the initial step in calculating a yield. When calculating a street rate, the periodic lease payments and the initial investment are the only cash flows considered in the analysis. From the assumptions of the case study, there are 16 quarterly payments of $6,600 and the equipment cost is $100,000.

Inception Cash Flows	Subsequent Cash Flows	Termination Cash Flows
($100,000) Equipment cost	16 payments at $6,600	Nothing

Based on these cash flows compute the street rate, using the following keystrokes for the HP-12C.

		g	END
100,000	CHS		PV
6,600			PMT
16			n
			i .6484

The quarterly yield is .6484%, and the annual yield is 2.5934%.

MODIFIED STREET RATE

A street rate represents the lowest deriveable rate and is, therefore, the rate most often quoted by lessors to lessees. Because a residual assumption is not included in the analysis, sometimes the yield even may be negative. Incorporating the impact of any advance payments into the analysis results in a more true and, understandably, higher yield.

Inception Cash Flows		Subsequent Cash Flows	Termination Cash Flows
($100,000)	Equipment cost	15 payments at $6,600	Nothing
6,600	Advance payment		
($ 93,400)	Net outflow		

The modified street rate is computed on the HP-12C as follows:

	g	END
93,400	CHS	PV
6,600		PMT
15		n
	i	.7368

The quarterly yield for the modified street rate is .7368%, or 2.9474% on an annual basis. By including the advance payment in the analysis, the yield increased 35.40 basis points. This modified street rate is considered by some lessors to be the most accurate street rate.

ALL-INCLUSIVE RATE

Although most lessors rarely quote an all-inclusive gross, pretax yield, it is well worth noting because, of the three types of gross, pretax yields, it most accurately portrays the true yield of the lessor. All cash flows at the lease inception are quantified in this yield and the pretax residual assumption is also included. Lease inception cash flows may consist of (in addition to any advance payments) a refundable security deposit, closing fees and any initial direct costs. The identification of the cash flows from the example reveals the following:

Inception Cash Flows		Subsequent Cash Flows	Termination Cash Flows	
($100,000)	Equipment cost	15 payments at $6,600	($ 4,000)	Deposit refund
6,600	Advance payment		20,000	Purchase option
4,000	Refundable security deposit		$16,000	Net inflow
(2,500)	Initial direct costs			
($ 91,900)	Net outflow			

The following HP-12C keystrokes are used to compute the all-inclusive gross, pretax yield:

91,900	CHS	g	CF_o
6,600		g	CF_j
15		g	N_j
16,000		g	CF_j
		f	IRR 2.5777

The quarterly yield for the all-inclusive gross, pretax yield is 2.5777% or 10.3108% on an annual basis. Note the significant difference in the three methods of computing the gross, pretax yields.

Street rate	2.5934%
Street rate including advance payments	2.9474%
All-inclusive gross, pretax yield	10.3108%

Net, After-tax ROA (IRR)

Refer to Table 1, column 6, and observe the after-tax cash flow generated by the base case lease. How valuable or profitable is this cash flow? IRR attempts to answer the question by solving for the discount rate that will equate the $91,900 net investment with the present value of the cash inflows and outflows generated by the investment. The IRR is the yield of the lease or the loan interest rate equivalent. The cash flows in column 6 include G & A as well as initial direct costs expense and are, therefore, net. Furthermore, tax timing has been included since all the tax expenses and benefits have been assigned to their appropriate quarterly estimated tax payment dates. There are 39 different cash flows in this lease, so use of the HP-18C is necessary (rather than an HP-12C), since the HP-12C has capacity for only 20 uneven cash flows. The keystrokes for solving for the IRR of these cash flows (once the calculator is in the FIN, CFLO mode) are shown in Table 3.

Thus, the lease is shown to be earning .637794 per month or 7.653531% per year, after-tax. Those not having access to an HP-18C also can prove the IRR by discounting the cash flows at .637794 (use of the HP-12C requires loading the cash flow in two groups). The HP-12C solution is presented in Table 4. The net present value will indeed be zero, because when the present value of the first group, –37,813.40, is added to that of the second group, + 37,813.40, the two net to zero, thereby proving that the .637794 per month IRR is accurate.

Net, After-tax, ROE (IRR)

The conversion of an ROA to an ROE requires additional information such as (1) the amount and cost of the debt used to finance the lease investment and (2) whether the debt will be paid back in a manner that maintains a constant debt-to-equity ratio in the lease (constant debt percentage funding), or in a manner such that loan payments are matched to lease payments (match funding).

CONSTANT DEBT PERCENTAGE FUNDING

Assume a lessor's debt cost is 8%, is fixed throughout the lease term and that 85% of the asset's net cash cost of $91,900 is funded with debt using constant debt percentage funding. A simple formula for constant debt percentage funding can be used to convert an ROA to an ROE, but it is only an approximation to a more accurate method described later.

$$ROD_w + ROE_w = ROA_t, \text{ where}$$

ROD_w = weighted, average after-tax return on debt
ROE_w = weighted, average after-tax return on equity
ROA_t = total after-tax return on assets

Table 3
Net, After-tax ROA (IRR) Solution
(HP-18C)

Cash Flow Number		Keystrokes		
0	91,900	+ / –	INPUT	
1	6,226		INPUT	INPUT
2	0		INPUT	
	2		INPUT	
3	6,949		INPUT	INPUT
4	467		INPUT	INPUT
5	0		INPUT	INPUT
6	6,942		INPUT	INPUT
7	0		INPUT	
	2		INPUT	
8	6,942		INPUT	INPUT
9	0		INPUT	
	2		INPUT	
10	6,942		INPUT	INPUT
11	0		INPUT	
	2		INPUT	
12	6,681		INPUT	INPUT
13	513	+ / –	INPUT	INPUT
14	0		INPUT	INPUT
15	5,962		INPUT	INPUT
16	0		INPUT	
	2		INPUT	
17	5,962		INPUT	INPUT
18	0		INPUT	
	2		INPUT	
19	5,962		INPUT	INPUT
20	0		INPUT	
	2		INPUT	
21	6,249		INPUT	INPUT
22	1,100	+ / –	INPUT	INPUT
23	0		INPUT	INPUT
24	5,375		INPUT	INPUT
25	0		INPUT	
	2		INPUT	
26	5,375		INPUT	INPUT
27	0		INPUT	
	2		INPUT	
28	5,375		INPUT	INPUT
29	0		INPUT	
	2		INPUT	
30	5,986		INPUT	INPUT
31	595	+ / –	INPUT	INPUT
32	0		INPUT	INPUT
33	5,880		INPUT	INPUT
34	0		INPUT	
	2		INPUT	
35	5,880		INPUT	INPUT
36	0		INPUT	
	2		INPUT	
37	10,922		INPUT	INPUT
38	0		INPUT	
	2		INPUT	
39	749	+ / –	INPUT	INPUT
	CALC			
	TOTAL		15,220	(Net undiscounted cash flow total)
	IRR		.637794	
	× 12		7.653531	

Table 4
Net, After-tax ROA (IRR) Solution
(HP-12C)

Cash Flow Number		Keystrokes		
		First Group		
	.637794			i
0	91,900	CHS	g	CF_o
1	6,226		g	CF_j
2	0		g	CF_j
	2		g	N_j
3	6,949		g	CF_j
4	467		g	CF_j
5	0		g	CF_j
6	6,942		g	CF_j
7	0		g	CF_j
	2		g	N_j
8	6,942		g	CF_j
9	0		g	CF_j
	2		g	N_j
10	6,942		g	CF_j
11	0		g	CF_j
	2		g	N_j
12	6,681		g	CF_j
13	513	CHS	g	CF_j
14	0		g	CF_j
15	5,962		g	CF_j
16	0		g	CF_j
	2		g	N_j
17	5,962		g	CF_j
18	0		g	CF_j
	2		g	N_j
19	5,962		g	CF_j
			f	NPV	−37,813.40
		Second Group		
			f	REG
	.637794			i
1	0		g	CF_j
	27		g	N_j
2	6,249		g	CF_j
3	1,100	CHS	g	CF_j
4	0		g	CF_j
5	5,375		g	CF_j
6	0		g	CF_j
	2		g	N_j
7	5,375		g	CF_j
8	0		g	CF_j
	2		g	N_j
9	5,375		g	CF_j
10	0		g	CF_j
	2		g	N_j
11	5,986		g	CFj
12	595	CHS	g	CF_j
13	0		g	CF_j
14	5,880		g	CF_j
15	0		g	CF_j
	2		g	N_j
16	5,880		g	CF_j
17	0		g	CF_j
	2		g	N_j
18	10,922		g	CF_j
19	0		g	CF_j
	2		g	N_j
20	749	CHS	g	CF_j
			f	NPV	37,813.40

More specifically, RODw equals the percentage debt in the capital structure times the debt cost percentage, times one minus the tax rate, and ROEw equals the percentage equity in the capital structure times the ROE. Thus, the transformed equation reads:

$$[\% \text{ debt} \times \text{debt cost } \% \times (1\text{-}t)] + (\% \text{ equity} \times \text{ROE}) = \text{ROA}_t$$

Filling in the equation, the ROE can be solved for:

$$[.85 \times .08 \times (1-.34)] + (.15 \times \text{ROE}) = 7.65353[8]$$

4.488	+ .15 (ROE)	=	7.65353
	.15 (ROE)	=	7.65353 – 4.488
	ROE	=	3.16553 ÷ .15
	ROE	=	21.1035%

The shortcomings of this approximation approach relate to the implicit assumptions that (1) the company constantly maintains debt at 85% of its total assets (most companies would do so only at month's end or quarter's end) and (2) the tax benefits on the interest expense are received concurrently with the payment of interest when, in fact, such benefits are spread over the lessor's five estimated tax payment dates.

An example of an ROE computation that deals with the two shortcomings just mentioned first requires an amortization of the lease using its after-tax interest rate. The amortization schedule will provide the net investment in the lease at the end of any monthly or, in this case, quarterly period (column 4, Table 5). From this schedule the loan balance can be derived since it is always assumed to be 85% of the net investment (column 5, Table 5). Given the loan balances, the assumed loan amortization is calculated, which provides sufficient information to solve for the after-tax, after-loan payment cash flow in the lease. This process is depicted in Table 5. First, however, the amortization must be set up on the HP-12C:

91,900		PV
.637794		i
6,226	CHS	PMT

When a company maintains a constant debt percentage in a lease it does not do so every second of every day. Rather, it does so generally when the regular lease payments are received. In this case, rentals are received quarterly and the loan balances on those payment dates are indicated by footnote 10 in Table 5. The loan amortization schedule can be derived by finding the difference between loan balances, as in Table 6. Given the loan payments required to maintain a relatively constant debt percentage (column 8, Table 6), the after-tax, after-debt payment cash flow in the lease is solved for, as shown in Table 7. Once the after-tax, after-debt payment cash flows are known, the net after-tax ROE (IRR) for a lease with constant debt percentage funding is determined using the HP-18C (Table 8).

Note that the more accurate ROE is 37.01 basis points higher than the approximate one (21.4736 – 21.1035). Had the lease payments been paid monthly, the actual ROE would have been lower rather than higher than the approximate one. Obviously, one would not spend this much effort to analyze every lease in a portfolio since a computer makes the task much easier. The purpose here is to describe the logic underlying what computers do in lease analysis.

---

[8] From Table 3.

Table 5
Amortization of the Lease

Month	1 Payment [9] (CHS PMT)	2 Interest (1 f AMORT)	3 Principal (X ≥ Y)	4 Balance (RCL PV)	5 Loan Balance (4 × .85)
0	0	0	0	91,900	78,115
1	6,226	586.13	5,639.87	86,260	73,321
		586.13			
2	0	550.16	(550.16)	86,810	73,789
3	0	553.67	(553.67)	87,364	74,259
4	6,949	557.20	6,391.80	80,972	68,826 [10]
5	467	516.44	(49.44)	81,022	68,868
6	0	516.75	(516.75)	81,538	69,308
7	6,942	520.05	6,421.95	75,116	63,849 [10]
8	0	479.09	(479.09)	75,595	64,256
9	0	482.14	(482.14)	76,078	64,666
10	6,942	485.22	6,456.78	69,621	59,178 [10]
11	0	444.04	(444.04)	70,065	59,555
12	0	446.87	(446.87)	70,512	59,935
13	6,942	449.72	6,492.28	64,019	54,417 [10]
		6,001.35			
14	0	408.31	(408.31)	64,428	54,764
15	0	410.92	(410.92)	64,839	55,113
16	6,681	413.54	6,267.46	58,571	49,786 [10]
17	(513)	373.56	(886.56)	59,458	50,539
18	0	379.22	(379.22)	59,837	50,861
19	5,962	381.64	5,580.36	54,257	46,118 [10]
20	0	346.05	(346.05)	54,603	46,412
21	0	348.25	(348.25)	54,951	46,708
22	5,962	350.47	5,611.53	49,339	41,939 [10]
23	0	314.68	(314.68)	49,654	42,206
24	0	316.69	(316.69)	49,971	42,475
25	5,962	318.71	5,643.29	44,328	37,678 [10]
	0	4,362.04			
26	0	282.72	(282.72)	44,610	37,919
27	0	284.52	(284.52)	44,895	38,161
28	6,249	286.34	5,962.66	38,932	33,092 [10]
29	(1,100)	248.31	(1,348.31)	40,280	34,238
30	0	256.91	(256.91)	40,537	34,457
31	5,375	258.54	5,116.46	35,420	30,108 [10]
32	0	225.91	(225.91)	35,647	30,300
33	0	227.35	(227.35)	35,874	30,493
34	5,375	228.80	5,146.20	30,728	26,119 [10]
35	0	195.98	(195.98)	30,924	26,285
36	0	197.23	(197.23)	31,121	26,453
37	5,375	198.49	5,176.51	25,945	22,053 [10]
		2,891.10			
38	0	165.47	(165.47)	26,110	22,194
39	0	166.53	(166.53)	26,277	22,335
40	5,986	167.59	5,818.41	20,458	17,389 [10]
41	(595)	130.48	(725.48)	21,184	18,006
42	0	135.11	(135.11)	21,319	18,121
43	5,880	135.97	5,744.03	15,575	13,239 [10]
44	0	99.33	(99.33)	15,674	13,323
45	0	99.97	(99.97)	15,774	13,408
46	5,880	100.61	5,779.39	9,995	8,495 [10]
47	0	63.75	(63.75)	10,058	8,550
48	0	64.15	(64.15)	10,123	8,604
49	10,922	64.56	10,857.44	(735)	(624) [10]
		1,393.52			
50	0	(4.69)	4.69	(740)	(629)
51	0	(4.72)	4.72	(744)	(632)
52	(749)	(4.75)	(744.25)	0	0 [10]
		(14.16)			
Total	107,120	15,220.00	91,900.00	0	0

[9] From column 6, Table 1.
[10] Loan balance on the payment date.

Table 6
Derivation of Loan Payment

1 Month Number	2 Beginning Loan Balance[11]	3 Interest Rate Per Month	4 Number of Elapsed Months	5 Interest (2×3×4)	6 Ending Loan Balance[11]	7 Principal Paid (2 − 6)	8 Total Loan Payment (5 + 7)
0	$ 78,115	.006667	0	$ 0	$ 78,115	$ 0	$ 0
4	78,115	.006667	4	2,083	68,826	9,289	11,372
7	68,826	.006667	3	1,377	63,849	4,977	6,354
10	63,849	.006667	3	1,277	59,178	4,671	5,948
13	59,178	.006667	3	1,184	54,417	4,761	5,945
16	54,417	.006667	3	1,088	49,786	4,631	5,719
19	49,786	.006667	3	996	46,118	3,668	4,664
22	46,118	.006667	3	922	41,939	4,179	5,101
25	41,939	.006667	3	839	37,678	4,261	5,100
28	37,678	.006667	3	754	33,092	4,586	5,340
31	33,092	.006667	3	662	30,108	2,984	3,646
34	30,108	.006667	3	602	26,119	3,989	4,591
37	26,119	.006667	3	522	22,053	4,066	4,588
40	22,053	.006667	3	441	17,389	4,664	5,105
43	17,389	.006667	3	348	13,239	4,150	4,498
46	13,239	.006667	3	265	8,495	4,744	5,009
49	8,495	.006667	3	170	(624)	9,119	9,289
52	(624)	.006667	3	(12)	0	(624)	(636)
Total				$ 13,518		$ 78,115	$ 91,633

[11] The beginning and ending loan balances are taken from Table 5, and represent those balances with footnote 10.

Table 7
Derivation of Net Equity Cash Flow

1 Payment Period	2 Date	3 After-tax Cash Flow[12]	4 Loan Payment[13]	5 Interest Tax Benefits[14]	6 Net Equity Cash Flow
0	11-15	($ 91,900)	$ 78,115	$ 0	($ 13,785)
Tax payment	12-15	6,226	0	0	6,226
1	3-15	6,949	(11,372)	(4,423)	
Tax payment	4-15	467	0	453	920
2	6-15	6,942	(6,354)	453	1,041
3	9-15	6,942	(5,948)	453	1,447
4	12-15	6,942	(5,945)	453	1,450
5	3-15	6,681	(5,719)	201	1,163
Tax payment	4-15	(513)	0	294	(219)
6	6-15	5,962	(4,664)	294	1,592
7	9-15	5,962	(5,101)	294	1,155
8	12-15	5,962	(5,100)	294	1,156
9	3-15	6,249	(5,340)	131	1,040
Tax payment	4-15	(1,100)	0	194	(906)
10	6-15	5,375	(3,646)	194	1,923
11	9-15	5,375	(4,591)	194	978
12	12-15	5,375	(4,588)	194	981
13	3-15	5,986	(5,105)	88	969
Tax payment	4-15	(595)	0	94	(501)
14	6-15	5,880	(4,498)	94	1,476
15	9-15	5,880	(5,009)	94	965
16	12-15	10,922	(9,289)	94	1,727
Tax payment	3-15	(749)	636	40	(73)
Total		$ 15,220	($ 13,518)	$ 4,600	$ 6,302

[12] From Table 1.

[13] From Table 6.

[14] The computation to derive the interest tax benefit for the first year is as follows. The same process occurs each year thereafter.

Quarter	Interest Expense
1	$ 2,083
2	1,377
3	1,277
4	1,184
Total	$ 5,921 × .34 = $2,013 tax benefit

Quarterly estimated tax receipts from the interest tax benefit

Quarter	
1	.225 × $2,013 = $453
2	.225 × 2,013 = 453
3	.225 × 2,013 = 453
4	.225 × 2,013 = 453
5	.100 × 2,013 = 201

Table 8
Net, After-tax ROE (IRR)
(constant debt percentage)

Cash Flow Number	Keystrokes			
0	13,785	+/−	INPUT	
1	6,226		INPUT	INPUT
2	0		INPUT	
	2		INPUT	
3	4,423	+/−	INPUT	INPUT
4	920		INPUT	INPUT
5	0		INPUT	INPUT
6	1,041		INPUT	INPUT
7	0		INPUT	
	2		INPUT	
8	1,447		INPUT	INPUT
9	0		INPUT	
	2		INPUT	
10	1,450		INPUT	INPUT
11	0		INPUT	
	2		INPUT	
12	1,163		INPUT	INPUT
13	219	+/−	INPUT	INPUT
14	0		INPUT	INPUT
15	1,592		INPUT	INPUT
16	0		INPUT	
	2		INPUT	
17	1,155		INPUT	INPUT
18	0		INPUT	
	2		INPUT	
19	1,156		INPUT	INPUT
20	0		INPUT	
	2		INPUT	
21	1,040		INPUT	INPUT
22	906	+/−	INPUT	INPUT
23	0		INPUT	INPUT
24	1,923		INPUT	INPUT
25	0		INPUT	
	2		INPUT	
26	978		INPUT	INPUT
27	0		INPUT	
	2		INPUT	
28	981		INPUT	INPUT
29	0		INPUT	
	2		INPUT	
30	969		INPUT	INPUT
31	501	+/−	INPUT	INPUT
32	0		INPUT	INPUT
33	1,476		INPUT	INPUT
34	0		INPUT	
	2		INPUT	
35	965		INPUT	INPUT
36	0		INPUT	
	2		INPUT	
37	1,727		INPUT	INPUT
38	0		INPUT	
	2		INPUT	
39	73	+/−	INPUT	INPUT
	CALC			
	TOTAL		6,302	
	IRR		1.789464	
	× 12		21.473566	

MATCH FUNDING

The previous ROE assumed debt remained at a constant percentage of the quarterly net investment in the lease. When a lessor match funds, the debt is repaid according to the amortization schedule required by the creditor, which is usually fixed equal payments over the lease term (with perhaps a balloon payment at lease termination matching a percent of the expected residual). The debt amortization seldom maintains a constant debt relationship to net assets.

In order to understand why match funding alters the debt relationship, another example is used. Using the same base case, the match funded loan payments are deducted from the lease cash flow and the interest tax benefits (from Table 9) are added back in the same manner as was done for ROE constant debt percentage funding. This process is illustrated in Table 10. The following assumptions are used to illustrate this point:

APR: 8% (or 2% quarterly)

Payments: 15 payments in arrears at $5,593 (loan payments coincide with lease payments)

Balloon payment: $9,300, which is about 85% of the expected residual value of $10,922

Total loan: $78,115 (85% of the $91,900 net investment).

Given the column 6, after-tax, after-match funded loan payment cash flows of Table 10, the lease's net, after-tax ROE (IRR, match funded) can be computed, as shown in Table 11. Notice the dramatic increase of 21.47% to 43.85% in the match funded ROE. Why this large difference? Both funding methods began with $78,115 of debt, both had similar balloon payments in the 49th month (constant debt percentage funding of $9,289, match funding of $9,300) and both loans had 8% interest rates. Why did one generate an additional 22.38% in yield? The answer is that match funding provides more financial leverage over the life of the lease than constant debt percentage funding does, even though the debt percentage of the net investment in the lease begins and ends the same as in constant debt percentage (CDP) funding. This greater financial leverage produces a much greater yield. Figure 3 and Table 12 describe the differing leverage amounts at the end of each quarter during the lease.

What creates the difference in financial leverage between the two methods? The primary cause has to do with the receipt of tax benefits under constant debt percentage funding. Tax benefits, when received, are assumed to pay off debt just like the regular rentals in the lease. This constant pay down of debt from all cash sources reduces debt more rapidly than match funding, since match funding payback is determined by the funding source, and is independent of any relationship to the net investment in the lease or to the receipt of leasing tax benefits. Notice in the constant debt percentage funding case that the receipt of a large tax benefit on December 15, one month after the lease's inception, caused the debt to be paid down rapidly, whereas the same $6,226 tax benefit under match funding was ignored.

Whether the 43.85% match funded IRR is meaningful is the subject of the section on NPV analysis in this chapter. Note that at the same time the ROE went from 21.47% to 43.85%, total net cash flow dropped from $6,302 to $5,267, respectively. Cash flow was sacrificed for yield, which creates an interesting dilemma for the analyst.

Table 9
Amortization of the Lease
(match funded)

Quarter	Payment	Interest	Principal	Balance
0	$ 0	$ 0	$ 0	$ 78,115
1st month	0	521	(521)	78,636
1	5,593	1,573	4,020	74,616
2	5,593	1,492	4,101	70,515
3	5,593	1,410	4,183	66,332
4	5,593	1,327	4,266	62,066
5	5,593	1,241	4,352	57,714
6	5,593	1,154	4,439	53,275
7	5,593	1,066	4,527	48,748
8	5,593	975	4,618	44,130
9	5,593	883	4,710	39,420
10	5,593	788	4,805	34,615
11	5,593	692	4,901	29,714
12	5,593	594	4,999	24,715
13	5,593	494	5,099	19,616
14	5,593	392	5,201	14,415
15	5,593	288	5,305	9,110
16	9,300	190	9,110	0
Total	$ 93,195	$ 15,080	$ 78,115	

Conversion to a Pretax IRR

It is difficult, if not impossible, to solve for the pretax yield in a lease directly without also valuing the tax benefits in a lease. Therefore, most software packages simply solve for a lease's after-tax yield and then convert it to a pretax equivalent through a gross-up procedure. If one attempts to solve directly for the pretax IRR of a lease, there will be an understatement of actual yield, due to the omission of the impact of MACRS depreciation. Using the HP-18C, the direct pretax IRR approximation would be as shown in Table 13.

The indirect computation of a pretax IRR is achieved by dividing the lease's after-tax yield by one minus the tax rate. This method is called the gross-up method and does provide a more accurate surrogate for the real pretax rate than the method immediately above. For example, using the data of the study case:

$$\text{After-tax ROA (IRR)} \quad \frac{7.653531}{(1-.34)} \quad = \quad 11.596\%$$

Table 10
Derivation of Net Equity Cash Flow

1	2	3	4	5	6
				Interest	Net
Payment		After-tax	Loan	Tax	Equity
Period	Date	Cash Flow[15]	Payment[16]	Benefits[17]	Cash Flow
0	11-15	($ 91,900)	$ 78,115	$ 0	($ 13,785)
Tax payment	12-15	6,226	0	0	6,226
1	3-15	6,949	(5,593)	0	1,356
Tax payment	4-15	467	0	484	951
2	6-15	6,942	(5,593)	484	1,833
3	9-15	6,942	(5,593)	484	1,833
4	12-15	6,942	(5,593)	484	1,833
5	3-15	6,681	(5,593)	214	1,302
Tax payment	4-15	(513)	0	339	(174)
6	6-15	5,962	(5,593)	339	708
7	9-15	5,962	(5,593)	339	708
8	12-15	5,962	(5,593)	339	708
9	3-15	6,249	(5,593)	152	808
Tax payment	4-15	(1,100)	0	226	(874)
10	6-15	5,375	(5,593)	226	8
11	9-15	5,375	(5,593)	226	8
12	12-15	5,375	(5,593)	226	8
13	3-15	5,986	(5,593)	101	494
Tax payment	4-15	(595)	0	104	(491)
14	6-15	5,880	(5,593)	104	391
15	9-15	5,880	(5,593)	104	391
16	12-15	10,922	(9,300)	104	1,726
Tax payment	3-15	(749)	0	48	(701)
Total		$ 15,220	($ 15,080)	$ 5,127	$ 5,267

---

[15] From Table 1.
[16] From Table 9.
[17] The computation to derive the interest tax benefit is the same as explained in footnote 14, of Table 7.

Table 11
Net, After-tax ROE (IRR)
(match funded)

Cash Flow Number	Keystrokes			
0	13,785	+/−	INPUT	
1	6,226		INPUT	INPUT
2	0		INPUT	
	2		INPUT	
3	1,356		INPUT	INPUT
4	951		INPUT	INPUT
5	0		INPUT	INPUT
6	1,833		INPUT	INPUT
7	0		INPUT	
	2		INPUT	
8	1,833		INPUT	INPUT
9	0		INPUT	
	2		INPUT	
10	1,833		INPUT	INPUT
11	0		INPUT	
	2		INPUT	
12	1,302		INPUT	INPUT
13	174	+/−	INPUT	INPUT
14	0		INPUT	INPUT
15	708		INPUT	INPUT
16	0		INPUT	
	2		INPUT	
17	708		INPUT	INPUT
18	0		INPUT	
	2		INPUT	
19	708		INPUT	INPUT
20	0		INPUT	
	2		INPUT	
21	808		INPUT	INPUT
22	874	+/−	INPUT	INPUT
23	0		INPUT	INPUT
24	8		INPUT	INPUT
25	0		INPUT	
	2		INPUT	
26	8		INPUT	INPUT
27	0		INPUT	
	2		INPUT	
28	8		INPUT	INPUT
29	0		INPUT	
	2		INPUT	
30	494		INPUT	INPUT
31	491	+/−	INPUT	INPUT
32	0		INPUT	INPUT
33	391		INPUT	INPUT
34	0		INPUT	
	2		INPUT	
35	391		INPUT	INPUT
36	0		INPUT	
	2		INPUT	
37	1,726		INPUT	INPUT
38	0		INPUT	
	2		INPUT	
39	701	+/−	INPUT	INPUT
	CALC			
	TOTAL		5,267	
	IRR		3.654049	
	× 12		43.848592	

Table 12
Leverage Derivation in Match Funding

Quarter	Match Funded Debt Balance		Net Investment		Leverage %
0	$ 78,115	÷	$91,900	=	85.00%
1	74,616	÷	80,972	=	92.15
2	70,515	÷	75,116	=	93.87
3	66,332	÷	69,621	=	95.28
4	62,066	÷	64,019	=	96.95
5	57,714	÷	58,571	=	98.54
6	53,275	÷	54,257	=	98.19
7	48,748	÷	49,339	=	98.80
8	44,130	÷	44,328	=	99.55
9	39,420	÷	38,932	=	101.25
10	34,615	÷	35,421	=	97.72
11	29,714	÷	30,728	=	96.70
12	24,715	÷	25,945	=	95.26
13	19,616	÷	20,458	=	95.88
14	14,415	÷	15,575	=	92.55
15	9,110	÷	9,995	=	91.15
16	0	÷	0	=	N/A

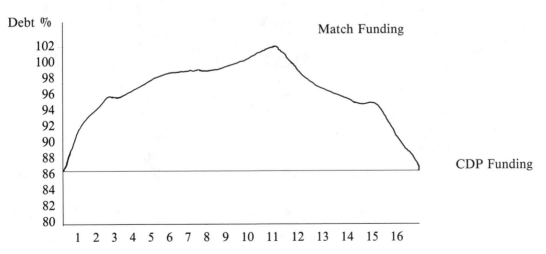

Figure 3
Debt as a Percentage of Investment

Table 13
Pretax IRR

Cash Flow Number		Keystrokes		
0	91,900	+ / −	INPUT	
1	2,000		INPUT	INPUT
2	0		INPUT	
	2		INPUT	
3	6,600		INPUT	INPUT
4	0		INPUT	
	2		INPUT	
5	6,600		INPUT	INPUT
6	0		INPUT	
	2		INPUT	
7	6,600		INPUT	INPUT
8	0		INPUT	
	2		INPUT	
9	6,600		INPUT	INPUT
10	0		INPUT	
	2		INPUT	
11	6,600		INPUT	INPUT
12	0		INPUT	
	2		INPUT	
13	6,600		INPUT	INPUT
14	0		INPUT	
	2		INPUT	
15	6,600		INPUT	INPUT
16	0		INPUT	
	2		INPUT	
17	6,600		INPUT	INPUT
18	0		INPUT	
	2		INPUT	
19	6,600		INPUT	INPUT
20	0		INPUT	
	2		INPUT	
21	6,600		INPUT	INPUT
22	0		INPUT	
	2		INPUT	
23	6,600		INPUT	INPUT
24	0		INPUT	
	2		INPUT	
25	6,600		INPUT	INPUT
26	0		INPUT	
	2		INPUT	
27	6,600		INPUT	INPUT
28	0		INPUT	
	2		INPUT	
29	6,600		INPUT	INPUT
30	0		INPUT	
	2		INPUT	
31	6,600		INPUT	INPUT
32	0		INPUT	
	2		INPUT	
33	16,000		INPUT	INPUT
	CALC			
	TOTAL		25,100	
	IRR		.902722	
	× 12		10.832667	

Although this method clearly reflects the value of MACRS depreciation omitted in the previous pretax computation (10.833%), it does not quite reflect the true yield, because dividing the after-tax yield by (1-t) implies that taxes are paid concurrently with all cash flows in the lease. This, of course, is not the case. Taxes are paid over each tax year's five estimated tax payment dates.

In order to properly integrate tax timing into a pretax conversion, a rather rigorous procedure must be followed. Surprisingly, only one software firm seems to follow this procedure, while all others appear to follow the indirect computation of a pretax IRR (gross-up method). Four steps are followed to convert the case study to its accurate pretax IRR.

STEP ONE

First, the after-tax cash flows must be amortized into their after-tax earnings and principal portions, using the after-tax IRR in the lease. This amortization is exactly the same as the one in columns 1, 2, 3 and 4 of Table 5.

STEP TWO

Next, convert each year's after-tax income to its pretax equivalent (divide by one minus the tax rate) and multiply it times the tax rate. This product equals the taxes that theoretically have been paid. Then determine the proper amounts and timing of these tax expenses relative to the estimated tax remittance dates, as shown in Table 14.

STEP THREE

The after-tax cash flows must be reinstated to their pretax equivalents by adding back the taxes assumed to have been paid (as computed in Table 14). This step is illustrated in Table 15.

STEP FOUR

Once the taxes have been reinstated to the after-tax cash flows, the IRR of the reinstated cash flows is computed. Computation of the IRR is shown in Table 16.

SUMMARY

The actual pretax ROA (IRR) is, therefore, 11.513% and can be compared to 11.596% (gross-up approach) and the 10.833% (direct computation approach). It may appear there is no material difference between these three yields. Although perhaps immaterial in this case, it must be realized other leases can show dramatic differences by as much as 200 basis points. For instance, larger discrepancies than in this example may occur when the lease term is longer than 49 months, lease payments are monthly, other tax benefits are involved, the lease is structured earlier in the tax year, the lease is budgeted and not incremental or when the tax rate is higher than 34%. The existence of all or any of these factors tends to exaggerate the impact of tax timing.

Table 14
After-tax to Pretax Conversion

1	2	3	4		
		Implied Tax			
	Implied	Expense			
Tax Year	Taxable Income	$(2 \times .34)$	Quarterly Allocations		
Inception year	$\dfrac{\$586.13}{(1 - .34)}$[17]	$=$ $ 302	$\times$ .900 $=$		$272
			$\times$ .100 $=$		30
1st year	$\dfrac{\$6,001.35}{(1 - .34)}$	$=$ 3,092	$\times$ .225 $=$		696
			$\times$ .100 $=$		308
2nd year	$\dfrac{\$4,362.04}{(1 - .34)}$	$=$ 2,247	$\times$ .225 $=$		506
			$\times$ .100 $=$		223
3rd year	$\dfrac{\$2,891.10}{(1 - .34)}$	$=$ 1,489	$\times$ .225 $=$		335
			$\times$ .100 $=$		149
4th year	$\dfrac{\$1,393.52}{(1 - .34)}$	$=$ 718	$\times$ .225 $=$		162
			$\times$ .100 $=$		70
5th year	$\dfrac{(\$14.16)}{(1 - .34)}$	$=$ $\dfrac{(7)}{\$ 7,841}$	(immediately due)		

---

[17] Yearly totals from column 2, Table 5.

Table 15
Reinstatement of After-tax Cash Flows

Payment Period	Date	After-tax Cash Flow[19]	Imputed Tax Expense[20]	Pretax Equivalent Cash Flow
0	11-15	($ 91,900)		($ 91,900)
Tax payment	12-15	6,226	$ 272	6,498
1	3-15	6,949	30	6,979
Tax payment	4-15	467	696	1,163
2	6-15	6,942	696	7,638
3	9-15	6,942	696	7,638
4	12-15	6,942	696	7,638
5	3-15	6,681	308	6,989
Tax payment	4-15	(513)	506	(7)
6	6-15	5,962	506	6,468
7	9-15	5,962	506	6,468
8	12-15	5,962	506	6,468
9	3-15	6,249	223	6,472
Tax payment	4-15	(1,100)	335	(765)
10	6-15	5,375	335	5,710
11	9-15	5,375	335	5,710
12	12-15	5,375	335	5,710
13	3-15	5,986	149	6,135
Tax payment	4-15	(595)	162	(433)
14	6-15	5,880	162	6,042
15	9-15	5,880	162	6,042
16	12-14	10,922	162	11,084
Tax payment	3-15	(749)	63	(686)
Total		$ 15,220	$ 7,841	$ 23,061

---

[19] From Table 1.
[20] From Table 14.

Table 16

Computation of the IRR

Cash Flow Number	Keystrokes			
0	91,900	+ / −	INPUT	
1	6,498		INPUT	INPUT
2	0		INPUT	
	2		INPUT	
3	6,979		INPUT	INPUT
4	1,163		INPUT	INPUT
5	0		INPUT	INPUT
6	7,638		INPUT	INPUT
7	0		INPUT	
	2		INPUT	
8	7,638		INPUT	INPUT
9	0		INPUT	
	2		INPUT	
10	7,638		INPUT	INPUT
11	0		INPUT	
	2		INPUT	
12	6,989		INPUT	INPUT
13	7	+ / −	INPUT	INPUT
14	0		INPUT	INPUT
15	6,468		INPUT	INPUT
16	0		INPUT	
	2		INPUT	
17	6,468		INPUT	INPUT
18	0		INPUT	
	2		INPUT	
19	6,468		INPUT	INPUT
20	0		INPUT	
	2		INPUT	
21	6,472		INPUT	INPUT
22	765	+ / −	INPUT	INPUT
23	0		INPUT	INPUT
24	5,710		INPUT	INPUT
25	0		INPUT	
	2		INPUT	
26	5,710		INPUT	INPUT
27	0		INPUT	
	2		INPUT	
28	5,710		INPUT	INPUT
29	0		INPUT	
	2		INPUT	
30	6,135		INPUT	INPUT
31	433	+ / −	INPUT	INPUT
32	0		INPUT	INPUT
33	6,042		INPUT	INPUT
34	0		INPUT	
	2		INPUT	
35	6,042		INPUT	INPUT
36	0		INPUT	
	2		INPUT	
37	11,084		INPUT	INPUT
38	0		INPUT	
	2		INPUT	
39	686	+ / −	INPUT	INPUT
	CALC			
	TOTAL		23,061	
	IRR		.959399	
	× 12		11.512791	

External Rate of Return Analysis (ERR)

There are occasions when, due to certain problems, the IRR approach to yield analysis is inadequate and ERR analysis is required. What problems does IRR present and how does ERR solve them? In order to answer this question an example is required. Assume a $4,500 lease investment generates the following six annual, after-tax cash flows:

Year	Cash Flows
0	($ 4,500)
1	4,000
2	2,000
3	1,000
4	1,000
5	(3,500)
6	1,000

To understand some of the problems that IRR presents, first compute the annual after-tax IRR on the above cash flows using an HP-12C.

4,500	CHS	g	CF_o
4,000		g	CF_j
2,000		g	CF_j
1,000		g	CF_j
2		g	N_j
3,500	CHS	g	CF_j
1,000		g	CF_j
		f	IRR
			ERROR 3

ERROR 3 will most likely appear in the display. This is because there is more than one answer to the problem and the calculator does not know which one is wanted. For illustrative purposes, negative answers are sought first by choosing a negative guess to the solution and then pressing RCL g PSE (in order to prompt the calculator to continue). The first guess will be negative 75.

　　75　CHS　RCL g　PSE

The calculator should give –65.857931 as a solution. A positive solution is sought next by guessing positive 75.

　　75　　　　RCL g　PSE

The calculator should display 25.442492 as another solution. This solution, however, is positive.

In a sixth degree polynomial (six cash flows) there are six answers. However, some are imaginary, others are real. Descartes' rule of signs states there will be a real solution for each sign change. Thus, there are three real solutions to this problem, two of which have been

THE HANDBOOK OF EQUIPMENT LEASING

calculated. The other solution may approach infinity, which is beyond the HP-12C's ability to locate. The third solution may be positive or negative also. Some analysts would view the existence of three IRRs in this example as a definite problem with using IRRs.

Another problem with using IRR is that positive cash flows are assumed to be immediately reinvested at the IRR. This assumption has two shortcomings: (1) the actual reinvestment rate available might be materially greater or less than the investment's IRR and (2) the actual reinvestment rates may vary from year to year. An example of how IRR might lead to a faulty conclusion due to its reinvestment assumptions follows.

Compare the above example (Alternative 1) with the following lease investment (Alternative 2) of the same amount, over the same lease term of 6 years.

Year	Cash Flows
0	($ 4,500.00)
1	1,368.07
2	1,368.07
3	1,368.07
4	1,368.07
5	1,368.07
6	1,368.07

The IRR on this lease is computed.

		g	END	
4,500	CHS		PV	
1,368.07			PMT	
6			n	
			i	20.4425

The IRR of Alternative 2 is 5% below Alternative 1's IRR of 25.4425%. Which alternative is best if cash flows can be reinvested only at 12%? Table 17 displays the future value of each cash flow reinvested at 12%. Notice that Alternative 2 has the higher future value of reinvested cash flows. Clearly if 12% were the real reinvestment opportunity, then Alternative 2 is superior even though it has a lower IRR. Were cash flows actually invested at 25.44%, then the future value of the Alternative 1 cash flows would exceed those of Alternative 2, whose cash flows would appreciate only at 20.44%. Therefore, it can be seen that the reinvestment assumption is another problem inherent in IRR analysis.

Another little-understood problem with IRR concerns the assumption of earnings on disinvestment balances in a lease. Leases with only positive cash inflows beyond the inception never have disinvestment balances, only normal investment balances. Disinvestment balances occur when there are sufficient negative cash flows in a lease to cause the normal investment balance to change signs (accounting viewpoint: change from a normal debit asset to a credit liability balance). An amortization of the cash flows of Alternative 1 demonstrates how a disinvestment balance occurs (see Table 18).

Notice during the third and fourth year that the investment balance in Table 18 went from negative to positive (debit to credit balances from the lessor's viewpoint). When this happens a

Table 17
Future Value of Cash Flows

	Alternative 1 (IRR: 25.44%)			**Alternative 2** (IRR: 20.44%)		
	Cash Flow	Years	Future Value at 12%	Cash Flow	Years	Future Value at 12%
1	$ 4,000	5	$ 7,049.37	$ 1,368.07	5	$ 2,411.01
2	2,000	4	3,147.04	1,368.07	4	2,152.68
3	1,000	3	1,404.93	1,368.07	3	1,922.04
4	1,000	2	1,254.40	1,368.07	2	1,716.11
5	(3,500)	1	(3,920.00)	1,368.07	1	1,532.24
6	1,000	0	1,000.00	1,368.07	0	1,368.07
Total	$ 5,500		$ 9,935.74	$ 8,208.42		$ 11,102.15

Table 18
Amortization of Alternative 1

Cash Flow Number	Cash Flow	Interest	Principal	Balance
0	$ 0.00	$ 0.00	$ 0.00	($ 4,500.00)
1	4,000.00	1,144.91	2,855.09	(1,644.91)
2	2,000.00	418.51	1,581.49	(63.42)
3	1,000.00	16.14	983.86	920.44
4	1,000.00	(234.18)	1,234.18	2,154.62
5	(3,500.00)	(548.20)	(2,951.80)	(797.18)
6	1,000.00	202.82	797.18	0.00
Total	$ 5,500.00	$ 1,000.00	$ 4,500.00	

disinvestment balance is said to occur. Disinvestments are also referred to in the leasing industry as sinking fund balances. When a disinvestment balance does occur, the amortization reflects the lessor owing interest the next year, rather than earning interest. In Table 18, in years 4 and 5, there was an interest expense of $234.18 and $548.20, respectively.

Actually, the disinvestment balance represents money set aside (invested in something else) to grow to an amount sufficient to cover future negative cash flows. In Table 18, the disinvestment balance provided sufficient cash flow to cover almost the entire $3,500 outflow in the fifth year. The $797.18 deficiency left in the fifth year came from the sixth year's cash flow. This phenomenon raises the issue of what rate money, assumed to be set aside to cover future cash reinvestments in a lease, earns or accumulates at. IRR assumes disinvestment balances earn at the lease's IRR, which might be far in excess of opportunity reinvestment rates.

Thus, it can be concluded that the use of IRRs has three drawbacks:

1. Multiple solutions (some positive, some negative)
2. Cash flows are reinvested at the IRR, which might materially exceed actual opportunity reinvestment rates, thereby leading to contradictions with future and present value analysis
3. Disinvestment balances earn at the IRR, which might exceed actual investment opportunities.

How does the external rate of return method deal with and solve these IRR problems? In the first place, there is no single ERR method; actually, there are six different types of ERRs. One attribute common to all ERR approaches, however, is reinvestment rates are externally imposed on the solution, hence, the name external rate of return. The six ERR approaches can be sorted into three groups.

1. Those methods that emphasize the reinvestment of positive cash flows. Negative cash flows as well as disinvestment balances are ignored
   a. Reinvested earnings ERR (RE ERR)
2. Those methods that dwell only on disinvestment balances and negative cash flow problems, to the exclusion of the reinvestment of positive cash flows
   a. Multiple investment sinking fund ERR (MISF ERR)
   b. Sinking fund ERR (SF ERR)
   c. Sinking fund with borrowing ERR (SFB ERR)
3. Combined methods that deal simultaneously with disinvestment balances, negative cash flows as well as the reinvestment of positive cash flows
   a. Sinking fund with reinvestment (SFR ERR)
   b. Opportunity reinvestment with limited borrowing (ORLB ERR).

REINVESTED EARNINGS ERR

This method imposes on the ERR solution an external reinvestment rate that affects all cash flows, both positive and negative. The total future value of all appreciated cash flows is used to find an IRR that equates the investment cost with that future total. Using the previous IRR case, and the information in Table 17 that assumes a 12% after-tax reinvestment rate, the RE ERR of Alternative 1 is solved for, as shown:

4,500	CHS	PV	
9,935.74		FV	
6		n	
		i	14.112

Obviously, being able to reinvest cash flows at 12% versus the IRR rate of 25.44% has heavily impacted the 14.112% RE ERR. The RE ERR of Alternative 2 would be calculated as follows:

4,500	CHS	PV	
11,102.15		FV	
6		n	
		i	16.243

Notice that the RE ERR results in the same decision as the future value analysis of Table 17 that showed Alternative 2 to be preferable. RE ERR has solved several of the objections to IRR.

1. There is only one unique solution to an RE ERR problem since there are only two cash flows (the future and present values) and one sign change
2. The RE ERR gives the same answer as NPV or future value analysis by considering the reinvestment of cash flows
3. The reinvested cash flows could have appreciated at any series of varying reinvestment rates, whereas IRR permits only one.

However, the RE ERR did not deal with the $3,500 negative cash flow in necessarily the best possible manner, for it was treated as a new investment that earned only 12%, and not the 14.112% the overall investment earned. This problem will be dealt with under SFR ERR and ORLB ERR.

MULTIPLE INVESTMENT SINKING FUND ERR

This method deals very conservatively with disinvestment sinking fund balances should they occur (as in Alternative 1). In effect, the MISF ERR approach assumes that disinvestment balances do not earn any interest at all; therefore, no interest expenses will occur in an MISF amortization. Table 19 is an amortization of the Alternative 1 cash flows according to a 15.256503% MISF ERR. This ERR was determined with software since neither the HP-12C nor the HP-18C can solve the problem without undue manual effort.

The 15.256503% MISF ERR rate is that rate that, when applied to the net investment in the years that it is normal (negative balance), will distribute the interest to those years. Years beginning with disinvestment balances do not receive any earnings. Notice, in Table 19, that a disinvestment balance occurred in year 2; thus, year 3 was precluded from receiving any negative earnings (interest expense, as occurs in the IRR amortization), because of the assumptions in MISF analysis.

Although this method acknowledges sinking fund or disinvestment balances, it does not allow any earnings on the fund. The net effect of this approach is to understate the real economics of the lease. However, the MISF ERR's lack of attention to positive cash flow reinvestment opportunities often creates a counterbalancing overstatement of yield. It is interesting to note that this yield has popular appeal because of the FASB 13 requirement that it be used for

Table 19
MISF ERR Amortization

Cash Flow Number	Cash Flow	Interest	Principal	Balance
0	$ 0.00	$ 0.00	$ 0.00	($ 4,500.00)
1	4,000.00	686.54	3,313.46	(1,186.54)
2	2,000.00	181.02	1,818.98	632.44
3	1,000.00	0.00	1,000.00	1,632.44
4	1,000.00	0.00	1,000.00	2,632.44
5	(3,500.00)	0.00	(3,500.00)	(867.56)
6	1,000.00	132.44	867.56	0.00
Total	$ 5,500.00	$ 1,000.00	$ 4,500.00	

leveraged lease accounting (not for single investor capital or operating leases), although FASB 13 does not require, or suggest, that MISF ERR be used to analyze the economics of a leveraged lease.

SINKING FUND ERR

This method is identical to the MISF ERR method, except the disinvestment balance is allowed to earn a conservative, liquid, sinking fund rate. Rates at or near the lessor's after-tax, short-term, money market rates are typical of sinking fund rates. In the following example (Table 20) of an SF ERR amortization, notice the disinvestment balance beginning the third year is $434.29. It has been assumed that disinvestment balances will earn 5% after-tax; therefore, the third year's sinking fund expense will be .05 × $434.29, or $21.71. Sinking fund earnings are shown as opposite from normal interest earnings. This method, too, requires software or hours of tedious iterations to solve for the SF ERR rate.

Although SF ERR has partially solved the problem of not recognizing earnings on disinvestment balances presented by the MISF ERR, nevertheless, it still has certain drawbacks:

1. Disinvestment balances earn at after-tax, money market rates instead of at the higher portfolio investment rates normally earned by lessors
2. Cash generated by most lease companies is invested back into the overall portfolio. Cash shortages on a given lease in a particular year are first paid out of current cash flow, second, from limited borrowings against future earnings (residual, etc.) and, third, from current liquidation of the portfolio. Sinking fund investments are rarely created in earlier years to cover a current year cash flow deficit
3. SF ERR assumes all positive cash flows are reinvested and earn at the SF ERR rate, which, like IRR, is internally calculated and remains constant over the lease term,

Table 20
SF ERR Amortization

Cash Flow Number	Cash Flow	Interest	Principal	Balance
0	$ 0.00	$ 0.00	$ 0.00	($ 4,500.00)
1	4,000.00	823.51	3,176.49	(1,323.51)
2	2,000.00	242.20	1,757.80	434.29
3	1,000.00	(21.71)	1,021.71	1,456.00
4	1,000.00	(72.80)	1,072.80	2,528.80
5	(3,500.00)	(126.44)	(3,373.56)	(844.76)
6	1,000.00	155.24	844.76	0.00
Total	$ 5,500.00	$ 1,000.00	$ 4,500.00	

whereas real reinvestment opportunities might differ from the SF ERR rate and continue to change over the lease term.

SINKING FUND WITH BORROWING

This technique solves sinking fund problems by borrowing from future positive cash flows (residual values, etc.) to the maximum degree possible. These borrowings are used to offset negative cash flows. If any negative difference still remains, a sinking fund is established in earlier years. The SFB ERR amortization (Table 21) is more complex than the previous ones because of the extra two columns to keep track of the borrowings. Money is assumed to be borrowed at a 4% after-tax cost and sinking funds are assumed to earn at a 5%, after-tax rate.

To understand the SFB ERR method, study the investment balance column of Table 21. The first year a normal investment balance earned at the SFB ERR rate of 19.8025%, resulting in earnings of $891.11 (.198025 × $4,500). The second year's investment balance was also normal, so it earned $275.48. The second year ended with a $333.41 disinvestment balance, however, that now must earn at the sinking fund rate of 5%. Thus, the next year's disinvestment interest expense is $16.67 (.05 × 333.41).

In the fifth year the limited borrowings come into play. The borrowed amount is $961.54, which represents the present value of the entire last positive cash flow discounted 1 year at the 4% after-tax borrowing rate. Therefore, the true cash flow of year 5 is ($3,500) + $961.54, from which $120.88 in interest expense was deducted, leaving a difference of $2,417.58. This difference is exactly the amount needed to eliminate the $2,417.58 disinvestment balance at the beginning of the fifth year. The last cash inflow in the sixth year, $1,000, is just sufficient to pay $38.46 in after-tax interest on the loan plus $961.54 in loan principal.

Although this method attempts to deal realistically with sinking funds through minimizing or eradicating such funds by borrowing from the future, it suffers from numerous defects.

Table 21
SFB ERR Amortization

Cash Flow Number	Cash Flow	Interest	Principal	Investment Balance	Interest on Borrowings	Principal on Borrowings
0	$ 0.00	$ 0.00	$ 0.00	($ 4,500.00)	$ 0.00	$ 0.00
1	4,000.00	891.11	3,108.89	(1,391.11)	0.00	0.00
2	2,000.00	275.48	1,724.52	333.41	0.00	0.00
3	1,000.00	(16.67)	1,016.67	1,350.08	0.00	0.00
4	1,000.00	(67.50)	1,067.50	2,417.58	0.00	0.00
5	(3,500.00)	(120.88)	(2,417.58)	0.00	0.00	961.54
6	1,000.00	0.00	0.00	0.00	(38.46)	(961.54)
Total	$ 5,500.00	$ 961.54	$ 4,500.00	$ 0.00	($ 38.46)	$ 0.00

1. Cash flow in a given year generated by a lease generally is derived from interest earned on past reinvested cash flows generated by the lease, and from current after-tax cash flow received under the terms of the lease. If these two sources of cash flow still result in a negative situation, borrowing against any future cash inflows would be reasonable. However, to allow unrestricted borrowing from the future (as the SFB ERR method permits) simply is using financial leverage to increase yield. The ORLB ERR method effectively deals with this problem
2. Sinking fund disinvestment balances still present the same problem discussed previously, since they occur any time borrowings are insufficient to fully cover the negative cash flow in any given year
3. Remaining positive cash flows after borrowings, loan paybacks, sinking funds, etc., are assumed to be reinvested at the SFB ERR rate, which again might vary in magnitude and constancy
4. This method tends to overstate the yield due to the acceleration of future cash flow recognition caused by the borrowing.

SINKING FUND WITH REINVESTMENT

This method adopts the sinking fund approach to negative cash flows, but imposes a proper reinvestment rate for remaining positive cash flows. In the example for SFR ERR, sinking funds earn at 5%, after-tax, and remaining positive cash flows will be reinvested at 12%, after-tax, which represents the portfolio's normal earnings rate. The amortization is quite complex, as shown in Figure 4. Figure 4 traces the initial cash inflow of $4,000 through its reinvestment growth (left to right) until its future value totals $9,578.42.

The following is a narrative description of what is occurring in the SFR ERR yield computation of Figure 4. The initial cash inflow of $4,000 in year 1 is reinvested at 12%. In year 2, $392.74 is set aside in an independent investment (sinking fund) earning at 5% in order to

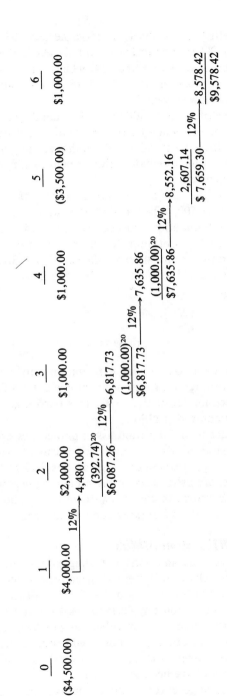

0	1	2	3	4	5	6
($4,500.00)	$4,000.00	$2,000.00	$1,000.00	$1,000.00	($3,500.00)	$1,000.00

$4,000.00 — 12% → 4,480.00

$(392.74)^{20}$

$6,087.26$

$6,087.26$ — 12% → 6,817.73

$(1,000.00)^{20}$

$6,817.73$

$6,817.73$ — 12% → 7,635.86

$(1,000.00)^{20}$

$7,635.86$

$7,635.86$ — 12% → 8,552.16

$2,607.14$

$7,659.30$ — 12% → 8,578.42

$9,578.42$

Figure 4
Derivation of the SFR ERR

[20] Current sinking fund contribution, such that in year 5, the $3,500 of negative cash flow is offset by the sinking fund balance, plus current earnings.

Sinking fund (5%)	$ 2,607.14
Year 5 earnings	916.30
	$3,523.44

provide the $2,607.14 required in the fifth year to offset the large negative $3,500 outflow. Additional sinking fund investments of $1,000 in the third year, plus $1,000 in the fourth year, also are invested at 5%. All these investments grow to $2,607.14, which, when combined with the $916.30 of reinvestment earnings generated on the $7,635.86 year 4 ending balance, completely offsets the $3,500 negative cash flow in year 5.

The second year, after-tax cash inflow of $2,000, added to the cumulative reinvestment balance of $4,480, less the sinking fund investment of $392.74, results in a new $6,087.26 reinvestment balance carryforward. The reinvestment balance from the second year, $6,087.26, when invested at 12%, grows to $6,817.73, which includes reinvestment earnings of $730.47. This process is repeated for each year thereafter.

The sinking fund balance is used to meet the cash flow requirement of year 5. In that year, the current year after-tax cash outflow of $3,500, offset against the cumulative reinvestment balance of $8,552.16, plus the sinking fund liquidation proceeds of $2,607.14, results in a new reinvestment balance carryforward of $7,659.30. Continuing to earn reinvestment earnings until the end of the investment results in the terminal reinvestment balance of $9,578.42. Using this future value amount, the SFR ERR is determined with an HP-12C, as follows:

4,500	CHS	PV	
9,578.42		FV	
6		n	
		i	13.417541

Though complex, the amortization and its accompanying explanation clarify how both the sinking fund concept and the reinvested earnings approach are combined. Thus far, this yield comes the closest to emulating the real economics of the lease. This particular yield, too, is similar to the RE ERR in that it does not contradict NPV.

The sole limitation of this method relates to sinking fund assumptions. Lessors seldom set aside investment funds to cover future cash outflows. Instead, they consume current earnings derived from carryforward reinvested earnings. If these earnings are insufficient, borrowings, limited to the future expected cash inflows, are used to cover any remaining negative outflows. Once borrowings are exhausted, part of the reinvested carryforward earnings is liquidated until the negative amount is consumed, but in no case is a sinking fund established.

OPPORTUNITY REINVESTMENT WITH LIMITED BORROWINGS

This method completely avoids sinking fund assumptions in dealing with negative cash flows occurring subsequent to the lease inception. Under this method, negative cash flows are offset with positive cash flows derived from the following three sources, listed in order of priority:

1. Current year earnings on the investment, and any carryforward reinvestment earnings received, are used to fund the cash outflow. (Remember, as positive cash flows are received in a lease, they are reinvested.) Earnings on these reinvested funds are used to offset cash outflows so as not to cause any liquidation of the overall portfolio, including any previously received cash flows that have been reinvested

2. If current year earnings are insufficient to cover negative outflows, the lessor borrows against expected future cash inflows. This is preferable to establishing sinking funds or

to liquidating portfolio assets to cover the balance of a negative outflow. Note that this is not indiscriminate borrowing used to leverage yield, as in the SFB ERR approach. Borrowing under the ORLB ERR occurs only if absolutely necessary

3. If numbers 1 and 2 are insufficient, previously invested cash inflows are liquidated. No sinking funds are established, however.

The amortization in Figure 5, which is similar to the one for SFR ERR, depicts the results of an ORLB ERR yield of 14.258750% and also assumes a 4%, after-tax, cost of debt. The amortization is explained in the same manner as the SFR ERR yield.

The $4,480 in year 2 represents the future value of $4,000, the first cash inflow, growing at 12%. Included in this amount is $480 of earnings. The current year after-tax cash inflow of $2,000, added to the cumulative reinvestment balance of $4,480, results in a new, $6,480 reinvestment balance carryforward. This process is repeated each year until year 5, at which time the negative $3,500 cash flow requirement is met.

The cumulative reinvestment carryforward balance from the fourth year of $10,248.51 generates earnings in the fifth year of $1,229.82. These earnings are used to help offset the $3,500 cash outflow occurring in the fifth year. When the earnings on the cumulative reinvestment carryforward of $1,229.82 are insufficient to fully offset the fifth year $3,500 negative cash outflow, a $2,270.18 deficit occurs. As discussed earlier, this deficit is offset first by borrowings and then by portfolio liquidation. The maximum borrowing amount available is $961.54 and is the present value of any net future positive cash flows discounted at the after-tax cost of debt (4% in this case).

After offsetting earnings and borrowings against the fifth year's $3,500 outflow, there still remains a $1,308.64 deficit, which causes a partial liquidation of the cumulative reinvestment carryforward that is part of the lessor's overall leasing portfolio. Liquidation is still a more reasonable assumption than establishment of a sinking fund in the previous 2 years.

Note that the cumulative reinvestment carryforward from the fourth year of $10,248.51 has not grown in size, since its earnings were fully consumed in offsetting the $3,500 outflow during the fifth year. The sixth year after-tax cash flow of $1,000, less the $1,000 loan payment, plus the $10,012.65 cumulative reinvestment carryforward totals $10,012.65. This future value total can now be used to compute the ORLB ERR, as follows:

4,500	CHS	PV
10,012.65		FV
6		n
		i 14.258737

The ORLB ERR comes closest to reflecting the actual economics of the transaction. Of course, this yield is only as good as the external reinvestment and loan rates imposed on its solution. Keep in mind, however, that the other alternatives had their own reinvestment assumptions far in excess of the 12% assumed in this problem. It should be noted that both the SFR ERR and the ORLB ERR yields come close to an actual depiction of the cash flow reality of a lease and both give the same answer as the NPV approach, which also imposes a 12% reinvestment rate on the cash flows.

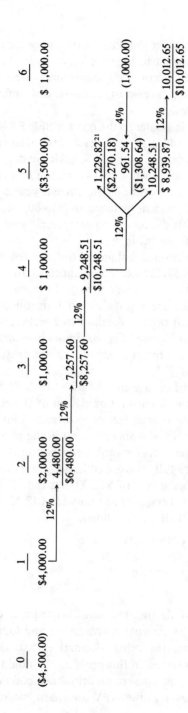

Figure 5
Derivation of the ORLB ERR

[21]$10,248.51 \times 12\% = \$1,229.82$

APPLICATION

Now net IRR and ERRs have been discussed, what are some general rules regarding their use? If a lease is a nonleveraged, single investor lease, it is highly unlikely there will be a negative cash flow sufficient in size or amount to cause a disinvestment balance; therefore, if the lease's IRR is approximately equal (plus or minus 1%, after-tax) to reinvestment opportunities, use IRR analysis. If the lease's IRR is greater than or less than the reinvestment opportunities (more than 1%), use RE ERR, which is not dependent upon sinking fund assumptions.

If the lease is leveraged, and does not have disinvestment balances, treat it as a nonleveraged lease. If the lease is leveraged, has disinvestment balances and the lease's IRR is approximately equal (plus or minus 1%, after-tax) to the reinvestment opportunities, use SF ERR. If the lease's IRR is greater than or less than the reinvestment opportunities (more than 1%), use SFR ERR or ORLB ERR.

The use of IRR versus ERR and the choice between the six ERRs is mainly a function of (1) the user's understanding, (2) available analytical software, (3) reinvestment, sinking fund and borrowing rate assumptions, (4) level of conservatism and (5) belief in the existence of sinking funds, etc.

PRESENT AND FUTURE VALUE ANALYSIS

NPV and future value analysis make use of discounted after-tax cash flows and are closely related to the ERR method of analyzing leases, since both approaches use externally imposed reinvestment rates. The modified NPV or dual rate technique closely mimics the SFR ERR technique. It is because of this reinvestment rate similarity that ORLB ERR, RE ERR and SFR ERR generally give the same investment decision answer as NPV analysis (modified NPV always gives the same answer).

The basic analytical decision methodology in NPV or future value analysis requires the present value (NPV analysis) of future cash inflows, when discounted at an externally imposed discount rate, to be equal to or greater than the investment cost; or, the future value of cash inflows, when appreciating at an externally imposed appreciation rate, to equal or exceed the future value of the investment cost. NPV or future value analysis always give the same answer when the discount rate equals the appreciation rate. This is necessarily so since NPV and future value analyses differ only in time perspective, or from which end of the investment time spectrum the investment decision is being made.

Net Present Value Method

This technique discounts the after-tax cash inflows (and subsequent outflows) of a lease to ascertain whether their present value is equal to or greater than the equipment's inception cost. Present value inflows are netted against outflows. If the difference is positive the lease is considered acceptable from an investment viewpoint. Discounting of cash flows removes the implied interest earnings from them. If earnings are deducted from a series of cash flows in some systematic fashion, that remaining is return of investment (not return on investment, which is eliminated through discounting). If the total of the recouped investment is equal to or greater than the cost of the investment, profitability is indicated and the investment is deemed acceptable.

Using the base case, along with an HP-12C calculator, the net present value of the cash flows is determined. The lease's cash flows are discounted in Table 22 using an assumed reinvestment rate (usually the lease company's weighted average, after-tax, cost of capital) of 6%. The cash flows must be loaded as two distinct groups to keep them within the capacity of the HP-12C.

Adding the first present value number, -$36,897.74, to the second, +$39,907.49, a net present value of $3,009.75 is arrived at. The number is positive, so it is concluded that the investment is acceptable, since, after removing the earnings (at 6%) from all cash flows, the remaining recoupment of investment is $3,009.75 greater than the equipment's net inception cost of $91,900.

Future Value Analysis

This technique is also known as the TVA method or net future value approach. TVA adds earnings to cash flows at an assumed reinvestment rate, whereas NPV analysis deducts them. For many, TVA analysis intuitively is more understandable. If the future value of cash inflows exceeds that of the inception investment, then the investment is deemed acceptable.

The HP-18C, unlike the HP-12C, can determine the future value of an uneven series of cash flows. Using the base case, the future value is determined, as shown in Table 23. In effect, this method begins with an investment of $91,900 and questions what it would be worth if it were invested at compound interest of 6% over the lease term. If the future value of the anticipated lease cash flows, together with their implied earnings, exceeds this amount, then the investment is worthwhile. As shown in Table 23, the future value of the cash flows does exceed the future value of the equipment cost by $3,900.92.

Present Value Payback Method

This investment analysis technique is a combination of normal payback and NPV analysis. In this method, the number of periods until the present value of the cash inflows exactly equals the inception investment is first determined (the modified payback period). Any cash flow beyond the modified payback period is present valued and shown as a remainder. Done in this manner the present value payback gives both the NPV of an investment plus the time required for the NPV to equal zero. As long as the technique is used in conjunction with the present valued remainder (thus equating it to the NPV technique), it is a useful evaluation tool.

An example of the technique, using the simplified cash flows of the previous ERR analysis, is shown in Table 24 (a 12% discount rate is deemed appropriate). The present value payback was in 2 years, with a remainder of $533.76 of net present value. If capital rationing is not a problem for the lessor, any investment that has a present value payback period is deemed acceptable. If an investment does not have a payback period, its net present value is negative and it should be rejected. However, if capital rationing is a problem and two projects are mutually exclusive, the present value payback with the greater present value remainder is preferable unless the remainder is exceptionally insignificant relative to the additional present value payback time required to obtain the present value remainder.

Table 22

Net Present Value Analysis

Cash Flow Number	Keystrokes				
				First Group	
	6		g	$12 \div$	
0	91,900	CHS	g	CF_o	
1	6,226		g	CF_j	
2	0		g	CF_j	
	2		g	N_j	
3	6,949		g	CF_j	
4	467		g	CF_j	
5	0		g	CF_j	
6	6,942		g	CF_j	
7	0		g	CF_j	
	2		g	N_j	
8	6,942		g	CF_j	
9	0		g	CF_j	
	2		g	N_j	
10	6,942		g	CF_j	
11	0		g	CF_j	
	2		g	N_j	
12	6,681		g	CF_j	
13	513	CHS	g	CF_j	
14	0		g	CF_j	
15	5,962		g	CF_j	
16	0		g	CF_j	
	2		g	N_j	
17	5,962		g	CF_j	
18	0		g	CF_j	
	2		g	N_j	
19	5,962		g	CF_j	
			f	NPV	−36,897.74
				Second Group	
			f	REG	
	6		g	$12 \div$	
1	0		g	CF_j	
	27		g	N_j	
2	6,249		g	CF_j	
3	1,100	CHS	g	CF_j	
4	0		g	CF_j	
5	5,375		g	CF_j	
6	0		g	CF_j	
	2		g	N_j	
7	5,375		g	CF_j	
8	0		g	CF_j	
	2		g	N_j	
9	5,375		g	CF_j	
10	0		g	CF_j	
	2		g	N_j	
11	5,986		g	CF_j	
12	595	CHS	g	CF_j	
13	0		g	CF_j	
14	5,880		g	CF_j	
15	0		g	CF_j	
	2		g	N_j	
16	5,880		g	CF_j	
17	0		g	CF_j	
	2		g	N_j	
18	10,922		g	CF_j	
19	0		g	CF_j	
	2		g	N_j	
20	749	CHS	g	CF_j	
			f	NPV	39,907.49

Table 23
Future Value Analysis

Cash Flow Number		Keystrokes		
0	91,900	+/−	INPUT	
1	6,226		INPUT	INPUT
2	0		INPUT	
	2		INPUT	
3	6,949		INPUT	INPUT
4	467		INPUT	INPUT
5	0		INPUT	INPUT
6	6,942		INPUT	INPUT
7	0		INPUT	
	2		INPUT	
8	6,942		INPUT	INPUT
9	0		INPUT	
	2		INPUT	
10	6,942		INPUT	INPUT
11	0		INPUT	
	2		INPUT	
12	6,681		INPUT	INPUT
13	513	+/−	INPUT	INPUT
14	0		INPUT	INPUT
15	5,962		INPUT	INPUT
16	0		INPUT	
	2		INPUT	
17	5,962		INPUT	INPUT
18	0		INPUT	
	2		INPUT	
19	5,962		INPUT	INPUT
20	0		INPUT	
	2		INPUT	
21	6,249		INPUT	INPUT
22	1,100	+/−	INPUT	INPUT
23	0		INPUT	INPUT
24	5,375		INPUT	INPUT
25	0		INPUT	
	2		INPUT	
26	5,375		INPUT	INPUT
27	0		INPUT	
	2		INPUT	
28	5,375		INPUT	INPUT
29	0		INPUT	
	2		INPUT	
30	5,986		INPUT	INPUT
31	595	+/−	INPUT	INPUT
32	0		INPUT	INPUT
33	5,880		INPUT	INPUT
34	0		INPUT	
	2		INPUT	
35	5,880		INPUT	INPUT
36	0		INPUT	
	2		INPUT	
37	10,922		INPUT	INPUT
38	0		INPUT	
	2		INPUT	
39	749	+/−	INPUT	INPUT
	CALC			
	.5 i			
	TOTAL		15,220	
	NFV		3,900.92	

Table 24
Present Value Payback Analysis

Cash Flow Number	Present Value Cash Flow	Cumulative at 12%	Present Value
0	($ 4,500)	($ 4,500.00)	($ 4,500.00)
1	4,000	3,571.43	(928.57)
2	2,000	1,594.39	665.82
3	1,000	711.78	1,377.60
4	1,000	635.52	2,013.12
5	(3,500)	(1,985.99)	27.13
6	1,000	506.63	533.76

Modified Net Present Value

This method is closely related to the ERR methods in that several reinvestment and sinking fund rate assumptions are integrated into the problem solution. The ERR method most closely resembled is the SFR ERR. In fact, the only difference is in modified NPV analysis, cash flows remaining after sinking fund offsets are present valued instead of future valued.

The actual process begins by discounting cash flows in reverse order — last to first. All positive cash flows are discounted at an assumed reinvestment rate (12%, the same rate that was used in the ERR example) and remaining negative cash flows are discounted at a sinking fund rate, 5% in this case. The present value of positive cash flows is offset against negative cash flows. Any remainder is discounted at a sinking fund rate until completely offset by earlier positive flows. Figure 6 is a diagram of the sequential discounting, starting from the right (last cash flow) and going to the left (inception flow).

The present value of the sixth year's cash flow of $1,000, discounted 1 year at the 12% normal discount rate, is $892.86. The fifth year's cash outflow of $3,500 is partially offset with the present value of the sixth year's cash flow. However, the $2,607.14 difference creates the need for a sinking fund to be paid out of the positive cash flows of prior years. The present value of the fifth year's net cash flow of $2,607.14, discounted 1 year at the 5% sinking fund rate, is $2,482.99. The $1,000 cash flow received in the fourth year is insufficient to meet the current year sinking fund requirement of $2,482.99. The difference between the two, $1,482.99, represents the balance of the sinking fund requirement to be created out of earlier cash inflows.

This process is repeated each year, with the discount rate to be used dependent upon whether or not a sinking fund must be created. The $4,852.73 represents the final present value of all cash flows, sinking fund and normal inflows, which is offset against the $4,500 net investment in the year of inception.

The modified NPV in this case is $352.73, which is $181.02 less than the normal NPV of $533.75 for the same cash flows. The existence of sinking funds lowers present values just as

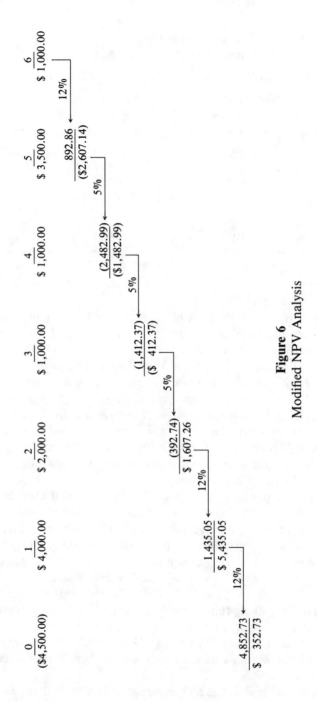

Figure 6
Modified NPV Analysis

ERR yields are lowered by them, since sinking funds are assumed to earn less (5% versus 12% in this case).

Relationship of Present Value Methods

Table 25 shows the present value counterpart of the various analytical yield methods. The last three yields (SFR, RE and ORLB) always give answers consistent with their present value counterparts. IRR may contradict NPV if reinvestment rates differ significantly from the IRR. As can be seen, MISF, SFB and SF do not have present value counterparts. Since they do not deal with reinvestment assumptions, but instead dwell on sinking fund issues, they might contradict NPV or future value analysis. When contradictions occur, NPV generally should be chosen.

MANAGERIAL-ORIENTED INDICES

Managerial yields relate primarily to the profitability results obtained by relating accounting book income (pretax or after-tax) to the balance sheet asset (net investment in the lease) that generates the income. Managerial yields reference the accounting book profit generated by the lease irrespective of its real economic yield. If the lease is not leveraged, but is a capital lease, there are three basic income recognition approaches to managerial analysis:

1. The implicit rate in the lease, which allocates income based on a pretax return on total assets, or an after-tax return on total assets
2. Rule of 78 interest recognition, which is a pretax return on total assets
3. Internal rate of return on an after-tax return on net assets basis.

For the leveraged lease there is only MISF, which gives an after-tax return on net assets. For nonleveraged operating leases, yield will be less meaningful unless the lessor employs either sinking fund depreciation or present value depreciation (see Chapter Fourteen).

Table 25
Relationship to Yield Methods

Yield	Present Value Counterpart
IRR	None
ERR	
MISF	None
SFB	None
SF	None
SFR	Modified NPV
RE	NPV, FV, PV Payback
ORLB	Modified NPV

Implicit Rates

Per FASB 13 an interest rate implicit in a lease is:

> . . . The discount rate that, when applied to (i) the minimum lease payments . . . and (ii) the unguaranteed residual value accruing to the benefit the lessor, . . . causes the aggregate present value at the beginning of the lease term to be equal to the fair value of the leased property to the lessor at the inception of the lease, minus any investment tax credit retained by the lessor and expected to be realized by him . . . [FASB 13, paragraph 5(k)].

An implicit rate, therefore, is simply a gross IRR that omits the impact of MACRS depreciation, refundable security deposits, G & A, tax timing, etc. Once an implicit rate is computed it can be compared against either the investment in the lease (total asset) or against the investment in the lease less any associated deferred tax credits. The procedures for computing the implicit rate, and the subsequent recognition of income, are explained in great detail in Chapter Fifteen; therefore, such computations are not presented in this chapter.

The implicit rate provides a pretax return on total assets that is constant throughout the lease term. Although this is a very common method used by management to evaluate a lease or portfolio, it is, nevertheless, deficient analytically. In the first place, the return is pretax, without any value being placed on such factors as tax timing, MACRS depreciation or refundable security deposits. In the second place, the net investment in the lease does not truly reflect the actual investment in the lease. If deferred tax credits are deducted from the net investment the lease's true, after-tax cash investment is known.

Rule of 78 Interest Recognition

This rule is a pretax allocation method and is based on a formula that determines each month's interest earned. The total pretax earnings in the base case lease of $25,100 are used in this illustration. The formula is:

$$\frac{\text{Number of months in reverse order}}{\dfrac{n(n+1)}{2}} \times \text{Total interest,}$$

where n = total number of months in the lease.

The first month's interest, therefore, would be:

$$\frac{49}{\dfrac{49(49+1)}{2}} \times \$25,100$$

$$\frac{49}{1,225} \times \$25,100 = \$1,004.00$$

The second month's interest would be:

$$\frac{48}{1,225} \quad \times \quad \$25,100 \quad = \quad \$983.51$$

To complete a full amortization, which is beyond the scope of this chapter, the numerator is decreased by one each month. Due to the methodology incorporated in the Rule of 78 method, income is overstated earlier in the lease and is understated later in the lease.

Internal Rate of Return

If the accounting under this method is done in a proper manner, the after-tax income represents a constant, after-tax return on the declining net asset investment of the lease, and the books will reflect the lease's actual earnings. Refer to Table 5 for an example of the amortization of the lease according to its actual .637794 per month, or 7.6535281 per year, after-tax rate.

MARKETING-RELATED TECHNIQUES

Marketing yields are used by sales personnel to quote to lessees. Although these yields generally understate significantly the real yield to the lessor, they have pragmatic value because they approximate the lessee's loan equivalent borrowing rate in the lease (assuming the lessee cannot use tax benefits and the asset is not purchased at the end of the lease term). They also give a valid comparison against competing leases as long as the other leases have exactly the same terms. The most common marketing yield is the street rate (stream rate, lessee effective rate, loan rate, apparent rate, etc.), although add-on (or discount interest) is occasionally quoted.

Add-on Interest

Add-on, or discount, interest rates seldom are quoted to lessees anymore except abroad and sometimes for certain agricultural equipment. Occasionally, however, lessees will request such quotes for comparative purposes. The following is a description of the computation of add-on interest in a lease.

First, the implied interest is computed:

Advance payment	$ 6,600
Interim rent	2,000
Remaining payments	99,000
Expected residual cost	20,000
Total costs to the lessee	$ 127,600
Less equipment cost	100,000
Implied interest	$ 27,600

Next, the implied interest is divided by the months in the lease

$$\frac{\$27,600}{49} \quad = \quad \$563.26 \text{ interest per month}$$

Finally, the monthly interest (times 12) is divided by the cost of the equipment

$$\frac{\$563.26}{\$100,000} \times 12 = 6.7592\% \text{ (add-on interest cost)}$$

There is an old financial adage that states when quoted add-on interest, double it and subtract one. This rule-of-thumb provides an approximate conversion rule to the true, pretax interest rate in the lease of 11.513%.

$$6.7592 \times 2 = 13.5184 - 1 = 12.5184\%$$

Street Rate

This rate is commonly quoted to lessees, and was discussed more fully earlier in the chapter. This rate, like add-on interest, significantly understates the real cost, or yield, but is compared to other leases with similar terms.

MAXIMIZATION VERSUS OPTIMIZATION

Along with a particular lease's NPV, IRR or ERR there must be an assessment of its total undiscounted cash flow. Two leases could have the same NPV but have significantly different cash flows. What is the importance of total cash flow in a lease? What are industry standards for appropriate cash flow? To answer these questions the relationship of cash flow to yield must first be understood. For example, examine the following two investments:

Investment A

0	1	2	3	4	5
($10,000)	$9,000	$2,000	$56	$56	$519

Investment B

($10,000)	$0	$0	$0	$0	$17,624

If the investments' IRRs and NPVs are computed, the following conclusions can be drawn:
1. Both have NPVs of 0 when discounted at 12% (the lessor's cost of capital)
2. Both have IRRs of 12%.

What is interesting in this situation is that Investment A provides total undiscounted cash flow of $1,631,

0	($10,000)
1	9,000
2	2,000
3	56
4	56
5	519
	$ 1,631

Investment B, on the other hand, provides $7,624 ($17,624 – $10,000) of net cash flow, which is 4.6744 times that of Investment A's. Certainly, such a significant difference in cash flow generation between two investments should somehow affect the decision regarding these two leasing alternatives. In order to choose between these two alternatives, additional information is required:

1. What are the reinvestment opportunities over the next 5 years? Will they be at 12%? Will they remain constant? What is the probability of both?
2. How difficult is it to locate new investments, irrespective of their potential yields?
3. What is the cost of finding new investments, in terms of staffing and overhead, etc.?
4. Are the two investments equal from a risk viewpoint (e.g., Investment B does not provide any returns for 4 years)?
5. How dependent are these cash flows on tax benefits that might be consumed too rapidly?
6. What cash flow needs exist in terms of having loanable funds available for current customer lease needs (e.g., Investment B does not provide any cash for 4 years)?

Ignoring questions 2 through 6, if reinvestment opportunities are estimable and highly probable at 12%, what should the lessor conclude? Theoretically, it should be indifferent between the two alternatives, because the early larger cash flows of Investment A, when reinvested at 12%, would grow to exactly $17,624, giving the same cash flow as Investment B.

Present Value	Years	Future Value at 12%
$ 9,000	4	$14,162
2,000	3	2,810
56	2	70
56	1	63
519	0	519
$11,631		$17,624

What if, however, reinvestment opportunities are expected to rise? Investment A should be chosen because its rapid recovery of investment makes cash available to be reinvested at higher rates. An ERR, or modified NPV with ever increasing discount rates, would demonstrate this.

If, on the other hand, reinvestment opportunities are expected to decline, Investment B should be chosen, because it has a larger investment outstanding over time. Investment B locks in the 12% earnings rate in much the same fashion as a zero coupon bond. Even if rates are expected to remain at 12%, any doubt about a shift in rates above or below 12% would tend to move the decision maker toward one or the other.

Even if reinvestment opportunities are estimable, constant and highly probable, Investment B still might be preferable if:

1. It is difficult to find the 3.6744 more Investment A investments required to generate the same cash flow
2. It is expensive to support the staff, etc., necessary to locate additional investments
3. Investment A results in too rapid a consumption of tax liabilities or creates an AMT position.

However, Investment A might be preferable given reasonable availability at low cost, the risk of the end-loading inherent in Investment B or the need for current cash to meet market demand or for unexpected opportunities.

Where does the trade-off occur between the portfolio churning of Investment A and the excessive end-loading residual risk of Investment B? There is no universal answer — it is a judgment call. However, the judgment can be improved by knowing how front-loaded or end-loaded an investment is through comparison to a standard. The cash flow standard used here is referred to as the equal payment liquidity standard (EPLS), and is defined as the net undiscounted cash flow an investment generates at a given IRR (or ERR), in equal installments over the full term of the investment. For example, the EPLS of the previous $10,000 investment is calculated as follows:

		g	END	
12			i	
10,000	CHS		PV	
5			n	
			PMT	2,774.10 (annual cash flows)
5			×	13,870.49 (total 5 years of cash flow)
10,000			–	3,870.49 (EPLS)

Given the $3,870 EPLS calculated above, each of the investments' net cash flow can be expressed as a percentage of the EPLS.

Investment A $\dfrac{\$1,631}{\$3,870}$ = 42.14% of standard

Investment B $\dfrac{\$7,624}{\$3,870}$ = 197.00% of standard

Thus, in a period of increasing expectations concerning lease yields, leases might be written with cash flows at 80% to 90% of standard, whereas during a period of declining expectations, cash flows might be in the range of 110% to 125% of standard (but never more, as too much residual emphasis increases risk inordinately). Generally, the larger the residual position taken in a lease, the greater the EPLS percentage, but other variables also influence large EPLS percentages. Large EPLS percentages should be investigated to see what the actual source of cash flow is.

In the leasing industry one occasionally hears of cash flow rules-of-thumb, such as the one-half percent rule in leveraged leasing. The one-half percent rule implies the lease should generate one-half percent per year of the equipment's cost in net cash flow. If the above investments represented 20% interests in $50,000 leveraged leases they should generate $1,250 in net cash flow (.005 × $50,000 × 5). This rule-of-thumb would result in 32.3% of the EPLS standard ($1,250 ÷ $3,870). The one-half percent rule, however, does not consider the end-loading, nor does it give an overall conceptual viewpoint of what standard cash flow should be.

The base case produced after-tax undiscounted net cash flow of $15,220. The EPLS cash would have been $15,397 at a .637794 per month interest rate.

		g	END	
.637794			i	
91,900	CHS		PV	
49			n	
			PMT	2,189.74
49			×	107,297.40
91,900			–	15,397.40

Thus, the base case lease generated cash flow equal to 98.85% of EPLS cash flow. Had the lease not produced so many tax benefits near its inception, its overall cash flow would have been around 110% of EPLS, due to its 20% residual position. Perhaps the best value of the EPLS approach is to identify leases that produce substandard cash flows (less than 50% EPLS) or above-standard cash flows (greater than 150% EPLS) indicating excessive residual dependence.

In leveraged lease syndication there are many investors who purchase an equity interest in a leveraged lease solely on the basis of yield, without paying any attention to the amount of cash flow generated. The lease may provide a 40% after-tax return with almost no cash flow, yet the lessor remains significantly at-risk throughout the lease term from two viewpoints: (1) unravel risk and (2) residual risk.

A low cash situation occurs by structuring the lease with so little equity that tax benefits the first tax year practically give back to the lessor its original investment. Subsequently, what little investment remains does in fact earn 40%, but the investment is so small its returns are insufficient to generate any cash flow. However, during this time period of minimal cash flow, the lessor is subjected to unravel risk, etc. Many leveraged lease investors would do well to compute the percentages of EPLS before investing.

CONCLUSION

The study of yield analysis is a critical aspect of every lease company's operations, since it is through yield analysis that the profitability of the company is determined. As has been illustrated, there are numerous yields (and combinations thereof) that may be calculated, ranging from a street rate to an after-tax, ORLB ERR. The yield that is used in any one situation is dependent upon the needs and sophistication of the user. The purpose of this chapter, therefore, has been to introduce the various alternatives available in computing portfolio, or single lease, yields.

CHAPTER EIGHT
STRUCTURING PRINCIPLES

Lease rate factors, like the great philosophers, are oft quoted, yet seldom understood. In this context, it safely can be said that few people have a true appreciation for all the complexities involved in structuring a lease that will be acceptable to the marketplace. Structuring (or pricing) integrates so many diverse variables into the process that putting together a well-structured lease indeed requires a great deal of skill and knowledge. The essential financial factors and principles that one should consider in profitably structuring leases will be explored in this chapter.[1] The principles of lease structuring are separated into the following sections:

- Primary Purpose of Structuring
- Structuring Theory
- Pretax Targeted Yield Structuring
- Pretax Versus After-tax Structuring
- Quantification of Structuring Variables
- After-tax Targeted Yield Structuring.

PRIMARY PURPOSE OF STRUCTURING

Everyone recognizes the importance of the role pricing plays in today's lease company. Without proper pricing of the company's lease transactions, either of two events may occur: (1) the transaction will be unacceptable to the marketplace, or (2) the transaction will not meet the profit requirements of the lease company. Both events can cause the demise of the entity.

---

[1]It should be noted that many of the principles involved in lease structuring will be illustrated by examples. These examples will be performed utilizing HP-12C keystrokes; therefore, it will be beneficial to have an advanced financial calculator available.

Given the importance of proper pricing to the company, what are its critical elements, and how is proper pricing accomplished?

Structuring incorporates so many variables, such as lessor requirements, lessee needs, marketplace constraints, funding constraints, lessee risk, etc., that each lease will be different. There are, however, certain characteristics fundamental to all lease structures. One of these, a twofold characteristic, is the primary purpose of lease structuring. For any lease written the company must obtain:

1. A return of the principal invested
2. A reasonable return on the principal invested. (What is reasonable is the subject of Chapter Ten.)

In this respect, leasing should be viewed as any other investment. For example, an investment of $1,000 in the bank today, earning at 10% interest, will return to the investor $1,100 ($1,000 return of principal and $100 return on principal) at the end of one year. This pervasive concept must be kept in mind at all times during the pricing process. The pricing specialist must always structure so as to recover the lease company's investment plus management's targeted rate of return, a principle that will be evident throughout this chapter and will underlie all the discussions of the many methods and techniques used to accomplish this goal.

STRUCTURING THEORY

If a return of principal invested plus a reasonable return on principal invested are the basic goals of structuring, then it is imperative to understand each concept. What is principal in a lease? The most obvious response would be simply the cost of the equipment, and that is true. Principal, however, goes well beyond just the cost of the equipment. In lease structuring we think of principal as being the total costs, or investment, in the lease. Investment principal, therefore, includes the many other costs being invested in the lease, such as commissions, legal fees and lease company general and administrative (G & A) expense. On the flip side, there are also many benefits generated to reduce the cost of the investment made, such as fees and tax benefits. All of these must be taken into account when determining principal for purposes of pricing. This principal must then be recovered through a combination of the lease payment and residual. (Some would consider residual to be a reduction, in the future, of principal to be recovered.)

For example, a lessor may lease equipment costing $10,000 for 48 months. Additionally, it will receive $1,800 in net tax benefits, a $250 closing fee, a $300 advance payment and will pay out $400 in initial direct costs. In this simple example, the lessor would need to recover $8,050 of principal (investment, or cost) through the remaining lease payments (see Table 1).

Investment need not be necessarily limited to actual cost. In the case of a dealer who recognizes gross profit on the leases being written, the equipment component of principal to be recovered would be fair market value. The dealer in this way would also recover the gross profit inherent in the transaction, through the lease payment.

The amount of principal required to be returned through the lease payment is only one side of the basic goal of structuring. The other side is the reasonable return on the principal invested. This return is generally referred to as the earnings, rate of return or simply the rate in the lease.

Table 1
Summary of Cash Flows

Description	Cash Flow	Nature of Cash Flow
Equipment cost	($ 10,000)	Outflow
Tax benefits	1,800	Inflow
Closing fee	250	Inflow
Advance payment	300	Inflow
Initial direct costs	(400)	Outflow
Principal to be recovered	($ 8,050)	Net Outflow

It is this rate of return, as typified by the interest rate, that, when applied to the principal to be recovered, generates the lease payment. Payments and lease rate factors are both a function of the rate of return in the lease. Lessors structure with it and lessees struggle with it.

There are many types of rates of return that can be used in pricing, all of which are covered in more depth later in the chapter. Several common rates are pretax return on assets (ROA), after-tax ROA and after-tax return on equity (ROE). The structuring in this chapter is done on an ROA basis. ROE structuring is discussed in Chapter Nine.

The rates used in structuring leases fall into two broad categories: cost accounting rates or market rates. Cost accounting rates of return can be capital budgeting returns, such as cost of capital or return on equity, or they can be derived from cost accounting inputs. These inputs would include the costs of working capital, uninvested capital, G & A, debt cost, debt payback method and deferred taxes, to name but a few. Based upon what the lease company must earn at (given the above factors), a hurdle rate is established. This hurdle rate then becomes the minimum acceptable rate at which the lease company must structure if the lease company is to continue to grow.

Market rates, on the other hand, are determined solely by what the market will support. Market rates may exceed or even be less than a company's hurdle rate. Because the market rates are so important, a company, when developing a rate to use in pricing, will attempt to establish a target rate. This target rate must be equal to or greater than the hurdle rate, yet still be acceptable in the marketplace. This concept is best shown through an illustration (see Figure 1).It is hoped, as in the illustration, the market rates will exceed the company's hurdle rate.

There are other earnings issues in addition to the choice of rate of return being used to price leases. These issues relate to the quality of the earnings generated by a lease and also the quantity of the earnings (i.e., cash flow sufficiency). An understanding of these issues is essential before proceeding any further.

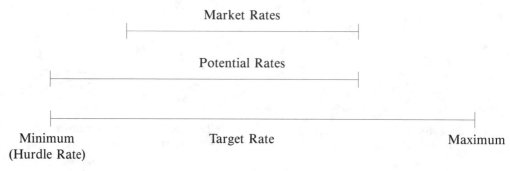

Figure 1
Lessor Rate Spectrum

Quality of Earnings

Earnings in a lease are generated through a mathematical application. As a result, if a lease company is to benefit from these earnings, they must be meaningful within the context of that application. Whether earnings are meaningful or not is determined through the quality of those earnings. Quality of earnings implies several conditions. Once these conditions have been assessed, the appropriate structuring technique for those conditions must be chosen. At this point, the conditions that must be dealt with in order to maintain quality of earnings are examined.

First, risk must be adequately addressed within the structure. Risk in a lease can take many forms — tax benefit risk, default exposure, residual risk, contingent rental risk and lessee credit risk. Certainly, if a lease company loses or cannot utilize its tax benefits the profitability of the structure has been adversely affected. Likewise, in case of default, the profitability is impacted. In those tax leases with nonrecourse debt, creditor repossession may create unsheltered tax liability. Such a disposition also can trigger recapture of tax benefits.

Another risk, that of residual, takes several forms. Technological obsolescence, poor maintenance by the lessee or oversupply of the equipment type can all lead to loss of residual value. If such a loss is incurred, either through loss on sale or lack of re-lease opportunities, the lease profitability again has been impaired.

All of the above risks should be dealt with through adjustment of inputs rather than increasing the targeted rate, since increasing the rate assumes risk increases over time. For instance, if residual remarketing is uncertain, the residual position could be reduced. Lessee risk can be dealt with through increases in yield, however, an approach that is consistent with traditional lending theory.

Second, earnings must meet either the company's hurdle rate or the targeted rate of return. Remember, the targeted rate should be equal to or greater than the hurdle rate, as the hurdle rate represents the absolute minimum rate of return at which the lease company must earn.

Third, reinvestment of cash flows and disinvestment balance sinking fund assumptions must have been properly addressed. The company's actual reinvestment opportunities must be accurately reflected in the structuring process and the appropriate sinking fund assumptions established. This necessitates the selection of a structuring technique appropriate for the reinvestment scenario.

Reinvestment assumptions are critical in any pricing scenario. When a lessor invests in equipment, that leased equipment generates cash flows. These cash flows typically are reinvested in other lease investments at a rate of return that may or may not be the same as the rate of return of the initial investment. To the extent the reinvestment rate is different, the return on the initial investment will be altered. This potential altering of rate of return must be considered in pricing. To more fully understand this concept it is necessary to examine how the reinvestment of cash flows occurs in the most common structuring methodology, internal rate of return (IRR) structuring.

Two basic assumptions of an IRR are that (1) all positive cash flows are immediately reinvested at the IRR of the investment and (2) any negative cash flow needs are met from sinking funds earning at the IRR of the investment. This is best illustrated by an example. Assuming the following cash flows, the IRR of 6.82% can be computed and the validity of the reinvestment assumptions proven (Figure 2).

From this example it is obvious that when the reinvestment rate (6.82% in this case) is equal to the IRR, the actual return will indeed be the IRR. To the extent, then, that a lease company's actual reinvestment opportunities differ from the IRR it is using in structuring, its actual rate of return will be altered. Thus, if a lessor were to write an atypical lease with an after-tax return

0	1	2	3	4
($1,000)	$500	$ 350	($100)	$ 400
		$(93.62)^3$ ←	100	
		$256.38	$ 0 —	→ 0
				→ 292.54^2
				→ 609.44^2
				$1,301.98

$$
\begin{array}{lll}
& 4 & n \\
& 1,000 \quad \text{CHS} & \text{PV} \\
& 1,301.98 & \text{FV} \\
& & i \qquad 6.82 \text{ (proof of original IRR in} \\
& & \qquad\qquad \text{investment of } 6.82\%)
\end{array}
$$

Figure 2
Reinvestment and Sinking
Fund Assumptions

[2] Cash flows reinvested at IRR of 6.82%
[3] Sinking fund earning at IRR of 6.82%

of 15%, yet could normally earn only 7% in its portfolio, a modification to the method of structuring should be used. These modified structuring methods are used to evaluate various structures of the same transaction to achieve the optimal structure. IRR, as a structuring methodology, is appropriate only when the cash flow from the lease can be reinvested at the IRR of that lease. The alternative methods of structuring are presented below and discussed further. Each methodology is dependent on the lessor's reinvestment opportunities (Figure 3).

Figure 3 indicates that a different method of structuring alternative is required for each situation. The reasons for these alternatives need to be developed next. The first to be discussed is the net present value (NPV) methodology. Again, an example is helpful in understanding this method.

NPV METHODOLOGY

Assume a lessor can make the following two investments and the lessor's reinvestment rate is 10%. Which investment should the lessor make?

Year	0	1	2	3	4	
A	($3,000)	$3,585	$3	$3	$18	IRR = 20%
B	($3,000)	$1,072	$1,072	$1,072	$1,072	IRR = 16%

Most lessors would choose Investment A because it has a higher IRR. This is an erroneous conclusion because the lessor cannot reinvest at the 20% rate, but only at the 10% rate. NPV analysis must be used because the reinvestment rate is substantially different from the IRR. Looking at the NPV, the lessor would choose B.

Investment	Net Present Value
A	$276
B	$398

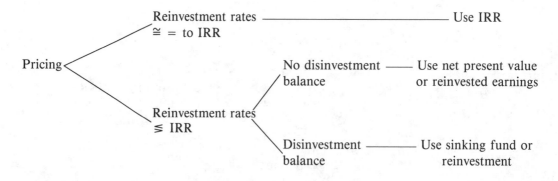

Figure 3
Structuring Methods

When NPV contradicts IRR, then NPV should be selected as NPV considers the reinvestment of cash flows at the true reinvestment opportunity. One must analyze cash flows using the rate at which they can be reinvested. Thus, if the reinvestment opportunity differs materially from the investment's IRR, then an NPV or reinvested earnings (RE) amount should become the structuring objective, as shown in Figure 3.

RE METHODOLOGY

The RE technique is an external rate of return (ERR) method of structuring and is an alternative to NPV structuring. It is expressed as a yield percentage, making it very easy to compare it to targeted ROAs or ROEs. The RE yield is calculated by reinvesting all the cash flows in an investment at the actual reinvestment rate and coming up with a terminal value. This appreciated terminal value is then compared to the original investment and a yield computed. This has been done for both Investment A and B from the previous example, using the 10% reinvestment rate (see Figure 4).

Again, after considering the effect of the actual reinvestment rate on the investment cash flows, B is the preferred investment. To reiterate, any time the reinvestment rate differs substantially from the IRR in the lease, and there is no disinvestment balance, net present value or reinvested earnings structuring should be utilized as a means of assessing various structuring alternatives.

DISINVESTMENT BALANCE

The discussion so far has centered on leases without a disinvestment balance. What about those instances when there is a disinvestment balance in the lease, as shown in Figure 3? First of all, what is a net disinvestment balance? What is its impact on structuring? From Figure 3 it is apparent a disinvestment balance requires a different structuring methodology.

A disinvestment balance occurs when the investment in the lease is recovered completely before the end of the lease, as in Table 2. As can be seen, there is a time (year 2) when the lessor, in essence, owes the investment $372.80. Earnings become negative (an expense). The key question becomes, however, at what rate should the earnings on the disinvestment balance be computed? It can be shown that not recognizing any earnings on the disinvestment will cause the principal balance to remain unamortized (Table 3).

This example serves to highlight the importance of utilizing the proper earnings assumptions on disinvestment (also known as sinking fund) balances. If these assumptions are incorrect, i.e., do not accurately reflect the economic earnings, then principal will not be recovered and the lease company's quality of earnings goal will not be met.

SINKING FUND WITH REINVESTMENT

A structuring technique used in solving the disinvestment balance problem is called sinking fund with reinvestment (SFR). Under this method, both reasonable reinvestment (as discussed earlier) and disinvestment earnings rates are imposed on the analysis.

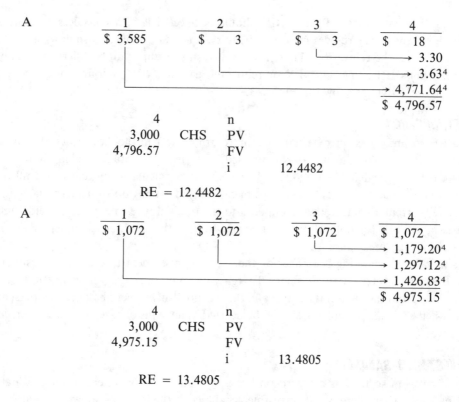

A

	1	2	3	4
	$ 3,585	$ 3	$ 3	$ 18

3.30

3.63[4]

4,771.64[4]

$ 4,796.57

	4		n
	3,000	CHS	PV
	4,796.57		FV
			i 12.4482

RE = 12.4482

A

	1	2	3	4
	$ 1,072	$ 1,072	$ 1,072	$ 1,072

1,179.20[4]

1,297.12[4]

1,426.83[4]

$ 4,975.15

	4		n
	3,000	CHS	PV
	4,975.15		FV
			i 13.4805

RE = 13.4805

Figure 4
RE (Terminal Value) Analysis

Table 2
Investment with a
Disinvestment Balance

Year	Cash Flows	Interest	Principal	Balance
0	($ 2,000)			($ 2,000.00)
1	1,800	$ 706.80	$ 1,093.20	(906.80)
2	1,600	320.40	1,279.60	372.80
3	(800)	(131.80)	(668.20)	(295.40)
4	400	104.60	295.40	0

[4] Reinvested at the reinvestment rate of 10%.

Table 3

Impact of a Zero Earnings Rate
on the Disinvestment Balance

Year	Cash Flows	Interest	Principal	Balance
2	$1,600	$320.40	$1,279.60	$372.80
3	(800)	0	(800.00)	(427.20)
4	400	151.00	249.00	(178.20)

Utilizing the previous example, the SFR yield can be calculated. The reinvestment rate on positive cash flows to be used is 18% and the earnings rate on disinvestment balances will be 12%. The SFR is computed in Figure 5.

SFR structuring simultaneously deals with disinvestment balances as well as reinvestment problems. SFR does not contradict NVP because, under both methods, the reinvestment rates have been considered. Net present value, reinvested earnings and sinking fund with reinvestment are all analytical methods used to evaluate various structures to determine which best meets the objectives of the company, given reinvestment and disinvestment balance parameters. They are used to ensure the quality of a lease company's earnings is maintained. A further discussion of lease yields is contained in Chapter Seven.

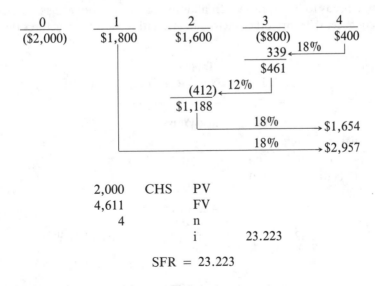

Figure 5

Computation of an SFR Yield

Quantity of Earnings

As was mentioned earlier in the chapter, there are two sides to the earnings issue, quality of earnings and the quantity of earnings. Quantity of earnings implies (1) sufficient cash flow has been generated and (2) the reported accounting profit is adequate, independent of any economic analysis or cash flow sufficiency concerns. A lessor, in structuring the lease, can choose to maximize either cash flow, net present value, yield, accounting income or some other variable. To do so, however, generally requires a trade-off in the other variables not being maximized. This is particularly true with the relationship between yield and cash flow (see Table 4).

In maintaining a comparable yield (15%), Investment A's net cash flow becomes seriously deficient in comparison to that of Investment B. Which investment should the lessor choose, given the above information? It again will depend, as in the other methods of evaluating structuring alternatives, upon the lessor's perception of reinvestment opportunities. If it is expected that reinvestment opportunities will remain at 15%, the lessor would be totally indifferent in regard to Investment A and B, because the net present value is the same (zero) for both.

If, on the other hand, reinvestment opportunities were expected to rise, Investment A would be the preferable investment since the rapid recovery of investment during the first year makes cash available to be reinvested at the expected higher rates. If reinvestment opportunity rates were expected to decline, however, Investment B would be the investment chosen. This is true because the investment in Investment B has been locked in at 15% and will continue to earn at that rate even if rates decline. (Notice Investment B is very similar to a zero coupon bond.)

When a lessor is faced with rising reinvestment opportunities, it should attempt to structure leases that are front-end loaded. In this way it is able to take advantage of those opportunities more quickly. The converse would be true in the case of declining rates. However, a caution about end-loading needs to be expressed. In addition to the additional risk in end-loading due to residual dependence, there are other factors in evaluating various structures that also should

Table 4
Cash Flow Versus Yield Comparison

Cash Flows

	0	1	2	3	4	5
A	($2,000)	$ 2,100	$ 30	$ 30	$ 30	$ 230
B	(2,000)	0	0	0	0	2,011

Analysis

	NPV 15%	IRR	Net Cash Flow
A	$ 0	15%	$ 420
B	$ 0	15%	$ 2,011

be considered. In the above example, a lessor would normally be indifferent in regard to Investments A and B if reinvestment opportunities were constant. Investment B may still be preferable, however, because choosing Investment A would cause the lessor to incur the additional costs and risks of locating four new investments to generate the same cash flow as Investment B. Another factor to be considered is the cash flow requirements of the lessor over the term of the investment, such as working capital needs. Investment B does not provide any interim cash flow.

In discussing cash flow adequacy one question that always arises is what is considered to be adequate cash flow. While the adequacy, or sufficiency, of cash flow must be answered by each lessor on a situation specific basis, a standard cash flow measurement may be developed. This measurement, termed here the standardized investment liquidity index (SLI), is defined as the cash flow an investment would generate (at a given IRR or ERR) in equal installments over the full term of that investment. Utilizing the previous $2,000 investment, the standardized investment liquidity index can be computed as follows:

0	1	2	3	4	5
($2,000)	$ 597	$ 597	$ 597	$ 597	$ 597

$$5 \times \$597 = \begin{array}{r} \$\ 2,985 \\ -2,000 \\ \hline \$\ \ \ \ 985 \end{array} \text{ is the standardized cash flow}$$

The SLIs on Investments A and B from the previous examples are then computed:

$$A \quad \frac{\$\ \ \ 420}{\$\ \ \ 985} = .43$$

$$B \quad \frac{\$\ 2,022}{\$\ \ \ 985} = 2.05$$

Purely in relation to the standard cash flow measure, Investment B should be selected as clearly being in excess of the standard and A as being less than the standard.

Of course, the next logical question regarding cash flow that is always asked is how to improve cash flow. The answer, like the answer so many times before, depends on the reinvestment rate. Cash flow may be enhanced by the following methods:

1. When reinvestment opportunities approximate the IRR
   a. If the IRR or ERR remains constant, end-loading will accomplish this objective. Emphasizing residuals or renewals, step-up leases and reducing front-end costs such as advance payments, closing fees, etc., are examples of methods to be used. Investment B in the previous example is an excellent example of cash flow enhancement
   b. If the IRR or ERR increases, cash flow should be added pro rata over the lease term to correspond with those increases
2. When reinvestment opportunities are greater or less than the IRR

a. If there is not a disinvestment balance, the same technique as method 1 should be used

b. If there is a disinvestment balance, method 1(a) may be used, or less debt should be used in structuring or the debt should be structured so that it is paid off more rapidly.

So far, the discussion regarding the quantity of earnings has centered on cash flow. The sufficiency of accounting earnings is the other element implied in adequate earnings quantity. Accounting earnings, and the sufficiency thereof, must be considered separately, for accounting earnings frequently do not reflect accurately an investment's true economics. There are many reasons for these differences, including Investment Tax Credit (ITC) flow-through accounting, deferred taxes, the use of implicit rates and residual understatement, to name but a few. The sufficiency of accounting earnings is one more decision that management must make based upon the lease company's established criteria.

PRETAX TARGETED YIELD STRUCTURING

There are probably as many ways to structure a lease as there are lease companies. These methods range from lease payment tables to sophisticated software, and utilize targeted yields ranging from pretax ROAs to after-tax ROEs. This section focuses on manual structuring using a targeted pretax ROA.

While a computer can certainly be used to structure any of the examples given in this section, there are important reasons for presenting them in the manner in which they are shown. It is just not good enough to be able to input and push buttons. To effectively structure, one must understand why a variable affects the pricing the way it does, how the payment is computed and how to alter it. There are also many lessors who price on a manual (as opposed to computer) basis. To those in the latter category, these examples will prove to be especially valuable.

Introductory Examples

A building block approach will be used to illustrate the structuring process beginning first with simple examples and then adding complexity. Before beginning, however, the assumptions to be used must be clarified. The following assumptions form the base case for the examples presented:

Equipment cost: $80,000
Annual pretax yield: 11%
Term: 48 months
Refundable security deposit: $3,500
Purchase option: $19,000
Initial direct costs: $1,500

As was discussed earlier in the chapter, the goal of structuring is to obtain a return of principal and a reasonable return on that principal. Therefore, it is imperative to consider all the cash flows in the transaction. This concept is illustrated throughout the examples. The examples themselves progress from simple structures that can be done using the white keyboard of the HP-12C to more complex structures.

EXAMPLE 1

Using the base case, structure a level payment lease for 48 months, with payments in arrears.

SOLUTION

The key to successful structuring is identifying the cash flows, not only as to their dollar amounts, but also as to the timing of the flows. When beginning to structure, the most effective means to achieve this is through use of a timeline. A timeline not only serves to organize the flows and place them in the proper period, but also is a graphic illustration of how those flows occur (see Figure 6). In this way, none is forgotten and proper timing is achieved.

Once the known cash flows have been identified, it becomes a simple matter of putting them in the proper registers in the HP-12C. The white keyboard may be used in this example because the payment stream is level and does not contain any multiple advance payments. With the calculator in the "END" mode:

78,000	CHS	PV	
15,500		FV	
48		n	
11	g	12 ÷	
		PMT	1,757.43

If it was required that this lease be structured with one payment in advance, then the above keystrokes would be the same except the calculator needs to be put in the "BEGIN" mode. Without clearing the registers:

g	BEG	
	PMT	1,741.47

With the lessons of Example 1 in mind, another example is presented.

	Unknown lease payments		
0			48
Time 0			Month 48
Cost	($ 80,000)	Residual	$ 19,000
Refundable security deposit	3,500	Refundable security deposit	(3,500)
Initial direct costs	(1,500)		
	($ 78,000)		$ 15,500

Figure 6
Timeline of Example 1 Cash Flows

EXAMPLE 2

Using the following assumptions, structure a level payment lease, with payments in advance:

Equipment cost: $130,000
Annual pretax yield: 12%
Term: 60 months
Refundable security deposit: $7,200
Purchase option: $20,000

SOLUTION

The solution steps are shown in Figure 7. It can be seen from the previous two examples that transactions with level payment streams and no more than one payment in advance can be easily structured using the white keyboard of the HP-12C. Many lessors find these to be the most common type of transactions encountered. Any different kind of structure, however, will require an alternative method.

One of the benefits of leasing, of course, is the creativity in structuring it allows. It is this creativity that necessitates using a method other than the white keyboard when structuring, one that will solve for a payment when there are multiple advance payments, skips, steps, etc. This method, using a pretax targeted yield, is discussed next.

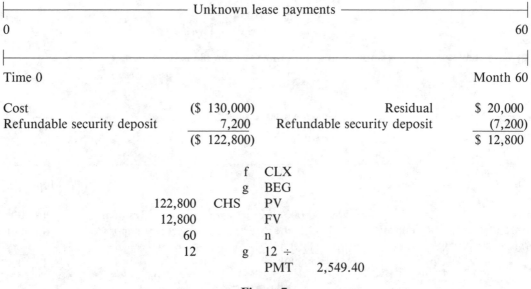

	Time 0			Month 60
Cost	($ 130,000)		Residual	$ 20,000
Refundable security deposit	7,200	Refundable security deposit	(7,200)
	($ 122,800)			$ 12,800

	f	CLX	
	g	BEG	
122,800	CHS	PV	
12,800		FV	
60		n	
12	g	12 ÷	
		PMT	2,549.40

Figure 7
Timeline of Example 2 Cash Flows

Structuring Steps

A lessor can manually structure any lease, on a pretax basis, by following three basic steps. These steps are followed whether the lease is a simple one with even payments or a complex multilevel skipped payment lease.

STEP ONE

Identify and present value all known cash flows in the transaction, using the targeted pretax yield as the discount rate. This step is very similar to the identification of all known cash flows, which was done in the previous two examples. Using this method, however, instead of leaving future events, such as the residual, at their future values, those future events will be present valued at the pretax targeted yield. These present value amounts then will be added or deducted, just as any other cash flow, from the initial net investment to be recovered through the lease payment.

This step can be illustrated using the numbers in Example 1. The net cash flow at inception in this example, without regard to future events, was $78,000. The future cash flow of $15,500 must now be present valued, at 11%, and added to the inception cash flow amount.

15,500		FV	
48		n	
11	g	12 ÷	
		PV	10,002.59

The present value of the residual events is now added to the other costs:

($ 78,000.00)	Net cash flow at inception
+ 10,002.59	Present value of future events
($ 67,997.41)	Net investment at time 0

All known cash flows now have been identified and present valued at the pretax targeted yield and the first step completed. The resultant $67,997.41 net investment is the amount of principal to be recovered through the lease payment at the given pretax return of 11%.

STEP TWO

Determine the present value of the payment stream, using the targeted pretax yield as the discount rate, and letting each payment equal one dollar. This step allows the lessor to see how much principal, on a present value basis, each dollar component of the payment will recover over the term. The amount of principal each one dollar of payment will recover can be thought of as an investment recovery unit (IRU). By knowing the amount of net investment to be recovered through the payment, as calculated in Step One, the lessor can compute the number of IRUs it will take to recover that net investment. Following the logical progression, since each IRU represents the amount of net investment to be recovered by a payment of one dollar over the lease term, the number of IRUs necessary to recover the lessor's net investment will represent the dollar amount of the payment the lessor is seeking. This concept is more easily understood when graphically illustrated.

If an IRU is equal to the present value of one dollar at the targeted yield (the amount of investment one dollar of payment over the lease term will recover at the targeted yield)

then $\dfrac{\text{NET INVESTMENT}}{\text{IRU}}$ will equal the desired payment.

Consider the following illustration:

A payment stream of one dollar per month for 36 months will recover, at 14%, $29.2589 of investment.

$$
\begin{array}{lll}
1 & & \text{PMT} \\
14 & g & 12 \div \\
36 & & \text{n} \\
& & \text{PV} \quad 29.2589
\end{array}
$$

If a lessor wanted to recover $29.2589 of investment over 36 months at 14%, what would the payment be? One dollar, of course, since it was just shown that one dollar of payment will recover $29.2589 of investment over 36 months at 14%. The $29.2589 represents one IRU. Alternately,

$$\frac{\$29.2589}{29.2589\ (\text{IRU})} = \$1\ (\text{payment})$$

If a lessor wanted to recover $58.5178 of investment over 36 months at 14%, what would the payment be?

$$\frac{\$58.5178}{29.2589\ (\text{IRU})} = \$2\ (\text{payment})$$

This concept can be applied to all net investments and payment structures, no matter how complex. Using the assumptions in Example 1 of a 48-month lease with level payments in arrears, at 11%, the IRU is calculated as follows:

$$
\begin{array}{lll}
 & g & \text{END} \\
1 & & \text{PMT} \\
11 & g & 12 \div \\
48 & & \text{n} \\
& & \text{PV} \quad 38.6914
\end{array}
$$

STEP THREE

Divide the net investment (from Step One) by the IRU (from Step Two). This, the third and last step, results in the pretax payment to be charged to the lessee. The logic behind this step should be apparent after carefully studying Steps One and Two. In Step One, the lessor determines the total net investment to be recovered through the payment, at a given rate and term. Step Two allows the lessor to determine exactly how much of that net investment will be recovered by a payment of one dollar over the lease term.

Alternatively, this concept can be viewed from an IRU viewpoint. The lessor determines how many IRUs are necessary to recover the net investment. Since an IRU is the present value of a payment of one dollar, the number of IRUs equals the dollar amount of the payment.

Given that the IRU for the lease in Example 1 is 38.6914, how many IRUs will it take to recover the net investment of $67,997.41 (also from Example 1)?

$$\frac{\$67,997.41 \quad \text{(Step One)}}{38.6914 \quad \text{(Step Two)}} = 1,757.43 \text{ IRUs}$$

An IRU, by definition, is equal to one dollar of payment over the lease term at the targeted yield; therefore, the 1,775.22 IRUs must be multiplied by the one dollar each IRU represents. This will equal the payment in dollars.

$$1,757.43 \times \$1 = \$1,757.43 \text{ monthly payment}$$

Notice this payment is exactly equal to the payment calculated in Example 1, using the white keyboard. This should provide confidence in the accuracy of this method. More complex transactions now can be structured.

If the answers are the same, though, why even bother to use this longer method? Why not go directly to the white keyboard? This is a valid question. The response to it lies in the complexity involved with each transaction. For those transactions involving level payments with no more than one advance payment, the white keyboard is adequate, but to manually structure a lease with uneven cash flows and/or multiple advance payments requires following the three steps described above.

Pretax Structuring Example

Another example is presented in order to illustrate all three pretax structuring steps together.

EXAMPLE 3

Structure a lease with multiple advance payments using the following assumptions:

Equipment cost: $37,000
Annual pretax yield: 15%
Refundable security deposit: $1,400
Purchase option: $4,600
Term: 54 months with three payments in advance

SOLUTION

The three steps in structuring the pretax payment are completed, in order.

Step One

Identify and present value all known cash flows in the transaction, using the targeted pretax yield as the discount rate.

The net residual proceeds first must be calculated and present valued since all the other cash flows are already stated at their present values:

Residual proceeds

Purchase option	$ 4,600
Refundable security deposit	(1,400)
Net residual proceeds	$ 3,200

3,200		FV	
54		n	
15	g	12 ÷	
		PV	− 1,636

All cash flows (at their present value) now have been identified in order to calculate the net investment in the lease at its inception:

Equipment cost	($ 37,000)
Refundable security deposit	1,400
Net residual proceeds	1,636
Net investment	($ 33,964)

Step Two

Determine the present value of the payment stream, using the targeted pretax yield as the discount rate and letting each payment equal one dollar.

In analyzing the payment stream, it can be seen that three payments will occur at inception (time "0"), followed by 51 remaining payments. Assigning each payment a value of one dollar, and utilizing the 15% pretax yield:

15	g	12 ÷	
3	g	CF_o	
1	g	CF_j	
51	g	N_j	
	f	NPV	40.5436

For every dollar of payment over the lease term, $40.5436 of net investment will be recovered.

Step Three

Divide the net investment (Step One) by the IRUs (Step Two).

The number of IRUs necessary to recover the net investment is equal to the desired payment.

$$\frac{\$33,964}{40.5436} = \$837.72$$

Thus, $837.72 is the payment necessary to provide the lessor with both the return of principal plus a 15% return on the principal. The accuracy of this payment may be verified by determining the IRR of all the cash flows in the lease. If this IRR or pretax yield equals 15%, the lease has been properly structured to provide a 15% return. Utilizing the cash flows in Figure 8, and the HP-12C, the IRR of 15% can be calculated, thereby proving the lease has been structured correctly.

33,086.84	CHS	g	CF_o	
837.72		g	CF_j	
51		g	N_j	
0		g	CF_j	
2		g	N_j	
3,200		g	CF_j	
		f	IRR	1.25
12			x	15.00

This structuring method can be used to structure any type of lease. The utility of the method is it allows the lessor total freedom and creativity in structuring the payment stream to meet the lessee's requirements. It is the basis for the after-tax structuring method discussed in this chapter and also for the specialty structuring topics discussed in Chapter Nine.

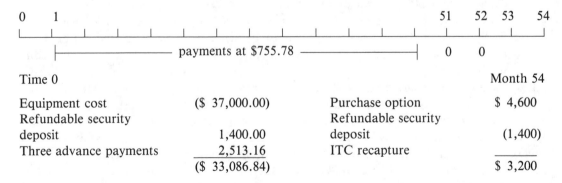

Time 0		Month 54	
Equipment cost	($ 37,000.00)	Purchase option	$ 4,600
Refundable security deposit	1,400.00	Refundable security deposit	(1,400)
Three advance payments	2,513.16	ITC recapture	
	($ 33,086.84)		$ 3,200

Figure 8
Identification of Cash Flows

PRETAX VERSUS AFTER-TAX STRUCTURING

All of the structuring examples to this point have been on a pretax targeted yield basis. Pretax structuring is widely used, relatively uncomplicated and easy to calculate and, for those companies who do not pay taxes, entirely accurate. For those lessors who do pay taxes, however, pretax structuring is a less accurate, although acceptable, method of pricing. Since taxes do play such a significant role in business, after-tax structuring, as it considers taxes, is a more accurate and, therefore, preferable level at which to structure.

Even after-tax structuring can be further stratified into a return on assets or return on equity structuring. ROE structuring, which is discussed in Chapter Nine, is the most sophisticated method of structuring. However, due to its sophistication and accuracy, it is the most complex and difficult to use. For this reason, ROE is not used on a widespread basis for pricing purposes. Before understanding any form of after-tax structuring, it is necessary to identify the conceptual differences between the pretax and after-tax structuring methodologies.

As the components included in pretax structuring have been illustrated previously, only those items impacting after-tax structuring now need to be identified. After-tax structuring includes the impact of:

1. Tax depreciation: The benefits of tax depreciation also must be included. Tax depreciation is not included in pretax structuring

2. Tax timing: The impact of an entity's method of paying taxes is included in after-tax structuring. The date the transaction is structured, the dates estimated taxes are remitted, the method of estimation, cash versus accrual taxpayer, etc., are all considered

3. Tax effect: All pretax cash flows are shown net of taxes, or the related taxes are shown separately. A cash outflow, such as interest expense for example, enters into the calculation at the net amount after any related tax benefits have been recognized. Cash inflows, conversely, are shown after any taxes paid on the inflow have been deducted

4. Targeted rate: The targeted yield used when structuring the payment must be on an after-tax basis, to be consistent with the after-tax basis of the cash flows. The development of targeted yields and hurdle rates is discussed in Chapter Ten

5. ITC: Although pretax structuring also may include ITC, the effect of any form of tax credit, when and if available, always must be included when calculating an after-tax payment. This would include also any recapture of ITC, or any other available credit, for that matter.

All of the above, plus any other tax benefits/constraints such as gross profit deferral or the alternative minimum tax, are included when structuring on an after-tax basis.

An ancillary aspect of after-tax structuring is the gross-up of an after-tax rate for pricing purposes. A company often will compute a targeted after-tax yield and then convert it to a pretax yield (sometimes referred to as "grossing up"). This pretax yield then is used by the marketing personnel when pricing transactions. There are many gross-up approximations, but these are sometimes materially at variance with the true pretax yield. The most common method is to simply divide the after-tax rate by one minus the tax rate. Thus, a 7% after-tax return would be converted to a pretax return as follows, assuming a 34% tax rate:

$$\frac{.07}{(1 - .34)} = 10.61 \text{ pretax equivalent}$$

There is a flaw in this method of conversion, however, and that is its failure to recognize that taxes on cashflows received are paid on a different basis than receipt of those cash flows. In short, the above method does not recognize the timing of tax payments. To achieve an accurate conversion of an after-tax to a pretax yield, one must incorporate the timing of the tax payments into the tax rate, developing, in essence, a timing effected rate. Once this is accomplished, the conversion would be:

$$\frac{\text{after-tax rate}}{(1 - t_e)} = \text{pretax equivalent, where } t_e \text{ equals the timing effected tax rate}$$

A full discussion and example of an accurate conversion of an after-tax yield to its pretax equivalent can be found in Chapter Seven.

QUANTIFICATION OF STRUCTURING VARIABLES

After-tax structuring is a more accurate and sophisticated method of structuring, and, as a result, is much more complex. While not for every lease company, the structuring of leases on an after-tax basis allows a company to be very competitive in its pricing and still know it is earning the return necessary to maintain growth. The inclusion of tax benefits in pricing is one of the reasons negative running rates are sometimes quoted.

The complexity involved in the pricing of a transaction on an after-tax basis necessitates understanding the impact of numerous variables beyond those discussed in the pretax section. For their effects to be recognized in the pricing of the lease payment, these variables must somehow be quantified, shown after-tax, put on a present value basis and included in the computation of the net investment at inception. The following variables are discussed in detail in this section:

1. Nominal versus effective rates
2. Budgeted versus incremental taxpayer
3. Present value of the tax effects of a lease on a given structuring (inception) date
4. Gross profit tax deferral
5. ITC carryforward issues
6. Miscellaneous variables.

Nominal Versus Effective Rates

More than 95% of the leases being written today incorporate monthly compounding of the yield. This is not to say all of these leases have monthly payments. Certainly there are quarterly, semiannual and annual payments being offered. The point is that although the payments may be on one of those bases, the yield still is being compounded monthly. When the cash flows or benefits occur on an other than monthly basis, an effective rate must be computed. First of all, what is an effective yield?

A nominal yield is the rate stated in the instrument. If the bank advertises a 5% earning on savings, 5% is the stated or nominal rate. An effective rate, on the other hand, includes the effects of any compounding. Since the interest earnings are also earning, in addition to the principal, the effective rate will always be higher. Using the same bank example, if the nominal 5% rate were to be compounded monthly, the effective rate would be 5.12%. The effective rate is higher due to the monthly compounding.

An annual effective rate is most commonly used in structuring to recognize the present value of tax depreciation. Since the allowable percentages are stated at an annual amount, the annual discount rate used must reflect monthly compounding. A monthly compounded annual effective rate accomplishes this. An annual effective rate can be computed a number of ways.

1. With a formula:

$$\left(1 + \frac{\left(\frac{i}{n}\right)}{100}\right)^n \qquad \text{where, i is the annual nominal rate and}$$
n is the number of compounding periods

Using the 5% bank example:

$$\left(1 + \frac{\left(\frac{5}{12}\right)}{100}\right)^{12} \quad =$$

$$(1.004167)^{12} \quad = 1.0512$$

$$(1.0512 - 1) = .0512 \text{ or } 5.12\%$$

The keystrokes to accomplish the above formula are as follows:

1	ENTER
5	ENTER
12	ENTER
100	x ÷ +
12	Y^x
1	— .0512, or 5.12%

2. The above method is a mathematical approach. An approach that makes more conceptual sense to most people is to use the white keyboard. Using this method, the future value of one dollar invested at the nominal rate for 12 months is computed. This is appropriate, for the effective growth rate (or earnings) is nothing more than the appreciated value (future value) of an investment less the original investment. To wit:

1	CHS	PV	(the original investment)
12		n	(the number of compounding periods)
5	g	12 ÷	(the nominal rate)
FV	g	1.0512	(the appreciated value)
1		−	(less the original investment)
		.0512, or 5.12%	

Both of these methods result in exactly the same answer: which to use depends on the individual lessor's discretion.

Effective rates have efficacy beyond finding the present value of tax benefits. They also can be used to compute nonmonthly payments, such as quarterly payments, and still maintain a monthly compounded yield. In the case of quarterly payments, a quarterly effective rate (with monthly compounding) must be computed. Using the methods previously discussed and the 5% bank example, the quarterly effective rate can be computed.

1. Formula:

$$\sqrt[4]{(1.004167)^{12}} \quad = \quad \text{(to reflect quarterly compounding)}$$

$$(1.004167)^3 \quad = \quad 1.0126$$

This formula compounds monthly the nominal monthly rate and then removes the subsequent quarterly compounding so there is not double compounding.

1.004167	ENTER
3	Y^x
1	−
	.0126, or 1.26%

2. White keyboard:

1		PV	(the original investment)
3		n	(the number of compounding periods)
5	g	12 ÷	(the nominal rate)
FV		1.0126	(the appreciated value)
1		−	(less the original investment)
		.0126, or 1.26%	

Effective rates are used extensively throughout the remainder of the structuring chapters.

Budgeted Versus Incremental Taxpayer

Whether or not a lease has been budgeted or is incremental will affect the timing, and, hence, the value of tax benefits. This necessarily impacts the structuring process.

Corporations pay taxes differently than most individuals. A corporation is allowed to estimate all its revenues and expenses for the coming year in arriving at what is termed its budgeted taxable income. Taxes must be computed on this estimated taxable income. These estimated taxes are then remitted over the five estimated tax remittance dates. For a calendar year taxpayer, these estimated rates will be paid on the following dates in accordance with the stated percentages:

April 15	.225	
June 15	.225	
September 15	.225	} 90%
December 15	.225	
March 15	.100	

Notice 90% of the taxes are paid prior to March 15. The tax benefits associated with a budgeted lease will be received over the five estimated payment dates, irrespective of when during the year it is funded. Conversely, any tax liabilities will be likewise recognized.

If a lease is not included in the budgeted tax remittances, it is termed an incremental lease. As such the tax benefits or liabilities will be recognized differently than for a budgeted lease. An incremental lease receives its tax benefits in a manner such that 90% of the tax benefits are recognized over the remaining tax remittance dates, and the balance of 10% on March 15 of the next year. (This is very similar in concept to a budgeted lease.) Thus, an incremental lease structured June 1 will receive its tax benefits as follows:

June 15	.30	
September 15	.30	} 90%
December 15	.30	
March 15	.10	

A fiscal year corporation remits taxes in the same sequence, except the first remittance date is 3.5 months into its fiscal year. Because of the timing of when tax benefits are recognized, a budgeted lease should be structured differently than an incremental lease.

Present Value of the Tax Effects of a Lease

When a lease is structured will impact the value of the tax benefits. Certainly, the tax benefits for a budgeted lease funded in December are worth more than the tax benefits of a lease funded in March. This is due to the fact that the tax benefits, and associated cash savings, are realized much earlier, and, hence, earn longer, for the lease written in December. These tax savings then can be reinvested for a period of time before any funds need to be expended for the lease. Naturally, the savings are invested for a longer period for a December lease than a March lease; thus, the tax benefits are inherently worth more. This phenomenon is seen each year at year-end when lease rates drop. While not the sole reason, it is certainly a contributing factor.

The impact of the structuring date on tax benefits can be quantified. Once quantified, it then can be incorporated into the structuring computation. The process by which this timing effect is quantified is to present value the tax benefits received on each remittance date to the date on which the lease is structured.

EXAMPLE 4

Assuming a company's monthly nominal cost of capital is 1% per month, calculate the value of the tax benefits for a lease that has a December 31 inception date, is part of the annual estimated tax budget and has $1,000 of after-tax benefits associated with it.

SOLUTION

In order to determine how much the after-tax benefits are actually worth (due to the December 31 structure date), the tax benefit on each of the remittance dates must be present valued to December 31, the inception date, as in Figure 9.

The present and future values of the estimated quarterly tax remittance dates are then calculated as in Table 5. The $1,000 of tax benefits are actually worth $1,041.55, due to this budgeted lease being structured on December 31.

Thus, tax benefits or liabilities in a lease structured on December 31 would be worth 104.2% of face value ($1,041.55 ÷ $1,000). This factor is referred to as the intraperiod present value factor (IPVF), and is utilized heavily throughout after-tax structuring. Intuitively, tax benefits from a lease structured in December, such as depreciation, should be worth more than face value since 90% of the lease value has been received and invested beginning in April of the current year. This concept of the IPVF must be applied to both tax benefits and liabilities.

Gross Profit Tax Deferral

If a manufacturing parent sells its products to its captive subsidiary, a tax benefit, gross profit deferral, is created. This benefit should be incorporated into the captive pricing. To amplify this concept, any gain realized by the parent on the sale of property to its captive lessor, in a deferred intercompany transaction, is not remitted by the parent at the time of sale. Instead, it is taken into income in proportion to the cost recovery on the financial instrument being recognized by the captive. It can be seen that the benefit of this tax deferral method is in receiving cash proceeds through match funding, yet paying taxes on those proceeds over the deferral period. (Gross profit deferral is further discussed and illustrated in Chapters Four and Seventeen.)

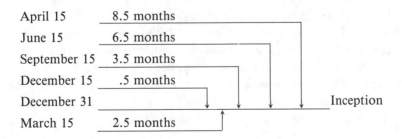

April 15	8.5 months
June 15	6.5 months
September 15	3.5 months
December 15	.5 months
December 31	Inception
March 15	2.5 months

Figure 9
Required Months of Appreciation and Discounting

Table 5
Inception Value of Tax Benefits

Date	Benefit Received	Present/Future Value of Benefit at Inception
April 15	$1,000 × .225 = $225	$ 244.86[5]
June 15	$1,000 × .225 = $225	240.04
September 15	$1,000 × .225 = $225	232.98
December 15	$1,000 × .225 = $225	226.13
March 15	$1,000 × .100 = $100	97.54
Total		$1,041.55

The benefit from gross profit tax deferral, which represents a reduction in taxes paid, then would be included in the calculation of the net investment at time 0 for purposes of computing the lease payment. Structuring to incorporate gross profit tax deferral is illustrated in Chapter Nine.

Investment Tax Credit Carryforward Issues

A point needs to be made regarding ITC carryforwards, which many lease companies have. This issue is the phenomenon known as ITC displacement. ITC displacement refers to the effect on ITC utilization that incremental expenses and revenues will have for a company with both an ITC carryforward and taxable income. Suppose a lessor had $20,000 of taxable income before entering the next lease, and the Modified Accelerated Cost Recovery System (MACRS) depreciation associated with the new lease will create $3,500 of additional deductions. Additionally, the lessor is in an ITC carryforward position that will reverse in 3 years, at which time the lessor will be able to fully utilize ITC. The effect of the MACRS depreciation as it relates to the new lease can be quantified as in Table 6.

Thus, the MACRS depreciation associated with the new lease would cause a reduction of taxes of $1,190 ($3,500 x 34%), but it would also impair the lessor's ability to use ITC by $893. The ITC impairment of $893 will be lost today, but will be added to the carryforward to be realized in the third year. The timing of these two differences causes an additional cost to the lessor due to the fact that recognition of ITC has been pushed to the future. This additional cost is quantified as follows using an 8% discount rate and the $893 computed in Table 6:

---

[5]

	225	PV
	1	i
	8.5	n
	FV	− 244.86

Table 6

ITC Displacement

	Before New Lease	After New Lease	Change
Prior taxable income	$ 20,000	$ 20,000	$ 0
Additional MACRS deduction	0	3,500	(3,500)
Subsequent taxable income	$ 20,000	$ 16,500	$ (3,500)
Taxes payable 34%	$ 6,800	$ 5,610	$ 1,190
Utilizable ITC	$ (5,100)	$ (4,207)	$ 893

8			i
893	CHS	g	CF_o
0		g	CF_j
2		g	N_j
893		g	CF_j
		f	NPV −184

The operating cost relating to the ITC pushed to the future due to the additional MACRS deduction will enter into the calculation of the net investment at time 0.

Miscellaneous Variables

Before finishing up this section on quantifying structuring variables, two other points need to be made. One is the impact of refundable security deposits, which are nontaxable. Refundable security deposits are included, therefore, at face value. The other issue is the Internal Revenue Service (IRS) uneven rent tests for guideline leases, and the Internal Revenue Code §467 uneven rent tests.

Creative structuring often results in an uneven rental stream, such as in a step-up or step-down pattern. The IRS has developed rules that are intended to preclude tax avoidance in structuring these kinds of leases. The IRS ordinarily will not raise any question about prepaid or deferred rent if the uneven rents in the payment stream meet either of two tests. These tests are sometimes referred to as the 10% tests and are discussed in Chapter Four, as are the §467 tests. When structuring tax leases, these criteria must be kept in mind. Uneven rent structuring is discussed more fully in Chapter Nine.

AFTER-TAX TARGETED YIELD STRUCTURING

Now that pretax structuring and the necessary preliminary steps have been discussed and explored, the next step is to price a lease on an after-tax basis. For purposes of illustration, and cementing conceptual understanding of this complex process, the examples given are computed manually using the HP-12C. While, as mentioned earlier, a computer certainly can be used to structure any lease, it is as important to know why a pricing variable affects a payment as it does, as it is to know how to run software.

Structuring Steps

After-tax structuring is predicated on the basic principles found in pretax structuring. Granted, there are more variables and a few special steps, but the core concept is exactly the same. In order to structure any lease to an after-tax targeted yield using the HP-12C, there are five steps that must be followed.

STEP ONE

Identify and present value all known cash flows in the transaction, including tax benefits, using the required after-tax IRR as the discount rate. This step is the same as Step One in pretax structuring. The only differences are the discount rate and the added and different nature of the variables, such as after-tax residuals, the effect of gross profit tax deferral, G & A expenses, etc.

STEP TWO

Determine the present value of the payment stream, using the targeted after-tax IRR as the discount rate, and letting each payment equal one dollar. This step is exactly equal to Step Two in pretax structuring.

STEP THREE

Determine the present value of the annual tax liabilities associated with the one dollar lease payments determined in Step Two. After computing the present value of the lease stream, it is necessary to compute the taxes on those payments being received, as they will generate a tax liability. This step is done in the same manner as Step Two, by letting one dollar equal the payment.

Taxes are paid on an annual basis over the five estimated payment dates; therefore, the present value of the payment stream will be calculated on an annual basis. This present value will then be multiplied by the tax rate to arrive at the associated taxes. The appropriate IPVF is applied to the present value of the taxes to reflect the five tax payment dates. By using this method of allocating the taxes on the payments to the tax year in which they are paid, the proper timing of the tax remittances is recognized. An annual effective rate must be utilized as a discount rate when computing the present value of the taxes. An example will help clarify this step.

The assumptions are for a lease structured on June 1, with two payments in advance, a 48-month term, an annual effective, after-tax discount rate of 9%, a 99.03 IPVF and a 34% tax rate. To calculate the taxes due on this payment stream, the payments must first be placed into the tax years in which they are taxed. Notice this 48-month lease spans five tax years:

Year	Number of Payments	
1	8	(six regular plus two advance payments)
2	12	
3	12	
4	12	
5	4	
Total	48	

The present value of the annual taxable income (payments) is computed and then multiplied by the tax rate to arrive at the taxes due. The IPVF is multiplied by the present value of the taxes to reflect the five estimated payment dates. The first year payments are placed at time 0 because the IPVF brings all payments to time 0.

9		i	
8	g	CF_o	
12	g	CF_j	
3	g	N_j	
4	g	CF_j	
	f	NPV	41.2092
.34	$\times$		14.0111
.9903	$\times$		13.8752

The total of 13.8752 represents the present value of the taxes payable on a payment stream of 48 months, with two in advance, discounted at an annual effective rate of 9%.

STEP FOUR
Deduct the results of Step Three from Step Two. This step puts the IRU on an after-tax basis so it can be applied to the after-tax net investment to arrive at the payment.

STEP FIVE
Divide the after-tax net investment (from Step One) by the after-tax IRU (from Step Four). This step results in the pretax payment computed on an after-tax basis. The logic behind this step is, again, exactly the same as Step Three in the pretax structuring section. It should be intuitively apparent that by reducing the IRU by the amount of taxes, the amount of the payment will be larger, so as to allow payment of the taxes, yet still return the lessor's targeted after-tax yield.

After-tax Structuring Example
The steps to be followed in structuring on an after-tax basis now have been explained. An example of how these steps are actually applied in structuring a lease will reinforce these concepts.

EXAMPLE 5
Structure a lease using the following assumptions:

Equipment cost: $100,000 (purchased June 1)

Refundable security deposit: $1,500

Tax depreciation: 5-year MACRS equipment placed in service June 1,
of a calendar year accrual basis taxpayer

Purchase option: $15,000, expected to be exercised after a 48-month
noncancellable lease term, which has two monthly rentals paid in advance

Pretax initial direct costs: $2,500

Incremental federal tax rate: 34%

Annual nominal after-tax yield required by the lessor: 8.04%
(.67% per month or 8.343% annual effective)

Monthly G & A expenses: $50, expected to increase due to
inflation at 1/2% each month throughout the lease. The lease is
considered part of the annual tax budget and not incremental.
The lessor currently can use all tax benefits.

SOLUTION

Before the five after-tax structuring steps can be completed, it is necessary to complete certain preliminary computations. The results of these computations then are used in the structuring steps.

Preliminary Computations

1. Convert the annual nominal IRR to its monthly nominal rate as well as its annual effective equivalent.
   (a) Monthly nominal: 8.04 ÷ 12 = .67%/month
   (b) Annual effective

$$\left(1 + \frac{.67}{100}\right)^{12}$$

   1.0067 ENTER 12y^x = 1.08343
   (Subtract one and move decimal two
   places to the right)

   8.343% annual effective

2. Compute the IPVF for a budgeted lease structured June 1 as in Table 7. Therefore, tax benefits or liabilities are worth 98.061% of face value for a lease structured on June 1.

Step One

Present value, at the required after-tax IRR, all known cash flows.
1. All the known cash flows must be identified and listed

Table 7
IPVF Computation

Remittance Date	Required Remittance %	Months From Inception	Present or Future Value of Quarterly % (.67% Discount Rate)
April 15	22.5%	−1½	.22727
June 1		0	0
June 15	22.5	+ ½	.22425[6]
Sept 15	22.5	+3½	.21980
Dec 15	22.5	+6½	.21544
Mar 15	10.0	+9½	.09385
			.98061

Equipment cost
Initial direct costs (after-tax)
Refundable security deposit
Residual value (net of taxes and deposit refund)
MACRS tax benefits
G & A costs

Net inception outflow

2. The present value of the equipment cost must be determined
   (a) Given at $100,000
   (b) Had the equipment been paid for at a later date (takedown date), present valuing would have been required
3. Any initial direct costs should be identified and expressed at their after-tax equivalent
   (a) After-tax conversion formula:
       Expense $\times [1 - (\text{tax rate} \times \text{IPVF})]$ = after-tax cost
   (b) $2,500 \times [1 - (.34 \times .98061)] = \$1,666.48$
4. The impact of the refundable security deposit must be identified
   (a) Given at $1,500, and is not adjusted for tax benefits since it is not tax deductible
   (b) Its refund will be considered as part of the net residual yet to be calculated
5. The residual value (net of taxes and the deposit refund) must be calculated and then present valued, as in Table 8. The present value of the net residual is then computed.

---

[6]

.67		i	
.225	CHS	FV	
.50		n	
		PV	.22425

.67		i	
48		n	
12,339.74	CHS	FV	
		PV	8,955.77

6. The value of the MACRS tax benefit is calculated

8.343		i
.20	g	CF_o
.32	g	CF_j
.192	g	CF_j
.1152	g	CF_j
.0576	g	CF_j
	f	NPV .7913
100,000	x	79,131.45 (equipment cost)
.34	x	26,904.69 (tax rate)
.98061	x	26,383.01 (IPVF)

The present value of the MACRS benfits is $26,383.01

7. G & A expenses must be converted to an after-tax basis and then present valued, incorporating the increasing nature of these costs

   (a) Convert the $50 G & A expense to its after-tax equivalent.

   $$\$50 \times [1 - (.34 \times .98061)] = \$33.33$$

   (b) Compute the present value of a growing annuity as follows:

		g	END	(months)
48			n	
1.005			ENTER	(enter 1 plus the decimal equivalent of the G & A growth rate)
1.0067	%	i	CLX	(enter 1 plus the discount rate's decimal equivalent)
33.33	X ≤ Y		÷	(enter the beginning G & A after-tax)
	PMT		PV	
	CHS		1,587.94	(present value of after-tax G & A expenses)

8. A summary of the present value of all known cash flows is as follows:

($ 100,000.00)	Equipment cost
(1,666.48)	Initial direct costs (after-tax)
1,500.00	Refundable security deposit
8,955.77	Residual value (net)
26,383.01	MACRS tax benefits
(1,587.94)	G & A costs
($ 66,415.64)	

Table 8
Calculation of Net Residual Proceeds

	Step	Amount
	Salvage proceeds	$ 15,000.00
−	Remaining tax basis	(11,520.00)
	(.1152 × 100,000)	
−	Salvage expenses	.00
	Taxable income (loss)	$ 3,480.00
×	Tax rate	× .34
	Tax benefit or (liability)	$ 1,183.20
×	IPVF	× .98061
	Net tax benefit or liability	($ 1,160.26)
+	Proceeds	15,000.00
−	Security deposit refund	(1,500.00)
	Net residual proceeds	$ 12,339.74

Step Two

Find the present value of the unknown lease payments, letting one dollar equal each payment.

The present value of this uneven cash flow stream is computed using the blue keyboard of the HP-12C.

.67		i
2	g	CF_o
1	g	CF_j
46	g	N_j
	f	NPV 41.474031

Step Three

Find the present value of the annual tax liabilities associated with the one dollar lease payments previously determined.

Since the payment is being structured on an after-tax basis, the tax impact of the unknown payments that will be received must be considered.

Tax Year	Lease Payments
1	8
2	+ 12
3	+ 12
4	+ 12
5	4

8.343		i	
8	g	CF$_o$	
12	g	CF$_j$	
3	g	N$_j$	
4	g	CF$_j$	
	f	NPV	41.637825
.34		x	14.156860
.98061		x	13.882359

The present value of 13.8824 represents the taxes associated with the payment stream.

Step Four

Deduct the present value of the tax liability from the present value of the payments. This step will place the structuring factor on an after-tax basis.

$$41.474031 \quad \text{(pretax structuring factor)}$$
$$\underline{13.882359} \quad \text{(tax liability present value)}$$
$$27.591672 \quad \text{(after-tax structuring factor)}$$

Step Five

Divide the 27.591672 after-tax structuring factor from above into the present value of all the known cash flows. The quotient is the required payment that will result in an 8.04% annual after-tax nominal return to the lessor.

$$\frac{\$66,415.64}{27.591672} = \$2,407.09$$

The structuring factor is shown as:

$$\frac{\$2,407.09}{\$100,000.00} = .024071$$

CONCLUSION

As can be seen, many diverse and complex variables must be incorporated into the lease structuring process. However, in spite of these complexities, lease pricing can be a stimulating and enjoyable experience. More importantly, however, is the critical role pricing plays in regard to the profitability of the lease company, in the context of its returns and the amount of business it can write. While relatively simple in approach, this chapter should have provided a solid background in the basics of lease pricing. Chapter Nine on advanced structuring delves into the mechanics of more innovative structures.

CHAPTER NINE
ADVANCED STRUCTURING

This chapter is based upon the structuring principles set forth in Chapter Eight. Those structuring principles are applied to the specialized problems that make up the following sections:

- Structuring Unusual Payment Streams
- Early Terminations of Leases
- Return on Equity Structuring (Match Funding)
- Operating Lease Structuring
- Gross Profit Tax Deferral Pricing
- Alternative Minimum Tax Considerations.

Because of the interrelationship between Chapters Eight and Nine, it is suggested that Chapter Eight be reviewed before reading this chapter.

STRUCTURING UNUSUAL PAYMENT STREAMS

Frequently, a lessor, in order to accommodate a lessee's unique cash flow requirements, will structure a lease with a varied or unusual payment pattern. These leases may offer skipped, step-up or step-down payment streams. At other times, the lessor will determine the rentals that must follow an earlier series of fixed payments determined by the lessee's needs. For example, if a lessee can pay only $1,000 per month for the first 12 months of a lease, the lessor must determine how much should be paid thereafter to earn a fair return on investment.

Another example of an unusual payment stream is the skipped payment lease. In the Northwest, there is an annual rainy season lasting about 3 months that causes a cessation in highway construction. Lessees of heavy road construction equipment, therefore, want leases that skip the payments during the rainy season when revenue is not being generated. These leases are also referred to as school teacher leases due to the annual skipping of three monthly payments. If the lessor does not meet this real lessee need through structuring a skipped payment lease, the lessee will seek other funding alternatives.

Step-up leases are required by lessees with cash flow constraints early in the lease, so the lease payments are increased once cash flow is expected to increase. Step-down leases are used by lessors to compensate for excess credit risk or for residual risk where an asset is expected to become technologically obsolete faster than normal. The lease begins with higher payments and then steps down to lower ones. The greater cash inflow to the lessor provides a hedge against both risks described above.

Review of Structuring Steps

The same structuring steps described in Chapter Eight are followed in structuring unusual payment stream leases except Steps Two and Three are slightly modified to include the impact of the unusual payment stream. Step Two must be changed by altering the assumed one dollar lease payments for the periods affected and Step Three must be modified to reflect the annual tax liability on the altered one dollar lease payment stream. The five structuring steps, as altered for a skipped payment lease, are shown here for review. Steps Two and Three would be altered, as appropriate, for other types of unusual payment stream leases.

STEP ONE

Identify and present value all known cash flows in the transaction, including tax benefits, using the required after-tax internal rate of return (IRR) as the discount rate. This step is the same as Step One in pretax structuring. The only differences are the discount rate, the added variables and the different nature of the variables, such as after-tax residuals, the effect of gross profit tax deferral, general and administrative (G & A) expenses, etc.

STEP TWO

Determine the present value of the payment stream, using the targeted after-tax IRR as the discount rate, and letting each regular payment equal one dollar and the skipped payments equal zero. This step is exactly the same as Step Two in the pretax structuring explained in Chapter Eight, except that a zero is used rather than one dollar for each skipped payment.

STEP THREE

Determine the present value of the annual tax liabilities associated with the one dollar lease payments determined in Step Two. After computing the present value of the lease payment stream in Step Two it is necessary to compute the taxes on those payments being received in each tax year since they will generate a tax liability. There is, of course, no liability on the skipped payments since they do not create taxable income. This step is done in the same manner as Step Two, by letting one dollar equal the regular payments and ignoring the skipped payments. Taxes are paid on an annual basis over the five estimated payment dates; therefore, the present value of the tax liability stream is calculated on an annual basis. This present value total is multiplied by the tax rate to arrive at the associated income tax liability. The appropriate intraperiod present value factor (IPVF) is applied to the present value of the tax liability to reflect the impact of paying taxes over the five estimated tax payment dates. By using this method of computing taxes on payments received in each tax year, the proper timing of the tax remittances is recognized. An annual effective rate must be used as a discount rate when computing the present value of any cash flows that occur on an annual basis.

STEP FOUR

Deduct the results of Step Three from Step Two. This step converts the investment recovery unit (IRU) to an after-tax basis so it can be divided into the after-tax net investment to arrive at the lease payment.

STEP FIVE

Divide the after-tax net investment (from Step One) by the after-tax IRU (from Step Four). This step results in the required lease payment that will achieve the targeted after-tax return on investment.

Structuring a Skipped Payment Lease

The base example from Chapter Eight, modified to reflect a skipped payment stream, is used to illustrate the structuring of a skipped payment lease.

EXAMPLE 1

Structure a skipped payment lease using the following assumptions:

Equipment cost: $100,000, purchased April 1, 19XX

Refundable security deposit: $1,500

Purchase option: $15,000, expected to be exercised after a 48-month noncancellable lease term

Pretax initial direct costs: $2,500

Incremental federal tax rate: 34%

Annual nominal after-tax yield: 8.04% (.67% per month or an 8.343% annual effective rate)

Monthly G & A expenses: $50, expected to increase due to inflation at ½% each month throughout the lease

Tax depreciation: 5-year Modified Accelerated Cost Recovery System (MACRS) equipment placed in service April 1, of a calendar year accrual basis taxpayer

Lease term: 48 months with payments in arrears, beginning May 1, 19XX, with the second, third and fourth payments (June, July, August) being skipped each year.

SOLUTION

Based on the modified assumptions from Chapter Eight, certain preliminary computations are performed after which the five structuring steps are completed, in order.

Preliminary Computations

First, convert the annual nominal IRR to its monthly nominal rate as well as its annual effective equivalent.

1. Monthly nominal: 8.04 ÷ 12 = .67% per month

2. Annual effective

$$\left(1 + \frac{.67}{100}\right)^{12}$$

1.0067 ENTER 12 y^x = 1.08343

The annual effective discount rate is 8.343% (subtract one and move the decimal two places to the right).

Next, the IPVF for a lease structured April 1, must be computed, as shown in Table 1. As Table 1 demonstrates, the tax benefits or liabilities are worth 96.76% of face value for a lease structured on April 1.

Step One

Identify and present value all known cash flows in the transaction, including tax benefits, using the required after-tax IRR as the discount rate.

1. Review of known cash flows:

Table 1
Computation of IPVF

Remittance Date	Quarterly Remittance Percentages	Months from Inception	Present Value of the Remittance Percentage
April 1	0.0%	0	.00000
April 15	22.5%	½	.22425
June 15	22.5%	2½	.22127
September 15	22.5%	5½	.21689
December 15	22.5%	8½	.21258
March 15	10.0%	11½	.09261
IPVF			.96760

---

¹

.67		i	
.225	CHS	FV	
5.5		n	
		PV	.21689

Equipment cost
Initial direct costs (after-tax)
Refundable security deposit (nontaxable)
Residual value (net of taxes and deposit refund)
MACRS tax benefits
G & A expenses (after-tax)
Net inception outflow

2. Equipment cost is given at $100,000. Had the equipment been paid for at a later takedown date, present valuing would have been required
3. Initial direct costs
   (a) After-tax conversion formula:
       (Expense × [1 − (tax rate × IPVF)] = after-tax cost
   (b) $2,500 × [1 − (.34 × .9676)] = $1,677.54
4. The refundable security deposit is given at $1,500, and is not adjusted for tax benefits since it is not tax deductible. Its refund will be considered as part of the net residual yet to be calculated
5. The residual value (net of taxes and deposit refund) is calculated as in Figure 1, and the present value of the net residual is then computed

.67	i	
48	n	
12,355.14 CHS	FV	
	PV	8,966.94

Salvage proceeds	$ 15,000.00
Remaining tax basis[2]	(11,520.00)
− Salvage expenses	0.00
Taxable income (loss)	$ 3,480.00
× Tax rate	× .34
Tax benefit or (liability)	($ 1,183.20)
× IPVF	× .9676
Net tax benefit or (liability)	($ 1,144.86)
+ Proceeds	15,000.00
− Security deposit refund	(1,500.00)
Net residual proceeds	$ 12,355.14

Figure 1
Residual Proceeds Schedule

---

[2] $\left[\left(\frac{.1152}{2} + .0576\right) \times \$100,000\right]$

6. MACRS tax benefits

8.343		i	
.20	g	CF_o	
.32	g	CF_j	
.192	g	CF_j	
.1152	g	CF_j	
.0576	g	CF_j	(one-half year depreciation in year of disposal)
	f	NPV	.7913
100,000		×	79,131.45 (equipment cost)
.34		×	26,904.69 (tax rate)
.9676		×	26,032.98 (IPVF)

The present value of the MACRS tax benefits is $26,032.98.

7. G & A expenses

(a) Convert the $50 G & A expenses to their after-tax equivalent

$$\$50 \times [1 - (.34 \times .9676)] = \$33.55$$

(b) Compute the present value of a growing annuity

	g	END	
48		n	(months)
1.005		ENTER	(enter 1 plus the decimal equivalent of the G & A growth rate)
1.0067	% i	CLX	(enter 1 plus the discount rate's decimal equivalent)
33.55	X≥Y	÷	(enters the beginning G & A after-tax)
	PMT	PV	
		CHS	1,537.81 (present value of the after-tax G & A expenses)

8. Summary of the present value of all known cash flows

Equipment cost	($100,000.00)
Initial direct costs	(1,677.54)
Refundable security deposit	1,500.00
Residual value (net)	8,966.94
MACRS tax benefits	26,032.98
G & A expenses	(1,537.81)
Net inception outflow	($ 66,715.43)

Step Two

Determine the present value of the payment stream, using the targeted after-tax IRR as the discount rate, and letting each regular payment equal one dollar and the skipped payments equal zero.

.67		i	
1	g	CF_j	
0	g	CF_j	
3	g	N_j	(three skipped payments)
1	g	CF_j	
9	g	N_j	
0	g	CF_j	
3	g	N_j	
1	g	CF_j	
9	g	N_j	
0	g	CF_j	
3	g	N_j	
1	g	CF_j	
9	g	N_j	
0	g	CF_j	
3	g	N_j	
1	g	CF_j	
8	g	N_j	
	f	NPV	30.458475

The present value of this skipped payment lease stream is 30.458475.

Step Three

Find the present value of the annual tax liabilities associated with the one dollar lease payments determined in Step Two.

Tax Year	Lease Payments Per Tax Year
1	5
2	9
3	9
4	9
5	4

8.343		i
5	g	CF_o
9	g	CF_j
3	g	N_j
4	g	CF_j
	f	NPV 30.954135
.34	×	10.524406
.9676	×	10.183415

The present value of the tax liability associated with this skipped payment lease stream is 10.183415.

Step Four

Deduct the results of Step Three from Step Two.

$$
\begin{array}{ll}
30.458475 & \text{(pretax structuring factor)} \\
- \underline{10.183415} & \text{(tax liability present value)} \\
20.275060 & \text{(after-tax structuring factor, or IRU)}
\end{array}
$$

Step Five

Divide the 20.275060 remainder from Step Four into the present value total from Step One. The quotient is the required payment that will result in an 8.04% annual after-tax nominal return to the lessor.

Payment:

$$\frac{\$\ 66{,}715.43}{20.275060} = \$3{,}290.52$$

Structuring factor:

$$\frac{\$\ 3{,}290.52}{\$100{,}000.00} = .0329052$$

The secret, therefore, of structuring skipped payment leases is to let zero equal the skipped payment when finding the present value of the one dollar payments and when computing the tax liability on the one dollar payments.

Structuring Step-up or Step-down Leases

Structuring step-up or step-down leases is similar to structuring skipped payment leases in that a modification of Step Two is required. In a stepped lease, however, the stepped-up or -down payment is expressed as a percentage of the base one dollar rental. This concept is illustrated in the following examples.

EXAMPLE 2

Structure a step-up lease consisting of 24 monthly base rentals, in arrears, followed by 24 rentals that are 12% higher than the base rentals.

SOLUTION

Step One is exactly the same as Step One in Example 1 ($66,715.43). Step Two is calculated by determining the present value of the payment stream, using the targeted after-tax IRR as the discount rate, and letting each regular payment equal one dollar. The stepped-up payments are set equal to 1.12, which is 12% higher than the base rental of one dollar.

.67		i	
1	g	CF_j	(base one dollar rentals)
24	g	N_j	
1.12	g	CF_j	(stepped-up rentals at 112% of the one dollar base)
24	g	N_j	
	f	NPV	43.189882

The present value of this payment stream is 43.189882.

Step Three

Determine the present value of the annual tax liabilities associated with the one dollar lease payments determined in Step Two. Based on the changes to Step Two, the following tax liability would result.

Tax Year	Total Rentals		
1	9 × 1	=	9.00
2	12 × 1	=	12.00
3	3 × 1	=	3.00
	9 × 1.12	=	10.08
			13.08
4	12 × 1.12	=	13.44
5	3 × 1.12	=	3.36

8.343		i	
9	g	CF_o	
12	g	CF_j	
13.08	g	CF_j	
13.44	g	CF_j	
3.36	g	CF_j	
	f	NPV	44.225703
.34	×		15.036739
.9676	×		14.549549

The present value of the tax liability associated with this payment stream is 14.549549.

Step Four

Deduct the results of Step Three from Step Two.

$$
\begin{array}{r}
43.189882 \\
-\ \underline{14.549549} \\
28.640333
\end{array}
$$ (after-tax structuring factor, or IRU)

Step Five

Divide the 28.640333 remainder from Step Four into the present value total from Step One of $66,715.43. The quotient is the required base payment. The stepped-up payment will be 112% of the base payment.

Base payment:

$$
\frac{\$66,715.43}{28.640333} = \$2,329.42
$$

Stepped-up payment:

$$
\begin{array}{r}
\$\ 2,329.42 \\
\times\ \underline{1.12} \\
\$\ 2,608.95
\end{array}
$$

EXAMPLE 3

In the situation where a lessee has requested a step-down lease, a similar procedure to the step-up lease is required. In this example, assume the lessee desires 36 base payments, one in advance, followed by 12 reduced payments that are 87% of the base payment.

SOLUTION

Step One, which is to identify and present value all the known cash flows, is exactly the same as Examples 1 and 2 ($66,715.43). The remaining steps must then be completed.

Step One

Identify and present value all known cash flows in the transaction, including tax benefits, using the required after-tax IRR as the discount rate (previously determined to be $66,715.43).

Step Two

Determine the present value of the payment stream, using the targeted after-tax IRR as the discount rate, and letting each regular payment equal one dollar and the stepped-down payments equal 87% of the one dollar base rental.

.67		i	
1	g	CF_o	(one advance payment)
1	g	CF_j	
35	g	N_j	
.87	g	CF_j	
12	g	N_j	
	f	NPV	40.021926

The present value of this payment stream is 40.021926.

Step Three

Determine the present value of the annual tax liabilities associated with the one dollar lease payments determined in Step Two.

Tax Year	Total Rentals			
1	10×1	=		10.00
2	12×1	=		12.00
3	12×1	=		12.00
4	2×1	=	2.00	
	$10 \times .87$	=	8.70	
				10.70
5	$2 \times .87$	=		1.74

8.343		i	
10	g	CF_o	
12	g	CF_j	
2	g	N_j	
10.7	g	CFj	
1.74	g	CF_j	
	f	NPV	40.975382
.34		$\times$	13.931630
.9676		$\times$	13.480245

The present value of the tax liability associated with this payment stream is 13.480245.

Step Four

Deduct the results of Step Three from Step Two. This step converts the IRU to an after-tax basis so it can be divided into the after-tax net investment to arrive at the lease payment.

```
   40.021926
 - 13.480245
   26.541681   (after-tax structuring factor, or IRU)
```

Step Five

Divide the 26.541681 remainder from Step Four into the present value total from Step One of $66,715.43. This step results in the required lease payments that will achieve the targeted after-tax return on investment.

Base payment:

$$\frac{\$66,715.43}{26.541681} = \$2,513.61$$

Stepped-down payment:

$$\begin{array}{r} \$\ 2,513.61 \\ \times\quad .87 \\ \hline \$\ 2,186.84 \end{array}$$

Structuring Leases With Known Initial Payments

Each lessee has a different set of needs, depending on its circumstances. In those situations where the lessee can pay only a limited amount of rent during the early months of a lease, there will be several changes in structuring methodology.

EXAMPLE 4

Using the assumptions of the preceding lease, and assuming additionally the lessee can pay only $1,800 per month in arrears for the first 12 months of the lease, structure the 36 remaining payments in order to provide the lessor its required after-tax, .67% monthly yield.

SOLUTION

The primary adjustment required is the inclusion of the known cash flows of $1,800 per month as part of Step One, where all known cash flows are identified and present valued. The following process reflects the necessary adjustments to the structuring steps.

Step One

Identify and present value all known cash flows in the transaction, including tax benefits, using the required after-tax IRR as the discount rate. The present value of the 12 payments of $1,800, less the present value of the tax liability associated with the payments, must be added to the $66,715.43 present value of known cash flows from the preceding examples. In standard lease structuring, of course, no known payments would exist.

First, present value the known lease payments

$$\begin{array}{rll} .67 & & i \\ 1,800 & g & CF_j \\ 12 & g & N_j \\ & f & NPV \quad 20,688.01 \end{array}$$

Next, present value the tax liability associated with the known payments

Tax Year	Total Taxable Lease Payments
1	$9 \times 1,800 = 16,200$
2	$3 \times 1,800 = 5,400$

8.343		i	
16,200	g	CF_o	
5,400	g	CF_j	
	f	NPV	21,184.17
.34		$\times$	7,202.62
.9676		$\times$	6,969.25

Finally, compute the net inception outflow

Previous present value net cash flows	($66,715.43)
Present value of the 12 rentals at $1,800 each	20,688.01
Present value of the tax liability on the rentals	(6,969.25)
Net inception outflow	($52,996.67)

Step Two

Determine the present value of the payment stream, using the targeted after-tax IRR as the discount rate, and letting each regular payment equal one dollar. This step is modified by using a zero in place of the twelve $1,800 payments already considered in Step One.

.67		i	
0	g	CF_j	(12 payments already considered)
12	g	N_j	
1	g	CF_j	
36	g	N_j	
	f	NPV	29.437088

The present value of the remaining payment stream is 29.437088.

Step Three

Determine the present value of the annual tax liabilities associated with the one dollar lease payments determined in Step Two, as adjusted by the 12 payments whose tax liability was previously dealt with.

Tax Year	Total Rentals		
1	9×0		0
2	3×0	=	0
	9×1	=	9
			9
3	12×1	=	12
4	12×1	=	12
5	12×1	=	3

8.343		i
0	g	CF_o
9	g	CF_j
12	g	CF_j
2	g	N_j
3	g	CF_j
	f	NPV

		NPV	30.143075
.34		$\times$	10.248646
.9676		$\times$	9.916589

The present value of the tax liability associated with the remaining payment stream is 9.916589.

Step Four

Deduct the results of Step Three from Step Two. This step converts the IRU to an after-tax basis so that it can be divided into the after-tax net investment to arrive at the lease payment.

$$
\begin{array}{r}
29.437088 \\
- \quad 9.916589 \\
\hline
19.520499 \quad \text{(after-tax structuring factor, or IRU)}
\end{array}
$$

Step Five

Divide the after-tax net investment (from Step One) by the after-tax IRU (from Step Four). This step results in the required lease payment that will achieve the targeted after-tax return on investment.

$$
\frac{\$52,996.57}{19.520499} = \$2,714.92 \text{ per month}
$$

Uneven or Step Payments (IRS Tests)

The lessor must take care not to run afoul of the Internal Revenue Service (IRS) uneven rent tests when structuring uneven rent leases. The purpose of these tests is to eliminate any potential tax avoidance through either acceleration of expense or deferral of revenue. The IRS ordinarily will not raise any question about prepaid or deferred rent if the uneven rents meet either of two tests:

1. The annual rent does not vary more than 10% above or below the average annual rent during the initial period
2. The annual rent during the first two-thirds of the lease is not more than 10% above or below the average annual rent during the initial period and the annual rent during the remaining period is no greater than the highest annual rent during the initial phase and no less than one-half of the average annual rent during the initial period.

If the uneven rent tests are not met, the IRS may designate portions of the rent as either prepaid or accrued in order to eliminate any tax avoidance. Prepaid rent would occur in a step-down lease where the IRS may deny the lessee an immediate deduction for some or all of the higher rentals paid in excess of the average rentals during the earlier part of the lease term (see Figure 2). Such excess rent would be considered prepaid and not yet incurred as an expense for tax purposes and, therefore, would not be deductible.

Accrued rent occurs in a step-up lease where the IRS requires the lessor to recognize revenue not yet received, but which has been deferred to the latter part of the lease term in the form of higher payments. The pattern of this payment stream is shown in Figure 3. Average annual rentals include rental holidays, other skipped payments, partial and stepped-up or stepped-down payments occurring within a given year. If the IRS test did not consider annual averages, a lease with only one skipped monthly payment per year would be in violation of the rule.

FORMULAE FOR DETERMINING STEP LEASE MAXIMUMS

When the low annual rents are equal to the high annual rents, the following formula is used to determine the maximum difference between the high and low rents the IRS test will allow.

$$L = .8182H, \text{ where L equals the low payment and H equals the high payment}$$

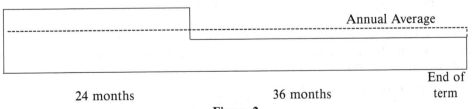

Figure 2
Prepaid Rent Expense Above Average

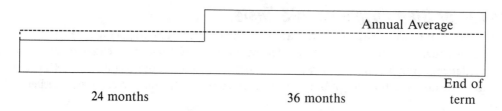

Figure 3
Accrued Rental Revenue Below Average

Thus, the low payments can be no lower than 81.82% of the high payments. This is proven by an example that assumes 3 years of high rentals at $20,000, followed by 3 years of low rentals at $16,364, which is equal to .8182 × $20,000.

$$\frac{(3 \times \$20,000) + (3 \times \$16,364)}{6} = \$18,182 \text{ average}$$

$18,182 ×.10   = $1,818
High limit $18,182 + $1,818 = $20,000
Low limit $18,182 - $1,818 = $16,364

Note the high and low payments are at the absolute limits of IRS acceptability.

When the number of low annual rents is greater than the number of high annual rents (L > H), the following formula is used (if a lease contains a partial year, as in a 42-month lease, the partial year should be annualized).

$$H = \frac{1.1\,L\,(X)}{X-.1\,(Y),}$$ where   L = Low payment
H = High payment
X = Number of annual low payments
Y = Number of annual high payments

Assuming 3 years of low rentals followed by 2 years of high rentals (step-up lease), the high rental can be calculated in relation to the low.

$$H = \frac{1.1\,L\,(3)}{3-.1(2)} = \frac{3.3\,L}{2.8} = 1.1786\,L$$

Thus, H = 1.1786 L, or, put into words, the high payments can be no higher than 117.86% of the low payments. If the annual low payments were $20,000, the high payment would be $23,572 ($20,000 x 1.1786).

$$\frac{3\,(\$20,000) + 2\,(\$23,572)}{5} = \$21,429 \text{ average}$$

$21,429 ×.10   = $2,143

| High limit | $21,429 + $2,143 = $23,572 |
| Low limit | $21,429 - $2,143 = $19,286 |

Note the high and low payments fall within the limits; however, the high payment is at the extreme limit, whereas the low payment is above the lower limit. There is no way the low payment can ever meet the lower limit as long as the number of low payment years are in excess of the high payment years. When the number of low annual rents equals the number of high annual rents, both the upper and lower limits can be met.

When the number of low annual rents is less than the number of high annual rents (L < H), the following formula is used:

$$L = \frac{.9\ H\ Y}{.1\ X + Y,} \qquad \text{where} \quad \begin{array}{l} L = \text{Low payment} \\ H = \text{High payment} \\ X = \text{Number of annual low payments} \\ Y = \text{Number of annual high payments} \end{array}$$

Assuming 3 years of high rentals followed by 2 years of low rentals (step-down lease), the low rental can be seen to be equal to 84.38% of the high rental.

$$L = \frac{.9\ H3}{.1\ (2) + 3} = \frac{2.7\ H}{3.2} = .8438\ H$$

If the annual low payments were $20,000, then the annual high rentals would be $23,702 $\left(\frac{\$20,000}{.8438} \right)$.

$$\frac{3\ (\$23,702)\ +\ 2\ (\$20,000)}{5} = \$22,222\ \text{average}$$

$22,221 × 110	= $2,222
High limit	$22,222 + $2,222 = $24,444
Low limit	$22,222 - $2,222 = $20,000

Note the high and low payments fall within the limits; however, the low payment is at the extreme limit, whereas the high payment is below the limit. There is no way the high payment can ever meet the higher limit as long as the number of high payment years are in excess of the low payment years.

When structuring unusual payment streams the lessor should be cognizant of the IRS uneven rent tests, and also of any alternative minimum tax (AMT) ramifications of the proposed structure.

EARLY TERMINATIONS OF LEASES

For various reasons, leases are sometimes terminated prior to the end of their noncancellable terms. For example, the lessee may want to purchase the equipment (payoff), or return the equipment to the lessor (early out or early termination) or the equipment may have been destroyed (stipulated loss value). Irrespective of the early termination cause, the lessor must compute how much the lessee owes at the termination date in order to make the lessor whole.

The basic problem in early termination calculations is defining what it means to make the lessor whole. Does it mean to maintain the original yield in the lease on a pretax or after-tax basis, or is the yield computed at the return on assets (ROA) or return on equity (ROE) level? Does whole mean being paid the then existing book value (remaining net investment) of the lease, or are associated deferred tax credits also considered? Then, too, how about Investment Tax Credit (ITC) recapture? How do lost interest earnings impact the value in the situation where the lease is paid off at a time when investment opportunities are paying 2% less per year than the interest structured in the existing lease being paid off? Or does whole mean assessing the customer with a Rule of 78 payoff? (Rule of 78 payoffs are basically penalties assessed the lessee for early termination, as they recognize more interest up front than an actuarial yield, thus causing the unpaid principal balance to be higher.) Keep in mind that the lessor has the liberty to compute terminations any way it desires (or agrees to in advance with the lessee) since there are no laws requiring the lessor to let a lessee out of a lease prematurely.

Basically, lessors attempt to achieve one of four basic objectives in computing payoffs, etc.:

1. Maintain the pretax yield in the lease
2. Maintain the after-tax yield in the lease
3. Maintain the accounting yield (avoid book loss)
4. Penalize the lessee.

In a payoff or early out the results of each of these objectives will not be the same, and, therefore, the lessor must decide in advance which goal is to be met.

The basic procedure employed in computing lease payoffs is to compute the present value of all costs and benefits that were incurred or received up to the date of the lease termination. Since all benefits will not have been received at this point, there will be a net unrecouped present value investment cost still remaining. The lease payoff will be the pretax equivalent of the future value of this unrecouped net investment.

Maintaining Pretax Yield

As an illustration, assume a $1,000 lease investment on which six lease payments of $20 in arrears have been received at the time of termination (there are 54 payments still due). If the lessor were attempting to earn a 10% return, the payoff would be calculated as follows. First, the present value of the benefits received is computed.

10	g	12 ÷	
20	g	CF_j	
6	g	N_j	
	f	NPV	116.58

The unrecouped investment would be $1,000 less $116.58, equaling $883.42 and the payoff, ignoring tax benefits or tax consequences, would be the future value of the $883.42, or $928.52.

$$\begin{array}{llll}
10 & \text{g} & 12 \div \\
883.42 & \text{CHS} & \text{PV} \\
6 & & \text{n} \\
& & \text{FV} & 928.52
\end{array}$$

Alternatively, the lease payoff amount may be looked upon as the remaining unpaid principal as of the payoff date. This amount can be determined through an amortization as shown in Table 2. The keystrokes for the first month of the amortization, using the above example, are:

$$\begin{array}{llll}
10 & \text{g} & 12 \div \\
1{,}000 & & \text{PV} \\
20 & \text{CHS} & \text{PMT} \\
6 & \text{f} & \text{AMORT} & 8.33 \\
& & \text{X} \gtrless \text{Y} & 11.67 \\
& \text{RCL} & \text{PV} & 928.52
\end{array}$$

Thus, the nontax adjusted payoff is $928.52, which is the future value of the unrecouped net investment at the lease inception, or the remaining principal at the time of the payoff.

Actual lease payoffs, however, would include additional items beyond the simple example just given. For instance, tax benefits received or ITC recapture, etc., would also be factored in. There also would exist, beyond the tax adjustments to the payoff, various penalties and other costs incurred by the lessor, such as:

1. Loan prepayment penalties on the lessor's debt used to fund the lease
2. Direct costs associated with removing the lease from the accounting system, etc.
3. Salvage and remarketing costs incurred to sell returned assets (early outs, etc.)
4. Opportunity cost when leases are cancelled during a period where reinvestment opportunities are not equal to the implicit rate in the lease being cancelled
5. Accrued rentals due, plus any accrued late fees.

Table 2

Pretax Amortization of Lease

Month	Payment	Interest	Principal	Remaining Balance
0	$ 0	$ 0	$ 0	$1,000.00
1	20	8.33	11.67	988.33
2	20	8.24	11.76	976.57
3	20	8.14	11.86	964.71
4	20	8.04	11.96	952.75
5	20	7.94	12.06	940.69
6	20	7.83	12.17	928.52

Other considerations include whether the lessor wants repeat business from the customer. Poor credit experience may prompt the lessor to use a Rule of 78 penalty payoff. Penalties of any kind tend to be ignored, however, if the cancelled lease is being replaced with a larger lease from a good customer.

Maintaining After-tax Yield

After-tax payoffs and early outs represent the most accurate form of termination valuation since the lessor maintains its original after-tax yield that was structured into the lease. It is also used when the lessor does not wish to penalize the lessee as a Rule of 78 payoff would. When lessors are involved in takeout-rollover financing with an existing customer, the takeout cost must be kept at a minimum, which would be achieved by an after-tax payoff.

EXAMPLE 5

Based on the following assumptions, the payoff procedures to maintain the after-tax yield in the lease will be described.

Equipment cost: $100,000, purchased June 1

Refundable security deposit: $1,500

Purchase option: $15,000, expected to be exercised after a 48-month noncancellable lease term

Pretax initial direct costs: $2,500

Incremental federal tax rate: 34%

Annual nominal after-tax yield: 7.00% (.5833% per month or a 7.2290% annual effective rate)

Payment: monthly payments of $2,332.03, with two rentals paid in advance

Monthly G & A expenses: $50, expected to increase due to inflation at 3% at the end of each calendar year throughout the lease

Tax depreciation: 5-year MACRS equipment placed in service June 1, of a calendar year accrual basis taxpayer

IPVF:.9831 (the lease is considered part of the annual tax budget and not incremental. Moreover, the lessor can currently use all tax benefits)

Lease cancellation date: March 15 of the third year of the lease after 21.5 months (i.e., 23 payments have been received, two in advance and 21 subsequently).

SOLUTION

The objective of a net after-tax actuarial payoff calculation is to maintain the after-tax ROA yield (7% in this case). There are six steps involved in computing a net after-tax actuarial payoff.

Step One

Compute the present value of all cash flows, including tax benefits, already received by the lessor up to the payoff date (include any expenses or cash flows such as ITC recapture or deposit refunds). Discount the cash flows at the.5833% monthly rate using the IPVF of .9831.

1. Present value the lease payments

.5833		i	
4,664.06	g	CF_o	(two advance payments)
2,332.03	g	CF_j	
21	g	N_j	(21 subsequent payments)
	f	NPV	50,630.20

2. Determine the present value of the deposit discounted from the date of its refund

.5833		i	
1,500	CHS	FV	
21.5		n	
		PV	1,323.68

3. Determine the amount of the refundable security deposit received at the lease's inception, which is given at $1,500.00

4. Convert the initial direct costs to an after-tax cost

$$\$2,500 \times [1 - (.34 \times .9831)] \quad = \quad \$ 1,664.37$$

5. Calculate the present value of the MACRS tax deductions and then convert them to cash inflow by multiplying the present value of the MACRS deduction times the lessor's tax rate times the IPVF factor

7.2290		i	
.20	g	CF_o	
.32	g	CF_j	
.096	g	CF_j	(.192 ÷ 2)
	f	NPV	.5819
100,000	×		58,191.91
.34	×		19,785.25
.9831	×		19,450.88

6. Determine the present value of the tax expenses (accrual basis) associated with the lease payments already earned by the lessor

Tax Year	Total Rentals		
1	8 × $2,332.03	=	$18,656.24
2	12 × 2,332.03	=	27,984.36
3	3 × 2,332.03	=	6,996.09
			$53,636.69

7.2290		i
18,656.24	g	CF_o
27,984.36	g	CF_j
6,996.09	g	CF_j
	f	NPV
.34	×	
.9831	×	

50,838.58	
17,285.12	
16,993.00	

7. Calculate the present value of the G & A expenses that had originally been allocated to the lease

   a) Present value the pretax G & A expenses

.5833		i
50	g	CF_j
7	g	N_j
51.50	g	CF_j
12	g	N_j
53.05	g	CF_j
2	g	N_j
26.53	g	CF_j
	f	NPV 1,030.94

   b) Calculate the present value of the tax benefits associated with the G & A expense by first determining the annual expenses

Year	Monthly Expense		Number of Months		Annual Expense
1	$50.00	×	7	=	$ 350.00
2	51.50	×	12	=	618.00
3	53.05	×	2.5	=	132.63
					$ 1,100.63

Next, present value the tax benefit created by the G & A deductions

7.2290		i
350	g	CF_o
618	g	CF_j
132.63	g	CF_j
	f	NPV 1,041.69
.34	×	354.17
.9831	×	348.19

c) Determine the present value, after-tax, of the G & A expenses

Pretax expense	$ 1,030.94
Tax benefits	(348.19)
After-tax expense	$ 682.75

8. Present value summary of benefits and costs already received or incurred

MACRS benefit	$ 19,450.88
Refundable security deposit	1,500.00
Deposit refund	(1,323.68)
Lease payments	50,630.20
Taxes on payments	(16,993.00)
Initial direct costs	(1,664.37)
G & A expenses	(682.75)
Net benefits received	$ 50,917.28

Step Two

Determine the present value of the amount of the asset's cost not yet received (the difference between the asset's cost and the total present value of benefits already received calculated above).

$100,000 – $50,917.28 = $49,082.72 (net unrecouped cost)

Step Three

Compute the after-tax future value at the payoff date of the net unrecouped cost from Step Two.

.5833		i
49,082.72	CHS	PV
21.5		n
	FV	55,620.76

Step Four

Convert the after-tax payoff from Step Three to its pretax equivalent by using the following formula:

X + (tax basis – X) r = after-tax future value,

where X is equal to the pretax future value and r is equal to the lessors effective tax rate (t x IPVF).

Conversion:

$$\text{Tax basis} = \left(\frac{.192}{2} + .1152 + .1152 + .0576 \right) \times \$100,000 = \$38,400$$

$$X + [(\$38,400 - X) \ (.34 \times .9831)] = \$55,620.76$$
$$X + [\$12,835.35 - .334254\ X] = \$55,620.76$$
$$.665746X = \$42,785.41$$
$$X = \$64,266.86 \text{ (pretax payoff)}$$

Step Five

The proof that $64,266.86 is the pretax equivalent of $55,620.76 is shown in the following computation:

Tax basis	$ 38,400.00
Less payoff proceeds	(64,266.86)
Taxable gain	$ 25,866.86
× effective tax rate (IPVF adjusted)	× .334254
Tax expense	($ 8,646.10)
Plus payoff proceeds	64,266.86
	$ 55,620.76

The $55,620.76 total is the same as the after-tax payoff computed above.

Step Six

The payoff is converted to an early out by deducting the after-tax salvage proceeds from the $64,266.86 payoff.

Maintaining Accounting Yield

Most lease companies account for leases using either the rate implicit in the lease or Rule of 78. For this example, if a lease payoff is computed that maintains the original accounting yield in the lease, the payoff would represent the accounting book value of the lease after the 21st month. This book value is determined by performing an amortization of the lease, either using the rate implicit in the lease or the Rule of 78, whichever is being used to recognize accounting yield. Many lessors use this method of calculating payoffs since it never results in a book loss and generally provides payoff proceeds that are greater than an after-tax payoff. The accounting approach thus creates a good in-between result. An accounting yield payoff, using the implicit rate (assumed to be .8766% per month), is computed by first determining the net inception cash flow.

Fair market value	($100,000.00)
Initial direct costs	(2,500.00)
Two advance payments	4,664.06
Net inception outflow	($ 97,835.94)

The amortization of the lease can then be completed, which will result in the remaining book value after the 21st month.

$$
\begin{array}{lll}
97,835.94 & \text{CHS} & \text{PV} \\
2,332.03 & & \text{PMT} \\
.8766 & & \text{i} \\
21 & \text{f} & \text{AMORT} \\
& \text{RCL} & \text{PV} \quad 64,003
\end{array}
$$

Add one-half month's accrued interest to the remaining book balance of $64,003 since 21.5 months have elapsed in the lease. This amount, $64,283, is the final payoff.

$$
\$64,003 \quad \times \quad \frac{.008765}{2} \quad = \quad \$280.49
$$

$$
\$64,003 + \$280 = \$64,283
$$

Penalty Payoffs

Rule of 78 payoffs are very common in the leasing industry, even though they create an economic penalty to the lessee in the sense that the lessee has paid more to the lessor than would have been required to maintain the original after-tax actuarial yield in the lease. The earlier in a lease a payoff occurs, the greater the Rule of 78 penalty, although payoffs occurring in the last third of a lease term will not create severe penalties. Penalty payoffs are often used in situations where no repeat business is expected with the customer or where the client is unaware of how payoffs are computed. (Bear in mind this is a cash flow discussion and does not consider the lessor's method of accounting.) They are also used to compute stipulated loss value tables where the penalty will be paid by an insurance company.

EXAMPLE 6

Using the same assumptions as in the previous after-tax payoff examples, compute a Rule of 78 payoff for a lease cancelled on March 15 in the third year of the lease (after 21½ months).

SOLUTION

Although this method does not maintain the specific targeted after-tax yield in the lease, the Rule of 78 payoff can be calculated on an after-tax basis. The computation of this payoff also requires six steps.

Step One

Compute the total implicit interest in the lease.

48 payments at $2,332.03	$ 111,937.44
Residual	15,000.00
Less initial direct costs	(2,500.00)
Gross proceeds	$ 124,437.44
Less equipment cost	(100,000.00)
Implicit interest	$ 24,437.44

Step Two

Determine the amount of the total interest earned using the Rule of 78 formula.

$$\frac{\dfrac{n_t\,(n_t+1)}{2} - \dfrac{n_r\,(n_r+1)}{2}}{\dfrac{n_t\,(n_t+1)}{2}} \times \text{total interest,}$$

where n_t = total months in the lease term

and n_r = remaining months in the lease (n_r does not usually include any partial months; thus, a lease paid off one day after a due date will be charged with a whole month's interest).

Applying the formula to the numbers in the example, the interest earned is computed.

$$\frac{\dfrac{48\,(49)}{2} - \dfrac{26\,(27)}{2}}{\dfrac{48\,(49)}{2}}$$

$$= \frac{1176 - 351}{1176}$$

$$= \frac{825}{1176}$$

$$= .70153$$

The total implicit interest of $24,437.44 times the interest earned factor of .70153 equals $17,143.61 of interest earned so far in the lease.

Step Three

Determine the proportion of the lease payments received that is principal by deducting the interest earned from items already received.

Two advance payments	$ 4,664.06
21 regular payments	48,972.63
Less initial direct costs	(2,500.00)
Less interest earned	(17,143.61)
Principal received	$ 33,993.08

Step Four
Determine the unpaid principal balance as the difference between the equipment's cost and the principal paid.

$$\$100,000 - \$33,993.08 = \$66,006.92$$

Note: ITC recapture (if applicable) should be added to the Rule of 78 payoff amount of $66,006.92.

Step Five
Deduct the value of any salvage proceeds from the Step Four payoff to convert the answer to an early out or stipulated loss value.

Step Six
Deduct from either the payoff or the early out any refundable security deposits due the lessee.

Review of After-tax Payoff Conclusions
Each payoff method requires a different computation and, therefore, will result in a different payoff amount. The payoff for each of the various methods is shown in Table 3. The Rule of 78 has a $1,740 penalty relative to the actuarial payoff amount required to earn a constant after-tax return on investment ($66,007 versus $64,267). It is interesting to note that the book value approach also created a slight penalty of $16. Had the preceding payoffs been early outs, where the leased asset was returned to the lessor, the preceding payoffs would have been reduced by the expected after-tax salvage value of the returned asset. Also, had the Rule of 78 payoff occurred earlier in the lease, the penalty would have been much greater in comparison to the others.

RETURN ON EQUITY STRUCTURING (MATCH FUNDING)
Certain lessors attempt to maintain constant debt-to-equity ratios in their leasing portfolios, or to fund their leases with known amounts of match funded debt with terms equal to their leases. In these situations, the targeted yield in the lease could be at the ROE level. ROE level structuring takes into consideration the known debt structure of the lessor and incorporates the amount of the debt, the cost of the debt and the way it is repaid. Those lessors that structure

Table 3
Summary of Payoff Methods

	Gross Payoff	Deposit Refund	Net Payoff
After-tax actuarial	$64,267	($1,500)	$62,767
Book value	$64,283	($1,500)	$62,783
Rule of 78	$66,007	($1,500)	$64,507

their leases on the ROE level do so for several reasons. One of the major reasons, however, is debt optimization, of which match funding is a subset.

Structuring Methodology

When structuring a lease to obtain a targeted ROE, assuming match funded debt, the same structuring procedures are followed as in ROA structuring except that all cash flows are discounted at the required ROE (rather than the ROA), the IPVF is recomputed using the ROE as a discount rate and the known cash flows now include loan proceeds, loan payments and the interest tax deduction benefits.

Using match funding means to fund the debt of a lease investment with a loan whose terms are the same as the lease. Therefore, a 48-month lease would have a loan requiring 48 monthly loan payments. Since at the inception of a lease the terms of the debt repayment are known (interest rate, payment amounts, etc.), the structuring process revolves around recouping the investment cost less debt proceeds, which difference is the same as equity. ROEs, of course, are higher than typical ROA returns since ROEs have the impact of financial leverage factored into their determination. Structuring match funded leases is much the same as structuring leveraged leases. The only difference is the debt in a leveraged lease would be nonrecourse to the lessor, whereas in a nonleveraged lease the debt is usually recourse to the lessor.

EXAMPLE 7

The following structuring techniques are used to structure a match funded single investor (nonleveraged), or leveraged lease. There are certain procedural modifications that must be made to the previously illustrated structuring steps in order to structure on an ROE, match funded level. This method of structuring will be demonstrated using the following ROA structuring assumptions:

Equipment cost: $100,000, paid for on April 15, one-half month after inception
Refundable security deposit: $1,500
Purchase option: $15,000 unguaranteed residual
Pretax initial direct costs: $2,500
Incremental federal tax rate: 34%

Monthly G & A expenses: $50, expected to increase due to inflation at $\frac{1}{2}\%$ each month during the lease

Match funded loan: $85,000, with interest at 7.9707% and 48 loan payments, in arrears, at $2,073.93 per month. Loan proceeds are obtained on April 1 (lease inception)

ROE required (annual effective): 17% (1.317% per month nominal)

IPVF: .9380

Tax depreciation: 5-year MACRS classlife equipment placed in service April 1

Lease term: 48-month lease with two payments in advance.

SOLUTION

The following steps must be followed in ROE, match funding structuring. They are exactly the same as the after-tax structuring steps previously discussed (except for the aforementioned modifications). Because of this repetition, each step will be presented in a highly abbreviated format.

Step One

Present value, at the required after-tax IRR, all known cash flows.

1. Review of known cash flows

> Equipment cost
> Initial direct costs
> Refundable security deposit
> Residual value (net of taxes and deposit refund)
> Loan proceeds ⎫
> Loan payments ⎬ Newly added cash flows
> Interest tax benefits ⎭
> MACRS tax benefits
> G & A expenses
> Net inception outflow

2. Equipment cost (with a delayed payment)

1.3170	i	
.5	n	(one-half month delayed payment)
100,000 CHS	FV	
	PV	99,345.81

3. Initial direct costs

$$\$2,500 \times [1 - (.34 \times .938)] = \$\,1,702.70$$

4. The refundable security deposit is given at $1,500

5. The residual value (net of taxes and deposit refund) is computed as in Figure 4. The present value of the net residual must then be determined

1.3170		i
12,390.16	CHS	FV
48		n
		PV 6,611.89

6. MACRS tax benefits

17		i	
.20	g	CF_o	
.32	g	CF_j	
.192	g	CF_j	
.1152	g	CF_j	
.0576	g	CF_j	
	f	NPV	.716429
100,000		×	71,642.86 (equipment cost)
.34		×	24,358.57 (tax rate)
.938		×	22,848.34 (IPVF)

7. G & A expenses

(a) Convert the $50 G & A expense to its after-tax equivalent

$$\$50 \times [1 - (.34 \times .938)] = \$34.05$$

Salvage proceeds	$ 15,000.00
− Remaining tax basis	(11,520.00)
− Salvage expenses	0.00
Taxable income (loss)	$ 3,480.00
× Tax rate	× .34
Tax benefit or (liability)	($ 1,183.20)
× IPVF	× .938
Net tax benefit or (liability)	($ 1,109.84)
+ Proceeds	15,000.00
− Security deposit refund	1,500.00)
Net residual proceeds	$ 12,390.16

Figure 4
Residual Proceeds Schedule

(b) Compute the present value of a growing annuity

		g	END
	48		n
	1.005		ENTER
	1.01317	% i	CLX
	34.05	X ≥ Y	÷
		PMT	PV
			CHS 1,342.06

8. The loan proceeds were given at $85,000
9. Present value the pretax loan payments

	1.3170	i
	2,073.93	PMT
	48	n
		PV 73,439.45

10. Present value the interest tax benefits associated with the loan payments
    (a) Loan amortization

Tax year	Payments	Interest Expense
1	7	$3,739.26
2	12	5,207.35
3	12	3,580.14
4	12	1,818.39
5	5	203.47

(b) Present value the loan interest per year

		i	
17			
3,739.26	g	CF_o	
5,207.34	g	CF_j	
3,580.14	g	CF_j	
1,818.39	g	CF_j	
203.47	g	CF_j	
	f	NPV	12,049.26
.34	×		4,096.75
.938	×		3,842.75

11. Summary of the present value of the cash flows

Equipment cost	($ 99,345.81)
Initial direct costs	(1,702.70)
Refundable security deposit	1,500.00
Residual value (net)	6,611.89
Loan proceeds	85,000.00
Loan payments	(73,439.45)
Interest tax benefits	3,842.75
MACRS tax benefits	22,848.34
G & A expenses	(1,342.06)
Net inception outflow	($ 56,027.04)

Step Two

Find the present value of the unknown lease payments, letting one dollar equal each payment.

1.3170		i	
2	g	CF_o	
1	g	CF_j	
46	g	N_j	
	f	NPV	36.336457

Step Three

Find the present value of the annual tax liabilities associated with the one dollar lease payments determined in Step Two above by first computing the taxable income.

Tax Year	Total Rentals
1	8
2	12
3	12
4	12
5	4

Next, calculate the present value of the liability

17		i	
8	g	CF_o	
12	g	CF_j	
3	g	N_j	
4	g	CF_j	
	f	NPV	36.649620
.34		×	12.460871
.938		×	11.688297

Step Four

Deduct the results of Step Three from Step Two.

$$
\begin{array}{r}
36.336457 \\
- \ 11.688297 \\
\hline
24.648160
\end{array}
$$

Step Five

Divide the remainder from Step Four into the present value total from Step One. The quotient is the required payment that will result in a 17% annual effective, after-tax ROE to the lessor.

Payment:

$$
\frac{\$56,307.20}{24.648160} = \$2,284.44
$$

Lease rate factor:

$$
\frac{\$2,284.44}{\$ 100,000} = .0228444
$$

Comparisons to ROA Structuring

Looking at Table 4, it can be seen that the ROE, match funding method of structuring results in a lower payment than the ROA method of structuring. The reason the match funded lease payment was lower than the ROA payment is that match funding provides a greater degree of financial leverage throughout the lease term than the ROA approach, which assumes a lower degree of leverage.

There are other debt structures that can be used in structuring leases at the ROE level. For example, a balloon payment equal to 85% of the $15,000 purchase option in the preceding example could have been assumed. The resulting lease payment would have been even lower due to the increase in financial leverage over the previous match funded example. Keep in mind that although the preceding examples are producing the same ROE, their net undiscounted cash

Table 4
ROA/ROE Comparison

Method	Targeted Return	Payment
Constant debt-to-equity	8.04% ROA	$ 2,419.39
Match funded	17.00% ROE	$ 2,284.44

flows differ. Refer to Chapter Seven for an in-depth discussion of yield versus cash flow trade-offs.

OPERATING LEASE STRUCTURING

The primary concern of the lessor in structuring an operating lease is not to take a residual position in a lease at the end of the lease term in excess of the asset's expected fair market value at the time. The term operating lease, in the context of structuring, refers to a lease in which the lessor has taken a significant residual position. Remember, in an accounting operating lease the present value of the minimum lease payments must be less than 90% of the leased asset's fair market value. Usually this 90% test is not a problem since lessors providing operating leases offer noncancellable lease terms that are short (2 to 4 years). These short-term leases cause the lessor to take large residual positions. (The larger the lessor residual position, the smaller the present value of the minimum lease payments.)

Special structuring problems are created in an operating lease, however. This is because the lessor usually does not salvage the equipment after the first firm-term lease, but, rather, expects to re-lease the equipment to the same lessee or to others. For instance, one problem that is created is the re-lease payments generally must be related to the fair market value of the equipment at that time. Thus, if the equipment had lost 60% of its value after a 36-month lease term, a renewal lease payment that is 60% lower than the first payment would be expected, assuming renewal after the initial lease term. Juggling that expectation with future residuals can be a difficult task.

Structuring Methodology

As has been pointed out, operating lease structuring incorporates a different set of variables into the structuring process. Therefore, in the situation where the lessor desires to structure an operating lease to meet lessee requirements, several additional procedures must be added to the basic structuring steps previously outlined. These additional procedures apply primarily to the relationship between residual value and the renewal rentals.

EXAMPLE 8

Structure an operating lease, but not for Financial Accounting Standards Board Statement No. 13 (FASB 13) purposes, using the following operating lease requirements and assumptions:

1. The lease will have 36 rentals with only one payment in advance
2. The equipment's fair market value after 36 months is expected to be $35,000 or 35% of the original asset's cost
3. The lease is expected to be renewed for an additional 24 months
4. The tax rate is 34%, the budgeted IPVF is 1.0175, the incremental IPVF is .9954 and the monthly discount rate is .5701%.

The lessor requires the 24 renewal payments to be based on the $35,000 fair market value at the end of the first 36 months. The present value of the renewal payments will be equal to the $35,000 fair market value (FMV) in order to avoid excessive residual speculation. Were the lessor to base renewals on a much higher residual value, there might not be any lessees who would be willing to lease used equipment at such a high rate.

Step One

The first step in structuring an operating lease is the same as structuring an ordinary capital lease; all known cash flows must be summarized. Assume that the net unrecouped investment in this example is equal to $65,063.96. This net investment reflects equipment cost, MACRS, residual proceeds and all other lease cash flows. From this point on, the lease structuring steps for operating leases are different.

Step Two

Determine the renewal rentals that would represent the after-tax equivalent of the expected fair market value at the end of the first firm term. It will be assumed the lessor would be indifferent between receiving the pretax FMV proceeds or the pretax renewal payments.

1. Convert the pretax expected residual to an after-tax basis

$$\text{FMV residual} \times [1 - (\text{tax rate} \times \text{IPVF})]$$

$$\$35,000 \times [1 - (.34 \times 1.0175)] = \$22,891.75$$

2. Find the present value of the unknown renewal lease payments, letting one dollar equal each payment

.5701		i
1	g	CF_o
1	g	CF_j
23	g	N_j
	f	NPV 22.498590

3. Determine the present value of the tax liability associated with the one dollar renewal payments

Tax Year	Total Renewal Rentals
1	2
2	12
3	10

7.06		i
2	g	CF_o
12	g	CF_j
10	g	CF_j
	f	NPV 21.933268
1.0175	×	22.317100
.34	×	7.587814

4. Deduct the results of 3 from the present value of the unknown lease payments

22.498590

−7.587814

14.910776 (structuring factor)

5. Divide the structuring factor into the after-tax residual FMV (from 1)

$$\frac{\$\ 22{,}891.75}{14.910776}\ =\ \$1{,}535.25\ \text{renewal payment}$$

Step Three

Determine the after-tax present value of the lease renewals and deduct from Step One. Note the present value of the renewal payments after-tax at the end of 36 months has already been determined in Step Two, part 1. However, this sum needs to be present valued over 36 more months.

22,891.75	CHS	FV
.5701		i
36		n
		PV 18,655.17

Unrecouped investment (Step One)	($65,063.96)
Less the present value of renewals	18,655.17
Recomputed unrecovered investment	($46,408.79)

Step Four

Calculate the present value of the unknown firm-term lease payments, letting one dollar equal each lease payment.

.5701		i
1	g	CF_o
1	g	CF_j
35	g	N_j
	f	NPV 32.647815

Step Five

Calculate the tax liability associated with the one dollar lease payments in Step Four.

7.06		i	
.338436	g	CF_o	(1 × .34 × .9954)
4.1514	g	CF_j	(12 × .34 × 1.0175)
2	g	N_j	
3.80545	g	CF_j	(11 × .34 × 1.1075)
	f	NPV	10.939166

Step Six

Deduct Step Five from Step Four and then divide this difference into the results of Step Three.

$$
\begin{array}{r}
32.647815 \\
- \ 10.939166 \\
\hline
21.708649 \ \text{(structuring factor)}
\end{array}
$$

$$
\frac{\$46,408.79}{21.708649} = \$2,137.80 \ \text{firm-term rentals}
$$

FASB 13 Test

Once the 36 firm-term rentals are known, a quick check for operating lease status should be completed from the lessee's viewpoint.

FASB 13 capital lease comparison base

$$
90\% \ \text{of} \ \$100,000 = \$90,000
$$

Present value the minimum lease payments (renewals are excluded). Assume the lessee borrows at 8.5%.

8.5	g	12 ÷	
2,637.80	g	CF_o	($2,137.80 advance rental plus $500 origination fee)
2,137.80	g	CF_j	
35	g	N_j	
	f	NPV	68,701.16

Since the present value of the minimum lease payments, $68,701.16, discounted at the lessee's pretax, incremental, coterminous borrowing rate was less than 90% of the leased asset's FMV ($90,000), the lease is also operating from an accounting perspective.

GROSS PROFIT TAX DEFERRAL PRICING

In a typical vendor lessor situation, the parent corporation remits to its captive subsidiary an amount equal to the taxes saved on the gross profit on equipment sold to the subsidiary. In turn, the subsidiary pays this interest free loan back to the parent in proportion to the rate at which the subsidiary depreciates the asset for tax purposes (MACRS, straight-line over the MACRS life, etc.). This is known as gross profit tax deferral. (The concept of gross profit tax deferral is discussed in Chapters Four and Seventeen.) What impact does the interest free loan have on pricing for the captive lessor?

Structuring Methodology

The value of gross profit tax deferral in structuring a lease is equal to the value of the loan proceeds from the parent less the present value of the loan repayments to the parent, discounted at the lessor's targeted after-tax yield or IRR. This value should be incorporated into the structuring process. The loan proceeds and subsequent repayments are not tax adjusted since they do not enter taxable income. The loan proceeds and repayments, however, are adjusted by the IPVF since the loan proceeds as well as payments are typically received and paid on the quarterly estimated tax payment dates of the parent corporation.

EXAMPLE 9

Incorporate the impact of gross profit tax deferral into the structuring process. Assume the gross margin in this December 15 intercompany transaction is $10,000, or 10% of the asset's cost to the captive. The parent, therefore, has deferred 34% of $10,000 in taxes, or $3,400. The $3,400 benefit in this incremental transaction will be received by the parent 90% on December 15 of the current year, and 10% on March 15 of the next tax year. For 5-year MACRS property, the $3,400 would be reduced by the current 20% MACRS depreciation taken by the captive. Thus, 80% of $3,400, or $2,720, would be the actual net amount of the parent's benefit. This amount is remitted to the captive as follows: .9 x $2,720 = $2,448 on December 15, and .1 x $2,720 = $272 on March 15 of the next tax year. The net $2,720 loan from the parent will then be repaid over the MACRS life of the asset on the quarterly tax remittance dates.

SOLUTION

The value of the net benefit, which is incorporated into the structuring process, is the result of the following present value calculation, using a 7.06% annual effective discount rate. This benefit represents the timing value of the $3,400 interest free loan paid back over the asset's MACRS life.

7.06			i	
2,707.49		g	CF_o	($2,720 ×.9954 incremental IPVF)
1,107.04	CHS	g	CF_j	($3,400 ×.3200 × 1.0175 budgeted IPVF)
664.22	CHS	g	CF_j	($3,400 ×.1920 × 1.0175)
398.53	CHS	g	CF_j	($3,400 ×.1152 × 1.0175)
398.53	CHS	g	CF_j	($3,400 ×.1152 × 1.0175)
199.27	CHS	g	CF_j	($3,400 ×.0576 × 1.0175)
		f	NPV	324.14

The present value of the net gross profit tax deferral is $324.14. In order to determine the impact of this gross profit tax deferral on pricing, further assume a base lease structuring factor of 34.08832. (Note the value of gross profit tax deferral impacts only the cash flows, not the structuring factor.) By dividing the $324.14 present value of the gross profit tax deferral by this base lease structuring factor, the reduction in lease payment is arrived at.

$$\frac{\$324.14}{34.088352} = \$9.51 \text{ per month reduction in the lease payment}$$

$$\frac{\$\ \ 9.51}{\$100,000} = .00095 \text{ reduction in the lease rate factor}$$

Since the $9.51 reduction is for a 10% gross profit margin, a company with a 70% margin would receive seven times the $9.51 amount, or a total reduction in lease payment of $66.57. Keep in mind the lessor does not have to lower the lease rate; it can charge whatever the market will bear and keep the gross profit tax deferral benefit as extra profit.

ALTERNATIVE MINIMUM TAX CONSIDERATIONS

In the event the lessor is in an AMT position, pricing and analysis become particularly onerous. This difficulty is a direct result of the unique tax attributes (as discussed in Chapter Four) caused by being in an AMT position. It is recommended that the AMT section of that chapter be referred to at this time, as this section will not discuss the AMT, but only its impact on structuring. A simple example, utilizing the following assumptions, will demonstrate the analytical and structuring difficulty of AMT.

1. The lease is a 4-year lease with annual payments of $2,500, in arrears
2. Taxes are paid (or benefits received) only on December 31 of this calendar year taxpayer
3. The lessor expects residual proceeds of $3,000 at the end of the lease
4. The equipment cost is $10,000 and there are not any initial direct costs
5. The equipment is 5-year MACRS classlife property and 5-year asset depreciation range (ADR) midpoint property
6. The lessor requires a 6.86% after-tax IRR (a 9.893% pretax implicit rate is used in accounting for the lease's income). Book earnings are as follows:

Year	Earnings
1	$989
2	840
3	676
4	495

7. The lease inception date is January 1, 19XX.

The cash flows (non-AMT) generated by this lease would appear as in Table 5. Now, assume the tax department of the lessor determines the company is currently in an overall AMT position (with or without the above lease), and that it will remain in that position until the third year of the lease. When such an AMT situation occurs, the lessor will pay the AMT on all incremental leases for the period the company is in AMT because the AMT is larger in amount than the regular tax liability. Once an overall company (versus an individual transaction) is in an AMT position, the next transaction will cause the AMT to be paid whether or not that transaction's regular tax liability is higher or lower than its AMT. The only time this would not be the case is where the next transaction was so large relative to the existing portfolio that its non-AMT attributes caused the whole portfolio to leave an AMT position.

The AMT impact on the preceding example, and the resultant cash flows, are shown in Table 6. As is readily apparent from analyzing Table 6, the computations associated with AMT are extremely complex and require several levels of supporting calculations. Table 7, as indicated, shows the AMT liability, but, in order to come up with that liability, preference schedules (Table

Table 5
Non-AMT Cash Flow Analysis

	0	1	2	3	4	Total
Cost	($ 10,000)	$ 0	$ 0	$ 0	$ 0	($ 10,000)
Rentals	0	2,500	2,500	2,500	2,500	10,000
Residual	0	0	0	0	3,000	3,000
MACRS	0	(2,000)	(3,200)	(1,920)	(1,152)	(8,272)
Tax basis	0	0	0	0	(1,728)	(1,728)
Taxable income	0	$ 500	$ (700)	$ 580	$ 2,620	$ 3,000
Taxes at 34%	0	(170)	238	(197)	(891)	(1,020)
Net income	0	$ 330	$ (462)	$ 383	$ 1,729	$ 1,980
MACRS	0	2,000	3,200	1,920	2,880	10,000
Cash flow[3]	($ 10,000)	$ 2,330	$ 2,738	$ 2,303	$ 4,609	$ 11,980

Table 6
AMT Cash Flow Analysis

	0	1	2	3	4	Total
Cost	($ 10,000)	$ 0	$ 0	$ 0	$ 0	($ 10,000)
Rentals	0	2,500	2,500	2,500	2,500	10,000
Residual	0	0	0	0	3,000	3,000
Taxes						
AMT[4]	0	(199)	(79)	(139)	N/A	(417)
Regular[5]	0	N/A	N/A	N/A	(891)	(891)
AMT reversal[6]	0	0	0	288	0	288
Net cash flow	($ 10,000)	$ 2,301	$ 2,421	$ 2,649	$ 4,609	$ 1,980

[3] The present value of these cash flows is zero, proving the 6.86% after-tax IRR.
[4] From Table 7.
[5] From Table 5.
[6] From Table 9.

Table 7
AMT Liability

	1	2	3	4	Total
Taxable income[7]	$ 500	($ 700)	$ 580	$ 2,620	$ 3,000
Depreciation preference[8]	500	650	135	(257)	1,028
Residual preference[8]	0	0	0	(1,028)	(1,028)
Other AMT income (AMTI)	$ 1,000	($ 50)	$ 715	$ 1,335	$ 3,000
Book/tax preference[8]	(5)	445	(20)	(420)	0
AMTI	$ 995	$ 395	$ 695	$ 915	$ 3,000
AMT at 20%	($ 199)	($ 79)	($ 139)	($ 183)	($ 600)

8) and the AMT reversal schedule (Table 9) must also be completed. The net cash flows after the AMT adjustments result in a new IRR, computed as follows:

10,000	CHS	g	CF_o
2,301		g	CF_j
2,421		g	CF_j
2,649		g	CF_j
4,609		g	CF_j
		f	IRR 6.777

Notice the AMT adjustments have caused the lease's yield to drop eight basis points (6.86 down to 6.78%). Had the AMT position been prolonged (5 or 6 years, etc.), a greater impact on yield would have occurred.

Assume the lessor desires to restructure the above lease to earn the required 6.86% after-tax return on investment. From a cash flow perspective, it is obvious the payment must go up to reimburse the lessor for the additional taxes paid under AMT. Since the amount of the additional taxes is known, this appears to be a simple solution. There are problems, however, that make this process much more difficult than it appears.

What are the problems AMT presents in restructuring the lease? It is not the depreciation preference. The amount of this preference remains constant, since changes in payment do not affect the depreciation of the asset. Instead, the primary difficulty encountered in restructuring a lease under an AMT situation arises from the pretax book income preference. Every dollar of increase in the lease payment causes a corresponding increase in the lease's pretax income,

---

[7] From Table 5.
[8] From Table 8.

Table 8
Preference Calculations

	1	2	3	4	Total
Depreciation preference					
MACRS	$ 2,000	$ 3,200	$ 1,920	$ 576	$ 7,696
150% declining balance	(1,500)	(2,550)	(1,785)	(833)	(6,668)
	$ 500	$ 650	$ 135	($ 257)	$ 1,028
Book/tax preference					
Book earnings	$ 989	$ 840	$ 676	$ 495	$ 3,000
Less other AMTI[9]	(1,000)	50	(715)	(1,335)	(3,000)
Difference	($ 11)	$ 890	($ 39)	($ 840)	$ 0
× ½	($ 5)	$ 445	($ 20)	($ 420)	$ 0
Residual preference					
MACRS basis	$ 8,000	$ 4,800	$ 2,880	$ 2,304	$ 2,304
AMT basis	8,500	5,950	4,165	3,332	3,332
	($ 500)	($ 1,150)	($ 1,285)	($ 1,028)	($ 1,028)

Table 9
AMT Reversal Computation

	1	2	3	4	Total
Normal liability[10]	($ 170)	$ 238	($ 197)	N/A	($ 129)
AMT liability[11]	($ 199)	(79)	(139)	N/A	(417)
Difference	($ 29)	($ 317)	$ 58	N/A	$ 288
AMT reversal	0	0	(288)	N/A	(288)
Cumulative	($ 29)	($ 346)	0	N/A	0

[9] From Table 7.
[10] From Table 5.
[11] From Table 7.

which, if different than the increase in other AMTI (as is the case for a capital lease), creates a tax preference. This increase in tax preference causes taxes to increase over the life of the lease. If the increase in pretax income were easily predictable, the restructuring would be easy, but, in fact, the process for capital leases requires successive iterations until the present value of the increases in the lease payments, less any AMT amounts, equals the desired present value increase in payments. As a practical matter, a computer is required to perform the numerous trial and error iterations necessary. This problem, however, is not encountered when structuring operating leases under AMT, because any increase in the operating lease rents causes a corresponding increase in other AMTI. As a result, a pretax book income preference is not created, and neither is a depreciation preference, as discussed earlier.

Another perplexing, yet interesting, issue concerning AMT arises when the date the lessor will eliminate its AMT position is beyond the termination of the lease term. In this prolonged case, the lessor will have paid taxes during the lease term at only 20%, instead of the normal 34% rate. This situation generates a deferred AMT liability that will not be paid until the lessor's overall portfolio reverses out of the AMT position. Therefore, it is very possible that a lease written today, given a lessor with a prolonged AMT problem, will actually generate more present value cash flow to the lessor, with a corresponding increase in after-tax yield, due to the deferral of the 14% tax rate differential (34% less 20%). This provides a false sense of security, however, for common sense dictates that the longer a company is in AMT (a penalty situation), the worse off it will be.

What are some of the remedies to the AMT problem? There is no single sine qua non solution; however, some of the following might help mitigate the AMT problem.

1. Increase the portfolio's proportion of accounting operating leases (assuming tax leases) while, at the same time, employing straight-line depreciation for tax purposes over the MACRS classlife. In this situation there are no new tax preferences created, since there is not any accelerated depreciation creating preferences and there is no difference between pretax book income and other AMTI. It should be noted in this case that, while solving or mitigating AMT, the lessor is also giving up substantial depreciation tax benefits by using straight-line depreciation

2. Become owned by a parent corporation that can absorb a sufficient amount of the subsidiary's AMTI such that the AMT position is nullified

3. Use straight-line depreciation over the MACRS classlife or ADR midpoint life, which minimizes the AMT problem. This approach may not fully eliminate the AMT problem since there will still exist a pretax book earnings preference when the lessor books a capital lease. Furthermore, as mentioned above, the lessor gives up substantial depreciation benefits, so a careful analysis should be performed before adopting this remedy

4. Become a broker and generate fee income through selling leases to lessors who do not have an AMT problem

5. Book low or zero residuals to minimize the book versus other AMTI difference. It is doubtful this practice will be acceptable to a company's external auditors

6. Diversify the product base

7. Attempt to pass on to lessees the increase in lease payments necessary to earn the required return on investment. If a majority of lessors have an AMT problem this will be a

common solution, although it currently is highly unlikely. The most likely scenario for those lessors with AMT problems, therefore, is they will either accept lower yields on the leases being written, or not write any tax leases.

The focus of this section has not been to teach and solve all the problems and intricacies of the AMT, for this aspect of tax law and pricing is much too complex and, therefore, beyond the scope of this work. It is suggested that those who desire to deal more extensively with this aspect of structuring (either through circumstances, or curiosity) seek additional resources.

CONCLUSION

It can be concluded that specialized lease structuring is not so different from standard lease structuring. The primary difference is how the one dollar lease payments are altered in the computation of the IRU. Leases can be structured to target ROE objectives as well as the ROA goals discussed in Chapter Eight. The ROE approach is used when debt-to-equity ratios are being held constant by the lessor or when match funding is an issue. Additional pricing concerns, such as operating leases, AMT structuring, integrating gross profit tax deferral into the pricing process and lease payoffs must also be considered in the structuring process. It should be noted that the intent of the chapter was not to supplant existing lease structuring software the reader might be using, but was intended, instead, to give the reader greater insight into the cash flow components that make up a lease.

CHAPTER TEN
CAPITAL BUDGETING AND FINANCIAL MANAGEMENT

Capital budgeting is the process of evaluating whether a particular investment has sufficient cash returns to meet a prespecified profitability objective. For a lease company, its investment in a lease must generate sufficient cash flow returns from rents, residual value and tax benefits to meet the company's profit goal. Capital budgeting is used also in the pricing, planning, forecasting and analyzing of budget variances. Capital budgeting methodology and its several uses are divided into five sections:

- Purpose and Nature of Capital Budgeting
- Capital Budgeting Methods
- Internal Rate of Return Method of Capital Budgeting
- Match Funding Techniques
- Sensitivity Analysis and Capital Budgeting.

PURPOSE AND NATURE OF CAPITAL BUDGETING

Should a lessor enter into a particular lease transaction? The answer depends upon whether anticipated lease payments, together with tax benefits and any expected residual value, will defray the lessor's equipment cost, initial direct costs, interest expense and operating expenses, plus provide a reasonable profit. In leasing, capital budgeting usually means pricing (lease payment determination) in such a manner that all the lessor's costs, expenses, losses, revenues and gains are considered.

Beyond pricing, capital budgeting is used in planning and forecasting. Will next year's anticipated new leasing volume together with the old existing leasing portfolio provide sufficient earnings to cover expected general and administrative (G & A) expenses? How should fixed costs be allocated to new leases written? Should fixed costs be allocated at all? These types of questions are answered as a result of using capital budgeting as a planning and forecasting tool.

Capital Budgeting and Pricing

There are three basic techniques to pricing: (1) price according to the going market rate, and then analyze the lease to ascertain if it has sufficient profit; (2) price to cover only the lessor's incremental costs and a targeted profit, and then establish whether the marketplace will accept the rate or (3) price to cover both incremental and allocated fixed costs plus a profit, and then determine whether it has market acceptance. The first pricing method is discussed in Chapter Seven. This chapter is devoted to the last two pricing methods, which are cost accounting approaches to pricing.

At the onset, cost accounting pricing methods should be placed in their proper perspective. A lease rate or rental payment, when determined under capital budgeting, establishes a hurdle rate only, which is a rate below which the lessor's profit objectives will not be met. However, to imply the lessor should price at this rate is dangerous. The lessor should price at what the market will bear while keeping in mind that the rate never can be below the hurdle rate. Above the hurdle rate, market permitting, of course, is where pricing should always occur. Thus, the cost accounting capital budgeting approach to pricing establishes a floor only, whereas the market pricing approach creates a ceiling. The only thing worse than letting a cost accountant set pricing is to let a marketing person price without first checking with a cost accountant.

As previously described, there are two other types of hurdle rates: (1) incremental and (2) fully absorbed. Incremental hurdle rates are used in highly competitive situations where a rock bottom lease price is required and occur where no fixed overhead has been allocated to the lease. Such marginal or incremental pricing is proper so long as there is high certainty that the remaining leases to be written will defray the fixed overhead costs whose allocation was avoided in the incremental lease. Marginal pricing is appropriate also when sufficient leases previously have been written to cover the lessor's fixed costs (above breakeven). On the other hand, fully absorbed pricing is the more common method of establishing lease rates. This method allocates a pro rata share of fixed overhead costs to each lease based on an estimate of the volume of new leases to be written, added to the remaining portfolio of previously written leases.

To the degree the lease company's actual volume is within its budget, the fully absorbed method of establishing hurdle rates insures the lessor that leases priced at this level will provide the previously budgeted amount of profit. Many lease companies provide extra compensation when their sales personnel structure leases above the fully absorbed hurdle rates, since the profit is higher on these leases.

Capital Budgeting and Planning

Capital budgeting is a useful tool in portfolio forecasting and planning. It allows the lessor to establish flexible budgets for various volumes of expected new leasing business. Each budget provides insight into the ability of the overall portfolio (old and new) to absorb fixed and variable expenses. Such flexible budgets for varying volume levels also can be adjusted for changes in other essential expenses and revenues of the company, such as:

Revenues:

Advance rentals
Normal rentals
Closing fees
Interim rent
Residuals
Tax benefits

Expenses:

G & A
Initial direct costs
Interest expense
Equipment cost

Flexible budgets, therefore, may provide the basis for sensitivity analysis regarding the many sources of revenue and expense.

Once an economic capital budget has been completed using net present value (NPV) or internal rate of return (IRR) analysis, etc., the impact on the related accounting financial statements can be readily ascertained. Under the Tax Reform Act of 1986, the accounting net income must be calculated, since it might create a tax preference impacting the lessor's alternative minimum tax (AMT) position.

Basic Nature of Capital Budgeting

Coupled with pricing and planning, capital budgeting is used to determine whether an investment's cash flow returns are truly sufficient to generate a profit. Applied to a lease investment, the first step in this process is to establish the actual investment cost and then ascertain whether the cash returns are sufficient to pay back the investment. Total lease investment cost has three components:

1. The fair market value of the equipment to be leased, which is usually its acquisition cost, unless the lessor is a manufacturer or merchandiser of equipment, in which case the fair market value would be the normal retail selling price were the lessee to pay cash to purchase the equipment. The equipment's takedown date is an important acquisition consideration also, since the actual investment cost is not incurred until this date. Usually the takedown date occurs after the equipment is delivered and accepted, at which time the lessor pays the manufacturer. It also usually coincides with the lessor's obtaining of funding for the lease

2. The additional incremental costs incurred to originate the lease, which are designated by Financial Accounting Standards Board Statement No. 91 (FASB 91) as initial direct costs and include:

Only those costs incurred by the lessor that are (a) costs to originate a lease incurred in transactions with independent third parties that (i) result directly from and are essential to acquire that lease and (ii) would not have been incurred had that leasing transaction not occurred and (b) certain costs directly related to specified activities performed by the lessor for the lease. Those activities are: evaluating the prospective lessee's financial condition; evaluating and recording guarantees, collateral, and other security arrangements; preparing and processing lease documents; and closing the transaction . . . [FASB 91, paragraph 24]

An additional incremental cost that would not be classified as an initial direct cost per FASB 91, but which is an important component of investment cost, is the increase in working capital (cash on hand, current lease payments receivable, etc.) that would come into being because of this lease

3. The certain allocated cost and expenses that are incurred in the lease investment. Two of these allocated costs and expenses are ignored under incremental pricing, but, necessarily, are allocated under fully absorbed pricing. The first is an allowance for doubtful accounts, usually ranging from .5% to 3% of the net investment in the lease. The second cost represents an allocated portion of what we refer to as uninvested capital. Lease companies, to greater or lesser degrees, have investments such as property, plant and equipment that do not earn profit for the lessor in the same direct method that its leasing portfolio does. However, each lease in the portfolio must earn sufficient extra profit to cover its pro rata share of uninvested capital. Uninvested capital allocations range from 10 to 30 basis points of the equipment's acquisition cost.

The second step in lease capital budgeting is to establish the pretax cash revenues and expenses expected to be generated by the lease. Pretax cash revenues include:

1. Closing, origination or commitment fees that are not refundable
2. Refundable security deposits
3. Interim rents
4. Lease rentals paid in advance
5. Regular lease rentals
6. Expected contingent rentals (extra rent paid as a function of excess usage, etc.)
7. Residual proceeds through lessee purchase of the equipment, lessee renewal of the lease or any salvage proceeds to the lessor if the asset is returned by the lessee and is not leased to others.

Pretax cash expenses, on the other hand, include:

1. G & A overhead expenses, including variable incremental costs as well as allocated fixed costs when deemed appropriate (fully absorbed pricing)
2. Costs of bundled services for full-service leases, when appropriate (maintenance, repairs, etc.)
3. Refurbishment and remarketing expenses expected to be incurred to realize residual value
4. Cost of interest expense on debt used to fund the lease together with the periodic reductions of the debt's unpaid principal balance. The cost is included only when the

lease is being analyzed on a return on equity (ROE) basis; otherwise, a return on asset (ROA) analysis is assumed.

The third step in capital budgeting is to determine the tax consequences of the previous two steps. These consequences generate additional cash inflows and outflows, such as depreciation tax benefits, that are an integral part of capital budgeting. The primary tax consequences of tax leasing that must be considered in capital budgeting are:

1. The Modified Accelerated Cost Recovery System (MACRS) depreciation tax deductions must be quantified. The cost of the equipment generally will equal the depreciation tax basis of the property for purposes of determining the annual MACRS deductions. Exceptions to this rule would be where trade-ins have occurred or where the lessor manufactured the equipment. In these cases, specific Internal Revenue Service (IRS) guidelines must be followed in order to determine the tax basis of the equipment

2. The initial direct costs must be identified. These costs have three different tax treatments (refer to Chapter Four): (a) those expenses that are immediately tax deductible, such as credit checking fees and documentation costs; (b) those expenses that are deferred and subsequently deducted pro rata over the term of the lease, such as sales commissions and attorneys' fees; and (c) those expenses that are capitalized and become part of the tax basis of the asset and are taken as tax deductions in the form of MACRS depreciation, such as bundled software and installation costs

3. The tax consequences of all other taxable revenues and expenses must be recognized. These taxable revenues and expenses include working capital, the allowance for doubtful accounts and uninvested capital expense allocations, which are not tax deductible. Bad debt expenses are deductible only when the actual lease is deemed uncollectible. (Current tax regulations no longer permit the allowance method. Only the direct write-off method is allowable.) While refundable security deposits are not normally taxed, step-up rents (low rents followed by higher ones) might be taxable before they are collected if their annual total deviates more than 10% from the annual average. Residual proceeds, of course, must be adjusted for any remaining tax basis

4. Gross profit tax deferral for dealers or manufacturers of equipment (see Chapter Seventeen) can be a significant tax benefit, depending upon the level of gross profit in the sales-type lease being considered. This benefit may or may not be considered in pricing

5. Any impact of the AMT, including additional liabilities, the lease company's AMT position and AMT position entry and exit dates must be incorporated into the capital budgeting process, along with the effects of the midquarter penalty. Investment Tax Credit (ITC) or net operating loss (NOL) carryforwards from previous tax years also must be considered.

The most difficult task embodied in these capital budgeting steps is the allocation of fixed and variable overhead expenses to any particular lease. There are numerous methods used to allocate these expenses, as is demonstrated using the information in Tables 1 and 2.

Table 1
Net Investment in Leases (Assumptions)

	Beginning of year	End of year	Average
Dollar amount of existing leases	$ 14,000,000	$ 12,000,000	$ 13,000,000
New leases	0	$ 4,000,000	$ 3,000,000
Number of existing leases	500	450	475
New leases	0	80	65

Table 2
Unearned Income (Assumptions)

	Beginning of year	End of year	Average
Existing leases	$ 4,200,000	$ 3,600,000	$ 3,900,000
New leases	0	$ 1,000,000	$ 750,000
Additionally, G & A expenses consist of:			
Variable expenses (accounting, billing and collecting)		$ 50,000	
Initial direct costs (documentation, pricing, commissions and credit checking and analysis)		$ 100,000	
Fixed expenses (remarketing, occupancy, miscellaneous administrative and allowance for doubtful accounts)		$ 110,000	

Since, by their very nature, initial direct costs are variable costs, the $100,000 would be divided by the total expected new leases written, giving the initial direct costs allocation as a percentage of the total net investment in new leases (net investment equals equipment fair market value).

$$\frac{\$\ 100,000 \text{ (total expected initial direct costs)}}{\$4,000,000 \text{ (total new leases)}} = \begin{array}{l} 2.5\% \text{ of} \\ \text{equipment cost} \end{array}$$

However, if most leases were of the same size, the total initial direct costs could be divided by the number of leases expected to be written.

$$\frac{\$100,000}{80} = \$1,250 \text{ per lease}$$

This method is invalid if the standard deviation of the average size lease is more than 20%. In fact, initial direct costs in leveraged leasing can be so large they must be allocated on a lease-by-lease basis.

The other nonfixed expenses of $50,000, which include the ongoing cost of billing, accounting and collecting, are considered variable costs and are usually allocated on a lease-by-lease basis without any allowance for lease size. These costs must be borne by the previously existing portfolio as well as by the new leases written; therefore, the average expected number of old and new leases outstanding is used in this computation.

$$\frac{\$50,000 \text{ (variable expenses)}}{475 \text{ (from Table 1)} + 65 \text{ (from Table 1)}}$$

$$\frac{\$50,000}{540} = \$92.59 \text{ per lease} \div 12 = \$7.72 \text{ per month, per lease}$$

Allocating such variable expenses on a lease-by-lease basis without regard to lease size is reasonable in that it costs just as much to account for a $100,000 lease as a $1,000,000 lease, and collecting and billing cost the same, too. Were there empirical evidence suggesting these costs were not the same for small as well as large leases, then other methods of allocation would be appropriate, such as allocating the variable overhead as a percent of the average net investment in the lease:

$$\frac{\$50,000 \text{ (variable expenses)}}{\$13,000,000 + \$3,000,000 \text{ (from Table 1)}}$$

$$\frac{\$50,000}{\$16,000,000} = .003125 \div 12 = .026\% \text{ of the monthly net investment in the leases}$$

Experience indicates that most variable expenses, as defined above, are allocated on a lease-by-lease basis without reference to the size of the lease. However, the fixed costs of $110,000 are seldom allocated on a lease-by-lease basis. If they were to be allocated on a lease-by-lease basis, then small leases would appear unprofitable. For example, if a $10,000 lease had to bear the same allocation as a $1,000,000 lease (100 times its size), the smaller lease would appear unprofitable. Fixed expenses, therefore, generally are allocated on the basis of either average expected net investment in the leasing portfolio or average expected unearned income in the leasing portfolio.

Allocating according to unearned income rather than net investment is justified on the basis that more profitable leases should absorb, proportionately, more of the leases' fixed costs than less profitable ones. This method keeps the preallocation yields in the same proportion as the postallocation yields. Both methods are described below.

A net investment allocation of fixed expenses would appear as:

$$\frac{\$110,000 \text{ (fixed expenses)}}{\$13,000,000 + \$3,000,000 \text{ (from Table 1)}}$$

$$\frac{\$110,000}{\$16,000,000} = .006875 \div 12 = .0573\% \text{ per month}$$

Thus, if a new lease were written with a $60,000 equipment cost, its allocated expenses for the first month would be:

Initial direct costs ($60,000 × .025)	$ 1,500.00
Variable costs, per the lease-by-lease method	7.72
Fixed costs, per the net investment method ($60,000 × .000573)	34.38
Total allocated costs	$ 1,542.10

However, if fixed costs were allocated according to the average expected unearned income in the leases, the same fixed expense allocation would be:

$$\frac{\$110,000 \text{ (fixed expenses)}}{\$3,900,000 + \$750,000 \text{ (from Table 2)}}$$

$$\frac{\$110,000}{\$4,650,000} = .02366 \div 12 = .1971\% \text{ per month}$$

Thus, if the same $60,000 lease had costs allocated to it using the unearned income percentage approach, its allocated expenses for the first month would be (assume the lease has $22,000 of unearned income):

Initial direct costs ($60,000 × .025)	$ 1,500.00
Variable costs, per the lease-by-lease method	7.72
Fixed costs, per the % of unearned income method ($22,000 × .001971)	43.36
	$ 1,551.08

Lease portfolios less than $500,000,000 in size typically are considered too small to gain economies of scale in terms of fixed cost allocations. In other words, the portfolio size is too small to absorb adequately all the fixed costs of running the typical lease company and, therefore, will not appear as profitable as a larger lease company. Typical overhead allocation ranges for (1) initial direct costs (excluding allowance for doubtful accounts) are 2 to 4% of the equipment's net cost, with 2.5% quite typical; (2) variable overhead per month (using the lease-by-lease method) are $5 to $25 per month, with $10 quite typical and (3) fixed overhead per month (using the % of net investment approach) are from .04 to .08%, with .05% quite common. As a note of caution, these rules of thumb are highly dependent upon portfolio size and average transaction size.

The last step in capital budgeting, once all cash inflows have been identified as in the previous three steps, is to analyze the cash flows using IRR, NPV, external rate of return (ERR), terminal value analysis (TVA), etc., to see if the benefits of leasing outweigh the costs.

CAPITAL BUDGETING METHODS

As Chapters Seven and Eight demonstrate, there are numerous methods to analyze the profitability of a lease or to structure its lease rents to meet a particular profit objective. Most lease companies employ IRR analytical techniques for nonleveraged leases, whereas ERR techniques with appropriate sinking fund assumptions are required for leveraged leases. The primary determinant of the analytical method to be used is the assumed reinvestment assumptions, as shown in Figure 1. Notice that in two out of the three cases, IRR analysis and structuring are used. Then, too, most of the time reinvestment assumptions will not deviate materially from the IRR of a lease so IRR structuring and analysis are required.

What is the appropriate IRR for a particular lease? The answer is that it should be an IRR equal to or greater than the lessor's after-tax, weighted-average incremental cost of capital. Lessor costs of capital typically are computed in one of three different methods, although there are more complex methods available (see any intermediate or advanced textbook on corporate finance.)

Targeted Growth Rate in Earnings Method

This technique assumes the sole source of growth in earnings is from internal sources, i.e., no mergers or acquisitions. It assumes also that the lessor maintains a constant ROE and the debt-to-equity ratio as well as the dividend payout ratio is held constant. With these assumptions of constancy, and through use of the following formula, the company's required

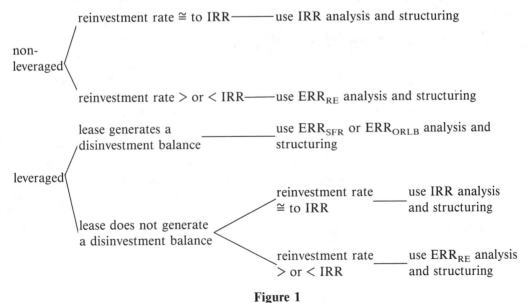

Figure 1
Methods to Analyze and Structure Leases

ROE can be solved for, given its targeted growth rate in earnings and dividend payout ratio. Since it is a basic axiom that

$$\text{ROE} = \frac{\text{growth rate in earnings}}{(1 - \text{dividend payout ratio}),}$$

once the ROE is known, the required IRR can be computed using the standard cost of capital derivation:

$$\frac{\% \text{ debt} \times \text{cost of debt} \times (1 - \text{tax rate})}{+ \% \text{ equity} \times \text{ROE}}{\text{Required IRR}}$$

For example, assume a payout ratio of 30%, a targeted growth rate of 12%, debt costing 8% and a tax rate of 34%. Debt is 85% of the capital structure and equity is 15%. Combining the above formula and derivation, what is the required after-tax IRR for the lease company?

$$\text{ROE} = \frac{12\%}{(1 - 30\%)} = \frac{.12}{.7} = 17.143\%$$

$$\frac{.85 \times 8\% \times (1 - .34) = 4.488\%}{+ .15 \times 17.143\% = 2.571}{\text{Required IRR} \qquad 7.059\%}$$

Other methods the lessor may use in arriving at an IRR utilize ROE derivations different from this method. Two of these methods are discussed in the next subsections.

Capital Asset Pricing Model (CAPM) Method

This method deals with the market-assessed risk of the company that leads to a minimum ROE a lease company should have to keep up with the leasing industry (see any intermediate finance textbook). Based on industry norms, lease companies leveraged with debt between 80 and 92% of their capital structure should expect ROEs of 15.46 to 22.23% with pretax debt costs in the range of 7.4 to 8.6%. The range is shown in Table 3.

It is assumed in Table 3 that a 7% after-tax IRR is typical of lease companies based on the CAPM approach. Also assumed is that the higher the leverage, the higher the cost of debt although the impact of greater debt percentages for larger companies might not be as great as that shown. Any changes from either a 34% tax rate, the stated costs of debt or a 7% CAPM risk would alter Table 3.

Using Table 3 to arrive at the required IRR, and given a company with 88% debt and 12% equity, the required IRR is computed as follows:

$$\frac{.88 \times 8.2\% \times (1 - .34) = 4.763\%}{.12 \times 18.65\% = 2.238}{\text{Required IRR} \qquad 7.001\%}$$

Table 3
Relationship of ROE to Leverage

Debt Percentage	Required ROE	Debt Costs at Various Debt Percentages
80%	15.46%	7.40%
82	16.04	7.60
84	16.72	7.80
86	17.57	8.00
88	18.65	8.20
90	20.10	8.40
92	22.23	8.60

Arbitrary ROE Designation Method

Many lease companies simply use averages of other companies or attempt to improve on their previous year's ROE. The pitfall with this method is that ROEs determined this way are frequently too small for the amount of lessor debt relative to equity. The required IRR would be determined in the same manner as previously discussed, using the cost of capital derivation.

INTERNAL RATE OF RETURN METHOD OF CAPITAL BUDGETING

A complete grasp of all the variables entering into the capital budgeting process is difficult to obtain due to the many complex and interrelated variables. Because of this, a comprehensive example describing the process required to solve a capital budgeting problem from the ground floor, all the way through determination of the lease payment, is be presented.

Structuring Process

In order to structure a lease for the purpose of determining either an incremental or fully absorbed hurdle rate, the following procedure is used. Refer to Chapter Eight for a complete discussion of the steps to be used in structuring. Once the four steps have been reviewed, an example will be presented.

Step One: Identify and present value, to the date of the lease inception, all known cash flows including tax benefits. Use the lessor's required monthly IRR previously calculated as the discount rate

Step Two: Calculate the present value of the unknown lease rentals, letting one dollar equal each lease payment

Step Three: Calculate the tax liability on the one dollar lease payment in Step Two

Step Four: Deduct the results of Step Three from Step Two. The difference is the structuring factor that is divided into the net unrecouped cash investment from Step One. The resulting quotient is the lease payment necessary to earn the required IRR. The lease rate factor is obtained by dividing the monthly lease payment by the equipment cost.

EXAMPLE 1

Using the preceding structuring steps, and given the following assumptions, calculate the lease rate factor this company can quote the lessee.

Equipment cost: $100,000 expected to be paid 2 weeks after a November 30, 19XX, lease inception. The equipment cost is considered equal to the equipment's tax basis as well as its fair market value

Initial direct costs: $2,500 or 2.5% of the equipment's cost. Allowance for doubtful accounts is not included. The total $2,500 initial direct costs are considered immediately tax deductible

Inception of the lease: the lease's inception for both tax purposes (placed in service date) as well as accounting is November 30, 19XX

Lease origination fee: $500 nonrefundable closing (origination, commitment, etc.) fee is to be paid by the lessee at the lease's inception

Interim rent: none

Contingent rentals: none

Lease rentals: 60 monthly rentals with two payments in advance at the inception of the lease

Refundable security deposit: $2,000 required of the lessee at the lease inception to be returned to the lessee at the end of the 60th month of the lease, given the lessee's faithful performance of the lease obligation

Working capital and uninvested capital: $300 is being allocated to the lease

Tax status of the lease: the lease qualifies as a tax lease, providing MACRS tax depreciation to the lessor on 5-year MACRS classlife equipment. The annual MACRS depreciation percentages are:

Year	Percentage
1	20.00%
2	32.00
3	19.20
4	11.52
5	11.52
6	5.76

Residual expectation:

Sale proceeds	$ 15,000
Refurbishment costs	(1,000)
Sales commissions	(1,500)
Net residual proceeds	$ 12,500

Note the lease contains a fair market value purchase option, but the lessor expects the lessee not to exercise the option. The returned equipment will, therefore, have to be remarketed as indicated above. Proceeds are expected to be received on November 30, 19XX at the lease termination

Lessor tax status: the lessor is in a 34% federal corporate tax bracket. No AMT problems are foreseen during the term of this lease. Moreover, the 40% midquarter penalty is not deemed applicable. The lessor treats the lease as incremental, such that the first year's tax benefits (and the residual proceeds) are received as follows:

90%	December 15	current tax year
10%	March 15	subsequent tax year

All other tax benefits and expenses are realized as follows:

22.5%	April 15	current tax year
22.5%	June 15	current tax year
22.5%	September 15	current tax year
22.5%	December 15	current tax year
10.0%	March 15	subsequent tax year

G & A expenses: variable overhead is allocated on a lease by lease basis and totals $10 per month. Fixed overhead is allocated on the basis of average annual net investment in the lease and totals the following for each month of the lease

First tax year	2 months at $30
Second tax year	12 months at $27
Third tax year	12 months at $23
Fourth tax year	12 months at $18
Fifth tax year	12 months at $12
Sixth tax year	10 months at $ 4

G & A expenses are assumed incurred at the end of each month of the lease (in arrears). G & A expenses were incurred during the last 2 months of the lease even though no lease payments were received (they were paid in advance). Note that the fixed overhead per month decreased quite rapidly in the later years of the lease because more principal was received by the lessor, causing the net investment in the lease to decrease rapidly

Required internal rate of return: the lessor uses the targeted growth rate in earnings approach assuming growth of 10% per year with a 44.5% dividend payout ratio. Debt-to-equity is 6:1, or 86% debt and 14% equity. Debt costs the lessor 8% over 5 years. The company expects to maintain, throughout the lease term, a constant 6:1 debt-to-equity ratio.

SOLUTION

Certain preliminary calculations must be performed in the IRR method of capital budgeting, after which the structuring steps are completed in order.

Preliminary Computations

The required rate of return the lease company will use in structuring must first be calculated, using the growth rate and dividend payout ratio to calculate the ROE.

$$\text{ROE} = \frac{10\% \text{ growth rate}}{(1 - 44.5\% \text{ payout ratio})}$$

$$= \frac{10\%}{55.5\%}$$

$$= 18\%$$

Once the ROE has been calculated, it is substituted for the after-tax, weighted cost of equity number in the cost of capital derivation. The required after-tax is then computed.

$$
\begin{array}{l}
\quad \text{after-tax weighted cost of debt} \\
+ \; \text{after-tax weighted cost of equity} \\
\hline
\quad \text{Required after-tax ROA}
\end{array}
$$

$$
\begin{array}{lll}
.86 \times 8\% \times (1 - .34) & = & 4.54\% \\
.14 \times 18\% & = & 2.52 \\
\hline
\text{After-tax ROA (or IRR)} & & 7.06\%
\end{array}
$$

The monthly nominal IRR to be used for structuring is then computed.

Monthly nominal IRR

$$\sqrt[12]{1 + \frac{7.06}{100}}$$

HP-12C solution

1.0706	ENTER	
12	1/x	
	y^x	
1	−	
100	×	.5701 per month nominal yield

Note the lessor's annual 7.06% IRR includes monthly compounding; therefore, the monthly rate is not 1/12 of 7.06%, but is the 12th root of the rate.

In order to save time discounting cash flows generated by tax deductions or expenses, a type of present value factor will be computed and applied to all situations involving taxes. The factor will be referred to as the intraperiod present value factor (IPVF). To compute the IPVF, present value the quarterly estimated tax payment percentages to the lease inception date using the monthly nominal IRR, as in Table 4. Budgeted tax date percentages occurring before the lease inception are future valued to the lease inception for budgeted IPVFs, also shown in Table 4.

Step One

Identify and present value to the date of the lease inception all known cash flows including tax benefits.

1. All the known cash flows must be identified and listed

> Equipment cost
> Initial direct costs
> Lease origination fee
> Refundable security deposit
> Working capital and uninvested capital
> Residual value (net of taxes and deposit refund)

Table 4
IPVF Calculations

	Months	Quarterly Tax Payment %	Present/Future Value	
Incremental IPVF				
November 30	0	.000	–	.0000
December 15	.5	.900	(FV)	.8974
March 15	3.5	.100	(PV)	.0980
IPVF (incremental)				.9954
Budgeted IPVF				
April 15	–7.5	.225	(FV)	.2348
June 15	–5.5	.225	(FV)	.2321
September 15	–2.5	.225	(FV)	.2282
November 30	0	.000	–	.0000
December 15	+ .5	.225	(PV)	.2244
March 15	+ 3.5	.100	(PV)	.0980
IPVF (budgeted)				1.0175

MACRS depreciation

G & A expenses

Net inception outflow

2. The present value of the equipment cost must be determined
   (a) $100,000 with a 2-week delayed takedown
   (b)

.5701		i
100,000	CHS	FV
.5		n (2-week delayed takedown)
		PV 99,715.76

3. Any initial direct costs should be identified and expressed at their after-tax equivalent
   (a) Expense × [1 – (tax rate × IPVF)]   =   after-tax cost
   (b) 2,500 × [1 – (.34 × .9954)]   = $1,653.91
   Note the incremental IPVF is used since the lease will be structured during the last tax quarter and will not be considered part of any earlier budgeted amount for tax purposes

4. The lease origination fee (LOF) is expressed at its after-tax equivalent
       $500 × [1 – (.34 × .9954)]   = $330.78

5. The impact of the $2,000 refundable security deposit, which is not adjusted for tax benefits since it is not tax deductible, must be identified. Its refund will be considered as part of the net residual yet to be calculated

6. The impact of the working capital and uninvested capital, given at $300, must be identified. There are no tax consequences to this cost

7. The value of the MACRS tax benefit is calculated

   1st tax year

20%	× $100,000	× .34	× .9954 =	$6,768.72
(MACRS %	× tax basis	× tax rate	× IPVF)	

   2nd through 6th tax year

7.06		i	(annual effective IRR)	
.32	g	CF$_j$		
.192	g	CF$_j$		
.1152	g	CF$_j$		
2	g	N$_j$		
.0576	g	CF$_j$		
	f	NPV	.68893	
100,000		x	(68,893.14)	
.34		x	(23,423.67)	
1.0175		x		
				23,833.58
Present value of the MACRS benefit				$30,602.30

8. The present value of the residual proceeds (after-tax) must be calculated. Since the asset will be fully depreciated during the sixth tax year, there will be no remaining tax basis of the asset and, therefore, all residual proceeds will be fully taxable

   (a) Net residual × [1 − (tax rate × IPVF incremental)]   =   after-tax cost

   (b) $12,500 × [1 − (.34 × .9954)]   = $ 8,269.55

      Less refund of deposit   (2,000.00)

      Plus return of working capital and uninvested capital   300.00

      Net residual proceeds $ 6,569.55

.5701		i	
6,569.55	CHS	FV	
60		n	
		PV	4,670.92

9. G & A expenses must be converted to an after-tax basis and then present valued.

Tax Year	Variable Expenses +	Fixed Expenses	Total	Number of Months
1	10 +	30	40	2
2	10 +	27	37	12
3	10 +	23	33	12
4	10 +	18	28	12
5	10 +	12	22	12
6	10 +	4	14	10

Pretax present value of G & A expenses

.5701		i
40	g	CF_j
2	g	N_j
37	g	CF_j
12	g	N_j
33	g	CF_j
12	g	N_j
28	g	CF_j
12	g	N_j
22	g	CF_j
12	g	N_j
14	g	CF_j
10	g	N_j
	f	NPV $1,441.50

Present value tax savings of G & A expenses

7.06		i	
27.07	g	CF_o	$(2 \times 40 \times .34 \times .9954)$
153.60	g	CF_j	$(12 \times 37 \times .34 \times 1.0175)$
137.00	g	CF_j	$(12 \times 33 \times .34 \times 1.0175)$
116.24	g	CF_j	$(12 \times 28 \times .34 \times 1.0175)$
91.33	g	CF_j	$(12 \times 22 \times .34 \times 1.0175)$
48.43	g	CF_j	$(10 \times 14 \times .34 \times 1.0175)$
	f	NPV	488.75
		After-tax basis	$ 952.75

10. Summary of the present value of all known cash inflows and outflows

Equipment cost	($ 99,715.76)
Initial direct costs	(1,653.91)
Lease origination fee	330.78
Refundable security deposit	2,000.00
Working capital and uninvested capital	(300.00)
MACRS depreciation	30,602.30
Residual proceeds	4,670.92
G & A expenses	(952.75)
Unrecouped investment	($ 65,018.42)

Step Two

Calculate the present value of the unknown lease payments, letting one dollar equal each lease payment.

.5701		i	
2	g	CF_o	(two advance payments)
1	g	CF_j	
58	g	N_j	(remaining 58 payments)
	f	NPV	51.267539

Step Three
Calculate the tax liability associated with the one dollar lease payments in Step Two.

7.06		i	
.676872	g	CF_o	$(2 \times .34 \times .9954)$
4.151400	g	CF_j	$(12 \times .34 \times 1.0175)$
4	g	N_j	
3.459500	g	CF_j	$(10 \times .34 \times 1.0175)$
	f	NPV	17.179187

Step Four
The results of Step Three are deducted from Step Two and the difference is divided into Step One.

51.267539
−17.179187
34.088352   (after-tax structuring factor)

$$\frac{\$65,018.42 \ \text{(unrecouped investment)}}{34.088352 \ \text{(structuring factor)}} = \$1,907.35$$

Therefore, the lease payment in this comprehensive example is $1,907.35 and the lease rate factor is computed to be .019074 ($1,907.35 ÷ $100,000).

MATCH FUNDING TECHNIQUES
The previously described methods of determining hurdle rates through capital budgeting assumed the lessor's debt-to-equity ratio remained constant throughout the lease term. When a lessor match funds a lease, the debt-to-equity ratio relative to that lease changes constantly (match funding is described in Chapter Seven). Match funding generally requires a loan used in funding a lease to be paid back in equal installments over the same term of the lease.

The technique of establishing a hurdle rate for a match funded lease is basically the same as that for a constant debt-to-equity lease. However, three additional cash flows are included in the first structuring step: (1) match funded loan proceeds, (2) loan payments and (3) tax benefits generated from interest expense, as shown in Table 5. Inclusion of debt proceeds, payments and interest tax benefits as part of the cost of leasing implies that the resulting cash flows inure to the benefit of the equity holders. Thus, all after-debt cash flows will be discounted at the lessor's cost of equity. Using the information in Table 5, and adjusting for the following assumptions, the lease payment of $1,810.12 and lease rate factor of .0181012 are calculated.

Table 5
Present Value Summary of all
Known Cash Flows

Equipment cost	($ 99,310.34)
Initial direct costs	(1,659.27)
Lease origination fee	331.85
Refundable security deposit	2,000.00
Working capital and uninvested capital	(300.00)
MACRS depreciation	26,736.20
Residual proceeds	2,883.22
G & A expenses	(799.19)
Loan proceeds	86,000.00
Loan payments	(71,079.26)
Interest tax benefits	4,572.48
Net unrecouped equity	($ 50,624.31)

Loan proceeds: $86,000 (6 to 1 debt-to-equity ratio)

Interest rate: 8% pretax

Terms: 58 payments in arrears at $1,792.73, with no balloon payment, although some lease companies might obtain one

Return on equity: 18% annual effective or 1.3889% per month nominal

IPVFs: Incremental   .9891
       Budgeted   1.0439

It is concluded that, without match funding, the lease rate factor and payment are .019074 and $1,907.35, respectively. With match funding, the lease rate factor and payment are .0181012 and $1,810.12, respectively, which represents a 5.1% decrease. In both cases, however, the lessor is earning an 18% ROE. The primary difference between the two techniques is that match funding has more debt outstanding over the lease term than the constant debt-to-equity method. More debt implies less equity — with less equity earning 18%, the payment can drop. Obviously, the lessor can charge the higher amount, $1,907.35, and still match fund, with the result that its ROE would be higher than 18%.

One difficulty with match funding is the appropriateness of earning a constant 18% return over the lease term during the period when the debt, as a percentage of the investment, is increasing as it does under match funding (see Chapter Seven). As Table 3 indicates, the higher the debt, the higher the required ROE; therefore, under match funding, higher and higher discount rates theoretically should be used as the match funded debt-to-equity ratio increases. The net lease payment resulting from this theoretical approach would be exactly the same as determined under the constant debt-to-equity method (refer to the Miller-Modigliani arguments concerning debt-to-equity ratios in any intermediate finance textbook). Nevertheless, many lessors structure match funded leases in the manner described above.

SENSITIVITY ANALYSIS AND CAPITAL BUDGETING

Once a lease has been structured to achieve a particular hurdle rate, it is very easy to perform sensitivity analysis if the lease term does not change, which would alter the structuring factor. Studying the impact of the security deposit — its deletion, exclusion, increase, etc., or changes in other lease structuring variables such as fees and residuals — is very easy if certain rules are kept in mind.

The first step is to divide any changes in the Step One net investment total by the Step Four lease structuring factor to determine the impact on lease payments or rates. Any increases in the unrecouped net investment (additional negative cash flows) will cause an increase in lease payments, while any decreases in the net investment will cause decreases in the lease payment. These steps are accurate as long as the number of advance payments and lease term remain constant; otherwise Steps Two through Four have to be repeated. Several examples of sensitivity analysis performed on the previous base lease appear in the following section.

Changes in Refundable Security Deposit

By how much would the lease payment increase were the $2,000 refundable security deposit removed from the lease?

The net adjustment to the unrecouped net investment first must be determined.

.5701			i	
2,000		g	CF_o	(deposit inflow)
0		g	CF_j	
59		g	N_j	
2,000	CHS	g	CF_j	(deposit refund outflow)
		f	NPV	578.01

Without the deposit, $578.01 of net investment value is lost, so the unrecouped net investment would increase by the $578.01 amount. The impact on pricing is found by dividing the $578.01 by the lease structuring factor as computed earlier in Step Four.

$$\frac{\$578.01}{34.088352} = \$16.96 \text{ or a } .0001696 \text{ rate increase}$$

Changes in Origination Fees

By how much would the lease payment increase without the $500 origination fee? Divide the after-tax value of the fee by the structuring factor.

$$\frac{\$330.78}{34.088352} = \$9.70 \text{ or a } .000097 \text{ rate increase}$$

Changes in MACRS Depreciation

Suppose the asset was 7-year MACRS classlife equipment, what would happen to the lease payment?

Recompute the present value of the MACRS depreciation using the 7-year percentages. Note that since this is a 5-year lease the last 2 years of depreciation will become part of the salvage value tax basis.

1st tax year

$$.1428 \times \$100,000 \times .34 \times .9954 = \qquad \$ 4,832.87$$

2nd through 6th tax year

7.06		i		
.2449	g	CF_j		
.1749	g	CF_j		
.1249	g	CF_j		
.0893	g	CF_j		
.0893	g	CF_j		
	f	NPV	.6146	
100,000		x	61,459.32	
.34		x	20,896.17	
1.0175		x		21,261.85

6th tax year, remaining tax basis present value

$$(.0893 + .0446) \times \$100,000 \times .34 \times .9954 = \$4,531.66$$

4,531.66	CHS	FV	
60		n	
.5701		i	
		PV	3,221.99

Total 7-year MACRS value $29,316.71

5-year MACRS value	$ 30,602.30
7-year MACRS value	29,316.71
Difference	$ 1,285.59

$$\frac{\$1,285.59}{34.088352} = \$37.71, \text{ or a } .000377 \text{ lease rate factor increase}$$

The lease payment would increase for the change in MACRS classlife.

Changes in Residual Amounts

What impact will an additional $2,500 in residual value have on the lease rate? First convert the increase in residual to its after-tax value.

$$\$2,500 \times [1 - (.34 \times .9954)] = \$1,653.91$$

Determine the present value of the after-tax increase in residual value.

1,653.91	CHS	FV
60	n	
.5701	i	
	PV	1,175.92

Divide the present value of the residual increase by the structuring factor.

$$\frac{\$1,175.92}{34.088352} = \$34.50 \text{ or a .000345 lease rate factor decrease for every \$2,500 increase in residual}$$

CONCLUSION

Capital budgeting for a leasing company is the process of determining whether a given lease rental generates sufficient profit to meet the lessor's income and growth objectives. More often, the process is used in reverse to solve for the hurdle rate or rental payment that generates the targeted income objective. Lease rates are fixed by what the market will bear, but never below the hurdle rate floor. It was illustrated that lease rentals coupled with residual values, origination fees and tax benefits must be sufficient to defray equipment cost, initial direct costs and G & A expenses. G & A expenses can be allocated on an incremental or fully absorbed basis to each individual lease. An additional cost allocation is the pro rata share of working capital and uninvested capital for which each lease must earn a return. Although many do not realize it, these are necessary steps in the overall structuring process.

CHAPTER ELEVEN
DEBT FUNDING TECHNIQUES

The use of borrowed funds to finance all or part of the cost of leased assets is standard practice in today's leasing industry; therefore, the funding aspects of a lease are an integral part of the transaction. This chapter deals with five important attributes of debt funding that should be considered by those involved in structuring and funding leases:

- Cost of Debt
- Amount of Debt Relative to Assets (Financial Leverage)
- Debt Payback Method (Debt Optimization)
- Tax Ramifications of Funding (Recourse Versus Nonrecourse)
- Accounting Implications of Debt (Sale or Pledge).

COST OF DEBT

Leasing companies earn profit primarily by maintaining a positive interest spread between the interest earned in a lease and the interest cost of the debt funding. In some tax-oriented leases this spread can be negligible, especially when the lessor depends upon tax benefits instead of the interest spread as the primary source of earnings.

Debt cost generally remains at a fixed rate over the lease term to avoid the problems associated with fixed returns being mismatched with increasing debt costs. Some lessors during the last recession attempted to solve this problem by writing variable payment leases whose lease payments would increase whenever borrowing rates increased, but variable rate leases never really became established. The trend now is to fund with fixed borrowing rates over the lease term.

Debt cost is such an important expense in operating a lease company that many managerial income statements for lessors appear with debt cost shown as the second line item, as in Figure 1.

Interest income	$ 10,000,000	
Interest expense	6,000,000	
Disposable interest spread		$ 4,000,000
Residual gains		180,000
Other income		40,000
Total income sources		$ 4,220,000

Figure 1
Income Statement

AMOUNT OF DEBT RELATIVE TO ASSETS (FINANCIAL LEVERAGE)

Due to the contractually agreed upon nature of lease company rental revenues, significant amounts of financial leverage are commonplace in equipment leasing. Typical amounts of debt relative to equity in single investor leases are six to one, or debt of 85.7% (86%) and equity of 14.3% (14%). At this leverage amount, typical returns on equity range from 16 to 19%. Higher amounts of debt would require greater returns on equity (see Chapters Seven and Ten).

Because of the high proportions of debt and the low risk (contractually agreed upon rentals), lease companies have weighted average costs of capital far below those of manufacturing companies. A typical lessor cost of capital would be computed as shown in Figure 2.

Debt at 86% of the capital structure, costing 8% pretax
Equity at 14% of the capital structure, costing 18% after-tax
Tax rate of 34%

Formula for the cost of capital:

$$\frac{\text{Cost of debt (\% debt} \times \text{debt cost} \times (1 - \text{tax rate}))}{+ \text{ Cost of equity (\% equity} \times \text{cost of equity})}$$
$$\text{Cost of capital}$$

Cost of debt	=	.86 × 8% × (1–.34)	=	4.541%
Cost of equity	=	.14 × 18%	=	2.520
Cost of capital				7.061%

Figure 2
Cost of Capital Computation

On the other hand, a manufacturing company with 45% debt, costing 8%, and 55% equity, costing 16%, would have the following cost of capital:

Cost of debt	=	$.45 \times 8 \times (1-.34)$	=	2.376%
Cost of equity	=	$.55 \times 16$	=	8.800
Cost of capital				11.176%

Notice there is a 4.115 percentage point spread between the two costs of capital caused primarily by the greater leverage of the lease company.

A common failure in leasing concerning financial leverage is the result of ignorance. As leverage increases so does the risk of the firm; therefore, as leverage increases, equity costs as well as debt costs should increase. Then, too, a given after-tax return on assets before debt funding, earnings before interest (EBI), should result in higher and higher returns on equity as debt funding levels are increased. Even without possible increases in the cost of debt that higher leverage amounts might cause, the return on equity (ROE) of a firm must increase as leverage grows. This relationship is shown in Table 1, where a constant 8% cost of debt is assumed.

Notice if a lessor increased its leverage from 86% (industry norm) to 93%, its ROE must increase significantly. In this example (based on industry norms), lessors settling for lower ROEs than 18% with leverage above 86% are accepting too little return for the level of financial leverage. Remember, too, that the required ROEs of Table 1 have not been adjusted for increases in debt cost at higher levels of debt.

Table 1
Relationship of ROE to Leverage
(based on preceding cost of capital formula where
cost of capital remains constant at 7.061%)

Leverage Amount	Required ROE
10%	7.3%
50	8.8
75	12.4
86	18.0
90	23.1
93	30.7
95	40.9

DEBT PAYBACK METHOD (DEBT OPTIMIZATION)

When lessors obtain debt funding from banks, commercial paper, bond markets, etc., they usually will be maintaining a constant debt-to-equity ratio. The debt-to-equity ratio might be imposed by the lender directly, or indirectly by Moody's, Standard and Poors or other rating agencies. On the other hand, the lessor might be unconstrained by second parties, but still might choose to maintain a particular debt percentage because it is deemed to be at an optimum level for that company. Whatever the reason for maintaining a constant debt percentage, the result will be that the debt used to fund a particular transaction will be paid back in a unique manner that will maintain the required debt-equity relationship. The following example demonstrates the unique manner in which debt is assumed to be repaid when a lessor maintains a constant debt-to-equity ratio.

Assume the following after-tax cash flows received on a lease (no debt payback or interest costs have been deducted). The equipment's cost is $5,447 and the after-tax return on assets, internal rate of return (IRR), is equal to 7%. Debt costs the lessor 8% pretax and represents 86% of the equipment's cost, with the loan equal to $4,685. The required return on equity is 17.59%.

Year	0	1	2	3	4	5
	($5,447)	$1,500	$1,500	$1,100	$1,100	$1,400

As this after-tax cash flow is received by the lessor it will be distributed according to the priority shown in Table 2 for the first year cash flow. Each year this process is repeated until the debt has been fully paid. The resulting cash flows appear as in Table 3.

Note in Tables 2 and 3 that the lessor's debt to equity relationship is always 86% debt; for example, at the end of the third year, debt is $1,936 or .86 × $2,250 of total assets. The net result of these schedules is that the lease's underlying debt has been amortized in a unique way in Table 4.

However, there are numerous other ways of paying down a debt. These other methods are referred to collectively as debt optimization techniques. For example, match funding is a common and very basic method of debt optimizing, where the debt is paid back in equal installment payments over a period matching the lease term. The primary result of debt optimization is to raise the lessor's ROE (although there are numerous other objectives that can be achieved with debt optimization — discussed later in this chapter).

To understand how the match funding method of debt optimization alters the lessor's ROE, the previous example will be adjusted for match funded debt that will be paid back in five equal installments of $1,173.39, as shown in Table 5.

In the match funding situation, the loan payback is determined by the lender without regard to the investment's after-tax cash flow or the impact on the lessor's debt percentage. A 5-year equal payment installment loan has its own unique amortization and resulting payback

Table 2
Distribution of Earnings (Year One)

Calculation	Distribution	Remaining Cash Flow Balance
		$ 1,500
1. Interest on debt, after-tax		
$4,685 \times .08 \times (1 - .34) =$	$ 247	1,253
2. Return on equity (return on assets – debt cost after-tax)		
($5,447 \times .07) – $247 \quad =	$ 134	1,119
or $762 \times .1759$, where $762 equals total beginning equity		
3. Debt payback (86% of cash flow balance)		
$1,119 \times .86 \quad\quad =	$ 962	157
4. Equity payback (remaining balance)	$ 157	0

schedule. What is interesting about the two debt repayment schedules (constant debt to equity versus match funded) is the difference in their ROEs, whose calculation is shown in Table 6.

The match funded ROE (IRR) is 4.3 full percentage points above the constant debt-to-equity funding method. How does one account for the difference since both were funded with the same amount of debt, were paid back over the same time period and incurred the same interest cost? The answer has to do with the amount of financial leverage associated with the two funding alternatives. The following figures show the difference in financial leverage over the lease term (Figure 3) and the difference between outstanding debt over the term (Figure 4).

Notice in Figure 3 the financial leverage debt percentages started at 86% for both the match funded and the constant debt-to-equity funding method, but the match funded debt percentage quickly increased and remained above that point for most of the lease term. This extra financial leverage accounted for the increase in ROE yield and decrease in the cash flow.

Other methods of debt optimization would include:

1. Solving for a debt payback schedule that would eliminate any disinvestment balances caused by numerous negative cash flows in a lease
2. Solving for a debt payback schedule that maximizes the lease's multiple investment sinking fund (MISF) return. MISF is used primarily in leveraged leasing
3. Solving for the maximum total cash flow given a particular MISF or IRR requirement
4. Solving for the maximum IRR or external rate of return (ERR) given a particular cash flow requirement.

Table 3
Loan and Equity Paybacks
(constant debt-to-equity)

Year	1	2	3	4	5
Earnings					
Interest	$ 247	$ 197	$ 142	$ 102	$ 59
Loan payback	962	1,029	758	811	1,125
Loan total	$ 1,209	$ 1,226	$ 900	$ 913	$ 1,184
Return on equity	$ 134	$ 106	$ 77	$ 55	$ 34
Equity payback	157	168	123	132	182
Equity total	$ 291	$ 274	$ 200	$ 187	$ 216
Total cash flow	$ 1,500	$ 1,500	$ 1,100	$ 1,100	$ 1,400
Debt, equity and investment balances					
Remaining debt balances	$ 4,685	$ 3,723	$ 2,694	$ 1,936	$ 1,125	$ 0
Remaining equity balances	762	605	437	314	182	0
Total investment	$ 5,447	$ 4,328	$ 3,131	$ 2,250	$ 1,307	$ 0

Table 4
Debt Amortization

Year	0	1	2	3	4	5
Debt principal payments	$ 0	$ 962	$ 1,029	$ 758	$ 811	$ 1,125
Remaining principal balances	$ 4,685	$ 3,723	$ 2,694	$ 1,936	$ 1,125	$ 0

Table 5
Loan and Equity Paybacks
(match funded)

Year	0	1	2	3	4	5
Interest	$ 0	$ 247	$ 205	$ 160	$ 110	$ 57
Loan payback	0	799	862	931	1,006	1,086
Loan total	$ 0	$ 1,046	$ 1,067	$ 1,091	$ 1,116	$ 1,143
Equity cash flow	0	454	433	9	(6)	257
Total cash flow	$ 0	$ 1,500	$ 1,500	$ 1,100	$ 1,100	$ 1,400
Declining debt balance	$ 4,685	$ 3,886	$ 3,024	$ 2,093	$ 1,086	$ 0
Debt %		86%	89.8%	96.6%	93.0%	83.1%	0

Table 6
Return on Equity Comparison

Constant Debt-to-Equity				Match Funded			
762	CHS	g	CF_o	762	CHS	g	CF_o
291		g	CF_j	454		g	CF_j
274		g	CF_j	433		g	CF_j
200		g	CF_j	9		g	CF_j
187		g	CF_j	6	CHS	g	CF_j
216		g	CF_j	257		g	CF_j
Total net cash flow		f	NPV 406			f	NPV 385
ROE (IRR)		f	IRR 17.6			f	IRR 21.9

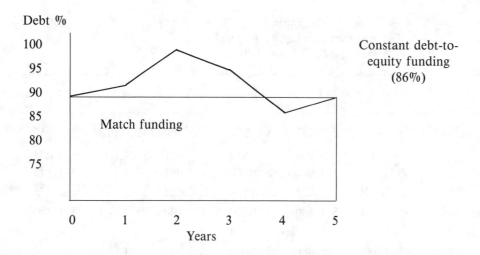

Figure 3
Differences in Financial Leverage
(debt expressed as a % of net lease investment)

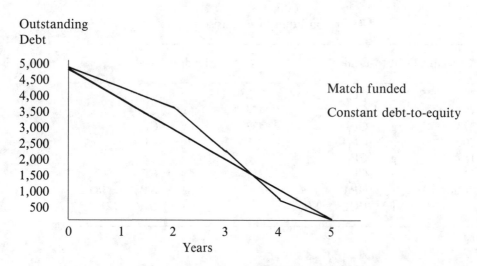

Figure 4
Differences in Financial Leverage
(outstanding debt balances)

TAX RAMIFICATIONS OF FUNDING (RECOURSE VERSUS NONRECOURSE)

There are three primary issues concerning the tax aspects of funding: (1) the at-risk provisions of Revenue Procedure (Rev. Proc.) 75-21 have been met when a lease has been funded with a large proportion of nonrecourse debt, (2) the tax consequences of a lessee default when a lease is funded with nonrecourse debt have been considered and (3) the treatment of the funding as a sale of property or as a collateralization of a loan has been proper.

At-risk Provisions of Revenue Procedure 75-21

When significant amounts of nonrecourse debt have been used to fund a leveraged lease, the lessor must be at-risk 20% at the lease's inception and throughout the lease term. At-risk investment includes equity plus any recourse debt used by the lessor to fund its direct investment in the lease, with the balance being funded with nonrecourse debt. The 20% rule comes from the guidelines published by the Internal Revenue Service (IRS) in Rev. Proc. 75-21, discussed more fully in Chapter Three. Numerous lessors do not feel it necessary to conform to the strict 20% guideline of Rev. Proc. 75-21, but still maintain an at-risk position of about 14% or more.

Tax Consequences of a Lessee Default on a Leveraged Lease

To the degree the nonrecourse debt assumed by the lender in a default of a leveraged lease exceeds the lessor's tax basis (remaining undepreciated cost), the resulting difference is taxable as ordinary income to the lessor. This is known in the industry as the unravel risk in leveraged leasing. Should a lease unravel or be taken apart because the nonrecourse lender repossesses the lessee's equipment, the above cited risk could have severe lessor consequences. Suppose, for example, that in the fourth year of a 10-year leveraged lease the remaining tax basis is 28.8% of the equipment's original cost (100% – 20% – 32% – 19.2%), when the nonrecourse debt balance is still 68.8% of the equipment's original cost. Should the nonrecourse funder repossess the equipment, the lessor would have to pay 34% (tax rate) of 40% of the equipment's adjusted cost (68.8% – 28.8 = 40%). Thirty-four percent of 40% is 13.6% of the equipment's cost. Thus, a million dollar equipment lease could cause a $136,000 tax liability for the lessor upon a lessee default, a liability that must be paid without the benefit of any rentals from the lease.

Sale versus Collateral Pledge

The borrowing of funds must not be deemed to be a sale of the equipment. Instead, the funding must be collateralized with the leased equipment without the assignment documents implying that a title transfer has, or will, occur except in the case of lessee default. Should the IRS treat a loan as a de facto sale the lessor would lose any Modified Accelerated Cost Recovery System (MACRS) depreciation, gross profit tax deferral and any other available tax benefits.

ACCOUNTING IMPLICATIONS OF DEBT (SALE OR PLEDGE)

Similar to the tax definitions of borrowing previously described, accounting rules also distinguish between the sale and pledge of lease receivables. In addition, the recourse versus nonrecourse status of debt transactions has importance. The many combinations of these two accounting aspects of debt require a fundamental knowledge of the sale versus pledge issue and the basic funding methods from an accounting viewpoint. As a result of the two accounting aspects of debt there are four basic situations encountered:

1. Sale of leases with recourse
2. Sale of leases without recourse
3. Collateral pledge of leases with recourse
4. Collateral pledge of leases without recourse.

Regardless of which funding techniques is used, there will be two primary accounting consequences:

1. Whether sale or loan accounting treatment will be accorded the transaction
2. Whether the remaining unearned income associated with the residual will be recognized over the remaining lease term if only the lease payments have been sold or pledged (not the residual).

If a transaction is accorded sale treatment the lessor, in substance, will treat the lease as having been sold and, therefore, the lease receivables (net of unearned income) will be removed from the balance sheet, resulting in a gain or loss recognized currently. Generally, when the implicit rate in a lease is higher than the lender's discount rate, a gain on the transfer of the lease will occur, which gives rise to the term sale treatment. On the other hand, a loss could occur if the lender's discount rate is higher than the implicit rate in the lease.

However, if the same transaction is given loan treatment, the net lease receivable will remain and the loan proceeds will be booked as a loan liability (rather than being offset against the net receivable). Furthermore, no gain or loss on the transaction will occur. In summary, sale or loan treatment results in the following:

Sale: Balance sheet - Loan proceeds are offset against the net investment in the lease. No loan liability appears. The residual may still appear if it was not sold as part of the transaction

Income statement - Gain or loss is shown immediately as part of income

Loan: Balance sheet - Loan proceeds appear as a liability separate from the net investment in the lease

Income statement - Nothing is shown — no gains or losses.

Sale Versus Loan Example

An example of sale versus loan treatment is shown for a direct financing capital lease in Figures 5 through 7.

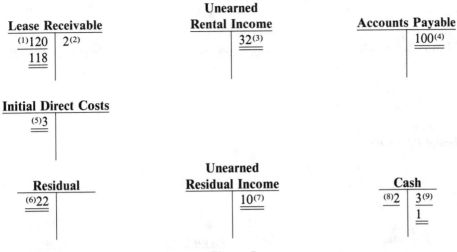

Figure 5
T-account Summary at Inception

ASSUMPTIONS

The following assumptions will be used:

        Payments: 60, in advance, of $2
        Residual: $22
        Initial direct costs: $3
        Equipment cost: $100
        Implicit rate in the lease: 12%
        Loan proceeds: $95 (10% lender discount rate).

The explanations of the entries of Figure 5 (by number) are as follows:

(1) 60 rentals at $2 equals $120
(2) One advance rental
(3) Portion of unearned income attributable to the rentals. This amount is equal to the difference between the lease receivable of $120 plus the initial direct costs of $3 less the present value ($91) of the sixty $2 rentals in advance, discounted at the lease's 1% per month implicit rate
(4) Equipment costs
(5) Capitalized initial direct costs (IDC) per Financial Accounting Standards Board Statement No. 91 (FASB 91) treatment, which no longer allows IDC to be an unearned income offset
(6) Unguaranteed residual estimated at $22

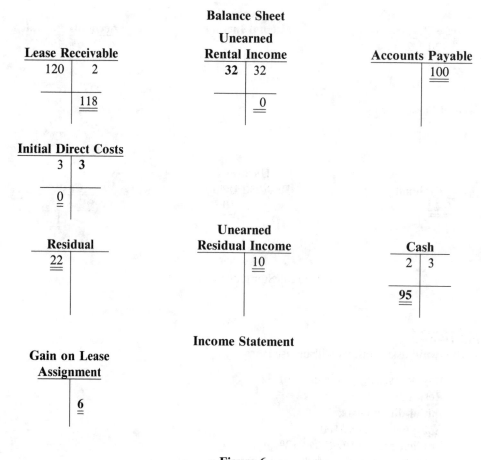

Figure 6
Sale Treatment

(7) Portion of overall unearned income attributable to the residual equal to the difference between the future $22 estimated value and its present value of $12 (discounted at the 1% per month implicit rate)

(8) One advance payment of $2 received at lease inception

(9) Cash payment of initial direct costs.

Note that the lease receivable, initial direct costs and the unearned rental income have been removed entirely from the books. This is consistent with the concept that the rental stream indeed has been sold. Since the net investment at the time of the sale was $89 ($118 + $3 – $32: lease receivable + initial direct costs – unearned rental income) and the loan or sale proceeds were $95, a $6 assignment gain resulted. The net residual of $12 ($22 – $10) remains on the

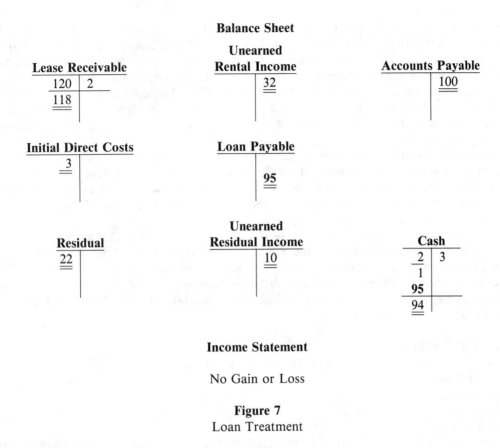

Balance Sheet

Lease Receivable	Unearned Rental Income	Accounts Payable
120 | 2	| 32	| 100
118		

Initial Direct Costs	Loan Payable	
3	| 95	

Residual	Unearned Residual Income	Cash
22	| 10	2 | 3
		1
		95
		94

Income Statement

No Gain or Loss

Figure 7
Loan Treatment

books until the termination of the lease. Its unearned income may or may not be recognized depending upon its conformity to FASB Technical Bulletin 86-2, discussed later. Note that the only balance sheet impact is the appearance of a loan liability equal to the loan proceeds, hence, the term loan treatment. In addition, there was no income statement impact.

Funding Nomenclature

Should a given leasing transaction be given sale or loan treatment? First, it must be ascertained whether the transaction is with or without recourse to the lessor. If the assignment of the leases (whether used to transfer rights in a sale or pledge) is with recourse, the lender can force the lessor-transferor to buy back the lease (or substitute a lease, or find a new lessee) should the lessee default. In a nonrecourse situation, the lender-transferee cannot look to the lessor-transferor upon lessee default.

Once the recourse status is determined, it must be ascertained whether the transaction was a collateral pledge or an outright sale. In a pledging situation the lease receivable is assigned to the lender solely as collateral for a loan. In the typical pledge, a company first enters into either a sales-type or direct financing capital lease. Subsequently, the lessor discounts the lease receivable at a bank (or other lender) and assigns the lease receivables (and possibly the residual, too) as collateral to the bank. The loan proceeds received equal the present value of the remaining lease rentals receivable discounted at the bank's lending rate. The company signs either a recourse or nonrecourse note payable secured by the lease receivable and equipment being leased. Lease rentals paid by the lessee may be received directly by the bank or received by the lessor and passed on to the lender. Such collateralized borrowings can occur on a lease-by-lease basis or include a pool of leases.

Collateral is not an issue in the sale situation since the lease payments are purchased outright. Even though the rentals and/or residual have been purchased, the buyer still may have recourse to the seller-lessor should the lessee default. Basically the difference between a sale and a pledge is a technical legal distinction that differentiates ownership of title from contingent interest in title (lien) for collateral purposes.

Another confusing aspect of selling versus pledging relates to the fact that any or all parts of a lease can be assigned in a sale or pledge situation. For example, lease rentals can be sold apart from the residual, sold together or the residual sold without the rentals. Perhaps the greatest difficulty in understanding the difference between sales versus pledges is lease assignment terminology or, the misuse of leasing terminology. Unfortunately, many terms are used to describe both sales and pledges.

SALES AND PLEDGES

These terms are used often to describe both sales and pledges:

1. Assignment
2. Transfer
3. Discounting
4. Factoring.

These terms refer primarily to the legal mechanism of transferring an interest in a lease receivable from the lessor to the lender whether the transaction is deemed a sale or pledge. Their use causes great confusion due to their inherent ambiguity. Use of these terms to describe the mechanism of transferring title is, perhaps, acceptable, but the sale versus pledge aspect should also be clarified at the same time.

SALES OF LEASE RECEIVABLES

These terms are often used to describe sales of lease receivables:

1. Sale
2. Sale by assignment
3. Transfer
4. Discounting
5. Factoring.

Note the misuse of terms used to describe the transfer mechanism.

COLLATERAL PLEDGES

These terms are often used to describe a collateral pledge:

1. Hypothecation
2. Loan
3. Collateralized loan or borrowing
4. Collateral pledge
5. Pledge
6. Assignment
7. Transfer
8. Factoring
9. Discounting.

It is preferable to say simply that funding transactions are either sales or collateralized pledges, both effectuated by legal documents called assignments. Unfortunately, accounting statements, etc., from the American Institute of CPAs (AICPA), Accounting Principles Board (APB) and FASB are replete with the misuse of these terms.

Accounting Alternatives for Various Funding Methods

Figure 8 identifies each transaction with a number (far right hand side). It also indicates whether a given leasing transaction will be afforded sale (S) treatment (off balance sheet financing with front-loaded profit from any assignment gains described above) or loan (L) treatment (on balance sheet funding without gains). The figure also differentiates between sales and pledges, as well as recourse and nonrecourse transactions and whether or not funding was obtained either at, or subsequent to, a lease's inception. This last circumstance will also impact the accounting treatment. Each of the 34 different accounting results will be described in terms of the nature of the transaction as well as the accounting consequences to the original lessor-transferor's viewpoint. The question marks after any accounting result indicate potential divergence in accounting thought as to treatment between sale and loan.

TRANSACTIONS 1 AND 2

Description of Transactions

Lessor enters into an operating lease (lessor's viewpoint) and subsequently sells a future interest in the lease residual effective after the end of the noncancellable lease term. The purchaser does not expect to lease the equipment on an operating lease basis to others in the future. Note the lease payment stream has not been sold, but is still retained by the lessor. In other words, only the future interest in the asset has been sold without the right to the lease payments. However, the purchaser may have the right to return the equipment at some future date.

Accounting References

FASB Statement No. 48 (FASB 48), paragraphs 6-8.

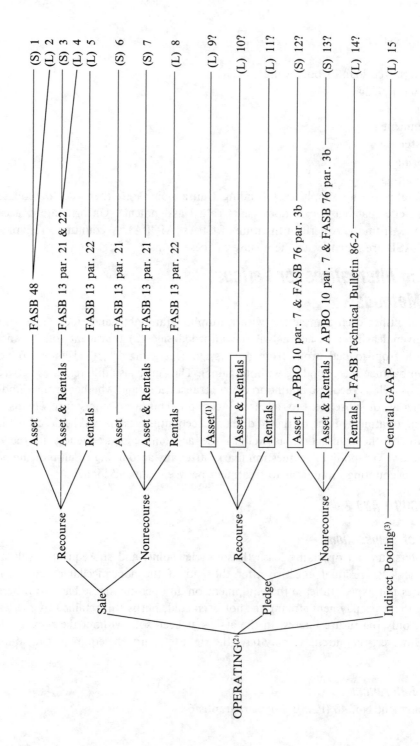

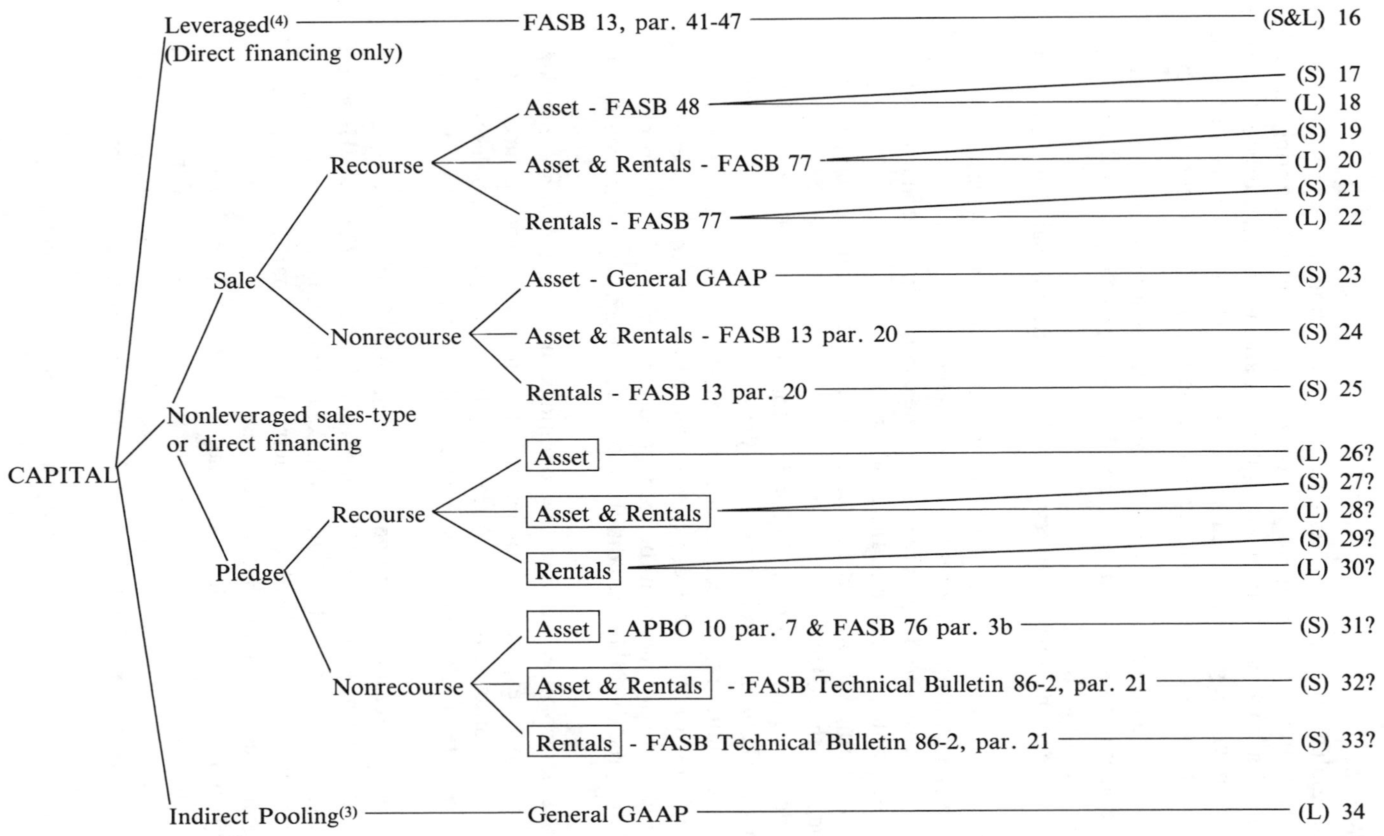

Figure 8

Accounting Alternatives for Various Funding Methods

(1) A box indicates that there is no concensus as to generally accepted accounting principles governing this type of transaction.

(2) Operating versus capital lease in this context is from the lessor's accounting viewpoint. See lessor capital lease criteria in Chapter Fifteen.

(3) Indirect pooling represents borrowing where the lender has only an indirect claim to a lease as collateral. Borrowing with bonds, commercial paper or bank borrowing based on overall net worth of the lessor, etc., are examples of pooling.

(4) Leveraged lease - represents a direct financing capital lease funded with nonrecourse debt plus it meets the other criteria of FASB 13, paragraph 42.

Accounting Consequences

If a lessor sells its residual (or future interests therein) (1) without it being subject to the operating lease, (2) without the buyer anticipating re-leasing the asset on an operating lease basis and (3) without recourse back to the lessor in terms of being able to return the asset (recourse sale), then the transaction will be given sale treatment. However, if a right of return (recourse sale) exists, then FASB 48 controls whether a sale or loan accounting treatment will occur.

If an enterprise sells its product but gives the buyer the right to return the product, revenue from the sales transaction shall be recognized at time of sale only if all of the following conditions are met:

a. The seller's price to the buyer is substantially fixed or determinable at the date of sale.
b. The buyer has paid the seller, or the buyer is obligated to pay the seller and the obligation is not contingent on resale of the product.
c. The buyer's obligation to the seller would not be changed in the event of theft or physical destruction or damage to the product.
d. The buyer acquiring the product for resale has economic substance apart from that provided by the seller.
e. The seller does not have significant obligations for future performance to directly bring about resale of the product by the buyer.
f. The amount of future returns can be reasonably estimated (paragraph 8).

Sales revenue and cost of sales that are not recognized at time of sale because the foregoing conditions are not met shall be recognized either when the return privilege has substantially expired or if those conditions subsequently are met, whichever occurs first.

If sales revenue is recognized because the conditions of paragraph 6 are met, any costs or losses that may be expected in connection with any returns shall be accrued in accordance with FASB Statement No. 5, Accounting for Contingencies. Sales revenue and cost of sales reported in the income statement shall be reduced to reflect estimated returns.

The ability to make a reasonable estimate of the amount of future returns depends on many factors and circumstances that will vary from one case to the next. However, the following factors may impair the ability to make a reasonable estimate:

a. The susceptibility of the product to significant external factors, such as technological obsolescence or changes in demand.
b. Relatively long periods in which a particular product may be returned.
c. Absence of historical experience with similar types of sales of similar products, or inability to apply such experience because of changing circumstances, for example, changes in the selling enterprise's marketing policies or relationships with its customers.
d. Absence of a large volume of relatively homogeneous transactions [FASB 48, paragraphs 6-8].

TRANSACTIONS 3, 4 AND 5

Description of Transactions

Lessor enters into an operating lease (lessor's viewpoint) and subsequently sells the residual (leased property) subject to the operating lease. In other words, both the asset and the operating lease rentals have been sold. If the asset is sold without the operating lease having been consummated, but with full knowledge that the buyer will lease it to others on an operating lease basis, then it will be treated as though the operating lease already exists. Transactions 3 and 4 describe these two situations. Transaction 5 describes the situation where the lessor enters into an operating lease and subsequently sells only the rental stream without any residual rights, but with certain recourse provisions should the lessee default.

Accounting References

FASB Statement No. 13 (FASB 13), paragraphs 21 and 22.

Accounting Consequences

The accounting treatment for Transactions 3 and 4 (sale of asset and rentals) is sale treatment if the seller does not retain substantial risks of ownership; otherwise, loan treatment is required. The accounting for Transaction 5 (sale of rentals only) is loan treatment only.

These conclusions are based on the following paragraphs from FASB 13:

> The sale of property subject to an operating lease, or of property that is leased by or intended to be leased by the third-party purchaser to another party, shall not be treated as a sale if the seller or any party related to the seller retains substantial risks of ownership in the leased property. A seller may by various arrangements assure recovery of the investment by the third-party purchaser in some operating lease transactions and thus retain substantial risks in connection with the property. For example, in the case of default by the lessee or termination of the lease, the arrangements may involve a formal or informal commitment by the seller to (a) acquire the lease or the property, (b) substitute an existing lease, or (c) secure a replacement lessee or a buyer for the property under a remarketing agreement. However, a remarketing agreement by itself shall not disqualify accounting for the transaction as a sale if the seller (a) will receive a reasonable fee commensurate with the effort involved at the time of securing a replacement lessee or buyer for the property and (b) is not required to give priority to the re-leasing or disposition of the property owned by the third-party purchaser over similar property owned or produced by the seller. (For example, a first-in, first-out remarketing arrangement is considered to be a priority.)
>
> If a sale to a third party of property subject to an operating lease or of property that is leased by or intended to be leased by the third-party purchaser to another party is not to be recorded as a sale because of the provisions of paragraph 21 above, the transaction shall be accounted for as a borrowing. (Transactions of these types are in effect collateralized borrowings.) The proceeds from the "sale" shall be recorded as an

obligation on the books of the "seller." Until that obligation has been amortized under the procedure described herein, rental payments made by the lessee(s) under the operating lease or leases shall be recorded as revenue by the "seller," even if such rentals are paid directly to the third-party purchaser. A portion of each rental shall be recorded by the "seller" as interest expense, with the remainder to be recorded as a reduction of the obligation. The interest expense shall be calculated by application of a rate determined in accordance with the provisions of APB Opinion No. 21, Interest on Receivables and Payables, paragraphs 13 and 14. The leased property shall be accounted for as prescribed in paragraph 19(a) for an operating lease, except that the term over which the asset is depreciated shall be limited to the estimated amortization period of the obligation. The sale or assignment by the lessor of lease payments due under an operating lease shall be accounted for as a borrowing as described above [FASB 13, paragraphs 21 and 22].

TRANSACTIONS 6 AND 7

Description of Transactions

Owner sells an asset with or without buyer's intent to release on an operating lease basis, or lessor enters into an operating lease and subsequently sells either the asset or the asset subject to the lease (asset only or asset plus rentals) without any recourse (buyer does not have the right to return the asset for whatever reason).

Accounting References

FASB 13, paragraph 21 and FASB 48, paragraph 6.

Accounting Consequences

Since both of the above described sales of assets (with or without rights to the rental stream) are totally without recourse, i.e., buyers have no rights to return purchased goods, etc., the transactions will be given sale treatment. Refer to FASB 13 and 48 for Transactions 3, 4 and 5.

TRANSACTION 8

Description of Transaction

Lessor enters into an operating lease and subsequently sells the rental stream without selling any interest in the leased asset or in its future residual value.

Accounting Reference

FASB 13, paragraph 22 (last sentence).

Accounting Consequences

Loan treatment is mandated whether the sale of the lease receivables is with or without recourse, which makes sense since there is no recorded rental receivable to sell like in a capital lease. Operating leases show only the equipment leased, not rentals receivable.

TRANSACTION 9

Description of Transaction

Lessor enters into an operating lease and pledges the leased property (not the rental stream) as collateral for a loan.

Accounting References

There are no official generally accepted accounting principles (GAAP); however, 'Accounting by Lease Brokers' AICPA Issues Paper and Emerging Issues Task Force Issue No. 84-25 shed some light on the subject. See Appendix A for relevant excerpts of both.

Accounting Consequences

Loan treatment probably would be given since recourse loans collateralized with property are similar to real estate mortgages, which are always shown as liabilities on the borrower's balance sheet. Furthermore, the right of offset, loan against the residual, is executory, which means it is a future event. Upon loan default the residual will belong to the lender, but not until then.

TRANSACTIONS 10 AND 11

Description of Transactions

Lessor enters into an operating lease and pledges the rental stream or the rental stream plus the leased property as collateral for a full recourse loan.

Accounting References

There is no official GAAP. Refer to Transaction 9 for unofficial references.

Accounting Consequences

Loan treatment probably would be accorded these transactions since they differ from Transaction 9 only in that additional collateral has been given to secure the loans.

TRANSACTIONS 12 AND 13

Description of Transaction

Lessor enters into an operating lease and subsequently pledges the rentals and the leased asset (or future rights to the leased asset alone) on a nonrecourse basis. Nonrecourse implies that a legal and binding right of offset exists against the pledged collateral should the lessee default.

Accounting References

APB Opinion 10, paragraph 7 and FASB Statement No. 76 (FASB 76), paragraph 3b.

Accounting Consequences

Since the asset or the asset along with the operating lease have been pledged in a manner that some deem to be a clear right of offset, there are those who contend sale treatment should be given as described in paragraph 7 of APB Opinion 10, which states "it is a general principal of accounting that the offsetting of assets and liabilities in the balance sheet is improper except where a right of setoff exists." Furthermore, FASB 76, paragraph 3b states that a debt is extinguished (offset against an asset) when "The debtor is legally released from being the primary obligor under the debt . . . by the creditor and it is probable that the debtor will not be required to make future payments with respect to that debt under any guarantees." Since the loan is nonrecourse to the lessor and the lender's sole recourse upon lessee default is the property, some view the transaction as if a de facto defeasance has occurred, thereby allowing sale treatment. However, on February 26, 1987 the FASB Emerging Issues Task Force (EITF) said this concerning such pledges:

> . . . an FASB staff representative commented that the FASB staff has received several calls about the effect paragraph 21 of FASB Technical Bulletin No. 86-2, Accounting for an Interest in the Residual Value of a Leased Asset: Acquired by a Third Party or Retained by a Lessor That Sells the Related Minimum Rental Payments," has on EITF Issue No. 84-25, "Offsetting nonrecourse debt with lease receivables." Some enterprises have apparently offset nonrecourse debt and the related lease receivable used as collateral, viewing the transaction, in substance, as a sale. Several comment letters on the proposed Technical Bulletin (86-2) inquired as to whether it is appropriate to increase the carrying amount of an interest in the residual value of a leased asset if they have offset nonrecourse debt and the related lease receivable. Other than FASB Technical Bulletin No. 85-2, Accounting for Collateralized Mortgage Obligations (CMOs), the staff of the FASB is not aware of any provision in existing pronouncements that allows nonrecourse debt to be accounted for as an in-substance sale, and it is doubtful that those transactions would meet the conditions of that Technical Bulletin. Accordingly, the intent of paragraph 21 of Technical Bulletin 86-2 is to clarify that nonrecourse financing is not considered a sale and that increasing the carrying amount of the residual value of a leased asset is appropriate in that circumstance because the entity would continue to apply lessor accounting as provided in FASB 13, Accounting for Leases. Paragraph 21 of Technical Bulletin 86-2 does reaffirm that paragraph 7 of APB Opinion No. 10, Omnibus Opinion − 1966, prohibits the offsetting of assets and liabilities unless a legal right of setoff exists. Therefore, the staff believes that Technical Bulletin 86-2 has resolved EITF Issue 84-25 and that accounting for nonrecourse financing as an in-substance sale or offsetting nonrecourse debt with lease receivables in which no legal right of setoff exists is not appropriate.

The Securities and Exchange Commission (SEC) observer added that the SEC has recently objected to the offsetting of nonrecourse debt and lease receivables by a registrant on the basis that Technical Bulletin 86-2 reaffirms generally accepted accounting principles with respect to the offsetting issue. In that registrant matter, the registrant asserted that the Technical Bulletin did not apply in this circumstance because the registrant subsequently sold all or a portion of the asset subject to the lease and the nonrecourse borrowing. The SEC staff did not believe that the registrant's subsequent sale of an interest in the asset changed the company's position with respect to either the lease receivable from the original lessee or the nonrecourse borrowing. Further, the SEC observer noted that the SEC Staff is in the process of preparing a Staff Accounting Bulletin to affirm the SEC staff's belief that collateralizing nonrecourse debt with lease receivables neither results in an accounting sale nor allows offsetting of nonrecourse debt against lease receivables [EITF Minutes, February 26, 1987].

SEC Staff Accounting Bulletin 70, incorporating the SEC staff's belief, has subsequently been issued, while the FASB is continuing to address this problem in its financial instruments project. Amembal & Isom's opinion is expressed in a letter to the FASB, which appears in Appendix A.

TRANSACTION 14

Description of Transaction

Lessor enters into an operating lease and subsequently pledges only the rental payment stream and not the leased property as collateral for a loan on a nonrecourse basis. In this situation the lender would have access to the leased property only if the lessee defaulted and the equipment was repossessed. Thus, no direct right of offset exists since the ownership of the property still vests with the lessor and appears on its balance sheet as leased equipment.

Accounting References

FASB Technical Bulletin 86-2, paragraph 21.

Accounting Consequences

Although FASB Technical Bulletin 86-2 and ABPO 10, paragraph 7, describe the right of offset as justifying offsetting liabilities against assets, it must be remembered in an operating lease there is no asset called lease receivable; only the leased equipment appears. Thus, the right of offset exists, but not against an asset that appears on the lessor's balance sheet. Remember, too, the offset right does not directly extend to the leased asset, only indirectly through a lessee default. Since the right of offset is inapplicable in this case loan treatment is required.

TRANSACTION 15

Description of Transaction

Lessor enters into an operating lease that is funded with debt that provides only an indirect collateral interest in the leased property. Bonds, commercial paper, commercial bank credit lines, etc., represent borrowings that do not affect specific transactions, although the total leasing portfolio is probably subject to some overall collateral requirement.

Accounting References

Reference is made to general GAAP, as no specific references exist; however, general debt obligations of any company must be shown as liabilities.

Accounting Consequences

Loan treatment must be given since the pooled debt would be a general obligation of the lessor.

TRANSACTION 16

Description of Transaction

Lessor enters into a direct financing capital lease, which meets all of the additional accounting criteria prescribed for a leveraged lease, and uses the leased equipment as well as the payment stream as collateral for a nonrecourse loan.

Accounting References

FASB 13, paragraphs 41-47.

Accounting Consequences

If the lease qualifies per FASB as a true leveraged lease, a combination of sale and loan treatment is used. The nonrecourse debt proceeds are used to offset the lease receivable similar to sale treatment, but no gain or loss on assignment is shown similar to loan treatment. Therefore, leveraged lease accounting is very unique. (Leveraged leasing, from an accounting perspective, is discussed in Chapter Sixteen.)

In order for a capital lease to be deemed an accounting leveraged lease it must have "all of the following characteristics" [FASB 13, paragraph 42]:

a. Except for the exclusion of leveraged leases from the definition of a direct financing lease as set forth in paragraph 6(b)(ii), it otherwise meets that definition. Leases that meet the definition of sales-type leases set forth in paragraph 6(b)(i) shall not be accounted for as leveraged leases but shall be accounted for as prescribed in paragraph 17.

b. It involves at least three parties: a lessee, a long-term creditor, and a lessor (commonly called the equity participant).

    c.   The financing provided by the long-term creditor is nonrecourse as to the general credit of the lessor (although the creditor may have recourse to the specific property leased and the unremitted rentals relating to it). The amount of the financing is sufficient to provide the lessor with substantial "leverage" in the transaction.

    d.   The lessor's net investment, as defined in paragraph 43, declines during the early years once the investment has been completed and rises during the later years of the lease before its final elimination. Such decreases and increases in the net investment balance may occur more than once [FASB 13, paragraph 42].

FASB Technical Bulletin 86-2, in paragraph 10, implies that all the above criteria be met at the inception of the lease before debt offsetting can occur: ". . . Therefore, offsetting the lease receivable with nonrecourse debt is appropriate only in those circumstances in which a legal right of offset exists or when, at the inception of the lease, the lease meets all of the characteristics of paragraph 42 of 13 and is appropriately classified as a leveraged lease. Otherwise, the guidance provided in paragraph 7 of Opinion 10 should be applied." For nonrecourse funding acquired after a lease's inception refer to Transactions 31, 32 and 33.

TRANSACTIONS 17 AND 18

Description of Transaction

Lessor enters into a capital lease (either sales-type or direct financing, but not leveraged) and subsequently sells a future interest in the lease residual effective after the end of the noncancellable capital lease term. Thus, the leased equipment has not been sold subject to the lease since it represents only a future interest in the property. In other words, only the asset has been sold without any current rights to the lease payments. However, the purchaser may have the right to return the equipment at some future date (recourse sale of a lease).

Accounting References

FASB 48, paragraphs 6-8.

Accounting Consequences

Either sale treatment or loan treatment will be accorded the transaction depending upon the severity of the buyer's right at some future time to return the equipment. FASB 48 provides for sale treatment:

    If an enterprise sells its product but gives the buyer the right to return the product, revenue from the sales transaction shall be recognized at time of sale only if all of the following conditions are met:

        a. The seller's price to the buyer is substantially fixed or determinable at the date of sale.

        b. The buyer has paid the seller, or the buyer is obligated to pay the seller and the obligation is not contingent on resale of the product.

    c. The buyer's obligation to the seller would not be changed in the event of theft or physical destruction or damage of the product.

    d. The buyer acquiring the product for resale has economic substance apart from that provided by the seller.

    e. The seller does not have significant obligations for future performance to directly bring about resale of the product by the buyer.

    f. The amount of future returns can be reasonably estimated [FASB 48, paragraph 6].

TRANSACTIONS 19, 20, 21 AND 22

Description of Transaction

Lessor enters into a capital lease (either sales-type or direct financing, but not leveraged) and subsequently sells either the rental payment stream along with the leased asset (Transactions 19 and 20) or the rental payment stream apart from the equipment leased (Transactions 21 and 22). In both cases the sale is subject to recourse by the purchaser of the leases.

Accounting References

FASB Statement No. 77 (FASB 77), paragraphs 5-8.

Accounting Consequences

A sale of a capital lease or of an asset plus rentals (effectuated by assignment, etc.) with recourse will be recorded as a sale if all of the following provisions are met:

    a. The transferor surrenders control of the future economic benefits embodied in the receivables. Control has not been surrendered if the transferor has an option to repurchase the receivables at a later date.

    b. The transferor's obligation under the recourse provisions can be reasonably estimated. Lack of experience with receivables with characteristics similar to those being transferred or other factors that affect a determination at the transfer date of the collectibility of the receivables may impair the ability to make a reasonable estimate of the probable bad debt losses and related costs of collections and repossessions. A transfer of receivables shall not be recognized as a sale if collectibility of the receivables and related costs of collection and repossession are not subject to reasonable estimation.

    c. The transferee cannot require the transferor to repurchase the receivables except pursuant to the recourse provisions.

If a transfer qualifies to be recognized as a sale, all probable adjustments in connection with the recourse obligations to the transferor shall be accrued in accordance with FASB 5, Accounting for Contingencies. The difference between (a) the sales price (adjusted for the accrual for probable adjustments) and (b) the net receivables shall be recognized as a gain or loss on the sale of receivables. If receivables are sold with servicing retained and the stated servicing fee rate differs materially from a current (normal) servicing fee rate or no servicing fee is specified, the sales price shall be adjusted to provide for a normal servicing fee in each subsequent servicing period, which shall not be less than the estimated servicing costs.

If a transfer qualifies to be recognized as a sale and the sales price is subject to change during the term of the receivables because of a floating interest rate provision, the sales price shall be estimated using an appropriate market interest rate at the transfer date. Subsequent changes in interest rates from the rate used at the transfer date shall be considered changes in the estimate of the sales price and not as interest cost or interest income. The effect shall be reported in income in the period the interest rate changes in accordance with paragraph 31 of APB Opinion No. 20, Accounting Changes [FASB 77, paragraphs 5-7].

If these provisions are not met, the transfer is recognized as a liability.

If any of the conditions in paragraph 5 are not met, the amount of the proceeds from the transfer of receivables shall be reported as a liability. A right of first refusal based on a bona fide offer by an unrelated third party ordinarily is not an option to repurchase. Some transfer agreements require or permit the transferor to repurchase transferred receivables when the amount of outstanding receivables is minor to keep the cost of servicing those receivables from becoming unreasonable. If those reversionary interests are not significant to the transferor, their existence alone does not preclude a transfer from being recognized as a sale [Ibid. paragraph 8].

In most cases, recourse sales of lease receivables (Transactions 21 and 22) or of rentals and the equipment (Transactions 19 and 20) will be accorded sale treatment since the three FASB 77 sale criteria are easily and typically met by lessors.

TRANSACTIONS 23, 24 AND 25

Description of Transaction

Lessor enters into a capital lease (either sales-type or direct financing, but not leveraged) and subsequently sells either the rental payment stream, the asset or the asset along with the rental stream on a nonrecourse basis.

Accounting References

FASB 13, paragraph 20.

Accounting Consequences

FASB 13, paragraph 20 accords such transactions sale treatment.

The sale or assignment of a lease or of property subject to a lease that was accounted for as a sales-type lease or direct financing lease shall not negate the original accounting treatment accorded to the lease. Any profit or loss on the sale or assignment shall be recognized at the time of the transaction except (a) if the sale or assignment is between related parties, the provisions of paragraphs 29 and 30 shall be applied or (b) if the sale or assignment is with recourse, it shall be accounted for in accordance with FASB 77, Reporting by Transferors for Transfers of Receivables with Recourse [FASB 13, paragraph 20].

Sale of residuals without the stream and without recourse are given sale treatment (Transaction 23) per general GAAP.

TRANSACTION 26

Description of Transaction

Lessor enters into a capital lease (either sales-type or direct financing, but not leveraged) and subsequently pledges a future interest in the equipment (after the noncancellable lease term) as collateral for a recourse loan to the lessor.

Accounting References

There is no official GAAP; however, the transaction is similar to normal borrowing where the lender has recourse to the borrower beyond any assets pledged as collateral for the loan.

Accounting Consequences

The probable accounting consequence will be loan treatment, especially since the pledged asset is not revenue producing until the end of the lease term, at which time it may be sold for a gain or loss.

TRANSACTIONS 27, 28, 29 AND 30

Description of Transaction

Lessor enters into a capital lease (either sales-type or direct financing, but not leveraged) and subsequently pledges either the equipment along with the rental payment stream, or the rental stream without the residual, as collateral for a full recourse loan to the lessor.

Accounting References

There is no official GAAP; however, 'Accounting by Lease Brokers' AICPA Issues Paper and EITF Issue No. 84-25 shed some light on the subject. See Appendix A for copies of both.

Accounting Consequences

If the FASB issues a statement it could possibly allow treatment similar to FASB 77 (see Transactions 19-22) requirements for transfers of lease receivables or lease receivables and leased equipment. Thus, either sales or loan treatment could be accorded the transactions depending upon the degree of recourse (refer to the reference to FASB 77 in Transactions 19, 20, 21 and 22). As yet, an official FASB pronouncement does not exist and, therefore, a conservative viewpoint would require loan treatment for these transactions.

TRANSACTION 31

Description of Transaction

Lessor enters into a capital lease (either sales-type or direct financing, but not leveraged) and subsequently pledges a future interest in the equipment (after the noncancellable lease term) as collateral for a nonrecourse loan to the lessor.

Accounting References

APB Opinion 10, paragraph 7 and FASB 76, paragraph 3(b).

Accounting Consequences

Since the future interest in the residual has been pledged in a manner where a clear right of offset exists, sale treatment would be given as described in APB Opinion 10, paragraph 7, which states "it is a general principle of accounting that the offsetting of assets and liabilities in the balance sheet is improper except where a right of setoff exists." Furthermore, FASB 76, paragraph 3b, states that a debt is extinguished (offset against the residual value in this case) when "the debtor is legally released from being the primary obligor under the debt . . . by the creditor and it is probable that the debtor will not be required to make future payments with respect to that debt under any guarantees." Since the loan is nonrecourse to the lessor and the right of offset exists then sale treatment would be accorded the transaction.

TRANSACTIONS 32 AND 33

Description of Transaction

Lessor enters into a capital lease (either sales-type or direct financing, but not leveraged) and subsequently pledges the lease rental stream without the asset (Transaction 33) or the asset subject to the lease rental stream (Transaction 32) as collateral for a nonrecourse loan to the lessor.

Accounting References

FASB Technical Bulletin 86-2, paragraph 21.

Accounting Consequences

Either of the above transactions is often accorded sale treatment since many lessors believe the right to offset exists in these cases because nonrecourse funding is involved. The general principles involved are:

> Some respondents expressed concern that paragraph 10 of the proposed Technical Bulletin would prohibit lessors from increasing the carrying amount of an interest in the residual value of a leased asset if they remove lease receivables from their balance sheet and retain an interest in the residual value of a leased asset, either (a) through sale of the related lease receivable or (b) by offsetting the lease receivable with nonrecourse debt. Some respondents who offset nonrecourse debt with the related

lease receivable used as collateral apparently view the transaction, in substance, as a sale. Paragraph 10, however, only addresses those transactions structured as a sale of the related lease receivable and is not intended to consider any circumstance in which nonrecourse debt is collateralized by a lease receivable. In that circumstance, recognizing increases in the carrying amount of an interest in the residual value of a leased asset is appropriate under Statement 13. However, paragraph 7 of Opinion 10 states:

> "It is a general principle of accounting that the offsetting of assets and liabilities in the balance sheet is improper except where a right of setoff exists."

Therefore, offsetting the lease receivable with nonrecourse debt is appropriate only in those circumstances in which a legal right of offset exists or when, at the inception of the lease, the lease meets all of the characteristics of paragraph 42 of Statement 13 and is appropriately classified as a leveraged lease. Otherwise, the guidance provided in paragraph 7 of Opinion 10 should be applied [Technical Bulletin 86-2, Paragraph 21].

Refer also to the discussion on operating leases under Transactions 12 and 13, to 'Accounting by Lease Brokers' and also to EITF Issue No. 84-25 for more insights.

TRANSACTION 34

Description of Transaction

Lessor enters into a capital lease (either sales-type or direct financing, but not leveraged) that is funded with debt that provides only an indirect collateral interest in the leased property. Bonds, commercial paper, bank commercial credit lines, etc., represent borrowings that do not affect specific transactions although the total leasing portfolio is probably subject to some overall collateral requirement.

Accounting References

Reference is made to general GAAP, as no specific references exist; however, general debt obligations of any company must be shown as liabilities.

Accounting Consequences

Loan treatment must be given since the pooled debt would be a general obligation of the lessor.

TRANSACTIONS 16, 21, 22, 25, 29, 30 AND 33

Description of Transaction

Lessor enters into a capital lease and subsequently sells or pledges the rental payment stream but still maintains on its books the present value of the originally booked unguaranteed or guaranteed residual.

Accounting References

FASB Technical Bulletin 86-2, paragraphs 9 through 12 and 21.

Accounting Consequences

The present value of the residual at the time of a sale in Transactions 16, 21, 22 and 25 would remain the same until the end of the lease term without recognizing (accreting) any residual income. However, when assignments are used to effectuate pledges, rather than sales, earnings on residuals are acceptable. This treatment also impacts transactions 29, 30 and 33. This issue is discussed as follows:

Question

9. If a lessor sells substantially all of the minimum rental payments associated with a sales-type, direct financing, or leveraged lease and retains an interest in the residual value of the leased asset, how should the lessor account for that asset over the remaining lease term?

Response

10. A lessor retaining an interest in the residual value of the leased asset should not recognize increases in the value of the lease residual to its estimated value over the remaining lease term. The lessor should report any remaining interest thereafter at its carrying amount at the date of the sale of the lease payments. If it is subsequently determined that the fair value of the residual value of the leased asset has declined below the carrying amount of the interest retained and that decline is other than temporary, the asset should be written down to fair value, and the amount of the writedown should be recognized as a loss. That fair value becomes the asset's new carrying amount, and the asset should not be increased for any subsequent increase in its fair value prior to its sale or disposition.

Question

11. If an interest in the residual value of a leased asset is guaranteed, does the guarantee change the nature of the asset or the accounting?

Response

12. No. A guarantee does not change the nature of an interest in the residual value of a leased asset or its historical acquisition cost [Technical Bulletin 86-2, paragraphs 9-12].

Refer also to Transaction 33 for the issue regarding the netting of nonrecourse debt.

CONCLUSION

It can be seen, therefore, that debt funding techniques are not simply methods of minimizing debt cost but also include concepts about optimal amounts of financial leverage, debt optimization, tax ramifications of funding and complex accounting issues. The objective in this chapter is not to make the reader into a CPA, but, rather, to present the sale versus pledge issues along with the many ramifications of recourse versus nonrecourse debt.

CHAPTER TWELVE

STRUCTURING FASB NO. 13 OPERATING LEASES

There are many reasons why lessees lease, one of which is the off balance sheet financing leasing provides. Because of the importance of this aspect of the decision process, this chapter approaches the structuring of operating leases from the lessee's viewpoint. The following topics are addressed in this chapter:

- FASB 13 and Operating Lease Structuring
- FASB 13 Operating Lease Test
- Operating Lease Structuring Methodology
- Structuring Operating Leases with the HP-12C.

Keep in mind that when a lease is operating from a financial reporting viewpoint, it will not appear as an asset or as a lease liability on the face of the lessee's balance sheet. This characteristic of the operating lease allows lessees to enhance their return on assets (ROA) as well as ostensibly improve many of their financial ratios. (There are numerous other reasons for choosing operating leases, as explained in Chapter Two.) The financial statement impact of a lease might be the single most important reason why a lessee wants to lease; because of this, lessors must understand how to achieve off balance sheet leasing through the structuring of operating leases. This knowledge is also extremely beneficial for the lessee seeking such leases. As a final note, the structuring methodology for operating leases relies heavily on the accounting definitions in Chapter Thirteen; therefore, it should be reviewed, as necessary, before reading this chapter.

FASB 13 AND OPERATING LEASE STRUCTURING

When a lessee requires a lease to be an operating lease, reference generally is made to the need for conformance to the operating lease classification criteria contained in Financial Accounting Standards Board Statement No. 13 (FASB 13). FASB 13 delineates the conditions that must be met in order for a lease to be capital. Somewhat clouding the definitional issues in operating lease structuring is the fact that FASB 13 does not actually define the operating lease. Rather, it defines the capital lease and states that anything not meeting the capital lease criteria will be, by default, an operating lease. When the capital lease criteria are met, and leases are material to the lessee, the lessee's auditor might be forced in an audit situation to issue a qualified opinion if the lessee allows the leases to improperly remain as off balance sheet operating leases.

There are many techniques described in this chapter that are used to structure operating leases. Overemphasis of any one of these techniques to the exclusion of the others, or any overt manipulation where only the form of the lease has been changed (rather than the substance), is not the educational objective of this chapter. Although substance over form is a basic tenet of accounting theory, there is, within a reasonably broad framework, sufficient room for structuring operating leases without unduly increasing the risk of improper classification.

Lessors should keep in mind that the operating lease structuring principles described herein must be acceptable to the audit firm of the lessee for whom the lease is being structured. The lessee's Certified Public Accountant (CPA) firm will have final say in regards to whether a transaction has operating lease status on the lessee's books.

Chapter Thirteen describes the capital lease criteria in depth. Apart from avoiding (1) an outright automatic transfer of title during or by the end of a lease term, (2) a bargain purchase option or (3) a lease term being $\geq 75\%$ of the equipment's economic life, a lease will be deemed operating only so long as the present value of the minimum lease payments is less than 90% of the leased equipment's fair market value (FMV) reduced by any lessor retained tax credits. In general, the problem of operating lease structuring is overcoming the 90% present value test. If this can be accomplished through the legitimate manipulation of lease structuring variables, without creating a substance-over-form problem, the lessor's mission of structuring an operating lease will have been achieved.

FASB 13 OPERATING LEASE TEST

In order to structure an operating lease, it is first necessary to understand how to prove whether a given lease is capital or operating. (A review of Chapter Thirteen, particularly in regards to minimum lease payments and lessee discount rates, may be appropriate before proceeding with the steps used in determining capital versus operating lease status.) There are three steps required in determining whether a lease is capital or operating.

Step One: Calculate the FASB 13 comparison base. The FASB 13 comparison base represents the amount that the present value of the minimum lease payments in a lease must be below in order for it to be classified as operating. The comparison base is defined as the FMV of the equipment less any tax credits retained by the lessor, times 90% [(.9 × (FMV − tax credits))].

Step Two: Determine the present value of the minimum lease payments. This step requires discounting the minimum lease payments with the appropriate discount rate. Remember, the payments are discounted to the lease inception date (the signing date of the lease or an earlier commitment), and not to the physical possession date or Internal Revenue Service (IRS) placed-in-service date.

The minimum lease payments basically represent the noncancellable lease payments a lessee is obliged to pay plus or minus certain deletion and addition adjustments. Executory costs, plus any profit thereon, must be deducted from the minimum lease payments. Executory costs are incremental costs incurred by a lessor that are reimbursed by the lessee through an increase in the periodic lease payments sufficient to defray the costs. They include bundled expenses that are part of an overall full-service lease payment such as maintenance, sales tax, insurance, etc. Furthermore, any anticipated contingent rentals per FASB Statement No. 29 (FASB 29) would be excluded from minimum lease payments because of their uncertain and speculative nature. Cash flows that are defined by FASB 13 as part of the minimum lease payments include, among others, bargain purchase options, lessee guaranteed residuals, nonrefundable origination, closing, processing fees, etc., required to be paid by the lessee at the lease's inception, lessor put purchase options and any interim rent paid before the regular lease payments begin.

The lessee is to use a discount rate that is the lower of the lessor's implicit rate in the lease, if known, or the lessee's pretax, coterminous, incremental borrowing rate. The lessee seldom knows the rate implicit in the lease (as it is difficult to obtain the lessor's residual assumptions); therefore, it generally will use its borrowing rate. Coterminous refers to a borrowing rate expressive of money costs for the same term as the lease, and incremental refers to today's borrowing rate rather than some past embedded borrowing rate (previous bond issuance, etc.).

Step Three: Compare the present value of the minimum lease payments (Step Two) to the FASB 13 comparison base (Step One). If the present value of the minimum lease payments is less than the FASB 13 comparison base, the lease will be deemed an operating lease from an accounting viewpoint. If the present value of the minimum lease payments is equal to or greater than the FASB 13 comparison base, the lease must be restructured using the techniques described in this chapter; otherwise it will remain an on balance sheet capital lease.

Examples of the FASB 13 Test

The preceding three steps will be applied to several examples using the FASB 13 capital lease criteria in determining whether a lease is capital or operating from the lessee's viewpoint.

EXAMPLE 1

Determine, from the lessee's perspective, whether the lease is a capital or an operating lease. Use the following assumptions:

Lessee's incremental borrowing rate: 8% (implicit rate unknown to the lessee)
Lease payments: 48 payments of $1,500, in advance
FMV of equipment: $70,000.

SOLUTION

The three steps for determining capital versus operating lease status must be completed, in order.

Step One

Calculate the FASB 13 comparison base.

Asset's FMV	$ 70,000
Less tax credits	0
Subtotal	$ 70,000
	× .90
FASB 13 comparison base	$ 63,000

Step Two

Determine the present value of the minimum lease payments at the lease inception date.

8	g	12 ÷	
1,500	g	CF_o	
1,500	g	CF^j	
47	g	N_j	
	f	NPV	61,852.49

Step Three

Compare the present value of the minimum lease payments to the FASB 13 comparison base.

FASB 13 comparison base	$ 63,000.00
Present value of the minimum lease payments	(61,852.49)
Difference	$ 1,147.51

The lease is operating since the present value of the minimum lease payments is less than the comparison base and, therefore, qualifies for off balance sheet treatment by the lessee.

EXAMPLE 2

Determine, from the lessee's perspective, whether the lease is a capital or an operating lease. Use the following assumptions:

Delivery and acceptance date: March 31, 19XX
Placed in service: April 15, 19XX
Date lease signed: January 1, 19XX
Implicit rate in the lease: 10% (unknown to the lessee)
Lessee's incremental borrowing rate: 9%
Lessee's embedded borrowing rate: 8%
Lease payments: 60 monthly payments at $1,696 (payments in advance)

Sales tax: $96 of each payment
Refundable security deposit: $1,000
Nonrefundable origination fee: $500
Unguaranteed residual: $20,000
FMV of equipment: $100,000
Energy tax credit retained by the lessor: $10,000.

SOLUTION

The three steps for determining capital versus operating lease status must be completed, in order.

Step One

Calculate the FASB 13 comparison base.

Asset's FMV	$ 100,000
Less energy tax credit	(10,000)
Subtotal	$ 90,000
	× .90
FASB 13 comparison base	$ 81,000

Step Two

Determine the present value of the minimum lease payments at the lease inception date. (The lease inception date is January 1, 19XX, the date the lease is signed.) The appropriate discount rate is 9%, the lessee's incremental, pretax, coterminous borrowing rate, since the implicit rate was unknown.

9	g	12 ÷
2,100	g	CF_o (advance payment plus fee)
1,600	g	CF_j (regular payments)
59	g	N_j
	f	NPV 78,155.48

Note that the minimum lease payment equals $1,600. This represents the base payment of $1,696 less $96 of executory costs (sales tax). The refundable security deposit of $1,000 is not included.

Step Three

Compare the present value of the lease payments to the FASB 13 comparison base.

FASB 13 comparison base	$ 81,000.00
Present value of the minimum lease payments	(78,155.48)
Difference	$ 2,844.52

Since the present value of the minimum lease payments is $2,844.52 below the comparison base, the lease is operating. Neither the refundable security deposit nor the unguaranteed residual impacts the solution since neither is designated by FASB 13 as part of the minimum lease payments.

EXAMPLE 3

Determine, from the lessee's perspective, whether the lease is capital or operating. Use the same assumptions as Example 2, except the lease contains a lessee guaranteed residual in the amount of $5,000.

SOLUTION

The result of Step One would be the same as in Example 2. Steps Two and Three, however, would be different.

Step One

No change from Example 2.

Step Two

Determine the present value of the minimum lease payments to the date of the lease inception. The lessee guarantee of the residual will become part of the minimum lease payments at the lease termination.

9	g	$12 \div$
2,100	g	CF_o (advance payment plus origination fee)
1,600	g	CF_j (regular payments)
59	g	N_j
5,000	g	CF_j (guaranteed residual)
	f	NPV 81,348.98

Step Three

Compare the present value of the lease payments to the FASB 13 comparison base.

FASB 13 comparison base	$ 81,000.00
Present value of the minimum lease payments	(81,348.98)
Difference	($ 348.98)

The lease has now changed from an operating lease, as in Example 2, to a capital lease since the present value of the minimum lease payments exceeds the FASB 13 comparison base.

OPERATING LEASE STRUCTURING METHODOLOGY

The beginning point in structuring operating leases is to choose the highest discount rate that is verifiable, as well as acceptable, to the lessee's auditor. The lessee discount rate must be a coterminous rate that reflects the same borrowing period as the lease. This equating of borrowing term to lease term is important because longer term borrowing usually costs more than shorter term. Prime rate, for example, is a short-term rate (typically less than a year) and would not be deemed appropriate as a discount rate for a 60-month lease. The reason for choosing the highest feasible discount rate is higher discount rates result in lower present value totals, thus facilitating operating lease structuring.

The next step would be to make certain the FASB 13 comparison base has been correctly determined. If the lessor is also the manufacturer of the equipment, most tax credits, if any, will be based on the manufacturing cost of the equipment and not on the retail sales price. Basing the tax credit in a lease on the lower manufacturing price results in a lower credit, which, in turn, results in a lower deduction from the equipment's cost, thereby creating a higher comparison base and making it easier to structure operating leases.

Next, attempt to decrease the minimum lease payments with a corresponding increase in other cash payments that are not considered part of the minimum lease payments. For example, lower the lease payments in exchange for a refundable security deposit, which is not considered part of minimum lease payments. A refundable security deposit generally should never exceed the total of three monthly lease payments; otherwise, a serious substance-over-form problem might or should occur. Recently, one Big 8 CPA firm advocated inclusion of deposits as part of minimum lease payments, but others have not yet taken such a stand. Prior to the issuance of FASB 91, closing, origination, documentation and commitment fees were sometimes used as a substitute for reductions in minimum lease payments. However, FASB 91 has reaffirmed that these fees are to be considered an integral part of the lessor's yield and, therefore, by analogy, should be included as part of minimum lease payments.

One of several substitution techniques is to replace part of the regular lease payment with a contingent lease payment per FASB 29. Contingent rentals are not considered part of the minimum lease payments. For example, assume a lessee has been quoted a $2,000 per month lease payment, but, in order for the lease to be operating, the payment must be reduced to $1,800. The lease agreement could be altered to include a requirement that if the machine is used more than 160 hours per month an extra $200 would be due; of course, it must be fairly certain the machine will be used more than 160 hours per month. The contingent payment could also be based upon numerous other indices such as revenue generated by the machine, prime rate, Consumer Price Index, etc.

Another substitution technique is to identify part of the minimum lease payments as an executory cost that would be excluded from minimum lease payments. For example, if the lessee is being provided a very complex monthly billing, including multiple leased assets at various locations, the lease might indicate that part of the payment is to defray the cost of this extra service being provided to the lessee. In a similar fashion, another company may provide a labor and repair warranty for 1 year at no additional cost to the lessee. The lessee should estimate what this warranty is worth in order to subtract it from the minimum lease payments.

Of course, if the lease is a full-service lease containing an already identified executory cost, such as maintenance, a simple shift in the stated lease payment cost from the finance portion to the maintenance portion of the rental payment will make the lease operating. This occurs because the executory cost portion of the payment must be excluded from minimum lease payments.

For example, assume a lessor quotes a lessee a lease payment of $2,000 per month, including $200 maintenance. The minimum lease payment portion of the total payment is $1,800 ($2,000 – $200). If a payment of $1,700 were required to make the lease operating, the lease could be requoted at $2,000 per month, including $300 maintenance. The total payment does not change, only the allocation of the maintenance amount. A full-service lease with bundled services is needed to use this technique; therefore, as many lessors are now beginning to offer full-service leases, this operating lease structuring method may be seen more often.

An easy but more risky approach for the lessor in structuring operating leases is to emphasize more residual in the lease, thereby causing a consequent reduction in monthly lease payments. Since increasing residual risk typically is avoided by lessors, this method is not very feasible, unless the lessor can obtain independent third-party residual insurance to cover the increase in residual risk.

A lessor also could provide the lessee with an early out to reduce the number of noncancellable lease payments a lessee must pay, which would lower the minimum lease payments. Again, if the lessee is likely to opt an early out, the lessor's risk will increase. For example, a 60-month lease may allow the lessee to get out of the lease after 48 months. Should this occur, the lessor will attempt to sell the returned equipment for enough to cover any unrecouped costs at that time, although this may or may not occur. This approach is considered risky; however, a similar approach to shortening the lease term is to structure the lease in the first place as a 48-month lease, but add a 12-month renewal option that, if not renewed, will trigger a nonrenewal penalty. True, the penalty cost (if not too exorbitant) will be included as part of the minimum lease payment, but will be much smaller in amount than the renewal payments would be.

Similar to increasing residual value is stepping up the lease payments (begin with smaller payments followed by higher ones). However, this approach may or may not work, depending upon the implicit rate in the lease relative to the lessee's borrowing rate. Table 1 describes the effect.

Note that only when the implicit rate in a lease is lower than a lessee's borrowing rate will stepping up of the lease payments cause a lowering of the present value of the minimum lease payments. Leveraged leases often have implicit rates that are lower than prevailing lessee borrowing rates, thus making a step-up lease a viable means of achieving operating lease status.

An interesting but rather complex method of structuring an operating lease is to create a short-term loan followed by a sale-leaseback. The leaseback is timed such that the present value of the leaseback payments would be less than 90% of the asset's FMV at the time of the leaseback. This technique works when the asset subject to the lease retains its value well. This permits the FASB 13 comparison base to remain high so that the present value of the remaining leaseback payments on the date of the leaseback will be less than the comparison base. The

Table 1
Impact of the Implicit Versus Borrowing Rate

Relationship	Impact on Minimum Lease Payments
Implicit rate > borrowing rate	Raises the present value
Implicit rate = borrowing rate	No effect on the present value
Implicit rate < borrowing rate	Lowers the present value

leaseback payments' present value will be small relative to the comparison base since the previous loan will have already amortized the balance due the lender.

Splitting the transaction is another unique but rather dubious method of achieving operating lease status. This method assumes there are two or more pieces of equipment under one lease contract. In effect, part of the overall lease payment is allocated to the more costly equipment in such a manner that it remains operating, whereas the balance of the payment is allocated to the remaining equipment, creating a capital lease. Sometimes the original lease is rewritten so two new leases result.

FASB 13 defines a lease's inception as the earlier of the signing of the lease document or a lease commitment (so long as it is signed by both parties and contains the major provisions of the lease). Because of this definition, an operating lease can be structured by delaying the time between the inception and the due dates of the subsequent lease payments. For example, suppose a lease has 60 monthly payments, in advance, of $2,000 each. By structuring 3 months of skipped payments immediately after the inception payment of $2,000, the present value of the 59 remaining payments will be lower, since they have to be discounted over 3 additional months (relative to a payment schedule with no skips). This method works if the lessor can wait 3 months to pay for the equipment. If the equipment were paid for at the inception, the remaining lease payments would have to increase to cover the lessor's interest cost during the skipped periods, or interim rents equal to the lessor's interest cost would be paid during those periods. Such increases would counteract the effect of the delay in subsequent payments. However, when interim rent is not required during the skipped period, a lag effect can assist in making a lease operating.

Once a lease has been structured as a capital lease, unless it is renegotiated, it will remain such until its termination. Thus, renegotiation could change a lease's status from capital to operating simply by agreement. Keep in mind that the new terms will be applied to the operating lease criteria as if they had been in effect at the lease inception. If the operating lease criteria are met, the accounting classification of the lease will change from capital to operating (see FASB 13, paragraph 9 for more information on amendments to existing leases).

Most lessors in their negotiations with lessees make use of several of the aforementioned techniques rather than depending upon only one method. This approach is preferable to overemphasis of one technique; otherwise, a substance-over-form problem might occur. The intent in describing operating lease structuring should not be construed to be one of converting a capital lease to an operating lease but, rather, how to structure an operating lease in the first place. These structuring techniques, when viewed in their proper perspective, should not be considered manipulative, but rather as legitimate operating lease structuring variables.

STRUCTURING OPERATING LEASES WITH THE HP-12C

The HP-12C calculator is useful in structuring and performing sensitivity analysis of operating leases. It can be used to determine the maximum rental a lessee can pay on a lease and still keep it operating, or, given a known lease payment, the maximum amount of a lessee guarantee required to maintain operating lease status. Finally, this financial calculator is also useful for determining the lag between a lease's inception and the commencement of subsequent payments necessary to achieve operating lease status.

Computing the Maximum Payment

Computation of the maximum operating lease payment that a lessee can pay and still keep the lease off balance sheet requires four structuring steps. Knowledge of this payment amount is important in order to apply several of the operating lease techniques previously described. For example, before maintenance expense can be substituted for rental expense in a full-service lease, the final lease payment that will achieve operating lease status must be known or else too much or too little may be substituted.

EXAMPLE 4

Utilizing the following assumptions, determine the maximum lease payment the lessee may be charged and still have the lease classified as a FASB 13 operating lease.

Safety margin for comparison base: $500
Lease term: 60-month lease with two payments in advance
FMV of equipment: $100,000
Nonrefundable commitment fee: $600
Tax credits taken by the lessor: none
Lessee guarantees of the residual: none
Lessee borrowing rate: 9%.

SOLUTION

Computation of the maximum operating lease payment is very similar to regular payment structuring. It is accomplished in four steps.

Step One

Compute the FASB 13 comparison base less (1) any nonrefundable commitment or closing fees, etc., (2) the present value of any lessee guaranteed residuals and (3) a safety margin.

Asset's FMV	$ 100,000
Less tax credits	0
Subtotal	$ 100,000
	× .90
FASB 13 comparison base	$ 90,000
Commitment fee	(600)
Present value of the guaranteed residual	0
Safety margin	(500)
Adjusted FASB 13 comparison base	$ 88,900

Step Two

Find the present value of the unknown operating lease payments, letting one dollar equal each payment. Use the lessee's borrowing rate (or the lessor's implicit rate, if lower and known) as the discount rate.

9	g	$12 \div$	(lessee's borrowing rate)
2	g	CF_o	(two advance payments)
1	g	CF_j	(remaining payments)
58	g	N_j	
	f	NPV	48.891184

Step Three

Divide Step One by Step Two, the quotient of which is the maximum payment the lessee can make to still maintain operating lease status, with a $500 safety margin.

$$\frac{\$88,900}{48.891184} = \$1,818.32 \text{ per month}$$

Step Four

Prove that the present value of the $1,818.32 monthly lease payments and the commitment fee of $600 equals $89,500 (FASB 13 comparison base of $90,000 less $500 safety margin).

9	g	$12 \div$	
4,236.64	g	CF_o	(2 × $1,818.32 + $600)
1,818.32	g	CF_j	
58	g	N_j	
	f	NPV	89,499.82

EXAMPLE 5

Utilizing the following assumptions, determine the maximum lease payment the lessee may be charged and still have the lease classified as a FASB 13 operating lease.

Lease term: 60-month lease with payments in advance
Safety margin for comparison base: $500
FMV of equipment: $50,000
Nonrefundable commitment fee: $750
Energy tax credit retained by the lessor: $5,000
Lessee guarantee of residual: $4,000
Lessee borrowing rate: 8%.

SOLUTION

Computation of the maximum operating lease payment is accomplished in four steps.

Step One

Compute the FASB 13 comparison base less (1) any nonrefundable commitment or closing fees, etc., (2) the present value of any lessee guaranteed residuals and (3) a safety margin.

Present value the lessee guaranteed residual using the lessee's borrowing rate as the discount rate.

8	g	12 ÷
4,000	CHS	FV
60		n
	PV	2,684.84

The FASB 13 comparison base is then computed.

Asset's FMV	$ 50,000
Less energy tax credit	(5,000)
Subtotal	$ 45,000
	× .90
FASB 13 comparison base	$40,500
Commitment fee	(750)
Present value of the guaranteed residual	(2,685)
Safety margin	(500)
Adjusted FASB 13 comparison base	$ 36,565

Step Two

Find the present value of the unknown operating lease payments, letting one dollar equal each payment. Use the lessee's borrowing rate as the discount rate.

8	g	12 ÷	
1	g	CF_o	
1	g	CF_j	
59	g	N_j	
	f	NPV	49.647223

Step Three

Divide Step One by Step Two, the quotient of which is the maximum payment the lessee can make and still maintain operating lease status, with a safety margin of $500.

$$\frac{\$\ 36{,}565}{49.647223} = \$736.50$$

Step Four

Prove that the present value of the $736.50 lease payments, the $4,000 lessee guarantee and the $750 commitment fee equals $40,000 (comparison base less $500 safety margin).

8	g	12 ÷	
1,486.50	g	CF_o	($736.50 + $750)
736.50	g	CF_j	
59	g	N_j	
4,000	g	CF_j	
	f	NPV	40,000.02

Computing the Maximum Guaranteed Residual

The computation of the maximum guaranteed residual, given a known lease payment, a lessee can pay and still keep the lease off balance sheet requires five structuring steps. This technique is commonly used in Terminal Rental Adjustment Clause (TRAC) leasing. For instance, a lessee guaranteed residual will occur, but the lessor will limit the amount of the guarantee to preserve operating lease status to the lessee.

EXAMPLE 6

Compute, from the lessee perspective, the maximum lessee guaranteed residual allowable in order to still maintain an operating lease.

Safety margin for comparison base: $500
Lease term: 60-month lease with monthly payments of $1,700 (two in advance)
FMV of equipment: $100,000
Nonrefundable commitment fee: $600
Tax credits available to lessor: none
Lessee borrowing rate: 9%, which is lower than the lessor's implicit rate in the lease.

Step One

Compute the FASB 13 comparison base, less a safety margin.

Asset's FMV	$100,000
Less tax credits	0
Subtotal	$100,000
	× .90
FASB 13 comparison base	$ 90,000
Safety margin	(500)
Adjusted FASB 13 comparison base	$ 89,500

Step Two

Calculate the present value of the minimum lease payments, including any commitment fees, etc., at the lessee's borrowing rate.

9	g	12 ÷	
4,000	g	CF_o	(2 × $1700 + $600)
1,700	g	CF_j	
58	g	N_j	
	f	NPV	83,715.01

Step Three

Subtract Step Two from Step One. This amount equals the present value of the maximum guarantee the lessor can require of the lessee and still maintain operating lease status for the lessee.

$ 89,500	
(83,715)	
$ 5,785	

Step Four

Find the future value at the end of the lease term of the difference from Step Three, using the lessee's borrowing rate (or the lessor's implicit rate, if lower) as the appreciation rate.

9	g	12 ÷	
5,785	CHS	PV	
60		n	
		FV	9,057.46

The $9,057.46 represents the maximum amount of residual value the lessee can guarantee and still have an operating lease, given lease rentals of $1,700, a $600 commitment fee and a $500 safety margin.

Step Five

Prove the lease has achieved operating lease status by finding the present value of the minimum lease payments, including the newly computed lessee guaranteed residual. The total should be $89,500 (Step One).

9	g	12 ÷	
4,000	g	CF_o	(2 × $1,700 + $600)
1,700	g	CF_j	
58	g	N_j	
0	g	CF_j	
9057.46	g	CF_j	
	f	NPV	89,500.01

Computing the Necessary Lag Time

The computation of how to increase the lag time between the inception of a lease and the beginning of the subsequent payments (and the date the equipment is paid for) for the lease to become an operating lease requires four structuring steps. Since many leases have a slight lag in them anyway, due to delayed delivery of the leased equipment, this technique simply increases the already standard delay.

EXAMPLE 7

Compute the lag time necessary for the following lease to be classified as an operating lease.
Lease term: 60-month lease with payments of $1,875 (two in advance)
FMV of equipment: $100,000
Nonrefundable lease origination fee: $800
Safety margin for comparison base: $500
Tax credits available: none
Lessee borrowing rate: 9%.

SOLUTION

There are four structuring steps required to compute the necessary lag time to achieve operating lease status.

Step One

Determine the FASB 13 comparison base less (1) any advance payments, (2) commitment or origination fees and (3) a safety margin.

Asset's FMV	$ 100,000
Less tax credits	0
Subtotal	$ 100,000
	× .90
FASB 13 comparison base	$ 90,000
Advance payments	(3,750)
Commitment fee	(800)
Safety margin	(500)
Adjusted FASB 13 comparison base	$ 84,950

Step Two

Determine the present value of the remaining minimum lease payments (including any lessee guaranteed residuals, etc.), in arrears, discounted at the lessee's borrowing rate of 9%.

9	g	12 ÷	
1,875	g	CF$_j$	
58	g	N$_j$	
	f	NPV	87,920.97

Step Three

Place the results of Step One as a present value figure (a negative outflow in the present value register) in the financial calculator. Place the results of Step Two in the future value register and then input the lessee's borrowing rate. Solve for "n," which represents the required lag time necessary to maintain operating lease status.

9	g	12 ÷	
84,950	CHS	PV	
87,920.97		FV	
		n	5

Note that the HP-12C rounds "n" up such that a whole number is always given as an answer to Step Three. This presents no problem since an additional safety margin beyond the $500 already assumed is automatically created by the rounding process.

Step Four

Prove that the present value of the minimum lease payments, due to the calculated lag time, is equal to or less than the FASB 13 comparison base, less a $500 safety margin.

FASB 13 comparison base	$ 90,000
Safety margin	(500)
Adjusted FASB 13 comparison base	$ 89,500

9	g	12 ÷	
4,550	g	CF_o	(2 × $1,875 + $800)
0	g	CF_j	
5	g	N_j	(lag period)
1,875	g	CF_j	
58	g	N_j	
	f	NPV	89,246.84

The present value of $89,246.84 is below the required $89,500, thereby proving 5 months is the appropriate lag time necessary to achieve operating lease status.

CONCLUSION

Lessees frequently favor operating leases because of the off balance sheet financing such leases generate. Because of this it is important to be familiar with the steps necessary to structure an operating lease. The primary criterion that must be met for purposes of structuring operating leases is the 90% test. Two of the means by which a lease is made operating involve minimizing the cash flows included in minimum lease payments or increasing the lessee's discount rate used to present value those payments. Various cash flow substitution techniques as well as alteration of cash flows through stepping up or down of lease payments, or creating skipped payments, etc., also can be used as viable means of creating operating leases. Development of the skills for structuring operating leases definitely will add another important selling tool to the lessor's marketing repertoire.

PART 4
ACCOUNTING

CHAPTER THIRTEEN
INTRODUCTORY LEASE ACCOUNTING

Accounting has long been considered the language of business, and continues to play an increasingly important role. Similarly, the importance of accounting in the leasing industry is becoming more evident each day, from both the lessor and the lessee viewpoint. It is not only the accountants, however, who need to understand accounting for leases. Managers, financial analysts, corporate planners and many others must also recognize and understand the impact of leases on the financial statements. With such a need in mind, this chapter provides, through the following topics, an understanding of the issues and basic concepts of accounting for leases.

- Accounting and Leasing
- Capital Versus Operating Leases
- FASB 13 Terminology
- Operating Versus Capital Lease Illustration.

ACCOUNTING AND LEASING

The American Institute of Certified Public Accountants has defined accounting as "the art of recording, classifying and summarizing in a significant manner, and in terms of money, transactions and events which are, in part at least, of a financial character, and in interpreting the results thereof." To properly account for leases, the various components of this definition must be applied to the already complex lease transactions of a company, all within the guidelines set forth by the accounting rule-making body, the Financial Accounting Standards Board (FASB).

Accounting Perspective

It is clear from the above definition that accounting amounts to a great deal more than the recording of transactions (i.e., bookkeeping). Note particularly the emphasis in the definition placed on the interpretation of the results of the accounting process. It is hoped the accounting information will be recorded in such a manner that interpretation of the results is possible, i.e., the information is useful in making economic decisions. There are two broad groups of decision-makers who may utilize accounting information — internal users and external users.

Internal decision-makers are the managers responsible for planning the future of the entity, implementing plans and controlling operations on a day-to-day basis. These users, therefore, require different and often more detailed information than do external users. Because of their internal relationship to the entity, they also can command whatever financial data they may need or desire, at dates of their choice. Further, the information is for their use and generally is not intended to be communicated to outsiders. The process of developing and reporting financial information to internal users is usually called management accounting, and the reports are referred to as internal management reports. Clearly, these reports should be structured to conform to the particular decision-making needs of the management team.

In contrast, the external decision-makers (i.e., the external users of financial information) make distinctly different types of decisions regarding the entity, such as to invest or disinvest, to loan funds and so forth. External decision-makers comprise present and potential investors and creditors, investment analysts, governmental units and the public at large. In view of the diverse range of external users of financial data, the accounting profession has developed general-purpose financial statements designed to meet their decision-making needs. These statements are developed in a phase of accounting known as financial accounting.

The external users, because of their detachment from the entity, cannot directly command specific financial information from the entity; therefore, they must rely primarily on general-purpose financial statements. The accounting profession, in order to serve external users, has developed a network of accounting standards designed to assure that external financial statements are fair representations of the economic circumstances of the company. These standards, which must be followed in financial statement presentation, are referred to as generally accepted accounting principles (GAAP). Outside auditors provide independent assurance to external users that GAAP has been followed in preparing the financial statements.

A logical question at this juncture is, "Who establishes GAAP?" GAAP is established through the practices of the accounting profession and formalized by the FASB. The FASB issues statements that outline the accounting principles to be followed in different situations. In November, 1976, the FASB issued Statement No. 13 (FASB 13), 'Accounting for Leases.' Much as the Internal Revenue Service (IRS) Code delineates how the tax aspects of leasing should be handled, FASB 13 details the manner in which leases are to be accounted for. The requirements of FASB 13 cover accounting for both lessors and lessees, and are the focus of this chapter.

Leasing Perspective

In general, a lease is viewed as a contract between a lessor (the owner of an asset) and a lessee (the user of the asset). The lessor grants the temporary possession and use of an asset to the lessee, usually for a specified period of time less than the asset's economic life, at a fixed periodic charge (rental).

This definition of a lease outlines the basic economics of a typical lease of equipment or other property and describes the main parties to the transaction. However, the process of describing or defining a lease for many other specialized purposes is much more involved. Beyond the basic economic lease definition, many other definitions must be considered when viewing a contract called a lease. These other definitions provide perspective for any attempt to define a lease from an accounting point of view.

The IRS has created an extensive set of rules used in determining whether a lease is a true lease or not. Even though the parties to a lease contract call the agreement a lease, it may be considered by the IRS to be a sale by the lessor, and a purchase by the lessee, of an asset, rather than the rental of the asset for a portion of its useful life.

When an asset is sold, the purchaser of the asset becomes both its owner and user and is, therefore, entitled to the tax benefits of ownership, including any applicable tax credits, cost recovery (depreciation), interest deductions, etc. When an asset is leased by a lessee (user), the ownership of the asset remains with the lessor. In this case, the lessor is considered to be the owner of the asset by the IRS and the tax benefits of ownership belong to the lessor. The IRS has issued guidelines for determining which party, the lessor or lessee, is the real owner for purposes of determining who is entitled to the tax benefits.

When a sale and purchase are disguised as a lease contract but more closely resemble an installment sale, the IRS may consider the contract to be what it terms a conditional sales contract rather than a true lease. When this is the case, the lessee is treated by the IRS as the owner-user of the asset and the lessee receives the tax benefits of ownership instead of the lessor.

It is important to be familiar, at this point, with the terminology used by the IRS in distinguishing between a lease and a purchase. A true periodic rental of an asset is called a true lease, whereas a disguised lease (one in which the asset has, in effect, been purchased by the lessee) is called a conditional sales contract. It is easy to confuse these terms with other terms used in the leasing industry, especially certain accounting terms; therefore, it is essential to understand the contrasting terminology used.

Not only does the IRS define a lease, but other legal entities do also. Other definitions and guidelines include those created by the Uniform Commercial Code, the Securities and Exchange Commission, federal bankruptcy laws, state laws and, of course, the general industry definitions of a lease.

As has been discussed, another entity that has defined a lease is the FASB. This rule-making body concerns itself with the proper accounting for, and reporting of, all leasing transactions as well as all other financial transactions of United States businesses. Certain rules of the FASB deal specifically with lease contracts and also distinguish between a true lease and a disguised lease.

Combining the Two Perspectives

A lease contract that is a true rental arrangement, where asset ownership is maintained by the lessor, and the lessee uses the asset for a portion of its useful life for a periodic rental charge, is called an operating lease for accounting purposes. However, a contract that is called a lease, but which, in fact, has transferred all or most of the characteristics and benefits of ownership to the lessee, is termed a capital lease by the FASB. It is called a capital lease because the transaction is similar to other asset acquisitions by the lessee where the asset is purchased and, therefore, recorded as an asset on the balance sheet of the purchaser. The act of recording the purchased asset on the balance sheet is called capitalizing the asset.

The terms used by the FASB in distinguishing between a usage agreement and an installment sale called a lease are different from those used by the IRS or the leasing industry. While these terms may be similar to the guidelines of the IRS, they are not, in all respects, the same. Different rules are used in defining the true IRS lease and the accounting operating lease. Similarly, just as a disguised lease that does not meet the IRS criteria of a true lease is called a conditional sales contract, the same category of leases from an accounting viewpoint is called a capital lease. Similar but different! The distinguishing criteria of the IRS and FASB vary slightly and must not be confused. For purposes of this chapter, leases from the IRS perspective are either true leases or conditional sales contracts; from an accounting point of view, leases are either operating or capital leases.

Lease Accounting Pronouncements

Much of the discussion in this chapter is derived from issues addressed in FASB 13. This statement describes the difference between capital and operating leases, details how to account for them in a firm's financial statements and defines many terms pertinent to the accounting classification of leases. While the bulk of lease accounting issues focuses on FASB 13, many other FASB pronouncements also affect leasing. Since its original issuance in 1976, FASB 13 has been amended and/or clarified by numerous Statements, Interpretations and Technical Bulletins (all of which are pronouncements of the FASB) and has become extremely complex. The pronouncements relating to leasing issued as of publication of this text are shown in Table 1. When the list from Table 1 is combined with the existing and constantly changing general body of accounting literature, the enormity of the task of properly accounting for leases becomes easy to appreciate.

CAPITAL VERSUS OPERATING LEASES

It is important to know at the onset of this discussion why the issue of distinguishing between operating and capital leases is so important. Of course, the technical accounting for each is different, but there is also a very real marketing reason. When a lease, from a lessee accounting point of view, is considered to be operating it is known in the industry as an off balance sheet lease. Many firms use this form of off balance sheet financing to their advantage. In the case of a capital lease, the leased asset is capitalized, or shown on the lessee's financial statements as an asset. At the same time, a corresponding liability of the same dollar amount as the capitalized asset is recorded. This liability is amortized over the life of the lease, in the same manner as the outstanding debt of an installment sale.

Table 1

Leasing-Related Pronouncements

Pronouncement	Topic
Statement No. 13	Accounting for Leases
Statement No. 17	Accounting for Leases — Initial Direct Costs
Statement No. 22	Changes in the Provisions of Lease Agreements Resulting from Refunding of Tax-Exempt Debt
Statement No. 23	Inception of the Lease
Statement No. 26	Profit Recognition on Sales-Type Leases of Real Estate
Statement No. 27	Classification of Renewals or Extensions of Existing Sales-Type or Direct Financing Leases
Statement No. 28	Accounting for Sales with Leasebacks
Statement No. 29	Determining Contingent Rentals
Statement No. 77	Reporting by Transferors for Transfers of Receivables with Recourse
Statement No. 91	Accounting for Nonrefundable Fees and Costs Associated with Originating or Acquiring Loans and Initial Direct Costs of Leases
Interpretation No. 19	Lessee Guarantee of the Residual Value of Leased Property
Interpretation No. 21	Accounting for Leases in a Business Combination
Interpretation No. 23	Leases of Certain Property Owned by a Governmental Unit or Authority
Interpretation No. 24	Leases Involving Only Part of a Building
Interpretation No. 26	Accounting for Purchase of a Leased Asset by the Lessee During the Term of the Lease
Interpretation No. 27	Accounting for a Loss on a Sublease
Technical Bulletin No. 79-10	Fiscal Funding Clauses in Lease Agreements
Technical Bulletin No. 79-11	Effect of a Penalty on the Term of a Lease
Technical Bulletin No. 79-12	Interest Rate Used in Calculating the Present Value of Minimum Lease Payments
Technical Bulletin No. 79-13	Applicability of FASB Statement No. 13 to Current Value Financial Statements
Technical Bulletin No. 79-14	Upward Adjustment of Guaranteed Residual Values
Technical Bulletin No. 79-15	Accounting for Loss on a Sublease Not Involving the Disposal of a Segment
Technical Bulletin No. 79-16	Effect of a Change in Income Tax Rate on the Accounting for Leveraged Leases
Technical Bulletin No. 79-17	Reporting Cumulative Effect Adjustments from Retroactive Application of FASB Statement No. 13
Technical Bulletin No. 79-18	Transition Requirement of Certain FASB Amendments and Interpretations of FASB Statement No. 13
Technical Bulletin No. 85-3	Accounting for Operating Leases with Scheduled Rent Increases
Technical Bulletin No. 86-2	Accounting for an Interest in the Residual Value of a Leased Asset

In the case of an operating (off balance sheet) lease, however, the leased asset is not capitalized nor is the corresponding liability recorded.[1] Both the asset and the obligation to pay for it are off balance sheet. Even though the obligation to pay the lease payments is real, and the term of the obligation often lasts for several years without opportunity to cancel, it is still not required to be shown on the face of the balance sheet. This ability to hide the existence of often substantial financial obligations has distinct advantages to a lessee who may be trying to borrow money, issue equity or acquire additional assets through other leases or loans. When the lessee can effectively remove a portion of its debt obligations from the balance sheet, it appears to others (users of the financial statement information) to be more liquid (or solvent) and less encumbered by debt.

As will be demonstrated later in this chapter, the reporting of a lessee's lease as operating enhances the lessee's financial statements in the early years of the lease term, and also tends to improve a company's apparent financial strength and ability to meet its financial obligations. There are many other advantages for the company, as discussed in Chapter Two, in addition to the favorable impact of operating leases on the balance sheet.

Capital Lease Criteria

FASB 13 provides for the classification of all leases into one of two types — capital or operating. It establishes criteria for determining how the lease will be classified and, once classified, how that lease should be recorded and subsequently accounted for. In determining the classification of a particular lease, FASB 13 considers the substance of the lease based on certain characteristics. For instance, does the agreement grant only usage of the asset, without any semblance of ownership, or does the lease provide for some form of effective ownership, such as asset exhaustion occurring in the hands of one user?

These are the type of factors that must be considered. Therefore, if the lease agreement does, in substance, transfer or resemble some form of ownership, the lease is deemed a capital lease for accounting purposes. If the lease agreement, in substance, provides only for usage of the asset and not ownership, the lease is classified as operating for accounting purposes. As shown in Figure 1, a capital lease connotes ownership, whereas an operating lease implies usage only.

FASB 13 establishes four criteria for determining whether a lease is capital (a purchase/sale agreement) or operating (usage agreement). If any one of the four criteria is met, the lease will be classified as a capital lease. If none is met, the lease becomes, by default, an operating lease. These criteria are applicable to both lessors and lessees and are applied at the inception[2] of the lease. Paragraph 7 of FASB 13 enumerates the four lease classification criteria.

1. The lease automatically transfers ownership of the property to the lessee by the end of the lease term

---

[1] It should be noted that even though an operating lease is not shown on the face of the lessee's financial statements, the lessee is still required to disclose, in notes to those statements, certain details concerning all leases, both capital and operating. This additional information is intended to enable the reader to discern the true impact of an operating lease, as if it had been included as an asset and a liability on the lessee's balance sheet.

[2] All terms presented are fully defined immediately following this subsection.

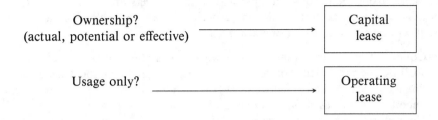

Figure 1
Ownership Versus Usage

2. The lease contains a bargain purchase option
3. The lease term is equal to 75% or more of the estimated economic life of the leased property
4. The present value of the minimum lease payments, at the beginning of the lease term, equals or exceeds 90% of the fair market value of the property, reduced by any Investment Tax Credit (ITC) retained and expected to be realized by the lessor (prior to determining the 90% base)
   a. The lessor's discount rate shall be the implicit rate in the lease
   b. The lessee's discount rate shall be the incremental borrowing rate, unless the lessor's implicit rate in the lease is known and that rate is lower. In this case, the lessee shall use the implicit rate.

Criteria three and four are ignored when used assets are leased during the last 25% of their economic lives.

A careful study of the above criteria indicates that a capital lease is recognized when any in-substance form of ownership occurs. The following relationships can be seen by correlating the above criteria to the narrow form of ownership:

1. Automatic transfer of ownership — **actual** ownership is obtained outright during the lease term
2. Bargain purchase option — **potential** ownership is available through the exercise of a bargain purchase option
3. Greater than 75% of the economic life — **effective** ownership occurs through use, or wearing out of the asset by using it for 75% or more of its economic life
4. Greater than 90% of the fair market value — **effective** ownership results when the present value of the price paid for use of the asset is 90% or more of the property's original fair market value.

As was mentioned, these criteria apply to both lessors and lessees. If none of the criteria is met, the lease is classified as an operating lease. Although implied earlier, it also goes without saying that the accounting treatment for a capital lease will be different from that of an operating lease, from both a lessor and lessee perspective.

Additionally, from the lessor's standpoint, if a lease meets any one of the preceding four criteria it must also meet both the following criteria in order to be classified as a capital lease; otherwise it will be classified as an operating lease.

 a. Collectibility of the minimum lease payments is reasonably predictable. A lessor shall not be precluded from classifying a lease as a sales-type lease or as a direct financing lease simply because the receivable is subject to an estimate of uncollectability based on experience with groups of similar receivables.

 b. No important uncertainties surround the amount of unreimbursable costs yet to be incurred by the lessor under the lease. Important uncertainties might include commitments by the lessor to guarantee performance of the leased property in a manner more extensive than the typical product warranty or to effectively protect the lessee from obsolescence of the leased property [FASB 13, paragraph 8].

FASB 13 TERMINOLOGY

FASB 13 contains numerous terms and definitions that must be understood by not only those in accounting, but also by individuals who deal with leasing on a day-to-day basis. This section addresses both the technical definitions and the terms used to describe various aspects of accounting for lease transactions.

Definitions[3]

In order to obtain a better understanding of the preceding classification criteria, and the subsequent accounting for operating leases (Chapter Fourteen), capital leases (Chapter Fifteen) and leveraged leases (Chapter Sixteen), there are certain terms that require definition. These definitions and explanations of the key aspects of FASB 13 are discussed in the following sections.

INCEPTION OF THE LEASE

The inception of the lease is defined as the date of the lease agreement or commitment, if earlier. A commitment must be in writing, be signed by all the parties to the transaction and specifically set forth the principal provisions of the transaction. If any of the principal provisions are yet to be negotiated, the date of such a preliminary agreement or commitment does not qualify as the inception date.

FAIR MARKET VALUE

The fair market value of the leased property is the price for which the property could be sold in an arms-length transaction between unrelated parties. When the lessor is a manufacturer or dealer, the fair value of the property at the inception of the lease will ordinarily be its normal

---

[3] The definitions in this section are based upon those of the FASB, and do not reflect direct quotes. For those desiring to review the actual text of the definitions, net of author comments and editorial changes, please refer to FASB 13, paragraph 5.

selling price, reflecting any standard volume or trade discounts that may be applicable. However, the determination of fair value must be made in light of market conditions prevailing at the time, which may indicate that the fair value of the property is less than the normal selling price and, in some instances, less than the cost of the property. When the lessor is not a manufacturer or dealer, the fair value of the property at the inception of the lease ordinarily will be its cost, reflecting any volume or trade discounts that may be applicable.

BARGAIN PURCHASE OPTION

A bargain purchase option is a provision in the lease allowing the lessee to purchase the leased property for a price that is sufficiently lower than the expected fair value of the property at the date of the option, such that exercise of the option appears, at the inception of the lease, to be reasonably assured.

BARGAIN RENEWAL OPTION

A bargain renewal option is similar to a bargain purchase option. It is a provision allowing the lessee to renew the lease for a rental sufficiently lower than the fair rental of the property at the date the option becomes exercisable, such that exercise of the option appears, at the inception of the lease, to be reasonably assured. Fair rental is defined as the expected rental for equivalent property, under similar terms and conditions.

LEASE TERM

The lease term consists of the fixed noncancellable term of the lease, bargain renewal option periods, renewal periods subject to a nonrenewal penalty that reasonably assures extension, ordinary renewal periods during which the lessee guarantees the lessor's debt, ordinary renewal periods preceding a bargain purchase option and lessor-forced renewal periods.

A lease that is cancellable (1) only upon the occurrence of some remote contingency, (2) only with the permission of the lessor, (3) only if the lessee enters into a new lease with the same lessor or (4) only upon payment by the lessee of a penalty in an amount such that continuation of the lease appears, at inception, reasonably assured, is considered noncancellable.

ESTIMATED ECONOMIC LIFE

The estimated remaining period during which the property is expected to be economically usable by one or more users, with normal repairs and maintenance, is defined as the estimated economic life. Additionally, the property must be used for the purpose for which it was intended at the inception of the lease, without limitation by the lease term, for purposes of this definition.

ESTIMATED RESIDUAL VALUE

The estimated residual value is the estimated fair value of the leased property at the end of the lease term.

UNGUARANTEED RESIDUAL VALUE

The unguaranteed residual value is defined as the estimated residual value of the leased property, exclusive of any portion guaranteed by the lessee, or by any party related to the lessee or by a third party unrelated to the lessor. Unguaranteed residuals result from closed-end leases (no purchase rights provided the lessee) and from leases containing either fair market value purchase options or fixed purchase options that are not considered bargains.

MINIMUM LEASE PAYMENTS

The definition of minimum lease payments consists of two parts: the lessee definition and the lessor definition. From the standpoint of the lessee, minimum lease payments include the payments that the lessee is obligated to make, or can be required to make in connection with the leased property. Contingent rentals are excluded from minimum lease payments, as is a guarantee by the lessee of the lessor's debt and the lessee's obligation to pay (apart from the rental payments) executory costs in connection with the leased property. If the lease contains a bargain purchase option, only the minimum rental payments over the lease term and the payment called for by the bargain purchase option are included. Otherwise, minimum lease payments include the following:

1. The minimum rental payments called for by the lease over the lease term
2. Any guarantee by the lessee, or any party related to the lessee, of the residual value at the expiration of the lease term, whether or not payment of the guarantee constitutes a purchase of the leased property. When the lessor can require the lessee to purchase the property at termination of the lease for a certain or determinable amount, that amount shall be considered a lessee guarantee. When the lessee agrees to make up any deficiency below a stated amount in the lessor's realization of the residual value, the guarantee to be included in the minimum lease payments is the stated amount, rather than an estimate of the deficiency to be made up
3. Any payment the lessee must make or can be required to make upon failure to renew or extend the lease at the expiration of the lease term. If the lease term has been extended because of a significant renewal penalty, the penalty is not included in minimum lease payments.

From the standpoint of the lessor, minimum lease payments include the payments described above, plus any guarantee of the residual value or of rental payments beyond the lease term by an unrelated third party, provided the third party is financially capable of discharging the obligations that may arise from the guarantee.

IMPLICIT RATE IN THE LEASE

The implicit rate in the lease is the discount rate that, when applied to (1) the minimum lease payments (excluding executory costs) and (2) the unguaranteed residual value accruing to the benefit of the lessor, causes the aggregate present value at the beginning of the lease term to be equal to the fair value of the leased property to the lessor at the inception of the lease, minus any ITC retained by the lessor and expected to be realized by it.

In simpler terms, the implicit rate in the lease is the internal rate of return (IRR) of the fair market value (less ITC), the minimum lease payments and the unguaranteed residual. This definition obviously does not, nor does it necessarily purport to, include all factors that a lessor might recognize in determining its true, economic rate of return. This rate is used as the lessor's discount rate for purposes of the 90% test.

LESSEE'S BORROWING RATE

The lessee's borrowing rate, for purposes of FASB 13, is the pretax, coterminous, incremental rate that, at the inception of the lease, the lessee would have incurred to borrow the funds necessary to purchase the leased asset, over a period similar to the lease term. This rate is used as the lessee's discount rate for purposes of the 90% test, if the lessor's implicit rate is either unknown or greater than the lessee's borrowing rate.

INITIAL DIRECT COSTS [4]

Only those costs incurred by the lessor that are (a) costs to originate a lease incurred in transactions with independent third parties that (i) result directly from and are essential to acquire that lease and (ii) would not have been incurred had that leasing transaction not occurred and (b) certain costs directly related to specified activities performed by the lessor for that lease. Those activities are: evaluating the prospective lessee's financial condition; evaluating and recording guarantees, collateral, and other security arrangements; negotiating lease term; preparing and processing lease documents; and closing the transaction. The costs directly related to those activities shall include only that portion of the employees' total compensation and payroll-related fringe benefits directly related to time spent performing those activities for that lease and other costs related to those activities that would not have been incurred but for that lease. Initial direct costs shall not include costs related to activities performed by the lessor for advertising, soliciting potential lessees, servicing existing leases, and other ancillary activities related to establishing and monitoring credit policies, supervision, and administration. Initial direct costs shall not include administrative costs, rent, depreciation, any other occupancy and equipment costs and employees' compensation and fringe benefits related to activities described in the previous sentence, unsuccessful origination efforts, and idle time [FASB 91, paragraph 24].

CONTINGENT RENTALS

Contingent rentals are the increases or decreases in lease payments that result from changes occurring subsequent to the inception of the lease in the factors (other than the passage of time) on which lease payments are based. Lease payments that depend on a factor directly related to the future use of the leased property, such as machine hours of use or sales volume, during the lease term, are contingent rentals and, accordingly, are excluded from minimum lease payments in their entirety. However, lease payments that depend on an existing index or rate, such as the consumer price index or the prime interest rate, are included in minimum lease payments based on the index or rate existing at the inception of the lease; any increases or decreases in lease payments that result from subsequent changes in the index or rate are contingent rentals.

---

[4] Initial direct costs are offset by nonrefundable fees that are yield adjustments, as prescribed in FASB Statement No. 91 (FASB 91), Accounting for Nonrefundable Fees and Costs Associated with Originating or Acquiring Loans and Initial Direct Costs of Leases.

RENEWAL OR EXTENSION

The continuation of a lease agreement beyond the original lease term, including a new lease under which the lessee continues to use the same property, is a renewal or extension.

EXECUTORY COSTS

Costs such as insurance, maintenance and taxes incurred for leased property, whether paid by the lessor or lessee, are executory costs. Amounts paid by a lessee in consideration for a guarantee from an unrelated third party of the residual value are also executory costs. If executory costs are paid by a lessor, any lessor profit on those costs is considered the same as executory costs.

Lease Types

Now that the essential terms have been defined, the discussion will focus on the various types of accounting leases. From the lessee's perspective, leases are accounted for as either operating or capital. A lessor also accounts for its leases as either capital or operating, but, additionally, a lessor's capital leases may be broken down into three subsets, as shown in Figure 2. At this point the various aspects of each type of lease will not be discussed, only the general characteristics of each (the details of these leases are discussed in Chapters Fourteen, Fifteen and Sixteen). The differences between the two classifications (operating and capital) are graphically shown in Table 2 (lessor) and Table 3 (lessee).

Given the comparisons in Tables 2 and 3, and the previous discussions regarding the difference between IRS and FASB lease classifications, the differences between tax and accounting terminology (an area of constant confusion) will now be addressed and clarified.

Although there are similarities between the two, it is important that the capital lease criteria, terminology and impact not be confused with that of taxation. As most individuals are aware, a company maintains two sets of books: one set for the shareholders and one set for the IRS. The rules governing each are different (although deferred taxes provide a bridge between the two). FASB 13 sets the guidelines for lease company shareholder reporting and the IRS sets those for tax reporting.

Taxes are computed based upon revenues and expenses, so the greatest misunderstanding occurs in regard to the income statement. There are similarities between a true lease for tax

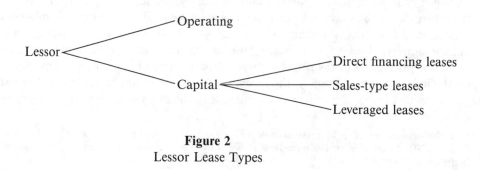

Figure 2
Lessor Lease Types

Table 2
Lessor Comparison

Classification	Balance Sheet Effect	Income Statement Effect
Operating lease	• Asset • Accumulated depreciation • Deferred initial direct costs	• Rental revenue • Depreciation expense • Initial direct costs expense
Capital lease	• Net investment in leases	• Net interest earned

Table 3
Lessee Comparison

Classification	Balance Sheet Effect	Income Statement Effect
Operating lease	• None	• Rental expense
Capital lease	• Capital leased asset • Capital lease obligation	• Depreciation expense • Interest expense

purposes and an operating lease for accounting purposes (and likewise for conditional sales contracts and capital leases), yet the occurrence of one does not necessarily demand the occurrence of the other. In fact, an extremely common lease is one that is a true lease for tax purposes, a direct financing capital lease to the lessor and an operating lease to the lessee. To reiterate, the tax consequences per se do not dictate accounting treatment, and vice versa. Table 4 details the terminology and characteristics of tax and accounting leases. Similarities, but also differences, between tax and accounting treatment can be clearly identified. As an illustration, assume a lease that is a tax lease to both parties, but is a direct financing capital lease to the lessor and an operating lease to the lessee. The tax and accounting treatment for both lessor and lessee would be as shown in Table 5.

An appreciation and understanding of the differences between taxes and accounting are valuable, and will aid in discussions with lessees and among company personnel. Having reviewed what constitutes a lease, lease terminology and the difference between capital and operating leases, an example illustrating the contrast between the impact of a capital and operating lease on the financial statements of the lessee is presented.

Table 4
Tax Versus Accounting Results

Classification	Lessor	Lessee
Accounting		
Capital	• Net interest earned	• Interest expense • Depreciation expense
Operating	• Rental revenue • Depreciation expense • Initial direct costs expense	• Rental expense
Tax		
Tax lease	• Rental revenue • Tax depreciation • Initial direct costs	• Rental expense
Conditional sales contract	• Interest earned • Initial direct costs	• Tax depreciation • Interest expense

Table 5
Tax/Accounting Comparison

Classification	Lessor (capital lease)	Lessee (operating lease)
Accounting	• Interest earned	• Rental expense
Tax	• Rental revenue • Tax depreciation • Initial direct costs	• Rental expense

OPERATING VERSUS CAPITAL LEASE ILLUSTRATION

The following comprehensive illustration contrasts the lessee's accounting and reporting for capital and operating leases by comparing a capital lease with the same lease accounted for as though it were operating. The financial statements of the lessee are examined since an operating lease provides off balance sheet financing only for the lessee. The illustration serves to demonstrate the difference in reporting for the two types of leases and highlights the impact of off balance sheet financing. The effects of off balance sheet lease financing are especially apparent because the dollar amounts involved in the lease being reported are substantial in relation to the other elements of the financial statements.

The impact on the balance sheet, as well as the other required financial statements, is shown, as are various financial ratios under the two different lease reporting techniques. Note that the net after-tax cash cost of leasing is the same whether the lease is classified as capital or operating because the accounting status of a lease does not impact its cash flows. This characteristic of leasing is shown in the statement of cash flows.

The following are the assumptions for the sample lease of the XYZ Company, a lessee, to be used in the illustration.

Lease payments: $3,484.19, due at the beginning of each month of the lease term

Lease term: 6 years (72 monthly payments)

Salvage value for accounting purposes: none

Depreciation: for accounting purposes the leased asset will be depreciated over 6 years, which corresponds to the lease term

Purchase option: fair market value

Lessee's pretax borrowing rate: 12%

The cash cost of the asset (were it purchased rather than leased): $200,000

Lease inception: January 1 of the current year.

Capitalization of the Leased Asset

In the case of the capital lease, even though the contract between the lessor and lessee is called a lease in form, it more closely resembles a sale and a purchase in substance and, therefore, the FASB requires that it be accounted for as a capitalizable purchase to the lessee. The capital lease accounting treatment will very closely resemble an installment purchase, in which the asset is paid for over a period of months or years through periodic payments consisting of principal and interest.

In a capital lease, the leased equipment is shown on the balance sheet as an asset separate from other types of property, plant and equipment of the lessee. A lease liability equal to the capitalized value of the leased equipment is also shown. The capital asset is depreciated according to the company's normal depreciation policy over either the lease term or the economic life of the equipment, depending upon which capital lease criteria caused the lease to be capital. Lease payments paid to the lessor are separated into principal and interest expense as though they are installment loan payments.

The amount that should be capitalized by the lessee in this illustration can now be determined, based on the preceding information. This amount should be shown as an asset on the balance sheet by the lessee as 'Capital Leased Equipment.' It is determined by calculating the present value of the minimum lease payments required by the lease contract (72 payments of $3,484.19).

In order to calculate the present value of these lease payments, an appropriate interest rate (discount rate) must be selected. FASB 13 requires the lessee to use its incremental, pretax cost of debt as the discount rate. This rate represents the rate of interest the lessee would have had to pay for a loan of equal term used to fund the acquisition of the equipment had it been purchased. The lessee's current borrowing rate is given at 12% in this example.

With the appropriate discount rate, the present value of the lease payments using the HP-12C can be calculated as follows:

	g	BEG (payments are in advance)
3,484.19		PMT
72		n
12	g	12 ÷
		PV 180,000 (rounded)

The present value of the lease payments discounted at the lessee's pretax borrowing rate is $180,000. This is the amount at which the leased asset will be capitalized on the lessee's balance sheet at the inception of the lease. This amount, however, cannot exceed the equipment's fair market value ($200,000 in this case).

Booking the Lease Liability

A corresponding liability equal to the capitalized asset is shown in the liability section of the balance sheet. Initially, the total liability is shown as $180,000. This total liability amount will be broken down, however, into its current and long-term components when the lessee classifies its balance sheet. The current portion of the total $180,000 debt is that portion of the total that will be paid off within the next 12 months of the lease. The balance of the debt is considered long-term and is shown accordingly on the balance sheet under Long-Term Leases Payable.

In order to separate the current from the long-term portions of the debt an amortization schedule of the lease payments must be prepared, as in Table 6. Using the HP-12C, the debt amortization is set up as follows:

	g	BEG
180,000	CHS	PV
3,484.19		PMT
12	g	12 ÷
0		n

As the lease obligation is amortized, the amount of the total $180,000 obligation paid off each year is shown. For example, in the first year, the principal portion of the payments will be $25,286. This is the portion of the total principal that will be recorded as current at the

Table 6
Amortization Schedule

Year	Interest (12 f AMORT)	Principal (X ≥ Y)	Balance (RCL PV)
1	20,009[5]	25,286	154,714
2	17,244	24,567	130,148
3	14,128	27,682	102,465
4	10,617	31,193	71,272
5	6,661	35,149	36,123
6	2,203	36,123	0
Total	70,862	180,000	

beginning of the first year. The long-term portion will be $154,714 ($180,000 - $25,286 = $154,714), and is shown in the balance column of Table 6.[5]

At the beginning of the second year the total remaining liability will be only $154,714, because $25,286 will have been paid off in the first year. The $154,714 will then be separated into its current and long-term components, which are found in the second year of the amortization schedule of Table 6. The liability breakdown between current and long-term in the second year is important because the comparative financial statements that follow are shown as of the end of the first year. Note in Table 6 that the interest expense relating to the lease payments for each year is found in the column entitled "Interest."

Depreciation

For accounting purposes, the capitalized leased asset of $180,000 is depreciated over the 6-year lease term according to XYZ Company's normal depreciation policy. FASB 13 requires that if the lease is capital because the present value of the lease payments is equal to or greater than 90% of the asset's fair market value, the lessee must depreciate the asset over the lease term. If, however, it is anticipated the lessee will acquire the asset at the end of the lease term because of automatic title transfer or the existence of a bargain purchase option, the lessee must follow its normal depreciation policy and depreciate the asset over its economic useful life.

In this example, the lessee has the option of purchasing the asset at the end of the lease at its fair market value. At the beginning of the lease it is not known what the asset's value will be 6 years later; therefore, the lessee is not certain whether it will exercise the purchase option. Since continued use of the asset after the lease term is uncertain, the lessee must depreciate it over the

---

[5] Payments are in advance so one extra payment is accounted for on the accrual basis during the first year. The keystrokes to accomplish this would be 13 f AMORT.

lease term. The yearly depreciation is calculated by dividing the capitalized leased asset amount of $180,000 by the 6 years of the lease term.

$180,000 ÷ 6 = $30,000 per year.

Accounting for the Operating Lease

Accounting by the lessee for the operating lease is much easier. The operating lease is treated the same as any other rental expense item. The rent expense is shown in the income statement, but the leased asset and the liability do not appear in the balance sheet. In this illustration the only impact on the financial statements is the lease expense each year of $41,810 ($3,484.19 for 12 months).

Financial Statement Comparison

All the information necessary to compile the lease portions of the financial statements has now been determined. The financial statements for XYZ Company for the sample lease are shown in Figures 3, 4 and 5. The operating lease treatment of the lease is described in the left hand column of numbers while the contrasting capital lease treatment is described in the right hand column. The comparative deferred tax computations are shown in Figure 6. An assessment of the differences between the two accounting treatments in the statements follows the presentation of the financial statements.

Analysis of Differences

The financial statements in Figures 3, 4 and 5 indicate definite differences between accounting for a lease as operating versus capital. The following is an analysis of the specific financial statement line items that gave rise to the differences.

BALANCE SHEET

The capital lease creates a $2,788 deferred tax charge (representing the difference between the books and the tax return). This deferred tax charge occurs because total depreciation and interest expense of the capital lease exceed the lease rental expense deduction on the tax return. Notice that the capitalized leased equipment appears as a separate category of property, plant and equipment when the lease is capital. Accumulated depreciation is shown as an offset to the capital leased equipment because it too must be depreciated like any other depreciable equipment.

The current portion of the lease liability consists of two parts:

(1)	Current portion of leases payable per Table 6	$ 24,567
(2)	Accrued lease rental for the last month of the first year, which is due the first day of the new fiscal year.	3,484
	Total liability	$ 28,051

The long-term portion of the lease liability is $130,148 and is shown only when the lease is capital. Operating leases are considered off balance sheet because they do not appear as either assets or liabilities. The current portion of retained earnings represents the impact of the

ASSETS

	Operating Lease	Capital Lease
Current assets		
Cash	$ 20,852	$ 20,852
Accounts receivable	21,270	21,270
Inventory	17,500	17,500
Total current assets	$ 59,622	$ 59,622
Fixed assets		
Deferred tax charge	$ 0	$ 2,788
Property, plant and equipment	174,000	174,000
Capital leased equipment	0	180,000
Less: accumulated depreciation	(36,000)	(66,000)
Total fixed assets	$ 138,000	$ 290,788
Total assets	$ 197,622	$ 350,410

LIABILITIES

	Operating Lease	Capital Lease
Current liabilities		
Accounts payable	$ 11,000	$ 11,000
Leases payable — current	0	28,051
Total current liabilities	$ 11,000	$ 39,051
Long-term liabilities		
Notes payable	$ 76,000	$ 76,000
Leases payable — long-term	0	130,148
Total long-term liabilities	$ 76,000	$ 206,148
Total liabilities	$ 87,000	$ 245,199

OWNERS' EQUITY

	Operating Lease	Capital Lease
Owners' equity		
Common stock	$ 30,000	$ 30,000
Retained earnings		
Prior	34,297	34,297
Current portion	46,325	40,914
Total owners' equity	$ 110,622	$ 105,211
Total liabilities and owners' equity	$ 197,622	$ 350,410

Figure 3
Balance Sheet
End of First Year Reporting

	Operating Lease	Capital Lease
REVENUE		
Sales	$ 480,000	$ 480,000
Cost of goods sold	(260,000)	(260,000)
Gross profit	$ 220,000	$ 220,000
OPERATING EXPENSE		
Selling expense	(6,400)	(6,400)
General and administrative expense	(67,600)	(67,600)
Lease expense	(41,810)	0
Depreciation expense	(16,000)	(46,000)
OPERATING INCOME	$ 88,190	$ 100,000
OTHER INCOME AND EXPENSES		
Interest expense	(18,000)	(38,009)
INCOME BEFORE TAXES	$ 70,190	$ 61,991
Income taxes 34%	(23,865)	(21,077)
NET INCOME	$ 46,325	$ 40,914

Figure 4
Income Statement
End of First Year Reporting

	Operating Lease	Capital Lease
SOURCES OF CASH		
Net income	$ 46,325	$ 40,914
Add depreciation expense	16,000	46,000
Deduct increase in deferred tax charge		(2,788)
Total sources	$ 62,325	$ 84,126
USES OF CASH		
Dividends	(15,000)	(15,000)
Purchase of equipment	(36,000)	(36,000)
Reduction of lease liability	0	(21,801)
Total uses	($ 51,000)	($ 72,801)
NET INCREASE IN CASH	$ 11,325	$ 11,325

Figure 5
Cash Flow Statement
End of First Year Reporting

OPERATING LEASE

	Tax Return	Books
12 regular payments	$ 41,810	$ 41,810
Tax rate	× .34	× .34
Tax benefit	$ 14,215	$ 14,215

CAPITAL LEASE

	Tax Return	Books
12 regular payments	$ 41,810	$ 0
Interest expense	0	20,009
Depreciation expense	0	30,000
Total	$ 41,810	$ 50,009
Tax rate	× .34	× .34
Tax benefit	$ 14,215	$ 17,003
Increase in deferred tax charge	2,788	0
	$ 17,003	$ 17,003

Figure 6
Deferred Tax Reconciliation

reported net income for the period presented. This difference is explained in the income statement discussion.

INCOME STATEMENT

Lease expense of $41,810 is the only lease related expense to appear under the operating lease. This figure does not appear at all under the capital lease because lease payments are treated as loan payments that generate interest expense rather than lease expense.

Depreciation expense is $30,000 greater under the capital lease alternative. This amount represents one year's depreciation of the $180,000 capitalized leased asset. Interest expense of $20,009 is incurred on the capital lease liability. Note that the sum of interest expense, $20,009, and depreciation expense, $30,000, results in total expense of $50,009 versus the total operating lease expense of $41,810. The difference of $8,199 ($50,009 - $41,810) is the reason net income and income before taxes are different under the two alternatives. Over time the difference between the two totals narrows and eventually reverses as the interest expense declines.

Income tax expense varies between the two alternatives because of the difference in income before taxes. Actual income taxes payable for both leases is $23,865, as shown under the operating lease alternative. The capital lease book tax expense is shown at $21,077, however, creating a $2,788 timing difference, which is shown as a deferred tax charge (see Figure 6).

CASH FLOW STATEMENT

All aspects of the cash flow statement have been previously explained. It should be clearly understood, however, that the net increase in cash is the same for both the capital lease and the operating lease. Only the accounting treatment is different. This concept is illustrated in Figure 5.

Financial Ratio Impact

As is illustrated in Table 7, the financial ratios portray the lessee as being financially healthier under operating lease treatment than when capital lease accounting is used. Explanations of the differences in ratios are also presented.

LIQUIDITY

The first three ratios ostensibly measure the firm's short-run ability to meet its debt obligations. Judging from these commonly used liquidity ratios, it appears the firm is in better condition to pay its short-term debt obligations when operating lease accounting is used, although the real cash position is identical in either case. The current and quick ratios, which show the availability of current assets to pay current liabilities, are both about three times greater under the operating lease. Since bills are paid with cash and not accounting accrual income, the apparent advantage of the operating lease is really artificial. However, those persons using the financial statements may still be mislead to favor firms where operating lease accounting is used. The apparent excess of "working capital" is also misleading because cash available for operations is the same with both accounting approaches.

SOLVENCY

The long-run ability of a firm to meet its debt obligations and interest expense is commonly measured with the times-interest-earned ratio. This measures the number of times the firm's interest bill could be paid with its available net income and is shown to be much greater for the operating lease. However, the actual ability of the firm to pay its ongoing interest bills on debt is the same as the same cash is available in either case.

FINANCIAL LEVERAGE

These ratios attempt to indicate a firm's dependence on debt by measuring the ratio of its total debt to either total equity or total assets. Because lease payment debt liability is hidden when operating lease accounting is used, these particular ratios can be very misleading. The actual contractual debt is really the same in both cases although it appears to be lower for the operating lease.

PROFITABILITY

Every measurement of profitability for the firm appears to favor the operating lease, including the bottom-line measurement of earnings per share, which is an important measure for financial analysts in assessing a firm's profitability because it directly affects stock price. The impact of operating lease accounting is evident from XYZ's financial statements and ratios. All of these tend to make the operating lease accounting approach more favorable. When operating lease accounting is used, a firm appears better able to service its debt and also less encumbered by debt. When this is the perception, it is usually much easier to acquire more debt, which is an advantage in great demand for many firms; hence, the demand for operating leases.

Although the financial statements make the operating lease look more favorable, FASB 13 requires additional information to be given in the footnotes to the financial statements that

Table 7
Financial Ratio Impact

Ratio	Formula	Operating Lease		Capital Lease	
Liquidity					
Current ratio	Current assets	$59,622	= 5.42	$59,622	= 1.53
	Current liabilities	$11,000		$39,051	
Quick or acid ratio	Quick assets	$42,122	= 3.83	$42,122	= 1.08
	Current liabilities	$11,000		$39,051	
Net working capital	Current assets - current liabilities	$59,622 (11,000)		$59,622 (39,051)	
	Net working capital	$48,622		$20,571	
Solvency					
Times-interest-earned	Interest + taxes + net income	$88,190	= 4.90	$100,000	= 2.63
	Interest	$18,000		$ 38,009	
Financial leverage					
Debt-to-equity	Debt	$87,000	= .79	$245,199	= 2.33
	Equity	$110,622		$105,211	
Percentage debt	Debt	$87,000	= 44%	$245,199	= 70%
	Assets	$197,622		$350,410	
Profitability					
Net profit margin	Net income	$46,325	= 9.7%	$40,914	= 8.5%
	Sales	$480,000		$480,000	
× Asset turnover	Sales	$480,000	= 2.429	$480,000	= 1.370
	Asset	$197,622		$350,410	
= Return on assets	Net income	$46,325	= 23.4%	$40,914	= 11.7%
	Assets	$197,622		$350,410	
× Leverage factor	Assets	$197,622	= 1.786	$350,410	3.331
	Equity	$110,622		$105,211	
= Return on equity	Net income	$46,325	= 41.9%	$40,914	= 38.9%
	Equity	$110,622		$105,211	
Earnings per share	Net income	$46,325	= $4.63	$40,914	= $4.09
	Total shares	$10,000		$10,000	

allow a user of those statements to be aware of the accounting differences. Enough extra information is required in the footnotes, in fact, that a knowledgeable user could effectively restate the financial statements showing operating lease data as if capital lease accounting had been used. Doing so would show the existence of the contractual lease obligation (debt) and prevent incorrect conclusions about the firm's liquidity, solvency or profitability.

The apparent advantages of off balance sheet operating lease accounting exist only in the early years of a lease. In later years these reporting advantages become disadvantages. Each of the financial statement impacts will reverse as total expenses (interest plus depreciation) for the capital lease become smaller than the operating lease expenses, thereby causing net income to be greater under the capital lease. Often this reversal of effect over the long run is ignored in favor of the short-run advantages, thereby making operating leases popular among today's lessees. Lessees also find they must commit to additional operating leases for new equipment as earlier operating leases mature, in order to offset the reversal of off balance sheet leasing advantages.

CONCLUSION

Accounting pervades every aspect of leasing; therefore, it is essential to have a basic understanding of the issues. What constitutes a capital, as opposed to an operating, lease, and how each differs from the tax treatment of the lease are examples of important accounting concepts. The issue of off balance sheet financing for lessees has always been one of interest, and for good reason, as has been illustrated.

With this background knowledge of lease accounting, and an understanding of lease terminology and definitions, one should be able to function more effectively in the industry. A full discussion of lease accounting topics beyond the introductory level is found in Chapters Fourteen, Fifteen and Sixteen.

CHAPTER FOURTEEN
OPERATING LEASES

Capital leases once dominated the portfolios of most lessors in the United States, but, of late, the proportion of operating leases in lessor portfolios has been growing. To the lessee, of course, operating leases have always been popular due to the off balance sheet financing they provide. Lessors are also concerned about operating leases, but for reasons unlike those of the lessee. Lessor operating leases, due to their dependence upon use of straight-line depreciation for book (not tax) purposes, usually show lower net earnings during the first half of the lease relative to capital leases, thereby impacting income statement results. This anomaly, plus other aspects of operating leases, will be explained in this chapter. The chapter is divided into the following sections:

- Lessor Operating Lease Accounting
- Lessee Operating Lease Accounting.

LESSOR OPERATING LEASE ACCOUNTING

All operating leases possess similar characteristics, whether they are viewed from the standpoint of the lessee or the lessor. There are certain aspects of each, however, that must be treated differently. This section will present the determination of, and subsequent accounting for, operating leases from the lessor's perspective.

Determination of Operating Lease Status

Before a lessor begins accounting for a lease, it must ascertain whether the lease is to be classified as capital or operating. For a lessor to have an operating lease, none of the four Financial Accounting Standards Board Statement No. 13 (FASB 13) capital lease criteria (as discussed in Chapter Thirteen) can be met. These four criteria are summarized below, as a review.

1. The lease automatically transfers title during, or by the end of, the lease term
2. A bargain purchase options exists
3. The noncancellable lease term is greater than or equal to 75% of the asset's economic life
4. The present value of the minimum lease payments, discounted at the lessor's interest rate implicit in the lease, is greater than or equal to 90% of the leased asset's fair market value reduced by any lessor retained tax credits.

Even if the lease is theoretically capital because it has met one or more of the above cited criteria, it will nevertheless be considered an operating lease if either (1) the collectibility of the minimum lease payments is not reasonably predictable or (2) important uncertainties surround the amount of unreimbursable costs yet to be incurred by the lessor under the lease. Because the last two criteria are lessor criteria only and are ignored by lessees in determining whether a lease is operating, a lease could be deemed operating on the lessor's books, but be considered capital to the lessee. Additionally, if criteria number three or four, and the two lessor criteria, are met, the lease could still be operating if the leased asset represents used equipment and is in the last 25% of its economic life.

Initial Entries and Subsequent Accounting

In order to explain the accounting for an operating lease, the following operating lease example will be used:

Equipment cost: $120,000

Lease term: 24 monthly lease payments at $4,000, due the first of each month (two payments in advance)

Refundable security deposit: $2,000

Initial direct costs: $2,880

Tax treatment: 5-year Modified Accelerated Cost Recovery System (MACRS) property

Tax rate: calendar year taxpayer in a 34% corporate tax bracket

Lease inception: August 1, 19XX

Unguaranteed residual: $48,000 (at the end of 24 months; however, the asset will be depreciated over its economic life of 5 years for book purposes, with an anticipated ultimate salvage value of $12,000).

As mentioned, the first step in accounting for an operating lease is to establish that, in fact, the lease is operating. Assuming the first three capital lease criteria were not met, this is achieved by ascertaining whether or not the present value of the minimum lease payments is less than 90% of the asset's fair market value reduced by any lessor retained tax credits. The lessor must use the rate implicit in the lease in performing the discounting.

PROOF OF OPERATING LEASE STATUS

Determine the FASB 13 comparison base, which establishes the floor that the present value of the minimum lease payments must be below in order for the lease to be operating.

Asset's fair market value (FMV)	$ 120,000
Less tax credits	0
Subtotal	$ 120,000
	×.90
FASB 13 comparison base	$ 108,000

Next, determine the lessor's interest rate implicit in the lease using the following steps (note that lessors must use the rate implicit in the lease to discount the minimum lease payments, whereas lessees must use the lower of the implicit rate, if known, or their pretax, incremental borrowing rate). In essence, implicit rates are simple internal rates of return (IRRs) that take into consideration the following cash flows:

1. Inception cash flows:

FMV	($120,000)
Initial direct costs	(2,880)
Two advance payments	8,000
Net inception cost	($114,880)

2. Subsequent cash flows: 22 months at $4,000 and 1 month at zero
3. Termination cash flows: $48,000 unguaranteed residual.

Calculation of the implicit rate is accomplished through the following keystrokes:

114,880	CHS	g	CF_o	(net inception outflow)
4,000		g	CF_j	(regular rentals)
22		g	N_j	
0		g	CF_j	
48,000		g	CF_j	(unguaranteed residual)
		f	IRR	1.0896

Finally, find the present value of the minimum lease payments using the implicit rate computed above as the discount rate, and compare the present value to the FASB 13 comparison base.

1.0896		i		(implicit rate)
8,000		g	CF_o	(two advance rentals)
4,000		g	CF_j	(regular rentals)
22		g	N_j	
		f	NPV	85,872.51

The present value of the minimum lease payments of $85,872.51 is less than the $108,000 FASB 13 comparison base; therefore, the lease is classified as operating.

FASB 13 REQUIREMENTS

Once the lease is clearly determined to be an operating lease from the lessor's viewpoint, the initial balance sheet accounting entries can be determined, followed by the accounting entries that occur subsequent to the inception of the lease. (Operating leases of the lessor are accounted for per FASB 13, paragraph 19.)

The leased property subject to operating leases must be included with or near property, plant and equipment in the balance sheet. The property is depreciated following the lessor's normal depreciation policy, and in the balance sheet the accumulated depreciation is deducted from the investment in the leased property. Lessors typically refer to this separate category of property as leased equipment, operating leased equipment or property subject to operating leases.

Rent from operating leases is reported as income over the lease term as it becomes receivable according to the provisions of the lease. However, even if the rentals vary from a straight-line basis, the income must still be recognized on a straight-line basis. An alternative method may be used only if it is systematic and rational and is more representative of the time pattern of use of the leased property.

Any initial direct costs incurred must be deferred and allocated over the lease term in proportion to the recognition of rental income (generally straight-line). However, initial direct costs may be charged to expense as incurred if they are not material. Lease commitment fees, closing fees, origination fees, lease bonuses, etc., received by the lessor from the lessee at the inception of the lease are generally deferred and allocated as revenue to the income statement on a straight-line basis over the noncancellable lease term. Refundable security deposits do not represent income so they are shown as a liability until they are refunded per the lease contract. Tax credits are accounted for completely separate from the operating leased asset.

JOURNAL ENTRIES

The initial entries, in general journal entry form, are shown below, followed by a T-account summary of the first 5 months of operation.

1. Leased equipment	$ 120,000	
Cash		$ 120,000

To record the acquisition cost of equipment to be leased on an operating lease basis

2. Cash	$ 10,000	
Refundable security deposit		$ 2,000
Deferred rentals		$ 4,000
Rental revenue		$ 4,000

To defer a refundable security deposit and one advance payment received at the inception of the lease

The other advance payment represents August's rental expense, which is recognized as August revenue.

3. Deferred initial direct costs	$ 2,880	
Cash (or accounts payable)	$ 2,880	

    To defer costs incurred to set up the operating lease at its inception

4. Cash	$ 120,000	
Contributed capital		$ 120,000

    To record the source of cash used to acquire the equipment

The journal entries to account for subsequent rentals are as follows, and will appear each month after the lease's inception.

Cash	$ 4,000	
Rental revenue		$ 4,000

    To record monthly rent

Depreciation expense[1]	$ 1,800	
Accumulated depreciation		$ 1,800

    To record depreciation expense for the month

Initial direct cost expense	$ 120	
Deferred initial direct costs		$ 120

    To recognize 1/24 of the $2,880 of deferred initial direct costs.

SUMMARY OF JOURNAL ENTRIES AT END OF FIRST YEAR

The T-accounts in Figures 1 and 2 summarize both the journal entries at the inception of the lease plus the recognition of earnings for August through December. The deferred tax credit entries will be explained after the presentation of the financial statements for this example. The numbers in parentheses next to the T-account entries correspond to the numbers of the initial journal entries presented earlier. The letters correspond to the first letter of the months in which the corresponding T-account entries are made (e.g., A = August entry, etc.).

Using the T-account balances in Figures 1 and 2, an income statement (Figure 3), a balance sheet (Figure 4) and a cash flow statement (Figure 5) can be prepared.

---

[1][($120,000 - $12,000) ÷ 60)] = $1,800. Cost recovery or depreciation for leased assets is generally straight-line over the expected economic life of the asset (neither the lease term nor the MACRS tax classlife). Anticipated salvage value also is deducted from the depreciable book value. In this case, the cost of $120,000 is adjusted for the anticipated salvage value of $12,000 at the end of 60 months, and the difference is divided by the total anticipated life (expressed in months). The quotient represents the monthly financial statement depreciation charge.

Leased Equipment		Accumulated Depreciation		Taxes Receivable	
(1)120,000			1,800 A	D 979	
			1,800 S		
			1,800 O		
			1,800 N		
			1,800 D		
			9,000		

Cash		Deferred Initial Direct Costs		Deferred Rentals	
(4)120,000	2,880(3)	(3)2,880	120 A		4,000(2)
(2)10,000	120,000(1)		120 S		
S 4,000			120 O		
O 4,000			120 N		
N 4,000			120 D		
D 4,000		2,880	600		
23,120		2,280			

Deferred Tax Credit		Refundable Security Deposit		Contributed Capital	
	4,515 D		2,000(2)		120,000(4)

Figure 1
Balance Sheet T-accounts

Rental Revenue		Initial Direct Cost Expense		Depreciation Expense	
	4,000 A(2)	A 120		A 1,800	
	4,000 S	S 120		S 1,800	
	4,000 O	O 120		O 1,800	
	4,000 N	N 120		N 1,800	
	4,000 D	D 120		D 1,800	
	20,000	600		9,000	

Income Tax Expense	
D 3,536	

Figure 2
Income Statement T-accounts

REVENUE

Rental payments	$ 20,000	
Less depreciation expense (5 months)	(9,000)	
Implicit lease interest		$ 11,000
Total lease income		$ 11,000

OPERATING EXPENSES

Initial direct costs	$ 600	
General and administrative	0	
Total operating expenses		600

OPERATING INCOME		$ 10,400
OTHER INCOME		0
OTHER EXPENSES		
Interest expense		0
INCOME FROM OPERATIONS BEFORE TAXES		$ 10,400
Current taxes	($ 979)	
Deferred taxes	4,515	
Income tax expense		3,536
NET INCOME		$ 6,864

Figure 3
Income Statement
End of First Year Reporting

INTERPERIOD TAX ALLOCATION

A deferred tax credit will be generated by the preceding operating lease because of the following book versus tax accounting differences:

1. Advance rentals beyond one are not shown as income on the accounting books, but are included in taxable income. More than one advance rental on the accounting books is deferred until earned, usually the last month of the lease. However, the Internal Revenue Service (IRS) will tax both advance payments

2. Initial direct costs may be fully tax deductible at a lease's inception, but are deferred for accounting purposes when material (typically greater than 1% of equipment cost). These deferred initial direct costs are then expensed over the lease term for accounting purposes

3. Depreciation for accounting book purposes is straight-line, whereas tax depreciation will most likely be MACRS according to the MACRS classlife.

ASSETS

Current assets
Cash		$ 23,120
Taxes receivable		979
Total current assets			$ 24,099

Fixed assets
Property, plant and equipment (net)		$ 0	
Leased equipment	$ 120,000		
Less: cost recovery	(9,000)		
Net leased equipment		111,000	
Total fixed assets			111,000

Deferred charges
Initial direct costs	2,280
Total assets	$ 137,379

LIABILITIES

Current liabilities
Taxes payable	$ 0

Long-term liabilities | 0

Deferred credits
Refundable security deposit	$ 2,000	
Deferred rental	4,000	
Deferred tax credit	4,515	
Total deferred credits		10,515
Total liabilities		$ 10,515

OWNERS' EQUITY

Contributed capital	$ 120,000	
Retained earnings (current net income)	6,864	
Total owners' equity		126,864
Total liabilities and owners' equity		$ 137,379

Figure 4
Balance Sheet
End of First Year Reporting

CASH FLOWS FROM OPERATING ACTIVITIES

Operating lease rentals	$ 15,000	
Security deposits received	2,000	
Initial direct costs paid	(2,880)	
Net cash provided by operating activities		**$ 14,120**

CASH FLOWS FROM INVESTING ACTIVITIES

Purchase of equipment to be leased	($120,000)	
Depreciation	9,000	
Net cash used in investing activities		(111,000)

CASH FLOWS FROM FINANCING ACTIVITIES

Proceeds from issuance of common stock	$ 120,000	
Net cash provided by financing activities		120,000

NET INCREASE IN CASH		$ 23,120
Cash at the beginning of the year		0
Cash at the end of the year		$ 23,120

RECONCILIATION OF NET INCOME TO NET CASH PROVIDED BY OPERATING ACTIVITIES

Net income		$ 6,864
Adjustments to net income		
Increase in security deposits	$ 2,000	
Increase in deferred tax credits	4,515	
Increase in deferred rentals	4,000	
Increase in taxes receivable	(979)	
Net increase in initial direct costs	(2,280)	
Total adjustments		7,256
Net cash provided by operating activities		**$ 14,120**

SUPPLEMENTAL SCHEDULE OF NONCASH INVESTING AND FINANCING ACTIVITIES $ 0

DISCLOSURE OF ACCOUNTING POLICY

The direct method of cash flow operating sources is shown on a gross basis, as promulgated in FASB Statement No. 95 (FASB 95).

Figure 5
Cash Flow Statement
(direct method presentation per FASB 95)
End of First Year Reporting

Based on the preceding differences between accounting books and the tax return, the interperiod tax allocation journal entry would be calculated by finding the difference between book and taxable income, as shown in Table 1.

Based on the information in Table 1, the December interperiod tax allocation journal entry would be:

1.	Taxes receivable	$ 979	
	Income tax expense	$ 3,536	
	Deferred tax credit		$ 4,515

To record the year-end tax provision

Special Problems

There are some operating leases in which skip payments, rent holidays or step payments exist. Although FASB 13 has always required straight-line income recognition, enough diversity in practice existed to prompt issuance of FASB Technical Bulletin No. 85-3 (TB 85-3). TB 85-3 requires straight-line recognition of revenue:

> Certain operating lease agreements specify scheduled rent increases over the lease term. Such scheduled rent increases may, for example, be designed to provide an inducement or 'rent holiday' for the lessee, to reflect the anticipated effects of inflation, to ease the lessee's near-term cash flow requirements, or to acknowledge the time value of money. For operating leases that include scheduled rent increases, is it ever appropriate for lessees or lessors to recognize rent expense or rental income on a basis other than the straight-line basis required by Statement 13?

Table 1
Book/Tax Differences

	Accounting Books	Tax Books
Advance rentals	$ 4,000	$ 8,000
Normal rentals (4 months)	16,000	16,000
Initial direct costs (5 months)	(600)	(2,880)
Depreciation/MACRS (5 months)	(9,000)	(24,000)
Taxable income	$ 10,400	($ 2,880)
Tax rate	× .34	× .34
Tax expense (benefit)	$ 3,536	($ 979)
Difference	$ 4,515	

The effects of those scheduled rent increases, which are included in minimum lease payments under Statement 13, should be recognized by lessors and lessees on a straight-line basis over the lease term unless another systematic and rational allocation basis is more representative of the time pattern in which the leased property is physically employed. Using factors such as the time value of money, anticipated inflation, or expected future revenues to allocate scheduled rent increases is inappropriate because these factors do not relate to the *time pattern* of the physical usage of the leased property. However, such factors may affect the periodic reported rental income or expense if the lease agreement involves contingent rentals, which are excluded from minimum lease payments and accounted for separately under Statement 13, as amended by Statement 29 [FASB Technical Bulletin 85-3, paragraphs 1 and 2].

Many of those lessors who did not use straight-line income recognition before TB 85-3 supported an interest imputation allocation approach, arguing that it reflects the economic substance of the transaction. They also indicated that the time value of money is an economic reality that warrants recognition.

The FASB recognizes that the time value of money is an important concept underlying the fundamental accounting in FASB 13 and that the initial measurements of capital leases are based on present value. However, FASB 13 views operating leases as executory contracts, not as financing transactions, for accounting purposes; therefore, the FASB has stated the interest imputation approach is unacceptable.

Disclosure Requirements

FASB 13 requires the following disclosure for lessor operating leases:

i. The cost or carrying amount, if different, of property on lease or held for leasing by major classes of property according to nature or function, and the amount of accumulated depreciation in total as of the date of the latest balance sheet presented.

ii. Minimum future rentals on noncancelable leases as of the date of the latest balance sheet presented, in the aggregate and for each of the five succeeding fiscal years.

iii. Total contingent rentals included in income for each period for which an income statement is presented.

b. A general description of the lessor's leasing arrangements . . . [FASB 13, paragraph 23].

Advanced Operating Lease Accounting

When lessors employ straight-line or accelerated depreciation methods for accounting purposes (not tax), their return on investment is materially understated during the early period of the lease, followed by overstatement during the latter period. This concept can be illustrated through an example of an operating lease that creates a significant distortion of earnings. The example is based on the following assumptions and the distortion of earnings is shown in Table 2.

Table 2
Return on Investment Analysis

Year	1	2	3	4	5
Revenue	$ 32,000	$ 32,000	$ 32,000	$ 32,000	$ 32,000
Residual	0	0	0	0	60,000
Depreciation	(16,000)	(16,000)	(16,000)	(16,000)	(16,000)
Book value	0	0	0	0	(60,000)
Implicit interest	$ 16,000	$ 16,000	$ 16,000	$ 16,000	$ 16,000
Beginning investment	$ 140,000	$ 140,000	$ 140,000	$ 140,000	$ 140,000
Accumulated depreciation	0	(16,000)	(32,000)	(48,000)	(64,000)
Year's beginning investment	$ 140,000	$ 124,000	$ 108,000	$ 92,000	$ 76,000
Return on beginning investment	11.43%[2]	12.90%	14.81%	17.39%	21.05%

Equipment cost: $140,000
Unguaranteed residual at the end of 5 years: $ 60,000
Lease term: 5-year operating lease with the following anticipated annual rentals (received in arrears):

1	$32,000
2	32,000
3	32,000
4	32,000
5	32,000

Implicit interest rate: 14.256%
Depreciation: 5-year, straight-line depreciation of $16,000 per year

$$\left(\frac{\$140,000 - \$60,000}{5}\right)$$

For this lease, with an actual implicit earnings rate of 14.256%, the first 2 years have significant understatements of reported earnings followed by overstatements of earnings in the third, fourth and fifth years.

There are two depreciation methods that are used to mitigate the impact of straight-line or accelerated depreciation. Each of these methods attempts to show interest earned at a constant

---

[2] $16,000 (implicit interest) ÷ $140,000 (beginning investment) = 11.43%

return on the declining net investment (equipment cost less accumulated depreciation). The two methods are present value depreciation and sinking fund depreciation.

PRESENT VALUE DEPRECIATION

The present value depreciation solution to earnings distortion is shown in Table 3. Present value depreciation is determined by performing an amortization of the lease using the interest rate implicit in the lease. The principal amortized column in Table 4 represents the present value depreciation of Table 3. The initial setup for the amortization is as follows:

14.256		i
140,000	CHS	PV
5		n
32,000		PMT

The present value method gives an exact constant return on the declining book value of the leased asset. The drawback of this method is that every asset in a portfolio would have its own depreciation schedule depending upon the interest rate implicit in each lease.

SINKING FUND DEPRECIATION

The sinking fund depreciation solution to earnings distortion is shown in Table 5. This method of depreciation is not directly dependent upon the implicit rate in any particular lease. Rather, the sinking fund method uses an average portfolio earnings rate as a surrogate for the actual earnings rate in any particular lease. Once the average pretax earnings rate is determined,

Table 3
Present Value Depreciation Returns

Year	1	2	3	4	5
Revenue	$ 32,000	$ 32,000	$ 32,000	$ 32,000	$ 32,000
Salvage value	0	0	0	0	60,000
Present value depreciation	(12,042)	(13,758)	(15,720)	(17,960)	(20,520)
Book value	0	0	0	0	(60,000)
Implicit interest	$ 19,958	$ 18,242	$ 16,280	$ 14,040	$ 11,480
Year's beginning investment	$ 140,000	$ 127,958	$ 114,200	$ 98,480	$ 80,520
Investment return	14.26%	14.26%	14.26%	14.26%	14.26%

Table 4
Present Value Amortization

Year	Interest (1 f AMORT)	Principal Amortized (X ≥ Y)
1	19,958	12,042
2	18,242	13,758
3	16,280	15,720
4	14,040	17,960
5	11,480	20,520

Table 5
Sinking Fund Depreciation Returns

Year	1	2	3	4	5
Revenue	$ 32,000	$ 32,000	$ 32,000	$ 32,000	$ 32,000
Salvage value	0	0	0	0	60,000
Sinking fund depreciation	(12,741)	(14,195)	(15,815)	(17,619)	(19,630)
Book value	0	0	0	0	(60,000)
Implicit interest	$ 19,259	$ 17,805	$ 16,185	$ 14,381	$ 12,370
Year's beginning investment	$ 140,000	$ 127,259	$ 113,064	$ 97,249	$ 79,630
Investment return	13.76%	13.99%	14.31%	14.79%	15.53%

an amortization of the lease is completed. The principal amortized column in Table 6 represents the depreciation charge.

In order to calculate sinking fund depreciation, the sinking fund payment (assuming an 11.41% pretax average portfolio earnings rate) must first be arrived at.

11.41		i	
140,000	CHS	PV	
5		n	
60,000		FV	
		PMT	28,715.32

Table 6
Sinking Fund Amortization

Year	Interest (1 f AMORT)	Principal Amortized (X ≥ Y)
1	15,974	12,741
2	14,520	14,195
3	12,901	15,815
4	11,096	17,619
5	9,086	19,630

The payment of $28,715.32 has no particular significance other than to aid in the completion of the necessary amortization schedule. Once it is determined, the payment is amortized, as shown in Table 6. Notice that this method gives results that are quite close to the actual 14.26% rate implicit in the lease.

Are either of these depreciation methods considered to be in accordance with generally accepted accounting principles (GAAP)? It can be argued that both methods are GAAP. Accounting Research Bulletin 43 requires that a depreciation method be cause and effect related (units of production) or otherwise systematic and rational. Systematic means determinable in advance, which has been demonstrated above, and rational means there is a logical basis for the method. It would appear that both criteria have been met with these depreciation methods, plus the two methods come very close to depicting the economic reality of the lease. Whether or not a Certified Public Accountant (CPA) firm will agree these depreciation methods are GAAP, however, is not as important as realizing that, at a minimum, these techniques should be used for managerial reporting. Frequently, use of straight-line depreciation in operating leases will result in losses being shown on the financial statements once interest expense, etc., has been deducted. The reality, of course, is that net income is being generated. For decision-making purposes, management should have financial statements that demonstrate the economic earnings of their leases.

Although there is a general lack of acceptance of either present value or sinking fund depreciation, there is another interesting way to achieve the same results as present value depreciation by converting an operating lease to a capital lease. Once a lease is capital, the interest rate implicit in the lease is used to generate interest earned, which will result in the same amount as if present value depreciation had been used to compute interest earned. How can an operating lease be converted to capital lease status without impacting the lessee or altering the tax status of the lease?

There are two common ways of making an operating lease capital without altering the monthly payments or the lease term, thereby leaving the lessee's operating lease status untouched. Each method makes use of residual guarantees that become part of the lessor's minimum lease payments, but not those of the lessee. The lessor solves mathematically for the precise amount of residual guarantee that would make the lease capital. The lessor will then purchase residual insurance equal to the guarantee or seek a manufacturer (vendor) guarantee. Such independent third-party guarantees are not prohibitively expensive since only part of the residual is being guaranteed. As these third-party guarantees do not impact the lessees minimum lease payments the lessee's operating lease status remains unaltered.

LESSEE OPERATING LEASE ACCOUNTING

As has been mentioned, all operating leases possess similar characteristics, whether they are viewed from the standpoint of the lessee or the lessor. This section will present the determination of, and subsequent accounting for, operating leases from a lessee's perspective.

Determination of Operating Lease Status

Before a lessee begins accounting for a lease, it must be ascertained whether the lease is classified as capital or operating. For a lessee to have an operating lease none of the four capital lease criteria (as discussed in Chapter Thirteen) can be met. These four criteria are summarized as a review.

1. The lease automatically transfers title during, or by the end of, the lease term
2. A bargain purchase options exists
3. The noncancellable lease term is greater than or equal to 75% of the leased asset's economic life
4. The present value of the minimum lease payments is greater than or equal to 90% of the leased asset's fair market value reduced by any lessor retained tax credits. The lessee uses as a discount rate the lower of its pretax, incremental, coterminous borrowing rate or the lessor's implicit rate in the lease, if known. Incremental means the current market rate and coterminous refers to a borrowing rate for a term equal to that of the lease. From a practical viewpoint, the lessee will generally use its borrowing rate since the lessee seldom, if ever, knows the rate implicit in the lease.

Even if number three or four is met, the lease would still be operating if the leased asset represents used equipment that is in the last 25% of its economic life.

Initial Entries and Subsequent Accounting

In order to explain the accounting for an operating lease, the following operating lease example will be used:

Lease term: 48-month lease with a 3-month rent holiday (three skipped payments at the beginning of the lease), followed by 45 rental payments at $3,960 per month

Lease inception: January 1, 19XX

Unguaranteed residual: $40,000, based on an FMV purchase option that the lessee does not expect to exercise

FMV of equipment: $160,000

Discount rate: lessee's incremental, pretax, coterminous borrowing rate is 11.5%. The lessor's implicit rate is known to be 11.95%

Executory costs: lessee pays executory costs

Tax status: the lease is a tax lease for IRS purposes.

As mentioned above, the first step in accounting for an operating lease is to ascertain that in fact the lease is operating. Assuming the first three capital lease criteria were not met, this is achieved by present valuing the minimum lease payments to establish whether their total is less than 90% of the asset's fair market value. The lessee would, in this example, use its borrowing rate for the discounting since it is lower than the lessor's implicit rate.

PROOF OF OPERATING LEASE STATUS

Determine the FASB 13 comparison base, which establishes the floor that the present value of the minimum lease payments must be below in order for the lease to be operating.

Asset's FMV	$ 160,000
Less tax credits	0
Subtotal	$ 160,000
	× .90
FASB 13 comparison base	$ 144,000

Next, find the present value of the minimum lease payments using the lessee's borrowing rate.

11.5	g	12 ÷	
0	g	CF_j	
3	g	N_j	(rent holiday)
3,960	g	CF_j	
45	g	N_j	
	f	NPV	140,132.17

The lease is operating since the present value of $140,132.17 is less than the $144,000 FASB 13 comparison base.

FASB 13 REQUIREMENTS

Once the lease is clearly demonstrated to be operating, the initial balance sheet accounting entries, if any, can be determined, followed by the accounting entries that occur subsequent to the inception of the lease. (Lessee operating leases are accounted for per FASB 13, paragraph 15.)

Rentals on an operating lease are normally charged to expense over the lease term as they become payable. If rental payments are not made on a straight-line basis, rental expense nevertheless must be recognized on a straight-line basis, unless another systematic and rational basis is more representative of the time pattern in which the use or benefit is derived from the leased property, just as in lessor accounting. Furthermore, lease commitment fees, closing fees, origination fees, lease bonuses and leasehold improvements paid at the inception of a lease by the lessee to the lessor are generally deferred and allocated as expenses to the income statement over the noncancellable lease term on a straight-line basis. Investment Tax Credits, etc., passed to the lessee are accounted for completely separate from the operating lease expenses.

JOURNAL ENTRIES

Since there is no balance sheet impact for an operating lease, the income statement entries representing the subsequent accounting for the lease expense will be shown.

1. Lease expense	$ 11,138	
Deferred lease liability	$ 11,138	
To record the first 3 months of lease expense		

Note that although no payments were paid by the lessee during the first 3 months of the lease, lease expense must still be shown. Each month would show 1/48th of the total lease obligation.

$$45 \times \$3,960 = \$178,200 \text{ (total lease obligation)}$$

$$\frac{\$178,200}{48 \text{ months}} = \$3,712.50 \text{ (pro rated straight-line lease expense)}$$

$$3 \times \$3,712.50 = \$11,138 \text{ (lease expense for 3 months)}$$

2. Lease expense	$ 33,418	
Deferred lease liability	$ 2,222	
Cash (9 × $3,960)		$ 35,640
To record the next 9 months of lease expense		

3. Taxes receivable	$ 12,118	
Deferred tax charge	$ 3,031	
Tax benefit		$ 15,149
To record the interperiod tax allocation (discussed later)		

4. Cash	$ 35,640	
Common stock		$ 35,640
To record the issuance of common stock to provide cash for the lease (used to make the balance sheet appear more realistic).		

SUMMARY OF JOURNAL ENTRIES AT END OF FIRST YEAR

The T-accounts in Figure 6 summarize the accounting activity for this lease through the end of the first year. The numbers in parentheses next to the T-account entries correspond to the numbers of the journal entries presented earlier. Using the T-account balances, an income statement (Figure 7), a balance sheet (Figure 8) and a cash flow statement (Figure 9) can be prepared.

INTERPERIOD TAX ALLOCATION

A deferred tax charge (debit balance) will be generated by this lease because of the following book versus tax accounting differences:

Lease Expense	
(1)11,138	
(2)33,418	
44,556	

Tax Benefit	
	15,149(3)

Deferred Lease Liability	
(2)2,222	11,138(1)
	8,916

Cash	
(4)35,640	35,640(2)
0	

Deferred Tax Charge	
(3)3,031	

Taxes Receivable	
(3)12,118	

Common Stock	
	35,640(4)

Figure 6
T-account Summary

REVENUE

Sales	$ 0	
Cost of goods sold	0	
Gross profit		$ 0

OPERATING EXPENSES

Selling	$ 0	
General and administrative	0	
Lease expense	44,556	
Depreciation expense	0	
Total operating expenses		44,556

OPERATING INCOME	($ 44,556)

OTHER INCOME AND EXPENSES

Interest expense	0

INCOME BEFORE TAXES		($ 44,556)
Current taxes	($ 12,118)	
Deferred taxes	(3,031)	
Income tax benefit		(15,149)

NET INCOME (LOSS)	($ 29,407)

Figure 7
Income Statement
End of First Year Reporting

ASSETS

Current assets		
Cash	$ 0	
Taxes receivable	12,118	
Accounts receivable (trade)	0	
Inventory (finished goods)	0	
Total current assets		$ 12,118
Fixed assets		
Deferred tax charge	$ 3,031	
Property, plant and equipment	0	
Capital leased equipment	0	
Less accumulated depreciation	0	
Total fixed assets		3,031
Total assets		$ 15,149

LIABILITIES

Current liabilities		
Taxes payable	$ 0	
Accounts payable (trade)	0	
Current portion leases payable	0	
Total current liabilities		$ 0
Long-term liabilities		
Deferred lease liability	$ 8,916	
Notes payable	0	
Long-term portion leases payable	0	
Total long-term liabilities		8,916
Total liabilities		$ 8,916

OWNERS' EQUITY

Common stock	$ 35,640	
Retained earnings (current net income)	(29,407)	
Total owners' equity		6,233
Total liabilities and owners' equity		$ 15,149

Figure 8
Balance Sheet
End of First Year Reporting

CASH FLOWS FROM OPERATING ACTIVITIES

Operating lease rentals paid	($ 35,640)	
Net cash used by operating activities		**($ 35,640)**

CASH FLOWS FROM INVESTING ACTIVITIES

	0

CASH FLOWS FROM FINANCING ACTIVITIES

Proceeds from issuance of common stock	$ 35,640	
Net cash provided by financing activities		35,640

NET INCREASE IN CASH

		$ 0
Cash at the beginning of the year		0
Cash at the end of the year		$ 0

RECONCILIATION OF NET INCOME TO NET CASH PROVIDED BY OPERATING ACTIVITIES

Net income		($ 29,407)
Adjustments to net income		
Increase in deferred tax charge	($ 3,031)	
Increase in taxes receivable	(12,118)	
Net increase in deferred lease rentals	8,916	
Total adjustments		(6,233)
Net cash used by operating activities		**($ 35,640)**

SUPPLEMENTAL SCHEDULE OF NONCASH INVESTING AND FINANCING ACTIVITIES

	$ 0

DISCLOSURE OF ACCOUNTING POLICY

The direct method of cash flow operating sources is used.

Figure 9
Cash Flow Statement
(direct method presentation per FASB 95)
End of First Year Reporting

1. Advance rentals (none in this case) are not shown as expenses on the accounting records, but are shown as expenses for tax purposes
2. Rental holidays or other forms of skipped or stepped payments are recognized on a straight-line basis for accounting purposes, but not for tax purposes.

Based on the preceding differences, the deferred tax charge would be calculated by finding the difference between book and taxable income, as shown in Table 7. The interperiod tax allocation journal entry, therefore, would be:

Taxes receivable	$ 12,118	
Deferred tax charge	$ 3,031	
Tax benefit		$ 15,149

Disclosure Requirements

FASB 13 requires the following disclosure for lessee operating leases:

   b. For operating leases having initial or remaining noncancelable *lease terms* in excess of one year:

      i. Future minimum rental payments required as of the date of the latest balance sheet presented, in the aggregate and for each of the five succeeding fiscal years.

      ii. The total of minimum rentals to be received in the future under noncancelable subleases as of the date of the latest balance sheet presented.

   c. For all operating leases, rental expense for each period for which an income statement is presented, with separate amounts for minimum rentals, *contingent rentals*, and sublease rentals. Rental payments under leases with terms of a month or less that were not renewed need not be included.

Table 7
Book/Tax Differences

	Accounting Books	Tax Books
9 regular cash payments (9 × $3,960)	$ 0	($ 35,640)
12 adjusted straight-line rentals (12 × $3,713)	(44,556)	0
Taxable income	($ 44,556)	($ 35,640)
Tax rate	× .34	× .34
Income tax benefit	($ 15,149)	($ 12,118)
Difference	($ 3,031)	

    d. A general description of the lessee's leasing arrangements including, but not limited to, the following:

        i. The basis on which *contingent rental* payments are determined.

        ii. The existence and terms of renewal or purchase options and escalation clauses.

        iii. Restrictions imposed by lease agreements, such as those concerning dividends, additional debt, and further leasing [FASB 13, paragraph 16].

CONCLUSION

Operating leases have always been popular from the lessee's perspective, and are becoming more frequent from the lessor's viewpoint. Operating leases are shown on the lessor's accounting books as assets owned subject to operating leases. These assets are generally depreciated according to the straight-line method. Operating lease accounting for the lessee is quite straightforward, since the operating lease is off balance sheet, and also less complex to account for than capital leases. As operating leases continue to grow in popularity it is essential to understand how to properly treat them for financial reporting purposes.

CHAPTER FIFTEEN
CAPITAL LEASES

Capital leases continue to constitute a significant portion of lessors' portfolios, in spite of the growing popularity of operating leases. Factors such as accelerated earnings curves and the profit recognition available in sales-type capital leases make capital leases a popular form of lease for lessors. Lessees, on the other hand, are finding the capital lease to be a means of limiting their alternative minimum tax (AMT) exposure.

The characteristics and various types of capital leases are discussed in this chapter. These discussions presuppose a working knowledge of the lease accounting principles of Chapter Thirteen; therefore, that chapter should be reviewed, as necessary, prior to reading this one. The chapter is divided into the following sections:

- Lessor Capital Lease Accounting
- Lessee Capital Lease Accounting.

LESSOR CAPITAL LEASE ACCOUNTING

Capital leases, from the standpoint of the lessor, may be divided into three categories: direct financing, sales-type and leveraged leases. Two of these capital leases, direct financing and sales-type, are discussed in this section. Leveraged leases are the subject of Chapter Sixteen.

Direct Financing Leases

A direct financing lease is a lease, other than a leveraged lease, that does not give rise to manufacturer or dealer profit (or loss) to the lessor, but that meets one or more of the capital lease criteria, and both of the criteria for a lessor capital lease, as promulgated by Financial Accounting Standards Board Statement No. 13 (FASB 13), as discussed in Chapter Thirteen. In such leases, the cost or carrying amount and the fair value of the leased property are the same at the inception of the lease. Direct financing leases are the most common capital lease written by lessors today.

The most prominent characteristic of this type of capital lease comes from its name — direct financing. The lease is just that: a pure financing in which no sale is involved (i.e., gross profit), only the financing of an acquired asset for the lessee. In the direct financing capital lease, interest income serves as the source of income to the lessor. Therefore, a direct financing capital lease is accounted for much as though the lessor had provided a loan to the lessee.

Of course, the accounting requirements are more complex than a simple interest installment loan because of the numerous variables that are frequently encountered in leasing, such as set-up fees, refundable security deposits, tax depreciation, residual values, initial direct costs, etc. Although similar in many respects, the direct financing lease should not be confused with the sales-type capital lease, which has both interest and gross profit as income sources.

Aside from the recognition of gross profit, perhaps the most subtle difference between the two types of leases is the treatment of initial direct costs. Initial direct costs are those costs necessary to consummate a lease. Under a sales-type lease, in which gross profit is recognized at the inception, initial direct costs are charged to income as a period cost. These costs are matched against the income (gross profit) generated. Initial direct costs incurred in a direct financing lease, however, are amortized to income over the life of the lease, as an adjustment to yield. Since there is no gross profit, the costs are matched against interest income as it is earned over the term of the lease. Other differences between the direct financing and sales- type capital leases are illustrated later.

Another complexity is caused by the fact that many direct financing capital leases are treated as true tax leases for purposes of reporting income to the Internal Revenue Service (IRS). Thus, direct financing capital leases, which do not reflect depreciation in the financial statements from a lessor perspective, are treated somewhat akin to conditional sales contracts for accounting purposes. For those leases that are tax leases, however, depreciation is recognized for tax purposes since the lessor retains tax ownership. Such completely opposite accounting and tax treatment gives rise to interperiod tax allocation, a concept that also is illustrated later in the chapter.

FASB 13 REQUIREMENTS

The best way to learn how to account for a direct financing lease is to study the requirements of FASB 13 and then walk through an example of those requirements, carefully illustrating each step. It should be noted that this process sets forth generally accepted accounting principles (GAAP) requirements, or those used for external financial reporting purposes. Management or internal financial reporting requirements are determined by the needs of each individual management team and, therefore, are not presented here. Useful aspects of reporting, or potential enhancements to the reporting process, however, will be pointed out and expanded upon as appropriate.

FASB 13, as amended by FASB Statement No. 91 (FASB 91), requires direct financing leases to be accounted for by the lessor as follows:

    a.   The sum of (i) the minimum lease payments (net of amounts, if any, included therein with respect to executory costs to be paid by the lessor, together with any profit thereon), (ii) the unguaranteed residual value accruing to the benefit of the lessor, and (iii) the initial direct costs shall be recorded as the gross investment in the lease. The estimated residual value used to compute the unguaranteed residual value accruing to the benefit of the lessor shall not exceed the amount estimated at the inception of the lease.

b. The difference between the gross investment in the lease in (a) above and the cost or carrying amount, if different, of the leased property shall be recorded as unearned income. The net investment in the lease shall consist of the gross investment less the unearned income. The remaining unearned income shall be amortized to income over the lease term so as to produce a constant periodic rate of return on the net investment in the lease. However, other methods of income recognition may be used if the results obtained are not materially different from those which would result from the prescribed method in the preceding sentence. The net investment in the lease shall be subject to the same considerations as other assets in classification as current or noncurrent assets in a classified balance sheet. Contingent rentals shall be included in the determination of income as accruable.

d. The estimated residual value shall be reviewed at least annually and, if necessary, adjusted in the manner prescribed in paragraph 17(d) [FASB 13, paragraph 18 (a), (b) and (d)].

From this definition it can be seen that future benefits (lease payments and residual) are shown as receivables. Any difference between future receipts and the cost of the asset (including initial direct costs) will be the total income to be recognized over the term of the lease. This total income to be earned is known on the first day of the lease. Appropriately enough, the net investment (as defined) at the inception of the lease is exactly equal to the net cash outflow of the lessor at that time.

Note that initial direct costs are treated as an adjustment to the yield of the lease. Because of this matching of costs to revenues over the term, it is important to include in initial direct costs only those costs that are proper. Prior to the issuance of FASB 91 (which amended the definition of initial direct costs) there was considerable debate as to the propriety of including the allowance for doubtful accounts as part of initial direct costs. Through a careful reading of the definition of initial direct costs provided in FASB 91, however, it is apparent that such an inclusion has been effectively precluded.

DIRECT FINANCING LEASE EXAMPLE

An example is the most effective method to illustrate the booking of a direct financing capital lease. The illustration is broken down into separate parts for clarity. The first part consists of the initial entries to set up the lease. The second part illustrates the accounting for subsequent interest income, including any related tax effects, and the third part presents the lease in financial statement form.

Assumptions

The following assumptions are utilized in the example illustrating the booking of a direct financing lease.

Inception date: July 1
Term: 48-month lease with one payment in advance
Equipment cost: $75,000
Monthly payment: $1,775
Unguaranteed residual: $11,250
Initial direct costs: $1,875
Tax lease: 5-year Modified Accelerated Cost Recovery System (MACRS) property
Disposition of equipment: $13,000 realized
Tax rate: 34%
Capital lease criteria: the first three are not met
Gross profit: none.

Initial Set Up

There are certain preliminary steps that must be completed before accounting for a lease, the first of which is determining the classification of the lease. Is the lease capital or operating? Since the assumptions stated that the first three criteria were not met, the remaining criterion to be evaluated is the 90% test. If the present value of the minimum lease payments is greater than or equal to 90% of the fair market value of the asset, less any lessor retained Investment Tax Credit (ITC), the lease will be capital. If not, it will be booked as an operating lease. The discount rate to be used is the implicit rate in the lease, which must be calculated. The implicit rate is defined as:

> . . . the discount rate that, when applied to (i) the minimum lease payments, and (ii) the unguaranteed residual value accruing to the benefit of the lessor, causes the aggregate present value at the beginning of the lease term to be equal to the fair value of the leased property to the lessor at the inception of the lease, minus any investment tax credit retained by the lessor and expected to be realized by him . . . [FASB 13, paragraph 5(k)].

The implicit rate, which is nothing more than the IRR of the lease cash flows (as shown in Table 1), is calculated as follows.

73,225	CHS	g	CF_o
1,775		g	CF_j
47		g	N_j
11,250		g	CF_j
		f	IRR	1.0031
12		×		12.0374

The annual implicit rate is calculated as 12.0374%. This rate is used to apply the 90% test to the minimum lease payments.

Table 1
Lease Cash Flows

	Inception Cash Flow	Subsequent Cash Flow	Residual Cash Flow
Equipment cost	($ 75,000)	47 payments of $1,775	$ 11,250
Advance payment	1,775		
Total	($ 73,225)		

Fair market value of the equipment	$ 75,000
	× .90
FASB 13 comparison base	$ 67,500

	g	BEG
1,775		PMT
48		n
12.0374	g	12 ÷
		PV 68,032.47

The present value of the minimum lease payments ($68,032.47) is greater than 90% of the fair market value; therefore, the lease is capital.

Now that the lease has been classified not only as capital but also as a direct financing capital lease (since there is no gross profit in the lease), it can be set up on the books of the lessor. The following entries are required to set up this direct financing capital lease on the lessor's books at the inception of the lease. Each journal entry is then elaborated upon.

1. Minimum lease payments receivable $ 85,200
   Unguaranteed residual $ 11,250
   Initial direct costs $ 1,875
        Unearned income $ 21,450
        Cash $ 76,875

   To record the minimum lease payments, unguaranteed residual and initial direct costs

Per FASB 13, the minimum lease payment receivable of $85,200 (48 × $1,775), the unguaranteed residual of $11,250 and the initial direct costs of $1,875 are recorded as the gross investment in the lease. The gross investment has been recorded by each of its component parts. This separation serves two purposes: (1) the lessor can now monitor its dependence on future residual values, an important aspect since such values are not as certain of realization as are the minimum lease payments, and (2) the unamortized balance of initial direct costs must be shown for disclosure purposes. If all components were shown in one gross investment account, these objectives would not be met.

The difference between the gross investment and the cost of the lease (equipment plus initial direct costs) is recorded as the unearned income. In this case unearned income is computed as follows:

Gross investment	$ 98,325
Equipment cost	(75,000)
Initial direct costs	(1,875)
Unearned income	$ 21,450

The equipment cost and initial direct costs are credited to either cash or accounts payable depending on the timing of the payments. As a practical matter, the amount of initial direct costs booked with each lease will represent the lessor's best estimate of such costs, based upon experience and historical data. The difference between the gross investment and the unearned income in the lease is the net investment. In general, this net investment is the only item shown on the face of the balance sheet and is separated into its current and long-term portions if the balance sheet is classified. The components of the net investment, however, must be shown in the footnotes to the financial statements.

Next, the receipt of the advance payment is recorded.

2. Cash	$ 1,775	
Minimum lease payments receivable		$ 1,775

To record the receipt of the advance payment as a reduction in the gross investment in the lease

With entries 1 and 2 completed the entire lease has been booked. A good check figure to ascertain whether the lease has been booked correctly is to compare the beginning net investment with the net cash outflow at the inception of the lease. They should be equal. The net investment of $75,100 is the net of the account balances:

Minimum lease payments receivable	$ 83,425	
Unguaranteed residual	11,250	
Initial direct costs	1,875	
Gross investment		$ 96,550
Unearned income		21,450
Net investment		$75,100

The lease has been booked correctly, since $75,100 is equal to the net cash outflow of the lease.

Equipment costs	($ 75,000)
Initial direct costs	(1,875)
Advance payment	1,775
Net cash outflow	($ 75,100)

Many companies prefer to further improve the informational value of their accounting records by also identifying the earnings associated with any unguaranteed residuals booked. This is the first step in the process referred to as accretion, or the walking up of income. It is easy to see that a leased asset generates earnings, as evidenced by the amount in the unearned income account. These earnings, however, come from two sources — the lease payments and any expected residual value. Because there are two different sources of income, proponents of this method prefer to monitor each source separately. This is accomplished by splitting the total unearned income into its separate components and then recognizing interest earnings on the minimum lease payments and on the unguaranteed residual.

To effectuate this separate income recognition involves presenting the unguaranteed residual at its present value, using the pretax earnings rate of the lease.

10.7995[1]	g	12 ÷
11,250		FV
48		n
		PV 7,318

The present value of the $11,250 residual value to be received in the future is $7,318. Therefore, the difference between the present and future values of $3,932 must represent the potential earnings on the residual; in effect, the unearned income to be recognized on the residual. The unearned residual earnings are journalized as follows:

Unearned income (minimum lease payments)	$ 3,932	
Unearned income (residual)		$ 3,932

> To record the unguaranteed residual at its present value and recognize the unearned income on the residual

It is apparent that one cannot change the total income to be recognized just by moving accounts around. Notice that, although the unearned income has been allocated to its various sources, the total remains the same.

Minimum lease payments receivable	$ 83,425
Unguaranteed residual	11,250
Initial direct costs	1,875
Gross investment	$ 96,550

---

[1] The pretax earnings rate is computed by considering all the pretax cash flows in the lease, including initial direct costs.

75,100	CHS	g	CF_o		
1,775		g	CF_j		
47		g	N_j		
11,250		g	CF_j		
		f	IRR	.9000	
		12	×	10.7995	

Unearned receivable income	$	17,518	
Unearned residual income		3,932	
Unearned income			21,450
Net investment			$ 75,100

The value of this methodology is that it allows a company to track its dependence on residual earnings. If the company has heavy residual dependence in a certain equipment category, and residuals begin to soften in that category, the impact on earnings is more easy to ascertain. It is interesting to note that as residual earnings are recognized, the unearned residual declines, serving to increase the net investment in residuals; hence the term accretion. By the end of the term the present value of the residual will have been accreted, or walked up, to its future value. This occurs whether the accretion method is used or not; the only difference is the accretion method identifies the specific increase.

Subsequent Earnings

The amount of unearned income booked at inception, less the full amortization of initial direct costs, is the total earnings to be recognized over the life of the lease. Each period interest earnings are computed on the net investment in the lease, utilizing a constant periodic rate of return, as required by FASB 13.

The use of different constant periodic rates of return or methods of recognizing income does not affect the total income to be recognized in a lease. Each method does allocate income in a different manner, however. What are these methods of income allocation and which one is most appropriate? There are currently four allocation methods that may be used to recognize income: (1) the pretax rate, (2) the Rule of 78, (3) an after-tax return on assets method and (4) an after-tax return on equity method. The latter two methods are highly sophisticated, have limited acceptance and are beyond the scope of this text; hence, only the pretax and Rule of 78 methods are discussed.

The pretax rate is perhaps the most common method of income allocation, although the Rule of 78 still remains popular. Under the pretax rate method, the rate that will amortize the cash flows (minimum lease payments, unguaranteed residual and initial direct costs) to the fair market value of the asset is applied against the net investment. This pretax rate is 10.7995%, as previously calculated. The monthly rate of .9000% (10.7995% ÷ 12) times the declining net investment in the lease equals the net interest earned for that month. For instance, the net interest earned for the first month for the example lease is $675.87 ($75,100 × .9000%). Unfortunately, this process is not as simple as it appears, due to the application of FASB 91 (relating to initial direct costs).

FASB 91 requires that initial direct costs be reflected as an adjustment to yield. Rather than being offset, or capitalized, to unearned income, initial direct costs are to be shown and amortized separately as a component of the gross investment in the lease. Under this method, interest earned on the investment is offset by the amortization of the initial direct costs, resulting in net interest earnings. To apply this quirk from a purely technical perspective, one must first compute the yield without including initial direct costs. This yield represents the gross interest earnings. Next the yield is computed with initial direct costs included. This yield represents the net interest earnings. The difference between the two becomes the amortization of initial direct costs against gross interest earnings. An illustration is needed to help clarify this concept.

The net interest earned of $675.87 shown earlier actually consists of gross interest earned less amortized initial direct costs. Following the methodology of FASB 91, the first step is to compute the yield without initial direct costs, which is the previously computed implicit rate of 1.0031% per month.

The yield of 1.0031% is applied to the "without" net investment to determine the gross interest earnings. Next, the yield with initial direct costs is computed. This yield also has been computed, and is .9000%, and is applied against the "with" net investment. The difference in earnings between the two will represent the amortization of initial direct costs. The monthly amortization amount will be credited against the initial direct cost component of the gross investment. These differences for the first month and over the term are shown in Table 2.

Literal application of the technically correct method of amortization of initial direct costs is burdensome and unwieldy. From a practical perspective, an allocation method such as the bonds outstanding or a pro rata method would be used. Under one pro rata method (pretax rate) the first month's initial direct cost allocation is $64.25.

$$\frac{\text{First month's earnings}}{\text{Total earnings}} \qquad \frac{\$\ \ 735}{\$21,450} \ = \ .0343$$

$$.0343 \times \$1,875 = \$64.25$$

Given the above discussion, and using the amortization of initial direct costs from Table 2, receipt of the payment and earnings recognition for the first month is theoretically journalized as follows:

Cash	$ 1,775	
Unearned income	$ 735	
Initial direct costs		$ 59
Interest earned		$ 676
Minimum lease payments receivable		$ 1,775

    To record receipt of the first month's payment and earnings
    recognition

The result of this entry is to reduce the net investment by the amount of principal received, or the difference between the payment and interest earned, as illustrated in Table 3. The implicit rate is multiplied by the new net investment each month until the end of the lease term, at which time the net investment will be equal to the expected unguaranteed residual.

If interest earnings were to be calculated using the Rule of 78, the gross earnings for the first month would be equal to $875.51. This represents an overstatement in earnings of 19.2% over the pretax method, which is an actuarial method. Because of its tendency to distort earnings (overstatement during the early phases of the term) the Rule of 78 is viewed by some as being an unacceptable method of income allocation.

Table 2
Amortization of Initial Direct Costs

	1 Without Initial Direct Costs	2 With Initial Direct Costs	Amortization of Initial Direct Costs (1 – 2)
Net investment	$ 73,225	$ 75,100	
× rate	× .010031	× .009000	
First month's earnings	$ 735	$ 676	$ 59
Full amortization over the term	$ 21,450	$ 19,575	$ 1,875

Table 3
First Month's Payment Allocation

	Gross Investment	Unearned Income	Net Investment
Beginning balance	$ 96,550	$ 21,450	$ 75,100
Payment	(1,775)	0	(1,775)
Initial direct costs	(59)	0	(59)
Gross interest earned	0	(735)	735
Ending balance	$ 94,716	$ 20,715	$ 74,001

Earnings for the first year (July 1 – December 31) are journalized as follows:

3.	Cash	$ 8,875	
	Unearned income	$ 3,567	
	Initial direct costs		$ 287
	Interest earned		$ 3,280
	Minimum lease payments receivable		$ 8,875
	To record receipt of the first year's payments		
4.	Tax expense	$ 2,366	
	Taxes payable	$ 865	
	Deferred taxes		$ 3,231
	To provide taxes on the first year's income		

End of First Year T-account Summary

The following T-accounts represent the balances on the books at year end for this direct financing capital lease. Some data (set in bold type so that they may be readily identified) have been added to present a more representative set of financial statements. T-account entries are annotated with the corresponding journal entry number for ease of reference. The T-account summaries for the balance sheet and income statement are shown in Figures 1 and 2, respectively.

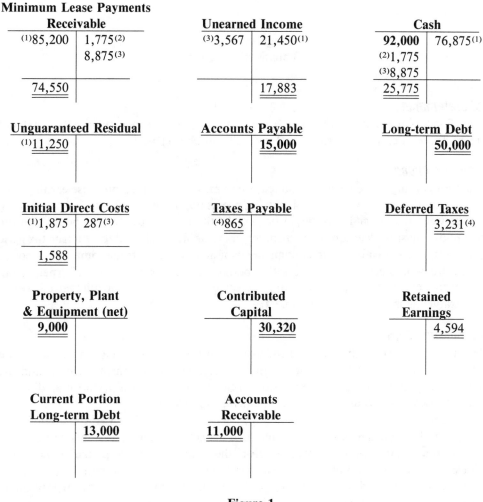

Minimum Lease Payments Receivable

[1]85,200	1,775[2]
	8,875[3]
74,550	

Unearned Income

[3]3,567	21,450[1]
	17,883

Cash

92,000	76,875[1]
[2]1,775	
[3]8,875	
25,775	

Unguaranteed Residual

[1]11,250	

Accounts Payable

	15,000

Long-term Debt

	50,000

Initial Direct Costs

[1]1,875	287[3]
1,588	

Taxes Payable

[4]865	

Deferred Taxes

	3,231[4]

Property, Plant & Equipment (net)

9,000	

Contributed Capital

	30,320

Retained Earnings

	4,594

Current Portion Long-term Debt

	13,000

Accounts Receivable

11,000	

Figure 1
Balance Sheet T-accounts

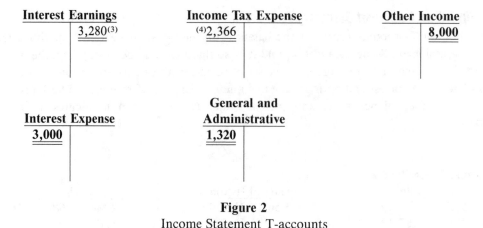

Figure 2
Income Statement T-accounts

Financial Statements

Using the T-account balances in Figures 1 and 2, an income statement (Figure 3), a balance sheet (Figure 4) and a cash flow statement (Figure 5) can be prepared.

Interperiod Tax Allocation

Once interest earnings have been ascertained, taxes must be provided on those earnings. To determine the interperiod tax allocation entries necessary to reflect the temporary timing differences between the tax and accounting books, the tax liability per the tax books and the accounting books must be determined. Remember, this lease is considered to be a true tax lease for tax purposes, in contrast to its direct financing capital lease status for accounting purposes. Based on the differences between the accounting books and the tax return, the interperiod tax allocation journal entry for the first year would be calculated by finding the difference between book and taxable income, as shown in Table 4.

Lease Termination Entries

A calculation of the yearly income and the associated taxes allows the example lease to be brought to full term, in order to present the fully amortized net investment account and the related taxes. Many find this type of illustration to be extremely helpful in understanding the booking and subsequent earnings of a direct financing capital lease.

In order to show this lease through termination, the first step is to display the T-accounts up until the last month (Figures 6 and 7) and summarize the net investment, as shown in Figure 8. The tax entries must be determined, however, before the summaries can be prepared. The taxes payable for each year are shown in Table 5. The yearly tax entries are determined by using the matrix in Table 6. The second, and final, step in this example is to illustrate the disposition of the residual at the end of the lease term. Only the accounts relevant to the lease termination are included.

REVENUE		
Interest earned		$ 3,280
OPERATING EXPENSES		
General and administrative		1,320
OPERATING INCOME		$ 1,960
OTHER INCOME		8,000
OTHER EXPENSES		
Interest on debt		3,000
INCOME FROM OPERATIONS BEFORE TAXES		$ 6,960
Current taxes	($ 865)	
Deferred taxes	3,231	
Income tax expense		2,366
NET INCOME		$ 4,594

Figure 3
Income Statement
End of First Year Reporting

Table 4
Book/Tax Differences

	Accounting Books	Tax Books
Advance rental	$ 0	$ 1,775
Interest earned	3,280	0
Normal rentals	0	8,875
Other income	8,000	8,000
Initial direct costs	0	(1,875)
General and administrative expenses	(1,320)	(1,320)
Depreciation (MACRS)	0	(15,000)
Interest expense	(3,000)	(3,000)
Taxable income	$ 6,960	($ 2,545)
Tax rate	× .34	× .34
Tax expense (benefit)	$ 2,366	($ 865)
Difference	$ 3,231	

ASSETS

Current assets
Cash $ 25,775
Accounts receivable 11,000
Total current assets $ 36,775

Net investment in leases
Minimum lease payments receivable $ 56,667
Unguaranteed residuals 11,250
Initial direct costs 1,588
Total net investment in leases 69,505

Fixed assets
Property, plant and equipment (net) 9,000
Total assets $ 115,280

LIABILITIES

Current liabilities
Accounts payable $ 15,000
Taxes payable (865)
Current portion long-term debt 13,000
Total current liabilities $ 27,135

Long-term liabilities 50,000

Deferred credits
Deferred taxes 3,231
Total liabilities $ 80,366

OWNERS' EQUITY

Contributed capital $ 30,320

Retained earnings 4,594
Total owners' equity 34,914
Total liabilities and owners' equity $ 115,280

Figure 4
Balance Sheet
End of First Year Reporting

CASH FLOWS FROM OPERATING ACTIVITIES

Net interest earned	$ 3,280	
Other income	8,000	
Operating expenses paid	(320)	
Interest expense paid	0	
Net cash from operating activities		**$ 10,960**

CASH FLOWS FROM INVESTING ACTIVITIES

Initial direct costs capitalized	($ 1,875)	
Principal received from capital leases	7,370	
Capital expenditures	(9,000)	
Investment in capital lease	(75,000)	
Net cash used in investing activities		(78,505)

CASH FLOWS FROM FINANCING ACTIVITIES

Proceeds from contributed capital	$ 30,320	
Proceeds from long-term debt	63,000	
Net cash provided by financing activities		93,320

NET INCREASE IN CASH

		$ 25,775
Cash at the beginning of the year		0
Cash at the end of the year		$ 25,775

RECONCILIATION OF NET INCOME TO OPERATING ACTIVITIES

Net income		$ 4,594
Adjustments to net income		
Increase in deferred taxes	$ 3,231	
Decrease in taxes payable	(865)	
Increase in accounts payable[2]	15,000	
Increase in accounts receivable	(11,000)	
Total adjustments		6,366
Net cash from operating activities		**$ 10,960**

Figure 5
Statement of Cash Flows
(direct method per FASB Statement No. 95)
End of First Year Reporting

---

[2] Includes $3,000 of interest payable and $1,000 of various accrued general and administrative items.

Table 5
Taxes Payable

Year	2	3	4	5
Revenue	$ 21,300	$ 21,300	$ 21,300	$ 10,650
MACRS	(24,000)	(14,400)	(8,640)	(4,320)
Taxable income	($ 2,700)	$ 6,900	$ 12,660	$ 6,330
Tax rate	× .34	× .34	× .34	× .34
Tax expense (benefit)	($ 918)	$ 2,346	$ 4,304	$ 2,152

Table 6
Deferred Taxes

Year	Tax Expense	Taxes Payable	Deferred Taxes
1	$ 2,366	($ 865)	$ 3,231
2	2,313	(918)	3,231
3	1,754	2,346	(592)
4	1,131	4,304	(3,173)
5	343	2,152	(1,809)
	$ 7,907	$ 7,019	$ 888

The net investment at the end of the lease term is equal to the booked unguaranteed residual of $11,250. Upon disposition of the asset for $13,000 at that time, the following journal entries are necessary.

Cash	$ 13,000	
Gain on sale		$ 1,750
Unguaranteed residual		$ 11,250

To record sale of the asset and zero out the net investment

Tax expense	$ 595	
Deferred taxes	$ 888	
Taxes payable		$ 1,483

To provide taxes on the sale of the asset

Minimum Lease Payments Receivable	
(1)85,200	1,775(2)
	8,875(3)
	21,300 **year 2**
	21,300 **year 3**
	21,300 **year 4**
	10,650 **year 5**
0	

Unearned Income	
(3)3,567	21,450(1)
year 2 7,427	
year 3 5,661	
year 4 3,671	
year 5 1,124	
	0

Cash	
92,000	76,875(1)
(2)1,775	
(3)8,875	
year 2 21,300	
year 3 21,300	
year 4 21,300	
year 5 10,650	
100,325	

Unguaranteed Residual	
(1)11,250	

Initial Direct Costs	
(1)1,875	287(3)
	625 **year 2**
	504 **year 3**
	346 **year 4**
	113 **year 5**
0	

Taxes Payable	
(4)865	
year 2 918	2,346 **year 3**
	4,304 **year 4**
	2,152 **year 5**
	7,019

Deferred Taxes	
year 3 592	3,231(4)
year 4 3,173	3,231 **year 2**
year 5 1,809	
	888

Figure 6
Balance Sheet T-accounts
(full term)

Interest Earnings		Income Tax Expense	
3,280[3]		[4]2,366	
6,802 **year 2**		**year 2** 2,313	
5,157 **year 3**		**year 3** 1,754	
3,325 **year 4**		**year 4** 1,131	
1,011 **year 5**		**year 5** 343	
19,575		7,907	

Figure 7
Income Statement T-accounts
(full term)

Gross investment:
Minimum lease payments receivable	$ 0
Unguaranteed residual	11,250
Initial direct costs	0
Total	$ 11,250
Unearned income	0
Net investment	$ 11,250

Figure 8
Net Investment Summary
(full term)

Note that the net investment has now been completely zeroed out, as has the deferred tax balance. Taxes were computed as follows:

Payable:

$ 13,000	Proceeds
(8,640)	Remaining basis
$ 4,360	Gain
× .34	
$ 1,483	Taxes payable

Expense:

$ 13,000	Proceeds
(11,250)	Remaining book value
$ 1,750	Gain
× .34	
$ 595	Tax expense

Deferred taxes:

$ 595	Tax expense
(1,483)	Taxes payable
($ 888)	Deferred taxes

Sales-Type Leases

The sales-type capital lease, as previously mentioned, has several characteristics that set it apart from a direct financing capital lease. The most prominent of these is the recognition of gross profit in the transaction. Due to this gross profit requirement, sales-type leases occur most commonly in the portfolios of manufacturers or dealers who use leasing as a means of marketing their products, although a capital lease written by a nonmanufacturer/dealer may result in a sales-type lease.

From the nature of these examples it can be concluded that a lease should be classified as a sales-type lease whenever the fair value of the lease property at inception of the lease is different from its cost or carrying amount. Be aware that in this definition such a difference could represent either a gain or a loss, either of which must be recognized when the lease is booked. The sales-type capital lease must also, of course, meet one of the general capital lease criteria and both of the lessor capital lease criteria as discussed in Chapter Thirteen. The determination of whether or not the lease is a capital lease is made first, and then its status as a direct financing or sales-type capital lease is ascertained.

A sales-type capital lease is viewed as a sale of a product; therefore, gross profit is recognized. The revenue on the sale is recognized immediately along with the associated cost of goods sold. FASB 13 requires different treatment of initial direct costs for sales-type than for direct financing capital leases. In a sales-type lease, initial direct costs are required to be charged against income in the period in which the sales revenue is recorded, under the premise these costs are incurred primarily to produce sales revenue. This is consistent with the practice of accounting for these types of costs for normal sales of goods.

Once the sales revenue has been recognized, the sales-type lease is treated the same as a direct financing lease. Interest income is recognized over the term of the lease, as though the lessor had provided normal loan financing for the sale of its product. As in the direct financing lease, though, the accounting requirements are more complex than a simple interest loan because of the numerous other variables that are frequently encountered.

FASB 13 REQUIREMENTS

Accounting for sales-type leases is most effectively learned through the use of examples in applying the requirements of FASB 13. The examples are presented in accordance with GAAP, but other useful aspects of reporting, or potential enhancements to the reporting process, are also pointed out and expanded upon as appropriate. The format to be followed is similar to the presentation of the direct financing capital lease.

FASB 13 requires sales-type leases to be accounted for by the lessor as follows:

a. The minimum lease payments (net of amounts, if any, included therein with respect to executory costs to be paid by the lessor, together with any profit thereon) plus the unguaranteed residual value accruing to the benefit of the lessor shall be recorded as the gross investment in the lease. The estimated residual value used to compute the unguaranteed residual value accruing to the benefit of the lessor shall not exceed the amount estimated at the inception of the lease.

b. The difference between the gross investment in the lease in (a) above and the sum of the present values of the two components of the gross investment shall be recorded as unearned income. The discount rate to be used in determining the present values shall be the interest rate implicit in the lease. The net investment in the lease shall consist of the gross investment less the unearned income. The unearned income shall be amortized to income over the lease term so as to produce a constant periodic rate of return on the net investment in the lease. However, other methods of income recognition may be used if the results obtained are not materially different from those which would result from the prescribed method. The net investment in the lease shall be subject to the same considerations as other assets in classification as current or noncurrent assets in a classified balance sheet. Contingent rentals shall be included in the determination of income as accruable.

c. The present value of the minimum lease payments (net of executory costs, including any profit thereon), computed at the interest rate implicit in the lease, shall be recorded as the sales price. The cost or carrying amount, if different, of the leased property, plus any initial direct costs, less the present value of the unguaranteed residual value accruing to the benefit of the lessor, computed at the interest rate implicit in the lease, shall be charged against income in the same period.

d. The estimated residual value shall be reviewed at least annually. If the review results in a lower estimate than had been previously established, a determination must be made as to whether the decline in estimated residual value is other than temporary. If the decline in estimated residual value is judged to be other than temporary, the accounting for the transaction shall be revised using the changed estimate. The resulting reduction in the net investment shall be recognized as a loss in the period in which the estimate is changed. An upward adjustment of the estimated residual value shall not be made [FASB 13, paragraph 17(a),(b),(c) and (d)].

From this definition it can be seen that the lessor in a sales-type capital lease receives income from two sources. The first is the gross profit on the sale of the leased asset. This gross profit is recognized immediately and represents the difference between the leased asset's fair value (retail) and its carrying amount (cost). The second component consists of financing income and represents the difference between future receipts and the net investment, which represents the fair value of the leased asset at the beginning of the lease term. The future benefits in the lease are shown as receivables, similar to the direct financing lease.

SALES-TYPE LEASE EXAMPLE

An example is the most effective method to illustrate the booking of a sales- type capital lease. The illustration is broken down into separate parts for clarity. The first part consists of the initial entries to set up the lease and the second part illustrates the accounting for subsequent interest income, including taxes and their related effects. The third part presents the lease in financial statement form.

Assumptions

The following assumptions are utilized in the example illustrating the booking of a sales-type lease.

    Inception date: July 1
    Term: 48-month lease with one payment in advance
    Equipment cost: $50,000
    Fair market value of the equipment: $75,000 at lease inception
    Monthly payment: $1,775
    Initial direct costs: $1,875
    Tax lease: 5-year MACRS property
    Disposition of equipment: $11,250
    Tax rate: 34%
    Capital lease criteria: the first three are not met.

Initial Set Up

There are certain preliminary steps that must be completed before accounting for a lease, the first of which is determining the classification of the lease. Since the assumptions stated that the first three criteria were not met, the remaining criterion to be evaluated is the 90% test. If the present value of the minimum lease payments is greater than or equal to 90% of the fair market value of the asset, less any lessor retained ITC, the lease will be capital. If not, it will be booked as an operating lease. The discount rate to be used is the implicit rate in the lease. This rate must be calculated, and is the same rate as computed in the previous subsection on direct financing leases.

In that subsection, the annual implicit rate was calculated as 12.0374%. This rate is used to apply the 90% test to the minimum lease payments.

Fair market value of the equipment	$ 75,000
	× .90
FASB 13 comparison base	$ 67,500

	g	BEG
1,775		PMT
48		n
12.0374	g	12 ÷
		PV 68,032.47

The present value of the minimum lease payments ($68,032.47) is greater than 90% of the fair market value; therefore, the lease is capital. The lease has been classified as capital and also as a sales-type capital lease because (per the assumptions) there is a gross profit component in the lease. The lease can now be set up on the books of the lessor.

The following entries are required to set up this sales-type lease on the lessor's books at the inception of the lease. Each journal entry then is elaborated upon. The entries to set up a sales-type lease are more complex than those of a direct financing lease; therefore, each component is explained separately.

1.	Minimum lease payments receivable	$ 85,200	
	Unguaranteed residual	$ 11,250	
	Cost of sales	$ 44,907	
	Unearned income		$ 21,450
	Cash		$ 1,875
	Sales		$ 68,032
	Inventory		$ 50,000

To record the minimum lease payments, unguaranteed residual, sales revenue and related costs

Per FASB 13, the minimum lease payment receivable of $85,200 (48 × $1,775) and the unguaranteed residual of $11,250 are recorded as the gross investment in the lease. The gross investment has been recorded by each of its component parts. This separation allows the lessor to monitor its dependence on future residual values, an important aspect since such values are not as certain of realization as are the minimum lease payments. If the two components were shown in one gross investment account, this objective would not be met.

Calculation of unearned income. The difference between the gross investment in the lease and the present value of its two components is equal to the unearned income of $21,450.

Gross investment		
Minimum lease payments receivable	$ 85,200	
Unguaranteed residual	11,250	$ 96,450
Present value		
Minimum lease payments receivable	$ 68,032	
Unguaranteed residual	6,968	75,000
Unearned income		$ 21,450

The present value of each component of the gross investment must be computed. The present value of the minimum lease payments receivable is computed as follows:

	g	BEG	
12.0374	g	12 ÷	
48		n	
1,775		PMT	
		PV	68,032

The present value of the unguaranteed residual is computed as follows:

12.0374	g	12 ÷	
11,250		FV	
48		n	
		PV	6,968

In a sales-type lease, the initial direct costs are not shown as a component of the gross investment. Per FASB 13, the difference between the gross investment and the unearned income in the lease is the net investment. In general, this net investment will be the only item shown on the face of the balance sheet and will be separated into its current and long-term portions in a classified balance sheet. The components of the net investment are disclosed in the footnotes to the financial statements.

Calculation of gross profit. The sales price is the present value of the minimum lease payments. The cost of the equipment plus the initial direct costs, less the present value of the unguaranteed residual, is the cost of goods sold. The present value of the minimum lease payments of $68,032 has already been computed.

Sales price		$ 68,032
Cost of goods sold	$ 50,000	
Initial direct costs	1,875	
Present value of the unguaranteed residual	(6,968)	
		44,907
Gross profit		$ 23,125

The revenue components of this sales-type lease have now been shown. The present value of the residual has not been counted in either sales or cost of sales, as it is unguaranteed. Since the unguaranteed residual represents a potential reversionary interest in the asset it is not recognized in either sales or in cost of goods sold. The $23,125 gross profit coincides with what one would expect it to be, e.g.,

Fair market value of the equipment	$ 75,000
Cost of the equipment	(50,000)
Initial direct costs	(1,875)
Total	$ 23,125

In order to complete the initial set up of the lease, the receipt of the advance payment must be recorded.

2. Cash $ 1,775

       Minimum lease payments receivable $ 1,775

       To record the receipt of the advance payment as a reduction in the gross investment in the lease

With the above two entries completed, the entire lease has been booked. The net investment at this point in time equals $73,225.

Minimum lease payments receivable	$ 83,425	
Unguaranteed residual	11,250	
Gross investment		$ 94,675
Unearned income		(21,450)
Net investment		$ 73,225

Viewed from an economic perspective, this net investment can be shown to consist of these elements:

Cost	$ 50,000
Gross profit	23,125
Initial direct costs	1,875
Advance payment	(1,775)
Total	$ 73,225

Many companies prefer to improve the informational value of their accounting records even further by also identifying the earnings associated with the unguaranteed residuals booked. This process is referred to as accretion, or the walking up of income, and is discussed in further detail in the direct financing lease subsection of this chapter.

Subsequent Earnings

The sales revenue, and attendant gross profit, of the sales-type lease can be easily identified from the journal entries. The other aspect of earnings in the lease, interest, is represented by the amount of unearned income booked at inception. This amount is the total interest earnings to be recognized over the life of the lease. Each period interest earnings are computed on the net investment in the lease, utilizing a constant periodic rate of return as required by FASB 13.

Although the use of various constant periodic rates of return, or methods of recognizing income, does not affect the total income to be recognized, each method will allocate income in a different manner.

The implicit or pretax rate is, perhaps, the most common method of income allocation, although the Rule of 78 remains popular. (Note that the implicit and pretax rate methods for sales-type leases are the same without ITC). Under the implicit rate method, the rate that amortizes the cash flows (minimum lease payments and unguaranteed residual) to the fair market value of the asset is applied against the net investment. This rate is the implicit rate of 12.0374% previously calculated. The monthly rate of 1.0031% (12.0374 ÷ 12) times the net investment in the lease equals the interest earned for that month. The amount of interest earned during the first month for the example lease is $734.52 ($73,225 × 1.0031%). This amount is higher than the corresponding amount for the direct financing lease because initial direct costs are treated differently.

Receipt of the payment and earnings recognition for the first month is journalized as follows:

Cash	$ 1,775	
Unearned income	$ 735	
Interest earned		$ 735
Minimum lease payments receivable		$ 1,775

    To record the first month's payment

The result of this entry is to reduce the net investment by the amount of principal received (the difference between the payment and interest earned). This allocation is shown in Table 7. The implicit rate is multiplied by the new net investment each month until the end of the lease term, at which time the net investment will be equal to the expected unguaranteed residual.

If interest earnings were to be calculated using the Rule of 78, the earnings for the first month would be equal to $875.51. This represents an overstatement in earnings of 19.2% over the actuarial method. Because of its tendency to distort earnings (overstatement during the early phases of the term) the Rule of 78 is viewed by some as being an unacceptable method of income allocation.

Earnings for the first year (July 1 – December 31) are journalized as follows:

3.	Cash	$ 8,875	
	Unearned income	$ 3,567	
	Interest earned		$ 3,567
	Minimum lease payments receivable		$ 8,875

    To record receipt of the first year's payments

4.	Tax expense	$ 10,326	
	Taxes payable		$ 835
	Deferred taxes		$ 9,491

    To provide taxes on the first year's income

Table 7
First Month's Payment Allocation

	Gross Investment	Unearned Income	Net Investment
Beginning balance	$ 94,675	$ 21,450	$ 73,225
Payment	(1,775)	0	(1,775)
Interest earned	0	(735)	735
Ending balance	$ 92,900	$ 20,715	$ 72,185

End of First Year T-account Summary

The following T-accounts represent the balances on the books at year end for this sales-type capital lease. Some data (which have been set in bold type so that they may be readily identified) have been added to present a more representative set of financial statements. T-account entries are annotated with the corresponding journal entry number for ease of reference. The T-account summaries for the balance sheet and income statement are shown in Figures 9 and 10, respectively.

Financial Statements

Using the T-account balances in Figures 9 and 10, an income statement (Figure 11), a balance sheet (Figure 12) and a cash flow statement (Figure 13) can be prepared.

Interperiod Tax Allocation

Once interest earnings have been ascertained, taxes must be provided on those earnings. In order to determine the interperiod tax allocation entries necessary to reflect the temporary timing differences between the tax and accounting books, the tax liability per the tax books and the accounting books must be determined. Remember, this lease is considered to be a true tax lease for tax purposes, in contrast to its sales-type capital lease status for accounting purposes. Based on the differences between the accounting books and the tax return, the interperiod tax allocation journal entry for the first year is calculated by finding the difference between book and taxable income, as shown in Table 8.

The example in the direct financing lease subsection was taken to termination and all the associated journal entries were shown. The process and journal entries for a sales-type lease are very similar; the only difference is the deferred taxes. The differences in deferred taxes between the two types of leases are due primarily to the treatment of gross profit and initial direct costs. In the sales-type lease initial direct costs do not create a timing difference. The timing difference

Minimum Lease Payments Receivable		Unearned Income		Cash	
(1)85,200	1,775(2)	(3)3,567	21,450(1)	17,000	1,875(1)
	8,875(3)			(2)1,775	
				(3)8,875	
74,550			17,883	25,775	

Unguaranteed Residual		Accounts Payable		Long-term Debt	
(1)11,250			15,000		50,000

Inventory		Taxes Payable		Deferred Taxes	
50,000	50,000(1)		835(4)		9,491(4)
0					

Property, Plant & Equipment (net)		Contributed Capital		Retained Earnings	
9,000			5,320		20,046

Current Portion Long-term Debt		Accounts Receivable	
	13,000	11,000	

Figure 9
Balance Sheet T-accounts

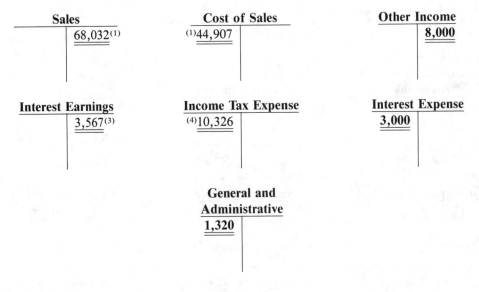

Figure 10
Income Statement T-accounts

REVENUE			
Sales		$ 68,032	
Interest earned		3,567	
Total revenue			$ 71,599
Cost of sales			(44,907)
OPERATING EXPENSES			1,320
OPERATING INCOME			$ 25,372
OTHER INCOME			8,000
OTHER EXPENSES			
Interest on debt			3,000
INCOME BEFORE TAXES			$ 30,372
Current taxes		$ 835	
Deferred taxes		9,491	
Income taxes			10,326
NET INCOME			$ 20,046

Figure 11
Income Statement
End of First Year Reporting

ASSETS

Current assets

Cash	$ 25,775	
Accounts receivable	11,000	
Total current assets		$ 36,775

Net investment in leases

Minimum lease payments receivable	$ 56,667	
Unguaranteed residuals	11,250	
Total net investment in leases		67,917

Fixed assets

Property, plant and equipment (net)		9,000
Total assets		$113,692

LIABILITIES

Current liabilities

Accounts payable	$ 15,000	
Taxes payable	835	
Current portion long-term debt	13,000	
Total current liabilities		$ 28,835

Long-term liabilities 50,000

Deferred credits

Deferred taxes		9,491
Total liabilities		$ 88,326

OWNERS' EQUITY

Contributed capital	$ 5,320	
Retained earnings	20,046	
Total owners' equity		25,366
Total liabilities and owners' equity		$113,692

Figure 12
Balance Sheet
End of First Year Reporting

CASH FLOWS FROM OPERATING ACTIVITIES

Net interest earned	$ 3,567	
Other income	8,000	
Operating expenses paid	(320)	
Initial direct costs incurred	(1,875)	
Interest expense paid	0	
Net cash from operating activities		**$ 9,372**

CASH FLOWS FROM INVESTING ACTIVITIES

Principal received from capital leases	$ 7,083	
Capital expenditures	(9,000)	
Investment in capital lease	(50,000)	
Net cash used in investing activities		(51,917)

CASH FLOWS FROM FINANCING ACTIVITIES

Proceeds from contributed capital	$ 5,320	
Proceeds from long-term debt	63,000	
Net cash provided by financing activities		68,320

NET INCREASE IN CASH		$ 25,775
Cash at the beginning of the year		0
Cash at the end of the year		$ 25,775

RECONCILIATION OF NET INCOME TO OPERATING ACTIVITIES

Net income		$ 20,046
Adjustments to net income		
Increase in deferred taxes	$ 9,491	
Increase in taxes payable	835	
Increase in accounts payable[3]	15,000	
Increase in accounts receivable	(11,000)	
Sales-type lease gross profit	(25,000)	
Total adjustments		(10,674)
Net cash from operating activities		**$ 9,372**

Figure 13
Statement of Cash Flows
(direct method per FASB Statement No. 95)
End of First Year Reporting

---

[3] Includes $3,000 of interest payable and $1,000 of various accrued general and administrative items.

Table 8
Book/Tax Differences

	Accounting Books	Tax Books
Gross profit	$ 23,125	$ 0
Advance rental	0	1,775
Interest earned	3,567	0
Normal rentals (5 months)	0	8,875
Other income	8,000	8,000
Initial direct costs	0	(1,875)
General and administrative expense	(1,320)	(1,320)
Depreciation	0	(10,000)
Interest expense	(3,000)	(3,000)
Taxable income	$ 30,372	$ 2,455
Tax rate	× .34	× .34
Tax expense (benefit)	$ 10,326	$ 835
Difference	$ 9,491	

due to the gross profit will turn around as the tax depreciation on the cost of $50,000 (rather than $75,000) is recognized.

Gross profit	$ 23,125	
Initial direct costs	1,875	(not a timing difference)
Gross profit (timing)	$ 25,000	

$75,000 – $50,000 = $25,000

Only the timing of the $25,000 gross profit is different between the tax return and the accounting books.

Other Issues

The steps involved in classifying capital leases, setting them up on the books and accounting for subsequent earnings have been explained. There are other issues, however, that one will encounter in accounting for leases. These include residual write-downs, renewals and extensions, terminations and subleases. Each of these aspects is now examined in more detail.

RESIDUAL WRITE-DOWNS

The residual in a capital lease is an integral part of the income of that lease, yet residual amounts (unless guaranteed) are subject to future market conditions, unlike minimum lease payments. Because of this, it is essential residual values are properly stated as to expected value. To this end, FASB 13 (as clarified by Technical Bulletin 79-14) states:

> The estimated residual value shall be reviewed at least annually. If the review results in a lower estimate than had been previously established, a determination must be made as to whether the decline in estimated residual value is other than temporary. If the decline in estimated residual value is judged to be other than temporary, the accounting for the transaction shall be revised using the changed estimate. The resulting reduction in the net investment shall be recognized as a loss in the period in which the estimate is changed. An upward adjustment of the estimated residual value shall not be made [FASB 13, paragraph 17(d)].

FASB 13 is clear in its mandate that declines in residual value be reflected in income. How this is accomplished is not quite so clear. From a practical perspective there are four methods, although some are more theoretically preferable than others. For purposes of the discussion of the mechanics and pros and cons of each, and using the example presented in the direct financing lease subsection, assume an other than temporary decline in the unguaranteed residual value from $11,250 to $6,250 at the end of the first year. Ignore the impact of initial direct costs.

The first method recognizes the entire difference between the original estimated residual and the revised estimate as a loss in the current period, in essence a total write-down. A new pretax earnings rate is calculated to amortize the remaining unearned income. The journal entry for this method is as follows:

Loss on residual write-down	$ 5,000	
Unguaranteed residual		$ 5,000

This entry complies with FASB 13 in that it recognizes the loss in the current period. Subsequent earnings, however, are overstated, since the unearned income account relating to the portion of the residual written down is not reduced. This method recognizes the future value of the write-down, in its entirety, today.

The second method reduces unearned income for the entire difference between the original estimated residual and the revised estimate, and also requires recalculation of the earnings rate to amortize the remaining unearned income. The associated journal entry is as follows:

Unearned income	$ 5,000	
Unguaranteed residual		$ 5,000

This method, while lowering income over time, does not comply with the FASB 13 requirement that a current loss be recognized in the period of the decline.

The first two methods both have problems theoretically. One recognizes a current loss per FASB 13, but does not reduce future earnings, while the other reduces future earnings, but does not recognize a current loss. The next methods presented recognize a current loss and reduce future earnings, both of which are theoretically desireable. The first of these methods is complex and requires much recomputation (and is also the most theoretically correct), while the second method is simpler, and easier to grasp conceptually.

The most theoretically correct write-down process is based upon the premise that the decline in the estimated residual value will occur in the future; therefore, only the previously recognized income relating to that decline should be reversed and shown as a loss in the current period. Furthermore, the net investment should be restated to reflect the decline in the unearned accounts and the unguaranteed residual (i.e., pull out any future income related to the decline that would have been recognized had the decline not occurred). A new pretax earnings rate must be computed to reflect the above changes. The associated journal entry is as follows:

Unearned income	$ 4,337	
Residual write-down loss	$ 663	
Unguaranteed residual		$ 5,000

The theory behind this method is to restate the net investment as if the residual had been $6,250 from the beginning of the lease term. This involves recomputing a new pretax earnings rate and then present valuing the remaining lease cash flows. The loss on write-down will represent the difference in the existing net investment (before write-down) and the new net investment (after write-down). This process is accomplished as outlined below.

First, compute the new earnings rate based on a $6,250 residual.

73,225	CHS	g	CF_o	
1,775		g	CF_j	
47		g	N_j	
6,250		g	CF_j	
		f	IRR	.8198

Second, compute the new net investment in the lease on the date of the write-down.

.8198			i	
1,775		g	CF_j	
42		g	N_j	
6,250		g	CF_j	
		f	NPV	67,254

Based on these computations, the change in the net investment in the lease can be calculated.

New net investment	$ 67,254	
Existing net investment	(62,917)	($69,505[4] – $1,588[4] – $5,000)
Debit to unearned income	$ 4,337	

The write-down loss of $663 represents the difference between the asset write-down of $5,000 and the debit to unearned income of $4,337.

Although complicated, this method is preferred, because it completely eliminates the effects of the write-down from future income, reverses previously recognized income and amortizes the remaining net investment. There is no bunching or under- or overstating of income in past or

---

[4] From Figure 4.

future years. With the exception of previously recognized income, this method acts as if the revised estimate has always been the residual estimate.

The last process for writing down residuals recognizes that the difference between the original estimated residual and the revised estimate is a future event; therefore, only the present value of that future loss is recognized in the current period. The journal entry for this method is as follows:

Residual write-down loss	$ 3,255[5]	
Unearned income	$ 1,745	
Unguaranteed residual		$ 5,000

This approach to residual write-downs is conservative in that it recognizes the total present value of the loss today, and reduces the future residual income associated with the loss. It does, however, overstate future income.

Finally, there is a different conceptual view of writing down residuals. Previous methods have dealt with individual leases. Some leasing companies view the residual evaluation process as a portfolio or pooled process, whereby only the net pool decreases are recognized. This methodology is, in reality, an in-substance write-up of certain leases in the portfolio, which is proscribed by FASB 13, and, therefore, is not acceptable.

RENEWALS AND EXTENSIONS

There are some cases where leases are renewed or extended. These renewals and extensions may result in a new lease agreement with a fixed term or they may be month-to-month. The first situation is one in which the lease term is extended for a fixed term beyond the original lease term, such as through the exercise of a lease renewal option (assuming it was not already included in the lease term). Per FASB 13, this is a new agreement and must be classified as either capital or operating as of the inception date of the renewal or extension. If the renewal or extension is classified as a capital lease, and the original lease was also a capital lease, then the balances of the minimum lease payments and residual value will be adjusted to reflect the changes, if any. This adjustment should be made through the unearned income account.

If the renewal or extension is classified as an operating lease, and the original lease was a capital lease, then the existing lease shall continue to be accounted for as a capital lease to the end of its original term. The renewal or extension then is accounted for as an operating lease.

There are several other cases that may arise due to renewals or extensions. One is where the renewal or extension of an existing operating lease is classified as a capital lease. In this instance, the renewal or extension would be prospectively accounted for as a capital lease. When a renewal or extension occurs in the last few months of an existing lease, and that renewal or extension is

---

[5]

5,000	FV
1.0031	i
43	n
	PV 3,255

classified as a sales-type capital lease, then the renewal or extension is accounted for as a sales-type lease. Otherwise, it would be accounted for as a direct financing capital lease.

Generally, lease agreements state that the lessee may, at the end of the lease term, continue to lease the equipment on a month-to-month basis until it either (1) signs a renewal or extension, (2) purchases the equipment or (3) returns it to the lessor. This automatic renewal becomes, in essence, an operating lease due to its month-to-month nature. Therefore, the proper accounting would be to evaluate the current residual estimate and record the asset at the lower of its fair market value, carrying cost or original cost. The lease then is accounted for as any other operating lease by recording rental revenue and depreciation expense.

In practice, though, several other methods are also used. One, which is not acceptable for GAAP and, therefore, not that common, is to recognize the revenues from the renewal as income, without any corresponding expense. This process is continued until disposition of the original lease. Another more common means of dealing with month-to-month renewals utilizes a cost recovery or sunk cost approach. Under this method, revenues are used to reduce the residual value each month until the residual is equal to zero. At this point, revenues would begin to be recognized. Although conservative, this method does not provide a proper matching of revenues and expenses either, particularly if the asset has a long remaining life. While not in technical compliance with FASB 13, this method, as was mentioned earlier, is used often, particularly when the effects are not material.

ACCOUNTING FOR SUBLEASES

Subleases (or similar transactions) occur throughout the leasing industry. One of the more common (for accounting purposes) is the sublease generated due to the sale-leaseback of equipment in a wrap transaction. FASB 13 defines three types of subleases, or similar transactions, where:

1. The leased property is re-leased by the original lessee to a third party, and the lease agreement between the two original parties remains in effect (a sublease)
2. A new lessee is substituted under the original lease agreement. The new lessee becomes the primary obligor under the agreement, and the original lessee may or may not be secondarily liable
3. A new lessee is substituted through a new agreement, with cancellation of the original lease agreement.

Accounting for these types of transactions can be further broken down into accounting by the original lessor and by the original lessee. An original lessee is any lessee who acts as sublessor on a sublease.

As far as the original lessor is concerned, in those cases where the original lessee enters into a sublease or the original lease agreement is sold or transferred by the original lessee to a third party, the original lessor should not change its accounting for the lease. If, however, the original lease agreement is replaced by a new agreement with a new lessee, the original lessor should account for the original lease as being terminated and then classify and account for the new lease as a separate transaction.

In regards to accounting for the transaction by the original lessee, the appropriate treatment will depend on the nature of the transaction, i.e., whether or not it is a true sublease or a similar transaction. The core issue is the obligations of the original lessee. If the original lessee is relieved of the primary obligation under the original lease, the treatment will be different from that of a sublease, where the original lessee remains the primary obligor. In this subsection, the accounting for an original lessee who has been relieved of the primary obligation under the original lease (2 and 3 above) is presented first, followed by that in which the original lessee enters into a sublease (1 above).

1. When an original lessee is relieved of its primary obligation under the lease, the original lease is treated as being terminated. If the original lease was a capital lease, the corresponding asset and obligation representing the original lease must be removed from the books and any gain or loss recognized for the difference, and, if the original lessee is secondarily liable under the original lease, a loss contingency must be provided for in accordance with FASB Statement No. 5 (FASB 5), 'Accounting for Contingencies.' If the original lease was an operating lease and the original lessee is secondarily liable under the original lease, then a loss contingency must be provided for in accordance with FASB 5

2. In a sublease transaction, the original lessee, as sublessor, must classify the new lease as either capital or operating, according to the criteria of paragraphs 7 and 8 of FASB 13, if the original lease met either criterion (a) or (b) of paragraph seven. The unamortized balance of the original lease is to be treated as the cost of the leased property. Irrespective of the classification of the new lease, the original lessee continues to account for the original lease as before the sublease. In those cases where the original lease met either the 75% or 90% tests (criterion (c) and (d) of paragraph 7, respectively) the original lessee should, with one exception, classify the new lease as capital or operating through application of the 75% of economic life criterion only. The unamortized balance of the original lease is to be used as cost and the original lease continues to be accounted for as before.

The exception referred to in 2 relates to sale-leaseback-subleases in which the timing of the cash flows and other considerations in the transaction are such that the original lessee is, in substance, serving only as a middleman. This type of situation occurs most commonly in what are known as wrap leases. When the original lessee is indeed serving the function of a middleman, then both the 75% and 90% tests are applied in classifying the new lease as either capital or operating. Because of the timing of this type of transaction, the fair market value the original lessee uses should be the fair market value to the original lessor at the inception of the original lease. Finally, if the original lease was classified as an operating lease, the original lessee must account for both it and the new lease as operating leases.

LESSEE CAPITAL LEASE ACCOUNTING

Capital leases from the lessee's viewpoint all result in an asset being capitalized or being shown on the lessee's balance sheet; hence, the name capital lease. In addition to causing capitalized assets, capital leases also create lease payables. This section presents the determination of, and subsequent accounting for, lessee capital leases.

FASB 13 Requirements

The best way to learn to account for a capital lease is to study the requirements of FASB 13 and then walk through an example of those requirements, carefully illustrating each step. FASB 13 describes capital lease accounting from the lessee's perspective as follows:

> The lessee shall record a capital lease as an asset and an obligation at an amount equal to the present value at the beginning of the lease term of minimum lease payments during the lease term, excluding that portion of the payments representing executory costs to be paid by the lessor, together with any profit thereon. However, if the amount so determined exceeds the fair value of the leased property at the inception of the lease, the amount recorded as the asset and obligation shall be the fair value. If the portion of the minimum lease payments representing executory costs, including profit thereon, is not determinable from the provisions of the lease, an estimate of the amount shall be made. The discount rate to be used in determining present value of the minimum lease payments shall be that prescribed for the lessee in paragraph 7(d) . . .
>
> Except as provided in paragraphs 25 and 26 with respect to leases involving land, the asset recorded under a capital lease shall be amortized as follows:
>
> a. If the lease meets the criterion of either paragraph 7(a) or 7(b), the asset shall be amortized in a manner consistent with the lessee's normal depreciation policy for owned assets.
>
> b. If the lease does not meet either criterion 7(a) or 7(b), the asset shall be amortized in a manner consistent with the lessee's normal depreciation policy except that the period of amortization shall be the lease term. The asset shall be amortized to its expected value, if any, to the lessee at the end of the lease term. As an example, if the lessee guarantees a residual value at the end of the lease term and has no interest in any excess which might be realized, the expected value of the leased property to him is the amount that can be realized from it up to the amount of the guarantee.
>
> During the lease term, each minimum lease payment shall be allocated between a reduction of the obligation and interest expense so as to produce a constant periodic rate of interest on the remaining balance of the obligation . . . In leases containing a residual guarantee by the lessee or a penalty for failure to renew the lease at the end of the lease term, following the above method of amortization will result in a balance of the obligation at the end of the lease term that will equal the amount of the guarantee or penalty at that date . . . [FASB 13, paragraphs 10, 11 and 12].

The preceding accounting procedures for the lessee capital lease can be summarized and broken into three groups:

1. Capitalization of the leased asset and the lease obligation. The capitalized amount is equal to the present value of the minimum lease payments. That amount, however, cannot exceed the equipment's fair market value

2. Depreciation of the asset. The capitalized asset is depreciated like any other asset in terms of method or length of time, and is not limited to the lease term when the lease is

capital because of either of the first two FASB 13 capital lease criteria. If, however, the lease is capital due to either of the last two criteria being met, the capitalized equipment is depreciated using normal methods but the depreciation period is limited to the lease term

3. Amortization of the capitalized lease obligation. The capitalized lease obligation is amortized as a loan with periodic loan payments separated into principal (and interest) per a constant interest rate over the lease term.

Lessee Capital Lease Example

In order to explain the accounting for a capital lease, the following capital lease example is used. (This is the same example as the direct financing capital lease used in lessor capital lease accounting at the beginning of this chapter.)

ASSUMPTIONS

The following assumptions will be utilized in the example illustrating the booking of a capital lease.

Inception date: July 1
Term: 48-month lease with one payment in advance
Equipment cost: $75,000
Monthly payment: $1,775
Unguaranteed residual: $11,250
Tax lease: 5-year MACRS property
Fiscal year: begins July 1
Tax rate: 34%
Capital lease criteria: the first three are not met
Discount rate: the implicit rate in the lease of 10.7995% is unknown to the lessee. The lessee's incremental, coterminous pretax borrowing rate is 10%
Closing fees: none.

INITIAL SETUP

The first step in accounting for a capital lease is to ascertain in fact that the lease is capital. Given that none of the first three FASB 13 capital lease criteria was met, the minimum lease payments must be discounted to establish whether the present value is equal to or greater than 90% of the leased equipment's fair market value at the leases inception. If so, the lease is capital.

The lessee uses its borrowing rate as the discount rate for the 90% present value test, since it is lower than the lessor's implicit rate. Implicit rates are seldom known by lessees nor can they be computed easily, since lessees do not know the lessor's residual and initial direct cost assumptions.

To apply the 90% test, first determine the FASB 13 comparison base. This base establishes the amount that the present value of the minimum lease payments must equal or exceed to be deemed capital.

Fair market value of the equipment	$ 75,000
	× .90
FASB 13 comparison base	$ 67,500

Next, calculate the present value of the minimum lease payments using the lessee's borrowing rate of 10%.

10	g	12 ÷
1,775	g	CF_o
1,775	g	CF_j
47	g	N_j
	f	NPV	70,568.19

The lease is definitely a capital lease since the present value of the minimum lease payments ($70,568.19) is in excess of the $67,500 FASB 13 comparison base.

Capitalization of Leased Asset

The capitalization amount of the asset is calculated by present valuing the minimum lease payments at the incremental borrowing rate. From the previous calculation, this amount is $70,568.19. Since this present value amount does not exceed the leased asset's $75,000 fair market value, it is used as the capitalized cost of the leased equipment. The lease payable obligation also is booked at $70,568 but is split into the current portion coming due during the next 12 months (irrespective of the fiscal year end), and the long-term portion due beyond the current period. This separation of the lease liability into its current and long-term portions is required only when the lessee classifies its balance sheet. Since most companies do classify their balance sheets into current and long-term liabilities, that method is described here.

The separation of the lease liability into its current and long-term portions is accomplished by performing an amortization of the lease using the HP-12C, as shown in Table 9. First, the calculator is set up to perform an amortization by inputting the following data:

		g	BEG
10		g	12 ÷
1,775			PMT
70,568	CHS		PV

Depreciation of the capitalized leased asset is over the lease term with no assumed salvage value, since the fourth capital lease criterion was met and the equipment is not used in the remaining 25% of its life. The capitalized value of $70,568 is divided by 48 months to arrive at the monthly depreciation expense.

$$\frac{\$70,568}{48} = \$1,470$$

Journal Entries

Based upon the preceding explanations and calculations, the initial setup general journal entries are booked.

Table 9

Amortization of the Obligation

Year	Interest Expense		Current Principal		Long-Term Principal	
1	13⁶ f AMORT	6,200	X ≥ Y	16,875	RCL PV	53,693
2	12 f AMORT	4,618	X ≥ Y	16,682	RCL PV	37,011
3	12 f AMORT	2,872	X ≥ Y	18,428	RCL PV	18,583
4	11⁶ f AMORT	942	X ≥ Y	18,583	RCL PV	0

1. Capital leased equipment $ 70,568
         Lease payable (current) $ 16,875
         Lease payable (long-term) $ 53,693

    To record a capital lease and an equal lease liability separated
    into its current and long-term portions

Next June 30, at the end of the fiscal year, the following additional journal entries are made to
complete the first year's accounting for a lessee capital lease.

2. Interest expense $ 6,200
    Lease payable (current) $ 16,875
         Cash $ 21,300
         Lease rental payable $ 1,775
    To record the payment of 12 lease payments (July 1 through
    June 1) plus one accrued payment for the last month of the fiscal
    year

3. Depreciation expense $ 17,640
         Accumulated depreciation $ 17,640

    To record 12 months of depreciation expense at $1,470 per
    month

    Lease payable (long-term) $ 16,682
         Lease payable (current) $ 16,682

    To transfer the lease liability currently due from the long-term
    liability

---

⁶ The fact that lease payments are in advance requires deviation from the standard 12 payments per year.

4. Taxes receivable $7,242
    Deferred tax charge $ 864
        Tax benefit $8,106

    To provide for taxes on the lease expense

END OF FIRST YEAR T-ACCOUNT SUMMARY

The following T-accounts represent the balances on the books at year end for this capital lease. The T-account entries are annotated with the corresponding journal entry number for ease of reference. The T-account summaries for the balance sheet and income statement are shown in Figures 14 and 15, respectively.

Capital Leased Equipment
(1)70,568

Lease Payable (Current)
(2)16,875 | 16,875(1)
          | 16,682(3)
          | 16,682

Lease Payable (Long-term)
(3)16,682 | 53,693(1)
          | 37,011

Accumulated Depreciation
17,640(3)

Cash
21,300(2)

Lease Rental Payable
1,775(2)

Deferred Tax Charge
(4)864

Taxes Receivable
(4)7,242

Figure 14
Balance Sheet T-accounts

Depreciation Expense
(3)17,640

Interest Expense
(2)6,200

Tax Benefit
8,106(4)

Figure 15
Income Statement T-accounts

FINANCIAL STATEMENTS

The financial statements depicting the preceding information are shown in Figure 16 (income statement), Figure 17 (balance sheet) and Figure 18 (cash flow statement). Assume the lessee corporation has other fixed assets of $20,000 and contributed capital of $20,000 in order to make a more complete presentation.

INTERPERIOD TAX ALLOCATION

Based on the preceding differences between the accounting books and the tax return, the interperiod tax allocation journal entry is calculated by finding the difference between the book and tax loss, as shown in Table 10. Remember this capital lease is considered a true lease for tax purposes.

Other Considerations

Sometimes leases are classified as capital because they contain bargain purchase options or guaranteed residuals. In either case, these residual obligations become part of the lessee's minimum lease payments. Such an inclusion creates a difference from the previous example; the present value of the minimum lease payments will be larger and might exceed the leased equipment's fair market value, which cannot be exceeded for purposes of booking the lease. If the leased asset is capitalized at the fair market value ceiling limitation, an interest rate must be computed that relates the present value of the lease payments to the capitalized equipment value. This internal rate of return (IRR) is used in the lease amortization.

An example clarifies best the changes in accounting brought about by the existence of a bargain purchase option or guaranteed residual where the present value total exceeds the leased

REVENUE		$ 0
OPERATING EXPENSES		
Depreciation expense		17,640
OPERATING INCOME		($ 17,640)
OTHER EXPENSES		
Interest on the capital lease		6,200
INCOME (LOSS) BEFORE TAXES		($ 23,840)
Current	$ 7,242	
Deferred	864	
Income tax benefit		8,106
NET INCOME (LOSS)		($ 15,734)

Figure 16
Income Statement
End of First Year Reporting

ASSETS

Current assets

Cash	($ 21,300)	
Taxes receivable	7,242	
Total current assets		($ 14,058)

Fixed assets

Capital leased equipment	$ 70,568	
Less: accumulated depreciation	(17,640)	
Net	$ 52,928	
Other property, plant and equipment (net)	20,000	
Total fixed assets		72,928
Deferred tax charge		864
Total assets		$ 59,734

LIABILITIES

Current liabilities

Lease rental payable	$ 1,775	
Lease payable (current)	16,682	
Total current liabilities		$ 18,457

Long-term liabilities

Lease payable (long-term)		37,011
Total liabilities		$ 55,468

OWNERS' EQUITY

Contributed capital	$ 20,000	
Retained earnings	(15,734)	
Total owners' equity		4,266
Total liabilities and owners' equity		$ 59,734

Figure 17
Balance Sheet
End of First Year Reporting

CASH FLOWS FROM OPERATING ACTIVITIES

Interest paid (capital leases)	($ 6,200)	
Net cash consumed by operating activities		**($ 6,200)**

CASH FLOWS FROM INVESTING ACTIVITIES   0

CASH FLOWS FROM FINANCING ACTIVITIES

Principal payments under a capital lease obligation		
($16,875-$1,775)	($ 15,100)	
Net cash used in financing activities		(15,100)

NET DECREASE IN CASH   ($ 21,300)

Cash at the beginning of the year	0
Cash at the end of the year	($ 21,300)

RECONCILIATION OF NET INCOME TO OPERATING ACTIVITIES

Net income		($ 15,734)
Adjustments to net income		
Depreciation	$ 17,640	
Increase in taxes receivable	(7,242)	
Increase in deferred tax change	(864)	
Total adjustments		9,534
Net cash consumed by operating activities		**($ 6,200)**

NONCASH INVESTING ACTIVITIES

The company acquired the use of equipment under a capital lease:

Present value of assets acquired		$ 70,568
Liabilities assumed		
Current	$16,875	
Long-term	53,693	
Total liabilities assumed		$ 70,568

Figure 18
Statement of Cash Flows
(direct method per FASB Statement No. 95)
End of First Year Reporting

Table 10
Book/Tax Differences

	Accounting Books	Tax Books
Lease rental (12 months)	$ 0	$ 21,300
Interest expense	6,200	0
Depreciation expense	17,640	0
Taxable loss	$ 23,840	$ 21,300
Tax rate	× .34	× .34
Tax benefit	$ 8,106	$ 7,242
Difference	$ 864	

assets fair market value. Assume that all assumptions are the same as the previous example except the $11,250 residual is guaranteed.

CAPITALIZATION OF LEASED ASSET

The capitalization amount is calculated by present valuing the minimum lease payments:

10	g	12 ÷
1,775	g	CF_o
1,775	g	CF_j
47	g	N_j
11,250	g	CF_j
	f	NPV 78,121.80

Since the $78,121.80 amount is in excess of the $75,000 fair market value of the leased equipment, the asset is capitalized at $75,000 and the lease payable obligation totals $75,000.

The separation of the $75,000 lease liability into its current and long-term portions is accomplished by first computing the implied borrowing rate (the IRR that equates the minimum lease payments to the equipment's fair market value) in the lease liability, followed by an amortization of the lease payments.

To calculate the implied borrowing rate of the lease, proceed as follows with an HP-12C:

		g	BEG
75,000	CHS		PV
1,775			PMT
48			n
11,250			FV
			i 1.00312

Using the implied borrowing rate, set up the calculator to perform the amortization of Table 11 by inputting the data shown below:

	g	BEG	(payments are in advance)
1.00312		i	(implied borrowing rate)
1,775		PMT	(lease payment amount)
75,000 CHS		PV	(fair market value and lease obligation total)

After the 48 monthly lease payments there will be a remaining lease liability of $11,137, which is made up of the bargain purchase option amount of $11,250 less $113 of interest for the last month.

Depreciation of the capitalized leased asset amount of $75,000 will be over the lease term since the fourth capital lease criterion was met. However, the asset will be depreciated only to its assumed salvage value of $11,250 per normal asset depreciation accounting. The monthly depreciation charge would be:

$$\frac{(\$75,000 - \$11,250)}{48} = \$1,328$$

At the end of the lease term there will be $11,250 of remaining asset book value and a lease payable liability of $11,137. If the purchase option is exercised or the lessee guarantee paid, and the lessee keeps the asset, the following journal entry results:

Lease payable	$ 11,137	
Interest expense	$ 113	
Cash		$ 11,250

To record the purchase of a capital leased asset

Table 11
Amortization of the Obligation

Year	Interest Expense		Current Principal		Long-Term Principal	
1	13 f AMORT	8,102	X ≥ Y	14,973	RCL PV	60,027
2	12 f AMORT	6,421	X ≥ Y	14,879	RCL PV	45,148
3	12 f AMORT	4,529	X ≥ Y	16,771	RCL PV	28,377
4	11 f AMORT	2,285	X ≥ Y	17,240	RCL PV	11,137
11,250 PMT	1 f AMORT	113	X ≥ Y	11,137	RCL PV	0

However, if the lessee does not keep the asset, the remaining equipment book value as well as the lease payable must be removed from the books as follows:

Accumulated depreciation	$ 63,750	
Lease payable	$ 11,137	
Interest expense	$ 113	
Capital leased asset		$ 75,000

> To remove the capital leased asset and the related obligation from the books

CONCLUSION

Accounting for capital leases can be a challenging, yet certainly not insurmountable task. As in any aspect of leasing, there are many complexities that must be considered. Careful study and review of the guidelines of FASB 13 provide the background necessary to understand the vast majority of lease transactions that one might encounter. Of course, the challenge lies in those transactions that are not ordinary, but there are resources available, in the form of accounting and consulting firms, the FASB and the various associations, to provide today's lease professional with answers to those difficult questions.

CHAPTER SIXTEEN
LEVERAGED LEASES

Although leveraged leases are, in essence, direct financing capital leases, they are accounted for in a very different manner. One of the reasons for the difference in accounting methodology is that leveraged lease income is recognized on an after-tax, after-interest expense basis, whereas nonleveraged capital lease accounting occurs on a pretax, preinterest expense basis. This, and the other unique aspects of leveraged leases, are discussed in this chapter, which contains the following topics:

- Leveraged Lease Definitions
- Initial Balance Sheet Entries
- Accounting for Leveraged Lease Income
- Disclosure Requirements
- Disinvestment Balances in the Financial Statements
- Significant Changes in Assumptions
- Avoiding Leveraged Lease Accounting.

LEVERAGED LEASE DEFINITIONS

Leveraged leases are commonly viewed in one of four ways: (1) the laymen's definition, (2) the Internal Revenue Service (IRS) viewpoint, (3) the lease assignment approach and (4) the Financial Accounting Standards Board (FASB) definition. In other words, a lease may be considered leveraged by the IRS, but may not necessarily be viewed the same from an accounting viewpoint. The FASB definition of a leveraged lease, as detailed in FASB Statement No. 13 (FASB 13), paragraph 42, requires that a lease, for it to be leveraged, must have all of the following characteristics:

1. The lease is a direct financing capital lease. Since only direct financing capital leases can be leveraged leases, rental programs, operating leases and sales-type capital leases cannot

be accounted for as leveraged leases. A direct financing capital lease differs from a sales-type capital lease in that the direct financing lease has no gross profit involved, whereas the sales-type lease does

2. There are at least three parties to the lease: (1) a lessee, (2) a long-term, nonrecourse creditor and (3) a lessor. However, there may be additional parties, such as a trustee (if the lease takes the legal form of a grantor trust), other equity participants, etc. The key is that in addition to the lessor and lessee, there must be a nonrecourse creditor providing debt financing for a specific lease transaction

3. The financing provided by the long-term creditor is nonrecourse to the general credit of the lessor. Nonrecourse to the lessor means that in the event of lessee default the lender cannot look to the lessor for payment of its loan. Nevertheless, the creditor has recourse to the equipment through repossession and can obtain a deficiency judgement against the lessee. The financing must also be intact at the inception of the lease, although actual take-down (disbursement of loan proceeds) may await equipment delivery. The Emerging Issues Task Force has also validated the use of delayed (or deferred) equity payments in leveraged leases. The important issue here is that the loan has been agreed to in writing by all parties thereto. Retroactive funding of a direct financing lease after the inception usually results in assignment accounting (as described in Chapter Fifteen) rather than leveraged lease accounting. Lastly, the financing must be significant in amount (usually assumed by the industry to be in excess of 50% of the equipment's cost, although the FASB does not specifically define significant)

4. The lessor's net investment (normally the at-risk investment including equity plus recourse debt, if any, less associated deferred tax credits) declines during the early years when Modified Accelerated Cost Recovery System (MACRS) depreciation tax benefits are available and rises during the later years when reinvestment is occurring due to negative cash flows created by the loss of tax benefits

   Such decreases and increases in the net investment may occur more than once and be so significant that a disinvestment, or credit investment, balance occurs prior to the period of increased investment. (Leases with terms equal to or less than an asset's MACRS classlife seldom display decreases and increases in the net investment.) Debt optimization, or the altering of the nonrecourse debt repayment schedule in a manner that eliminates disinvestment balances, may also eliminate the increases and decreases in the net investment

5. The deferral method of accounting for the Investment Tax Credit (ITC) must be used. Use of the flow-through method requires direct financing capital lease accounting, which requires that any nonrecourse debt be shown as a liability. Leveraged lease accounting, on the other hand, allows nonrecourse debt to remain off balance sheet

It can be seen that the accounting definition of a leveraged lease is quite complex, and should not be confused with either the lay sense of the term, the IRS definition or lease assignments. For instance, the lay sense of the term leveraged lease would include any lease that has been funded with debt. The technical accounting use of the term leveraged is more restrictive and includes only leases funded with a significant amount of nonrecourse debt, plus the other attributes cited above.

The IRS, on the other hand, views a leveraged lease as one meeting the guidelines of Revenue Procedure 75-21. These guidelines include certain at-risk levels that must be met and a proscription against bargain purchase options, among others. IRS leveraged leases also often incorporate many of the lay and accounting characteristics of leveraged leases. Note, too, that for IRS purposes, leveraged leases do not have to be considered leveraged from an accounting viewpoint.

Lease assignment accounting (collateralized pledges or outright sales of leases) is used when nonrecourse debt funding has been obtained subsequent to the lease's inception. When a direct financing lease's rental stream and residual have been assigned as collateral for a nonrecourse loan, the transaction might have all the attributes of FASB 13's definition of a leveraged lease except that such funding occurred after the lease's inception. FASB Technical Bulletin 86-2, paragraph 21, provides further clarification of the importance of the date on which a lease is leveraged (inception or later).

It is obvious, from the preceding discussion, that leveraged leases can be defined in several different ways, whether it be from a tax, lay or accounting perspective. For purposes of this chapter, however, the only definition used is the one contained in FASB 13.

INITIAL BALANCE SHEET ENTRIES

Leveraged leases usually appear on a lessor's balance sheet as a single line item entitled 'Net Investment in Leveraged Leases.' In reality, the net investment represents the netting together of five components. FASB 13 describes the initial balance sheet recording of a leveraged lease as follows:

> The lessor shall record his investment in a leveraged lease net of the nonrecourse debt. The net of the balances of the following accounts shall represent the initial and continuing investment in leveraged leases:
>
> a. Rentals receivable, net of that portion of the rental applicable to principal and interest on the nonrecourse debt.
> b. A receivable for the amount of the investment tax credit to be realized on the transaction.
> c. The *estimated residual value* of the leased asset. The estimated residual value shall not exceed the amount estimated at the inception of the lease.
> d. Unearned and deferred income consisting of (i) the estimated pretax lease income (or loss), after deducting initial direct costs, remaining to be allocated to income over the lease term and (ii) the investment tax credit remaining to be allocated to income over the lease term [FASB 13, paragraph 43 (a), (b), (c) and (d)].

The initial setup of a leveraged lease on a lessor's balance sheet begins with booking the lease as if it were a direct financing capital lease (see Chapter Fifteen). Once booked as a direct financing capital lease, the nonrecourse debt borrowed to fund the transaction is netted against the direct financing lease through certain offsetting entries (e.g., the total debt payments, both principal and interest, are offset against the gross lease rentals receivable of the direct financing lease, etc.). Once the netting process is complete, the balance sheet will show only the net investment in the leveraged lease.

In order to explain the preceding elements of the initial balance sheet recording of a leveraged lease, an example is given based on the following assumptions:

Cost of leased equipment: $1,000,000

Lease term: 10 years, beginning January 1, 19XX

Lease rental payments: $150,000 per year, payable in advance on the first day of each year

Residual value: $100,000, estimated to be realized at the termination of the lease (end of the 10th year)

Lessor equity investment: $300,000

Long-term nonrecourse debt: $700,000, with interest at 10%, payable on the last day of each year in 10 annual installments of $113,922 (last payment of $113,917 due to rounding)

Depreciation allowable for IRS tax purposes: 5-year MACRS property

Lessor's federal tax rate: 34%, assumed unchanged throughout lease term

ITC: not applicable

Initial direct costs: $35,000, assumed incurred at lease inception and fully tax deductible at that time

Lease origination fee (nonrefundable): $10,000.

Based on these assumptions, the initial balance sheet recording of the lease appears as follows, using general journal entries. The T-accounts and financial statement presentation, including footnote disclosure, are then shown.

Journal Entries

The first four journal entries in this section set up the lease as a direct financing capital lease. The next two journal entries are used to book the nonrecourse debt used to fund the acquisition cost of the leased asset.

1.	Lease rentals receivable	$ 1,500,000	
	Unguaranteed residual	$ 100,000	
	Cash	$ 300,000	
	Contributed capital		$ 300,000
	Accounts payable		$ 1,000,000
	Unearned income		$ 600,000

    To record 10 annual rentals of $150,000, residual, equipment cost and equity cash inflow of $300,000

2.	General and administrative (G & A) expense	$ 35,000	
	Fee income		$ 10,000
	Cash		$ 25,000

    To record payment of initial direct costs and receipt of the origination fee

3. Deferred initial direct costs $ 25,000

    Fee income $ 10,000

        G & A expense $ 35,000

To capitalize net initial direct costs per FASB Statement No. 91 (FASB 91).

The various G & A accounts that contained the initial direct costs could have been credited instead of a general G & A control account as shown above.

4. Cash $ 150,000

    Lease rentals receivable $ 150,000

To record receipt of the advance rental

The next two journal entries book the nonrecourse debt borrowed to fund the acquisition of the leased equipment.

5. Unearned income $ 439,215

    Cash $ 700,000

        Lease rentals receivable $ 1,139,215

To record total nonrecourse debt ($1,139,215) as an offset to the lease receivable and to offset the $439,215 interest expense portion of the debt against unearned income

6. Accounts payable $ 1,000,000

    Cash $ 1,000,000

To record purchase of the equipment subject to the leveraged lease

Once the initial balance sheet entries have been journalized, the net investment in the leveraged lease would appear as an asset and would include the net of the preceding journal entries:

Lease rentals receivable (less debt)	$ 210,785
Capitalized initial direct costs	25,000
Unguaranteed residual	100,000
ITC receivable	0
Gross investment in leveraged lease	$ 335,785
Unearned and deferred items	(160,785)
Net investment in leveraged lease	$ 175,000

The net investment in leveraged leases does not include an offset of deferred taxes; however, deferred taxes will be included as an integral part of the net investment for purposes of computing net income from the lease. The computation of leveraged lease income is described in the next subsection.

A T-account summary of the initial balance sheet entries appears in Figure 1. The numbers in parentheses next to the T-account entries correspond to the applicable journal entries presented earlier.

Lease Rentals Receivable	
(1)1,500,000	150,000(4)
	1,139,215(5)
210,785	

Unearned Income	
	600,000(1)
(5)439,215	
	160,785

Accounts Payable	
(6)1,000,000	1,000,000(1)
	0

Unguaranteed Residual	
(1)100,000	

Cash	
(1)300,000	25,000(2)
(4)150,000	1,000,000(6)
(5)700,000	
125,000	

Fee Income	
(3)10,000	10,000(2)
	0

Deferred Initial Direct Costs	
(3)25,000	

Contributed Capital	
	300,000(1)

G & A Expense	
(2)35,000	35,000(3)
0	

Figure 1
T-account Summary

ACCOUNTING FOR LEVERAGED LEASE INCOME

Pretax, reported leveraged lease income is allocated on an after-tax cash flow basis, unlike nonleveraged leases, in which reported income is allocated on a pretax basis. Because of this unique method of reporting income, certain additional steps must be followed in arriving at the pretax, reported earnings in a leveraged lease. The derivation of pretax earnings consists of a three-step process.

1. Determine the after-tax cash flows in the lease. This determination takes into consideration cash flows such as lease rentals receivable, advance rentals, interim rent, nonrefundable closing and origination fees (per FASB 91), ITC (if and when available), tax depreciation, initial direct costs and any residuals
2. Allocate the after-tax cash flows to earnings and investment using the multiple investment sinking fund (MISF) method of income allocation
3. Derive the pretax earnings for the leveraged lease, based upon the after-tax, MISF earnings allocation performed in the second step.

Using the lease example in the previous section, and the steps just discussed, the determination of the pretax, reported income is now illustrated.

Determination of After-tax Cash Flows

In order to determine a leveraged lease's reported earnings, its total net, after-tax cash flow per earnings period must be determined. This is accomplished by first calculating the annual taxable income in a lease, and then the resultant tax liability. Once the tax liability is known, all the cash flows are summed by period, and in total, as shown in Table 1 (which also displays the determination of the tax liability).

Determination of MISF Earnings

Once a leveraged lease's after-tax cash flows have been determined (usually on a monthly basis, unlike the simplified annual example above), the earnings component of the after-tax cash flows can be determined in the manner specified by FASB 13:

> Given the original investment and using the projected cash receipts and disbursements over the term of the lease, the rate of return on the net investment in the years in which it is positive shall be computed. The rate is that rate which when applied to the net investment in the years in which the net investment is positive will distribute the net income to those years . . . and is distinct from the interest rate implicit in the lease . . . [FASB 13, paragraph 44].

This unique type of earnings recognition does not provide earnings in those periods beginning with disinvestment balances, allocates earnings only to periods beginning with normal investment balances and is known in the industry as the MISF or separate phase method. The MISF allocation of the after-tax cash flows (from Table 1), to earnings and investment, is shown in Table 2.

The interest, or after-tax earnings, in Table 2 is recognized as 18.865076% of the unrecovered investment at the beginning of each year in which the net investment is normal (years 0 through 3). The rate for allocation used in Table 2 is calculated by a trial and error, or iterative, process. The allocation is calculated based upon an initial estimate of the rate as a starting point. If the total thus allocated to interest differs under the estimated rate from the net after-tax cash flow (column 8 of Table 1), the estimated rate is increased or decreased, as appropriate, to derive a revised allocation. This process is repeated until a rate is selected that develops a total amount allocated to income that is precisely equal to the net cash flow from Table 1 (another check is to make certain the balance at the end of the term is zero). As a practical matter, a computer program is used to calculate MISF earnings under successive iterations until the correct rate is determined.

FASB 13, in the discussion of the FASB's basis for conclusions, describes why MISF was selected for leveraged lease reporting:

> . . . This method recognizes the separate investment phases and the reversing cash flow pattern of a leveraged lease. By recognizing income at a level rate of return on net investment in the years in which the net investment is positive, it associates the income with the unrecovered balance of the earning asset in a manner consistent with the investor's view of the transaction. In the middle years of the lease term, the investment balance is generally negative, indicating that the lessor has not only recovered his initial investment but has the temporary use of funds that will be reinvested in the later years.

Table 1
Computation of Annual After-Tax Cash Flow

	1	2	3	4	5	6	7	8
Year	Lease Rentals/ Residual	MACRS	Initial Direct Costs (Net)	Loan Interest Expense	Taxable Income (Loss) (1-2-3-4)	Income Tax (Benefit) or Expense[1]	Loan Principal	Annual Net Cash Flow[2]
0	$ 150,000	$ 0	$ 25,000	$ 0	$ 0	$ 0	$ 0	($ 175,000)[3]
1	150,000	200,000	0	70,000	5,000[4]	1,700	43,922	34,378
2	150,000	320,000	0	65,608	(235,608)	(80,107)	48,314	116,185
3	150,000	192,000	0	60,776	(102,776)	(34,944)	53,146	71,022
4	150,000	115,200	0	55,462	(20,662)	(7,025)	58,460	43,103
5	150,000	115,200	0	49,616	(14,816)	(5,037)	64,306	41,115
6	150,000	57,600	0	43,185	49,215	16,733	70,737	19,345
7	150,000	0	0	36,111	113,889	38,722	77,811	(2,644)
8	150,000	0	0	28,330	121,670	41,368	85,592	(5,290)
9	150,000	0	0	19,771	130,229	44,278	94,151	(8,200)
10	100,000	0	0	10,356	89,644	30,479	103,561	(44,396)
	$ 1,600,000	$ 1,000,000	$ 25,000	$ 439,215	$ 135,785	$ 46,167	$ 700,000	$ 89,618

[1] Column 5 ×.34.
[2] Column 1 – 3 – 4 ± 6 – 7.

[3]
Investment	($ 300,000)
Advance payment	150,000
Origination fee	10,000
Initial direct costs	(35,000)
Net investment at inception	($ 175,000)

[4]
Advance rental	$ 150,000
First year rental payment	150,000
Less: MACRS	(200,000)
Initial direct costs (net)	(25,000)
Interest expense	(70,000)
Taxable income	$ 5,000

Table 2
Multiple Investment Sinking Fund Earnings
(MISF rate: 18.865076%)

Year	Cash Flow	Interest	Principal	Balance
0	$ 0.00	$ 0.00	$ 0.00	($ 175,000.00)
1	34,378.00	33,013.88	1,364.12	(173,635.88)
2	116,185.00	32,756.54	83,428.46	(90,207.42)
3	71,022.00	17,017.70	54,004.30	(36,203.12)
4	43,103.00	6,829.88	36,273.12	70.00
5	41,115.00	0.00	41,115.00	41,185.00
6	19,345.00	0.00	19,345.00	60,530.00
7	(2,644.00)	0.00	(2,644.00)	57,886.00
8	(5,290.00)	0.00	(5,290.00)	52,596.00
9	(8,200.00)	0.00	(8,200.00)	44,396.00
10	(44,396.00)	0.00	(44,396.00)	0.00
	$ 264,618.00	$ 89,618.00	$175,000.00	$ 0.00

The earnings on these temporary funds are reflected in income as and if they occur in the years in which the investment is negative. The income that is recognized at a level rate of return in the years in which the net investment balance is positive consists only of the so-called "primary" earnings from the lease, as distinct from the earnings on temporary funds to be reinvested, sometimes referred to as "secondary" earnings. The lessor-investor looks upon these secondary earnings for the temporarily held funds as one of the economic benefits inherent in the transaction [FASB 13, paragraph 109(c)].

Certainly this method of income recognition is conservative in that no benefits derived from secondary earnings are directly recognized as part of the after-tax cash flow amortization. Ignoring secondary earnings might be acceptable from an accounting viewpoint since secondary earnings will be recognized anyway as they occur; nevertheless, use of MISF interest rates may distort actual economic returns (see Chapter Seven). The actual internal rate of return (IRR) of this lease, on an after-tax basis, is 22.517541%, and its amortization appears in Table 3.

The amortization in Table 3 of the lease at its IRR, rather than its MISF (Table 2), demonstrates that, indeed, the MISF rate is not necessarily indicative of the lease's real economic yield (an 18.9% accounting recognition rate (MISF) versus a 22.5% economic rate (IRR)). Notice, in either case, a total of $89,618 in interest earned is reported. The difference is that the IRR method would show the earnings such that a 22.5% IRR is reported versus the lower 18.9% MISF rate. Note, too, that the IRR method shows negative earnings in the sixth through the tenth year, whereas the MISF method never shows negative earnings.

Table 3
Internal Rate of Return Earnings
(IRR: 22.517541%)

Year	Cash Flow	Interest	Principal	Balance
0	$ 0.00	$ 0.00	$ 0.00	($ 175,000.00)
1	34,378.00	39,405.70	(5,027.70)	(180,027.70)
2	116,185.00	40,537.81	75,647.19	(104,380.51)
3	71,022.00	23,503.92	47,518.08	(56,862.43)
4	43,103.00	12,804.02	30,298.98	(26,563.45)
5	41,115.00	5,981.44	35,133.56	8,570.11
6	19,345.00	(1,929.78)	21,274.78	29,844.89
7	(2,644.00)	(6,720.34)	4,076.34	33,921.23
8	(5,290.00)	(7,638.23)	2,348.23	36,269.46
9	(8,200.00)	(8,166.99)	(33.01)	36,236.45
10	(44,396.00)	(8,159.55)	(36,236.45)	0.00
	$ 264,618.00	$ 89,618.00	$ 175,000.00	$ 0.00

Derivation of Pretax Earnings

The next step in accounting for leveraged lease income is to gross up the MISF earnings calculated in Table 2 into their pretax income, ITC (when applicable) and income tax expense components, as depicted in Table 4. Note that there is not an ITC allocation since ITC did not exist in this lease. Even though earnings in a leveraged lease are computed on an after-tax basis, they are converted to their pretax equivalent through use of the gross-up method. The derivation of the pretax earnings and associated taxes for the first year of $50,021 and $17,007, respectively (from Table 4), is as follows:

Total income	$ 89,618
ITC component	0
After-tax, after-ITC income	$ 89,618

$89,618 ÷ (1 – tax rate) = grossed-up pretax earnings

$89,618 ÷ (1 – .34) = $135,785[5] earnings

$$= \frac{\$ 135,785}{\$ 89,618} = 1.515153\% \text{ gross-up factor}$$

Thus, the first year's grossed-up, pretax earnings are $50,021 (1.515153 x $33,013.88 = $50,021). The tax expense on $50,021.09 of $17,007 would be calculated as $50,021.09 x 34%.

---

[5] Total unearned income of $160,785, less the amortization of the net initial direct costs of $25,000.

Table 4
Pretax Income Allocation

Year	MISF Earnings	Pretax Income	Income Tax Expense	Investment Tax Credit
0	$ .00	$ 0	$ 0	$ 0
1	33,013.88	50,021	17,007	0
2	32,756.54	49,631	16,875	0
3	17,017.70	25,785	8,767	0
4	6,829.88	10,348	3,518	0
5	.00	0	0	0
6	.00	0	0	0
7	.00	0	0	0
8	.00	0	0	0
9	.00	0	0	0
10	.00	0	0	0
	$ 89,618.00	$ 135,785	$ 46,167	$ 0

INTERPERIOD TAX ALLOCATION

Deferred tax credits occur because of the differences between reported book expenses (benefits) and tax liabilities (benefits). Table 5 shows, in column 1, the actual tax liability of the lessor as taken from Table 1. Column 2 indicates the accounting reported tax expense from Table 4. Column 3 represents the difference between columns 1 and 2, resulting in the deferred tax credit (charge) for any given year. Column 4 reveals the cumulative impact of the deferred tax credit account. Of course, by the end of the lease the deferred tax credit account will be zeroed out.

FIRST YEAR JOURNAL ENTRIES

Based on the MISF earnings separation into pretax earnings and tax expense, and the above interperiod tax allocation schedule, the first year journal entries are as follows.

7. Income tax expense	$ 17,007	
Unearned income	$ 59,231	
Interest earned		$ 50,021
Income taxes payable		$ 1,700
Deferred taxes		$ 15,307
Deferred initial direct costs		$ 9,210

To record first year's earnings

Pretax earned income of $50,021 is net of the impact of the initial direct costs that must be amortized to expense each year. In effect, total pretax unearned income is $135,785 (from Table

Table 5
Deferred Tax Computation

Year	1 Income Tax (Benefit) Liability	2 Book Tax (Benefit) Expense	3 Deferred Tax Credit (Charge)	4 Cumulative Deferred Tax Credit
0	$ 0	$ 0	$ 0	$ 0
1	1,700	17,007	15,307	15,307
2	(80,107)	16,875	96,982	112,289
3	(34,944)	8,767	43,711	156,000
4	(7,025)	3,518	10,543	166,543
5	(5,037)	0	5,037	171,580
6	16,733	0	(16,733)	154,847
7	38,722	0	(38,722)	116,125
8	41,368	0	(41,368)	74,757
9	44,278	0	(44,278)	30,479
10	30,479	0	(30,479)	0
	$ 46,167	$ 46,167	$ 0	$ 0

4) plus $25,000 of initial direct costs. Thus, total unearned income before the impact of initial direct costs is $160,785, as shown in the initial T-account balances in Figure 1.

Theoretically, the amortization of the initial direct costs should be recognized using the effective yield methodology as described in FASB 91. As a practical matter, and for purposes of this example, a simple pro rata amortization can be used. Based on such a pro rata amortization, the first year amount would be $9,210. The debit to unearned income is the sum of the net interest income and the initial direct cost amortization.

$$\frac{\text{Net interest (year 1)}}{\text{Total interest}} \qquad \frac{\$ 50,021}{\$135,785} \quad = \quad .368384$$

$$\$25,000 \times .368384 = \$9,210$$
$$\$50,021 + \$9,210 = \$59,231$$

8. Income taxes payable $ 1,700
    Cash $ 1,700

    To record payment of actual tax liability

9. Cash $ 36,078
    Lease rentals receivable $ 36,078

    To record receipt of rental at year end ($150,000 – $113,922 = $36,078)

END OF FIRST YEAR T-ACCOUNT SUMMARIES

A complete T-account summary of the accounts at the end of the first year is presented in Figures 2 and 3. The numbers in parentheses next to the T-account entries correspond to the applicable journal entries presented earlier.

The net investment in the leveraged lease at the end of the first year would appear as follows:

Net lease rentals receivable	$ 174,707	
Capitalized initial direct costs	15,790	
Unguaranteed residual	100,000	
Gross investment in leveraged lease	$ 290,497	
Unearned and deferred items	(101,554)	
Net investment in leveraged lease		$ 188,943
Less related deferred tax credits		(15,307)
Net adjusted investment in leveraged lease		$ 173,636

Note that although the $188,943 'Net Investment in Leveraged Leases' appears as an asset on the balance sheet, it is not the same amount ($173,636) that appears as the investment balance in the MISF Earnings Summary (Table 2). Only when the associated deferred taxes are deducted from the net investment in leveraged leases is the net adjusted investment in leveraged leases

Lease Rentals Receivable		Unearned Income		Accounts Payable	
(1)1,500,000	150,000(4)		600,000(1)	(6)1,000,000	1,000,000(1)
	1,139,215(5)	(5)439,215			0
	36,078(9)	(7) 59,231			
174,707			101,554		

Unguaranteed Residual		Cash		Contributed Capital	
(1)100,000		(1)300,000	25,000(2)		300,000(1)
		(4)150,000	1,000,000(6)		
		(5)700,000	1,700(8)		
		(9) 36,078			
		159,378			

Deferred Initial Direct Costs		Deferred Taxes		Income Taxes Payable	
(3)25,000	9,210(7)		15,307(7)	(8)1,700	1,700(7)
15,790					0

Figure 2
Balance Sheet T-accounts

arrived at that was used in the MISF earnings determination. FASB 13 indicates that the investment in leveraged leases, less any associated deferred taxes, is the net investment to be used for purposes of computing periodic net income, not the balance sheet net investment.

The same process previously illustrated for recognizing pretax earnings would be followed each year until lease termination. As in an unleveraged capital lease, the asset remaining on the books at the end of the lease term will be the unguaranteed residual. Using the T-accounts for this leveraged lease an income statement (Figure 4), a balance sheet (Figure 5) and a cash flow statement (Figure 6) can be prepared.

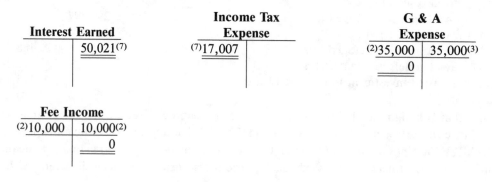

Figure 3
Income Statement T-accounts

REVENUE

Leveraged lease income . . . $ 50,021

OPERATING EXPENSES

General and administrative . . . 0

OPERATING INCOME . . . $ 50,021

OTHER INCOME . . . 0

OTHER EXPENSES

Interest expense . . . 0

INCOME FROM OPERATIONS BEFORE TAXES . . . $ 50,021

Current taxes . . . $ 1,700

Deferred taxes . . . 15,307

Income tax expense . . . 17,007

NET INCOME . . . $ 33,014

Figure 4
Income Statement
End of First Year Reporting

ASSETS

Current assets		
Cash		$ 159,378
Funds and leveraged lease investments		
Lease rentals receivable	$ 174,707	
Residual values	100,000	
Initial direct costs	15,790	
Gross lease investment		$ 290,497
Unearned and deferred items		(101,554)
Net leveraged lease investments		188,943
Total assets		$ 348,321

LIABILITIES

Current liabilities		$ 0
Long-term liabilities		
Deferred taxes		15,307
Total liabilities		$ 15,307

OWNERS' EQUITY

Capital		
Contributed capital		$ 300,000
Retained earnings		33,014
Total owners' equity		333,014
Total liabilities and owners' equity		$ 348,321

Figure 5
Balance Sheet
End of First Year Reporting

DISCLOSURE REQUIREMENTS

FASB 13 requires the following disclosures that impact both the face of the balance sheet, as well as the footnotes:

For purposes of presenting the investment in a leveraged lease in the lessor's balance sheet, the amount of related deferred taxes shall be presented separately (from the remainder of the net investment), as prescribed in APB Opinion No. 11, *Accounting for Income Taxes*, paragraphs 57, 59, and 64. In the income statement or the notes thereto, separate presentation (from each other) shall be made of pretax income from the leveraged lease, the tax effect of pretax income, and the amount of investment tax credit recognized as income during the period. When leveraged leasing is a significant part of the lessor's business activities in terms of revenue, net income, or assets, the

CASH FLOWS FROM OPERATING ACTIVITIES

Net rental payments	$ 34,714	
Taxes paid	(1,700)	
Net cash provided by operating activities		**$ 33,014**

CASH FLOWS FROM INVESTING ACTIVITIES

Advance rentals	$ 150,000	
Principal received	1,364	
Nonrefundable fees	10,000	
Initial direct costs	(35,000)	
Purchase of leased equipment (net)	(300,000)	
Net cash used in investing activities		(173,636)

CASH FLOWS FROM FINANCING ACTIVITIES

		0

NET DECREASE IN CASH

		($ 140,622)
Cash at the beginning of the year		300,000
Cash at the end of the year		$ 159,378

RECONCILIATION OF NET INCOME TO NET CASH PROVIDED BY OPERATING ACTIVITIES

Net income	$ 33,014	
Net cash provided by operating activities		**$ 33,014**

SUPPLEMENTAL SCHEDULE OF NONCASH INVESTING AND FINANCING ACTIVITIES

Borrowed $700,000 nonrecourse debt to fund a leveraged lease. (Although the cash account was impacted no debt appears and, therefore, the transaction has the same effect as a noncash investment.)

DISCLOSURE OF ACCOUNTING POLICY

The direct method of cash flow operating sources is shown on a gross basis, as promulgated in FASB Statement No. 95 (FASB 95).

Figure 6
Statement of Cash Flows
(direct method per FASB 95)
End of First Year Reporting

components of the net investment balance in leveraged leases as set forth in paragraph 43 shall be disclosed in the footnotes to the financial statements . . . [FASB 13, paragraph 47].

An illustration of the presentation of a leveraged lease in the balance sheet, income statement and cash flow statement has been presented. Footnote disclosure of the same leveraged lease, regarding the lessor's investment in leveraged leases, might appear as follows.

The company is the lessor in a leveraged lease agreement entered into January 1, 19XX, under which manufacturing equipment, having an estimated economic life of 12 years, was leased for a noncancellable term of 10 years. The company's at-risk investment in the lease represented 30% of the equipment's $1,000,000 purchase price. The remaining 70% of the purchase price was provided by third-party financing in the form of a long-term (10-year) note payable that is nonrecourse to the company and is secured by a first lien on the equipment. At the end of the lease term, the equipment is expected to be returned to the company (although the lessee has the option to purchase the equipment for its then established fair market value). The residual value at its return is estimated to be 10% of the original $1,000,000 cost. The company will not utilize any ITC and has the benefit of the following tax deductible expenses: 5-year MACRS deductions on the entire equipment cost, initial direct costs and interest expense on the nonrecourse debt. During the early years of the lease, the cash flow benefits derived from those deductions, as well as the net lease rentals (rentals less nonrecourse debt service), allow the company's initial investment to be totally recouped, plus a substantial excess. In the later years of the lease, when all tax deductions, except interest expense, have been exhausted, rental income will be almost completely unsheltered. Rental income less nonrecourse debt payments at this point will be insufficient to cover the associated tax liabilities, resulting in negative cash flows. In effect, negative cash flows represent reinvestment in the lease, which will counterbalance any excess returns received in earlier years.

The company's net investment in leveraged leases is composed of the following elements.

Rentals receivable (net of principal and interest on the nonrecourse debt)	$ 174,707
Deferred initial direct costs	15,790
ITC receivable	0
Estimated residual value of leased equipment	100,000
Gross investment in leveraged leases	$ 290,497
Less: Unearned and deferred income	(101,554)
Investment in leveraged leases	$ 188,943
Less deferred tax credits arising from leveraged leases	15,307
Net investment in leveraged leases	$ 173,636

DISINVESTMENT BALANCES IN THE FINANCIAL STATEMENTS

During the life of a leveraged lease, the lessor's net investment frequently will decline to the point of becoming a disinvestment (credit balance). By the end of the lease, the disinvestment balance usually returns to zero or to a normal (debit) balance. This section is concerned with the cause of disinvestment balances, their financial statement impact and the use of debt optimization as a means of eliminating them.

The Cause of Disinvestment Balances

It is erroneously assumed by many of those who analyze leveraged leases that disinvestment balances are caused solely by the loss of tax benefits in the later years of a lease, when MACRS deductions are gone and interest expense is at a minimum. Although such loss of tax benefits reduces net after-tax cash inflows, it is really the debt repayment schedule that causes negative cash flows, which then lead to disinvestment balances. Note in Table 6, based on the preceding lease, that there are no negative cash flows before the lease is funded with nonrecourse debt. Hence, it must be assumed that the funding caused the negative cash flows. In fact, it easily can be shown that a debt repayment schedule can be contrived that eliminates negative cash flows (although the lease's yield would be altered and certain IRS tests no longer may be met). Since negative cash flows did not exist before funding, and since certain funding methods also avoid creating negative cash flows, it follows that the debt funding method, and not loss of tax benefits, causes negative cash flows and their resultant disinvestment balances.

A disinvestment balance occurs in the balance sheet when, on a given date, the deferred tax credit associated with a particular lease exceeds the leveraged lease's net investment (without considering the credit). For example, at the end of the fifth year the net investment in the leveraged lease example of this chapter would appear as follows:

Lease rentals receivable (net of nonrecourse debt)	$ 30,395	
Deferred initial direct costs	0	
Unguaranteed residual	100,000	
Gross investment in leveraged lease	$ 130,395	
Unearned and deferred items	0	
Net investment in leveraged lease	$ 130,395	(debit)
Less related deferred tax credits	(171,580)	(credit)
Net adjusted investment in leveraged lease	($ 41,185)	(credit)

Note that if the relatively large $171,580 deferred tax credit were not offset against the net investment in the lease, there would not be a disinvestment balance.

Table 6
Cash Flows Before Debt Funding

	1	2	3	4	5	6
					Income Tax	
	Lease Rentals		Initial Direct	Taxable	(Benefit)	Annual Net
Year	/Residual	MACRS	Costs (Net)	Income (Loss)	Expense[6]	Cash Flow[7]
0	$ 150,000	$ 0	$ 25,000	$ 0	$ 0	($ 875,000)[8]
1	150,000	200,000	0	75,000[9]	25,500	124,500
2	150,000	320,000	0	(170,000)	(57,800)	207,800
3	150,000	192,000	0	(42,000)	(14,280)	164,280
4	150,000	115,200	0	34,800	11,832	138,168
5	150,000	115,200	0	34,800	11,832	138,168
6	150,000	57,600	0	92,400	31,416	118,584
7	150,000	0	0	150,000	51,000	99,000
8	150,000	0	0	150,000	51,000	99,000
9	150,000	0	0	150,000	51,000	99,000
10	100,000	0	0	100,000	34,000	66,000
	$ 1,600,000	$ 1,000,000	$ 25,000	$ 575,000	$ 195,500	$ 379,500

Financial Statement Treatment of Disinvestment Balances

Since generally accepted accounting principles do not allow deferred tax credits to be offset against the assets that give rise to them, a disinvestment balance per se will seldom appear on the balance sheet. Although leveraged lease income is allocated only to those years that begin with a normal (debit) investment balance, and not to years with disinvestment balances, this disinvestment balance never appears as such on the balance sheet. It is only when the associated deferred tax credits are offset against the net investment (for analytical and income allocation purposes), and the deferred tax credit exceeds the lease receivable, that an overall disinvestment

---

[6] Column 4 × .34.

[7] Column 1 – 3 ± 5.

[8]
Investment	($1,000,000)
Advance payment and fee	150,000
Initial direct costs	(25,000)
	($ 875,000)

[9]
Advance rental	$ 150,000
First year rental payment	150,000
Less: MACRS	(200,000)
Initial direct costs (net)	(25,000)
Taxable income	$ 75,000

balance occurs. Table 7 shows the end of year investment balances of the preceding leveraged lease. The first column of Table 7 represents the net investment in leveraged leases as shown on the face of the balance sheet. The last column is the lessor's true, economic investment in the lease.

Note that only at the end of the ninth year was there a disinvestment balance that was not caused by the deferred tax credit offset. Practically speaking, the ninth year's financial statement disinvestment balance would be offset against the normal investment balances of other leveraged leases in the portfolio of the lessor. However, if there were no other leases, the disinvestment credit balance would appropriately appear as a deferred credit (not a long-term liability, but, rather, as a separate element of the liability section of the balance sheet).

If disinvestment balances are considered a problem (as they are in the minds of some analysts), they can be eliminated by paying off the debt in such a manner that no negative cash flows occur. This technique of arranging the way debt is repaid is commonly referred to as debt optimization. An example of such a loan, along with its payment amortization, appears in Table 8. Based on the loan in Table 8, the after-tax, after funding net cash flow in the leveraged lease is shown in column 8 of Table 9.

Table 7
Investment/Disinvestment Balances

Year	Unadjusted Net Investment in Leveraged Lease	Cumulative Deferred Tax Credit[10]	Adjusted Net Investment (Disinvestment)[11]
0	$ 175,000	$ 0	$ 175,000
1	188,943	15,307	173,636
2	202,496	112,289	90,207
3	192,203	156,000	36,203
4	166,473	166,543	(70)
5	130,395	171,580	(41,185)
6	94,317	154,847	(60,530)
7	58,239	116,125	(57,886)
8	22,161	74,757	(52,596)
9	(13,917)	30,479	(44,396)
10	0	0	0

[10] From Table 5.
[11] From Table 2.

Table 8
Optimized Debt Repayment

Year	Loan Payment	Interest	Principal Paid	Remaining Loan Balance
1	$ 70,000	$ 70,000	$ 0	$ 700,000
2	70,000	70,000	0	700,000
3	162,657	70,000	92,657	607,343
4	158,818	60,735	98,083	509,260
5	155,483	50,926	104,557	404,703
6	132,344	40,470	91,874	312,829
7	109,636	31,283	78,353	234,476
8	106,973	23,448	83,525	150,951
9	104,132	15,095	89,037	61,914
10	68,105	6,191	61,914	0
	$ 1,138,148	$ 438,148	$ 700,000	$ 0

An amortization of the annual net cash flow reveals there is no longer a disinvestment balance. Although the problem of the disinvestment balance has been eliminated, the solution has altered several other analytical aspects of the lease.

For instance, Table 10 shows how the IRR is altered when the disinvestment balance is changed. When there are no disinvestment balances in a lease, its IRR will be equal to its MISF. The IRR equals 26.685834% and the MISF is the same.

Notice that the IRR of the investment in this leveraged lease (with optimized debt) is 26.685834%, whereas the IRR of the lease with negative cash flows was 22.517541%, with an MISF of 18.865076%. Do not be misled by this seemingly significant improvement of investment return, since the present values of the cash flows tell a different story if the company can only reinvest its cash flow at an after-tax rate of below 6.600708% but above 1.046276% (see Table 11).

Refer to Chapter Seven for a complete explanation of the proper investment choice between these two alternatives. Even though the new funding method has eliminated disinvestment balances and negative cash flows, improved net undiscounted cash flows and increased the investment's IRR, it still may be the less desirable alternative when considered in light of the lessor's reinvestment opportunities, as the net present values in Table 11 indicate. At reinvestment rates less than 6.600%, but greater than 1.046%, the present values of cash flows for the lease with negative cash flows are greater than the debt optimized cash flows.

Table 9
Optimized Leveraged Lease Cash Flows

Year	1 Lease Rentals/ Residual	2 MACRS	3 Initial Direct Costs (Net)	4 Loan Interest Expense	5 Taxable Income (Loss)	6 Income Tax (Benefit) or Expense	7 Loan Principal	8 Annual Net Cash Flow
0	$ 150,000	$ 0	$25,000	$ 0	$ 0	$ 0	$ 0	($175,000)
1	150,000	200,000	0	70,000	5,000	1,700	0	78,300
2	150,000	320,000	0	70,000	(240,000)	(81,600)	0	161,600
3	150,000	192,000	0	70,000	(112,000)	(38,080)	92,657	25,423
4	150,000	115,200	0	60,735	(25,935)	(8,818)	98,083	0
5	150,000	115,200	0	50,926	(16,126)	(5,483)	104,557	0
6	150,000	57,600	0	40,470	51,930	17,656	91,874	0
7	150,000	0	0	31,283	118,717	40,364	78,353	0
8	150,000	0	0	23,448	126,552	43,028	83,525	0[12]
9	150,000	0	0	15,095	134,905	45,868	89,037	0
10	100,000	0	0	6,191	93,809	31,895	61,914	0
	$1,600,000	$1,000,000	$25,000	$438,148	$136,852	$46,530	$700,000	$ 90,323

[12] Rounding error.

Table 10
Amortization (IRR) of Optimized Cash Flows

Year	Cash Flow	IRR Interest	Principal	Balance
0	$ 0.00	$ 0.00	$ 0.00	($ 175,000.00)
1	78,300.00	46,700.21	31,599.79	(143,400.21)
2	161,600.00	38,267.54	123,332.46	(20,067.75)
3	25,423.00	5,355.25	20,067.75	0.00
4	0.00	0.00	0.00	0.00
5	0.00	0.00	0.00	0.00
6	0.00	0.00	0.00	0.00
7	0.00	0.00	0.00	0.00
8	0.00	0.00	0.00	0.00
9	0.00	0.00	0.00	0.00
10	0.00	0.00	0.00	0.00
	$ 265,323.00	$ 90,323.00	$175,000.000	$ 0.00

Table 11
Net Present Value of Cash Flows

Reinvestment Rates	Lease with Optimized Debt	Lease with Negative Cash Flows	
0.000000%	$ 90,323	$ 89,618	
1.046276	85,401	85,401	(breakeven point)
3.000000	76,609	77,206	
4.000000	72,298	72,912	
5.000000	68,108	68,586	
6.600708	61,646	61,646	(breakeven point)
7.000000	60,078	59,918	
10.000000	48,836	47,103	

SIGNIFICANT CHANGES IN ASSUMPTIONS

Changes in any important assumptions affecting the estimated total net income to be derived from a leveraged lease, such as residual assumptions, income tax rate assumptions, depreciation deductions, etc., require a revision in the accounts affecting the net investment in the lease. The revisions will be similar to those required of a company that changes an accounting principle, i.e., the new principle will be applied retroactively and the catch up effect (cumulative effect) of applying the new accounting principle will be shown as a gain or loss in the current income statement. This cumulative effect approach differs from a change in accounting estimate where no immediate income statement impact is shown. FASB 13 mandates the cumulative effect approach:

> . . . If during the lease term the estimate of the residual value is determined to be excessive . . . or if the revision of another important assumption changes the estimated total net income from the lease, the rate of return and the allocation of income to positive investment years shall be recalculated from the inception of the lease . . . The accounts constituting the net investment balance shall be adjusted to conform to the recalculated balances, and the change in the net investment shall be recognized as a gain or loss in the year in which the assumption is changed . . . [FASB 13, paragraph 46].

FASB Technical Bulletin No. 79-16, concerning the effect of a change in tax rates on leveraged leases, reaffirms the requirement for the cumulative effect approach when a change in tax rate occurs, since a tax rate alteration is deemed to be a change in important assumptions. Note that residual values cannot be written up even though tax rates can be lowered. This seems inconsistent since both result in gains; nevertheless, residual write-up gains are not allowed.

An example of the cumulative effect approach procedure appears in Table 12 where the same lease example (with negative cash flows) used in the preceding sections undergoes two important changes in assumptions: (1) the estimated unguaranteed residual value is reduced to $50,000 and (2) the income tax rate at the beginning of the fifth year of the lease is increased from 34% to 40%, where it remains for the duration of the lease. The first step is to recalculate the net after-tax cash flow in the lease given the changed assumptions, followed by a recalculation of the MISF earnings, as shown in Table 13.

Having established the newly expected after-tax cash flows and consequent MISF earnings, the adjusting entries that will result in an immediately recognized gain or loss must be determined. The adjusting entries are determined by subtraction. The elements of the new net investment in the lease are subtracted from the corresponding elements of the old net investment. The difference results in the adjusting entry, as computed in Table 14.

Table 12
Recalculation of After-tax Cash Flows

	1	2	3	4	5	6	7	8
Year	Lease Rentals/ Residual	MACRS	Initial Direct Costs (Net)	Loan Interest Expense	Taxable Income (Loss)	Income Tax Benefit or (Expense)	Loan Principal	Annual Net Cash Flow
0	$ 150,000	$ 0	$ 25,000	$ 0	$ 0	$ 0	$ 0	($ 175,000)
1	150,000	200,000	0	70,000	5,000	1,700	43,922	34,378
2	150,000	320,000	0	65,608	(235,608)	(80,107)	48,314	116,185
3	150,000	192,000	0	60,776	(102,776)	(34,944)	53,146	71,022
4	150,000	115,200	0	55,462	(20,662)	(7,025)[13]	58,460	43,103
5	150,000	115,200	0	49,616	(14,816)	(5,926)	64,306	42,004
6	150,000	57,600	0	43,185	49,215	19,686	70,737	16,392
7	150,000		0	36,111	113,889	45,556	77,811	(9,478)
8	150,000	0	0	28,330	121,670	48,668	85,592	(12,590)
9	150,000	0	0	19,771	130,229	52,092	94,151	(16,014)
10	50,000	0	0	10,356	39,644	15,858	103,561	(79,775)
	$ 1,550,000	$ 1,000,000	$ 25,000	$ 439,215	$ 85,785	$ 55,558	$ 700,000	$ 30,227

[13] The tax rate increases from 34% to 40% during the 5th year on.

Table 13
Multiple Investment Sinking Fund Earnings
(MISF rate: 7.950839%)

Year	Cash Flow	Interest	Principal	Balance
0	$ 0.00	$ 0.00	$ 0.00	($ 175,000.00)
1	34,378.00	13,913.97	20,464.03	(154,535.97)
2	116,185.00	12,286.91	103,898.09	(50,637.88)
3	71,022.00	4,026.12	66,995.88	16,358.00
4	43,103.00	0.00	43,103.00	59,461.00
5	42,004.00	0.00	42,004.00	101,465.00
6	16,392.00	0.00	16,392.00	117,857.00
7	(9,478.00)	0.00	(9,478.00)	108,379.00
8	(12,590.00)	0.00	(12,590.00)	95,789.00
9	(16,014.00)	0.00	(16,014.00)	79,775.00
10	(79,775.00)	0.00	(79,775.00)	0.00
	$ 205,227.00	$ 30,227.00	$ 175,000.00	$ 0.00

The journal entry required to restate the lease on the balance sheet is:

Loss on leveraged lease	$ 59,391	
Unguaranteed residual		$ 50,000
Deferred tax credit		$ 9,391

To record a loss due to a reduction of residual estimate
from $100,00 to $50,000, and an increase in tax rates from
34% to 40% in the 5th year

The loss on the lease makes sense since before the changes the total after-tax earnings were expected to be $89,618, but the changes lowered the expectation to $30,227 (see the cash flow analysis in Table 12). The difference between the two earnings totals is $59,391. Since the total earnings in the leveraged lease had already been recorded per the MISF amortization, there was no alternative but to show a cumulative effect catch-up loss of $59,391. From the time of this adjustment on normal leveraged lease, accounting is followed, but the new MISF earnings table is consulted. In this case, however, since all earnings have already been recorded, the only entries remaining affect the lease receivable and the deferred tax credit accounts. At the termination of the lease the residual account would be closed out.

Table 14
Adjusting Entry Computation
Beginning of Fifth Year

	Old Net Investment	Newly Adjusted Net Investment	Difference	
Lease receivable	$ 66,473	$ 66,473	$ 0	
Residual	100,000	50,000	50,000	Credit
Initial direct costs	0	0	0	
ITC receivable	0	0	0	
Gross investment	$ 166,473	$ 116,473	$ 50,000	Credit
Unearned income	0	0		
Net investment	$ 166,473	$ 116,473	$ 50,000	Credit
Deferred tax credit	(166,543)	(175,934)	9,391	Credit
Adjusted net investment	($ 70)	($ 59,461)	$ 59,391	Debit

AVOIDING LEVERAGED LEASE ACCOUNTING

There are seven common methods of avoiding the required FASB 13 MISF accounting for leveraged leases. MISF accounting frequently understates, for book purposes, the true economics of a leveraged lease. This is due to its zero sinking fund earnings assumption, which means the net investment in leveraged leases does not show any earnings in disinvestment balance years. Note that avoidance of MISF accounting may result in improved income statement treatment, but may simultaneously result in the nonrecourse debt appearing on the balance sheet.

1. Convert the direct financing leveraged lease to a sales-type capital lease. Sales-type capital leases are precluded from leveraged lease treatment. Without leveraged lease status, MISF income recognition is eliminated and actuarial methods replace it; however, the nonrecourse debt would appear as a liability on the lessor's balance sheet. Moreover, it is difficult to make a lease into a sales-type lease since the equipment must be purchased at less than fair market value to create a sales-type lease

2. Consolidate a captive leveraged lease lessor with its parent. Previously, if a captive finance company had purchased parent manufactured equipment at retail, a direct financing lease at the captive level would have resulted, causing leveraged lease treatment (assuming all other leveraged lease criteria had been met). However, if the captive subsidiary is consolidated as required by FASB Statement No. 94 (FASB 94), the lease would become a sales-type lease. Sales-type leases resulting from consolidation will not qualify for leveraged lease treatment, as indicated by FASB 94

3. Employ the ITC flow-through method of accounting for ITC, if and when available. Leveraged lease accounting requires the deferral method of accounting for ITC. Use of

the flow-through method causes the lease to revert to direct financing capital lease status. Direct financing leases are accounted for actuarily, but their nonrecourse debt is required to appear as a lessor liability

4. Fund the direct financing lease subsequent to its inception. Leases funded after their inception are considered either sales or pledges, depending upon the nature of the assignment agreement that transfers rights to the buyer or lender (see Chapter Eleven for an in-depth discussion). Lease assignments frequently result in the disappearance of the nonrecourse debt from the balance sheet. Furthermore, the assignment may result in the entire leveraged lease's income (net interest income less nonrecourse interest expense) being recognized in total in the income statement on the date of the assignment

5. Debt optimize the lease to remove negative cash flows. The lease's debt can be structured in such a manner that negative cash flows no longer exist in the lease. Elimination of all negative cash flows automatically eliminates disinvestment balances as well as prevents the net investment from undulating. Without the ebb and flow of the net investment balance, the lease no longer qualifies as leveraged, per FASB 13. Even if it were still considered a leveraged lease, the MISF interest rate in it would be equal to its after-tax IRR, since there would be no sinking fund assumptions, earnings or balances

6. Shorten the noncancellable lease term to equal the asset's IRS depreciation life. Equating of a lease's term with its MACRS or other IRS depreciation lives eliminates most negative cash flows and consequent disinvestment balances in the same manner as number 5

7. Convert the lease to an operating lease by employing some of the same techniques described in Chapter Twelve on structuring operating leases. Such operating leases to the lessor are not given leveraged lease accounting treatment, which is reserved exclusively for direct financing capital leases.

CONCLUSION

Leveraged leases are defined many different ways (tax, industry or accounting) by many different people, depending upon the perspective of the one defining the lease. Although leveraged lease accounting is related to that of direct financing capital leases, leveraged leases are accounted for on an after-interest expense, after-tax basis. The direct financing lease is accounted for on a preinterest, pretax basis. In addition, leveraged leases employ MISF interest recognition for accounting purposes. Due to the large size and, hence, impact of leveraged leases on the financial statements, many lessors also structure leveraged leases using MISF. While leveraged lease accounting is complex, the large ticket size, variety of transactions and interaction of accounting and financial theory make this an exciting area of leasing.

PART 5
SPECIAL TOPICS

CHAPTER SEVENTEEN
CAPTIVES AND VENDOR PROGRAMS

When manufacturing companies, distributors or equipment merchandizing dealers employ leasing as a means of selling their products, they are known as vendor lessors. Frequently a manufacturer or dealer will establish a wholly-owned subsidiary to perform the leasing function. These subsidiary leasing companies are referred to as captive lessors. Since the majority of vendor lessor companies use this subsidiary approach in structuring their vendor leasing programs, the terms vendor leasing and captive leasing sometimes are used interchangeably, a fact that causes some confusion. In this chapter, the term vendor leasing refers to any program, including captives, in which a manufacturer, distributor or dealer employs leasing as a means of selling its product.

This chapter has five major divisions:

- Reasons for Establishing Vendor Leasing Programs
- Impact of Consolidating Captives with Their Corporate Parents
- Techniques for Transferring Tax Benefits to Captives
- Methods of Minimizing and Identifying Leasing Risks
- Methods of Servicing Vendor Lessors by Third-Party Lessors.

REASONS FOR ESTABLISHING VENDOR LEASING PROGRAMS

There are numerous reasons prompting the establishment of vendor leasing programs. In this chapter the various reasons have, somewhat arbitrarily, been sorted into seven groups. It should be understood that few, if any, companies have established vendor programs for all the reasons that will be described. Most were established primarily for marketing reasons, while a few were created for the tax benefits that vendor leasing programs generate. The seven major groups of reasons for the creation of vendor leasing programs, of which captives are a subset, are:

- Market Control
- Market Enhancement
- Ancillary Income
- Tax Benefits
- Financial Leverage
- Services to the Parent
- Miscellaneous Reasons.

Market Control

It has been said that:

> He who controls the past controls the future.
> He who controls the present controls the past.

Although this epigram has been applied to the communist control over written history, it can also apply to vendor leasing. If an equipment sale can be controlled at its inception, and subsequently during the lease term, the future disposition of the leased equipment also will be controlled. It is hoped such control will result in a new sale.

Control over the initial acquisition of equipment is important and can be achieved through leasing. Assume, for example, that a potential customer has just decided to acquire some equipment, but is unwilling to sign a purchase order until financing has been obtained (whether lease or loan financing). Without on-the-spot financing offered by a vendor financing program, any of the following events may occur:

1. While seeking financing, the potential customer might lose interest in the equipment — a type of premature buyer's remorse
2. A funding source of the potential customer might dissuade the customer from leasing the equipment, and in turn persuade it to acquire another competing product. Remember, many lessors own dealerships that promote their own products
3. The potential customer might become discouraged, not with the product, but with the hassle involved in obtaining financing
4. During the time period required to search for financing, a competitor might convince the potential customer that its product is superior.

Once a customer is sold on the merits of a product, it is best to close the sale immediately to avoid any risks of a lost sale. A vendor program offering on-the-spot financing can facilitate and expedite a closing. Another reason for control over the initial acquisition process is the manufacturer or dealer would not want to lose any potential financing profit or any of the other control advantages provided by a lease's ongoing contractual relationship with the customer.

Once customer financing has been initially provided through leasing, another important control function begins and continues through the lease term. Ongoing control throughout the lease term influences the purchase by the lessee of additional lessor products and services. Since the lessee has constant monthly contact with the lessor (remitting of monthly rental payments), should a lessee need arise for additional services or products, the lessor will have an advantage in winning the sale. Some leasing companies also include advertising with their monthly billings to promote additional services. Typical products and services provided by vendor lessors during the lease term include equipment parts, supplies (chemicals, reagents, lubricants), maintenance, software, human resources and upgrades to increase efficiency or capacity.

Perhaps the most critical control juncture occurs at the termination of the initial non-cancellable lease term when the lessee must usually choose between three equipment disposition alternatives:

1. Purchase the equipment
2. Renew the lease
3. Return the equipment.

In most cases, the lessee will be contractually bound to inform the lessor in writing, usually 30 to 90 days before the end of the lease term, as to which alternative will be selected. Once the lessee's intentions are known, a salesperson is dispatched to the lessee to attempt to control any future equipment purchases. Even if the lessee intends to purchase or renew the lease on the old equipment, there is potential for upgrading the existing capacity or efficiency without switching to brand new equipment. The lease creates a virtual contractual obligation on the part of the lessee to inform the lessor as to the lessee's future equipment needs. Without this obligation, tracking of changes in a client's equipment needs is much more difficult.

Control over used equipment market prices and availability is provided through vendor leasing programs. Used equipment becomes available to vendor lessors from three basic sources:

1. Equipment returned at the end of the noncancellable lease term
2. Repossessed equipment on defaulted leases
3. Trade-ins on new equipment.

It is important to control the resale price of used equipment to insure that used equipment sales prices are not so low that (1) cross-elasticity problems arise where new equipment sales are reduced, (2) yields in existing vendor leases are reduced because equipment returned at the end of leases is sold for less than the residual values originally used in structuring the leases and (3) operating lease programs are rendered infeasible due to the lessor's inability to realize reasonable residual values.

Low resale values on used equipment result primarily from two causes. The first is technological obsolescence from the customer's viewpoint, and the second is the disposal of equipment by customers at low fire sale prices. Obsolescence is caused by lack of capacity and inefficiency. Capacity obsolescence is relative — what is lack of capacity to one company is not to another. Leasing, with its automatic reversion of equipment to the lessor, allows the lessor to find that other customer whose capacity problems can be met. Were the customer allowed to dispose of the equipment, it might be sold at too low a price. Leasing solves the low resale or fire sale price problem in the same way. When equipment is no longer needed by the lessee, the disposal problem shifts to the lessor who has a greater understanding of the marketplace due to its already in-place marketing organization. Such understanding leads to more objective (usually higher) prices. Then, too, the cross-elasticity problems are solved through market control since the lessor can sell returned equipment in noncompeting foreign markets (economic dumping).

It can be seen that lessor disposal of residuals has several benefits. As resulting resale prices are pushed higher, vendor lease yields will be better maintained. Improved achievability of residual values will make operating leases easier to structure. It is important to note that as manufacturing companies establish vendor leasing programs, it will be in the parent company's best interest to manage the introduction of new equipment in a manner that will not render existing equipment obsolete, thereby diminishing the value of the residual values structured into the vendor's leases. Thus, control over used equipment prices is important to the parent. Where vendor lessors take aggressive stances in reselling returned equipment, rather than viewing the disposal task as a relegated burden, the resulting control will help alleviate problems of low resale value described above.

The last control consideration relates to multiple product acquisition. Equipment users frequently purchase equipment in bundles — one brand of central processing unit, a disc drive from another company and other brands of peripheral equipment all packaged together. The user, of course, does not want to obtain separate financing for each component; therefore, what is known as a blanket lease will probably be sought. Vendor blanket leases generate an element of control, resulting in increased sales (or avoidance of lost sales) since the lessor insures that its product will be part of the bundle. To lose a sale because another independent lessor offered a different product package excluding the vendor's product would be frustrating. Blanket leases are gaining in popularity because they save time by consolidating financing otherwise needed for each individual member product of the group, assure fixed lease rates for multiple pieces of equipment acquired over a prolonged shipment period and lower financing costs due to economies of scale.

In conclusion, vendor programs are created in part to exercise control over critical junctures occurring during the useful life of equipment that affect acquisition, upgrading, disposal and replacement. The primary control objectives achieved through vendor leasing include:

1. Control over the initial acquisition to prevent loss of a sale during the time needed to locate funding
2. Control during the noncancellable lease term to provide for upgrades maintenance, parts, supplies and any other service or product
3. Control over disposition of the equipment, in a manner such that, at lease termination, when the lessee must inform the lessor as to its intent to purchase, renew or return the equipment, the vendor lessor is able to influence the decision towards acquiring the lessor's new equipment
4. Control over the resale prices of used equipment repossessed, returned or traded-in to support lease yields, operating lease programs, and avoid cross-elasticity problems with competing new products
5. Control over blanket leasing to insure that the lessor's product is part of the multiple product package.

Market Enhancement

Both the size and quality of a manufacturer's sales market can be enhanced through leasing. The quality of the market is improved by obtaining increases in gross profit margins. How are profit margins improved? Increased margins result from avoidance of list price discounting. If the only tool a salesperson is given to achieve a sale is discounting of list price, it is certain the tool will be well-worn. On the other hand, if the product attributes and financing services are combined in such a manner that the financial package is differentiated from those of competitors (while better meeting the equipment user's needs), a sale might occur without excessive discounting of list price. Avoidance of list price discounting occurs because the combined product and financial package diverts the customer's attention from the primary emphasis of purchase price. The elements of a lease (term, rate, purchase options, etc.) provide the salesperson with additional marketing tools that serve to distract the lessee. In many instances, where financing costs are not fully understood by the lessee, such diversion away from list price discounting is easily attainable. However, many lessees are astute and distraction is difficult. Nevertheless, when full-service leasing is used, where other services such as maintenance are bundled in the lease, it is difficult for even astute lessees to determine the real cost of leasing. In summary, differentiated financial product packages that better meet customer needs result in both a preservation of profit margin and an expansion of sales volume.

The use of rental programs (or rent-to-buy programs) that entice lessees to purchase equipment by allowing part of each rental payment to accrue towards the purchase price is another technique vendors use to expand sales volume. This "try it, you'll like it" approach is valuable for both parties. Although the lessee may return the equipment at any time, the lessor has received at least partial investment recovery from the rentals received. Furthermore, changing the equipment's status from inventory to that of leased equipment provides the lessor with three tax benefits not otherwise available had the equipment remained idle as inventory awaiting sale:

1. Modified Accelerated Cost Recovery System (MACRS) depreciation tax deductions
2. Investment Tax Credit (ITC) based on the manufacturer's cost (when and if available)
3. Gross profit tax deferral.

Operating lease programs designed to provide the lessee with a reasonable hedge against obsolescence as well as off balance sheet financing are an extension of the rental programs just described. In the operating lease, the noncancellable period is greater than that typically available in a rental program (1 to 6 months), but is still less than a capital lease. Frequently, for example, computers will be leased on a 36-month basis, which usually results in the lease being classified as operating from an accounting viewpoint. The operating lease is the only method of financing certain customers will consider. If the manufacturer does not provide an operating lease program, and assuming third-party lessors will not provide them due to uncertainty concerning residual values, etc., a sale might be lost. Thus, where operating lease and rental programs meet important legitimate financing needs of the lessee, sales volume will be increased.

Another method of expanding sales volume is through takeout-rollover leasing programs. A takeout is where the lessor takes out of the customer's possession existing equipment so that the lessor's new equipment can be installed. Takeouts are performed by lessors in several ways:

1. If the existing equipment is subject to an existing lease or loan, the vendor lessor may:
   a. Pay an early out penalty and return the equipment to the lessor
   b. Purchase the equipment by paying off the lease and either salvage it or re-lease it to others, or take the equipment as a trade-in on new equipment

    c. Continue, extend or renew the existing lease, but take out the equipment and sublease to others

    d. Pay off any existing loan plus prepayment penalties, if any, and salvage, re-lease to others or trade in on new equipment

  2. If the existing equipment is debt or lease free the lessor may:

    a. Salvage the equipment for the customer

    b. Lease the equipment to others

    c. Take the equipment as a trade-in on the lessor's new replacement equipment.

If the equipment once purchased by the lessor cannot be sold or re-leased for an amount sufficient to defray the takeout cost, a deficiency will be incurred by the lessor. Such deficits are reimbursed to the lessor by rollovers where the deficits are financed (rolled over) by one of several methods:

  1. Lessor adds the deficit to the new equipment's cost, resulting in a higher lease payment over the term of the new lease

  2. Same as 1 above except the lease is a step-down lease where, for example, the lessor recoups the deficit over 24 months after which lease payments are reduced during the remaining 36 months of a 60-month lease term

  3. An installment loan apart from the lease is provided the lessee.

Sales volume as well as asset turnover are increased since the customer has been induced to acquire the new equipment now rather than waiting until the end of an existing lease or loan arrangement. Note that the take-out-rollover approach also can be used to remove the vendor's own equipment to facilitate replacement with newer more expensive equipment.

Market penetration for new products is achieved through leasing by (1) lease subsidy programs and (2) rental programs. Lease subsidy programs provide financing at such low rates the customer is tempted to buy the product now rather than later and this product rather than another. Rental programs, described earlier, allow the lessee to try out a piece of equipment before making a long-term commitment.

One technique related to subsidizing leases employs full-service leasing. The equipment is given an extremely low rental payment coupled with an extended maintenance or supplies purchase agreement. The lessor recoups its costs from profit on the bundled services instead of from the rental payments.

Vendor guarantee programs also can result in increased sales volume through assisting others in providing financing to the manufacturer's customers. In the situation where the manufacturer is reluctant to finance its sales due to constraints such as limited borrowing capacity, or lack of leasing knowledge concerning credit, accounting, legal and managerial procedures, etc., third-party lessors might provide the required equipment financing and other services at attractive rates, thus promoting and increasing sales. Frequently, however, these independent lessors will require vendor guarantees to mitigate lessor residual risk on high-tech equipment that is deemed too risky and difficult to resell. To overcome such perceived risk on the part of the independent lessor, vendors offer several types of guarantees, which include the following:

  1. Priority remarketing agreements that require priority effort from the manufacturer in the reselling of the returned equipment ahead of new equipment

2. Repurchase agreements that require the vendor to repurchase lessor equipment that has been returned or repossessed

3. Net loss indemnity agreements that provide for loss reimbursements by vendors to independent lessors for losses of any sort (repossessions, salvaging, etc.) up to a certain percentage (say 3 to 5%) of a block of leases funded over a fixed time period by the independent lessor.

Vendor guarantees also can be used to assist wholesalers or distributors who aid the manufacturer in making sales. To the degree these parties require financing on behalf of their customers, the manufacturers can assist by providing vendor guarantees on products they have financed for their customers.

In conclusion, market enhancement results from:

1. Reduction or elimination of discounts off list price by directing attention to other financial considerations of a lease

2. Improvement of sales volume through product differentiation obtained by the unique combination of product attributes, financial services and other bundled services

3. Enhancement of sales volume through the offering of operating lease and rental programs that meet certain lessee needs not met by other financing alternatives

4. Expedition of asset turnover through takeout-rollover programs that result in removal of competitor's equipment before the end of the equipment's lease term

5. Expansion of market penetration for new products through rental programs and lease subsidies

6. Improvement of dealer sales through vendor guarantee programs that offer incentives for others to offer financing for customers.

Ancillary Income

In addition to the primary sale of the parent's products, the vendor leasing program may generate additional ancillary profits and benefits. These income and benefit sources are grouped into interest spread, sales-type lease gross profit, full-service leasing and residual profit.

INTEREST SPREAD

Whether a vendor lessor is leasing its parent's products or noncompeting products manufactured by others, there generally will be a difference between the interest earned in the lease and the interest expense incurred on the debt used to fund the lease. This spread between interest income and interest expense is an important source of profit for vendor programs. Interest earned, in this context, does not include the value of tax benefits associated with the lease.

Interest spread appears in the lessor's financial statements as income over the life of the lease when the vendor lessor retains the lease in its portfolio. Should the vendor lessor choose to sell the lease or pledge it as collateral for a match funded loan, the interest spread may or may not be shown as income over the lease term, depending upon whether the assignment of the lease is deemed a sale or pledge, and whether the sale or pledge is with recourse or not.

Outright sales of leases are governed, from an accounting point of view, by Financial Accounting Standards Board Statement No. 13 (FASB 13), paragraphs 20-22, and FASB Statement No. 77 (FASB 77). (Refer to Chapter Eleven for a more in-depth analysis of funding techniques.) Some view FASB 13, paragraph 20, as stating that the sale of a direct financing or sales-type capital lease without recourse (the buyer of the lease may not look to the seller upon lessee default) and between unrelated parties will result in the total interest spread being shown all at once at the time of the sale without any proration over the lease term. An example of sales treatment of a lease is shown in Table 1.

The $4,910 difference between the lease's net investment of $100,000 and the sale proceeds of $104,910 represents the interest spread between the lease's $44,000 unearned interest income and the loan's $39,090 interest expense. Sales treatment requires the $4,910 of interest spread to be shown, in total, as income as of the transaction date. Sometimes the lessor sells only the rental payment stream without the residual being sold. This transaction still might result in immediate gain recognition, in which case the residual would remain on the lessor's books until the end of the lease term.

If, however, the sale of the lease is with recourse, the sales treatment just described may or may not be afforded the transaction. FASB 77 provides for sales treatment if all of the following three criteria are met:

> The transferor surrenders control of the future economic benefits embodied in the receivables. Control has not been surrendered if the transferor has an option to repurchase the receivables at a later date. A right of first refusal based on a bona fide offer by an unrelated third party ordinarily is not an option to repurchase.

Table 1
Sale of Capital Lease

	Lessor Viewpoint		Purchaser Viewpoint	
Gross investment	$ 129,000[1]	Purchaser proceeds		$ 144,000
Unguaranteed residual	15,000			
Less unearned interest	(44,000)	Interest expense		(39,090)
Net investment	$ 100,000[2]	Sale proceeds		$ 104,910[3]

[1]60 rentals at $2,150, in arrears.
[2]Equipment cost of $100,000, which is equal to the net investment.
[3]Present value of the lease rentals and expected $15,000 residual discounted at the buyer's required 12% annual yield requirement.

1		i	
2,150	g	CF_j	
59	g	N_j	
17,150	g	CF_j	
	f	NPV	104,910

The transferor's obligation under the recourse provisions can be reasonably estimated. Lack of experience with receivables with characteristics similar to those being transferred or other factors that affect a determination at the transfer date of the collectibility of the receivables may impair the ability to make a reasonable estimate of the probable bad debt losses and related costs of collections and repossessions. A transfer of receivables shall not be recognized as a sale if collectibility of the receivables and related costs of collection and repossession are not subject to reasonable estimation.

The transferee cannot require the transferor to repurchase the receivable except pursuant to the recourse provisions. Some transfer agreements require or permit the transferor to repurchase transferred receivables when the amount of outstanding receivables is minor to keep the cost of servicing those receivables from becoming unreasonable. If those reversionary interests are not significant to the transferor, their existence alone does not preclude a transfer from being recognized as a sale [FASB 77, paragraph 5(a), (b) and (c)].

Thus, if all of the preceding criteria are met, even though the transfer or assignment of the lease is with recourse, the transfer will be treated as a sale. Remember, sales treatment front-loads all the $4,910 of interest spread at the time of transfer. If any or all of the FASB 77 criteria are not met, then the transfer is accorded loan treatment where the sale proceeds are shown as a loan and the interest spread is taken into income over the life of the lease, even though it has been assigned to the purchaser.

Typically, in the outright sale of leases or receivables, the lessor/transferor would probably lose any tax benefits such as MACRS or gross profit tax deferral. Many lessors, however, structure their transfers or assignments of leases as collateral pledges instead of outright sales. If the appropriate tax laws, rulings and regulations (at-risk provisions, etc.) have been met in the collateral pledge, the lessor may generally retain the tax benefits. Thus, the collateral transfer is not deemed a sale, but merely a pledge of a lease to secure the repayment of a loan whose term matches the assigned lease. From an accounting viewpoint, pledges pose a problem. There are no authoritative, generally accepted accounting principles that cover such arrangements. Many lessors use sale treatment if the pledge is without recourse and employ loan treatment when the collateralization is with recourse. Refer to Chapter Eleven for a more in-depth coverage of lease assignment accounting.

In the case of a sale of a lease, there might be additional profit for the lessor/transferor beyond the interest spread, as the MACRS tax benefits can be transferred to the purchaser. Since lease benefits have significant value, the purchaser typically pays a brokerage or finder's fee for the tax benefits in addition to any interest spread. Then, too, the lessor/transferor may continue to service the lease (billing, collections, etc.) for which it would charge a service fee to the purchaser.

Thus, leasing may provide a significant amount of profit to a vendor lessor in the form of interest earned, representing the net interest received over any interest expense incurred in funding leases. This interest spread may be shown in total at the time of a subsequent transfer when the lease is sold, but meets the three criteria of FASB 77, the lease is sold nonrecourse or the lease is pledged on a nonrecourse basis. The interest spread is shown over the term of the lease (usually as a constant return on the declining net investment) when the lease is either retained by the vendor lessor, sold recourse (but fails any or all of the three FASB 77 criteria) or pledged on a full recourse basis. Profit, too, derives from brokerage fees from the sale of tax benefits (when available) and from service fees when the lessor continues to service the lease.

SALES-TYPE CAPITAL LEASE GROSS PROFIT

There are two sources of profit in addition to the gross profit recognized on leases of parent manufactured products: (1) profit derived from purchasing noncompeting equipment at a dealer's wholesale price and (2) profit obtained from lease renewals that qualify as capital leases and meet the criteria of FASB Statement No. 27 (FASB 27), controlling gross profit recognition on lease renewals.

Frequently, vendor lessors, particularly captives, will attempt to become dealers in equipment that is used in conjunction with (but not competing against) their own equipment. Such dealerships create sales-type capital leases and result in a form of horizontal product integration. In addition to replacing lost tax benefits, the sales-type lease makes economic sense when leasing is viewed as fulfilling a service/usage function as opposed to a pure financial function. Buying equipment at a lower cost allows the lessor to take more aggressive residual positions, resulting in more meaningful rentals and operating lease programs.

Another little known source of the sales-type lease is from capital lease renewals that occur at or near the end of their noncancellable terms. If the renewal is a capital lease and not an operating lease and meets the criteria of FASB 27, then any significant difference between the remaining book value of the earlier lease (remaining residual value) and the then established fair market value (assumed to be greater than the book value, resulting in gross profit) will be shown as gross profit at the inception of the lease renewal. Note the lease renewal can be with the original lessee or a new lessee.

Thus, vendor lessors that specialize in particular types of equipment, and thereby become dealers, are able to generate gross profit as another important ancillary source of profit for the parent. Additionally, certain renewals of leases on equipment whose fair market values are above their booked values generate gross profit.

FULL-SERVICE LEASING

The full-service lease, wherein additional products and services are bundled with the lease, increases ancillary income to the degree that these services and products represent incremental sales to the parent. In other words, leasing must generate new sales of bundled services and products, otherwise there would be no net benefit to the parent since these services and products are generally sold to the customer anyway, whether it leases or not.

RESIDUAL PROFIT

To the degree returned equipment can be sold for more than its remaining book value at the end of a lease, residual profit will be earned. Unfortunately there are two ways this might occur — one legitimately and the other expediently. Obvious underbooking of expected residual values at the inception of a lease for the sake of conservatism will lead to gains on the disposal of leased assets. Such understating of expected residuals creates future residual gains, but, at the same time, understates interest earned during the period prior to the termination of the fixed noncancellable term. On the other hand, overbooking of residuals creates losses on equipment disposals preceded by months of overstated interest earned. Only when residuals have been recorded in the accounting records at the lease inception at their anticipated future fair market values (without bias) will true residual speculation gains be known. The residual risk taken by a lessor in rental and operating lease programs deserves a legitimate reward, which will be a gain on the ultimate sale, disposal or salvaging of the equipment. Industry statistics for the past several years have shown that 80 to 85% of lessors sell their equipment for amounts greater than their originally booked residual values.

Tax Benefits

The tax benefits of leasing have been described in detail in Chapter Four; therefore, only those tax benefits germane to vendor leasing will be described here. The primary tax benefits are MACRS and gross profit deferral. The value of MACRS, which is worth one-half to three after-tax, present value percentage points of the equipment's retail selling price, increases the later in the tax year the lease is structured.

Gross profit tax deferral varies in worth depending upon the magnitude of the gross profit, the discount rate applied and the MACRS classlife of the equipment leased. Gross profit tax deferral is approximately worth 58.9 basis points (.59%), present value, after-tax, for each 10% of gross margin on 5-year MACRS equipment, using a 12% parent, after-tax, weighted average cost of capital as a discount rate. Thus, equipment with a 40% gross margin would generate tax savings worth about 2.4% of the equipment's retail sales price.

INSTALLMENT SALE GROSS PROFIT TAX DEFERRAL

When the parent sells equipment on the installment basis to a joint venture in which its captive leasing company owns less than 80%, the parent will receive actuarial gross profit tax deferral worth about 30% more than tax deferral generated by MACRS deductions.

A summary of vendor leasing tax benefits appears in Table 2, along with comparisons with third-party lessors and various approaches to vendor leasing. (All values are expressed as a percent of retail sales price, based on an after-tax present value computation.)

The value of tax benefits to a vendor program can be quite significant, as Table 2 depicts. To a two-party leasing company in a 34% federal tax bracket, total tax benefits worth 6.497% are equivalent to raising the pretax sales price of the product 9.84%. Realize, too, that the impact of financial leverage relative to tax benefits has not been considered in the previous analysis. Were the leases to be funded with 86% debt (six to one leverage), then the tax benefits relative to the true equity investment in the leased equipment would be rather substantial. The tremendous value of tax benefits available under vendor programs emphasizes the importance of the manufacturer being able to use tax benefits. In the absence of this ability, the vendor lessor should consider joint venturing with a partner who can use the tax benefits. Brokering and/or syndicating of tax leases also can provide partial reimbursement of unusable tax benefits through the fees these techniques provide. Then, too, joint venturing the vendor program might

Table 2

Third-party Versus Two-party Lessor Tax Benefits

	Third-party Lessor	Two-party Lessor	79% Owned Joint Venture	Installment Sale to 79% Owned Joint Venture
MACRS	4.141%	4.141%	3.271%	3.271%
Gross profit tax deferral	0.000	2.356	0.000	3.063
Total	4.141%	6.497%	3.271%	6.334%

Assumptions:
   (1) 40% gross margin
   (2) 12% parent discount rate (values would be lower were a typical captive discount rate of 6 to 8% used in the present value analysis)
   (3) December 15 structuring date
   (4) 5-year MACRS classlife
   (5) 34% corporate tax rate

avoid or alleviate an alternative minimum tax (AMT) problem of the parent by minimizing the creation of tax preferences.

Financial Leverage

Although the use of financial leverage does not, in and of itself, create ancillary income, it nevertheless enhances a company's return on equity to the degree the interest rate implicit in the lease is greater than the cost of the debt used to leverage the lease.

Large degrees of financial leverage are quite common in leasing due to the lower investment risk involved. Normal investments do not have predictable, steady, contractually agreed upon revenue sources. Leasing, on the contrary, does provide a predictable revenue source during the noncancellable period of the lease. Captive lessors use large amounts of debt to fund their leasing portfolios in order to receive as much cash as possible.

In addition to financial leverage's ability to enhance return on equity, another benefit may occur, depending on how it is treated for accounting purposes. When debt does not appear on the balance sheet, the lessor's financial ratios will appear more favorable. Such off balance sheet funding of leases occurs when the following funding techniques are used:
   1. Use of a partially owned subsidiary ($\leq 50\%$) to perform the leasing function rather than using a wholly-owned captive subsidiary or division. Since $\leq 50\%$ owned financial subsidiaries or joint ventures of manufacturing companies are not currently consolidated for accounting purposes (the equity method is used instead), the debt of the partially

owned subsidiary will not appear on the balance sheet of the parent. Note, however, that FASB Statement No. 94 (FASB 94) does require greater than 50% owned subsidiaries to be consolidated with their parents

2. Use of leveraged leasing in the technical accounting sense. Although most leases are leveraged in the lay sense of the term they are, nevertheless, not leveraged in the technical accounting sense unless the funded debt is significant in amount relative to the cost of the equipment, intact at the inception of the lease, nonrecourse to the lessor, such that any lessee default would not cause the lessor to be liable for the nonrecourse funding provided, and coupled with other accounting attributes, including:

   a) The ITC deferral method is used rather than the flow-through method

   b) The lease is a capital direct financing lease, thus excluding sales-type and operating leases from being technical leveraged leases. Note, however, when a parent sells a product to its wholly-owned subsidiary it becomes a direct financing lease. If the captive, however, is consolidated with the parent, the lease will be a sales-type lease per FASB 94, thus preventing its status as a leveraged lease

   c) The investment in the lease, net of nonrecourse debt and deferred tax credits, drops during the earlier phase of the lease and then rises (this may occur several times). Such undulation in the net investment is caused by loss of tax benefits after the end of the MACRS depreciation life. See Chapter Sixteen for an in-depth discussion

   In the true technical leveraged lease for accounting purposes, the nonrecourse debt does not appear on the accounting records of the lessor

3. Selling of lease receivables by assigning or transferring them to buyers (or lenders). The selling of leases is not to be confused with the pledging or hypothecating of leases where the lease is not sold, but, instead, is given as collateral to a lender. In both cases, the lease is assigned or transferred, but the one is a sale, the other a pledge. A sale of a capital lease, not between related parties, requires removal of the lease from the books. To the degree the sale proceeds exceed the book value of the lease (net investment in the lease including or excluding residual), a profit will be recognized.

   If the sale is with recourse the same off balance sheet treatment of the sale proceeds will be given along with immediate recognition of profit as long as the three FASB 77 criteria discussed earlier are met

4. Pledging leases on a nonrecourse basis. Where the leases are given as collateral for loans and the lender has recourse only to the lessee and leased equipment, the debt may or may not be shown on the leasing company's balance sheet. The FASB has not yet issued a definitive statement in this regard, but many lessors would argue that a lease funded with nonrecourse debt is in essence a leveraged lease and, thus, subject to netting treatment. This problem is discussed further in Chapter Eleven.

Services to the Parent

Beyond marketing objectives achieved by the vendor program and tax benefits supplied the parent, vendor programs can provide several additional valuable services, which include:

1. Controlling the parent's equipment financing and leasing requirements

2. Disposing of used, returned, repossessed and slow moving inventoried equipment of the parent

3. Decreasing the parent's accounts receivable days outstanding

4. Diversifying the parent's income sources.

CONTROLLING THE PARENT'S EQUIPMENT FINANCING AND LEASING REQUIREMENTS

Since the vendor program specializes in the structuring, negotiating and funding of leases, it makes sense to allow the vendor program to utilize its expertise in arranging for financing and leasing of equipment to be used by the parent and its subsidiaries. The vendor program becomes, in effect, a specialized purchasing agent for the parent. The financial rewards of such specialization can be significant. The following discussion examines several sources of the financial benefits of control over the acquisitions of the parent.

Lease and loan rates can be minimized through better negotiating, volume purchasing and mass financing (financial packages funded through one source). Furthermore, equipment is acquired in the least costly manner when control over the lease versus buy decision is exercised through proper understanding of the issues involved and by using proper analytical techniques. The cost of refinancing, or of sale-leasebacks, can be minimized, as sale-leasebacks of the parent's equipment or buildings can be quite costly if not properly evaluated from an income tax as well a funding viewpoint. Vendor programs usually employ personnel that are especially adept in specialty leasing financial analysis.

Although off balance sheet operating leases often serve valid purposes, they are nevertheless frequently used for expediency reasons not in the best interests of the overall consolidated company. For example, certain divisions or subsidiaries of the parent company may employ the operating lease as a ploy to enhance their return on assets (ROA). Some divisions will budget a piece of equipment as part of the capital acquisitions budget and then switch the acquisition to the operating budget through leasing. The newly available portion of the capital budget can now be used for another acquisition. Then, too, some abuse occurs when the parent's overhead is allocated to divisions on the basis of assets under its control. Since operating leases do not appear as assets, a portion of the division's overhead charge allocation is avoided. Operating leases whose monthly rentals are less than the sum of a capital lease's depreciation and interest expense charges serve also to increase a division's ROA. These abuses need to be curtailed or at least controlled — the vendor program can easily perform this function through its negotiating ability or by leasing the equipment directly to the parent. Control over renewals and exercising of purchase options under leases that the parent or its subsidiaries have entered into as lessees are other benefits. All too often a lease is repeatedly renewed at exorbitantly priced renewals when the equipment should have been purchased or returned to the lessor. The vendor program again can negotiate better renewals or offer other equipment financing alternatives such as takeouts and rollovers.

DISPOSING OF USED, RETURNED, REPOSSESSED AND SLOW MOVING INVENTORIED EQUIPMENT OF THE PARENT

There are several sources of parent equipment requiring disposition. Examples include equipment originally purchased but no longer needed, equipment returned to the vendor lessor at the termination of the lease (purchase options not exercised), equipment under existing parent leases that can be favorably acquired due to bargain purchase options or built-up accruals under rental programs, slow moving inventory of the parent that might be rented or leased and repossessions of equipment financed or leased.

Disposition of the equipment obtained from the preceding sources could take the form of salvaging, reselling, renting or leasing. Again the vendor program or captive might be in a better position to perform these functions since it is part of the normal operational activities of a lease company. The lease company specializes in equipment disposition. The result of this specialization will be better profit margins on salvaging or other disposition of the equipment, based on the following benefits provided by the vendor program or captive:

1. Understanding used equipment values and the secondary marketplace results in higher salvage prices
2. Negotiating adeptness results in higher proceeds. The parent is not normally in the business of equipment disposal, but the captive is
3. Economies of scale serve to minimize disposition costs such as storage, advertising and marketing expenses
4. Time spent by the leasing company on equipment disposal is less disruptive to operations than if the operating divisions of the parent were to dispose of the equipment
5. Early equipment disposal minimizes equipment losses and avoids abandonment of equipment resulting from procrastinating the disposal of obsolete equipment
6. Better tax management is accomplished such that MACRS and ITC recapture can be avoided
7. Controlling disposal and redistribution of unneeded equipment within the same company more effectively utilizes the resources of the company. For example, one division will salvage a computer for $850,000 and the purchaser will resell or re-lease it to another division of the same company a week later for a $1,400,000 sales price.

DECREASING THE PARENT'S ACCOUNTS RECEIVABLE DAYS' OUTSTANDING

When manufacturing companies sell their equipment directly to customers without providing financing, they frequently must wait 15 to 45 days or more before receiving payment. Vendor programs or captives can usually pay the parent within 15 days, thus reducing the day's outstanding on uncollected parent receivables. Vendor programs or captives are able to remit payments to the parent rapidly due to their preestablished credit lines and borrowing sources that fund the captive almost as soon as a lease is written. Reduction of the parent's outstanding receivables has a significant value since the required investment in receivables is permanently reduced. The resulting savings are equal to the company's cost of capital times the permanent reduction in the capital tied up in receivables.

DIVERSIFYING THE PARENT'S INCOME SOURCES

The value of diversification of earnings sources to a parent derives from two sources: (1) leasing of the parent's products and (2) leasing of noncompeting products manufactured by others. Should the parent's income based on sales of its primary products suffer in a given year, the interest earned on its leasing portfolio could fill in the gap. Since a leasing portfolio might consist of leases in various stages of maturity, reduction in current year sales would not affect the portfolio's interest earning for several years and possibly never significantly affect interest earned to the degree the portfolio consists of earnings on other's products.

In addition, to the degree the vendor lessor leases noncompeting equipment manufactured by others that is countercyclical, downturns of the parent would not impact the third-party leasing of the vendor lessor or captive. Diversification through the vendor lessor or captive is a natural form of horizontal and vertical integration. It represents vertical integration in the sense the parent's marketing efforts are enhanced and horizontal integration to the vendor lessor or captive when noncompeting equipment is leased.

Miscellaneous Reasons

There are several miscellaneous reasons for forming vendor and captive leasing programs that, although important, are not significant enough to merit a separate major category.

ALTERNATE INVESTMENT FOR CORPORATE CASH MANAGEMENT

In situations where the parent has temporary excess liquid funds, it may invest them in the vendor program or captive at after-tax rates generally higher than money market investments. Frequently, the captive generates municipal leases that are tax-exempt. Parents that purchase municipal leases of the captive can expect to enjoy after-tax yields ranging significantly above alternative money market rates.

SOURCE OF SHORT-TERM LIQUIDITY TO PARENT
THROUGH PORTFOLIO LIQUIDATION

Portfolios of leases are easily liquidated (without incurring losses) due to the financial instrument nature of leases. Such readily available cash can serve to solve an emergency liquidity problem of the parent. In fact, many parents view the leasing program as a savings bank providing a liquidity security blanket for the parent.

GENERAL APPEAL TO INVESTMENT BANKERS

The many benefits that vendor leasing programs offer their corporate parents are being understood and appreciated by investment bankers, leading to market appeal for those companies that have successfully managed vendor programs or captives.

IMPACT OF CONSOLIDATING CAPTIVES WITH THEIR CORPORATE PARENTS

FASB 94, 'Consolidation of All Majority-owned Subsidiaries,' requires consolidation of captive lease companies with their corporate parents for fiscal years ending after December 15, 1988. This FASB statement has had a great impact on captive leasing, which results from the following accounting changes:

1. There will not be any leveraged lease accounting for products manufactured by the parent. FASB 13, paragraph 42(a), states that sales-type capital leases cannot be treated as leveraged leases, even if they otherwise meet normal tax and accounting criteria defining leveraged leases. The net result of this prohibition against leveraged lease accounting for sales-type leases is that the nonrecourse debt in the lease will be required to appear on the lessor's balance sheet, whereas, formerly, nonrecourse debt did not appear on the balance sheet. Prior to the issuance of FASB 94, sales-type leases did not occur since the parent would sell the equipment to the captive at retail, creating a direct financing capital lease at the captive level. Direct financing capital leases that are funded with nonrecourse debt generally are accorded leveraged lease accounting treatment with its consequent off balance sheet treatment of the nonrecourse debt. Under the FASB 94 mandate of consolidation, no direct financing capital leases on parent manufactured equipment will exist, since any intercompany sales will be eliminated in consolidation. This causes the direct financing lease to become a ''nonleveraged'' sales-type capital lease

2. There will not be any gross profit recognition on operating leases. Prior to the issuance of FASB 94, parents would sell manufactured equipment to their captive at retail (generating gross profit) and the captive, in turn, would lease the equipment on an operating lease basis. Under consolidation, the intercompany sale to the captive is eliminated, leaving the consolidated entity with an operating lease. Of course, operating leases do not allow gross profit to be recognized immediately; rather, gross profit is recognized as part of lease revenue over the lease term. Technically, prior to consolidation, the intercompany profit still should have been eliminated under the equity method when the subsidiary entered into an operating lease — but many parent companies ignored, overlooked or disregarded this rule

3. Recourse debt of the captive will appear on the consolidated balance sheet. Before FASB 94, the recourse debt of the captive did not appear on the parent's books. Under consolidation, of course, all the debt of the captive appears as part of the parent's consolidated statements. The appearance of the captive's debt on the consolidated balance sheet represents the most significant impact of consolidation. In fact, many manufacturing companies want to avoid consolidation primarily for this reason. There are some methods of avoiding the appearance of recourse debt on the balance sheet, as described earlier under the financial leverage advantages of leasing. For example, FASB 77 allows qualifying recourse debt to remain off balance sheet. Other than this method, or the use of leveraged leasing, which is not available for the parent's products, there will be great difficulty in avoiding having the captive's debt appear on the parent's books

4. Certain transfers of assets to the captive subsidiary will no longer result in sales treatment. For instance, transfers of inventory to the captive would not result in a sale. Since intercompany sales are eliminated under consolidation, neither profit on the sale to the captive, nor avoidance of inventory write-downs to lower of cost or market by selling to the captive, would be available.

   The transfer of doubtful accounts or unwanted receivables will no longer aid the parent. Selling of receivables to the captive in the same manner as inventory transfers will not result in a sale since such transfers are eliminated in consolidation

5. Sales-type capital lease accounting will replace direct financing capital lease accounting. In consolidation, the sale of products at retail to the subsidiary will appear as sales-type capital leases. There are three consequences of sales-type lease accounting: (1) leveraged lease accounting is not permitted as explained above, (2) initial direct costs are not capitalized, but are written off as a current expense and (3) revenue and cost of goods sold on the transfer to the captive will be reduced by the present value of any unguaranteed residual booked by the captive.

   In direct financing capital leases, leveraged leases and operating leases, initial direct costs as defined in FASB Statement No. 91 (FASB 91) are capitalized and amortized as expenses over the lease term. FASB 13, paragraph 17(c), however, requires initial direct costs in sales-type leases to be written off in total at the inception of the lease. The impact of this accounting treatment will be to lower earnings on captive portfolios in the year in which sales-type leases are written.

   FASB 13, paragraphs 17(b) and (c), also require the sales revenue and associated cost of goods sold to be reduced by the present value of any unguaranteed residuals booked by the captive, since such value represents a reversionary value, or the portion of the asset not sold in the sales-type lease transaction. Many divisions and affiliate subsidiaries of parent companies have incentives based on gross revenue generated. These incentives, of course, will be impacted since revenue will be started lower due to the FASB 13 rule governing sales of products under capital leases

6. There will be a limitation on the advantage of off balance sheet leases from captives to their parents. Without FASB 94's consolidation rule, a captive could structure an operating lease with its parent and the asset and debt would remain doubly off balance sheet — once since the parent was the lessee under an operating lease and twice because the lessor captive was unconsolidated. Although operating leases will still remain off the balance sheet of a division or subsidiary of the parent, the asset and corresponding debt will nevertheless appear as part of the consolidated property, plant and equipment. However, the asset and debt will probably not be allocated to any particular division, etc., thereby still permitting off balance sheet financing for the division

7. There is a potential for classification of the captive's unclassified balance sheet. If the parent presents its financial statements on a classified basis, then so must the captive subsidiary. This requires a good deal of effort since the net investment in every lease will have to be separated into its current and long term portion. Lease companies typically do not classify their financial statements

8. There will be continued disclosure of Accounting Principles Board Opinion (APBO) 18 required disaggregated information. For those captives that were unconsolidated prior to the issuance of FASB 94, certain disaggregated information about revenue, expenses, etc., per APBO 18 still must be included in the consolidated footnotes. However, those companies that were already consolidated do not have to disclose that data, resulting in two different disclosure approaches.

TECHNIQUES FOR TRANSFERRING TAX BENEFITS TO CAPTIVES

In the situation where a captive leasing company generates MACRS deductions and ITC (when and if available), and creates gross profit tax deferral for the parent, some reimbursement or transfer device to the captive is necessary. Without the transfer of these tax benefits the captive might not remain competitive.

Excess MACRS Depreciation

MACRS deductions generated beyond a captive's ability to utilize them create a net operating loss (NOL), which in turn generates cash flow (but not earnings like excess ITC) at the parent level since it files a consolidated tax return with the captive. The cash flow generated by the NOL is equal to the parent's incremental tax rate times the MACRS generated NOL.

EXAMPLE 1

Assume a captive generates a $300,000 NOL from a tax lease as follows. Compute the value of the NOL to the parent.

Rental revenue	$ 300,000	
MACRS	(450,000)	(.2 × $2,250,000 cost)
General and administrative (G & A) expense	(50,000)	
Interest expense	(100,000)	
Net operating loss	($ 300,000)	

SOLUTION

The $300,000 NOL generates $102,000 in cash flow ($300,000 × .34 tax rate). The accounting book tax liability and net income are calculated on the direct financing capital lease in Table 3 and the journal entries are shown in Table 4.

Although the captive's income has not increased, its cash flow has, enabling it to reinvest in other leases that will have been funded with an interest free loan. The cash remitted to the captive will be returned to the parent as the deferred tax credit account reverses. However, if the captive continues to grow so will the deferred tax credit account; thus, the cash may never be returned to the parent.

Table 3
Net Income Calculation

Interest earned on direct financing capital lease	$ 210,000
G & A expense	(50,000)
Interest expense	(100,000)
Taxable income	$ 60,000
Tax expense 34%	(20,400)
Net income	$ 39,600

Table 4
Excess MACRS Journal Entries

Journal Entries on Captive's Books

Tax expense	$ 20,400	
Taxes receivable - parent	$ 102,000	
Deferred tax credit		$ 122,400
Cash (from parent)	$ 102,000	
Taxes receivable		$ 102,000

Journal Entries on Parent's Books

Taxes payable	$ 102,000	
Cash (to captive)		$ 102,000

Gross Profit Tax Deferral

The tax benefits generated by gross profit tax deferral originate at the parent level, unlike the MACRS and any potential ITC that is generated at the subsidiary level. The methods of transferring the cash flow created by gross profit tax deferral are extremely important. If no cash flow or very little is transferred to the captive subsidiary, it will not be able to structure its leases in a competitive manner. There are nine common methods of dealing with gross profit tax deferral.

INTEREST FREE LOAN TO THE CAPTIVE THAT IS PAID BACK TO THE PARENT IN PROPORTION TO REVERSALS OF DEFERRED TAXES ON GROSS PROFIT

In order to illustrate this method, assume 5-year MACRS equipment retails for $200,000, with manufacturing costs of $80,000 resulting in $120,000 gross profit. This gross profit would generate a $40,800 tax liability (.34 × $120,000 = $40,800). A $40,800 interest free loan to the subsidiary would be paid back as in Table 5.

The advantages of this method are that it:

1. Is the most common
2. Avoids undue distortion of the captive's debt-to-equity ratio, although some interest free debt will generally always be outstanding. Such debt would usually be subordinate to any outstanding bank borrowings
3. Avoids a permanent loan to the captive
4. Avoids manipulation by the parent on cash created by the subsidiary. It is better to let the captive use the cash flow at its earnings rate than to let the parent earn less on invested cash flow if the cash were to be invested only in the money market, etc.

The disadvantages of this method are that it:

1. Is difficult to account for due to the constant reversals of deferred tax credits
2. Causes temporary distortion of the debt-to-equity ratio, depending upon the captive's portfolio growth rate.

INTEREST FREE LOAN THAT IS SYSTEMATICALLY FORGIVEN, OR A FEE FOR LEASE SERVICES RENDERED

This method consists of a lump sum distribution to the captive in an amount equal to the present value of the gross profit tax deferral savings. The lump sum is treated as a loan and then systematically forgiven over the lease term or treated as a fee for lease services rendered.

Table 5
Interest Free Loan and Payback

Year	Loan to Subsidiary	Loan Repayment	Net Cash Flow
1	$ 40,800	$ 8,160 (20.00% of $40,800)	$ 32,640
2	0	13,056 (32.00% of $40,800)	(13,056)
3	0	7,834 (19.20% of $40,800)	(7,834)
4	0	4,700 (11.52% of $40,800)	(4,700)
5	0	4,700 (11.52% of $40,800)	(4,700)
6	0	2,350 (5.76% of $40,800)	(2,350)
	$ 40,800	$ 40,800	$ 0

Sometimes the fees are paid over the lease term in order to prevent a distortion of earnings in the first year.

The advantages of this method are that it:

1. Simplifies accounting
2. Is not subject to parent manipulation, other than in the original computation of the lump sum distribution amount
3. Never has to be repaid to the parent.

The disadvantages of this method are that:

1. Lump sum distributions treated as interest free loans cause temporary distortions in the captive's debt-to-equity ratio
2. Loan forgiveness is difficult to sell to the parent
3. Lump sum fees distort the captive's earnings during the inception year of a lease.

EQUITY INFUSION TO THE SUBSIDIARY EQUAL TO THE PRESENT VALUE OF THE GROSS PROFIT TAX DEFERRAL SAVINGS

This method is similar to the previous method in that a single lump sum distribution is made; however, in this case the transfer of cash is to purchase additional equity in the captive.

The advantages to this method are that it:

1. Is easily accounted for
2. Is not subject to manipulation, except for the determination of the original transfer amount.

The disadvantages to this method are that it:

1. Lowers the return on equity of the captive
2. Distorts the captive's debt-to-equity ratio during the early months of the lease
3. Bypasses the income statement, which understates the real earnings value of gross profit tax deferral.

INTEREST PAID TO THE CAPTIVE BASED ON IMPLIED EARNINGS ON THE CASH FLOW GENERATED BY THE GROSS PROFIT TAX DEFERRAL

This technique allows the parent to retain the cash flow benefits generated by gross profit tax deferral, but requires the parent to pay interest to the captive for the use of cash generated by the captive.

The advantages to this method are that:

1. It is theoretically the best treatment since the real value of gross profit tax deferral is represented by the opportunity investment returns that gross profit tax deferral cash flow can earn. These earnings are simply passed on to the captive by the parent
2. The debt-to-equity ratio is properly stated
3. There are no debts to repay
4. It is fairly easy accounting treatment
5. It properly impacts the earnings of the captive.

The disadvantages to this method are that it:

1. Is subject to manipulation by the parent. Furthermore, it is difficult for the parent to accept that such cash flow can generate after-tax earnings equal to the parent's cost of capital. Thus, future earnings policy is subject to change. Theoretically, the appropriate rate that the parent should pay is the captive's opportunity investment rate after-tax (usually the captive's cost of capital)
2. Requires a fair amount of accounting and computational time.

TRANSFERRING EQUIPMENT TO THE CAPTIVE AT A DISCOUNTED PRICE

The complexity of determining appropriate discounts from list price and the lost revenue to manufacturing divisions or affiliate corporations render this method virtually infeasible. If, however, the captive actually makes a practice of marketing the parent's equipment and is normally entitled to earn a profit margin, equipment could be sold at an even lower wholesale price to the captive to compensate for the gross profit tax deferral.

PARENT ABSORBS COSTS OF CAPTIVE SUBSIDIARY

Having the parent absorb or subsidize costs of the captive creates control problems and distorts the parent's operating results and is, therefore, considered unacceptable. For example, the parent may elect not to charge the captive the same overhead charge applicable to all other operating subsidiaries and divisions under its control.

LOWER THE CAPTIVE'S COST OF CAPITAL OR REQUIRED RETURN ON EQUITY TO COMPENSATE FOR CASH NOT REMITTED

If a captive's capital structure, on the average, consisted of 10% interest free loans due the parent (as previously discussed) then, instead of loans being made to the captive, the captive's required return on equity (ROE) will be lowered to compensate for the increased debt cost without those loans, as shown in Table 6.

Thus, a captive's required ROE could be lowered from 18% to 14.67% for the same degree of financial leverage (85%), as a means of compensating for the cash transfer.

The advantages to this method are that it:

1. Permits the parent to retain cash that might be put to more profitable use elsewhere (this cash must provide greater than a leveraged 18% ROE, however)
2. Requires little accounting or computational effort.

The disadvantages to this method are that it:

1. Removes the captive's ability to compare itself to competitors within the industry
2. Is difficult for the parent to leverage the cash flow created by gross profit tax deferral in a manner to earn 18 to 22%, which is typical for captives.

MEMO ENTRY ONLY

No cash transfers are made to the captive. Instead, the captive's performance is based on what might have happened had the cash been transferred (similar to the discussion above). The disadvantage of this method is that it is subject to manipulation.

Table 6
Change in Captive's Cost of Capital

	Interest Free Loans			Lowered Cost of Capital		
	% of Total	After-tax Cost	Weighted Average Cost	% of Total	After-Tax Cost	Weighted Average Cost
Debt	75.00%	5.00%	3.75%	85.00%	5.00%	4.25%
Debt	10.00	0.00%	0.00	0.00%	0.00%	0.00
Equity	15.00	18.00%	2.70	15.00%	14.67%	2.20
	100.00%		6.45%			6.45%

IGNORE TAX BENEFITS GENERATED BY THE CAPTIVE

Without proper accounting for, and transfer of, tax benefit earnings (MACRS, ITC and gross profit tax deferral), a captive will not be able to support marketing adequately as its lease rates could be uncompetitively high. It also will not appear as a profitable stand-alone financial subsidiary.

METHODS OF MINIMIZING AND IDENTIFYING LEASING RISKS

There are numerous risks associated with vendor leasing that must be understood in order to mitigate their impact on the vendor program's profitability. The 14 primary risks that confront the manager of a vendor leasing program will be discussed in this section.

Residual Risk

Lessors normally depend upon the realization of future residual values in order to receive their required yields. Without this dependence, lease rate factors might be unduly high for the lessee, as higher, expected residuals used in structuring leases will result in lower rentals. Unduly high residual expectations create the risk that the lessor might not realize the anticipated residual amount. Deflation or technological obsolescence are two factors that could lower future residual values. Residual realization depends primarily on whether the lessee will exercise a purchase option at the end of the noncancellable lease term. The lessee's failure to exercise a purchase option forces the lessor to re-lease the equipment or salvage it, which increases the risk of not receiving the originally anticipated residual value.

There are several factors that are utilized in mitigating residual risk:

1. Residual value insurance is purchased

2. Manufacturers of equipment have sales personnel and previously established markets to facilitate reselling of returned equipment
3. Vendor lessors can better predict expected residual values due to their experience with sales of the product
4. Manufacturer lessors are more efficient at refurbishment, maintenance and minimizing remarketing costs
5. Conservative underbooking of residual values serves as a hedge against accounting losses on residuals
6. Joint ventures with funders are entered into in order to share risk
7. Probability and decision tree payoff theory are used in arriving at expected residual values where precision and confidence levels are established
8. Vendor guarantees are obtained on noncompeting equipment manufactured by others.

Customer Risk

Lessee defaults attributed to inability to pay, or refusal to pay until the equipment is properly manufactured, maintained or repaired represent the primary types of customer risk that vendor lessors must deal with. Proper creditworthiness screening is a difficult task to perform, but necessary if customer risk is to be avoided. Techniques and procedures that might be implemented to counter customer risk include additional collateral, additional cosigners, a parent guarantee if the lessee is an affiliate or subsidiary and the charging of late payment fees on delinquent payments. If the lessee will not pay the late fee, the fee may be deducted from a refundable security deposit.

Cyclical Risk

The industry in which the lessee works could be highly susceptible to cyclical downturns in the economy, or credit shortages. Irrespective of the lessee's intent to pay, or its managerial expertise, the lessee may not be able to survive a recession. To hedge against credit crunches and cyclical economic downturns a vendor lessor can restrict the relative proportion of its leasing portfolio devoted to lessee's whose businesses are vulnerable to such economic events.

Tax Benefit Utilization Risk

Should a captive's parent incur an NOL or go into an AMT position such that the tax benefits provided by the captive lose most of their value, the captive's lease yields will plummet. Then, too, excessive deferred tax credits could create a significant strain on cash flow were the parent to eliminate or reduce its commitment to leasing, as reversals of deferred tax credits represent tax liabilities that are being paid. Tax utilization risks can be mitigated by indirectly transferring excess unused tax benefits to others through the selling of equity interests in leases or portfolios (lease syndication) or through joint venturing. Deferred tax credit reversals do not all happen in one year, which also somewhat mitigates these tax utilization risks.

Financial Leverage Risk

The danger created by use of financial leverage in funding leases is the large fixed obligation that is incurred to service both the interest and principal payback on the debt. Loan payments are due the creditor whether lease payments are delinquent or not, or whether operating income is sufficient for debt service. In other words, the leasing company's collection or operating problems cannot be passed off to the creditors. Bad debt, residual losses and operational inefficiencies all render the use of financial leverage risky. The greater the proportion of the capital structure that is debt, the greater the fixed charges required to service debt and, therefore, the greater the financial leverage risk.

Another related risk concerns consolidation of the captive with its parent (whether required by FASB or by Moody's or Standard and Poors, etc.). If the resulting consolidated debt-to-equity ratio is deemed excessive by rating agencies, the parent's credit rating might be lowered, causing an increase in its interest expense on new debt offerings.

Although risky, financial leverage still is not overly dangerous due to the contractually agreed upon revenue sources from the lessee. Then, too, few circumstances would prevent a lessor from reducing the amount of debt it uses to fund its portfolio. In addition, rating agencies would give advance warning to companies required to be consolidated. Sufficient lead time would allow adjustments to be made by the captive to avoid credit downgrading. Finally, a bank or other financial institution can be allowed to bear the leverage burden through nonrecourse funding, joint venturing or by allowing them to run the vendor program.

Managerial Risk

"Managing a manufacturing company is difficult enough without the added burden of worrying about running a lease company," is a frequent expression of the hassle and risk associated with management of a vendor leasing program. A working knowledge of lease structuring, credit, collections, lease accounting, residual valuation and disposal, etc., is necessary to insure the proper administration of a vendor leasing program. Is all this added responsibility worth the trouble? As with other risks, management of a vendor leasing program can be brought under control by hiring experienced personnel who are already adept at managing a lease company or by subcontracting or joint venturing with lending institutions who are very willing to provide services on behalf of the manufacturer.

Documentation, Billing and Collection Processing Risk

Even the best management cannot achieve effective results in a lease company without adequate lease documentation (lease documents, subsequent filings, etc.) and an accounting, billing and collections system. Fortunately, there are several lease operating and accounting systems available to the public that are very efficient in lowering this type of risk.

Misallocation of Scarce Resources Risk

When a manufacturing company establishes a vendor leasing program there may be a scarce resource allocation problem. Should cash be used to fund research and development, new property, plant and equipment or working capital, or should it be used for a vendor leasing program? If resources are limited, investment in leasing could be an impediment to expansion of the parent's main line of business.

Countering the misallocation of scarce resources risk is the fact that vendor programs or captives might provide the highest return on equity of all divisions of the parent; therefore, even though funds are being diverted away from manufacturing needs, creation of a vendor program or captive might be fully justified. Joint venturing or using nonrecourse debt also could reduce the parent's funding requirements to the vendor program or captive.

Stagnation From Inaction Risk

Manufacturing parents that are unwilling to make up their minds in regards to the establishment of a vendor leasing program stagnate or regress relative to the programs currently being offered by competitors. This risk is easily overcome by simply making a decision to use vendor leasing.

Manipulation of Earnings Risk

There are numerous ways to manipulate or overstate the earnings of the captive. For example, ITC flow through, Rule of 78's interest recognition, excessive initial direct cost capitalization, etc., all can mislead the parent in its attempt to ascertain the real economic status of its financial subsidiary. Such risk, of course, can be easily overcome with education. Proper education has done much to reduce the risk of being mislead by creative financial reporting by the captive.

Intermediate Wholesalers and Representatives Risk

Lending or leasing directly to end-user customers creates its own risk, but lending to marketing intermediaries creates another. These wholesalers and manufacturers' representatives frequently must offer financing to their own customers. If their financing programs are not properly managed, then direct loans to them from the vendor leasing program or captive could be imperiled. Again this risk can be allayed by using outside lenders to perform the funding function. Joint venturing with the marketing intermediary also promotes a certain degree of control over their leasing programs.

Lack of Parent Support and Understanding Risk

In terms of whether a vendor leasing program will succeed or fail, one of the greatest risks is based upon lack of the parent's understanding or support of what vendor leasing is all about. All too often a mental fixation as to a vendor leasing program's purpose, such as tax sheltering or marketing, without adequate consideration of its other purposes, might doom its progress. Again, ignorance can be overcome only through education and experience.

Casualty Loss Risk

As a title holder of equipment subject to a lease, there could be casualty loss risk exposure to the captive lessor. Two basic approaches are taken to reduce this exposure: (1) obtain casualty insurance in order to protect the lessor from loss of the equipment and (2) operate the vendor leasing program as a properly funded, wholly-owned subsidiary to isolate the parent from any uninsured losses.

Cost of Funding Risk

When a captive is funded by pooling (as opposed to fixed-rate match funding), the ebb and flow of interest costs cause real funding risks. Should the funding costs rise above the rates fixed in the lease contracts, substantial losses could occur. To reduce this exposure, a vendor lessor can match fund all or part of the portfolio with fixed rate funding, sell off the portfolio once funding costs rise to a certain level, purchase financial instruments that permit hedging against future interest rate increases, attempt to obtain fixed-rate financing on a pooling basis or borrow long, through the use of bonds, etc., during a period of low interest costs.

METHODS OF SERVICING VENDOR LESSORS BY THIRD-PARTY LESSORS

There are numerous ways in which a third party can service vendor lessors. As was discussed previously, the term vendor leasing has a much broader connotation than captive leasing, especially since it is the noncaptive vendor lessors who generally have the greatest need for these services (although more and more captives are sourcing various functions externally).

Why would a captive or vendor lessor seek the services of a third-party lessor? Although there are numerous reasons, some of which may be unique to a particular manufacturer, the primary motivations for seeking outside services can be grouped as follows:

- Lack of resources/in-house expertise
- Capital/funding constraints
- Risk diversification
- Excess tax benefits
- Inadequate size.

One of the most important motivators is the lack of in-house leasing expertise. Leasing is a specialized field, with its own unique accounting, legal and tax complexities. Most companies do not have the time or the resources to either develop this expertise internally or to hire leasing experts. In addition, many companies are unwilling to divert capital away from their primary business to fund and support a leasing portfolio, or may find their cost of capital too high to be competitive with the lease rates offered by third-party finance companies.

Even for companies with adequate resources and sufficient leverage to establish a full-fledged, competitive leasing program, concerns about managing the many risks associated with leasing (e.g., residual risk, credit risk, interest rate risk) or an excess tax benefit position may cause these companies to seek an outside leasing partner. Lastly, vendors may find it more cost-effective to purchase services from an entity specializing in equipment leasing, whose size and leasing concentration enable it to achieve certain economies of scale.

There are quite a large number of third-party participants in the vendor leasing market and the type of services they provide is quite varied. The participants include lease brokers, financial institutions, independent leasing companies and captive companies. One way to classify these participants is by the level of services provided. Many participants function solely as lenders and provide funding only, typically to captives seeking alternate and/or cheaper financing sources. Alternatively, there are other specialty niche players who provide or broker some unique service(s), such as remarketing, to the vendors. The next layer of participants provides funding and a limited range of support services (e.g., billing, collecting, credit review, etc.) to the vendors. In addition to funding, the last layer of participants engages in full-service leasing and provides the vendors with an extensive array of services from lease origination through equipment disposition.

In addition to the above roles, the third-party lessor also can serve as a joint venture/equity partner. Under such an arrangement, the third party invests directly in the leasing subsidiary or, more commonly, the vendor and an outside party jointly establish a separate company to lease the vendor's products to customers. The joint venture route is usually taken by vendors desiring to retain a portion of the financing profit and tax benefits in-house, but unwilling to bear all of the risks or allocate all of the capital required to establish a full-fledged captive. As mentioned earlier in the chapter, joint ventures are also used by vendors looking to sell (or outplace) their excess tax benefits.

Services Provided

The services that third-party lessors offer vendors are too numerous to list in a comprehensive manner and are, perhaps, limited only by the vendors' needs or the imagination and determination of third-party leasing companies. In general, however, these services can be grouped around the following categories:

- Sales-aid/training
- Lease structuring/documentation
- Credit review
- Outplacement/investment syndication
- Funding
- Administrative services
- Remarketing/asset management.

SALES-AID/TRAINING

The range of sales-related services provided by a third-party lessor varies, again depending on the vendor's needs and the extent of its in-house leasing expertise. Generally, for vendors in the early stage of developing a lease program, the sales-aid services can include sales force training, joint customer calls, customized lease documentation and marketing materials, jointly-sponsored advertising and pricing support. In this stage, the leasing company is utilizing its expertise to help the vendor establish an effective leasing program; the focus is on educating the vendor's sales force in the use of leasing as a sales tool and on packaging a saleable lease product. As a vendor grows in size and its leasing knowledge increases, third-party lessors tend to provide less in the way of point-of-sales help and training, and more in the way of on-going sales support in the form of structuring and customizing deals. Regardless of the stage, most of this sales support is transparent to the customer, who continues to deal directly with the vendor.

LEASE STRUCTURING/DOCUMENTATION

An area where third-party lessors offer a great deal of added value is in structuring, documenting and pricing the financing transaction. Although the documentation is often standard in format, the third-party leasing company will work with a vendor to customize a transaction to a particular lessee's needs. In this way, the vendor can capitalize on the leasing company's expertise in structuring a variety of financial products (e.g., operating leases, finance leases, municipal leases, etc.). Often the documentation, structure and pricing are negotiated up front between the vendor and the lessor, thereby providing the vendor with a "bag" of easy-to-use lease products.

The vendor can also look to the third-party lessor for assistance in processing and tracking the lease documentation prior to closing. The third-party lessor will assume responsibility for preparing the lease documents, completing any ancillary paperwork such as Uniform Commercial Code filings and bills of sale and following up with the customer on any missing and incomplete data. Some lessors even offer computerized systems that enable the vendor to track the status of its customers' pending lease transactions.

CREDIT REVIEW

Vendors often rely on a third party's expertise in assessing a customer's creditworthiness. The vendor will look to the leasing company to determine which customers should be approved for financing. Usually, this credit review process involves researching the customer's prior credit history, analyzing the customer's current financial statements and checking bank and trade references. Sometimes, in an effort to gain greater control over the lease origination process, a vendor elects to make the final credit decision (and retain the credit risk) and relies on the third party to merely provide the underlying credit analysis. More often than not, credit authority and risk reside with the third-party leasing company.

OUTPLACEMENT/INVESTMENT SYNDICATION

As already stated, one of the primary reasons for a vendor to seek the services of a third-party lessor is a lack of capital. Often, instead of seeking an equity partner, a vendor will look to a lease broker to sell off its equity investment in leases. Sometimes the investor will buy the entire lease (i.e., assume the credit and residual risk); other times the vendor will elect to sell only the rental stream or the residual. The outplacement can take the form of a single, direct purchase or some type of investment syndication.

FUNDING

Most often vendors look to a third party to arrange and/or provide the funding for the lease transactions, not only for the initial equipment purchase, but also for any upgrades, add-ons or replacements. A more detailed discussion of various funding methods follows this subsection.

ADMINISTRATIVE SERVICES

Economies of scale and/or existing expertise often make it more beneficial for a third party to administer the leases once the transaction has been funded and the equipment has been installed. The administrative services a third-party lessor might provide include: booking the transaction, billing and collecting the monthly lease payments (and/or accompanying maintenance, service contracts, etc.), processing customer service complaints, filing, collecting and remitting sales, use and property taxes and preparing financial statements and tax returns. The billing and collecting (as well as initial lease documentation) can be done on either a direct or private-label basis. In a private-label program, all of the documentation and correspondence (including billing) are sent out under the vendor's name, even though the leasing company actually provides the services and owns the equipment.

REMARKETING/ASSET MANAGEMENT

As a way to raise equity or reduce its residual risk, a vendor lessor may sell outright its entire (or a partial) interest in the equipment residual to a third party. Even if the vendor has elected to retain the residual risk, it will often seek outside help in remarketing the asset at the end of the lease term or in the event of a customer default. Additionally, a vendor may choose to utilize the asset tracking systems offered by many leasing companies. In general, these systems alert the lessor as to which assets are coming off lease, report on the status of any off-lease equipment and process any subsequent sales or re-leases of any expired equipment.

Funding Methods

Before proceeding to a detailed discussion on the various funding methods, it is important to note that vendor leasing is not restricted to any one type of lease. Indeed, any of the various lease products (operating or rental leases, finance leases, sale-leasebacks, leveraged leases, municipal or tax-exempt leases) can be utilized, with the actual choice dictated by a variety of factors such as market needs, tax considerations, obsolescence concerns and residual risk.

There are numerous ways third parties provide funding for a vendor leasing program. An important distinction is whether the funding is done on an indirect or direct basis. Indirect funding involves loans to the captive or vendor, who then utilizes the borrowed funds to lease the equipment directly to the customer (i.e., the vendor remains the lessor and the third party functions as a banker). Under direct funding methods, the third party is the lessor and provides the financing directly to the customer. Since, in the former case, the vendor generally retains title to the equipment and the funding source remains invisible to the lessee, the vendor's sales organization often prefers indirect funding. However, capital constraints and cost considerations, such as lack of competitive financing rates and an inability to manage an extensive lease portfolio, often make direct funding the preferred financing route.

Vendors usually obtain indirect funding in two ways: either (1) on a pooled or (2) a match funded basis. In a pooling, a financial institution lends to the vendor or captive on a formula basis against its entire portfolio of leases (e.g., as a percent of the vendor's total capital, a percent of its gross or net investment in leases, etc.). Under the pooled method, the third-party funding source is looking to the general creditworthiness of the vendor or captive for repayment.

In a match funding situation, the third-party source lends against a particular lease transaction (or portfolio of leases); that is, the lender looks to a designated stream of lease obligations for its repayment. The most common form of match funded financing is discounting. Here, a vendor discounts or pledges a specific rental stream with a financial institution. The financial institution then advances the vendor the present value of the future lease payments and collects the lease payments directly from the customer. (Title to the equipment remains with the vendor.) As already mentioned, one of the primary benefits of match funding is elimination of the interest rate risk associated with acting as a financial intermediary. By match funding a lease, the vendor can lock in its interest cost, and, hence, its financing profit up front.

Direct funding most commonly occurs when the third party provides the funding directly to the customer from the inception of the lease. Here the third-party lessor buys the asset from the vendor and leases it directly to the customer. Direct funding can also be accomplished through a third party purchasing existing leases (either individually or on a portfolio basis) from a vendor; in this case, the third party steps into the vendor's shoes once the lease has been put in place and title generally passes to the third-party lessor. Whether the vendor, third-party lessor or the customer retains the residual and tax rights to the asset depends on how the initial sale and lease of the equipment is structured and the type of lease entered into (i.e., capital versus operating). As with match funding, direct funding allows a vendor to pass on the interest rate risk to an outside party.

Another important distinction among the various funding methods is whether the vendor retains any or all of the credit risk. As already discussed, the credit retention decision involves balancing the vendor's desire to maintain control over the entire lease process with its ability to manage the attendant risk. Credit risk retention usually is accomplished through some type of recourse arrangement between the vendor and the third-party lessor, under which the vendor agrees to stand behind the customer's lease payments. Alternatively, the vendor elects, as a way to raise funds, to sell its interest in the residual only, thereby retaining the lease payment stream and associated credit risk.

Whether the funding is done on a recourse or nonrecourse basis can have important accounting considerations. In particular, providing recourse in a sale or discounting situation can result in the lease receivable remaining on the vendor's books and the loan proceeds being booked as a liability, as discussed in Chapter Eleven.

In summary, there are numerous ways to fund a vendor leasing program or captive — either directly or indirectly, with or without recourse, with or without an equity partner, etc. The particular method chosen depends primarily on the desired tax and accounting consequences such as off balance sheet versus sales treatment, as well as the individual vendor's capital constraints and creditworthiness.

CONCLUSION

Captive leasing companies and vendor programs are created for numerous reasons: market control, market enhancement, ancillary income, tax benefits, financial leverage, services to the parent and various other miscellaneous reasons. The recent consolidation rules of FASB 94 have eliminated many of the accounting reasons justifying the creation of captive lease companies. Furthermore, leveraged leases and direct financing leases on the parent's manufactured products will now become sales-type capital leases that do not allow capitalization of initial direct costs.

Once captives have been established, it is necessary and important for the parent to transfer to the captive cash flow derived from any and all tax benefits created by the captive vendor program. There are numerous means by which tax benefit cash flow can be transferred to the captive. Without the transfer of these tax benefits the captive's marketing efforts could fail. Residual risk taken by captive lessors can be minimized by appropriate planning and remarketing techniques. Then, too, outside financial institutions can help mitigate residual risk along with providing funding and numerous other vendor services.

CHAPTER EIGHTEEN
LEASE CREDIT ANALYSIS

The topic of credit is one of great importance to both the lessor and the lessee. The lessor aggressively pursues credit analysis in an attempt to manage bad debt losses; the lessee is equally aggressive in order to qualify for additional asset financing. Thus, the vested and material interests of each party suggest substantive attention be directed to credit analysis. This chapter divides credit analysis into the following sections:

- Financial Statement Analysis
- Risk Assessment
- Cash Flow Analysis
- Modeling.

FINANCIAL STATEMENT ANALYSIS

Financial statement analysis traditionally has assumed major proportions in credit analysis. However, financial statements impart many things to varied users. The income statement communicates profitability for a given period of time and the balance sheet illustrates balances or economic residuals at the end of such a period. The newly required cash flow statement presentation of Financial Accounting Standards Board Statement No. 95 (FASB 95) informs the user where cash came from, where it went and what was left over. Each of these financial statements is useful for credit purposes; each has limitations.

Income Statement Analysis

Income statement analysis takes many forms and its components can be broken down, or decomposed, either vertically or horizontally. Sales, the top-most figure in vertical analysis, is equated to 100%, after which each successive income statement line item is expressed as a percent of sales. A horizontal decomposition, however, assumes a totally different strategy, that of trending. Each line item in year 1 is defined as the base year and is, therefore, equal to 100%. Each successive year, the various line items of the income statement are expressed as a function of the base year. The dynamic, or time-spanning nature of the income statement, is most readily apparent in a horizontal decomposition.

Balance Sheet Analysis

Horizontal and vertical decomposition of the balance sheet is every bit as important as it is with the income statement. Horizontal decomposition pushes the analyst to trend, whereas vertical encourages the comparison of one classified line item to another. Regardless of which focus is desired, the static nature of the balance sheet is apparent. Each balance sheet is an economic snapshot of the company at a particular time.

Cash Flow Analysis

Generally accepted accounting principles (GAAP) dictate that income statements and balance sheets be prepared on an accrual basis. Thus, sales may be recorded as revenue before they are received and expenses may be recorded before they are paid. The resultant accrual financial statements accurately reflect the matching of income and expense within the time frame in which they were incurred. It has been said, however, that accrual accounting is nothing more than an accounting convention; cash flow is reality. Salaries, invoices and dividends are not paid with accrual net income, but, rather, with cash. In other words, the prudent credit analyst has learned that the accrual statements must be massaged and manipulated to arrive at cash flow figures, both cash in and cash out. The FASB also agrees with the importance of cash flow analysis, which is why it has issued FASB 95, which requires a statement of cash flows in the financial statements. Due to the importance of cash flow analysis, it will be discussed as a separate topic later in this chapter.

Standard Ratio Analysis

Standard textbook and traditional ratio analyses trace their genesis to accrual financial statements. Many decades ago, prior to the ever expanding nature of accrual accounting (deferred income tax liabilities, for example), cash accounting and accrual accounting were much closer financial relatives. Today they are related, but appear to be distant cousins rather than the identical twins so often assumed by unsophisticated financial statement users. Thus, although the traditional usage of ratios continues, prudence dictates that the credit analyst employ an arsenal of not only standard financial ratios, but also of other nontraditional cash flow ratios, which have been slow in evolving. Standard cash flows will be addressed at this time and cash flow ratios will be covered in the cash flow analysis section. Standard noncash ratios used to ascertain a company's financial well-being are typically grouped into six categories, each of which depicts a particular aspect of the financial condition of the company. The following are the six categories:

1. Profitability and earnings growth
2. Liquidity and working capital
3. Investment utilization and activity

4. Solvency and risk
5. Financial leverage
6. Owner's equity.

Each ratio within the category gives a different view of whether the goal of the particular category is being met. These ratios are used for comparative analysis, interrelationship study and input to forecasting models. Table 1 contains a side-by-side description of how ratios are used and what the effect of ratio analysis has on the decision process.

The year-end financial information in Figures 1 and 2 will be used to illustrate (by category) how these ratios are computed and how they are used in the decision process. Additional information to be used in the illustration includes (1) an average price per share for ABC Company stock of $35 during 1993 and (2) $28,000 of dividends paid.

PROFITABILITY AND EARNINGS GROWTH

If it is assumed the goal of management is to maximize shareholders' worth, then there is a dual objective: (1) maximize profits so continual dividends will be paid and (2) maintain steady growth in earnings so the investor's stock price will grow (capital gains). These two objectives are interrelated, for a company that pays proportionately high dividends compared to amounts retained each year from net income will find it difficult to grow as fast as another company that retains more earnings. The following seven ratios have been developed into a model (Figure 3) that not only describes a company's profit, but also describes the effect of dividend payout on potential growth rate in earnings.

Note that, whether or not the model is used, each factor in the model can stand alone and still have significance. However, the model does show the effect of a change in any one factor on both (1) return on equity (ROE) and (2) potential growth rate, which are two objectives that management should be especially concerned about in their planning. Following are examples of this category of ratios, based on the information in Figures 1 and 2.

Net Profit to Net Sales (Net Profit Margin)

The formula for computing this ratio is as follows:

$$\frac{\text{Net income (after taxes)}}{\text{Net sales (after returns and allowances)}} = \frac{\$\ 65,000}{\$1,500,000} = 4.33\%$$

Net profit margin indicates what percentage net income is of sales. Stable or growing net profit margins are favorable indicators so long as asset turnover has not been inordinately reduced. Remember it is net profit margin times asset turnover that really indicates profitability.

Net Sales to Total Assets (Asset Turnover)

The formula for computing this ratio is as follows:

$$\frac{\text{Net sales}}{\text{Total assets (beginning of year)}} = \frac{\$1,500,000}{\$1,679,000} = 89.34\%$$

Table 1

Ratios and the Decision Process

How Ratios are Used	Effect on the Decision Process
Comparisons	
1) Currently established ratios are compared with the same ratios of prior periods for the same firm	1) Trends are established by looking at a series of ratios over time
2) Industry ratios are compared with similar companies within an industry	2) Relative standing is established within an industry. Relative standing could highlight strengths or weaknesses
Interrelationships	
1) In-depth analysis finds logical causal relationships among various items on the balance sheet and income statement. Ratios reflect these interrelationships	1) Pinpointing of the causes of weaknesses is facilitated by the use of ratios causally related to a problem
2) Ratios are categorized according to common objectives of financial management	2) Common financial objectives that must be met to maximize profit, insure growth in share price and maintain liquidity are highlighted, along with serious weaknesses in one category that could ultimately lead to a weakening of another major category
Models	
1) Simulation models are developed from interrelated ratios to show the simultaneous effects of changes in these ratios	1) The overall effect of component variables can be observed from the use of simulation models
2) Forecasting models are developed by using regression analysis techniques on particular ratios	2) Planning is facilitated by the use of forecasting models. Budgets can be established as the result of a particular forecast of certain ratios

	1993	1992
Assets		
Cash	$ 106,000	$ 192,000
Accounts receivable	566,000	483,000
Inventories	320,000	250,000
Plant and equipment (net)	740,000	716,000
Patents	26,000	26,000
Other intangible assets	14,000	12,000
Total assets	$ 1,772,000	$ 1,679,000
Liabilities and equity		
Accounts payable	$ 170,000	$ 126,000
Federal income tax payable	32,000	13,000
Miscellaneous accrued payables and dividends payable	38,000	45,000
Bonds payable (4%, due 1996)	300,000	300,000
Preferred stock ($100 par, 7% cumulative, nonparticipating and callable at $110)	200,000	200,000
Common stock (no par, 20,000 shares authorized, issued and outstanding)	400,000	400,000
Retained earnings	720,000	683,000
Treasury stock - 800 shares of preferred	(88,000)	(88,000)
Total liabilities and equity	$ 1,772,000	$ 1,679,000

Figure 1
ABC Company
Balance Sheet

	1993	1992
Net sales	$1,500,000	$ 1,100,000
Cost of goods sold	900,000	710,000
Gross margin on sales	$ 600,000	$ 390,000
Operating expenses (including interest)	498,000	355,000
Income before federal income taxes	$ 102,000	$ 35,000
Income tax expense	37,000	13,000
Net income	$ 65,000	$ 22,000

Figure 2
ABC Company
Income Statement

	1.	Net profit to net sales (net profit margin)
×	2.	Net sales to total assets (asset turnover)
=	3.	Return on investment or assets
×	4.	Financial leverage advantage (assets to equity ratio)
=	5.	Net income to owners' equity (return on equity)
×	6.	Retention ratio (1 – dividend to net income ratio)
=	7.	Potential growth rate in earnings.

Figure 3
Profitability Model

Asset turnover indicates the amount of sales that each dollar invested in assets can generate. Thus, in this example, each dollar of assets is able to generate $.8934 of sales revenue. Increases in asset turnover are considered favorable so long as profit margins are not unduly sacrificed to generate volume increases.

In order to use asset turnover as part of the profitability growth model, two changes must be made: (1) use beginning of the year assets rather than an average and (2) use total assets rather than net fixed assets, which are commonly used for asset turnover computations.

Return on Assets (Return on Investment)

The formula for computing this ratios is as follows:

Net profit margin x Total asset turnover, or

$$\frac{\text{Net income}}{\text{Total assets}} = \frac{\$\ 65,000}{\$1,679,000} = 3.87\%$$

Return on assets (ROA) demonstrates the after-tax interest equivalent return on assets invested. Thus, assets are earning 3.87% after-tax. Steady or growing ROA percentages are important indices of financial health in a potential lessee.

Financial Leverage Advantage (Assets to Equity Ratio)

The formula for computing this ratio is as follows:

$$\frac{\text{Total assets (beginning of year)}}{\text{Owners' equity (beginning of year)}} = \frac{\$1,679,000}{\$1,195,000} = 1.405$$

Strictly speaking, this ratio is not one that indicates profitability directly; rather, it indicates the effect of financial leverage on profit. In effect, when a company earns more than enough on its assets to pay interest on debt, the balance goes to equity. This ratio, when multiplied times ROA, shows the effect on equity when leverage is employed.

Thus, assets are 1.405 times equity and the ROA, when converted to an ROE, will be 140.5% higher, as the next ratio demonstrates.

Return on Equity (Net Income to Owners' Equity)

The formula for computing this ratio is as follows:

$$\text{ROA} \times \text{Financial leverage advantage} = 3.87\% \times 1.405 = 5.44\%, \text{ or directly}$$

$$\frac{\text{Net income (after taxes)}}{\text{Net worth (beginning of year)}} = \frac{\$\ \ 65,000}{\$1,195,000} = 5.44\%$$

A company's ROE should be steady or growing and be relatively close to other industry competitors. However, increased ROEs that stem from increased financial leverage, rather than from a growing ROA, should not be considered a favorable indicator of creditworthiness.

Retention Ratio

The formula for computing this ratio is as follows:

$$1 - \frac{\text{Dividends}}{\text{Net income}} = 1 - \frac{\$28,000}{\$65,000} = 56.92\%$$

This ratio indicates the percentage of net income that remains after dividend payment. Sudden or systematic declines in the retention ratio could indicate an impending profitability crisis.

Potential Growth Rate

The formula for computing this ratio is as follows:

$$\text{ROE x Retention ratio} = 5.44\% \times 56.92\% = 3.10\%$$

A company can grow from internal sources no faster than the product of its retention ratio times its ROE. To grow faster, either ROE has to be increased or dividend payout reduced. Therefore, if leases are to be paid out of anticipated future earnings derived from increased growth, that growth should be justified.

Price Earnings Ratio

The formula for computing this ratio is as follows:

$$\frac{\text{Market price per share (average may be used)}}{\text{Net income (previous 4 quarters) per share}} = \frac{\$\ \ 35}{\left(\dfrac{\$65,000}{20,000}\right)} = \$10.769 \text{ per share}$$

Sudden decreases in the price/earnings ratio relative to the price/earnings ratios of the Standard and Poors 500 could indicate an impending profitability problem.

Gross Margin

The formula for computing this ratio is as follows:

$$\frac{\text{Gross profit on sales}}{\text{Total sales revenue}} = \frac{\$\ \ 600,000}{\$1,500,000} = 40\%$$

Gross profit margin indicates what percentage of sales is gross profit. Steady or increasing gross profit margins are favorable so long as asset turnover is not being reduced too fast or general and administrative expenses are not increasing too rapidly.

Dividend Yield

The formula for computing this ratio is as follows:

$$\frac{\text{Dividend per share}}{\text{Average price per share}} = \frac{\left(\frac{\$28,000}{20,000}\right)}{35} = 4\%$$

Dividend yields usually remain fairly constant within a narrow range of 2 to 4%. Ratios above 4%, or sudden reductions in a ratio when the general stock market is constant, could indicate upcoming profitability problems.

LIQUIDITY AND WORKING CAPITAL

In addition to profitability, another vital concern of the financial analyst is liquidity, or the ability of the firm to meet its maturing obligations (current liabilities). Following are four ratios that indicate liquidity, and the composition of working capital in terms of inventory and accounts receivable.

Current Ratio

The formula for computing this ratio is as follows:

$$\frac{\text{Current assets}}{\text{Current liabilities}} = \frac{\$992,000}{\$240,000} = 4.13 \text{ times}$$

Current assets are, therefore, 4.13 times as large as the current liabilities. Keep in mind, however, that a significant portion of current assets may not be liquid enough to be able to pay liabilities when due.

Acid-Test Ratio (Quick Ratio)

The formula for computing this ratio is as follows:

$$\frac{\text{Quick assets (cash, securities, accounts receivable)}}{\text{Current liabilities}} = \frac{\$672,000}{\$240,000} = 2.8 \text{ times}$$

Quick (readily convertible to cash) assets are, therefore, 2.8 times current liabilities, which is perhaps a more realistic index of liquidity than current ratio.

Inventory-to-Net Working Capital

The formula for computing this ratio is as follows:

$$\frac{\text{Inventory (end of period or average)}}{\text{Net working capital}} = \frac{\$285,000}{\$992,000 - \$240,000} = 37.90\%$$

Note that net working capital is not the same as current assets, but consists of current assets minus current liabilities. This ratio indicates what percentage of working capital is comprised of inventory, which is its most nonliquid component. An increasing inventory-to-net working capital ratio indicates movement towards a nonliquid position.

Accounts Receivable-to-Net Working Capital

The formula for computing this ratio is as follows:

$$\frac{\text{Accounts receivable (end of period or average)}}{\text{Net working capital}} = \frac{\$525,000}{\$752,000} = 69.81\%$$

A growing accounts receivable to net working capital ratio is favorable because it indicates a more liquid working capital than if inventory were the predominant component.

INVESTMENT UTILIZATION (ACTIVITY)

Investment utilization or activity ratios measure how effectively the firm employs the resources at its command. One method to measure investment utilization is to review the total operating cycle, which is an analysis of the time required to convert cash into merchandise, then into accounts receivable and ultimately back into cash again. There are five common ratios that aid in an analysis of investment utilization, which follow.

Days' Receivables (Collection Period)

The formula for computing this ratio is as follows:

$$\frac{365}{\text{Accounts receivable turnover}} \left\{ \frac{\text{Credit sales}}{\text{Average accounts receivable}} \right.$$

$$\left[\frac{365}{\left(\dfrac{\$1,500,000}{\left(\dfrac{\$566,000 + \$483,000}{2} \right)} \right)} \right] = 127.628 \text{ days}$$

If credit sales are not available, total sales may be used. In addition, year end accounts receivable may be used. This ratio indicates it takes, on the average, 128 days to collect ABC Company's receivables. If this time period is growing, a red flag is raised indicating liquidity problems such as bad debts, evading collection policy, etc.

Days' Inventories (Sales Period)

The formula for computing this ratio is as follows:

$$\frac{365}{\text{Inventory turnover}} \left\{ \frac{\text{Cost of goods sold}}{\text{Average inventory}} \right.$$

$$\left[\frac{365}{\left(\dfrac{\$900,000}{\left(\dfrac{\$320,000 + \$250,000}{2} \right)} \right)} \right] \quad = \quad 115.583 \text{ days}$$

If cost of goods sold is not available, total sales may be used. Furthermore, ending inventory may be used instead of average inventory. This ratio indicates the time required to convert inventory into a sale. A growing ratio could indicate sales slowdown or manufacturing inefficiencies, or a new product mix, all of which should be investigated and understood.

Total Operating Cycle

The formula for computing this ratio is as follows:

Days' receivables + days' inventories = 127.628 + 115.583 = 243.2 days

This ratio represents the total time to convert inventory into a sale, then into a receivable and back into cash. Growth of this conversion time period could indicate poorer overall utilization of resources.

Days' Payables and Accounts Payable Turnover

The formula for computing this ratio is as follows:

$$\frac{365}{\text{Payable turnover}} \quad \left\{ \quad \frac{\text{Cost of goods sold}}{\text{Average payable}} \right.$$

$$\left[\frac{365}{\left(\dfrac{\$900,000}{\left(\dfrac{\$170,000 + \$126,000}{2} \right)} \right)} \right] \quad = \quad 60.022 \text{ days}$$

This ratio represents the average time taken to pay trade payables. The time period should be less than both days' receivables or days' inventories. Growth in the days' payable could indicate forthcoming liquidy and profitability problems since trade creditors are being forced to increase their waiting period for payment.

Accounts Payable to Inventory

The formula for computing this ratio is as follows:

$$\frac{\text{Accounts payable}}{\text{Inventory}} \quad = \quad \frac{\$170,000}{\$320,000} \quad = \quad 53.125$$

Net Sales to Owners' Equity

The formula for computing this ratio is as follows:

$$\frac{\text{Net sales}}{\text{Owners' equity (average)}} \quad = \quad \frac{\$1,500,000}{\$1,195,000} \quad = \quad 1.26 \text{ times}$$

This indicates how dependent sales are on owners' equity (assuming constant financial leverage). Increased sales might require equity infusions if this ratio has held constant. Without equity infusions expansion might be limited. Increases in the ratio could indicate improvement in operational efficiencies.

Net Sales to Working Capital

The formula for computing this ratio is as follows:

$$\frac{\text{Net sales}}{\text{Average net working capital}} = \frac{\$1,500,000}{\$\ 747,000} = 2.01 \text{ times}$$

Net sales to average net working capital indicates the degree to which sales are dependent upon working capital. If this ratio increases, working capital inefficiencies are occurring or a new product with slower turnover is being sold.

FINANCIAL LEVERAGE

A lessor granting credit should always be concerned with the debt burden a potential lessee is carrying, for if the lessee is too highly leveraged it may not be able to pay the lease payment. Financial leverage ratios aid the analyst in determing the risk associated with debt.

Total Liabilities to Total Assets (Debt Ratio)

The formula for computing this ratio is as fllows:

$$\frac{\text{Total liabilities (or long-term liabilities)}}{\text{Total assets}} = \frac{\$\ 540,000}{\$1,772,000} = 30.47\%$$

This ratio describes what percentage debt is of the total capital structure. If a company's ROE is relatively constant while this ratio is growing, inefficiencies are occurring.

Current Liabilities to Owners' Equity

The formula for computing this ratio is as follows:

$$\frac{\text{Current liabilities}}{\text{Owners' equity}} = \frac{\$\ 240,000}{\$1,232,000} = 19.48\%$$

This ratio indicates relative commitment to the company: trade creditors (current liabilities) versus owners' equity. A growing ratio could indicate forthcoming liquidity needs.

Interest-to-Net Income Before Interest

The formula for computing this ratio is as follows:

$$\frac{\text{Interest}}{\text{Interest + Net income}} \quad \text{or} \quad \frac{\text{Interest } (1 + t)}{\text{Interest } (1 - t) + \text{Net income}}$$

$$= \frac{\$120,000}{\$185,000} = 64.86\%$$

Whereas total liabilities to total assets indicate total leverage, this ratio indicates both total leverage and the cost of the leverage relative to net income. A growing ratio without corresponding increases in ROE would indicate a profitability problem and possible forthcoming credit squeeze.

Total Liabilities to Owners' Equity

The formula for computing this ratio is as follows:

$$\frac{\text{Total liabilities}}{\text{Owners' equity}} = \frac{\$\ 540,000}{\$1,232,000} = 43.83\%$$

This ratio indicates the liabilities relative to the investment commitment of the company; all creditors (trade and long-term) versus owners' equity. A growing percentage could indicate forthcoming liquidity problems.

SOLVENCY AND RISK

The ability of a lessee to meet the carrying costs on its existing debt provides a good idea of its potential ability to make the lease payment. This ratio measures that capability.

Times Interest Earned

The formula for computing this ratio is as follows:

$$\frac{\text{Net income} + \text{taxes} + \text{interest}}{\text{Interest}} = \frac{\$222,000}{\$120,000} = 1.85 \text{ times}$$

Interest could have been paid 4.64 times before income is exhausted.

OWNERS' EQUITY

The amount of equity the owners are retaining in the business is another important measure of financial stability.

Net Fixed Assets to Owners' Equity

The formula for computing this ratio is as follows:

$$\frac{\text{Fixed assets (net of depreciation)}}{\text{Owners' equity}} = \frac{\$\ 740,000}{\$1,232,000} = 60.06\%$$

This ratio indicates the reliance of property, plant and equipment on equity. Increases in this percent indicate permanent capital requirements as opposed to short and intermediate term funding. Too rapid an increase could indicate a forthcoming liquidity problem as well a cutback on property, plant and equipment expansion.

Book Value per Common Share

The formula for computing this ratio is as follows:

$$\frac{\text{Total book value of common stock}}{\text{Shares outstanding}} \quad = \quad \frac{\$1,012,000}{\$\quad 20,000} \quad = \quad \$50.60$$

The liquidation value of callable preferred stock, cumulative preferred dividends in arrears and treasury stock is deducted from the total owners' equity in order to obtain the total book value of common stock.

Return on Common Equity

The formula for computing this ratio is as follows:

$$\frac{\text{Net income} - \text{preferred dividends currently due}}{\text{Total book value of common stock}} \quad = \quad \frac{\$65,000 - \$14,000}{\$1,012,000} \quad = \quad 5.04\%$$

So long as financial leverage is held constant, increases in ROE are the ultimate measure of profitability. Decreases in this percent indicate problems worthy of further inquiry.

RISK ASSESSMENT

Analysis of the risk components in a lease suggests there are at least four major categories or groupings of lease variables: (1) lessor risk assessment variables, (2) lessor requirement variables, (3) lessee need variables and (4) lease structuring variables. The lessor is obviously interested in the first two categories of leasing variables; the lessee focuses attention upon the latter two categories of variables. It is impossible, however, for either the lessor or the lessee to ignore the needs and requirements of the other. The lessor will be much more successful if the lessee variables and needs are anticipated in structuring the lease. By the same token, lessees are becoming increasingly sophisticated in lease analysis, which has led them to anticipate the requirements that a lessor must embrace in structuring the lease. It is important, therefore, that risk assessment is understood by both the lessee and the lessor as the risk resulting from the creditworthiness of a lessee is discussed.

The evaluation and assignment of the risks inherent in a lease transaction are primarily decisions centering around creditworthiness. Lessors have aggressively borrowed techniques employed by other grantors of credit as they seek to evaluate these risks. The techniques of risk assessment will be presented in this chapter as the 30 Cs of lease credit, and will be categorized into three groups representing the basic analytical functions performed, and types of risk identified, when assessing and evaluating risk. These three broad groups are lessor specific risk analysis, lessee specific risk analysis and lease specific risk analysis.

Lessor Specific Risk Assessment

There are eight Cs of credit that relate specifically to lessors. For the most part, they represent steps the lessor may take in assessing the lessee's credit, as opposed to a characteristic of the lessee or of the lease environment.

CONFIRMATION

The first element, confirmation, refers to the ability of the lessor to obtain information upon which a quantitative and/or qualitative risk evaluation can be based. Since it is imperative the lessor be able to confirm information supplied by the lessee, the primary sources of confirmation available will be examined.

A prime source of information is the audit report from an auditing firm. Inasmuch as audited financial statements are prepared according to GAAP, there is a traditional high level of reliance thereon. Although certain limitations, such as the use of historical cost rather than current market valuation techniques are inherent in GAAP, these statements universally provide an excellent starting point in risk assessment.

A compilation or disclaimer is another source of financial information, but care must be taken when such reports are utilized. If financial statements have not been audited, but merely compiled by an accounting firm, a disclaimer such as the following is likely to appear in the cover letter or on the face of the financial statements themselves: " . . . We have not audited or reviewed the accompanying financial statements and, accordingly, do not express an opinion or any other form of assurance on them."

Such a disclaimer on compiled figures does not necessarily invalidate the financial statements as a source of information. It does, however, present the lessor with an extended risk exposure. A sophisticated accountant can form many opinions about compilations by ascertaining that information presented in the financial statements assumes traditional reporting norms. It is, however, possible the financial statements appear reasonable when, in fact, the underlying figures are tainted. In conclusion, a disclaimer is a warning sign that lessor risk has been extended.

Somewhere between the audited financial statement and the disclaimer is a review or limited review of financial statements. Accounting firms are increasingly avoiding the use of such limited reviews because it has increased the audit risk to the firm. Occasionally, special or limited reviews are encountered, especially in circumstances where a complete audit is not necessary. An example is encountered when a bank or factory requires periodic reviews on receivables or inventories.

Tax returns also provide excellent information on which to evaluate lessor risk. Tax returns are prepared according to tax legislation, not according to GAAP; therefore, considerable differences can and usually do exist between financial statements and tax statements. When utilizing tax statements, it is prudent to carefully examine reconciliation schedule M-1, which explains the differences between net income according to GAAP and net income according to tax legislation.

Other special reports may exist that can assist the lessor in risk evaluation. Most public companies are required to provide periodic reports with the Securities and Exchange Commission (SEC). The 10-K (annual report), 10-Q (quarterly reports), 8-K (significant events), etc., are all examples of public information available from the SEC, the lessee or special reporting services. Certain special reports are sometimes required in specialized industries, such as the airline and broadcast industries. These industries are regulated by public agencies such as the

Federal Aviation Administration and the Federal Trade Commission; therefore, the information is readily available for credit purposes.

CORROBORATION

The second C, corroboration, is the lessor specific activity in which the lessor validates the credit information supplied by the prospective lessee. Bank references, for instance, should be obtained and properly evaluated. Usually this necessitates a letter of authorization from the lessee authorizing the bank to disclose any and all information that may impact the lessor's risk position. Proper documentation of bank corroboration would include the following:

1. Name and location of the bank
2. Loans outstanding
3. Loan amounts
4. Collateralization
5. Payment history
6. Length of the credit relationship
7. Highest amount of debt extended
8. Contingent debt
9. Leases with that bank.

Another important corroborative source is prior leasing commitments with other lessors. Due to burgeoning legal difficulties caused by negative replies to corroboration requests, many banks and lessors are becoming skilled at complying with credit requests while at the same time avoiding disclosure of information that may provoke subsequent litigation. Since the lessee is providing the lessor with a list of historical credit relationships, it is logical that the lessee, to the extent possible, will provide only references that will result in positive corroboration. Alternative corroborative sources will be discussed under a subsequent C, entitled credit.

CATASTROPHE

Catastrophe in risk evaluation dictates that the lessor adequately assess absolute down-side risk. The lessor should identify the worst practical down-side possibility and then evaluate the probability and amount of exposure. Two tools that can be utilized are modeling techniques and decision trees, which will be discussed later in this chapter. The final element of risk assessment in this category involves providing adequate protection against down-side risk once it has been identified, and its probability assessed.

CONCATENATION

Concatenation is the interrelating and choosing of those credit variables that will impact the credit decision. In other words, the lessor must determine what is important in the credit decision-making process.

CLASSIFICATION

Classification is the process of ranking credit variables or components from the most important to the least important. This results in a prioritization or relative ranking of credit variables.

CONSIDERATION

Consideration is the degree to which a credit standard is met. For example, once a concatenation occurs and the classifications of credit variables are chosen, the lessor subjectively scores each variable on a predetermined scale.

COMPUTATION

Computation is the multiplication of the classification value just discussed by the consideration, as illustrated in Table 2. For purposes of illustration, an example using a scoring system of 0 to 10, and incorporating concatenation, classification, consideration and computation, will be presented (see Table 2). If the credit variable is important, it is assigned a value of 8 to 10. If it is unimportant, it is assigned a value of 0 to 3, thus leaving a value of 4 to 7 for those variables in between.

COMPILATON

Compilation is the arithmetic process of adding all the computed products from the computation step, and is the decision rule for reaching a credit decision. This weighted average total is then used in a decision matrix. While this may be difficult to appreciate at this point, Table 2 adequately illustrates the meaning of compilation. Decision matrices, which are being utilized in increasing numbers, should be accompanied by narrative comment from the lease credit investigator. Figure 4 is a sample decision matrix worksheet used to incorporate the effects of all 30 Cs of credit into the overall credit decision. Note that one C, compilation, represents the overall process, four of the Cs (the column heads) are subprocesses of compilation and the remaining 25 Cs of credit are grouped according to the six concatenation subheads shown in Table 2.

The formatting of the credit matrix is subject to a high degree of subjectivity on the part of the lessor. Each lessor is swayed by different factors, which result in varying concatenations, fluctuating classification values and varying consideration values. Thus, the resulting computation varies considerably from lessor to lessor. It is important to note, however, that much of the subjectivity is resolved to very tolerable limits when historical leases (existing leases in a lessor's portfolio and paid-off leases) are subjected to a matrix analysis. Once a lessor has an historical trend of which leases were good, average and bad, the question of assigning values for the above matrix becomes quite plausible. Since this can be computerized rather easily, a large number of historical leases can be analyzed to provide classification values and consideration weightings. The use of such evaluative matrices is especially valuable in lease credit departments that are growing rapidly, as it enables the credit manager to maintain a fair degree of uniformity and consistency within the credit evaluation team. Conversely, lessors that have not developed a matrix system have traditionally reported a lesser degree of uniformity and consistency within the credit analysis team.

Table 2
Computation Worksheet

Concatenation	Classification		Consideration 0 –10		Computation
Future potential	.30	×	7	=	2.10
Independent verification	.20	×	6	=	1.20
Past experience	.15	×	8	=	1.20
Additional risk factors	.15	×	1	=	.15
Product and diversification risk	.10	×	4	=	.40
Mitigating considerations	.10	×	3	=	.30
Expected value					5.35

Compilation (correlation)

Reject	0 – 4
Accept (charge premium rate)	4.1 – 5
Accept	5.1 – 7
Accept (give preferential rate)	7.1 –10

Lessee Specific Risk Assessment

There are 12 Cs of credit that relate specifically to lessees. For the most part these lessee specific risks represent characteristics or traits of the lessee that the lessor will be investigating and evaluating.

CHARACTER

The first element, character, refers to the potential lessee's apparent or historically demonstrated integrity, honesty and commitment to honor its financial responsibilities, even during hard times. Short of previous experience with the lessee, this component is difficult to ascertain. Certainly, some degree of character assessment can be obtained from a personal interview or through checking with other lease companies, bankers and creditors from whom the potential lessee has obtained leases or other credit. Previous experience with the lessee is excellent evidence, either of a positive or a negative nature. If no previous experience with the prospective lessee exists, alternative indicators must be utilized.

Care should be taken to ascertain that proper financial communication occurs regarding existing leases on the income statement and balance sheet of a prospective lessee. For example, positive character indicators would dictate that a lessee properly disclose off balance sheet financing arrangements, such as sale-leaseback and defeasance arrangements. On the other

Concatenation	Classification Percentage	Consideration (0 – 10)		Computation
Future potential:				
Capital		×	=	
Capacity		×	=	
Cash flow		×	=	
Course		×	=	
Constraints	.	×	=	
Subtotal	.			
Past experience:				
Competence		×	=	
Control		×	=	
Chronological age		×	=	
Character	.	×	=	
Subtotal	.			
Equipment and diversification:				
Collateral		×	=	
Category		×	=	
Countercyclical	.	×	=	
Subtotal	.			
Additional risk factors:				
Capability		×	=	
Competition		×	=	
Cross border		×	=	
Currency		×	=	
Complexity		×	=	
Catastrophe	.	×	=	
Subtotal	.			
Independent verification:				
Credit		×	=	
Confirmation		×	=	
Corroboration		×	=	
CAPM – Beta	.	×	=	
Subtotal	.			
Mitigating considerations:				
Copartner		×	=	
Concealed value		×	=	
Circumstances	.	×	=	
Subtotal	.			
Total	1.00			

Figure 4
Decision Matrix Worksheet

hand, discovery by the lessor of off balance sheet financing may suggest flawed character. Good character is generally reflected by historical performance.

CAPITAL

Capital is a term that has been widely interpreted. Accordingly, three broad meanings of the term will be used here. In its broadest sense, capital refers to the total resources available for a firm's usage. This, by definition, includes all assets and balance sheet resources and has even been interpreted by some to include nonbalance sheet resources such as people, experience and other factors normally not quantified as resources. Narrower in its definition of capital is the definition of capital assets, which is generally regarded as property, plant and equipment. An even still narrower definition regards capital as cash. It is imperative for the credit analyst to properly define this term before communicating with the debtor concerning questions of a capital nature.

For risk assessment purposes, a creditor usually looks for strong net worth coupled with limited financial leverage. A strong capital position represents the assets available to satisfy a judgement in the event that a default should occur. This concept is communicated in the accounting formula of assets equal liabilities plus equity. The left-hand side of the equation represents all quantified asset values while the right-hand side of the equation indicates the source of financing for those assets.

There are only two methods of obtaining assets. Either money is borrowed to purchase them or equity funds are invested to purchase them. Careful analysis of the balance sheet equation, therefore, indicates not only the degree of the net worth, but also the extent of financial leverage. It is also necessary to determine the degree to which assets may be encumbered. It is possible for a company to have a high net worth but have an inordinate amount of assets placed as collateral with other creditors, thus leaving insufficient protection for a new lease. Many lessors, however, disregard encumbered assets, maintaining they will not enter into a lease if there is an intolerable likelihood that repossession may occur. These lessors reason that strong earning capacity and a secured position in the leased equipment adequately protect the lessor. If the asset has a questionable residual value or is rapidly wasting, however, the lessor is well-advised to obtain additional unencumbered capital protection.

With smaller companies, this may be resolved by requesting additional collateral from the lessee and/or personal guarantees. If the personal guarantees, however, have no merit (e.g., the personal guarantee is based upon a balance sheet of negligible net worth), the personal guarantee may be worthless. Consequently, the capital position of both the lessee's business and the lease guarantor must be examined and evaluated. In larger lease transactions and in most public companies, personal guarantees cannot or will not be given. The lessee net worth stands alone. Ratios that can be used to analyze capital include debt-to-equity, assets-to-net worth, ROA and ROE, all concepts that were discussed earlier in this chapter in the ratio section.

CAPACITY

Capacity refers to the lessee's ability to pay. Typical credit analysis involves income statement review, inasmuch as this is the primary source of repayment funds for the typical lessee. Lessors should ascertain that net income is adequate and, further, should trend historical net income figures to determine the pattern of growth. If net income is growing but at a declining rate, there is reason to question future indicators of paying ability. On the other hand, steady growth of net income or, even better yet, growth at an increasing rate, would normally reflect a decreased risk of capacity. If a sizable portion of the net income is realized through a limited number of customers, the lessor should ascertain the probability of continued sales by written or verbal confirmation with them.

It is also prudent to track not only historical net income, but also historical trends of gross profit or gross operating margin. For credit purposes, this determines if net income growth is occurring through controlling the cost of goods sold or through controlling the expenses. The best situation, of course, is to have an increasing gross and net profit margin. A traditional approach utilized to analyze capacity limitations, that of adequate fixed payment coverage (times interest earned), was pioneered by financial institutions and has been borrowed widely by the leasing industry. The assumption is made that the larger the net income, the more will be available to cover the next lease transaction that is entered into, as illustrated by the formula

$$\frac{\text{Net income} + \text{interest} + \text{taxes}}{\text{Incremental lease payment}}$$

The logic of this calculation suggests the larger the pretax, preinterest net income, the easier it will be to pay for the lease. There are several caveats, however, that the lessor should remember. First of all, when this formula was popularized decades ago in the banking industry, accrual net income and cash net income were much closer than they are today. It is possible today to have a positive net income, but a negative cash flow. Likewise, it is possible to have a negative net income and a positive cash flow. The former is illustrated by growth companies who have very favorable net incomes, but who invest large amounts in assets. Hence, they have a lot of net income, but no cash. Conversely, firms that have a negative net income often liquidate assets and can be cash rich, despite the fact they are net income poor. Therefore, there is a growing tendency today to substitute cash flow for the accrual net income that has traditionally appeared in the numerator of the above equation. Keep in mind also that FASB 95 now requires cash flow statements, which will bring about many changes in traditional ratio analysis.

If the information is available, it may be wise for the lessor to calculate the lessee's break-even point from both an accrual and a cash standpoint. In order to calculate the break-even, it is necessary to separate all costs into either fixed or variable portions. Once this is done, it is easy to perceive a conceptual basis inherent in break-even analysis. As long as it is possible to cover the variable costs (such as cost of goods sold) and make a contribution towards fixed costs (such as the president's salary), it makes economic sense to operate. Logically, the lower the break-even point and the higher the contribution rate, the more desirable the situation. Sophisticated lessees often will have done the analysis or have the information necessary to make the calculations. Smaller companies, however, who do not have the requisite analytical capabilities may not be able to comply with this request for break-even information. Should this be the case, or should a large, sophisticated lessee refuse to provide the information, there is a quick and dirty method of approximating the break-even point. Since an income statement will have been provided, this approximation can be accomplished by considering the cost of goods sold section to be variable costs (product costs) and the operating expenses to be fixed costs (period costs). Sales are then divided into the gross margin to arrive at a sales/profit relationship. This calculation is next divided into fixed costs. To illustrate, assume

Sales	$ 1,000,000
Cost of goods sold	(600,000)
Gross margin	$ 400,000
Expenses (fixed)	(300,000)
Net income	$ 100,000

$$\frac{\text{Gross margin}}{\text{sales}} = \frac{\$\ \ 400,000}{\$\ 1,000,000} = 40\%$$

$$\frac{\text{Fixed costs}}{\text{Gross margin/sales}} = \text{Break-even point}$$

$$\frac{\$300,000}{.40} = \$\ \ 750,000$$

The validity of this method of approximation can be proven.

Sales	$ 750,000
Cost of goods sold (60%)	(450,000)
Gross margin	$ 300,000
Expenses (fixed)	(300,000)
Net income (break-even)	$ 0

This approach is obviously quick and dirty since some of the expenses may be variable, but, in the absence of better data, it works as an indicator of risk. If better information is available, it should be used to determine which of the expenses are fixed and which variable.

Capacity in its broader interpretation includes not only the current ability of a lessee to earn, but also lessee ability to maintain adequate liquidity, cash flow and to sustain solvency. Liquidity typically is assessed by examination of the current assets and the current liabilities, as is indicated by measures such as the current ratio, working capital and the quick or acid test ratio.

In the event that a lessee's cash flow position deteriorates or is threatened, the question of liquidity may arise and, therefore, the firm's capacity may be compromised. Therefore, a cash budget or forecast should demonstrate adequate cash for at least one-half of the lease term. This will be discussed in more detail later in this chapter under cash flow. Finally, net income must grow at a rate sufficient to sustain and indeed strengthen solvency.

CREDIT

Credit experience should be investigated to determine historical trading policies and practices of the lessee. Dunn & Bradstreet is a common source that typically reports major credit phenomena; they report size of capital and payment trends (how big a company is and how fast it pays). Typically, the assumption is that the bigger a company is and the faster it pays, the better the creditor situation. Conversely, a smaller company that pays slowly would normally be determined less worthy of credit. Care should be taken to properly interpret this information.

Some firms choose not to provide Dunn & Bradstreet with the financial information requested to determine the rating. In these circumstances, the information is either estimated or a comment is placed in the rating that the company does not choose to be rated. Typically either of these alternative approaches casts a negative shadow upon the credit granting process.

Credit checks are frequently obtained on selected officers, owners and principals of a lessee seeking credit. This may be particularly revealing where the lessee is a closely-held company or has little historical background due to its short life. The lessor will feel more comfortable about extending credit if the principals have a superior track record in their individual credit files, especially for a start-up company.

Trade associations are a frequent source of credit information. These associations tend to be a close-knit club where the informal dispersion of credit information is widely shared with those who have privileged membership. Additionally, formal rating agencies, such as Moody's and Standard and Poor's, have research arms that formally rate most large and some small companies. TRW and National Credit Information Services (NACIS) are two other players in the independent credit verification business.

CASH FLOW

Cash flow analysis should indicate the lease can be serviced without impinging upon the liquidity of the lessee. Refer to the detailed discussion of cash flow in this chapter for further information on this aspect of risk assessment.

CHRONOLOGICAL AGE

The chronological age of the company should be noted, as a company with a relatively recent history presents increased risk to the lessor. In the case of start-up companies, the lessor should look to the historical successes and failures of the principals involved. For established firms the lessor should trend relevant income and figures to provide a basis for evaluation of forecasted data.

CAPM-BETA COEFFICIENT

The capital asset pricing model (CAPM), with its attendant beta coefficient, is a computational approach for the measurement of risk in capital budgeting. Since leasing is basically a capital expenditure consideration, it is logical to understand this conceptual approach to capital asset and risk evaluation.

Typically, interest rates received by investors vary according to the risks they bear. Within this context of risk perception, a mathematical model has been developed highlighting the impact of perceived changes in corporate risk; this approach makes use of the beta coefficient. At the risk of oversimplification, financial texts separate risk into two components, risk-free investments and a risk premium. The return on risk-free investments can be measured at any time by reviewing the return on government securities. A risk premium can be assigned to each lessee analyzed (risky lessees dictate higher risk premiums, low-risk lessees dictate lower risk premiums and leases such as those to the federal government would have no risk premium).

To illustrate this concept, assume that a risk-free return is 7%. Furthermore, due to the normal risk factor attendant to the lessee, an additional risk premium of 5% has been assigned. Thus, the total expected return on the lease investment would be 12% (7% + 5%) to compensate for both types of risk. At this point, the concept of the beta coefficient must be introduced into the example. Merrill Lynch, Standard and Poor's and many other financial organizations publish "beta books," in which the industry average for risk premium is assigned a value of one. Individual companies with a perceived risk premium of less than one would appear more stable and those with a beta in excess of one would be perceived as less stable. To complete the example begun above, assume the beta coefficient is one, as illustrated below:

$$7\% + (1)(5\%) = 12\%$$

If one of the financial reporting services, however, determines the beta coefficient in the capital model as having increased to 1.8, the formula is revised to yield an answer of 16% [7% + (1.8)(5%)].

The beta coefficient is the educated assessment of the financial risk premium of individual companies compared to their industry averages. Those lessors leasing to listed corporations would, therefore, find it wise to subscribe to a beta book, such as Merrill Lynch's, for the beta coefficients of all large public companies. For those lessors desiring to calculate a beta coefficient for unlisted lessees, they should be referred to the relevant chapters in most graduate-level finance texts. If there is a material adjustment in a beta coefficient for a particular company, it is evident there has been a change in the risk level of the company and lease terms should be adjusted accordingly.

CAPABILITY

Capability is the lessee's level of management expertise. New management frequently has a lower level of capability than experienced management. A proper assessment should be made of a managerial staff to ascertain that they possess requisite skills, training and experience. Numerous studies have indicated that this is one of the most important factors in predicting corporate success (see Table 3).

COMPETENCE

Competence refers to the concept of productivity and stewardship. These terms relate to the relationship between resource input and profitable output. How well has management done with the capital and labor resources entrusted to it? Financial reporting is moving towards the disclosure of more productivity information that will be very helpful to the credit analyst.

CONTROL

Control refers to existing feedback systems such as standard cost accounting systems, budget variance systems, zero base budgeting systems, etc. If there are no feedback systems in place, the decision-making process is hampered. On the other hand, superior feedback mechanisms aid the decision-making process. Attention should be paid to the type of cost system that is in place. For a manufacturing facility, it is imperative that feedback be obtained to correct or confirm past actions. This can be a job lot cost accounting system or a process costing system and

Table 3
Importance of Factors in Determining
Quality of Management
(base: total portfolio managers)

	1975	Total 1973	1972
Ranked as very important:			
Top management has extensive experience and knowledge of the specific business in which the company is involved	86%	85%	na%
Management is willing to admit its mistakes	64	75	79
There are identifiable successors to the top executive	53	60	66
Management has a strong incentive compensation program	41	50	na
Top executives have a strong financial background	39	35	33
Top management is concentrated in the hands of a few strong executives	21	20	23
Top management has a significant ownership position or stock options in the company	18	21	24
Top management comes from within the company rather than being brought in from outside	17	17	na
Top management receives a high level of compensation	15	25	31
Top management creates a high-pressure, performance-oriented environment	12	9	na
Top management has a real social awareness	9	22	23
Top management is relatively young	2	3	3

na = not asked

Source: Summary from *Major Institutional Investor, the Fourth Survey,* conducted by Louis Harris & Associates, Inc., New York, November 1975, p. 87.

typically involves the use of standard costs. Although service companies do not have as complex a system as a manufacturing company, it is still likely a standard system will be present.

In addition, a budgeting process should be in place. The budgeting process begins with the determination of a strategic, long-term, objective plan. By its very nature, the strategic plan is long-term, usually 3 to 5 years in today's economic arena, and should be very broad in nature. Historically, strategic plans have evolved around the word growth, and are evidenced by geographical, product line, diversification and total sales growth. More recently, however, strategic plans have begun to shift from these towards a growth of bottom-line profitability.

Once the strategic plan has been adopted by a company, it dictates the formation of a capital plan (balance sheet), which will enable the company to be strategically successful. In other words, the company must decide what assets it must gather and how these assets are to be financed. This balance sheet planning process is a long-term function, typically with the same time horizon as the strategic plan.

The next logical step in the budgeting process is the adoption of an operating plan, commonly referred to as the budget. The operating plan is an income statement plan, and, unlike the strategic plan and the capital plan, is a short-term one, typically of one year's duration, with a great deal of detail. The budget is an item-by-line item plan of what the income statement should be for the coming year. The point of concern for the lessor is the proper determination of what kind of lessee is applying for credit and what kind of budgetary or feedback tools that lessee is utilizing. If the lessee does not have a budget or feedback tools, beware! Credit risk has grown dramatically.

COURSE

Course is the direction in which the lessee is sailing its financial ship and also relates to the direction from which the ship has come. The lessor should ascertain that a proper trend analysis is available for cash flow, financial ratios and capacity indicators. This can be compared to the strategic plan of a company to see if historical trends have substantiated historical plans. Next, forecasts should be examined to ascertain the propriety of future positioning in the market. In forecasting, it is normally assumed that past trends will continue unless sufficient evidence exists to warrant a change in course. Therefore, compare the forecast course with historical trends to see if they are congruous. For example, if historical trending indicates a lease applicant has traditionally experienced a ROA of 11 or 12%, but the financial forecasts indicate an expected ROA of 20%, there must be evidence in the strategic plan, the capital plan and the operating plan of changes that will accommodate this growth. If not, it is likely to be wishful thinking at best and, perhaps, deception at worst.

CONSTRAINTS

Constraints are those unique business, governmental and social requirements that impede or promote a potential lessee's success. It has been said that, irrespective of a company's ambitions or goals, if the constraints and parameters of its environment can be identified, its outcome can be predicted. This is a truism in business; for example, the best product idea is doomed to failure if it is not marketed correctly. Thus, extending credit on the basis of product potential without demonstrated lessee marketing experience would be to ignore an important constraint.

The credit analyst most determine the unique characteristics of the potential lessee that strengthen or weaken its ability to perform on a lease contract. Easy competitive entrance to a marketplace, for example, may represent a characteristic that could constrain a lessee such that, without adequate resources to maintain market share, it fails. Dependence upon one customer as a major source of revenue is another example of a constraint that could weaken a lessee's creditworthiness.

Lease Specific Risk Assessment

There are 10 Cs of credit that relate specifically to the lease environment itself. For the most part these lease specific risks represent external factors that may impact the decision to extend lease credit.

COLLATERAL

Collateral is important since the lessor must first look to the equipment in case of default prior to obtaining any legal remedy directly against the lessee. Equipment that maintains value over time due to inflation and other causes is obviously superior to equipment that does not maintain resale value due to technological obsolescence. For example, commercial airplanes and jets frequently are worth as much after being leased 7 years as they were at the inception of the lease. In contrast, computers may lose a significant amount of their value even between the time they are ordered and the time they are delivered to the lessee. Collateral with questionable resale value requires the lessor to structure the lease in a manner to minimize this risk. Rather than offering the lessee a purchase option or no option at all (closed-end lease), a guaranteed residual can be required, which minimizes the risk to the lessor (but, unfortunately, may also cause the lessor to lose tax benefits).

Collateral subject to excessive wear and tear will require the lessor to enforce strict preventative maintenance clauses, coupled with excess-use penalties in order to mitigate the effect of impaired collateral value. Because the question of collateral is so important in many leases, it is wise for the lessor to compare an actuarial investment recovery curve to the economic obsolescence curve as in Figure 5. The shaded area in Figure 5 represents the area of increased risk to the lessor.

Whenever the economic obsolescence curve falls below the actuarial investment recovery curve, there is increased risk to the lessor, and the lease proposal should be adjusted accordingly. One adjustment method is to obtain a residual guarantee, which may fall into one of a number of categories. If the lessee guarantees the total residual, risk is removed from the lessor. FASB Statement No. 13 (FASB 13) dictates that most total lessee guarantees preclude treatment as an operating lease.

If the lessor still desires some type of collateral guarantee, it is possible to look elsewhere. Increasingly, vendors are concluding agreements with lessors in which the vendor manufacturer will make partial or full guarantees of the residual value. Vendors find this economically feasible due to (1) the increased sales volume of equipment generated through such policies and (2) because of expertise in the remarketing of their own equipment, either new or used, in the event of repossession or nonperformance. Since they can resell their own equipment with greater efficiency and increase new sales volume, there are increasing numbers of vendor guarantees

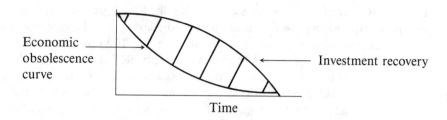

Figure 5
Obsolescence/Recovery Curves

being offered. It is important to note that a lease with this type of guarantee can still qualify as an operating lease under FASB 13 from the lessee's viewpoint, but not that of the lessor. Another type of guarantee that is encountered today is that offered by insurance companies. Although an additional cost to the lessor, an insurance company collateral guarantee may reduce the risk exposure of a questionable lease to the point where it becomes a very desirable lease, albeit one with less profit.

Remarketing agreements are agreements in which the vendor does not guarantee the residual equipment value, but does agree to assist in the remarketing of the equipment. The vendor either guarantees priority remarketing efforts or simply states in the remarketing agreement that best efforts will be used in assisting the lessor in remarketing the equipment. Best efforts is inferior to priority remarketing agreements, but comes at a cheaper price. Some of the priority remarketing agreements state that the lessor-owned equipment will actually be sold prior to the vendor's own new and/or used equipment. Finally, the lessor is always in a superior collateral position if it is possible to have additional collateral placed on a lease.

COMPLEXITY

Complexity refers to the inherent or designed intricacy of the equipment, the lease agreement, the tax law or any bundling of services. Equipment sophistication has increased considerably, especially in high technology equipment. If leased equipment subsequently proves operationally inappropriate, it is unlikely the revenue generated by the lease will be sufficient to sustain the lease, in which case the lease payments would be paid from other operating revenues. Thus, with the increased risk of high technology equipment, it must be ascertained that there is a proper and adequate engineering study with specifications, and the lessee must sign an equipment indemnification agreement stipulating that the equipment received is as ordered and the order was based upon adequate studies, specifications, etc. This does not eliminate the risk, but it causes the lessee to carefully rethink and review the lease agreement.

Lease agreements have become increasingly more detailed. The lessor should specify any security interests. Lessors also should require an insurance binder naming the lessor and/or the financing source as the insured parties of interest. Likewise, the lease agreement should specify what contingent lease agreements exist, such as excess miles on a leased automobile, excess copies on a copy machine, etc., how they are calculated and how the lessor is to be compensated.

During the last tax reform act, it became evident that the lease agreement also may contain restrictive provisions delineating the responsibilities of the lessor and the lessee regarding the effect of changing tax legislation upon the cash flow of the lessor. Therefore, tax indemnification clauses are becoming a common provision in the lease agreement. For the lessor, this provision should state the lessor will be made whole should the tax law change adversely. Because there are a great many definitions of what constitutes whole, the indemnification should indicate how the adjustment is to be made. A common approach would specify that the lessor's after-tax cash flow return on investment prior to the tax law change remain constant after the tax law change.

An additional area of complexity in the field of leasing is that of alternative minimum tax (see Chapter Four). Because it has changed the after-tax cost of leasing so dramatically for lessees, the lessor should aggressively address the situation by discussing it with all prospective lessees.

The competitive nature of leasing has pushed a number of old concepts into new perspectives. One of these is lease bundling, or full-service leasing. It has existed since the early days of the Phoenicians, as they leased not only the ship, but also the crew, the provisions and any other necessities attached to a successful voyage. Due to increasing competition in the leasing arena, there is a marked increase in bundling. Supplies, repairs, service, personnel, insurance and training may be attached to the equipment lease, making it that much more difficult for lessees to ascertain the true cost of the lease. This is not lessor subterfuge, but merely the reality of solving additional problems for a client and getting paid for doing it. The lessor, however, must calculate carefully the profitability of the various portions of the bundled lease in order to determine that the over all package provides adequate financial reward for the inherent complexity.

CURRENCY

Currency rates, restrictions, fluctuations and translations all increase credit risk to the lessor. Traditionally, contracts, including leases, have been denominated in US dollars. As a result, the major trading nations of the world have become the currency experts, highly trained and gifted in the area of hedging and arbitrage. As a result, lessors should continue to denominate their leases in terms of dollars unless they are prepared to pay the price for hedging expertise, inasmuch as the lessor would be competing against the acknowledged experts. If a lease is denominated in a foreign currency that is subsequently translated into a balance sheet and income statement, a translation gain or loss may also occur, a risk unforseen by many in the leasing business.

CATEGORY

Category impacts risk assessment in several unique ways. Certain types of equipment assume additional risk because they cannot be easily moved, such as elevators, air conditioning systems and even wallpaper. Other types of assets are subject to a high degree of abuse, such as certain rental cars, construction equipment and carpeting. If the equipment is substantially abused, considerable financial outlays are necessary to restore the asset to re-lease or sale condition. Sometimes, the asset is completely beyond reuse or sale. Thus, this credit risk must be quantified and worked into the lease proposal.

CROSS-BORDER

Cross-border leasing is the leasing of equipment in one geographical jurisdiction with utilization in another. Whereas currency risk touches upon this topic, the primary risk in currency was the monetary unit itself. In cross-border situations, the risk rests upon political and economic conditions. Cross-border leasing is growing dramatically and as it does so, risks are changing. During the 1970s, political and economic situations in Mexico were stabilizing and cross-border leasing witnessed a dramatic increase. American lessors participated widely in that increase. When the economic conditions changed in the early 1980s, many of the lessors were forced to feast upon the generous portions of risk they had unknowingly served themselves.

Another cross-border risk is the constant state of flux associated with property and income taxes. Cross-border lease opportunities lure many lessors into certain jurisdictions, but subsequent changes in local tax policies, often at the whim of a single individual, can force many of these lessors to rethink their cross-border policies. Several major players have withdrawn from that market entirely. Political and religious conditions may also alter the degree of risk inherent in cross-border leasing. This type of risk is especially damaging, inasmuch as after a cross-border lease goes bad (an underwater lease), it is frequently not possible to repatriate the asset in any way, shape or form.

COMPETITION

Competition involves the lessee's markets, market shares and trends. It is sometimes not enough just to grow. Proper analysis may indicate the lessee cannot adequately compete in its market. Accordingly, the lessor should determine if the lessee has:

1. A growing share of a growing market, a growing share of a stable market or a growing share of a declining market
2. A stable share of a growing market, a stable share of a stable market or a stable share of a declining market
3. A declining share of a growing market, a declining share of a stable market or a declining share of a declining market.

The growing internationalization of the business community has introduced many new competitive players. Japan, Germany and Great Britain, as well as a host of other countries, have gained access to US markets and are utilizing their respective comparative strengths (such as lower interest rates) to gain a strong foothold. This portends a dramatic metamorphosis in international competition in the years to come. Thus, both domestic as well as foreign competition of the lessee must be understood.

CYCLICAL AND COUNTERCYCLICAL

Cyclical and countercyclical risks refer to the type of economic behavior a company portrays in reaction to general economic conditions. If a lessee's business exhibits a high degree of elasticity with the economy in general, it is normal to classify that business as a cyclical business. For example, if interest rates rise dramatically, the housing industry typically experiences difficulty; if interest rates drop to abnormally low levels, car sales accelerate dramatically. There are other companies, however, that react in a countercyclical nature. When the economic climate deteriorates, grocery store sales are better than ever because as times get bad, people are forced to do more of their own cooking. Conversely, when economic indicators improve, restaurant business increases. From a lessor standpoint, a proper analysis would indicate what type of cyclical or countercyclical risk is expected.

COPARTNER

Copartner involves an amelioration of risk through the acceptance of some type of relationship with a second investing party. Typically, the introduction of a partner into a lease dilutes the profitability, as is the case with a genuine partner. If a lease company is undercapitalized, this may be the only avenue available for high growth. If, however, the need is not for additional capital but, rather, for risk mitigation, other types of copartnership arrangements are available that may not dilute earnings. An example of this is a vendor guarantee. Another vehicle for the mitigation of risk is that of the joint venture. Many of the cross border leases being written are utilizing this economic vehicle to avoid partnership liability as well as to gain additional expertise. Within certain political jurisdictions, however, joint ventures are regarded as partnerships and risk to the lessor is not mitigated.

CONCEALED VALUE

Concealed value is a risk concept arising because of validity problems inherent within the audited balance sheet. Because balance sheets are prepared according to GAAP, fixed assets reflect historical cost less accumulated depreciation (book value). Many pieces of equipment, however, retain a high market value and, therefore, vary considerably from the lower amount shown on the balance sheet. A good example of this is large aircraft. An aircraft may be fully depreciated on the balance sheet after 10 years, yet the fair market value may be a material portion of its original cost. Credit analysis, therefore, dictates the inclusion of sufficient fair market values on fixed assets. Both the lessee and the lessor would also want to project the fair market value and the book value of a piece of equipment at the expiration of the lease period.

An additional valuation, and, hence, risk situation, arises with intangible assets. Many lease applicants have considerable unreported goodwill, patents, copyrights, trade marks, etc., that represent assets dependent upon the successful continuation of the company, but that are not normally included on the balance sheet. Some lessees have considerable undervalued and unreported hidden assets (assets in the barn), while others are tempted to include intangible assets of questionable value.

CIRCUMSTANCES

In the situation where a potential lessee's creditworthiness appears suspect based on an evaluation of the previous 29 Cs of credit, there may, nevertheless, be mitigating circumstances sufficient to justify extending credit. For example, the equipment to be leased or used may be part of a profitable, self-liquidating investment or project that is not dependent upon other less profitable operations of the business.

Another situation might be where a start-up company is just entering a period of normal profit after having incurred losses during the development stage. Some potential lessees have been growing so fast that liquidity has been a problem, but with anticipated slowing of sales, working capital needs might reverse, making more cash available. Circumstances represent a last subjective, yet optimistic, view of a company to ascertain whether any conditions exist that might justify extending credit when most other credit indicators suggest credit refusal.

CASH FLOW ANALYSIS

Cash flow analysis is considered by many credit analysts to be the best tool to assess a potential lessee's creditworthiness, as available cash represents the resource the lessee will use to pay the lease payments. Cash flow analysis was once a cumbersome task since GAAP did not specifically require a cash flow statement as an integral part of a set of financial statements (most companies used an analysis of working capital). With the issuance of FASB 95, requiring cash flow statements as an integral part of a set of financial statements, the credit analyst's task in cash flow analysis has been greatly reduced, but not eliminated. Unfortunately, the FASB 95 cash flow format does not present cash flow data in a manner that demonstrates whether cash flow problems exist. However, the required information is presented in a fashion very amenable to being transformed into a credit analysis format.

Statement of Cash Flows

The cash flow statement required by FASB 95 is presented in Figure 6. After the cash flow statement, a worksheet for cash flow analysis, that has been found to be useful in credit analysis, is presented in Figure 7. Each element of the worksheet will be explained and expanded upon in terms of how it facilitates the making of a good lease credit decision.

Figure 6 presents a statement of cash flows for the year ended December 31, 19XX for Company M, a US corporation engaged principally in manufacturing activities. This statement of cash flows illustrates the direct method of presenting cash flows from operating activities, as encouraged in FASB 95. This method reflects increases and decreases in cash and cash equivalents. The numbers in Figure 7 represent the same cash flow information as in Figure 6, restated in a form that is more amenable to credit analysis.

The advantage of this worksheet presentation is that operating sources of cash flow are separated into gross operating sources and working capital sources. This allows the analyst to determine the degree to which net operating cash generation is dependent upon working capital as opposed to actual operations. In the long run, only operational cash flow is important since there is a limit to which working capital can generate cash flow through increasing trade payables, accrued expenses, etc.

Nondiscretionary cash requirements are deducted from net operating cash generation ($1,365 from Figure 7) to arrive at disposable net operating cash flow. It is from disposable cash flow that any future leases or loans would be repaid. Therefore, the computation of disposable cash flow is the whole purpose of the cash flow analysis worksheet. If a company cannot demonstrate that there will be sufficient disposable cash flow, then credit probably should not be extended. To arrive at disposable net operating cash flow ($444 from Figure 7), total nondiscretionary requirements of $921 must be subtracted from net operating cash generation of $1,365.

Nondiscretionary cash requirements generally include the following cash uses:

1. Common stock dividends. These cash requirements, although discretionary in the

CASH FLOWS FROM OPERATING ACTIVITIES

Cash received from customers	$ 13,850	
Cash paid to suppliers and employees	(12,000)	
Dividend received from affiliate	20	
Interest received	55	
Interest paid (net of amount capitalized)	(220)	
Income taxes paid	(325)	
Insurance proceeds received	15	
Cash paid to settle lawsuit for patent infringement	(30)	
Net cash provided by operating activities		**$ 1,365**

CASH FLOWS FROM INVESTING ACTIVITIES

Proceeds from sale of facility	$ 600	
Payment received on note for sale of plant	150	
Capital expenditures	(1,000)	
Payment for purchase of Company S, net of cash acquired	(925)	
Net cash used in investing activities		(1,175)

CASH FLOWS FROM FINANCING ACTIVITIES

Net borrowings under line-of-credit agreement	$ 300	
Principal payments under capital lease obligation	(125)	
Proceeds from issuance of long-term debt	400	
Proceeds from issuance of common stock	500	
Dividends paid	(200)	
Net cash provided by financing activities		875
NET INCREASE IN CASH AND CASH EQUIVALENTS		$ 1,065
Cash and cash equivalents at the beginning of the year		600
Cash and cash equivalents at the end of the year		$ 1,665

**RECONCILIATION OF NET INCOME TO NET CASH
PROVIDED BY OPERATING ACTIVITIES**

Net income		$ 760
Depreciation and amortization	$ 445	
Provision for losses on accounts receivable	200	
Gain on sale of facility	(80)	
Undistributed earnings of affiliate	(25)	
Payment received on installment note receivable for sale of inventory	100	
Change in assets and liabilities net of effects from purchase of Company S:		
Increase in accounts receivable	(215)	
Decrease in inventory	205	
Increase in prepaid expenses	(25)	
Decrease in accounts payable and accrued expenses	(250)	
Increase in interest and income taxes payable	50	
Increase in deferred taxes	150	
Increase in other liabilities	50	
Total adjustments		605
Net cash provided by operating activities		**$ 1,365**

SUPPLEMENTAL SCHEDULE OF NONCASH INVESTING AND FINANCING ACTIVITIES

The Company purchased all of the capital stock of Company S for $950. In conjunction with the acquisition, liabilities were assumed as follows:

Fair value of assets acquired	$ 1,580
Cash paid for the capital stock	(950)
Liabilities assumed	$ 630

A capital lease obligation of $850 was incurred when the Company entered into a lease for new equipment.
Additional common stock was issued upon the conversion of $500 of long-term debt.

DISCLOSURE OF ACCOUNTING POLICY

For purposes of the statement of cash flows, the Company considers all highly liquid debt instruments purchased with a maturity of three months or less to be cash equivalents.

Figure 6
Statement of Cash Flows[1]

---

[1] FASB 95, paragraph 133.

NET OPERATING CASH GENERATION
  Gross operating cash generation

Add:	Net income	$	760
	Depreciation		445
	Other noncash amortizations		
	Increase in deferred tax credits		150
	Increase in security deposits		
	Residual sale proceeds		
	Payment received on installment note		100
	Fixed asset losses (residuals and assignments)		
	Residual write downs		
	Bad debt expense (allowance method)		200
	Subsidiary dividends (equity method)		
	Principal portion of lease payments		
	Gross operating sources	$	1,655
Deduct:	Gains on the sale of fixed assets (residuals, etc.)	($	80)
	Allocated sale-leaseback gains	(	)
	Decrease in deferred tax credits	(	)
	Increase in leasing initial direct costs	(	)
	Gross profit on sales-type capital leases	(	)
	Uncollected late fees	(	)
	Assignment gains	(	)
	Decreases in security deposits	(	)
	Subsidiary income (equity method)	(	25)
	Miscellaneous	(	)
	Gross operating uses	($	105)
	Gross operating cash generation	$	1,550

Working capital cash generation (usage)

Add:	Increase in accounts payable	$	
	Increase in accrued expenses		50
	Increase in taxes payable		50
	Decrease in inventory		205
	Decrease in accounts receivable		
	Decrease in prepaid expenses		
	Working capital sources	$	305
Deduct:	Decrease in accounts payable	($	250)
	Decrease in accrued expenses	(	)
	Decrease in taxes payable	(	)
	Increase in inventory	(	)
	Increase in accounts receivable	(	215)
	Increase in prepaid expenses	(	25)
	Working capital uses	($	490)
	Working capital cash generation (usage)	($	185)

NET OPERATING CASH GENERATED $ 1,365

NONDISCRETIONARY CASH REQUIREMENTS

Dividends	($	200)
Replacement property, plant and equipment	(	445)[3]
Inflationary property, plant and equipment	(	151)[3]
Short-term debt repayment	(	)
Long-term debt repayment	(	)
Principal payments on capital lease		(125)
Total nondiscretionary requirements	($	921)

DISPOSABLE NET OPERATING CASH FLOW $ 444

DISCRETIONARY CASH NEEDS

Additional property, plant and equipment	($	404)[3]
Other investments (subsidiaries)	($	925)
Reduction of permanent debt (bonds, etc.)	(	)
Reduction of equity	(	)
Total discretionary needs	($	1,329)

NET CASH NEEDS   ($ 885)

NONOPERATING CASH SOURCES

Short-term debt increase	$	300
Long-term debt increase		400
Permanent debt increase (bonds)		
Sale of equity		500
Sale of fixed assets proceeds		600
Sale leaseback proceeds		
Payment on note receivable sale of plant		150
Nonoperating cash sources	$	1,950

NET INCREASE (DECREASE) IN CASH $ 1,065

Figure 7
Cash Flow Analysis Worksheet

---

[3] Total capital investment for the year split into component parts:

Replacement property, plant and equipment	
(equal to current year's depreciation)	$ 445
Inflation adjustment	151
Discretionary property, plant and equipment investment	404
	$1,000

strictest legal sense, are not so from a practical viewpoint. Companies are reluctant to eliminate or cut dividends lest they cause stock prices to go down. Preferred stock dividends might also be considered nondiscretionary

2. Principal payments due on short-term, intermediate and long-term debt (excluding accounts payable, etc.) and principal payments on capital lease liabilities
3. Capital expenditures for maintenance of existing property, plant and equipment capacity. These cash requirements are considered to be nondiscretionary, since to spend less than this amount would imply the systematic liquidation of the company. Capital expenditures beyond the going concern level that represent expansion of capacity are considered to be discretionary.

How are total capital expenditures split into their nondiscretionary and discretionary components? To avoid liquidation, a company would have to invest capital each year in an amount equal to its annual depreciation charge (assuming a noninflationary economy), which was $445 in Figure 7. If inflation is occurring, an additional amount of capital investment would be required to compensate for inflation. This assures that in real dollars the property, plant and equipment of the company is neither growing, nor shrinking in capacity. The determination of the inflation adjustment required for nondiscretionary property, plant and equipment is based on four steps.

First, determine the average depreciable life remaining for the property, plant and equipment by dividing the current year's depreciation charge into the average net investment in property, plant and equipment. Assume the beginning of the year net investment in property, plant and equipment was $2,340 and the year-end net investment in property, plant and equipment is $3,000.

Beginning of year net investment	$ 2,340
End of year net investment	3,000
Total	$ 5,340
	÷ 2
Average investment	$ 2,670

$$\frac{\$2{,}670 \text{ (average investment)}}{\$445 \text{ (current year's depreciation)}} = 6 \text{ years depreciable life remaining}$$

Second, determine the replacement value of the net investment in property, plant and equipment at the end of the previously computed depreciable life. Use the expected average inflation rate over the time period as the appreciation rate (assume 5% in this case).

5		i	(appreciation rate)
2,670	CHS	PV	(average remaining net book value)
6		n	(average remaining depreciable life)
		FV	3,578.06

Third, determine the average investment in property, plant and equipment required each year to maintain constant capacity in real dollars by dividing the replacement cost by the average remaining depreciable life.

$$\frac{\$3,578.06}{6} = \$596.34 \text{ (\$596 rounded)}$$

Finally, deduct the current year's actual depreciation charge from the annual property, plant and equipment investment determined in the third step. The difference represents the incremental investment in property, plant and equipment above investment equal to the current year's depreciation necessary to maintain constant capacity in real dollars.

Property, plant and equipment investment including inflationary impact	$ 596
Property, plant and equipment investment (current year's depreciation)	(445)
Inflationary property, plant and equipment	$ 151

Discretionary cash needs generally include the following expenses that are made, not out of necessity (contractual or otherwise), but according to management's desire.

1. Additional property, plant and equipment required for expansion of existing capacity. Expansion for growth in capacity is considered discretionary, whereas maintaining existing capacity is considered nondiscretionary. Additional property, plant and equipment is calculated by taking total property, plant and equipment investments for the year and subtracting from it replacement property, plant and equipment and the inflationary adjustment

Total property, plant and equipment investment	$ 1,000
Less replacement property, plant and equipment	(445)
inflationary property, plant and equipment	(151)
Discretionary property, plant and equipment	$ 404

2. Other investments, including joint-ventures, subsidiaries, etc. These cash requirements would be considered discretionary since they were not required to maintain existing capacity, but were instead required for expansion

3. Reduction of principal on debt or capital leases and the reduction of equity beyond that required by the legal contract. These cash requirements are considered discretionary. Contractually required reductions on debt and leases are considered nondiscretionary.

In Figure 7, the nonoperating cash sources on the cash flow worksheet disclose the sources of cash that provided for the $885 cash needs, plus the $1,065 increase in cash. Again, the advantage of the preceding cash flow analysis worksheet is to source cash inflows and outflows as a function of management discretion and nondiscretion since only disposable cash flow will be available to pay off future debt or lease obligations.

Cash Flow Ratios

Historical ratio analysis relates income statement data to balance sheet data, income statement to income statement and balance sheet to balance sheet. In the same manner, cash flow data will be related to income statement, balance sheet and other cash flow information. The ratios will be illustrated using the data in Figure 7.

INCOME STATEMENT TO CASH FLOW RATIOS

There are four cash flow ratios that are used in identifying trends in relationships between the income statement and cash flow.

$$1. \quad \frac{\text{Net income}}{\text{Gross operating cash flow}} \quad = \quad \frac{\$ \ 760}{\$1,550} \quad = \quad 49.03\%$$

This ratio demonstrates the proportion of gross operating cash flow derived from net income. If this percentage increases, less cash flow is being generated for each dollar of net income. If such a trend continues, liquidity problems might arise.

$$2. \quad \frac{\text{Net income}}{\text{Net operating cash flow}} \quad = \quad \frac{\$ \ 760}{\$1,365} \quad = \quad 55.68\%$$

This ratio is similar to 1 above, however, the impact of working capital sources and uses is factored into this ratio. To the degree this ratio is growing or exceeds 1 above, working capital requirements are consuming gross operating cash flow. A continuation in this trend would indicate a forthcoming liquidity problem. However, a decline in this percentage indicates favorable cash flow generation.

$$3. \quad \frac{\text{Net operating cash flow}}{\text{Interest and lease rentals}} \quad = \quad \frac{\$1,365}{\$220 + \$0} \quad = \quad 6.2045\%$$

This ratio is similar to times interest earned, except that the cash flow has not been adjusted for tax expenses or interest. The importance of the ratio is that interest expense was covered 6.2 times by net operating cash flow.

$$4. \quad \frac{\text{Disposable net operating cash flow}}{\text{Interest and lease rentals}} \quad = \quad \frac{\$444}{\$220} \quad = \quad 2.018$$

This cash flow ratio is similar to times interest earned also; however, this key ratio deals with disposable cash that is available to pay existing or future interest expense. Without a ratio greater than one, any proposed interest expense or rental expense would not appear feasible, due to a lack of disposable cash.

CASH FLOW TO CASH FLOW RATIOS

There are three cash flow ratios that are used in identifying trends in relationships between different cash flows.

$$1. \quad \frac{\text{Net operating cash generation}}{\text{Disposable net operating cash flow}} \quad = \quad \frac{\$1,365}{\$ \ 444} \quad = \quad 3.074$$

This ratio demonstrates the impact of nondiscretionary cash needs. If needs are few, the ratio would be closer to one. High or growing ratios indicate greater cash flow commitments, which reduce cash available to pay off future loan or lease payments.

2. $\dfrac{\text{Gross operating cash flow}}{\text{Disposable net operating cash flow}}$ $=$ $\dfrac{\$1,550}{\$\ \ 444}$ $=$ 3.491

This is the same as 1 above, except the impact of working capital cash use or generation has been removed. Increases in this ratio indicate greater cash flow commitments trending towards less cash available to pay future loans or leases.

3. $\dfrac{\text{Discretionary cash flow}}{\text{Net operating cash flow}}$ $=$ $\dfrac{\$\ \ 885}{\$1,365}$ $=$ .648

This ratio indicates the percent of net operating cash flow that is being spent on discretionary requirements. Increases in the percentage or a high percentage could indicate excess or run-away growth, which is hampering the creation of disposable cash flow.

CASH FLOW TO BALANCE SHEET RATIOS

There are three cash flow ratios that are used in identifying trends in relationships between the balance sheet and cash flow.

For purposes of these ratios, assume the following information:

Assets: $5,000
Equity: $2,300
Net working capital: $500

1. $\dfrac{\text{Net operating cash flow}}{\text{Assets}}$ $=$ $\dfrac{\$1,365}{\$5,000}$ $=$ 27.3%

This ratio is the same as the standard ROA, except it represents the total cash flow ROA. Decreases in this ratio indicate a decrease in the company's profitability.

2. $\dfrac{\text{Net working capital}}{\text{Net operating cash flow}}$ $=$ $\dfrac{\$\ \ 500}{\$1,365}$ $=$ 36.63%

The percentage that net working capital is of net operating cash flow should remain steady. Increases could indicate inefficiencies in working capital management.

3. $\dfrac{\text{Net operating cash flow}}{\text{Equity}}$ $=$ $\dfrac{\$1,365}{\$2,300}$ $=$ 59.35%

This ratio is the same as the standard ROE except this represents the total cash flow ROE. This percentage should remain relatively constant. Increases in the percentage would be considered favorable so long as financial leverage remains constant.

MODELING

A model may be defined as an inexpensive estimate of reality. Models can be used in trend analysis, sensitivity analysis and in forecasting. Earlier, in ratio analysis, a simple model was used to depict a company's profitability. A similar model, known as the DuPont Equation, appears in Figure 8.

The gross profit margin indicates the percentage margin of total sales revenue that is left after deducting cost of goods sold. The dollar difference is referred to as the gross margin on the income statement.

OPERATING EXPENSE FACTOR

The formula for computing this ratio is as follows:

$$1 - \frac{\text{Operating expenses}}{\text{Gross profit}} \quad = \quad 1 - \frac{\$50}{\$80} \quad = \quad 37.5\%$$

Operating expenses are those general and administrative and other overhead costs required to run a business (advertising, accounting, salaries, etc.). The operating expense factor is multiplied times the gross profit margin to arrive at earnings before interest and taxes (EBIT). In this example, EBIT equals $30 ($80 – $50), and the EBIT margin is 15% (40% × 37.5%). Notice that the 40% gross margin is diminished to a net margin of 15% when operating expenses are considered. Using sensitivity analysis, the effect of operating expenses as they use up a portion of the gross margin is isolated.

INCOME TAX FACTOR

The formula for computing this ratio is as follows:

$$1 - \frac{\text{Income taxes}}{\text{EBIT}} \quad = \quad 1 - \frac{\$10}{\$30} \quad = \quad 67\%$$

This factor isolates the effect of income taxes on EBIT. The 15% EBIT is reduced to earnings before interest (EBI) of 10% when income taxes are considered. Referring to Figure 9, it can be seen that the EBI of 10% is the product of the income tax factor multiplied by EBIT (67% × 15%).

INTEREST FACTOR

The formula for computing this ratio is as follows:

$$1 - \frac{\text{Interest}}{\text{EBI}} \quad = \quad 1 - \frac{\$5}{\$20} \quad = \quad 75\%$$

Interest to service the company's debt has consumed 25% (1 –.75) of EBI. Interest is often a costly expense in running a company so its effect on earnings is shown in this analysis. The net profit margin (after operating expenses, income taxes and interest costs) is shown to be 7.5% by multiplying the interest factor times EBI (75% × 10%).

ASSET TURNOVER

The formula for computing this ratio is as follows:

$$\frac{\text{Sales}}{\text{Total assets}} \quad = \quad \frac{\$200}{\$100} \quad = \quad 2$$

Asset turnover is measured by dividing total sales by total assets to determine how many times assets have been sold, in effect, during the year. The higher the turnover, the higher the company's profits will be, since more sales were generated with the same amount of assets. Often this factor would be more accurate if average total assets throughout the year were used as the denominator rather than total year-end assets as in this example. If average total assets is used (a better measure if total assets fluctuate significantly during the year), the same average total assets must be used throughout the sensitivity model. The asset turnover factor is multiplied by the net profit margin to determine ROA, which in this example is 15% (2 × 7.5%).

Once the ROA of a firm is known, it can be used as a measuring device against which to compare the ROA of individual investments of the company. Similarly, the ROA of potential investments or divisions of the firm may be compared with the overall ROA computed above. For example, a potential investment with an ROA of only 12% in this illustration should be scrutinized more closely, since it is less than the overall ROA of 15%. Such an investment would tend to pull down the firm's ROA since the investment would utilize assets less efficiently. The ROA of the investment also can be computed as an internal rate of return (IRR) or an external rate of return (ERR), depending on the reinvestment assumption made regarding cash inflows from the investment (see Chapter Seven). Only the appropriate yield (IRR or ERR) should be compared with the firm's ROA.

FINANCIAL LEVERAGE ADVANTAGE

The formula for computing this ratio is as follows:

$$\frac{\text{Assets}}{\text{Equity}} = \frac{\$100}{\$40} = 2.5$$

This factor shows the multiplying effect of financial leverage on earnings. Whatever ROA has been earned to this point in the model will be multiplied by the financial leverage advantage factor to convert ROA to ROE. In this example, ROE is equal to 37.5% (2.5 × 15%). Note that a firm with a greater percentage of debt would generate higher ROE yields. In our example, if debt and equity were $80 and $20, respectively, the financial leverage factor would be five ($100 ÷ $20) and, therefore, ROE would have been much higher (5 × 15% = 75%). It can be seen in this analysis how the use of debt or financial leverage can improve ROE yields.

RETENTION FACTOR

The formula for computing this ratio is as follows:

$$\frac{\text{Net income} - \text{dividends}}{\text{Net income}} = \frac{\$15 - \$7.5}{\$15} = 50\%$$

In this example, the firm retains 50% of net income. This leaves another 50% of net income to be paid out as dividends to shareholders. The more a company retains, the faster its earnings can grow, due to the expanded earnings base. In fact, an important rule in finance is that a company's earnings per share can grow no faster than the product of its ROE times the retention factor (given that no other sources of capital, debt or equity are available). Growth rate in earnings is important since stock prices are heavily influenced by the company's ability to

Gross profit margin	$\left(\dfrac{\text{Revenue}}{\text{Sales}}\right.$ $=$ $\left.\dfrac{\$80}{\$200}\right)$		$=$	40%
× Operating expense factor	$\left(1 - \dfrac{\text{Operating expenses}}{\text{Gross profit}}\right.$ $=$ $\left.1 - \dfrac{\$50}{\$80}\right)$		$=$	37.5%
= Net profit margin before interest and taxes			$=$	**15%**
× Income tax factor	$\left(1 - \dfrac{\text{Income taxes}}{\text{EBIT}}\right.$ $=$ $\left.1 - \dfrac{\$10}{\$30}\right)$		$=$	67%
= Net profit margin before interest			$=$	**10%**
× Interest factor	$\left(1 - \dfrac{\text{Interest expense}}{\text{EBI}}\right.$ $=$ $\left.1 - \dfrac{\$\ 5}{\$20}\right)$		$=$	75%
= Net profit margin			$=$	**7.5%**
× Asset turnover	$\left(\dfrac{\text{Sales}}{\text{Assets}}\right.$ $=$ $\left.\dfrac{\$200}{\$100}\right)$		$=$	2
= ROA			$=$	**15%**
× Financial leverage advantage	$\left(\dfrac{\text{Assets}}{\text{Equity}}\right.$ $=$ $\left.\dfrac{\$100}{\$\ 40}\right)$		$=$	2.5
= ROE			$=$	**37.5%**
× Retention factor	$\left(\dfrac{\text{Net income–Dividends}}{\text{Net income}}\right.$ $=$ $\left.\dfrac{\$15 - \$7.5}{\$15}\right)$		$=$	50%
= Potential growth rate in earnings			$=$	**18.75%**

Figure 10
Expanded Profitability Model Summary

goods sold. Assume also that the change would mean an increase of 12% in taxes and 5% in interest expense. Total assets, equity, operating expenses and dividends remain the same.

SOLUTION

Reconstruct the sensitivity model to reflect the above changes and multiply the factors to arrive at the new potential growth rate in earnings, as shown in Figure 11. The net effect on growth rate in earnings is to increase it from 18.75% in Figure 10 to 36% in Figure 11. Therefore, a 10% increase in sales will increase growth rate in earnings by 17.25 percentage points, even after taking into account the increase in income taxes and interest expense caused by the sales increase. Similarly, other variables could be changed for purposes of projecting or forecasting the effect such changes would have on all the variables and profitability yields.

Gross profit margin	$\left(\dfrac{\$220 - \$132}{\$200}\right)$	=	40%
× Operating expense factor	$\left(1 - \dfrac{\$50}{\$88}\right)$	=	43%
= Net profit margin before interest and taxes		**=**	**17%**
× Income tax factor	$\left(1 - \dfrac{\$11.20}{\$38}\right)$	=	71%
= Net profit margin before interest		**=**	**12%**
× Interest factor	$\left(1 - \dfrac{\$5.25}{\$26.80}\right)$	=	80%
= Net profit margin		**=**	**10%**
× Asset turnover	$\dfrac{\$220}{\$100}$	=	2.2
= ROA		**=**	**22%**
× Financial leverage advantage	$\dfrac{\$100}{\$40}$	=	2.5
= ROE		**=**	**55%**
× Retention factor	$\left(\dfrac{21.55 - 7.5}{21.55}\right)$	=	65%
= Potential growth rate in earnings		**=**	**36%**

Figure 11
Revised Sensitivity Model

EXPANDING THE PROFITABILITY MODEL

The basic profitability model can be easily expanded to include other factors that are pertinent to the firm. Looking at the profitability model, it can be seen that the factors emphasized are gross profit, operating expenses, income taxes, interest expense, asset turnover, financial leverage advantage and retention factor. The seven factors are useful especially in analyzing a manufacturing firm. Other types of companies may want to isolate certain other factors, such as advertising expenses or maintenance expenses. In order to add these additional factors to the model, they must be inserted into the model at a meaningful level in the form of a multiplier, so that all the variables in the model will still relate to each other. Example 2 will illustrate how a variable could be added to the model.

EXAMPLE 2

Refer to the base sensitivity model presented earlier. In addition to the seven variables considered so far, add an eighth variable, advertising expense. In this company advertising is a large part of total expenditures and it is desirable to measure it in relation to other key expenses and to be able to project what effect an increase in advertising would have on the ROA, ROE and potential growth rate in earnings of the company. Assuming advertising expenses are $15, reconstruct the model, including the additional factor.

SOLUTION

Prior to isolating advertising as a separate factor, it was part of operating expenses. It seems appropriate, therefore, to consider its effect on earnings after other operating expenses, but before taxes and interest. Adding this additional factor will create another measure of profitability that will be called earnings before advertising, interest and taxes (EBAIT).

Gross profit margin	$\dfrac{\$80}{\$200}$	= 40%
× Operating expense factor	$\left(1 - \dfrac{\$35}{\$80}\right)$	= 56%
= EBAIT		= 23%
× Advertising expense factor	$\left(1 - \dfrac{\$15}{\$45}\right)$	= 67%
= Net profit margin before interest and taxes		= 15%

From this point on the model would remain unchanged.

The gross profit margin is reduced from 40% to 23% when operating expenses other than advertising expenses are considered. Advertising expenses reduce the gross profit margin even further, to 15%. Therefore, of the total difference between 40% and 15%, which is 25%, a large portion of it is due to advertising expenses. Having included another variable in the model it would now be possible to project the effects on all the other variables and profitability yields of a change in the new variable (advertising expense).

CONCLUSION

Credit analysis throughout the financial services industry is a juggling act between granting sufficient credit so as not to hurt sales, yet still maintain high enough standards that profitability is not impaired. Credit analysis in leasing is viewed as being more complex due to the additional risks associated with leasing. However, the basic approach is similar to loan credit analysis in that financial statement analysis is still performed. The 30 Cs of lease credit analysis give insight into risk assessment, while the emphasis on cash flow analysis, required by FASB 95, requires new thinking on the part of the credit analyst. Because of this change, cash flow ratios will soon be developed that will assist in the analyst's task. Finally, modeling is another tool the credit analyst can use in the continual struggle to extend sound credit.

CHAPTER NINETEEN
LEASE DOCUMENTATION

Today, leasing is corporate America's largest and fastest growing exogenous form of equipment finance. The increasing popularity of leasing is due, in part, to the flexibility of lessors in tailoring the lease transaction to meet the exacting needs of each lessee. This innovativeness by lessors is, however, somewhat restricted by the tax statutes, guidelines and regulations and by the promulgations of the Financial Accounting Standards Board, among others. To further complicate matters, Congress has kept the leasing industry on the edge of its seat with ever-changing tax legislation, which is sure to continue to refocus the attention of lessors and lessees alike.

Given this environment, it is imperative for the parties to make known and to negotiate their often conflicting demands and expectations, and to express the resulting mutuality of understanding through as clear, cogent and unambiguous language as is feasible. With the magnitude of dollars involved in the average lease transaction, thorough lease documentation is an absolute necessity. Documentation in the leasing transaction is discussed from two perspectives:

- Lease Documents
- Loan Documents.

One must recognize there are numerous ways to structure a lease transaction, whether it be a leveraged lease, single investor lease, consumer lease, municipal lease or otherwise. With each different type of lease transaction the lease documentation can vary dramatically, from an extremely complex set of documents to a more simple snap-out form. Even the dollar volume of the equipment influences the complexity of the documentation.

Recognizing the numerous types of documents, this chapter focuses on the documentation for a leveraged lease transaction, the provisions of which should have general application to other types of lease transactions. The various documents involved in a leveraged lease transaction will be outlined and then some insight into the language and purpose of pertinent provisions of some of the lease documents will be provided. Exhibits I through XI of Appendix B represent samples of the lease documents discussed in this chapter. These documents are offered as examples only and the parties are urged to seek competent legal advice in structuring and documenting each lease transaction.

LEASE DOCUMENTS

Given the diversity of lease transactions, the leveraged lease documentation could include:

- Lease/Credit Application
- Master Lease
- Tax Indemnification Rider
- Equipment Schedule Fair Market Value Purchase Option Rider
- Fair Rental Value Renewal Option Rider
- Certificate of Acceptance
- Casualty Value Schedule
- Officer's Certificate or Corporate Resolution
- Opinion of Lessee's Counsel
- Certificate of Insurance
- Precautionary Form UCC-1.

In this section the nature and purpose of these documents is examined and the pertinent provisions of each explained. In several instances, language from the document is used as part of the explanation.

Lease/Credit Application

The Lease/Credit Application is a one page, two-sided document that is generally used in equipment leasing transactions involving smaller ticket items of $150,000 or less. It is a fill-in-the-blank type of document and is used by lessors to gather necessary information about the prospective lessee and the equipment desired to be leased. The information gathered includes: business information (i.e., nature and duration of the business, form of the business and principals of the business); trade, bank and credit references, including prior lessors; insurance information; and equipment information (i.e., manufacturer, description of equipment, list price and purchase price). With this information, the lessor is able to assess the creditworthiness of the prospective lessee and the desirability of the proposed lease transaction.

Master Lease

In smaller ticket lease transactions, the Master Lease generally is not used. Rather, a form lease agreement is likely to set forth all of the terms and conditions of the lease transaction, including a description of the equipment, the lease term and the lease payment amount. In a lease transaction involving large ticket equipment or involving one lease transaction of many to come, the Master Lease is often used. The Master Lease generally will set forth all of the major terms and conditions that will be common to all of the successive lease transactions. The variable terms and conditions of each lease transaction (i.e., description of equipment, lease term, and payment amount and terms) will then be set forth in each succeeding Equipment Schedule. By using a Master Lease with successive Equipment Schedules, the lessor and lessee may do numerous leasing transactions involving various types of equipment and different lease terms without having to execute a Master Lease for each transaction. Each Equipment Schedule will specifically incorporate by reference the terms and conditions of the Master Lease. Furthermore, once the lessee has had its attorneys review the lease documentation for the first Equipment Schedule, it is unnecessary for the lessee's attorneys to review the documents for the second Equipment Schedule, because the documents will be identical except for the fill-in-the-blank information. This can result in substantial savings to the lessee. The major terms and conditions of a Master Lease should include the following items.

DATE, NAMES OF THE PARTIES, ADDRESS OF EACH PARTY'S PRINCIPAL PLACE OF BUSINESS

This aspect of the Master Lease serves to identify the parties to, and date of, the agreement.

Master Lease dated as of _____ September 30 _____ 19 87 by and between Sentry Financial Corporation (Lessor), having its principal office and place of business at 3450 South Highland Drive, Suite 104, Salt Lake City, Utah 84106 and _____ Bono & Company: (Lessee), having its principal office and business at 2732 South 2140 East, Salt Lake City, Utah 84105 .

Where both the lessor and the lessee are clearly designated, there is little chance for mistake as to the parties to, and bound by, the contract. In addition, the date allows the Master Lease to be easily identified, and the full mailing addresses of the parties facilitate communications between the parties. The date also has significant implications for tax purposes and for Uniform Commercial Code (UCC) purposes.

EQUIPMENT DESCRIPTION, LEASE TERM, LEASE PAYMENT AMOUNT

The equipment description, lease term and lease payment amount will be set forth in each succeeding Equipment Schedule, as they are variable terms and conditions. By setting forth the variable terms in the Equipment Schedule, the parties maximize flexibility and minimize duplication of documents on succeeding lease transactions.

INSPECTION AND ACCEPTANCE OF THE EQUIPMENT

The inspection, testing and acceptance provisions are also variable terms and conditions and will be contained in each succeeding Certificate of Acceptance.

LIMITATION OF LIABILITY, DISCLAIMER OF WARRANTY

The following limits the lessor's liability as to certain events.

Lessee represents and agrees that the Equipment is of a size, design, capacity and manufacturer selected by Lessee and that Lessee takes the Equipment "AS IS". Lessor shall have no liability to Lessee for any claim, loss or damage caused or alleged to be caused directly, indirectly, incidentally or consequentially by the Equipment, by an inadequacy thereof or deficiency or defect therein, by any incident whatsoever in connection therewith, arising in strict liability, negligence or otherwise, or in any way related to or arising out of this Master Lease Agreement. LESSOR MAKES NO EXPRESS OR IMPLIED WARRANTIES OF ANY KIND, INCLUDING THOSE OF MERCHANTABILITY, DURABILITY AND FITNESS FOR A PARTICULAR PURPOSE OR USE WITH RESPECT TO THE EQUIPMENT AND EXPRESSLY DISCLAIMS THE SAME. Notwithstanding the foregoing, Lessee will be entitled to the benefit of any applicable manufacturer's warranties and, to the extent assignable, such warranties are hereby assigned by Lessor for the benefit of Lessee, and Lessee shall take all reasonable action to enforce such warranties where available to Lessee.

Under this provision, the parties acknowledge the lessee has selected both the particular equipment and the supplier of the equipment from whom the lessor is to purchase, based on the lessee's judgment. Therefore, the lessor should disclaim it has made any representations or warranties to the lessee with respect to the equipment. As discussed in Chapter Twenty, exclusion of such implied warranties requires a specific, conspicuous statement to that effect. These disclaimers reduce the risk of legal action against the lessor by the lessee for malfunctions, etc., of the equipment. A statement that the lessee has selected both the equipment and the supplier, and that the lessee takes the property "AS IS," and has not relied on any of the lessor's statements or representations, reinforces the lessor's disclaimer.

Under the UCC, two types of warranties exist, namely, express and implied. Express warranties generally arise from statements and representations of the seller or from a seller's description of the equipment, which becomes the basis for the bargain. On the other hand, two types of implied warranties exist: fitness for a particular purpose of the purchaser and merchantability. The extent and nature of warranties are discussed in greater detail in Chapter Twenty. Under the above provision, the warranty exclusions should effectively insulate a lessor from liability that could flow from express or implied warranties under the UCC. However, in the leasing of consumer goods, there seems to be a trend in favor of consumer protectionism and away from *caveat emptor* (i.e., "let the buyer beware"). Evidence of this trend is the growing potential subjection of a lessor to product liability claims. For that reason, insurance coverage is imperative.

In most leases there typically is an additional statement to the effect that the manufacturer's warranty is the only warranty made or deemed to have been made. In addition, to the extent assignable, the lessor assigns any manufacturer's warranties to the lessee so the lessee can utilize these warranties. The practical effect of this provision is to require the lessee to pursue any remedies directly against the manufacturer or supplier without affecting the lessee's obligations under the Master Lease.

INSTALLATION, MAINTENANCE, REPAIR

Language of this provision may include:

Lessee shall, at its expense, be responsible for the delivery, installation, deinstallation, redelivery, maintenance and repair of the Equipment by a party

> acceptable to Lessor. Lessee agrees, at all times during the term of each Equipment Schedule, at its sole expense, to keep the Equipment in good repair, condition, and working order and to furnish all parts, mechanisms or devices that may be required in the course of so doing. Lessee will at all times during the term of each Equipment Schedule maintain in force a maintenance agreement covering the Equipment with the manufacturer thereof or such other party as may be acceptable to Lessor. Lessee shall not make any alterations, additions or improvements to the Equipment without Lessor's prior written consent. Lessor or an Assignee of Lessor ("Assignee") will have the right, but not the obligation, to inspect the Equipment during reasonable business hours. Lessee shall permit manufacturer access to the Equipment to install "no charge" engineering changes in order to keep the Equipment at current engineering levels.

This provision clearly defines the party obligated to keep the equipment in good and proper working condition. Generally, the lease will be a net lease and, therefore, the burden of maintenance and repair rests with the lessee. This provision is important to the lessor because it provides some assurance to the lessor that the value of the equipment will be protected from excessive deterioration. In leases of high technology equipment, there is typically a statement requiring the lessee to obtain a maintenance agreement from the manufacturer or supplier. This statement provides the lessor with an additional level of comfort. The requirement of the lessor's prior written consent regarding alterations, additions or improvements to the equipment protects the lessor from changes to the equipment, which would be harmful to the equipment or which would decrease the value of the equipment. The requirement regarding installation of engineering changes further maintains the market value of the equipment.

OBLIGATION TO PAY RENT

This provision details the lessee's obligation under the agreement to pay the rentals.

> This Master Lease is a net lease and Lessee agrees that its obligation to pay all Basic Rent and other sums payable hereunder (collectively "Rent"), and the rights of Lessor and Assignee in and to such Rent, are absolute and unconditional and are not subject to any abatement, reduction, setoff, defense, counterclaim or recoupment due or alleged to be due to, or by reason of, any past, present or future claims which Lessee may have against Lessor, Assignee, the manufacturer or seller of the Equipment, or against any person for any reason whatsoever.

Under this provision, the lessor is protected from a withholding of the lease payment by the lessee for any reason. This provision is commonly referred to as the hell or high water clause. It derives this nickname from the fact that the lessee's obligation to make the lease payments in full to the lessor is absolutely unconditional. For example, the lessee is precluded from withholding or reducing the lease payment on the basis of a malfunction in the equipment or a breach of warranty by the manufacturer. Essentially, this provision provides assurance to the lessor that the lease payments will be made and requires the lessee to pursue its claims against the proper party — the manufacturer.

REPRESENTATIONS AND WARRANTIES

The lessee will warrant certain representations.

Lessee represents and warrants for the benefit of Lessor and, if requested by Lessor, will provide an opinion of counsel and other supporting documents to the effect that:

(a) Lessee is a legal entity, duly organized, validly existing and in good standing under the laws of the jurisdiction of its organization and in each jurisdiction where the Equipment will be located and has adequate power to enter into and perform this Master Lease and each Equipment Schedule executed hereunder.

(b) This Master Lease and each Equipment Schedule executed hereunder have been duly authorized, executed and delivered by Lessee and together constitute a valid, legal and binding agreement of Lessee, enforceable in accordance with its terms.

(c) The entering into and performance of this Master Lease and each Equipment Schedule executed hereunder will not violate any judgment, order, law or regulation applicable to Lessee or any provision of Lessee's Articles of Incorporation or Bylaws or result in any breach of, or constitute a default under, or result in the creation of any lien, charge, security interest or other encumbrance upon any assets of Lessee or on the Equipment pursuant to any instrument to which Lessee is a party or by which it or its assets may be bound.

(d) There are no actions, suits or proceedings pending, or to the knowledge of the Lessee threatened, before any court, administrative agency, arbitrator or governmental body which will, if determined adversely to the Lessee, materially adversely affect Lessee's ability to perform Lessee's obligations under this Master Lease or any related agreement to which Lessee is a party.

(e) Lessee is not a tax exempt organization.

(f) Lessee is not in any material default under any loan or other lease agreements.

Under this provision, the lessee makes numerous representations to the lessor, the falsity of which would constitute an event of default under the lease. To further substantiate the lessee's representations, the lessor can, and usually does, require the lessee to provide the lessor with an Opinion of Counsel and other supporting documents.

When doing business with entities other than individuals, it is necessary that the lessee be duly organized and authorized to do business in the jurisdiction where the equipment will be located. In addition, the lessor must be assured that the individual representing the lessee is authorized to execute the pertinent documents and to bind the lessee. The lessor must also be confident that the lessee is not prohibited from entering into the lease transaction by the lessee's Articles of Incorporation or Bylaws, any judgment or court order or any other obligation or agreement to which the lessee is bound. These representations are absolutely necessary to protect the lessor from engaging in contracts that may be unenforceable against the lessee.

ASSIGNMENT

The purpose of this provision is to protect the lessor's interest in the equipment itself and in the rentals flowing from it.

Without Lessor's prior written consent, Lessee shall not (i) assign, transfer, pledge, hypothecate or otherwise dispose of this Master Lease, and Equipment Schedule, the Equipment or any interest therein, or (ii) sublet or lend the Equipment or permit the Equipment to be used by anyone other than Lessee or Lessee's employees. Lessor may assign or sell all or a portion of Lessor's right, title and interest in and to the Equipment or this Master Lease or any Equipment Schedule and/or grant a security interest in the Equipment to one or more lenders or equity sources or other Assignees. Lessee hereby (i) consents to such assignments and/or grants, (ii) agrees to promptly execute and deliver such further acknowledgements, agreements and other instruments as may be reasonably requested by an Assignee to effect such assignments and/or grants, from time to time as each Equipment Schedule is executed, and (iii) agrees to comply fully with the terms of any such assignments and/or grants. In the event of an assignment, Lessor shall notify Lessee of such assignment and thereafter all references herein to Lessor shall include Assignee; provided, however, that Assignee shall not be obligated to perform the obligations of Lessor hereunder unless Assignee expressly agrees to do so in writing.

In entering into the lease transaction with the lessee, the lessor has the opportunity to evaluate the creditworthiness of the lessee. The prior written consent requirement permits the lessor to maintain control of the lease transaction by allowing the lessor to assess the creditworthiness of the lessee's transferee in terms of such transferee's ability to make the rentals and to properly care for the equipment. Even if the lessor consents to the assignment of the lessee's interest in the lease, the lessee remains liable to the lessor to make the lease payments under the lease, unless a novation occurs. A novation in this context is an agreement whereby the lessor agrees to relieve the lessee of liability on the lease and to substitute in the lessee's place the lessee's transferee. Thus, absent a novation, the lessor would be able to look to the lessee and the lessee's transferee for payment of the lease rentals.

It is fundamental contract law that one may assign his rights but not his duties under a contract. He may delegate his duties to a third party, but this does not relieve him of those duties. In the event the third person fails to perform, the delegator is liable. Under the above provision, the lessor is given the express right to assign its interest in the lease transaction and the lessee has given its prior consent to such an assignment. This provision enhances the financial flexibility of the lessor without prejudicing the lessee. This flexibility permits the lessor to obtain debt financing and to secure such financing with the lease payment stream and the equipment. The lack of prejudice to the lessee is further illustrated by the lessor's warranty of quiet use and enjoyment of the equipment.

RISK OF LOSS AND DAMAGE

Under this provision, the lessee bears the risk of damage or destruction of the equipment, as well as the risk of a theft or governmental taking of the equipment. Most of these risks can be mitigated by the lessee by obtaining the appropriate insurance coverage. Since most lease transactions are net leases (i.e., lessee bears the burden of maintenance, insurance and taxes), the lessee is obligated to obtain insurance on the equipment, insuring against damage, destruction, loss and theft.

(a) Lessee agrees to bear the risk of loss with respect to any damage, destruction, loss, theft or governmental taking of any Equipment, whether partial or complete and whether or not through any default or neglect of Lessee. Except as provided in this Section, no such event shall relieve Lessee of its obligation to pay Rent hereunder.

(b) If any Equipment is damaged, Lessee must promptly notify Lessor and within 60 days of such damage shall, at Lessee's expense, cause such repairs to be made as are necessary to return such Equipment to its previous condition. Lessee shall then be entitled to receive from Lessor or Assignee, as the case may be, any insurance proceeds received in connection with such damage.

(c) In the event that any Equipment is destroyed, damaged beyond repair, lost, stolen or taken by governmental action for a stated period extending beyond the term of the Equipment Schedule to which such Equipment is subject (an "Event of Loss"), Lessee must promptly notify Lessor and Assignee and pay to Lessor or Assignee, as the case may be, on the next Basic Rent payment date following the Event of Loss, an amount equal to the Casualty Value set forth in Exhibit C of such Equipment Schedule in effect on the date of the Event of Loss and all Rent accrued on such item up to the date of payment. Upon payment of such amounts, Lessee's obligation to pay further Rent will cease with respect to that Equipment (but not with respect to any remaining Equipment) and Lessee will be entitled to receive any insurance proceeds or other recovery received by Lessor or Assignee in connection with such Event of Loss.

(d) In the event of a governmental taking of any Equipment for an indefinite period or for a stated period which does not extend beyond the term of the applicable Equipment Schedule(s), all obligations of the Lessee with respect to such Equipment (including payment of Rent) will continue. So long as Lessee is not in default hereunder, Lessor will pay to Lessee all sums received by Lessor by reason of such governmental taking up to the amount paid by Lessee during such period.

The lessee's obligation to make the lease payments and to repair or replace the equipment depends on the extent of the loss to the equipment. The lessee's obligation to make the lease payments continues despite a loss to, or taking of, the equipment unless the loss is a total loss or the governmental taking exceeds the unexpired term of the lease. Where the loss is a total loss or the taking exceeds the unexpired term of the lease, the lessee must pay to the lessor all accrued lease payments plus the amount specified in the Casualty Value Table. Upon payment of this amount, the lessee would then be entitled to the insurance proceeds or the condemnation award, as the case may be.

Where the equipment is only partially damaged or the governmental taking is less than the unexpired term of the lease, the lessee remains obligated to make the lease payments to the lessor. In the event of a partial loss, the lessee must restore the equipment to its previous condition. Upon such restoration the lessee would be entitled to any insurance proceeds. In the event of a partial governmental taking, the lessee would be entitled to the condemnation award as long as the lessee was not in default under the terms of the lease.

INSURANCE

The objective of this provision is twofold: (i) to protect the lessor's investment in the equipment and (ii) to protect the lessor, the lessor's assignee and the lessee from liability to a third party for injury to persons or property.

> Lessee shall, at its expense, insure the Equipment against all risks and in such amounts as Lessor reasonably requires (but not less than the Casualty Value as identified on each Exhibit C with respect to each corresponding Equipment Schedule) with carriers acceptable to Lessor, shall maintain a loss payable endorsement in favor of Lessor and Assignee affording them such additional protection as they reasonably require, and shall maintain liability insurance satisfactory to Lessor. All such insurance policies must name Lessor, Lessee and Assignee as insured and loss payees and must provide that the insurance coverage may not be cancelled or altered without at least 30 days' prior written notice to Lessor and Assignee. Upon the written consent of Lessor and Assignee, Lessee may act as a self-insurer in amounts acceptable to Lessor and any Assignee.

The casualty insurance policy should be for the full replacement value of the equipment. Otherwise, the insurer would be bound to indemnify the lessor only for the lesser of (i) the fair market value of the equipment or (ii) the original cost of the equipment less accumulated depreciation. In most situations, the latter approach is far less desirable than full replacement value coverage. The liability insurance policy should be for at least $1 million, depending on the type of equipment leased. Obviously, liability coverage for computer equipment can be dramatically less than liability coverage for an airplane.

Generally, as stated in the insurance provision, the lessor requires that it be named as a loss payee on the policy of insurance. As a loss payee, the lessor protects itself from cancellation of coverage by the lessee. Additionally, the lessor has the right to procure insurance upon the lessee's failure to do so. In such an event, the lessor may pass the expense of such insurance to the lessee through increased lease payments, plus interest. This ensures insurance coverage will always exist and the cost thereof will be borne by the lessee. In addition to the coverages discussed above, the lessor may consider carrying its own insurance against product liability.

INDEMNITY

This provision provides the lessor with protection in addition to the insurance coverage.

> Lessee agrees to indemnify Lessor and Assignee against, and to hold Lessor and Assignee harmless from, any and all claims, actions, suits, proceedings, costs, expenses, damages and liabilities, at law or in equity, including attorney's fees, arising out of, connected with, or resulting from this Master Lease or the Equipment, including, without limitation, the manufacture, selection, purchase, delivery, possession, condition, use, operation or return thereof. Lessee's obligations hereunder will survive the expiration of this Master Lease with respect to acts or events occurring or alleged to have occurred prior to the return of the Equipment to Lessor at the end of the term of the applicable Equipment Schedule(s).

Essentially, the lessor is seeking protection against any claims or causes of action arising out of, or related to, the purchase, use and ownership of the equipment. Given the exorbitant costs of litigation, indemnification for attorneys' fees and costs of court is an absolute necessity from the lessor's perspective. The survival of the lessee's obligations under this provision is required in the event that a claim or cause of action is based on events that occurred during the term of the lease, but is not brought until after the termination of the lease.

LIENS AND TAXES

Under a net lease, the lessee is required to pay all license and registration fees and all taxes arising out of, or related to, the equipment, with the sole exception of any taxes incurred by the lessor based on the lease payment income. This provision sets forth the lessee's obligation to pay the taxes.

> Lessee will, at its expense, keep the Equipment free and clear of all levies, liens and encumbrances. Lessee shall not assign or otherwise encumber this Master Lease, any Equipment Schedule, any Equipment or any of Lessee's rights hereunder without the prior written consent of Lessor. Lessee will declare and pay when due all license fees, registration fees, assessments, charges and taxes, whether municipal, state or federal, including, but not limited to, sales, use, excise and property taxes, and penalties and interest with respect thereto, excluding, however, any taxes based on or measured solely by Lessor's net income. Lessee shall provide evidence of any payment hereunder upon request of Lessor.

In addition, this provision prohibits the lessee from assigning, transferring or otherwise encumbering the lease transaction or the equipment without the lessor's prior written consent. By conditioning the lessee's assignment, transfer or encumbrance of the lease transaction, or the equipment, upon the lessor's consent, the lessor maintains control of the lease transaction and the equipment.

LESSEE'S FAILURE TO PERFORM

In addition to the other remedies discussed, this provision grants to the lessor one additional and significant remedy. Under this provision, if the lessee fails to perform an obligation under the lease, the lessor may perform for the lessee and then charge the lessee for all expenses incurred, plus interest.

> Should Lessee fail to make any payment or to do any act required herein, Lessor has the right, but not the obligation and without releasing Lessee from any obligation hereunder, to make or do the same, and to pay, purchase, contest or compromise any encumbrance, charge or lien which, in the judgment of Lessor appears to affect the Equipment, and in exercising any such rights, incur any liability and expend whatever amount in Lessor's absolute discretion Lessor may deem necessary therefor. All sums so incurred or expended by Lessor shall be, without demand, immediately due and payable by Lessee, shall be considered Rent hereunder and will bear interest at the lesser of 2% per month or the highest interest rate legally permissible.

Generally, the remedy under this provision is invoked by the lessor where the lessee has failed to pay for insurance or taxes or has permitted a judgment or execution to be rendered against the equipment. In such circumstances, the lessor may obtain the necessary insurance, pay the accrued taxes or take any necessary action to remove a judgment or execution, rather than risk losing the equipment. The sums expended, plus interest, are immediately collectible from the lessee. This permits the lessor to place a priority on protecting the equipment, knowing the lessee will ultimately be held liable for the costs.

PERSONAL PROPERTY, LOCATION OF EQUIPMENT

An issue that arises frequently is whether the equipment has become so related or attached to real property that it becomes a fixture. As discussed in Chapter Twenty, the basic test of whether the equipment is personal property or a fixture is the intent of the parties. This provision establishes that intent.

> Lessee covenants and agrees that the Equipment is, and will at all times be and remain, personal property. If requested by Lessor, Lessee will obtain, prior to delivery of any Equipment, a certificate in a form satisfactory to Lessor from all parties with a real property interest in the premises wherein the Equipment may be located, waiving any claim with respect thereto.
>
> Lessee will not move any Equipment nor permit any Equipment to be moved from the address set forth in the Equipment Schedule attached as Exhibit A without Lessor's prior written consent, which consent will not be unreasonably withheld; provided however, that in no event will any Equipment be moved to a location outside the United States of America or to any jurisdiction within the United States of America which has not adopted the Uniform Commercial Code.

The fact that the parties agree the equipment is and shall remain personal property demonstrates the clear intent of the parties. As such, the equipment should remain classified as personal property. However, as an added precaution, the lessor is given the power to require the lessee to obtain waivers of claims to the equipment from land owners, landlords and mortgagees.

The second facet of this provision prohibits the lessee from moving or relocating the equipment without the lessor's prior written consent. As discussed in Chapter Twenty, a lessor will file a UCC-1 Financing Statement (UCC-1) as a precautionary measure to give the lessor a first priority security interest in the equipment in the event the lease transaction is reclassified as other than a true lease. The location of the equipment is important to the lessor for two reasons: (i) as the owner of the equipment, the lessor has the right to know where the equipment is located; and (ii) the moving or relocating of the equipment may jeopardize the lessor's security interest in the equipment under the lessor's precautionary UCC-1 filing. In addition, if the lessee moves the equipment to a jurisdiction that has not adopted the UCC (Louisiana is the only such state), the security interest of the lessor under its UCC-1 may be rendered completely null and void. Thus, this provision provides the lessor with additional assurance.

DESIGNATION OF OWNERSHIP

The wording of this provision substantiates the lessor's status as the owner of the equipment for tax and UCC purposes.

> If at any time during the term hereof Lessee is supplied with labels, plates or other markings stating that the Equipment is owned by Lessor or is subject to any interest of Assignee, Lessee agrees to affix and keep the same prominently displayed on the Equipment. Lessee agrees to execute and file Uniform Commercial Code financing statements and any and all other instruments necessary to perfect the interest of Lessor or Assignee in this Master Lease, the Equipment Schedule(s), the payments due hereunder and/or the Equipment. Lessor may file a copy of this Master Lease and appropriate Equipment Schedules as a financing statement.

In addition, by placing labels, plates or other markings on the equipment, the lessor is able to further protect its interest in the equipment in the event the lessee attempts to assign, transfer or otherwise encumber the equipment without the lessor's prior written consent. In such event, the assignee, transferor or other encumbrancer would take the equipment with full notice of the lessor's interest in the equipment. Accordingly, such parties would take the equipment subject to the lessor's interest. Again, the lessor protects its interest in and to the equipment.

USE

By requiring the lessee to use the equipment in a careful and proper manner, the lessor is providing itself with further protection in the event that the lessee misuses the equipment and thereby injures a third party or damages the equipment.

> Lessee shall use the Equipment in a careful and proper manner in conformance with manufacturer's specifications and shall comply with and conform to all federal, state, municipal and other laws, ordinances and regulations in any way relating to the possession, use or maintenance of the Equipment.

Under such a provision, and in the event of injury to a third party, or damage to the equipment, the lessor would have a claim or cause of action against the lessee for any liability arising out of, or related to, such misuse.

SURRENDER OF EQUIPMENT

As in the designation of ownership provision, the wording of this provision substantiates the lessor's status as the owner of the equipment for tax and UCC purposes.

> Upon the expiration or earlier termination of each Equipment Schedule with respect to any Equipment, Lessee shall, unless Lessee has paid Lessor in cash the Casualty Value of the Equipment pursuant to this Section, return the same to Lessor in good repair, condition and working order, ordinary wear and tear resulting from proper use thereof alone excepted, to the location specified on the Equipment Schedule attached as Exhibit A. All costs of deinstallation, packaging, insurance and transportation of the Equipment will be borne by Lessee.

The provision also requires the lessee to bear the expense of returning the equipment to the lessor. In addition, the lessor is protected from excessive wear and tear or depreciation of the equipment by the lessee. In the event the lessee abused or overused the equipment, the lessor is given a claim or cause of action against the lessee for such abuse or overuse.

EVENTS OF DEFAULT

The event of default is always a potentiality, so this provision should always be included.

The occurrence of any of the following events shall constitute an Event of Default and shall, at the option of Lessor, terminate the applicable Equipment Schedule(s) issued pursuant to this Master Lease and Lessee's right to possession of the Equipment:

(a) The nonpayment by Lessee of any item of Rent within 10 days of the date on which it is due.

(b) The failure by Lessee to perform or observe any other term, covenant or condition of this Master Lease or any Equipment Schedule, which is not cured within 10 days after notice thereof from Lessor or Assignee.

(c) Any affirmative act of insolvency by Lessee, or the filing by Lessee of any petition or action under any bankruptcy, reorganization, insolvency arrangement, liquidation, dissolution or moratorium law, or any other law or laws for the relief of, or relating to, debtors.

(d) The filing of any involuntary petition against Lessee under any bankruptcy, reorganization, insolvency, arrangement, liquidation, dissolution or moratorium law, or any other law for the relief of or relating to debtors which is not dismissed within 60 days thereafter, or the appointment of any receiver, liquidator or trustee to take possession of any substantial portion of the properties of Lessee, unless the appointment is set aside or ceases to be in effect within 60 days from the date of said filing or appointment.

(e) The subjection of a substantial part of Lessee's property or any Equipment to any levy, seizure, assignment or sale for or by any creditor or governmental agency.

(f) Any representation or warranty made by Lessee in this Master Lease or in any Equipment Schedule or in any document furnished by Lessee to Lessor or Assignee in connection with this Master Lease or any Equipment Schedule or with respect to the acquisition or use of the Equipment shall be untrue in any material respect.

A breach or default of an agreement results when one of the parties fails to perform one or more of its promises encompassed by the agreement. The UCC does not define what events constitute a default. Thus, the determination as to what actions of the lessee constitute a default should be defined in the lease agreement with extreme and explicit care. In addition, by defining in the lease agreement precisely which events constitute a default, the lessee is put on notice that any deviation from the terms of the lease may result in the lessor pursuing one or more of the remedies available to the lessor. As discussed in Chapter Twenty, the event of default premised upon the filing of a petition in bankruptcy by or against the lessee is generally unenforceable under the current Bankruptcy Act. Despite that restriction, most leases include such a provision

QUIET ENJOYMENT

Under this provision, the lessee is entitled to the unfettered use and enjoyment of the equipment provided the lessee has not breached the lease agreement. This provides the lessee with a certain level of comfort (as well as an enforceable legal right) that it will be permitted to use the equipment without interference by the lessor or any of its assignees.

Provided that no Event of Default has occurred or is continuing hereunder, Lessor, Assignee or their agents or assigns shall not interfere with Lessee's right of quiet enjoyment and use of the Equipment.

SUSPENSION OF OBLIGATIONS OF LESSOR

Absent this provision, the lessor could still be bound to perform under the terms of the lease agreement even though the equipment was not, or could not be, delivered due to, among other things, acts of God, strikes or failure of the supplier or manufacturer of the equipment. This provision, therefore, permits the lessor to escape from this potential liability. Additionally, since the lessor may terminate the lease agreement at its option, the lessor may be able to overcome the obstacle and deliver the equipment. Again, this provision protects the lessor, while also providing the lessor with maximum flexibility.

The obligations of Lessor hereunder will be suspended (or, at Lessor's option, terminated) to the extent that Lessor is hindered or prevented from complying therewith because of labor disturbances, including but not limited to strikes and lockouts, acts of God, fires, storms, accidents, failure of the manufacturer to deliver any item or Equipment, governmental regulations or interference or any cause whatsoever not within the sole and exclusive control of Lessor.

ATTORNEYS' FEES

In today's world, the costs of litigation are prohibitive; therefore, as such the only way a non-breaching party can be rendered whole is to require the breaching party to reimburse the nonbreaching party for its legal fees and costs. This provision is a powerful negotiating tool and provides a strong impetus for the parties not to breach the lease agreement. This provision is an absolute necessity in all lease agreements, as well as all other contracts.

In the event any action at law or suit in equity is brought by either party hereto against the other in relation to this Master Lease, any Equipment Schedule or any Equipment, the prevailing party will be entitled to a reasonable sum for its attorneys' fees and costs.

SPECIAL TERMS

This provision provides the parties with the maximum flexibility to tailor each lease transaction to the exacting needs of the parties. Under this provision, the parties can structure each equipment schedule to satisfy the needs of the parties that are unique to that particular transaction. Given the complexities of today's business environment, the parties need the flexibility to address the problems and intricacies of each transaction.

Any special terms set forth in one or more Exhibits, Schedules or Riders to this Master Lease as they apply to the applicable Equipment Schedule(s) will be applicable as though fully set forth herein.

MISCELLANEOUS PROVISIONS

Miscellaneous provisions are those legal provisions that appear in almost all legal documents.

(a) Effect of Waiver. No delay or omission to exercise any right or remedy accruing to Lessor upon any breach or default of Lessee will impair any such right or remedy or be construed to be a waiver of any such breach or default, nor will a waiver of any single breach or default be deemed a waiver of any other breach or default theretofore or thereafter occurring. Any waiver, permit, consent or approval on the part of Lessor of any breach or default under this Master Lease, or any Equipment Schedule, or of any provision or condition hereof, must be in writing and will be effective only to the extent specifically set forth. All remedies, either under this Master Lease, or at law or in equity or otherwise afforded to Lessor, are cumulative and not alternate.

(b) Notices. Any notice required or permitted to be given by the provisions hereof must be in writing and will be conclusively deemed to have been received by a party hereto on the day it is delivered to such party at the address indicated below (or at such other address as such party specified to the other party in a similar notice) or, if sent by certified or registered mail, on the fifth business day after the day on which mailed, addressed to such party at the following address:

IF TO LESSOR: 3450 South Highland Drive
Suite 104
Salt Lake City, UT 84106
Attn: General Counsel

IF TO LESSEE: 2732 South 2140 East
Salt Lake City, UT 84105
Attn: Vice President, Leasing

(c) Security Interest.

(i) Each executed copy of this Master Lease and each Equipment Schedule will be an original. To the extent, if any, that this Master Lease (or such Equipment Schedule) constitutes chattel paper (as such term is defined in the Uniform Commercial Code as in effect in any applicable jurisdiction) no security interest herein or therein may be created through the transfer or possession of any counterpart other than an original.

(ii) There shall be only one original of each Equipment Schedule to the Master Lease, and it shall be marked "Original," and all other counterparts will be duplicates. To the extent, if any, that any Equipment Schedule(s) to this Master Lease constitutes chattel paper (as such term is defined in the Uniform Commercial Code as in effect in

solely to the creditworthiness of the lessee. In order to facilitate the lender's credit decision, it is necessary that the lessor be able to obtain the necessary financial information of the lessee. Additionally, if the lessor is concerned about the lessee's current financial condition, the lessor has the right to obtain the pertinent information necessary to satisfy the lessor's concern.

One of the main purposes of reducing to written form an agreement between parties is to avoid future disputes regarding the terms of the agreement. The entire agreement provision protects each party from a claim by the other that there exists a side agreement between the parties or that the terms of the agreement are different from those set forth in the written agreement. Therefore, if the parties subsequently modify the terms of the original agreement, the parties should reduce such modifications to written form and should sign the written modification. This should help eliminate a future dispute regarding the agreement of the parties.

When a court or legislature determines a certain type of provision or clause is unlawful or unenforceable, a legal issue arises as to whether that renders the entire contract unenforceable. In order to avoid this issue, the parties should include a severability provision in their lease agreements. Under such a provision, the parties generally are able to enforce their agreements despite the unenforceability of a particular provision.

In most contracts, section headings are provided for the convenience of the parties and other persons (i.e., lawyers and judges) in reading the contract. However, the parties to a transaction want their rights and obligations to be determined by the language of the agreement rather than from the section headings. Accordingly, the headings provision is included in most contracts.

The last four miscellaneous provisions are added to lease agreements to give the lessor and lessee additional flexibility, particularly where the parties are unsure of their future needs or of subsequent developments with respect to the equipment. Under these provisions, the lessor can substitute equivalent equipment for the equipment originally leased or the lessee can upgrade the leased equipment with the new developments of the manufacturer. This added flexibility permits the parties to endure a lasting and long-term relationship.

SIGNATURE OF THE PARTIES

The Master Lease should contain the duly executed signatures of both parties. Where both the lessor and lessee are clearly designated there is little chance for mistakes as to the parties to, and binding provisions of, the contract. Under general contract law, the word "By" is significant in that it clearly indicates that the individual is signing on behalf of an organization rather than in an individual capacity.

IN WITNESS WHEREOF, Lessor and Lessee have caused this Master Lease to be duly executed all as of the date first above written.

LESSOR:	LESSEE:
Sentry Financial Corporation,	Bono & Company,
a Utah corporation,	a Utah corporation,
By: _____	By: _____
Print Name: _____	Print Name: _____
Title: _____	Title: _____

Tax Indemnification Rider

Due to the significance of tax benefits in leasing transactions (even where the investment credit is unavailable), the loss of these benefits could turn a very profitable agreement into a seriously undesirable contract. Lessors frequently enter into leases intending to take advantage of the tax shelter benefits, namely, the investment tax credit (when and if it is available), accelerated cost recovery system deductions and interest deductions. In light of the almost continuous changes to the tax law, the risk of the loss or the mitigation of these tax benefits has increased dramatically. Accordingly, lessors are carefully drafting tax indemnification provisions and insisting that these provisions be a part of the lease contract. The tax indemnification provisions may be either a separate provision of the lease agreement or may be attached to the lease agreement as a rider. An example of a Tax Indemnification Rider is attached as Exhibit V of Appendix B.

The purpose of a tax indemnification provision is to place the lessor in the same after-tax position (yield or cash flow) it would have been in had the loss not occurred. Generally, there are only three ways that a tax loss will occur. First, the lessor may cause the loss by its own acts or omissions that are inconsistent with the lessor's attainment or retention of the tax benefits. For example, where the investment credit exists, the lessor may prematurely dispose of the equipment and thereby trigger a recapture of some of the credit. Second, the lessee, by its acts or omissions, may cause the loss of tax benefits to the lessor. For example, the lessee may use the equipment before it is subject to the lease or may use the equipment outside of the United States. Finally, a loss of tax benefits may be caused by exogenous factors that are outside of the control of lessor and lessee. Such factors include an involuntary conversion or a change in the tax laws by Congress.

If the lessor is the cause of the lessor's tax loss, the lessee should not be required to compensate the lessor for it. On the other hand, if the lessee is the cause of the lessor's tax loss, then the lessee should be required to compensate the lessor for such loss. Originally, the main objective of a tax indemnification provision was to protect the lessor against tax losses caused by the lessee. However, given the present political environment, an equally important purpose of a tax indemnification provision is to protect the lessor from a tax loss caused by a change in the tax laws by Congress. Lessors should consider negotiating the effect of the lease transaction of a subsequent change in the tax rates. In other words, if the tax rates change, the prospective lease payments should similarly change (either up or down) to maintain the after-tax yield the lessor originally anticipated (using the same residual value assumption originally used).

Equipment Schedule

The purpose of an Equipment Schedule is to set forth all of the variable fill-in-the-blank information regarding a particular lease transaction. By using Equipment Schedules, the lessor and lessee may do numerous leasing transactions involving various types of equipment and different lease terms without having to execute a Master Lease for each transaction. Each Equipment Schedule will specifically incorporate by reference the terms and conditions of the Master Lease. Furthermore, once the lessee has had its attorneys review the lease documentation for the first Equipment Schedule, it is unnecessary for the lessee's attorneys to review the documents for the second Equipment Schedule because the documents will be identical except for the fill-in-the blank information. This can result in substantial savings to the lessee. An example of an Equipment Schedule is attached as Exhibit II of Appendix B.

As indicated in the example Equipment Schedule, the lessor and lessee are clearly identified, as well as the specific location of the equipment. As discussed in Chapter Twenty, the location of the equipment is significant for purposes of protecting the lessor's interest in the equipment under the UCC and in the event of bankruptcy of the lessee. Additionally, identifying the location of the equipment makes it easier for the lessor to periodically check on the equipment and to repossess it in the event of a default by the lessee. The most important information set forth in an Equipment Schedule is the description of the equipment, including the quantity, manufacturer, model/feature number, serial number, short textual description and estimated cost.

The most critical information contained in an Equipment Schedule is that regarding the lease payments. The amount of the lease payment, the commencement date and the lease term are essential to avoid misconceptions by either party. The number and amount of advance payments and the payment due dates are necessary for the same reason. In addition, an Equipment Schedule must contain a mechanism to adjust the lease payment up or down in the event the actual cost of the equipment differs from the estimated cost. This will provide the parties with the necessary certainty while also providing the necessary flexibility.

Typically, the first lease payment will be due on the first day of the month following the date the lessee accepts the equipment as being satisfactory (the acceptance date). The lessor should be compensated for the use of the equipment between the acceptance date and the due date of the first lease payment. This payment is commonly referred to as interim rent or stub rent. The provision regarding payment of interim rent should be drafted with care. If a security deposit is required, it should be specifically designated as such and should not be classified as an advance payment because a security deposit is normally not taxable as income to the lessor. This allows the lessor to utilize these funds free of taxes. The mechanism for assessment of late charges and interest penalties also should be clearly delineated and enforced by the lessor. Consistent enforcement of these charges by the lessor will preclude any argument by the lessee (on future defaults) that the lessor waived its rights to late charges and interest penalties. These charges are utilized to compensate the lessor for its out-of-pocket expenses incurred as a result of the delinquent payment by the lessee, namely, telephone calls and employee time as well as lost interest. The lessor should make sure the late charges and interest penalties do not exceed the amount allowed by law.

Fair Market Value Purchase Option Rider

Most lessors are willing to provide their lessees with the option to purchase the equipment at the end of the lease term at the equipment's then current fair market value. Where the option is only exercisable at fair market value, the parties should be able to avoid the lease transaction being classified as a conditional sale for federal income tax purposes or, from the lessee's perspective, as a capital lease for accounting purposes (assuming the lease transaction does not violate the other relevant criteria). The difficulty arises in determining what amount constitutes fair market value. The mechanism can be structured like the example found as Exhibit III of Appendix B, whereby fair market value is designated by the lessor and subject to agreement by the lessee. Alternatively, the mechanism could provide that each party obtain an appraisal and that the value as established by the appraisers constitutes the fair market value of the equipment. Either approach is acceptable as well as any other alternative that satisfies the objective of the parties.

Fair Rental Value Renewal Option Rider

Like the purchase option, most lessors are willing to provide their lessees with the option to re-lease the equipment for its then current fair rental value. The difficulty that arises is in setting the parameters of the renewal period such that they are acceptable to both parties. Again, like the purchase option, where the renewal option is only exercisable at fair rental value, the parties should be able to avoid having the lease transaction characterized as a conditional sale for federal income tax purposes or, from the lessee's perspective, as a capital lease for accounting purposes (again assuming the lease transaction does not violate the other relevant criteria). The alternative mechanisms for ascertaining the fair rental value of the equipment are virtually identical to those available for calculating fair market value under the purchase option. An example of a Fair Rental Renewal Option Rider is attached as Exhibit IV of Appendix B.

Certificate of Acceptance

The purpose of a Certificate of Acceptance is to obtain specific representations from the lessee upon delivery of the equipment. The important representations made by the lessee include, but are not limited to, the following. First, the lessor should obtain from the lessee a representation that the equipment has been delivered to the lessee, properly installed, inspected by the lessee, found to be in good working order and condition and accepted by the lessee. Second, the lessee should reconfirm all of the representations and warranties made by the lessee in the Master Lease and in the applicable Equipment Schedule. Third, the lessee should represent that no event of default has occurred or is continuing under the Master Lease or in the applicable Equipment Schedule. Finally, the lessor must obtain a representation from the lessee that the lessee has procured insurance coverage on the equipment in accordance with the terms of the Master Lease and the applicable Equipment Schedule. An example of a Certificate of Acceptance is attached as Exhibit VI of Appendix B.

The Certificate of Acceptance also requires the lessee to confirm the location of the equipment. As discussed in Chapter Twenty, the location of the equipment is significant for purposes of the UCC with respect to the precautionary filing of a Form UCC-1. In addition, upon delivery of the equipment, the lessor is able to verify and obtain a more accurate description of the equipment. For example, the lessor will be able to verify the serial numbers and will know the exact cost or basis of the equipment. With the exact cost or basis of the equipment, the lessor and lessee will be able to adjust the lease payment, if necessary, to reflect any difference in the actual cost of the equipment from the parties' estimated cost of the equipment. Thus, the parties will specify the exact lease payment and thereby avoid any misunderstanding.

Most importantly, the Certificate of Acceptance sets forth the acceptance date for purposes of that particular Equipment Schedule. The acceptance date is extremely important because of the tax and UCC ramifications. In addition, it marks the beginning of the lessee's obligation to make the lease payments. As discussed in Chapter Twenty, the acceptance date has important implications regarding the equipment's being placed in service for accelerated cost recovery system deductions. The acceptance date is also very important with respect to the perfection of the lessor's security interest under the UCC. Furthermore, from the practical perspective, a lender will not provide the funding necessary for the lessor to acquire the equipment until the lessee has properly executed the Certificate of Acceptance.

Casualty Value Schedule

The objective of the Casualty Value Schedule is to establish the value of the lease and the equipment to the lessor for purposes of payment by the lessee to the lessor upon the loss, destruction or condemnation of the equipment. The Casualty Value Schedule also is used sometimes as a measure of damages incurred by the lessor upon early termination by the lessee. The value is based upon an analysis of several factors including, among others, the projected declining value of the equipment each month during the lease term; the declining outstanding balance of any underlying loan used by the lessor to purchase the equipment; the loss or recapture of tax benefits by the lessor, particularly the investment tax credit; and a portion of the lessor's profit. All of these factors are incorporated into a complex formula, which is then used to compute the value at various time periods over the term of the lease. The value established through this procedure will usually also contain a fluff factor, which slightly increases the established value in order to provide the lessor with additional protection. An example of a Casualty Value Schedule is attached as Exhibit VII of Appendix B.

Officer's Certificate or Corporate Resolution

An Officer's Certificate or Corporate Resolution is a formal, but rather simple, document. One of these documents is necessary for a corporation that is a party to a lease transaction. The purpose of the Officer's Certificate or Corporate Resolution is to ensure the lease has been accepted by each corporation's Board of Directors and the agent signing the lease documents is authorized and empowered to do so on behalf of the corporation. If either of the parties is a partnership, a document akin to an Officer's Certificate or Corporate Resolution, indicating the lease is within the partnership's authority, should be signed by all of the partners or by the managing general partner. An example of an Officer's Certificate is attached as Exhibit IX of Appendix B.

Opinion of Lessee's Counsel

The purpose of an Opinion of Lessee's Counsel is to discover potential problems of the lessee and to provide additional security to the lessor that the lessee is able to enter into, and to perform, the obligations under the lease. If the lessee is unable to produce an Opinion of Counsel, it may serve as a red flag to the lessor (although many Fortune 500 lessees simply refuse to issue opinions because of the administrative hassles involved). The items opined upon by the lessee's counsel mirror, for the most part, the representations and warranties made by the lessee in the Master Lease. Those topics include (i) whether the lessee, as an entity, is properly organized and in good standing; (ii) whether the lessee has complied with the pertinent state doing business requirements (this usually involves nothing more than registering with the Secretary of State of each state in which the entity conducts business); (iii) whether the Master Lease and attendant documents constitute a valid and binding obligation of the lessee, enforceable according to their terms; (iv) whether the entering into and performance of the Master Lease and attendant documents will violate the lessee's Articles of Incorporation or Bylaws, loan restrictions, judgments, orders or regulations; and (v) whether there exist any actions, suits or proceedings against the lessee that would materially adversely affect the lessee's ability to perform under the Master Lease and attendant documents. An example of an Opinion of Lessee's Counsel is attached as Exhibit X of Appendix B.

Certificate of Insurance

The purpose of the Certificate of Insurance is to provide the lessor with assurance the lessee has fulfilled its insurance obligations under the lease agreement by obtaining the appropriate insurance coverage. This document should provide the lessor with information regarding the amount and extent of insurance coverage and should identify the lessor as the loss payee. As the loss payee, the insurance company usually must give the lessor reasonable notice before cancelling coverage. This notice requirement provides the lessor with additional comfort. An example of a Certificate of Insurance is attached as Exhibit VIII of Appendix B.

Precautionary Form UCC-1

As discussed in Chapter Twenty, it is unnecessary for the lessor to perfect a security interest in equipment that it owns and has leased to a third party. However, a lessor generally would be foolish not to file a precautionary Form UCC-1 to protect itself in the event that a court or other authoritative body were to construe the transaction as other than a lease agreement. The pertinent information contained in a Form UCC-1 is the name and address of the lessee and the lessor and a description of the leased property. The accuracy of the name of the lessee is absolutely critical and a mistake could render the Form UCC-1 ineffective. A sample description of the leased property is as follows:

> All [insert specific manufacturer or brand name of the Equipment] and related equipment under lease to Lessee pursuant to Equipment Schedule No. 1, dated as of September 30, 1987, issued pursuant to Master Lease dated as of September 30, 1987, between Sentry Financial Corporation, as original Lessor, and Bono & Company, as Lessee. This UCC-1 is filed pursuant to Section 9-408 of the Uniform Commercial Code for informational purposes only. The transaction covered by this UCC-1 is intended by the Lessor and Lessee to be a true lease.

The purpose of a Form UCC-1 is to provide notice to third parties that the lessor has an interest in the equipment. The precautionary Form UCC-1 acts as an inexpensive form of insurance that the lessor will have a priority claim in the equipment regardless of the transaction's classification by a court or other authoritative body as either a lease or security interest. An example of a Form UCC-1 is attached as Exhibit XI of Appendix B.

Lease Documents Conclusion

The preceding documents are examples of fairly standard lease transaction documentation. Most of the pertinent provisions can be adapted to most lease transactions. Some of the documents protect the lessee, but most are drafted to protect the lessor's interest. Depending on the magnitude and complexity of the transaction, there is, of course, a variety of additional documents that may be required, such as a Guaranty and Waiver, a Landlord/Mortgage Waiver and a Security Agreement or Deed of Trust. Generally, it is a good idea to seek the advice of competent legal counsel who is well-versed in the leasing field whenever entering into a leasing transaction.

LOAN DOCUMENTS

In leveraged lease transactions there are numerous documents that outline the duties and responsibilities by, and between, the lessor and the lender. Even though the loan documents may be drafted and prepared by the lessor, they will usually be more oriented toward protecting the interests of the lender. As with the lease transaction, but to a lesser extent, there are numerous ways to structure the loan transaction. The loan documentation can vary dramatically from one financial institution to another, and from an extremely complex set of documents to a more simple snap-out form. Even the dollar volume of the loan influences the complexity of the documentation. Recognizing that, this section focuses on one type of documentation, the provisions of which have general application to other types of lease transactions.

Generally, in a leveraged lease transaction, the loan documents would include:

- Secured Note
- Security Agreement
- Pay Proceeds Letter
- Officer's Certificate/Corporate Resolution
- Opinion of Debtor's Counsel
- Form UCC-1 Notice of Assignment Letter.

Examples of these documents are attached as Exhibits XII through XXI of Appendix B. Pertinent provisions of these documents and the nature and purpose of each particular document will be subsequently reviewed. These documents are offered as examples only and the parties are urged to seek competent legal advice in structuring and documenting each loan transaction.

Secured Note

The Secured Note (Note) and Security Agreement are the two essential documents involved in any loan agreement. Often, the Note will refer to and incorporate the provisions of the Security Agreement. Accordingly, the Note is a relatively short document. The caption of the Note should clearly indicate the principal amount and the interest rate of the obligation. This allows for easy identification of the Secured Note and avoids any disagreement between the parties. An example of a Note is attached as Exhibit XII of Appendix B. The major terms and conditions of the Note should include the following items.

NAMES OF PARTIES, PRINCIPAL AMOUNT AND INTEREST, TERMS OF PAYMENT

Like the Master Lease, clear identification of the parties substantially reduces any mistake as to the parties to, and binding provisions of, the Note. This provision also sets forth with particularity the principal amount of the loan, the rate of interest accruing on the principal and the number and terms of repayment. This loan and payment information must be set out with clarity so the lessor cannot be mistaken as to its obligations. For this reason, the attachment of an amortization schedule should preclude all uncertainty.

> Sentry Financial Corporation, a Utah corporation ("Debtor"), for value received, hereby promises to pay to Last National Bank ("Payee"), or assigns on or before _____, 19____, as hereinafter provided, the principal sum of _____Dollars and _____Cents ($_____) and to pay interest on the unpaid principal amount thereof from the date hereof to maturity at the rate of _____ percent (_____%) per annum, computed as if each year consisted of 360 days and each month consisted of 30 days. Such principal and interest shall be payable without presentation of this Note, in lawful money of the United States, at Bank, Salt Lake City, Utah, in _____ consecutive payments of principal and interest (the "Installment Payments") in and at the following amount and times: _____ on the first day of each month beginning on _____, 198____, and continuing for _____ (_____) consecutive months thereafter. The amortization schedule attached hereto reflects the payment of interest and amortization of principal under this Note by the Installment Payments.

In a leveraged lease transaction, which secures the loan obligation, the amount of the lease payments and the lease term generally will equal the loan payments and the loan term (i.e., the lease transaction is match funded). Accordingly, the lessor usually will assign the lease payment stream to the lender and direct the lessee to make its lease payments directly to the lender. In this scenario, the loan would be paid in full upon receipt of the last lease payment under the lease agreement. Thus, both the loan obligation and the lease agreement would expire at the same time and the lessor would be entitled to the equipment free and clear of any claim of the lender or the lessee.

INCORPORATION OF TERMS OF SECURITY AGREEMENT

This provision clearly indicates that the obligation evidenced by the Note is secured by collateral. It also specifically incorporates the terms and conditions of the Security Agreement. By incorporating the terms of the Security Agreement into the Note, the parties avoid duplicity and simplify the otherwise lengthy documentation.

> This Note is secured as provided in, and subject to, the provisions of a Security Agreement of even date herewith between Debtor and Payee and the terms used in this Note and not hereinabove defined have the meanings indicated in Article V of the Security Agreement. The parties incorporate by this reference all of the terms and conditions of the Security Agreement of even date herewith as fully as though completely set forth herein.

ATTORNEYS' FEES

In today's world the costs of litigation are prohibitive; therefore, the only way a lender can be rendered whole is to require a breaching debtor to reimburse the lender for its legal fees and costs. This provision provides a strong impetus for the debtor not to breach the Note.

> Should any of the indebtedness represented by this Note be collected in any Proceeding, or this Note be placed in the hands of attorneys for collection after default, Debtor agrees to pay, in addition to the principal and interest due and payable hereon, all costs of collecting this Note, including reasonable attorneys' fees and expenses.

An attorneys' fee provision is an absolute necessity in all documents. However, unlike the Master Lease, this provision is not reciprocal, but rather is one-sided in favor of the lender. This usually evidences the relative negotiating power between the lender and the lessor. However, in spite of its apparent one-sidedness, the legislators and/or courts of many states have adopted statutes or rules that automatically render such provisions reciprocal so as to put both parties on an equal footing.

NONRECOURSE

Under this provision, the parties clearly establish that, in the event of a breach, the lender's sole recourse is the collateral (i.e., the lease and the equipment) and that the lessor is not personally bound on the Note.

> No recourse shall be had for the payment of the principal of, or any interest or any other sums payable on, this Note against Debtor personally or against any incorporator, shareholder, officer or director of Debtor. Payee agrees (and shall cause any assignee hereof to agree) that all such obligations are nonrecourse obligations enforceable only against the Collateral. The foregoing shall not be deemed to bar or prohibit Payee from asserting a claim against Debtor in the event any material representation, covenant or warranty contained in this Note or in the Security

Agreement (other than the obligation to make the Installment Payments) shall prove to be untrue or to have been breached.

In entering into a nonrecourse note in a leveraged lease transaction, the lender enters the arrangement with full knowledge that it cannot seek collection of the payments from the lessor. Therefore, the lender's decision to loan the monies will be based on two primary factors. First, the lender will examine the creditworthiness of the lessee. Since the lessor assigns the lease payment stream to the lender as security for the Note, the lender has the right to collect the lease payments directly from the lessee. Second, the lender will evaluate the value of the leased equipment. Since the lessor is not personally obligated on the Note and in the event that collection is not likely from the lessee, the lender will have to look to the equipment to recoup the amount remaining owing under the Note. As discussed in Chapter Three, however, this nonrecourse provision could reduce the tax benefits available to a lessor subject to the at-risk rules of Internal Revenue Code §465.

SIGNATURE OF THE DEBTOR

As with all other documents, the Note should contain the signature of the party to be bound. By clearly designating the debtor, there is little chance for mistake as to who is bound by the Note. Under general contract law, the word "By" is significant in that it clearly indicates that the individual is signing on behalf of an organization rather than in an individual capacity.

IN WITNESS WHEREOF, Debtor has duly executed this Note this _____ day of _____, 198____.

SENTRY FINANCIAL CORPORATION
A Utah Corporation

By: _____
Print Name: _____
Title: _____

Security Agreement

The purpose of the Security Agreement is to secure repayment of the Note. In a leveraged lease transaction, the lessor has two forms of collateral to offer to the lender as security for the Note, namely, the lease agreement itself and the equipment. The lease agreement constitutes chattel paper and, depending on the nature of the equipment, the equipment may be classified as consumer goods, equipment, farm products, inventory or fixtures. An example of a Security Agreement is attached as Exhibit XIII of Appendix B. The major terms and conditions of the Security Agreement should include the following items.

DATE, NAMES OF THE PARTIES

As with all other legal documents, clear identification of the parties to the agreement substantially reduces any mistake as to who the parties are to the contract. In addition, the date allows the Security Agreement to be easily identified.

THIS SECURITY AGREEMENT (the "Agreement") is made and entered into this __30th__ day of __September__ , 198 _7_ , by and between Sentry Financial Corporation, a Utah corporation, as debtor (the "Debtor"), and Last National Bank (the "Secured Party").

PRELIMINARY STATEMENT

The Preliminary Statement sets the stage or background regarding the reasons and purpose of the Security Agreement. This provision essentially acts as the recitals section of a document. It provides a reader with some factual background as to why the parties are entering into the Security Agreement and specifically refers to the Note that is being secured.

Pursuant to a Secured Note of even date herewith, Debtor is borrowing a sum of money from Secured Party and granting to Secured Party a security interest in the Collateral as security for the payment of all sums payable and the performance of all obligations under the Secured Note and hereunder. Debtor is entering into this Agreement, and Secured Party is accepting the grant made hereby, for good and valuable consideration, the receipt and sufficiency of which are hereby acknowledged. Certain terms used in this Agreement, and not defined elsewhere, are defined in Article V herein.

GRANTING CLAUSE

Under this provision, the debtor grants to the lender a security interest in both forms of collateral, namely, the lease agreement and the equipment.

Debtor hereby Grants to Secured Party all of Debtor's right, title, interest, claim and demand in, to and under (a) the Equipment, (b) the Lease (other than amounts payable to Debtor pursuant to the tax and indemnification provisions of the Master Lease and the Equipment Schedules thereof), (c) After-Acquired Property, and (d) all proceeds (other than proceeds of a transfer permitted by Section 2.02 hereof [see Transfer of Collateral provision discussed below]) or the conversion, voluntary or involuntary, of the foregoing into cash or other liquidated claims, including, without limitation, all insurance proceeds and condemnation awards to which Debtor is or may be entitled for the benefit and security of the Note, and for the enforcement of the payment of the principal of, and interest on, the Note in accordance with its terms, and all other sums payable under this Agreement, or on the Note, and compliance with the provisions of this Agreement, all as herein provided, subject, however, to Permitted Encumbrances existing on the date hereof.

IT IS HEREBY COVENANTED, DECLARED AND AGREED that the Note is to be issued and secured, and the Collateral is to be held, dealt with and disposed of by Secured Party, upon and subject to the provisions of this Agreement.

Frequently, this granting clause will be confirmed or elaborated upon by other provisions in the Security Agreement. By having a security interest in, or an assignment of, the lease agreement, the lender is entitled to all payments from the lessee that the lessor otherwise would have been entitled. This includes not only the periodic lease payments, but also late charges, insurance proceeds and condemnation awards. If the lessee were to breach the lease agreement, the lender would be entitled to pursue any of the remedies specified in the lease agreement, including a cause of action against the lessee. Essentially, the lender steps into the shoes of the lessor for the duration of the term of the Note.

In addition, the lender is given a security interest in the equipment itself, subject to the lease agreement. As such, the lender would be entitled to such things as money damages and return of the equipment in the event of a default under the Note. A default under the Note generally arises only when the lessee has failed to make the appropriate lease payment. In such a case, the lender can request that the lessor make the payment but cannot require the lessor to make the payment because the Note is nonrecourse. The lender must, therefore, pursue its remedies under the lease against the lessee and the equipment.

WARRANTY OF TITLE

The purpose of this provision is to obtain an affirmative representation from the debtor that the debtor owns the equipment free and clear of all liens and encumbrances, except the lease agreement. The falsity of this representation would constitute a default under the Security Agreement.

> Debtor hereby warrants that: (i) Debtor owns the Equipment free and clear of all liens, charges and other encumbrances, except Permitted Encumbrances, and that this Agreement constitutes a valid lien on the Equipment, subject only to Permitted Encumbrances, and (ii) Debtor has and enjoys all right, title and interest in and to the Lease, free and clear of all liens, charges and other encumbrances, except Permitted Encumbrances. Until payment in full of the Note and all of its other obligations secured hereby, and except as otherwise specifically permitted hereby, Debtor will warrant and defend its title in and to the Equipment and its interest in the Lease against the claims and demands of all persons and will maintain the lien created under this Agreement. Debtor has full power and lawful authority to grant the security interest in the property granted by this Agreement.

This representation is extremely important to the lender because the lender may have to resort to the equipment to satisfy the Note. As a result, the lender must have a first priority security position. In addition, the lender also requires the debtor to represent that it has the power and authority to grant to the lender a security interest in the equipment. A breach of any of these representations would give the lender a cause of action against the debtor despite a nonrecourse provision in the Note or Security Agreement.

PAYMENT OF TAXES

The lessor must be assured through a provision such as this that any and all taxes will be paid by the lessee.

> Debtor will pay or cause to be paid all taxes respecting the Equipment and the Lease (including franchise and gross receipts taxes) which are at any time or from time to time levied upon or assessed against it. The foregoing sentence shall not prevent Debtor from contesting any such tax by appropriate proceedings so long as (a) such proceedings shall suspend the collection thereof, (b) no part of the Collateral would be subject to sale, forfeiture or diminution and (c) Debtor shall have furnished such security as may be required in the proceedings or reasonably requested by Secured Party. Debtor will conduct such contests in good faith and with due diligence and will, promptly after the final determination of each such contest, pay all amounts which shall be determined to be payable in respect thereof.

As discussed in the Lease Document section, the lessee is required to pay to the lessor the agreed upon periodic lease payment, plus any and all taxes attributable to the equipment and to the lease. In leveraged lease transactions the lease payments are assigned to the lender. Generally, the lessee will either make its entire payment (including the amount due for taxes) to the lender or will make the lease payment to the lender and the tax payment to the lessor. If the tax portion of the lessee's payment is made to the lender, the lender will remit it to the lessor. In either event, the lessor receives the money necessary to pay all taxes accruing by reason of the equipment. Accordingly, the lender needs assurance that the taxes are being paid.

The purpose of this provision is to provide the lender with that assurance without depriving the debtor of the right to properly contest the imposition of any tax. The concern of the lender is that the taxing authority may assert a lien against the lease payments or on the equipment. The assertion of such a lien could severely jeopardize the priority of the lender's security interest in the lease and the equipment. Accordingly, the lender imposes an affirmative obligation upon the debtor to pay all taxes respecting the lease and the equipment.

COLLECTION OF MONIES

This provision is confirmatory of the debtor's assignment of the lease to the lender as security for the Note.

> Secured Party shall receive and collect all Monies and other property payable to or receivable by the Secured Party pursuant to this Agreement or any Security Instrument, commencing with the rental payments due under the Lease on _____, 198____. Secured Party shall apply the Monies as provided in this Agreement. If any default occurs in the making of any payment or performance under any Security Instrument, Secured Party may take such action as it shall have power to take as may be appropriate to enforce such payment or performance, including the institution and prosecution of appropriate legal proceedings. Any such action shall be without prejudice to any right to claim a Default or Event of Default under this Agreement and to proceed thereafter as provided in Article IV.

Under this provision, the lender is given the right as well as the affirmative obligation to collect the lease payments from the lessee. Specific identification of which lease payment is the first lease payment to which the lender is entitled should minimize any subsequent misunderstanding between the parties. Such identification is necessary because the loan payment term may be less than the lease term. This situation arises frequently when the lessor does not put the financing in place until sometime after the first or second lease payment has been made. Along with the right to collect the lease payments, the lender is given the power to enforce collection from the lessee in accordance with the terms and conditions of the lease agreement. The ability to enforce the payment by the lessee of the lease payments is absolutely crucial to the lender.

TRANSFER OF COLLATERAL/CONDEMNATION

This transfer provision protects the lender in that it prevents the debtor from transferring by any means whatsoever any interest in the collateral unless such transfer is done in accordance with specific terms; however, this provision also gives the debtor the flexibility necessary in the event that the debtor wants to broker the lease transaction.

> Debtor will not sell, lease, transfer, exchange or otherwise dispose of any of the Collateral except in accordance with the provisions of this Section. Debtor may sell, transfer or assign its interest in the Collateral, or any part thereof, to one or more third parties who may sell, transfer or assign their interest in the collateral, or who, along with their successors, may make further sales, transfers and assignments. Any such sale, transfer or assignment shall be permitted if: (a) such sale, transfer or assignment is expressly subject and subordinate in all respects to the rights and interests of Secured Party, and (b) the purchaser, transferee or assignee (a "Transferee") delivers to Secured Party an agreement, in substantially the form attached hereto as Exhibit A, to Secured Party evidencing such subordination. Upon compliance with the foregoing, no further consent from Secured Party shall be required. No such sale, transfer or assignment shall relieve Debtor of any of its obligations hereunder.
>
> Debtor shall notify Secured Party of any condemnation or other eminent domain proceedings with respect to the Equipment immediately upon Debtor's obtaining knowledge thereof. Secured Party may participate in any such proceedings. Debtor shall use its best efforts to provide Secured Party with all instruments required by it to permit such participation upon obtaining actual knowledge thereof.

Quite frequently, a debtor (lessor) will want to sell or transfer its interest in the lease agreement. By doing so the debtor is able to recover its equity insertion and to immediately realize its profit on the transaction. A debtor may broker a lease transaction for various reasons. The debtor may have limited funds such that generating lease transactions and then selling them to investors permits it to expand its business. Such a debtor generally will not generate a lease transaction for its own account. Sometimes a debtor (lessor) will broker a lease transaction because it no longer has a tax appetite. The debtor may have satisfied its tax appetite with prior lease transactions. If so, the debtor may sell the lease transaction to a third party who can utilize the tax benefits.

A lender will usually not object to a transfer of the debtor's interest so long as the transferee's interest is clearly subordinate to the lender's interest. The lender protects itself by requiring the transferee to acknowledge in writing that any interest it receives from the debtor is subordinate to that of the lender. Typically, a sample form document of such an acknowledgement is attached to the Security Agreement as an exhibit. Under these circumstances, the lender has maximum protection and the debtor retains the necessary flexibility.

The condemnation provision is necessary to protect the lessor from a loss of its security interest in the collateral. In the event of condemnation proceedings, a lender will usually want the right to participate in such proceedings in order to protect its interest in the lease and the equipment. By imposing an affirmative obligation upon the debtor to notify the lender of such proceedings, the lender protects itself and provides the lender with the opportunity to participate in the proceedings.

EVENTS OF DEFAULT

This lengthy provision is set out in its entirety in the Security Agreement attached as Exhibit XIII of Appendix B. Generally, a breach or default of an agreement arises when a party fails to perform one or more of its promises set forth in the agreement. Because the UCC does not define what events constitute a default, the determination as to what actions of the debtor constitute a default should be defined in the Security Agreement with extreme and explicit care. By defining the events of default in the Security Agreement, the lender puts the debtor on notice, thereby avoiding any future misunderstandings.

Obviously, the most critical breach is the failure by the debtor to make the payments required under the terms of the Note. Other events of default typically include, among others, the following: (i) failure of the debtor to perform obligations other than making the payments, i.e., maintaining insurance and paying taxes on the equipment; (ii) permitting a lien or other encumbrance to be placed on the equipment; (iii) making a representation or warranty that is materially incorrect; and (iv) filing of a petition in bankruptcy by or against the debtor or lessee. A breach based upon a petition in bankruptcy is generally unenforceable under the Bankruptcy Act. However, most Security Agreements contain such a provision in the event that the Bankruptcy Act is subsequently modified.

Because the default and remedies provisions are probably the most important provisions of the Security Agreement, they should be drafted with utmost care. Simply using an outdated form contract or copying from a form book is likely to be inadequate. The parties should seek competent legal counsel to assure that the Security Agreement is adequately and properly drafted.

REMEDIES

Like the events of default provision, the remedies provision is rather lengthy and is therefore set forth in its entirety in the Security Agreement. As with the events of default provision, specifying with particularity in the Security Agreement the remedies available to the lender puts the debtor on notice of what options the lender may elect to follow. However, mere specification in the Security Agreement of the available remedies does not ensure that those options will be upheld in a court of law.

On a default by the debtor arising from a failure to make a payment as required under the Note, the lender has the right to accelerate and immediately call due all future payments not yet due. Absent such a provision, the lender would have to file successive actions for each payment that the debtor failed to make. Accordingly, the remedy of acceleration is crucial to the lender. Other remedies available to the lender include, without limitation, the following: (i) filing of an action for specific performance requiring the debtor to perform in accordance with the terms of the Security Agreement (i.e., to pay the necessary sales/use tax); (ii) performing for the debtor, for example, obtaining the requisite insurance and holding the debtor responsible for the monies so expended; and (iii) repossession and sale of the collateral to satisfy the amounts owing under the terms of the Note.

In the event of a sale of the collateral by the lender, the Security Agreement, as well as the UCC, allocate and prioritize the disbursement of the proceeds of the sale of the collateral. First, the proceeds are utilized to reimburse the lender for the expenses incurred in repossessing the collateral, including attorneys' fees. Second, the proceeds are applied to pay the lender all interest, all principal and all other sums due and payable on the Note. Finally, the balance, if any, of the proceeds will be remitted to the debtor or other persons legally entitled thereto.

In addition, one paragraph of the remedies provision puts the debtor on notice that the specified remedies are not exclusive. The lender may, therefore, pursue any other available remedies whether provided for by the UCC, other statutes, the common law or otherwise. This permits the lender to select the best remedy available to put the lender in the same position as it would have been had the debtor not committed a breach of the loan agreements.

DEFINITIONAL SECTION

The definitional section is used by attorneys primarily as a drafting aid. By defining a term in one place in an agreement, the document is simplified in that the defined term can then be used throughout the agreement without having to define or elaborate upon it each time it is used. The definitional section provides for a less cumbersome document that is easier to comprehend. Of the numerous definitions, the most important terms are those regarding the Note, the Installment Payments, the Collateral, the Lease and the Lessee.

DISCHARGE OF AGREEMENT

This provision of the loan documentation typically reads:

> This Agreement and all agreements contained herein shall cease and terminate when all principal, interest and other amounts payable under or in respect of this Agreement shall have been paid in full, whether at the end of the term of the Note, by acceleration, by prepayment or otherwise.
>
> Upon the termination of this Agreement, Secured Party shall execute and deliver such instruments as Debtor shall furnish and which shall be reasonably required to satisfy and discharge the lien of this Agreement.

As one would suspect, the Security Agreement is discharged upon performance by the debtor of all of its obligations under the Note and the Security Agreement. This primarily involves payment to the lender of all principal and interest under the terms of the Note. Upon payment in full, the debtor should obtain two things from the lender. First, the lender should return to the debtor the original Note marked paid in full or other words of similar import. Second, the lender should release its security interest in both the lease agreement and the equipment. Under the above provision, the debtor is entitled to those items from the lender.

MISCELLANEOUS PROVISIONS

Miscellaneous provisions are those legal provisions that appear in almost all loan documents, and include:

(a) Nonrecourse Obligations. No recourse shall be had against the Debtor personally, or against any incorporator, shareholder, officer or director of Debtor under or in respect of this Agreement or the Note. It is expressly understood that all such obligations are nonrecourse obligations enforceable only against the Collateral. The foregoing shall not be deemed to bar or prohibit Secured Party from asserting a claim against Debtor in the event any material representation, covenant or warranty contained in the Note or this Security Agreement (other than the obligation to make the installment payments) shall prove to be untrue or to have been breached.

(b) Notices. All notices and demand hereunder shall be in writing and shall be deemed to have been given upon receipt by Debtor or Secured Party, said notice to be accomplished by registered or certified mail, return receipt requested, postage prepaid, and addressed in each case as follows: (a) if to Secured Party, at Last National Bank, 310 South Main, Salt Lake City, Utah 84111, or (b) if to debtor at Sentry Financial Corporation, 3450 South Highland Drive, Suite 104, Salt Lake City, Utah 84106. Either party may change its address for notice hereunder by giving notice of such change to the other party in accordance with the provisions of this Section.

(c) Severability. No provision hereof, or of the Note, shall require the payment or permit the collection of interest in excess of the maximum permitted by the applicable law, any contrary provision herein or in the Note notwithstanding. Any provision hereof or of the Note, which is prohibited or unenforceable in any jurisdiction will, as to such jurisdiction, be ineffective to the extent of such prohibition or unenforceability without invalidating the remaining provisions hereof, or of the Note, and any such prohibition or unenforceability in any jurisdiction will not invalidate or render unenforceable such provision in any other jurisdiction. To the extent permitted by law, the parties hereto waive any provision of law which renders any such provision prohibited or unenforceable in any respect.

These boilerplate clauses are those provisions that have general application to virtually all contracts and, as such, are included in all contracts. The above provisions are only a few of the typical clauses and are discussed in the order they appear above.

If a nonrecourse provision is included in the Note, it should also be mirrored in the Security Agreement so that the documents are consistent. Accordingly, under this provision, the parties clearly establish that, in the event of a breach, the lender's sole recourse is to the collateral (i.e., the lease and the equipment) and that the debtor is not personally bound on the Note. Thus, if the lessee fails to make the payments, the debtor (lessor) has the option to make the payments or to risk losing its interest in the equipment.

Under various circumstances, the parties are required to give notice in one form or another to the other party. The notice provision sets forth the address of each party to which notice may be sent and establishes the mode of delivery. This provision minimizes a dispute between the parties regarding whether a given notice is proper and effective.

The severability provision has applications to virtually every contract. When a court or legislature determines that a certain type of provision or clause is unlawful or unenforceable, a legal issue arises as to whether that renders the entire contract unenforceable. In order to avoid this issue the parties should include a severability provision in their Security Agreement. Under such a provision, the parties are able to enforce their agreements despite the unenforceability of a particular provision.

SIGNATURE OF THE PARTIES

As with all agreements, the Security Agreement should contain the duly executed signatures of both parties. This will minimize the chance for mistake as to who are the parties to, and binding provisions of, the contract.

IN WITNESS WHEREOF, Debtor and Secured Party have caused this Security Agreement to be executed, all as of the day and year first above written.

SECURED PARTY: DEBTOR:
LAST NATIONAL BANK   SENTRY FINANCIAL CORPORATION
By: _____   By: _____
Name: _____   Name: _____
Title:_____   Title:_____

Pay Proceeds Letter

In most leveraged lease transactions, the lender will pay the proceeds of the Note not to the debtor (lessor), but directly to the manufacturer or vendor. By paying the proceeds of the Note directly to the manufacturer or vendor of the equipment, the lender knows the manufacturer or vendor has been paid. As such, the lender minimizes the risk the manufacturer or vendor will assert a claim against the equipment. Accordingly, the lender protects its first priority security position in the equipment. The purpose of the Pay Proceeds Letter is to receive authority from the debtor to pay the proceeds of the loan directly to the manufacturer or vendor. An example of a Pay Proceeds Letter is attached as Exhibit XVI of Appendix B.

Officer's Certificate or Corporate Resolution

An Officer's Certificate or Corporate Resolution is a formal, but rather simple, document. One of these documents is required of the debtor by the lender. The purpose of these documents is to ensure that the loan has been accepted by the debtor's board of directors and that the agent signing the loan documents is authorized and empowered to do so on behalf of the corporation. If the debtor is a partnership, a document akin to an Officer's Certificate or Corporate Resolution, indicating that the loan is within the partnership's authority, should be signed by all the partners or by the managing general partner. An example of an Officer's Certificate is included as Exhibit XVII of Appendix B.

Opinion of Debtor's Counsel

As with the Opinion of Lessee's Counsel, the purpose of an Opinion of Debtor's Counsel is to discover potential problems of the debtor and to provide additional security to the lender that the debtor is able to enter into, and to perform the obligations under, the Note and Security Agreement. If the debtor is unable to produce an Opinion of Counsel, it should serve as a red flag to the lender. The items opined upon by debtor's counsel include, among others, the following: (i) that the debtor, as an entity, is properly organized and in good standing; (ii) that the Note, Security Agreement and attendant documents constitute a valid and binding obligation of the debtor, enforceable according to their terms; (iii) that the entering into and performance of the loan documents will not violate the debtor's Articles of Incorporation or Bylaws, loan restrictions, judgments, orders or regulations; and (iv) that there are no actions, suits or proceedings against the debtor that would materially adversely affect the debtor's ability to perform under the loan documents. An example of an Opinion of Debtor's Counsel is attached as Exhibit XVIII of Appendix B.

Form UCC-1

A secured party will generally perfect its security interest in the lease and the equipment by filing the appropriate Form UCC-1. As with the precautionary Form UCC-1 filed by the lessor, the accuracy of the name of the debtor is absolutely critical and a mistake could render the Form UCC-1 ineffective. A sample description of the collateral is as follows:

> LEASE: Equipment Schedule No. 1 dated as of September 30, 1987, issued pursuant to Master Lease dated December 31, 1985, between Sentry Financial Corporation, as original Lessor, and Bono & Company, as Lessee.
> EQUIPMENT: All [insert specific manufacturer or brand name of the Equipment] and related equipment under lease to Bono & Company: Lease Education and Consulting pursuant to Equipment Schedule No. 1 described above.

The purpose of a Form UCC-1 is to put all third parties on notice that the lender claims a security interest in the lease and the equipment. In order to perfect the lender's first priority security interest, the lender must file a proper Form UCC-1 with the appropriate governmental authority. An example of a Form UCC-1 is attached as Exhibit XXI of Appendix B.

Notice of Assignment Letter

A Notice of Assignment Letter serves numerous purposes. First, the letter provides the lessee with notice that the lease has been assigned to the lender and that the lender has been granted a security interest in the equipment. Second, it directs the lessee to make the lease payments directly to the lender rather than to the lessor. Third, the letter puts the lessee on notice that no changes may be made to the lease documents by the lessor and the lessee without the consent of the lender. Finally, it requires the lessee to acknowledge receipt of the Notice of Assignment

Letter and to consent to compliance with its terms. A lender usually insists that such a letter be sent to the lessee and signed by the lessee. Again, the lender uses this document to minimize any misunderstandings between the parties. An example of a Notice of Assignment Letter is attached as Exhibit XIV of Appendix B.

Loan Documents Conclusion

The preceding documents are examples of those that normally accompany a loan transaction in the context of a leveraged lease. Although the documents may be drafted by the lessor, they will be drafted primarily to protect the lender's interests. Of course, depending on the magnitude of the transaction, there is a variety of additional documents that may be required, e.g., a Guaranty and Waiver and a Deed of Trust. Generally, it is a good idea to seek the advice of competent legal counsel who is well-versed in the leveraged leasing field whenever entering into such a transaction.

CONCLUSION

As discussed above, lease transactions, both leveraged and nonleveraged, involve a multitude of complex legal and practical issues ranging from tax guidelines to UCC restrictions. Because of this, and the diversity of practices, the documentation presented herein should not be relied upon as being adequate and appropriate for any given situation or transaction. This chapter was designed solely to provide (i) an understanding of the documentation complexities surrounding a lease transaction, (ii) some insight as to how the documents and their provisions attempt to address the concerns of the parties and (iii) samples of various provisions. The sample documents and provisions are offered as examples only and the parties are urged to seek competent legal advice in structuring and documenting each lease transaction.

CHAPTER TWENTY
LEGAL ISSUES

The commercial law encompasses a wide array of topics, only a few of which can be addressed here. While such areas of law as product liability, securities, corporations, antitrust, consumer protection and the like are important, the limited scope of this chapter allows a focus on only those areas of the commercial law having the most direct, day-to-day impact on a leasing business. This chapter will address the following topics, from a legal perspective:

- What is a Lease?
- Application of the Uniform Commercial Code
- Bankruptcy
- State Tax Considerations
- Article 2A-Leases.

WHAT IS A LEASE?

Throughout the various chapters of this book, the term lease has been defined many times, and in many different ways. Accounting, tax, industry and even finance definitions have all been spelled out. The legal aspects of leasing are no different, so in this section the lease will be defined again, but this time from a commercial law perspective.

Historical Perspective

Leases are different from sales and loans in their commercial law treatment; however, modern jurisprudence has had a difficult time addressing what distinguishes a true lease. If the word lease had been mentioned 50 years ago, the context would have been almost invariably that of a real estate transaction. It is telling that the first definition for lease in *Black's Law Dictionary* is "[a]ny agreement which gives rise to relationship of landlord and tenant." However, the law has not kept pace with the development of the major form of the modern personal property lease transaction — the finance lease. The finance lease is a lease that has as its purpose the financing of the use of property for a major portion of the property's useful life. Too often, the courts have considered these types of transactions as merely disguised sales, without analysis of the economic substance of the transaction to see if, indeed, the lessor has transferred all interest in the property, and thus has really sold it, or whether the lessor has retained an interest in the property (and one that is not nominal), and, thus, has leased it.

Even the Uniform Commercial Code (UCC) has provided modest guidance. As the rise of modern personal property leasing has been subsequent to the formulation of the UCC in the late 1940s and early 1950s, personal property leasing was given little attention.[1] Although nowhere in the UCC is a lease defined, the most frequently considered "definition" of a lease is set forth in the UCC as part of the definition of a security interest.

> (37) "Security interest" means an interest in personal property or fixtures which secures payment or performance of an obligation. The retention or reservation of title by a seller of goods notwithstanding shipment or delivery to the buyer (Section 2-401) is limited in effect to a reservation of a "security interest." The term also includes any interest of a buyer of accounts or chattel paper which is subject to Article 9. The special property interest of a buyer of goods on identification of such goods to a contract for sale under Section 2-401 is not a "security interest," but a buyer may also acquire a "security interest" by complying with Article 9. *Unless a lease or consignment is intended as security, reservation of title thereunder is not a "security interest" but a consignment is in any event subject to the provisions on consignment sales (Section 2-326). Whether a lease is intended as a security is to be determined by the facts of each case; however, (a) the inclusion of an option to purchase does not of itself make the lease one intended for security, and (b) an agreement that upon compliance with the terms of the lease the lessee shall become or has the option to become the owner of the property for no additional consideration or for a nominal consideration does make the lease one intended for security* (emphasis added) [UCC§1-201(37)].

Please note that §1-207(37) defines only when a lease is not a lease, but is a lease intended as security. It does not define what is a lease. A lease intended as security is governed by Article 9-Secured Transactions, of the UCC, whereas a true lease is not.

As will be discussed later, most courts have failed to first define a lease before trying to determine whether or not a given transaction involves a lease. The issue arises because of a difference in legal treatment for lease transactions and secured transactions. Additionally, the courts have often failed to consider that some secured transactions by a lessor may involve a sale while others may involve a loan. This confused state of affairs points dramatically to a need for a true and workable definition of what constitutes a lease transaction.

---

[1] See, Coogan, Hogan, Vaghts & McDonnell, *Secured Transactions* (Matthew Bender Supp. 1984) Chap. 4.1-2. See also *In re Loop Hospital Partnership*, 35 B.R. 929 (Bk. N.D. Ill. 1983), which contains a good discussion of some of the issues involved in the lease versus security interest analysis.

The distilled essence of those definitions of a lease that can be found in the case law might best be stated as a transfer of possession and use of property for a term for consideration. However, such a definition fails to address the distinguishing factor of a lease transaction that makes it neither a sale nor a loan — the retention by the lessor, as of the inception of the lease, of a significant residual interest in the leased property.

UCC §1-201(37) implies such a definition by giving security interest status to transactions where the lessor has no significant residual interest because upon compliance with the terms of the lease, the lessee shall become, or has the option to become, the owner of the property for no additional consideration or for nominal consideration. Peter Coogan, a noted commercial law commentator, has also focused upon the significance of the retention of a significant residual interest:

> The lessor must retain the right to regain possession at a time and in a manner that the residual is a thing of not insubstantial value.[2]

Other commentators have agreed:

> Where no such meaningful residual is anticipated, true lease treatment is inappropriate. *The existence of a meaningful residual is a touchstone of a true lease* (emphasis in original).[3]

Although it is rare to find the essence of a lease transaction articulated in either the case or statutory law,[4] such is the true source of the definitional guidelines available.

Case Law Perspective

Whether or not a lease is a true lease or a lease intended as security is an issue that has generated voluminous litigation with wildly unpredictable and confused results.[5] Some of the factors considered by the courts in deciding whether the lease is a true lease or a lease intended for security are presented in this subsection.

INTENT OF THE PARTIES

In determining whether a particular transaction is a lease, the courts have often focused upon the intent of the parties.[6] As stated in a 1955 case:

> It seems well settled that calling such a transaction a "lease" does not make it such, if in fact it is something else. . . . However, the test should not be what the parties call

---

[2] Coogan, *supra*, at p. 4.1-7.

[3] Harris and Mooney, *Recent Cases Relating to Equipment Leases*, Equipment Leasing 1985, PLI Handbook, p. 338.

[4] See, *In re Marhoefer Packing Co.*, 674 F.2d 1139, 1145, 33 UCC Rep. Serv. 370 (7th Cir. 1982), where the court stated: "An essential characteristic of a true lease is that there be something of value to return to the lessor after the term." See also *In re Loop Hospital, supra,* at 933.

[5] See Harris and Mooney, *supra.*

[6] See, e.g., *In re Velasco*, 13 Bankr. 872 (Bankr. W.D. Ky. 1981); *In re Catamount Dyers*, 43 B.R. 564 (Bankr. D. Vt. 1984); *Oesterreich v. Commissioner*, 226 F.2d 798 (9th Cir. 1955).

the transaction or even what they mistakenly believe to be the name of such transaction. What the parties believe the legal effect of such a transaction to be should be the criteria. If the parties enter into a transaction which they honestly believe to be a lease but which in actuality *has all the elements* of a contract of sale, it is a contract of sale and not a lease no matter what they call it or how they treat it on their books (emphasis added).[7]

In short, in an analysis of the true legal character of the transaction, the elements of the transaction must be examined.

Much mischief has been done in the case law by casual reference to the intent of the parties.

[T]he cases as a whole reflect much flailing about in futile attempts to ascertain the "intention" of the parties. It is this approach as much as any other which accounts for the various spurious factors and criteria relied upon by the courts. To the extent that the intentions of parties are an appropriate consideration in attempting to determine the precise terms and conditions of their agreement under applicable law, the factor may be relevant. But, this approach generally has served to cloud and distort rather than clarify the appropriate considerations and analyses.[8]

However, the biggest problem in analyzing a purported lease transaction has not been the mere recitation of the principle that intention of the parties controls, but the failure of the courts to engage in a meaningful analysis of what factors or what elements of the transaction distinguish a lease from a sale or a loan. The case law reveals a litany of allegedly relevant considerations:

1. The mere existence of a purchase option by a lessee
2. The existence of a nominal purchase option:
   a. as compared to the original cost of the equipment
   b. as compared to the estimated fair market value of the equipment at the time the option is exercisable, as estimated at the inception of the lease
   c. as compared to the actual fair market value of the equipment determined at the time the option is exercised
   d. as compared to the total lease payments
   e. that will clearly be exercised because of economic compulsion or the lack of a sensible alternative
3. The transfer of title at the end of the lease for no additional consideration
4. The creation of an equity in the equipment in favor of the lessee
5. Total lease payments by the lessee substantially equal to or greater than the purchase price of the equipment
6. Periodic lease payments that do not reflect reasonable rental value

---

[7] *Oesterreich, supra*, at 801-02.

[8] Mooney, *Recent Cases Relating to Equipment Leases*, Equipment Leasing 1983, PLI Handbook, p. 67. See also, Coogan, Hogan, Vaghts, McDonnell, *Secured Transactions* (Matthew Bender); Chap. 4A, "Leases of Equipment and Some other Unconventional Security Devices: An Analysis of UCC Section 1-201(37) and Article 9" (1981).

7. How the lessor conducts its business
8. How other lessees have dealt with the lessor, e.g., how many lessees exercised their purchase options, how many returned the equipment, etc.
9. The filing of a financing statement by the lessor
10. How the lessor treats the transaction on its books
11. What the parties understood the transaction to be
12. Whether the lessee was responsible for paying the taxes and insurance on the equipment and keeping it maintained and repaired
13. Who bears the risk of depreciation in estimated residual value.

The courts have not always been clear in citing which factors have been given the greatest weight in reaching their decisions. The usual style is a recital of a number of the above followed by a conclusion.[9] However, the greatest attention in most cases has been focused on the matter of a purchase option.

Purchase Options

Courts have long focused on the terms of any purchase option as highly informative as to whether or not a given transaction is a true lease. The UCC states in language often recited by the courts:

> Whether a lease is intended as security is to be determined by the facts of each case; however, (a) the inclusion of an option to purchase does not of itself make the lease one intended for security, and (b) an agreement that upon compliance with the terms of the lease the lessee shall become or has the option to become the owner of the property for no additional consideration or for a nominal consideration does make the lease one intended for security [UCC §1-201(37)].

Mere Existence (or Absence) of an Option to Purchase

Although courts have occasionally mentioned the mere existence of an option to purchase as suggestive of a lease, the law is clearly to the contrary. The mere existence of an option to purchase is not determinative of whether an agreement is a lease or a lease intended as security. In and of itself, without further information, the existence of a purchase option does not indicate whether or not the lessor has retained a significant interest in the equipment after the lease term has expired.

Similarly, the mere absence of a purchase option is not indicative of the existence of a lease transaction if indeed the lessor has leased the property for a term that substantially equals or exceeds the economic life of the equipment.[10] It might be noted that the proposed Article 2A-Leases expressly provides that a secured transaction is created when:

> . . . the lessee is to pay the lessor for the right to possession and use of the goods is an obligation for the term of the lease not subject to termination by the lessee, and

---

[9] See, e.g., *In re Alpha Creamery Co., Inc.*, 4 UCC Rep. Serv. 794 (W.D. Mich. 1967).
[10] *In re Loop Hospital Partnership, supra.*

(a) the original term of the lease is equal to or greater than the remaining economic life of the goods[.][11]

Purchase Option Comparisons

If the consideration required to exercise a purchase option is significant, then it would not follow that a transfer of the lessor's residual interest was made to the lessee at the inception of the lease, for it is entirely possible that the consideration may not be paid and no transfer may occur. However, significant may be difficult to quantify.

Significant implies an analysis of the relationship between two compared items. The consideration of a purchase option is one such item, but the courts have been unable to agree on the other item. They have compared the consideration of a purchase option to:

1. The original equipment cost
2. The fair market value of the equipment at the time the option is exercisable, as estimated at the inception of the lease
3. The fair market value of the equipment at the time the option is exercised, as actually determined at that time
4. The total lease payments.

The outcome of such a comparison is supposedly a determination of whether or not the purchase option is nominal, for if the purchase option is nominal, the lessee has become the owner of the entire economic value of the equipment from the beginning, because no consideration of any significance will have to be transferred to the lessor at the end of the lease term. In short, the lessor transferred all value in the property at the inception of the lease.

Purchase option compared to the original equipment cost. Some cases compare purchase options to the original equipment cost[12] because the original equipment cost is a useful basis upon which to project future value, e.g., "the equipment will likely be worth 25% of its original cost 5 years from now." Original cost may be used to measure whether or not a lessor has retained a significant residual interest in the equipment as of the inception of the lease when it is the basis for formulating estimates of future value, but it is the future value itself that is the real focus of such an analysis.

The courts have not agreed on what percentage of original equipment cost a purchase option should be if a lessor is to avoid nominality. Purchase options of 5% have been held to be substantial and purchase options of 25% nominal. What is important in those analyses is how such purchase options, stated in terms of original cost, compare to the value of the leased property at the time the option is to be exercised, as estimated at the inception of the lease.

Purchase option compared to the fair market value of the equipment at the time of exercisability, as estimated at the inception of the lease. Some courts have compared the fair market value of the equipment at the time of the purchase option's exercisability, as estimated

---

[11] Proposed "Article 2A-Leases," recommended amendment to UCC §1-201(37). The National Conference of Commissioners on Uniform State Laws and the Permanent Editorial Board of the UCC have proposed an amendment to the Uniform Commercial Code entitled "Article 2A-Leases," which would apply to all personal property leasing transactions.

[12] See, e.g., *In re AAA Machine Co. (Equilease Corp. v. AAA Machine Co.)*, 30 B.R. 323 (Bankr. S.D. Fla. 1983).

at the inception of the lease, to determine if the lessor has retained a significant residual interest.[13]

The comparison of that estimated fair market value to the purchase option can indicate whether or not the lessor retained, at the inception of the lease, a significant residual interest in the equipment. If the lessor has agreed to a purchase option that, in comparison to the estimated fair market value, is considered such a bargain that its exercise is assured, the option would be nominal. Thus, a comparison of the estimated fair market value at the time of exercisability, as estimated at the inception of the lease, to the purchase option price is a valid test for ascertaining whether or not a purchase option is nominal, and whether a purported lease is a lease intended as security. This is actually the most relevant test and, accordingly, is gaining increasing acceptance in the cases.

Purchase option compared to the actual fair market value at the time of exercisability as determined at the time of exercise. Some courts compare the purchase option to the fair market value as actually determined at the time of exercise. Such hindsight analysis is inconsistent with the generally accepted judicial philosophy of determining the character of an agreement by the facts and circumstances as they existed at the time the agreement is made. To apply a hindsight analysis is to effectively force the market to allow only fair market value purchase options, i.e., an option that has no specific purchase price other than the fair market value of the equipment determined at the time of exercisability (usually through a specified appraisal program). This hindsight analysis restricts the parties' freedom to contract regarding purchase options and puts the true character of the transaction into suspense until some time in the future. Additionally, the exercise of a fair market value option itself may be nominal if the estimated future value is nominal.[14]

Purchase option compared to the total lease payments. A comparison of the purchase option to the total lease payments provides no indication whatsoever as to whether or not the option is nominal. This analysis compares how much the lessee paid for the value of the lease over the term to the value of the residual interest as perceived by the lessor. Such a comparison does not address the issue of whether or not the lessor, at the inception of the lease, retained a significant residual interest. More importantly, a purchase option for equipment that has seen use for a major portion of its useful life almost always will be small in comparison to a stream of rental payments for that equipment usage. This is a test with an almost guaranteed conclusion. Nevertheless, courts have considered this comparison.[15]

A purchase option that will clearly be exercised because of economic compulsion or lack of a sensible alternative. The courts sometimes state that a purchase option is nominal because it will clearly be exercised because of economic compulsion or the lack of a sensible alternative.[16] However, the courts are not by any means consistent in analyzing what constitutes economic compulsion or what makes the exercise of the option the only sensible alternative. All in all, this

---

[13] See, e.g., *In re Marhoefer Packing Co., supra.*

[14] See, *In re Berge*, 370 B.R. 370 (Bankr. W.D. Wis. 1983).

[15] See, *McGalliard v. Liberty Leasing Co.*, 534 P.2d 528 (Alaska 1975).

[16] See, e.g., *In re Berge, supra, Bonczek v. Pasco Equipment Co.*, 450 A.2d 75, 34 UCC Rep. Serv. 1362 (Pa. Super. Ct. 1982); *In re Alpha Creamery Co., Inc., supra.*

test has not been any more useful in providing a benchmark for reasoned analysis than has been the intent of the parties.

The Transfer of Title at the End of the Lease

The transfer of title at the end of the lease for no additional consideration is clear evidence of a lease intended as security.[17] The lessor has, at the inception of the lease transaction, transferred all of its interest in the property for its entire useful life. It is also expressly covered by the UCC:

> . . . (b) an agreement that upon compliance with terms of the lease the lessee shall become or has the option to become the owner of the property for no additional consideration . . . does make the lease one intended for security [UCC §1-201(37)].

Whether a one dollar purchase option is considered nominal consideration or no consideration, it is evidence of a lease intended as security.[18]

The Creation of an Equity in the Equipment

By definition, a lessee does not have equity in property that is the subject of a true lease. The lessee may or may not have an equity in property that is the subject of a secured transaction. As *Mooney* aptly notes:

> This factor was recited as determinative in the early and oft-cited case of *In re Royer's Bakery, Inc.*, 56 Berks. Co. L.J. 48, 1 UCC Rep. Serv. 342 (Bankr. E.D. Pa. 1963). (Note that the *Royer's Bakery* case appears to have been wrongly decided, in that the lessee had an option to terminate the lease on short notice and lacked the requisite "obligation" for a lease intended as security.) Of course, this concept was derived from an owner's "equity of redemption" in a mortgage context. As the term is commonly understood, a lessee (debtor) in a lease for security will always be acquiring an "equity" in the property. Although a number of the recent cases cited herein have inquired as to whether the purported lessee was acquiring an "equity" in the property, the cases have given little analysis to this factor and its articulation. In and of itself it provides little guidance for analysis of a given factual situation.[19]

Total Payments by the Lessee Equal to or Greater than the Purchase Price

Courts sometimes hold that a purported lease is a security agreement because the lessee is required to pay an amount equal to or greater than the cost of the equipment.[20] These types of leases are known as full-payout leases. However, although the existence of an obligation by the

---

[17] See *Hervey v. Rhode Island Locomotive Works*, 93 U.S. 664 (1876).

[18] See *Clune Equipment Leasing Corp. v. Spangler*, 615 S.W.2d 106, 31 UCC Rep. Serv. 268 (Mo. Ct. App. 1981).

[19] Mooney, supra, p. 65.

[20] See, e.g., *Leasing Service Corp. v. American National Bank & Trust Co.*, 19 UCC Rep. Serv. 252 (D.N.J. 1976), criticized in Note, 56 Nebraska L. Rev. 354 (1977).

lessee to pay the initial value of the goods is essential to the existence of a sale or a loan, it is not inconsistent with true lease status.[21]

Article 2A-Leases (Exhibit A) recognizes this and specifically provides that:

> A transaction does not create a security interest merely because it provides that . . . (2) the present value of the consideration the lessee is obligated to pay the lessor for the right to possession and use of the goods is substantially equal to or is greater than the fair market value of the goods at the time the lease is entered into[.]

It also follows that if the lessee has an option to terminate the lease before such full payment has been made, the lease is not one intended as security.[22]

Periodic Payments That Do Not Reflect Reasonable Rental Value

The courts occasionally comment on whether or not the periodic lease payments reflect a reasonable rental value. Implicit in consideration of such a factor is an assumption that with an unreasonably high periodic lease payment, a lessee is paying for more than the value of the use of the property and may even be acquiring an equity in the property.

There is nothing inherent in a high, even unreasonably high, periodic lease payment that creates an equity. Rather, this test is a court imposed determination of reasonable lessor profit and is a hindsight analysis focusing on the lessee's decisional model of whether to lease or buy and at what terms. Furthermore, if rents are artificially high as disguised equity payments and the transaction is really a sale, there will have to be a nominal purchase option, the passage of title at the conclusion of the lease for no additional consideration or some similar mechanism (e.g., planned abandonment) for the lessee to end up with title to the property. That factor is the proper focus for characterizing the transaction as a lease intended as security.

How the Lessor Conducts its Business

A few courts have considered how a lessor generally conducts its business in deciding whether or not a specific transaction is a lease or a sale.[23] Some decisions have focused on the lessor's typical transaction. (Presumably, if the majority of a lessor's transactions are sales, the transaction at hand is likely to be a sale; conversely, if the majority of a lessor's transactions are leases, the transaction at hand is a lease.) Courts have also looked at whether or not a lessor is in the financing business, carries an inventory and the like.

---

[21] See Coogan, et al. *supra*, at §4.1–8: "In a long-term lease, lessor will often look to lessee's rent for a "full payout" of all costs, including costs of money plus profit. This may be true even where the item must be returned to lessor at a time when a substantial portion of useful life remains and the item has a substantial residual value." See also, *In re Loop Hospital, supra*, at p. 933; Harris & Mooney, *supra*, at p. 337.

[22] *Arnold Machinery Co. v. Balls,* 624 P.2d 678, 34 UCC Rep. Serv. 236 (Utah 1981); Article 2A-Leases (Exhibit A) also recognizes this by inclusion of the underscored language in the following:

> . . . a transaction creates a security interest if the consideration the lessee is to pay the lessor for the right to possession and use of the goods is *an obligation for the term of the lease not subject to termination by the lessee.*

[23] See, e.g., *McGalliard v. Liberty Leasing Co., supra.*

The nature of a given transaction must be determined by the attributes of that transaction alone. The fact that a party may be involved in transactions of a different nature, even for a majority of the time, is irrelevant and immaterial to any specific transaction's characterization. The worthlessness of this line of reasoning is well-illustrated by *In re Boling*, 13 Bankr. 39, 32 UCC Rep. Serv. 549 (Bankr. E.D. Tenn. 1981), where the court noted that since the lessor was *not* in the business of manufacturing or selling the equipment, a true lease was indicated, and *Clune Equipment Leasing Corp.*, *supra*, at pp. 107-08 where the court noted that the lessor "keeps no inventory and just purchases items at the request of others" as indicating a lease intended as security.

How Other Lessees Dealt with the Lessor

A few courts have considered how other lessees have dealt with the lessor, e.g., how many lessees exercised their purchase options, how many returned the equipment, etc. The difficulty with such factors is that of the same nature as set forth above: rejection of the analytically sound principle that the nature of a given transaction must be determined by the attributes of that transaction. A premise that a transaction shall be known by the company it keeps is as logically invalid, and of as dubious ethicality, as guilt by association.

The Filing of a Financing Statement by Lessor

Most lessors file a financing statement as a precaution against loss of a perfected status for their security interest if their lease transaction should subsequently be held to be a secured transaction. As the 1972 amendments to the UCC preclude consideration of such a filing in determining the character of the transaction,[24] this item should no longer be a factor.

How the Lessor Treats the Transaction on its Books

Financial Accounting Standards Board Statement No. 13 (FASB 13) deals with lease accounting and is arguably the single most complicated accounting standard. It has been the subject of numerous amendments, interpretations and complaints, and has generated requests for revision.

The accounting issues in leasing bear little relation to the legal issues, particularly as regards a determination of whether or not a transaction purporting to be a lease is indeed a lease. Generally speaking, the accounting standards' focus is on insuring that financial statements accurately report financial conditions. How a lessor treats a transaction in its financial statements is generally not indicative of whether or not it has the characteristic elements of a lease for other than accounting purposes.

The issue of whether or not a transaction is considered a lease, loan or sale for taxation purposes (whether federal, state or local) also has a different focus than does the private commercial law. The analysis of the transaction for taxation purposes may or may not be helpful to commercial law analysis. Although commercial law allows parties the freedom to contract in the manner of their choosing (so long as they do not violate public policy), tax laws,

---

[24] UCC §9-408.

particularly federal tax laws, are frequently designed to not only raise revenue but to affirmatively direct social conduct. (For example, the Investment Tax Credit was designed to encourage acquisition of capital assets, while the designation of tax preference items is designed to discourage certain investments.) While the tax laws may draw heavily from commercial law analysis in a determination of tax liability, the tax laws' service of different concerns (revenue and social policy) may complicate use of tax law analysis for commercial law purposes. Tax law analysis is usually best kept separate from commercial law analysis and some courts have done so.[25]

What the Parties Understood the Transaction to Be

Some courts have referenced what the parties understood the transaction to be as indicative of the nature of the transaction.[26] Of course, as stated previously, the mere calling of a transaction a lease will not make it one if it is indeed not.

Whether the Lease is a Net Lease

A number of decisions have focused upon whether or not the lessee was responsible for paying the taxes and insurance on the equipment and keeping it maintained and repaired. In short, these courts have considered the existence of net terms to be indicative of a lease intended as security and have reasoned that these "badges of ownership" are inconsistent with true lease treatment.[27] However, such a conclusion does not follow, as such costs must be borne by one party or another, and their direct allocation to a lessee simply reflects the lessor's bargaining power or the lessee's desire to have a lower stated rent. (If the lessor paid those items, a higher rent would have to be charged.)[28]

In the real estate industry it has been customary for a number of years to provide for net terms or even triple net terms. Real estate landlords might be surprised to learn that the existence of a real estate lease with net terms indicated that the landlord had transferred fee title in the property to the tenant.

Article 2A-Leases (Exhibit A) specifically rejects net terms as factors to be considered inconsistent with true lease treatment:

> A transaction does not create a security interest merely because it provides that . . .
> (b) the lessee assumes risk of loss of the goods, or agrees to pay taxes, insurance, filing, recording, or registration fees, or service or maintenance costs with respect to the goods.

---

[25] See, *In re Mitchell*, 44 B.R. 485 (Bank. N.D. Ala. 1984).

[26] See, e.g., *Leasing Service Corp. v. River City Construction, Inc.*, 743 F.2d 871 (11th Cir. 1984); *U.S Armament Corp. v. Charlie Thomas Leasing Co.*, 661 S.W.2d 197 (Tex. Ct. App. 1983).

[27] See, e.g., *In re Tulsa Port Warehouse Co.*, 690 F.2d 809 (10th Cir. 1982).

[28] See, *In re Marhoefer Packing Co.*, *supra*, p. 1146; *Rainier National Bank v. Inland Machinery Co.*, 29 Wn. App. 725, 631 P.2d 389 (1981); *In re Loop Hospital*, *supra*, at 935-36.

Who Bears the Risk of Depreciation in Estimated Residual Value

Some courts have found a transaction to be a lease intended as security if, at the end of the lease, the lessee is liable either for any deficiency in the agreed-upon estimated residual value of the equipment, or receives any surplus over and above the agreed-upon estimated residual value.[29] However, the federal consumer leasing act clearly recognizes open-end leases as true leases.[30]

Definitions of a Finance Lease

One of the reasons the courts have had, and still have, such difficulty in reaching a proper analysis of modern personal property lease transactions has to do with *stare decisis*[31] and the difficulties that doctrine creates for dealing with new types of transactions. There is a tendency to try and fit new items into old boxes. However, traditional bailment law and real estate lease law do not graft well onto the major form of modern personal property leasing, the finance lease.

The finance lease is a lease that has as its purpose the financing of the use of property for a major portion of the property's useful life. The term is typically used in reference to leases written by third-party lessors, i.e., a lessor who is not in the business of selling the equipment it leases and that functions essentially as a financier. A finance lease may or may not be a true lease, depending upon whether or not the lessor has retained, as of the inception of the lease, a significant residual interest.

Contrasted with the finance lease may be the more traditional rental, wherein the lessor typically deals in goods of the kind leased, or otherwise by occupation holds itself out as having knowledge or skill particular to the practices or goods involved in the transaction. In short, the lessor in a traditional rental has a close relationship with the leased property and is not involved primarily to finance the acquisition of its use.

Some courts have recognized the distinction between the finance lease and the more traditional rental.

> A finance lease is a transaction in which the lessor is essentially a financier; the financing lessor has no expertise in the type of equipment it leases, the lessee operates and maintains the equipment, and the lessor usually has no contact with the equipment. In contrast, the operating lessors act more like sellers: they include lessors which are in the business of renting personalty and which make available to lessees the use of that personalty for a portion of its useful life. The operating lessee relies on the operating lessor's expertise and the lessor is in a position to control the equipment.[32]

---

[29] *In re Tulsa Port Warehouse Co.*, *supra*;

[30] 15 U.S.C. §1667 et seq.; see §1667b re the "three payment rule" for open-end leases.

[31] The doctrine that once a court has laid down a principle of law as applicable to a certain state of facts, the court will apply that principle in all future cases when the facts are substantially the same.

[32] *Equico Lessors v. Tow*, 34 WnApp. 333, 661 P.2d 597 (1983).

Article 2A-Leases creates statutory recognition of the finance lease. However, it attaches certain conditions for achievement of statutory finance lease status that go above and beyond the common law status afforded by the current cases that recognize finance leases. If Article 2A-Leases becomes a new article to the UCC, there will be essentially two different types of finance leases: (1) the common law finance lease and (2) the statutory finance lease.

Article 2A-Leases defines a finance lease as:

> . . . a lease in which (i) the lessor does not select, manufacture or supply the goods, (ii) the lessor acquires the goods or the right to possession and use of the goods in connection with the lease, and (iii) either the lessee receives a copy of the contract evidencing the lessor's purchase of the goods on or before signing the lease contract, or the lessee's approval of the contract evidencing the lessor's purchase of the goods is a condition to the effectiveness of the lease contract [UCC §2A-103(1)(g)].

Provisions (i) and (ii) of Article 2A-Leases's finance lease definition reflect what is typical of a modern finance lease transaction and are those factors that distinguish it from the more traditional rental. However, provision (iii) is not descriptive of modern finance lease transactions and is, effectively, a "price of admission" to statutory finance lease status.

In drafting Article 2A-Leases, a policy decision was made very early on that freedom of contract would be preserved. Nothing in the Article restricts the parties' abilities to achieve finance lease status through their own contractual agreement. However, because statutory finance lease status confers certain legal consequences to a transaction as a matter of law, it was felt certain lessee protections were in order. In short, provision (iii) provides the lessee with some protection that the transaction that it has negotiated, with the vendor it has selected, has not been changed in the acquisition of the selected property by the lessor for lease specifically to the lessee. This is accomplished by requiring that either (1) the lessee receive a copy of the contract evidencing the lessor's purchase of the goods, on or before signing the lease contract, or (2) the lessee approve the contract evidencing the lessor's purchase of the goods as a condition to the effectiveness of the lease contract. The two-pronged approach of provision (iii) is necessary because the contract evidencing the lessor's purchase of the goods often will not be in existence on or before signing the lease contract. In such instances, the lessee's approval of the contract evidencing the lessor's purchase of the goods will be necessary for the lease contract to be effective.

APPLICATION OF THE UNIFORM COMMERCIAL CODE

Technically, at the present time leases are not covered by the UCC. However, provisions from the UCC have been applied to lease transactions, particularly provisions from Article 9-Secured Transactions and certain provisions from Article 2-Sales. In fact, as previously discussed, the "definition of a lease" that exists in the UCC is a definition of whether a lease is intended as security. If a lease is intended as security, the lease transaction will be a secured transaction and will be directly covered by the provisions of Article 9.

Article 9

While it is beyond the scope of this chapter to provide a detailed discussion of Article 9, certain provisions merit a lessor's attention. In the simplest terms, Article 9 addresses a creditor-debtor relationship and the quality of that relationship. A secured transaction is created when a debtor (lessee) gives a creditor (lessor) a security interest in certain property. Such security interest is granted by a security agreement. To make that grant of a security interest enforceable against third parties, the security interest must be perfected. The security interest is perfected by filing a record of it, in the required form, in the required place. Such filing gives notice to the world of the existence of that interest. Without such notice, the interest is generally good only as between the creditor and debtor. The method by which the grant of a security interest is made valid against third parties is called perfection. Thus, a creditor can have an unsecured interest, an unperfected secured interest and a perfected secured interest. Obviously, the perfected secured interest is the most desirable.

By definition, a true lease is not a secured transaction and is not subject to any filing or perfection requirement. However, because so much litigation has occurred over the issue as to whether or not a transaction creates a lease or creates a security interest, a prudent lessor will always make a UCC filing to protect its interests should a subsequent determination be made that the transaction was indeed a secured transaction, and not a true lease. The filing fee is cheap insurance against an expensive legal battle that could cost the lessor all its remaining value in the leased property.

A security interest is generally perfected by filing a financing statement with the proper state authorities, usually a centrally located state entity such as a Secretary of State, department of licensing or the like. Some filings are made locally, and some states require both a central and local filing. Fixture filings must be filed with the county recorder in the county where the real property to which the fixtures are attached is located.

REQUIREMENTS OF A FINANCING STATEMENT

A financing statement is sufficient if it gives the names of the debtor and the secured party, is signed by the debtor, gives an address of the secured party from which information concerning the security interest may be obtained, gives the mailing address of the debtor and contains a statement indicating the types, or describing the items, of collateral.[33] A financing statement may be filed before a security agreement is made or a security interest otherwise attaches.[34] A copy of the security agreement is sufficient as a financing statement if it contains the above information and is signed by the debtor.[35] A carbon, photographic or other reproduction of a security agreement or financing statement is sufficient as a financing statement if the security agreement so provides or if the original has been filed with the state.[36] Most states have approved forms that can be purchased in bulk for use by creditors and the use of the

---

[33] UCC §9-402.
[34] Id.
[35] Id.
[36] Id.

approved forms is recommended. The failure to use an approved form may result in payment of an additional fee for use of a nonstandard document.

A financing statement sufficiently shows the name of the debtor if it gives the individual, partnership or corporate names of the debtor, whether or not it adds other trade names or names of partners;[37] however, it is a good idea to list all names known to the secured creditor so as to give as extensive a notice as possible. The filing of a new financing statement is necessary within 4 months of any change of a debtor's name, identity or corporate structure that makes the financing statement seriously misleading, if a perfected security interest in collateral acquired by the debtor more than 4 months after the change is to be perfected.[38]

There are some instances when the financing statement signed by the secured party only, and not the debtor, is still sufficient to effectively perfect a security interest in the following (assuming the aforementioned requirements are met):

(a) the collateral was already subject to a security interest in another jurisdiction when it is brought into this state or when the debtor's location is changed to this state (however, such a financing statement must state that the collateral was brought into this state or that the debtor's location was changed to this state under such circumstances)

(b) proceeds (i.e., whatever is received upon the sale, exchange, collection or other disposition of collateral) if the security interest in the original collateral was perfected, but such a financing statement must describe the original collateral

(c) collateral as to which the filing has lapsed or

(d) collateral acquired after a change of name, identity or corporate structure of the debtor [UCC §9-402(2)].

Amendments to a financing statement must be by a writing that is signed by both the debtor and secured party and, if the amendment adds collateral, it is effective as to that additional collateral only from the filing date of the amendment.[39] Amendments do not extend the period of effectiveness of a financing statement.[40]

A financing statement that substantially complies with the requirements is effective even though it contains minor errors that are not seriously misleading.[41] Additionally, a filed financing statement remains effective with respect to collateral transferred by the debtor, even though the secured party knows of or consents to the transfer.[42] Thus, any person searching the condition of title as to certain property of a debtor must make inquiry as to the debtor's source of title to the property, and must search in the name of a former owner if the circumstances require it.

---

[37] Id.

[38] UCC §9-402-7.

[39] UCC §9-402(4).

[40] Id.

[41] UCC §9-402(8).

[42] UCC §9-402(7).

Some lessors have been reluctant to file financing statements for fear the filing of such a statement indicates the lease is not a true lease. In states that have adopted the 1972 amendments to the UCC (i.e., most states) this concern has been alleviated by Section 9-408, which specifically provides that the fact of the filing, in and of itself, shall not be a factor in determining whether or not a lease is intended as security, and that, if it should be so determined the lease is not a true lease, the filing is effective to perfect the security interest.

Fixture Filings

A fixture is an item of personal property that becomes so related to real property that it becomes treated as part of the real property, a definition that admittedly does not provide great guidance. Traditionally, the determination of whether or not an item of property was a fixture was made on the basis of how attached and how integrated it became to the real estate. Such an evaluation is still relevant; however, more recent cases have placed a stronger emphasis on the intent of the parties. Probably the best approach for a lessor is to treat any item of property that may be significantly attached to the real estate, or difficult to remove, as a fixture for purposes of perfecting a security interest in such items. Such security interests are perfected by a fixture filing, which is, in essence, a financing statement with the addition of a legal description of the real property upon which the fixtures will be located, and the name of the record owner of the real property if the debtor does not have an interest of record in the real estate. Additionally, fixture filings are to be filed in the real estate records of the county wherein the real property is located. In most instances, the lessor will achieve better protection if it files both a financing statement with the appropriate authorities and a fixture filing within the real estate records, as to any items of property that could remotely be considered fixtures.

Priority of Financing Statements and Fixture Filings

Generally, the filing system for security interests in equipment and fixtures is a "first in time, first in right" system. A filing party will have a position junior to those that have filed before, but senior to those filing after. However, there are some important exceptions to this general rule. The most important exception involves purchase money security interests. A purchase money security interest is a security interest that is taken and retained by a seller in its goods sold, or the security interest taken by a person who finances the purchase of such goods.[43] A party possessing a purchase money security interest "can cut in line" and obtain a first place position for its security interest in that property, even though other parties may be ahead of it because of broad blanket filings or provisions that automatically create security interests in after-acquired property. However, to obtain the benefits of a purchase money security interest perfection, a party must file or otherwise perfect its security interest before the debtor receives possession of the collateral, or within 10 days thereafter.[44] (Some states allow 20 days.) The priorities of security interests in fixtures are somewhat complex and beyond the scope of this chapter.[45]

---

[43] See UCC §9-107.

[44] UCC §9-312(4).

[45] See UCC §9-313.

MULTISTATE TRANSACTIONS

Transactions involving a number of states create a number of problems as to the perfection of security interests. Problems can arise also when equipment is moved from one jurisdiction to another.

The general rule is that the perfection, and the effect of perfection or nonperfection of a security interest in collateral, is governed by the law of the jurisdiction where the collateral is when the last event occurs on which is based the assertion that the security interest is perfected or unperfected.[46] However, if the parties to the transaction understand at the time the security interest attaches that the goods will be kept in another jurisdiction, then the law of that other jurisdiction governs the perfection, and the effect of perfection or nonperfection of the security interest, from the time it attaches until 30 days after the debtor receives possession of the goods, and thereafter if the goods are taken to the other jurisdiction before the end of the 30-day period.

When collateral is brought into, and kept in, a state while subject to a security interest perfected under the law of another state, the security interest remains perfected for only 4 months after the collateral is brought into the state, unless action is taken to continue it. Lessors and secured creditors must continually monitor the location of their leased property and collateral lest they lose their security interest. This loss of security interest can occur by having the property removed to another state for a period exceeding 4 months without their knowledge and their ability to preserve their perfected status.

GOODS SUBJECT TO CERTIFICATES OF TITLE

The perfection of security interest in goods subject to certificates of title is usually governed by the applicable certificate of title statutes. Those statutes usually require that the interest of a secured party appear on the document itself, as in the case of lienholders appearing on certificates of title to automobiles. Matters can get extremely complex with multistate transactions involving certificated property, and with the movement of certificated property from one jurisdiction to another.

SECURED TRANSACTION REMEDIES

In addition to the rights a secured creditor may have by contract upon a debtor's default, Aritcle 9 also provides certain rights and remedies, as well as certain limitations of their free exercise that legislative policy requires for the protection of not only the defaulting debtor but of other creditors.

Repossession

Unless otherwise agreed between the parties, a secured party has on default the right to take possession of its collateral.[47] The secured party may proceed without judicial process, if this can be done without a breach of the peace, or may proceed through the use of the courts.[48] A

---

[46] See UCC §9-103.

[47] UCC §9-503.

[48] Id.

secured party can also require the debtor to assemble the collateral and make it available to the secured party at a designated place that is reasonably convenient to both the parties, if the security agreement so provides.[49] The secured party may also render the equipment unusable and may dispose of it on the debtor's premises.[50]

Disposition of Repossessed Property

Any disposition of the property must be done in a commercially reasonable manner.[51] Although the requirement of a commercially reasonable disposition technically does not apply to a true lease, most courts that have considered the issue (and many without analyzing it) have extended this requirement to true leases. All prudent lessors, whether involved in true leases, conditional sales or lending, should always be prepared to prove their dispositions of leased property or collateral were done in a commercially reasonable manner. What is commercially reasonable must be determined by the facts and circumstances of each case. The mere fact that a better price could have been obtained by sale at a different time, or in a different method from that selected by the secured party, is not, in and of itself, sufficient to establish the sale was not made in a commercially reasonable manner.[52] However, every aspect of the disposition, including the method, manner, time, place and terms of the disposition, must be commercially reasonable.[53]

Notices of Disposition

Secured transactions require certain notices be sent to the debtor; such notices are not required for true leases. However, a prudent lessor will send such notices in case the transaction is subsequently recharacterized. Additionally, some courts (some by analogy, some without analysis) have applied the notice requirements to true lease transactions.

There are basically two different types of disposition: (1) public and (2) private. For public sales, unless the collateral is perishable and threatens to decline speedily in value, or is of a type customarily sold on a recognized market, reasonable notification of the time and place of any public sale must be given to the debtor. If the sale is a private sale, reasonable notification of the time after which any private sale or other intended disposition is to be made must be sent by the secured party to the debtor. Parties other than the debtor may be entitled to such notice if they have requested it of the secured party in writing.[54]

The secured party may buy at any public sale.[55] At a private sale, the secured party may buy if the collateral is of a type customarily sold in a recognized market or is of a type that is the subject of widely distributed price quotations.[56] The secured creditor must account to the debtor

---

[49] Id.
[50] Id. and §9-504.
[51] UCC §9-504.
[52] UCC §9-507(2).
[53] UCC §9-504(3).
[54] Id.
[55] Id.
[56] Id.

for any surplus and, unless otherwise agreed, the debtor is liable for any deficiency.[57] This rule should not apply in a true lease transaction; however, many lease documents may provide otherwise, particularly with respect to liability for a deficiency.

Failure to Comply with Notice and Other Requirements

If a secured party has disposed of collateral in violation of the requirements of Article 9, it may be liable to the debtor or other parties whose interests are damaged thereby. In some states, this noncompliance generates an offset for such damages. However, in other states, this noncompliance operates as a complete bar to the recovery of a deficiency from the debtor.

Article 2-Sales

Although Article 2-Sales does not technically apply to the lessor-lessee relationship in a true lease transaction, some of its provisions have been applied either directly, or by analogy, by the courts. (Article 2-Sales would apply to the supplier-lessor transaction by which the lessor bought the goods leased to the lessee.) Most notable has been the application of the implied warranties of merchantability and fitness for a particular purpose.

IMPLIED WARRANTIES

Section 2-314 of the UCC provides that, unless excluded or modified, a warranty that the goods shall be merchantable is implied in a contract for their sale if the seller is a merchant with respect to goods of that kind. To be merchantable, goods must at least:

1. Pass without objection in the trade under the contract description
2. Be of fair average quality within the description in the case of fungible goods
3. Be fit for the ordinary purposes for which such goods are used
4. Run, within the variations permitted by the agreement, of even kind, quality and quantity within each unit and among all units involved
5. Be adequately contained, packaged and labeled as the agreement may require
6. Conform to the promises or affirmations of fact made on the container, or label, if any.

Unless excluded or modified, other implied warranties may arise from the course of dealing or usage of trade.

An implied warranty of fitness for a particular purpose can be created when the seller, at the time of contracting, has reason to know any particular purpose for which the goods are required and the buyer is relying on the seller's skill or judgment to select or furnish suitable goods. The implied warranty is that the goods shall be fit for such purpose.[58]

Most lessors exclude such implied warranties by provisions in their lease agreement. However, to exclude or modify the implied warranty of merchantability or any part of it, the language must mention merchantability and, in case of a writing, must be conspicuous.[59] To exclude or modify any implied warranty of fitness, the exclusion must be by writing and conspicuous. However, some states have added additional requirements if implied warranties

---

[57] UCC §9-504(2).
[58] UCC §2-315.
[59] UCC §2-316.

are to be successfully excluded or modified. For example, it has been additionally required that the particular characteristics that are being excluded must be set forth in detail, and the exclusion or modification of warranties must be specifically bargained for between the parties.

Many lessors involved in multistate operations have documentation that will be unenforceable in states imposing these or other additional requirements.

EXPRESS WARRANTIES

In addition to implied warranties, express warranties can be created by lessors, whether the lessor is involved with secured transactions or true leases. Express warranties are specific promises respecting the equipment and its use, function, operation or other characteristics. They can be created in different ways,[60] and can be created by the seller as follows:

1. Any affirmation of fact or promise made by the seller to the buyer that relates to the goods, and becomes part of the basis of the bargain, creates an express warranty that the goods shall conform to the affirmation or promise
2. Any description of the goods that is made part of the basis of the bargain creates an express warranty that the goods shall conform to the description
3. Any sample or model that is made part of the basis of the bargain creates an express warranty that the whole of the goods shall conform to the sample or model.

It is not necessary to use such formal words as warrant or guarantee or to even have a specific intention to make a warranty in order to create one, but an affirmation merely of the value of the goods or a statement purporting to be merely the seller's opinion or recommendation of the goods does not create a warranty.[61] Lessors must be especially careful to protect themselves against express warranties that might be made by vendors, lease salespersons, brokers or others not ultimately responsible for the financing and enforcement of transactions. Proper documentation is essential.

Other Aspects of the Uniform Commercial Code

Leases are commercial transactions, whether categorized as true leases or secured transactions. Other provisions in the UCC, such as the obligations of good faith and fair dealing, have been, and will continue to be, applied to leases. If Article 2A-Leases is ultimately adopted in a number of states, leasing will be squarely covered by the UCC and rules specific to leasing will apply. Until that time, prudent lessors must continue to expect provisions in the UCC to continue to be applied either directly or by analogy.

BANKRUPTCY

As the term is commonly used today, bankruptcy indicates a debtor has filed a petition in the United States bankruptcy courts. The most commonly filed petitions are as follows:

1. Chapter 7 — Liquidation ("I give up")
2. Chapter 11 — Reorganization ("I want a time out so I can reorganize my affairs")

---

[60] UCC §2-313.
[61] Id.

3. Chapter 12 — Reorganization (A family farmer who says "I want a time out so I can reorganize my affairs")
4. Chapter 13 — Reorganization (A wage earner or similar individual with regular income who says, "I want to pay my creditors as much as I can over the next 3 to 5 years").

Various Bankruptcy Chapters

Although an in-depth examination of bankruptcy law is beyond the scope of this chapter, a general overview of these various bankruptcy chapters is presented.

CHAPTER 7

In a Chapter 7 filing, a trustee is appointed to collect and liquidate the assets of the debtor. From the assets of the debtor, creditors are paid according to the priorities established by the Bankruptcy Code.[62] The debtor generally leaves behind its prepetition debts and other obligations and starts a new life the day after the petition is filed, although it may take a number of months before the debtor formally receives its discharge of those prior obligations. (When given, the discharge is retroactive to the date of the petition's filing.)

CHAPTER 11

Most businesses faced with significant economic difficulties will file a Chapter 11 in an effort to obtain a time out from the pressure of their creditors, so they can have an opportunity to reorganize their affairs and rehabilitate their business.

Upon filing a petition in Chapter 11, the debtor becomes a debtor in possession and has the rights, powers and duties of a trustee in bankruptcy.[63] Typically, the debtor will continue to operate the business as it has before, with some degree of court supervision. Usually, that supervision amounts to no more than the obligation to file a monthly financial report with the court and the obligation to seek court approval for affairs that are outside the ordinary course of business.

While a business is in a Chapter 11, action against the business by its creditors is stayed.[64] The purpose of the stay is to allow the company to turn its attentions to formulating a reorganization plan that is likely to succeed. During the first 120 days after the filing of the petition, the debtor is the only party entitled to file a plan of reorganization. However, the debtor does not have to file such a plan within that 120 days. After the expiration of that 120-day exclusivity period, any creditor or party in interest can propose a plan of reorganization.[65]

Typically, a plan of reorganization will divide the creditors of the debtor into various classes according to the creditors' claims or interests, and then specify the treatment to be accorded the claims or interests in that class. The proposed treatment of the claims or interests in a class may involve 100% payment of those claims or interests, a reduced payment of those claims or interest, or no payment at all.

---

[62] 11 U.S.C. § §101, et seq., hereinafter "Bankruptcy Code" or "Code."
[63] Id. §1107.
[64] Id. §362.
[65] Id. §1121.

The plan must also provide adequate means for the plan's implementation such as:[66]

1. Retention by the debtor of all or any part of the property of the estate
2. Transfer of all or any part of the property to any one or more other entities
3. Merger or consolidation of the debtor with another party
4. Sale of all or any part of the property either subject to, or free of, any lien encumbering that property or the distribution of such encumbered party to those parties having the encumbrance
5. Satisfaction or modification of any lien
6. Cancellation or modification of any indenture or similar instrument
7. Curing or waiving of any default
8. Extension of a maturity date, or a change in an interest rate or other term of outstanding securities
9. Modification of the business' capital structure, including the issuance of new stock or other securities
10. Other items that will assist the plan's implementation.

A plan can propose to impair (i.e., pay less than the full value of a claim or interest) a class of claims or interest and still be an approvable plan. The plan may be approved over the objection of a class of claims or interests of any party, as long as each holder of a claim or interest of such class has accepted the plan, or will receive or retain under the plan an amount equal to or greater than what the creditor would have received had the debtor been liquidated under Chapter 7.[67] Since in many cases unsecured creditors would receive nothing in a Chapter 7 liquidation, unsecured creditors in a Chapter 11 proceeding are often powerless to enforce significant payments on their claims.

After a plan is formulated, a disclosure statement is developed, which is then approved by the court and disseminated to those parties having claims or interests. The purpose of the disclosure statement is to provide sufficient information to creditors so that they can intelligently decide whether or not to vote for the plan.[68] The holder of each claim or interest is entitled to vote on the plan. A class of claims is considered to have accepted the plan if such plan has been accepted by creditors that hold at lease two-thirds of the amount, and more than one-half of the number of allowed claims of the class.[69] The two-thirds and the one-half requirements are computed based on a denominator that equals the amount or number of claims that have actually been voted for or against the plan, rather than the total number and amount of claims in the class.

A class of equity securities has accepted a plan if at least two-thirds of the amount of the outstanding securities actually voted vote for the plan;[70] the one-half the number requirement is dispensed with. No acceptance is required from any class whose claims or interests are unimpaired.[71] If a class is denied receipt or retention of any property under the plan, it is

---

[66] See §1123.
[67] Id. §1129(a)(7).
[68] See Id. §1125.
[69] Id. §1126(c).
[70] Id. §1126(d).
[71] Id. §1126(f).

deemed to have rejected the plan.[72] (Of course, a class receiving nothing under the plan is not likely to vote in favor of it.) After the votes are tallied, a confirmation hearing is held respecting the plan and, it is hoped, the plan is approved by the court. Of course, parties in interest may object to the confirmation of the plan and such objection may result in a modification or rejection of the plan.[73]

Upon confirmation of the plan, the plan replaces all of the old debt structure of the debtor and creates new obligations that are enforceable by the debtor's creditors. The automatic stay is lifted and the debtor is revested with its assets and new liabilities.[74]

CHAPTER 12

Most farm families have too much debt to qualify for relief under Chapter 13, but find Chapter 11 too unworkable and expensive for farming operations. Chapter 12 was enacted in 1986 (effective November 26, 1986) to give family farmers a "fighting chance to reorganize their debts and keep their land."[75]

Only family farmers with regular annual income qualify for Chapter 12. A family farmer is defined as:

> An individual (or individual and spouse) engaged in a farming operation whose aggregate debts on the date the case is filed do not exceed $1,500,000, with not less than 80% of the aggregate noncontingent, liquidated debts, excluding principal residence debt (unless such debt arises from a farming operation) arising from farm operations, and such individual (or individual and spouse) received more than 50% of its (their) income from the preceding taxable year from such farming operation.
>
> A corporation or partnership in which one family and its relatives own more than 50% of the outstanding stock or equity and conducts the farming operations and more than 80% of the value of the entity's assets consists of assets related to the farming operation and the debt requirements set forth above are met [§101(17)].

Chapter 12 generally provides more favorable treatment to family farmers than is available under Chapter 11. Although the Act is relatively new and its administration and enforcement do not have a track record, it is expected to have a major impact on lessors involved in the leasing of agricultural equipment.

CHAPTER 13

Chapter 13 involves the adjustment of debts of an individual with regular income. It is somewhat like a mini-Chapter 11, except that a court appointed trustee takes an active role in the administration of the Chapter 13 plan. (However, a debtor engaged in business usually

---

[72] Id. §1126(g).

[73] See Id. § §1127 and 1128.

[74] Id. §1141.

[75] Conference Report (H.R. Rept. 99-958, Cong., 2d Sees., p. 48 (1986), Bankruptcy Judges, United States Trustees and Family Farmer Bankruptcy Act of 1986 (the "Act"); all references to sections within this heading are to sections of the Act.

performs the duties of the Chapter 13 trustee. A debtor that is self-employed and incurs trade credit in the production of income from such employment is engaged in business.[76])

Under Chapter 13 only the debtor has the right to file a plan of reorganization.[77] Generally, the plan shall provide for the submission of all or such portion of future earnings or other future income of the debtor to the supervision and control of the trustee as is necessary for the execution for the plan, provide for full payment and deferred cash payments of all priority claims and, if the plan classifies claims, provide the same treatment for each claim within a particular class.[78] The plan is limited to a 3-year repayment period unless the court for cause permits a longer period; however, in any event the plan shall not exceed 5 years.[79]

A Chapter 13 debtor may also, among other things, divide unsecured claims not entitled to priority into classes in the manner of Chapter 11, modify the rights of holders of secured and unsecured claims (except claims wholly secured by real estate that is the debtor's principal residence), cure any defaults, propose payments on unsecured claims concurrently with payments on any secured claim, provide for payment of postpetition claims and assume or reject executory contracts of unexpired leases.[80]

Confirmation of a Chapter 13 plan binds the debtor and each creditor to the plan and revests the property of the bankruptcy estate in the debtor free and clear of any claim or interest of any creditor. As soon as practicable after completion by the debtor of all payments under the plan, the debtor generally will be granted its discharge.

Issues for Lessors

As one of the debtor's creditors, a lessor may be interested in all aspects of a debtor's bankruptcy. However, some issues should almost always merit a lessor's attention.

PROOFS OF CLAIM

A creditor or any other party in interest may file a proof of claim.[81] (Proofs of claim generally must be filed in Chapter 7 and Chapter 13 cases.)[82] If the debtor has properly listed the creditors and its debt in its schedules of assets and liabilities, the filing of a proof of claim may not be necessary in some instances; however, a prudent lessor will almost always file a proof of claim.

The proof of claim is the creditor's or other interested party's statement of what it is owed by the debtor, how such obligation is calculated and may include supporting documentation. Most courts provide a standard form that they prefer to see used for the filing of proofs of claims. These forms can create problems for lessors because they rarely have the necessary blanks or boxes for lessors, and are written in terms of secured creditors and unsecured creditors. Some

---

[76] Id. §1304.

[77] Id. §1321.

[78] Id. §1322.

[79] Id.

[80] Id.

[81] Id. §501.

[82] B.R. 3002.

modification of those forms is often necessary to properly set forth the lessor's true lease interest and its contingently perfected security interest.

MOTIONS TO ASSUME OR REJECT EXECUTORY CONTRACTS AND UNEXPIRED LEASES

A lessor receiving notice of a bankruptcy petition filing by one of its lessees should determine a course of action without delay, especially if the lessee is in arrears on its lease payments or has otherwise defaulted on its lease (for example, through its failure to maintain insurance on the leased property). If the lease is a true lease, a motion to require assumption or rejection of the unexpired lease will be appropriate.

A trustee or debtor in possession, subject to the court's approval, may assume or reject any executory contract or unexpired lease of the debtor.[83] Generally speaking, the trustee has until the filing of a plan in any Chapter 11 to decide whether or not to assume or reject an unexpired personal property lease unless the court, upon a lessor's or other party's motion, has established an earlier deadline. (However, the deadline is only 60 days for real property leases.) In a Chapter 7, if the trustee does not assume or reject an executory contract or unexpired lease, of either residential real property or personal property, within 60 days after the filing of the petition (or such additional time as the court for cause allows), then such contract or lease is deemed rejected.[84]

If the executory contract or unexpired lease is in default and the trustee desires to assume it, at the time of the assumption, the trustee must:

1. Cure or provide adequate assurance that the trustee will promptly cure such default
2. Compensate or provide adequate assurance that the trustee will promptly compensate a party (e.g., the lessor) for any actual pecuniary loss resulting from the default
3. Provide adequate assurance of future performance under such contract or lease.[85]

These cure requirements give the lessor a powerful tool for use in lessee bankruptcy filing. The cure may even include payment of attorneys' fees and costs, additional advance payments and other types of compensation and assurance. However, in many instances, it is unlikely that all of these payments will be paid immediately upon the assumption of the lease; the court may order them satisfied over a period of time. Nevertheless, in many instances the lessor will have readily determined the debtor's intentions toward the lease and either had payments resumed or its property returned.

THE AUTOMATIC STAY AND ADEQUATE PROTECTION

The ability to pursue a motion for assumption or rejection of an unexpired lease will not be available to a lessor who does not have a true lease, but has instead a conditional sale or loan. Rather, such a lessor is a secured creditor who will need to pursue a motion to lift the automatic stay or, in the alternative, to provide adequate protection.

---

[83] 11 U.S.C. §365.

[84] Id.

[85] Id.

Upon the filing of a petition for relief under the bankruptcy laws, almost all actions against the debtor to collect, enforce or otherwise obtain satisfaction of obligations that the debtor has to its creditors are stayed. Parties who proceed with such efforts may be cited for contempt by the bankruptcy court and will find their actions void. However, there are circumstances in which a creditor can obtain relief from the automatic stay.

The stay is actually composed of two stays: (1) a stay of actions against the debtor and (2) a stay of actions against the property of the debtor (now property of the bankruptcy estate). A stay of actions against the property of the estate continues until such property is no longer property of the estate. A stay against activities against the debtor continues until the earliest of the closing of the case, the dismissal of the case or the granting or denial of a discharge.

Relief Under the Stay

Upon request of a party in interest, after notice and hearing, the court shall grant relief from the stay if certain conditions are met.[86] Relief can comprise the termination, annulment, modification or conditioning of the stay. The court shall grant relief from the stay with respect to acts against property of the estate if (1) the debtor does not have an equity in such property and (2) such property is not necessary to an effective reorganization. As to other stayed actions, the court shall grant relief from the stay for cause, including the lack of adequate protection of an interest in property of such party requesting relief.

Of course, in a true lease, a debtor has no equity in the property; however, the property may be necessary for an effective reorganization. A lessor moving for relief from the automatic stay should expect an argument by the debtor that it has both equity in the property and that the property is necessary for an effective reorganization. The equity issue usually turns upon the factual evidence as to the value of the property and as to payments made by the debtor for that value, and in the case of a lease, whether the lease is a true lease or lease intended as security. As to the "necessary for effective reorganization" issue, it can be difficult for a lessor or other secured creditor to show that the property is not necessary for an effective reorganization when a debtor argues strenuously that it is. Challenges to the necessity standard usually involve a challenge to the ability of the debtor to effectively reorganize at all. (Of course, there is no reorganization in a Chapter 7 case and this particular requirement would not apply.)

Adequate Protection

The term adequate protection is not defined in the Bankruptcy Code as such, and has been left to the development of the case law. However, the Code does give some indication of how adequate protection may be provided: (1) by requiring a trustee to make a cash payment or periodic cash payments to a creditor to the extent that the use, sale or lease of the property or the granting of any lien against the property under the Code results in a decrease in the value of the creditor's interest in the property, (2) by providing the creditor with an additional or replacement lien to the extent that there is a decrease in the value of the creditor's interest in such property or (3) by granting such other relief as will result in the realization by such entity of the

---

[86] Id. §362.

indubitable equivalent of such entity's interest in such property.[87] The foregoing list is not exhaustive and the court has significant freedom to fashion creative solutions to the need for adequate protection.

The concept of adequate protection is based both upon constitutional grounds (the Fifth Amendment protection of property rights), and public policy grounds that secured creditors should not be deprived of the benefit of their bargains. However, there remains a balancing between the protection of those property rights, the needs of a debtor in bankruptcy and the public policy behind the bankruptcy laws. Adequate protection is a mechanism to help achieve a balance between those conflicting interests and policies.

The focus of adequate protection is upon the creditor's interest in such property. Such focus implies evaluation of such interest; however, the Code does not provide for a mechanism to determine such value. Such value will depend upon the facts and circumstances in each case, but the determination of such value can be critical to the quality and quantity of adequate protection that the creditor will receive. Value is a flexible concept that, in some cases, may involve liquidation value and, in other cases, may involve going concern value. In many instances, the value issue will be resolved by negotiations between the debtor's counsel and the creditor's counsel. If the parties cannot agree, the court will decide.

Special Provision Regarding Aircraft Equipment and Vessels

There is a special provision in the Bankruptcy Code dealing with certain interests in aircraft equipment and vessels.[88] This section modifies the automatic stay and the court's ability to prevent lessors, conditional vendors and secured parties with purchase money security interests in aircraft transferred to certified air carriers, and vessels transferred to certified water carriers under the Federal Aviation Act and the Ship Mortgage Act, respectively, from repossessing their property or collateral unless the trustee takes certain actions within 60 days after the bankruptcy petition is filed.

Before the expiration of those 60 days, the trustee, subject to the court's approval, must agree to perform all obligations under the security agreement, lease or conditional sale contract, and any default occurring before the filing of the petition must be cured before the expiration of the 60 days. Any default occurring after that date must be cured before the latter of 30 days after the date of the default or the expiration of the 60-day period.

STATE TAX CONSIDERATIONS

The following summary has been provided for informational purposes and as a quick, and very simplistic overview of an extremely complicated subject where the rules change frequently. Specific liabilities for specific activities must turn upon the facts and circumstances of each

---

[87] Id. §361.

[88] Id. §1110.

individual situation. The need for competent legal advice on state taxation issues cannot be overstated.

Sales/Use Tax Distinction

Generally speaking, sales and use taxes can be considered two sides of the same coin. Sales tax can be assessed only on intrastate transactions because of the federal constitution's commerce clause and due process clause complications attendant to taxation of interstate transactions; however, states utilize a use tax to accomplish the same result by taxing the privilege of utilizing property within the state. The sales/use taxes usually mirror one another in terms of rate, timing and other facets.

The vast majority of states assess sales/use taxes upon the gross lease receipts, collectible as each lease payment is received by the lessor. Some states allow for an election as to whether or not the sales/use tax will be paid up front on the purchase price of the goods, or on the gross lease payments as the payments are received. A few states require that a sales/use tax be paid both on the purchase price of the goods acquired by the lessor and upon the gross lease receipts.

Special sales/use tax problems can arise in the case of sale-leasebacks. Since title is transferred, many states will take the position that a sales/use tax is due. Some do not, if the transaction is clearly just a financing. Since the liability for the tax will often turn upon the particular facts and circumstances of the transaction, a general rule cannot be stated. A lessor involved in a sale-leaseback should carefully investigate the applicable state's position.

Personal Property Taxes

Personal property taxes are taxes on the ownership of property and thus a tax on the lessor. However, many lessors pass this tax on to the lessee as part of the lease's net terms. Because a lessee's liability for payment of personal property taxes can be considered just an additional item of rent, a number of states require the payment of sales/use tax upon personal property tax.

Most personal property tax assessments are made at the county level, although at least one state assesses at the state level and several New England states assess at the town or township level. The mechanism for taxpayer compliance is usually the preparation of an affidavit, or a similar such statement, as to the personal property owned by that taxpayer. The states divide as to whether or not personal property is taxed in the county of the residence of the owner (which for a business would be its place of business) or where the property is actually located. As a general rule, motor vehicles and other titled items of property are not taxed as part of the personal property taxation system, but are taxed as part of the registration system for such property.

Income Tax and Lessors

The vast majority of states assess a tax on the net income of corporations; however, a few do not, and one state's income tax is a gross tax that is combined with the sales tax as a single tax on gross receipts. Another state also assesses a tax on gross receipts in lieu of an income tax (but still assesses a sales tax).

A corporation "doing business" within a state will be liable for that state's corporate income tax.[89] If the activities of the corporation do not rise to the doing business level, the business will still have an income tax liability if it has a sufficient nexus with the state to justify that liability. (If a business is receiving significant revenue from a state, it can expect the state's taxing authorities to pursue taxation of that revenue.)

Almost all states with taxes on net income tie the basic taxation scheme to the federal income tax code. However, most states also make some changes, excluding or including certain items of income and allowing or disallowing additional or different types of deductions. Given the recent tax reform at the federal level, it can be expected that a number of changes in state income taxation will continue to occur in the near future.

As a general rule, a corporation liable for income taxes in a number of states will be able to apportion that tax liability on a state-by-state basis. However, the apportionment formulae vary from state to state and may thus result in overlapping tax liabilities. A majority of states apportion according to the arithmetic average of a corporation's sales, property and payroll within the taxing state as compared to all other jurisdictions. For most states, only sales, property and payroll within the United States are included in the apportionment formula, but a few states include such activities worldwide. Some of the states using the sales, property and payroll formula may weight one factor more strongly than another. Some states have abbreviated formulae: payroll and sales only, property and payroll only, or sales only.

Unitary taxation involves the taxation of the combined operations of related business enterprises (i.e., parent-subsidiary, affiliated corporations, etc.) as a single entity. A state may require, prohibit or allow an election as to unitary taxation. Almost half of the states do not allow unitary taxation. Approximately a dozen states require it. Of those that require it, the majority do not require unitary taxation outside of the US, but a few require unitary taxation on a worldwide basis. The other dozen or so states provide that unitary taxation may either be required by the state or elected by the taxpayer. Even with such a requirement or election, most of those states do not provide for unitary taxation on a worldwide basis but stop "at the water's edge."

Most states require corporations operating either under domestic or foreign license to pay a franchise tax for permission to operate in a corporate form. The bases for that tax vary from state to state. The largest number of states tie the franchise tax to the capital structure of the corporation. Approximately 16 states utilize this structure. Approximately a dozen states simply charge a flat fee. At least one state utilizes a capitalization approach for its domestic corporations and a flat fee approach for its foreign corporations. A few states use a complicated formula involving net worth and net income as a basis for calculation of a franchise tax. However, in approximately a dozen states, the franchise tax and corporate income tax are one in the same such that a separate franchise tax does not truly exist. However, such states will still

---

[89] The general definition of doing business has been stated as follows:

"It is established by well considered general authorities that a foreign corporation is doing, transacting, carrying on, or engaging in business within a state when it transacts some substantial part of its ordinary business therein." *Royal Insurance Co. v. All States Theatres*, 6 So.2d 494 (Ala. 1942).

usually require the payment of a fee with the filing of the corporation's annual report to the state.

ARTICLE 2A-LEASES

A new article for the UCC has been proposed that will, for the first time, provide a statutory codification of leasing law. It is called Article 2A-Leases (the Article). While an in-depth discussion of this lengthy law is beyond the scope of this chapter, some of the Article's more important points deserve mention.

Scope of Coverage

The Article applies to any transaction, regardless of form, that creates a lease. It does not apply to conditional sales or loans that may appear documented as a lease. It covers all leasing transactions, whether business or consumer, daily rental or multimillion dollar leveraged lease transactions. There are no exemptions or exceptions from coverage of the Article. However, there are differences in treatment in certain areas for finance leases and consumer leases.

The Finance Lease

Most importantly, the Article recognizes that a modern finance lease is different from a traditional rental or bailment and creates a statutory definition of a finance lease that will provide a qualifying finance lessor with several major benefits:

1. As a matter of law, after acceptance of the leased property, the lease is not revocable and the lessee must pay rent without excuse
2. As a matter of law, a finance lessor does not make any implied warranties such as merchantability or fitness for a particular purpose as a matter of law.

A finance lease is defined as follows:

"Finance lease" means a lease in which (i) the lessor does not select, manufacture or supply the goods, (ii) the lessor acquires the goods in connection with the lease, and (iii) either the lessee receives a copy of the contract evidencing the lessor's purchase of the goods on or before signing the lease contract, or the lessee's approval of the contract evidencing the lessor's purchase of the goods is a condition to effectiveness of the lease contract [UCC, §2A-103(1)(g)].

Freedom of Contract

The lessor and lessee can still contract for treatment different from that provided by the Article. Although some courts may be confused by the detail of the Article (which can, depending upon typesetting, exceed 180 pages), it is fundamental to the Article's creation that freedom of contract be preserved. The Article's provisions will come into play when the parties have failed to address any particular matter by contract or when specific contract terms are unenforceable or otherwise fail.

Time Value of Money

The Article recognizes the time value of money concept and requires that future lease payments accelerated upon default must be discounted to present value. Some recent court cases have held that such an acceleration without a discount to present value constitutes a penalty and is unenforceable. The Article accepts such findings.

Remedies and Damages

The Article provides a complex and convoluted remedies and damages scheme for those parties who have not specified damages by contract, or whose contract provisions are unenforceable or otherwise fail. The Article provides for different damage calculations depending upon whether or not the lessor leaves the leased property with the lessee for the duration of the lease, repossesses the property and, after repossession, disposes of it by re-lease by a lease that is substantially similar, or by one that is not substantially similar, or by sale or other disposition. The basic underlying principle of damage computation is that the lessee's original rent will be compared to fair market rent. The result will be that the parties having to use the remedies provision of the Article will find their simple collection actions converted to expensive expert witness battles.

True Lease versus Secured Transaction

The Article also clarifies those factors to be considered and not considered in determining when a lease is not a true lease but, rather, a secured transaction. The Article provides that net lease terms (such as the lessee assumes the risk of loss of the goods or agrees to pay taxes, insurance, filings, recordings or registration fees, or service or maintenance costs with respect to the goods), or the fact that the lease is a full-payout lease or that the lease has a fixed price renewal or purchase option, do not, in and of themselves, indicate a transaction purporting to be a lease is a secured transaction. However, the Article still does not state in a positive fashion what constitutes a true lease.

CONCLUSION

The legal considerations in leasing are many and complex. By its nature this overview has had to be simple and basic. All parties to a lease transaction should always seek competent legal advice respecting their business activities.

CHAPTER TWENTY-ONE
COMMERCIAL VEHICLE LEASING

Although this book focuses on the many aspects of equipment leasing, there is a large and viable vehicle leasing industry that deserves mention. The basics of the equipment leasing and vehicle leasing industries are very similar, yet due to certain unique characteristics of vehicle leasing, they are usually addressed separately. Because of the many similarities between the two industries, the majority of the concepts presented earlier can be applied to vehicle leasing; however, there are differences. These differences and the unique characteristics of vehicle leasing are presented in this chapter. Topics discussed include:

- Vehicle Leasing Today
- Taxation
- Pricing
- Truck Leasing.

VEHICLE LEASING TODAY

The practice of leasing vehicles developed around the turn of this century, although it was not until after World War II that significant growth and interest (primarily regarding automobiles) in the industry were generated. This growth in leasing was a function of the pent-up demand for vehicles after the war, and the ability of leasing companies to utilize prewar relationships with the manufacturers in obtaining a scarce product. The influx of returning veterans into the workforce, many as salespeople requiring transportation, added to demand. After this initial impetus, the vehicle lease industry continued to grow.

Industry Statistics

Total leasing revenue since the war has increased an average of 24% annually. Total lease revenues for 1986 were approximately $53.4 billion dollars, compared to $15.7 billion in 1975; this represents an increase in dollar volume of 240% over the last decade.

The following segments comprise total lease revenue for 1986 ($53.4 billion):

Cars (fleet leased)	59%
Trucks (leased)	21%
Car and truck (rental)	20%

Nationwide, 4,578,000 cars and 913,000 light trucks were leased in 1986 for a total of 5,491,000 vehicles. This compares with a total of 3,985,000 cars and trucks in 1975. The growth in the number of vehicles leased is shown in Figure 1. An *Automotive Fleet* magazine survey outlines the composition of the fleet leasing market (Tables 1 and 2).

As indicated in Tables 1 and 2, the business/corporate sector represents the majority of the car and truck leasing market in the US. It is interesting to note that the second largest segment of the market for cars is the daily rental sector, while the second largest segment of the truck leasing market is the utility sector.

Currently, approximately 10,000 vehicle lessors throughout the country serve the vehicle needs of lessees. Of this group, the top 10 leasing companies in the nation write between 50,000 and 275,000 vehicle leases (each) per year. In 1986 alone, the top 10 lessors wrote approximately

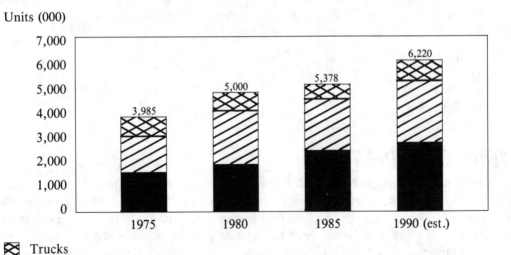

Figure 1
Number of Vehicles Leased

Table 1
Composition of Automobile Fleets

Sector	Portion
Business/corporate	59.0%
Utilities	11.6%
Government	11.3%
Daily rental	16.7%
Police/taxi	1.4%
Average annual mileage	27,500
Average trade-in time (months)	30.2

Source: *Automotive Fleet 1987 Fact Book.*

Table 2
Composition of Light Truck/Van Fleets

Sector	Portion
Business/corporate	57.1%
Utilities	27.8%
Government	12.6%
Rental/police/taxi	2.5%
Average annual mileage	18,500
Average trade-in time (months)	60.5

Source: *Automotive Fleet 1987 Fact Book.*

1,164,000 vehicle leases. This is almost double the number of leases written by the top 10 in 1979.

The average capitalized cost of automobiles leased in 1986 was $15,969. This represents a 26% increase over the prior 3-year period. In contrast, a recent survey conducted by the National Automobile Dealers Association indicates the average selling price of an automobile in 1986 was $12,800. This difference is mitigated somewhat by the addition of tax and licensing costs to the sales price of the car. However, the difference remains approximately $2,200 to $2,500, indicating additional profit taking through mark-ups by lessors. Research estimates forecast vehicle leasing revenues will exceed $62 billion in 1990, as the vehicle leasing industry continues as a viable and competitive financing alternative for consumers and corporations alike.

Reasons for Vehicle Leasing

There are many reasons for the popularity of vehicle leasing, most of which are the same as those discussed for equipment leasing in Chapter Two. Some, however, are specific to vehicle leasing. For instance, vehicle leasing provides a better allocation of resources than purchasing. Lessees do not want to be in the vehicle business. Leasing removes the hassle of the acquisition and disposition of fleets, maintenance, etc. This frees personnel to conduct the normal business of the company. Additionally, vehicles are more likely to be well-maintained when the lessor is responsible for maintenance (since it is in the lessor's best interest to do so). This, of course, also benefits the lessee, who has a well-maintained fleet without the headaches and scheduling problems associated with ownership.

Conservation of capital is a major reason for companies to lease all types of property. This is particularly true for a company that has seasonal transportation needs. Rather than expend funds to purchase vehicles that will be utilized for only part of the time, a company can lease those vehicles, thereby matching costs with usage. By the same token, lessees may attempt to pass the costs associated with heavy usage of a vehicle to a lessor by leasing those vehicles the lessee expects to take a beating. This is not always successful if the lessor builds appropriate over-use fees and residual positions into the leases.

Residual reliability also plays an important role in vehicle leasing. Automobile residuals are well-established and there is an efficient wholesale market. Because of this, the lessor is exposed to less risk than in, for instance, a lease of high technology equipment. This, in turn, gives the lessee more flexibility in requesting various structures, exercising purchase options, etc.

Types of Leases

There are some differences in terminology between equipment and vehicle leasing. A closed-end lease in vehicle leasing, for instance, relates to the risk associated with the residual, not the availability of ownership, as in equipment leasing. In vehicle leasing, a closed-end lease is one in which the lessee can walk away from the lease at the end of the term, without any additional obligations (except, of course, for any unique wear and tear charges). Residual risk is closed to the lessee in this type of lease.

In an open-end lease, on the other hand, the lessee is open to residual risk. The lessee in an open-end lease guarantees a certain value to the lessor at the end of the lease term. This value can be received by the lessor either through the selling price, an amount paid by the lessee or a combination of both. Ownership is neither required nor precluded under either of these leases. If the lessee decides to buy, the purchase price would be fair market value in the closed-end lease, and the amount of the guarantee in the open-end lease. Another type of lease with a guaranteed residual, the Terminal Rental Adjustment Clause (TRAC) lease, is discussed later in the chapter.

The concepts of net leases and full-service (maintenance) leases in vehicle leasing are the same as in equipment leasing. Full-service leases may run the gamut of truly full-service leases to partial-service leases. For many lessors (particularly dealers), a full-service lease makes good sense because the lessors have service facilities and ready markets for well-maintained used cars. As mentioned earlier, the full-service lease also benefits the lessee. Lessors can often offer corporate lessees better rates on these services than those available to the lessee, due to lessor economies of scale.

The many tax lease products discussed in previous chapters are also available in vehicle leasing. Furthermore, the accounting guidelines apply equally to vehicle leasing. Whether a lease is capital or not, from an accounting perspective, is generally more clearcut in vehicle leasing, due to the size of the residuals. Open-end leases are, for the most part, capital, while closed-end leases are generally operating leases, depending, of course, on the vehicle being leased.

TAXATION

Vehicle leasing tax law is predicated upon general tax law; therefore, the precepts and principles of Chapters Three and Four apply here also. Differences applicable to vehicle tax law, however, are highlighted and discussed in this section.

Modified Accelerated Cost Recovery System

Vehicles are depreciated under the Modified Accelerated Cost Recovery System (MACRS). Over-the-road tractor units are 3-year classlife property with a 4-year Asset Depreciation Range (ADR) life, automobiles and light duty trucks are 5-year classlife property with 5-year ADR lives and trailers are 5-year classlife property with a 6-year ADR life. The standard conventions and methodologies apply to vehicle lease depreciation. There are unique depreciation characteristics in vehicle leasing, however.

LUXURY CAR PROVISIONS

Automobiles are considered listed property (business property subject to private use by taxpayers). Depreciation on listed property is limited for owners, other than lessors, of certain passenger automobiles classed as luxury automobiles. A luxury automobile is any passenger automobile with a cost greater than or equal to $12,800. A passenger automobile is defined as any four-wheeled vehicle that is manufactured primarily for use on public streets, roads and highways, and rated at 6,000 pounds unloaded gross vehicle weight or less. (In the case of a truck or van, gross vehicle weight is substituted for unloaded gross vehicle weight.)

The term passenger automobile does not include any (1) ambulance, hearse or combination ambulance-hearse used by the taxpayer directly in a trade or business, (2) vehicle used by the taxpayer directly in the trade or business of transporting persons or property for compensation or hire, (3) commuter highway vehicle or (4), under regulations, any truck or van.

The limitation on the MACRS deduction available for luxury automobiles is in the form of a ceiling on the annual deduction. As an example, assume a company purchases and places in service an automobile for $22,000 and the automobile is used 100% for business purposes. Table 3 illustrates the amount of the annual MACRS deduction for an user/owner and for a lessor/owner who is not affected by these rules. Any MACRS deduction is further reduced by the percent of nonbusiness use, making the maximum depreciation available equal to the percent business use for the asset.

For example, a taxpayer buys a $16,000 automobile, which is subject to the luxury car limitations. In year 1 the business use is 70%, in year 2 75%, in year 3 80%, in year 4 60%, in

Table 3
Luxury Car Limitations

Year	User/Owner MACRS	Lessor/Owner MACRS
1	$ 2,560	$ 4,400
2	4,100	7,040
3	2,450	4,224
4	1,475	2,534
5	1,475	2,534
6	1,475	1,268
7	1,475	0
8	1,475	0
9	1,475	0
10	1,475	0
11	1,475	0
12	1,090	0
Total	$ 22,000	$ 22,000

year 5 65%, in year 6 60%, in year 7 55% and in year 8 55%. The MACRS recovery deductions, assuming no inflation, are shown in Table 4.

If listed property is not used predominantly in a qualified business use for any taxable year (greater than 50%), the MACRS deduction for that year (which includes the §179 deduction) and subsequent years is determined in accordance with the Alternative Depreciation System. Therefore, if, in the previous example, business use was less than 50%, the taxpayer would be required to utilize 5-year straight-line depreciation, with the half-year convention, also subject to the business use limitations. If business use falls below 51%, any excess of MACRS deductions over straight-line depreciation must be recaptured in the year the drop occurs.

In an attempt to maintain parity between the use of equipment, either through ownership or through leasing, Congress issued a set of complex rules. Under these rules, lessees are entitled to deduct only a portion of the lease payments. This portion, through its impact on the lessee's tax position, is intended to be the lease equivalent of the limitations associated with ownership. As a result, lessees of luxury automobiles must include an amount in income (the inclusion amount). This amount is based on fair market value, the quarter the automobile is placed in service, the percent of business use and the number of days the automobile is in use during the year. This amount is determined through reference to tables issued by the Internal Revenue Service. When business use drops to less than or equal to 50%, an additional inclusion amount must be computed in the year of the drop.

Table 4
Business Use Limitations

Year	Maximum MACRS Deductions	Percentage of Business Use	Allowable MACRS Deductions
1	$ 2,560	70%	$ 1,792
2	4,100	75	3,075
3	2,450	80	1,960
4	1,475	60	885
5	1,475	65	959
6	1,475	60	885
7	1,475	55	811
8	990		544
	$ 16,000		$ 10,911

TRAC Leases

As a general rule, a lease most likely will not be considered a true lease if it contains a lessee guaranteed residual. In a TRAC lease, however, and if the lease otherwise qualifies as a true tax lease, the existence of a guaranteed residual (the TRAC) will not be cause to disallow the tax lease treatment. It should be noted that the mere existence of a TRAC does not imply true tax lease status.

TRAC leases may be written on automobiles, trucks and trailers. To be considered a TRAC lease, a lease on any of the foregoing vehicle types must be a true tax lease and also meet the following three criteria:

1. The lessor must maintain a minimum at-risk position equal to the borrowings used to fund the vehicle (in essence no nonrecourse financing)
2. The lessor must obtain a lessee certification that the lessee will use the vehicle more than 50% for business
3. The lessor must not know the foregoing certification is false.

TRAC leases serve as a stimulus to the vehicle economy, due to the inherent pricing flexibility in these leases. TRAC leases should, theoretically, be priced lower than conventional tax leases due to elimination of the lessor's residual risk.

PRICING

The basic principles of vehicle lease pricing are identical to those of equipment leasing, particularly for the larger transactions. However, there are some differences in pricing methodologies between the two industries, depending upon the size and sophistication of the lessor.

Depreciation is one of the key concepts in vehicle lease pricing. In early pricing models the payment consisted of three components — depreciation, interest and lessor profit. Depreciation from a pricing perspective is different from either tax or accounting depreciation. In this context, depreciation represents the difference between the capitalized cost and the lessor's residual position. This amount is the principal to be recovered in the lease. Each month the payment returns a portion of the depreciation (principal) to the lessor.

The other components of the payment consist of interest on the outstanding balance in the lease (unrecovered depreciation plus the residual) and profit to the lessor. This profit component should be sufficient to cover all overhead plus provide a reasonable return to the lessor. A common worksheet format to compute a payment using this method (on a level yield basis) is shown in Figure 2. Many smaller lessors use the worksheet approach because it provides documentation of the decision, allows for a logical flow in the rate development and provides an organized format so that all items are considered. When attempting to price to a targeted hurdle rate, however, this approach cannot be considered an accurate pricing method. Reference should be made to the accurate methods of pricing discussed in Chapters Eight and Nine.

TRUCK LEASING

The truck leasing market has origins as far back as the automobile leasing market. Truck leasing, however, was well-accepted long before the leasing of cars in high volume occurred. This acceptability was due to several factors. First, truck leasing was business oriented. Businesses were far more amenable to leasing than were consumers, and, early on, trucks were utilized much more extensively in business than were cars.

More importantly, however, the truck leasing industry was able to provide a complete transportation service, including maintenance, insurance, taxes and, in many cases, a driver. This full-service approach to leasing has long been a hallmark of the truck leasing industry and continues today. This is not to say that leasing as a pure financing tool is not being used also, for it is. Many lessors, though, still find the traditional full-service approach a valuable means of product differentiation.

The leasing of trucks is very similar to the leasing of automobiles. The pricing of residuals, however, poses some unique concerns since the resale market (i.e., standard and widespread sources of resale prices, auctions, etc.) is not as established as in the automobile market. Additional problems are created by the specialized nature of certain trucks such as those built to specifications, refrigeration or other sole use bodies and/or equipment.

The entrance of manufacturers into leasing has not been limited to equipment. Truck manufacturers also play an integral role in the financing of their products either through captives or vendor leasing programs. The manufacturers, along with the fleet lessors and many independent lessors, provide a creative financing alternative to meet the growing transportation needs of the country.

CAPITALIZED COST

1. Vehicle cost (includes preparation, options and dealer markup) $_____
2. Lease company profit   _____
3. Adjusted vehicle cost (1 + 2) $_____
4. Credit to adjusted vehicle cost (trade-in or capitalized cost reduction)   _____
5. Sales tax _____ %   _____
6. Other (insurance, service contract)   _____
7. Total capitalized cost (3 + 4 + 5 – 6) $_____

RESIDUAL VALUE

8. Guidebook _____ $_____
9. Excess mileage   _____
10. Market adjustment   _____
11. Reconditioning   _____
12. Inflation adjustment   _____
13. Estimated residual value (8 – 9 ± 10 + 11 + 12) $_____

DEPRECIATION

14. Total capitalized cost (line 7) $_____
15. Estimated residual (line 13)   _____
16. Total depreciation (7 – 13) $_____

INTEREST

17. Total capitalized cost $_____
18. Estimated residual value   _____
19. Total (17 + 18) $_____
20. Simple interest rate _____
21. Lease term _____
22. Money factor _____
23. Total interest (19 × 22) $_____

LEASE PAYMENT

24. Depreciation $_____
25. Interest   _____
26. Total $_____
27. Base payment (26 ÷ term) $_____
28. Sales tax (tax rate × 27)   _____
29. Subtotal (27 + 28) $_____
30. Other: Insurance $_____
                  Taxes   _____
                  Maintenance   _____
31. Lease payment (29 + 30) $_____

Figure 2
Standard Worksheet

CONCLUSION

Vehicle leasing, for the most part, is very similar to equipment leasing. The basic principles of finance apply to both vehicle and equipment leasing, as do the principles of accounting and taxation. Lease portfolio analysis is the same, as is the lease versus buy decision. Of course, as previously discussed, the residual plays a much greater role in vehicle leasing than in equipment leasing, a fact that impacts the analysis, tax and accounting provisions.

Although traditionally viewed as two distinct industries, the equipment and vehicle leasing industries are actually companion industries, each complementing the other. Many vehicle lessors find equipment leasing to be the next logical step in the development of their businesses as they recognize the profit and growth potential equipment leasing has to offer. Regardless of initial focus, with proper study and preparation, lessors can understand either industry, and find profits and opportunities in both.

CHAPTER TWENTY-TWO
TRENDS IN LEASING

During the past decade, we have had the opportunity to meet many people, see diverse practices, encounter some thorny problems and enjoy a broad range of experiences. Through our daily contact with all segments of the leasing industry — lessees, captives, independent lessors, lease brokers, managers and sales, accounting, tax and credit personnel, etc. — we have been able to keep our finger on the pulse of the industry. By combining this feel for the industry with our vast knowledge, experience and judgment, we have been able to identify and predict important trends developing within the leasing industry. Over the years, many of these predictions have come true, while others are still in the formative stage.

After having presented a wealth of information concerning leasing as it is today, it is only appropriate at this point that we look toward the future of leasing by outlining and discussing several key trends that are, or will be, significantly influencing the leasing industry in the years ahead. These key trends are:

- Increase in Demand For Leasing
- Increase in Mergers and Acquisitions
- Proliferation of Vendor Leasing
- Growth of Full-service Leasing
- Increase in Operating Leases
- Importance of Lessor Niches
- Greater Foreign Competition (Domestically)
- Increased Opportunities for US Companies Abroad
- Emergence of a Comprehensive Financial Theory of Leasing
- Greater Uniformity of Laws Regarding Leasing
- Increased Interest in Consumer Leasing.

Some of these trends are ongoing; others represent subtle shifts in prior trends, but the majority represent fresh, new insights — a direct result of the many changes that have occurred recently in tax, financial reporting and industry practices.

INCREASE IN DEMAND FOR LEASING

The leasing industry has experienced enviable growth in recent years, and this trend will continue, due to a number of significant factors. First, the growing sophistication of the lessee populace through their awareness and understanding of leasing will play a critical role in the increased demand for lease financing. Much of this awareness can be attributed to the lessors who have taken the time and effort to become knowledgeable of the many facets of the industry. This knowledge has benefitted both them and their lessees, and, hence, furthered the growth of the industry. Acquirers of equipment can no longer afford to blindly continue purchasing equipment as they may have done in the past. Due to complex tax changes, the economics of equipment financing have been altered substantially, and a full understanding of leasing has become essential.

Over time, as increasingly sophisticated lessees more closely assess the tax impact and resulting economic benefits of leasing versus buying, they will also gain a greater appreciation for, and be influenced by, the many qualitative benefits of leasing. In many instances, such factors as cash flow availability, transfer of technological obsolescence risks, off balance sheet financing and service, flexibility and convenience have swayed the lease versus buy decision to favor the lease. Therefore, a greater understanding of leasing by astute lessees will cause them to more properly analyze the economic and qualitative benefits of leasing, and, hence, more readily opt for the lease alternative.

The tax benefits of equipment ownership have changed dramatically. The many new tax issues facing potential acquirers of equipment now tend to favor the use of equipment through leasing, as opposed to actual ownership. The alternative minimum tax (AMT), for example, is here to stay, for it has become a politically acceptable means of raising revenue without increasing tax rates. Under AMT, the purchase of equipment has been made more costly for many taxpayers, due to the accelerated depreciation preference. In addition, other quirks, such as the midquarter depreciation convention, have made taxpayers very concerned about the tax impact of equipment acquisition.

These two tax considerations, as well as others such as the impact of equipment financing on a corporation's foreign tax credit position, have caused many profitable companies to reassess their need to purchase and own equipment, and to more seriously consider equipment leasing. Of course, companies that could not effectively utilize the tax benefits associated with equipment ownership in a given period have, for some time, recognized the value of equipment leasing. Leasing, therefore, will be used increasingly by both profitable and less profitable companies alike.

Aside from tax considerations and increasing lessee sophistication, there are also the over 30 other reasons for leasing presented in Chapter Two. The continued popularity of leasing after the Tax Reform Act of 1986 further validated the importance of these nontax benefits, all of which will contribute to the increase in demand for leasing.

INCREASE IN MERGERS AND ACQUISITIONS

The major force behind the future increase in mergers and acquisitions is that many leasing companies will realize or project fundamental shifts in their competitive advantages in the marketplace. Obviously, the same tax considerations that will cause more lessees to lease, versus purchase, equipment, such as AMT and the midquarter convention, will have similar impact on lessors of equipment. Leasing companies faced with adverse tax situations may find themselves uncompetitive in the leasing marketplace, as tax laws will not affect all companies in the same manner, or to the same extent. Many of these companies will seek a buyer willing to purchase all or a portion of their company. As the leasing industry has matured, exhibiting staying power and profitability, many companies also have become ripe for acquisition.

As owners of depreciable equipment, leasing companies, in general, should be concerned with AMT. Bank lessors, however, are owned by large parents (a bank or bank holding company) who tend to have less depreciable assets than more capital-intensive industries. Thus, although the bank lessor could, in and of itself, have a severe AMT problem, the larger parent may very well be able to shelter it. This is a good illustration of one of the factors driving some of the merger and acquisition activity, and of course, could be analogized to captive lessors as well.

Many firms attempting to hedge against, or plan for future, yet unforeseen changes in the leasing industry will diversify their businesses. Leasing companies will diversify from either an equipment, a marketplace (small, middle, large ticket) and/or a geographic standpoint. While growth in diversified areas can be accomplished internally, many firms will move to a quicker resolution of strategic issues through external means, such as mergers and acquisitions.

As competition becomes more fierce and tax benefits play a diminishing role in leasing, lessors will be forced to seek alternative sources of profit. Vertical integration (control over the means of production and/or distribution) shows signs of becoming a lucrative alternative source of profit. To control costs, a lessor could become a dealer and purchase the equipment to be leased at wholesale prices. The lessor already has the product and marketing knowledge, and the skills and resources that readily qualify it as a dealer.

Nonfinancial firms are also acquiring leasing companies (conglomerate integration) for a variety of reasons. Diversification is often cited by these firms as a reason for entering into the financial services industry, as is the need to develop financing capabilities and expertise for related companies. A nonfinancial firm simply may be interested in increasing its corporate-wide return on equity as it considers the profitability of the leasing industry. Other firms still may be interested in the tax benefits that an equipment lessor, as an equipment owner, is capable of generating. Leasing companies will attempt to improve their operational economies of scale through mergers and acquisitions, thereby causing an increase in mergers and acquisitions.

PROLIFERATION OF VENDOR LEASING

Manufacturers and dealers will continue to see a need to provide leasing services in order to boost sales of their products, either through setting up their own internal financing organization or through vendor leasing agreements with independent third-party lessors. Numerous other reasons support this prognostication of increased vendor leasing. First, vendor lessors are in a superior position to manage the inherent residual risk in equipment leasing. They work very closely with the manufacturer or dealer and, therefore, have a better understanding of the equipment, its residual value, maintenance and repair requirements and other factors. Since equipment vendors are in the business of selling equipment, national and international marketing organizations already exist. Such residual knowledge and marketing expertise permit vendor lessors to offer very attractive, competitive lease programs.

Vendor leasing also aids equipment vendors in enhancing market size and in creating market control. Leasing, due to the contractual relationship between lessor and lessee, allows the vendor — through its captive leasing arm or through an independent vendor program — to control the critical junctures that impact the original sale, subsequent servicing and future sales of replacement products. Furthermore, many leases give the lessor inspection rights regarding repair and maintenance, thus providing the vendor with a legally sanctioned opportunity to exploit maintenance and other marketing opportunities.

The most important control point for a vendor lessor occurs at the end of the lease when the lessee has a legal obligation to inform the lessor whether it will exercise a purchase option and buy the equipment, renew the lease, return the equipment or upgrade the equipment for efficiency, capacity or by product line. Obviously, this legal obligation of the lessee to divulge to the lessor its intent regarding end-of-term options provides the equipment vendor with advance marketing information that can be used by its sales representatives. This, plus the many other benefits, will cause a proliferation of vendor leasing.

GROWTH OF FULL-SERVICE LEASING

Full-service leasing, and the bundling of services, will grow in popularity, as lessees take advantage of the convenience, and lessors realize additional profits from this creative form of lease contract. Captive leasing companies can very readily provide additional services, such as maintenance and insurance; however, independents also provide full-service leases by subcontracting for services that are then bundled into the lease.

Types of services being bundled or conducive to bundling include maintenance, performance guarantees, swaps of working equipment for nonworking equipment during repair, repair parts, supplies, chemicals, additives, reagents for medical equipment and software. Other types of services that potentially may be bundled are casualty insurance, property taxes, sales tax, human labor, installation and delivery charges, deinstallation charges, architectural, engineering and design assistance for potential equipment.

The ascendance of bundled leasing is a logical result of the service nature of leasing. If a lease is viewed as a service arrangement, adding extra services as part of a service package makes sense, especially if the lessor can lower the overall cost of the bundled services. Lessors that specialize in certain equipment types, for example, may be able to offer maintenance at a low price due to economies of scale resulting from volume and their specialization.

Captive lessors have taken the lead in full-service leasing, but independent third-party lessors will shortly follow suit. Growth in full-service leasing can be expected because it facilitates product differentiation and provides the lessee with a convenient and affordable product.

INCREASE IN OPERATING LEASES

A variety of tax, economic and financial reporting considerations will add to the number of operating leases in the marketplace. One overriding factor necessary for, and contributing to, the increase of operating leases from a lessor perspective is a strong secondary market for used equipment.

There are several factors that support a strong secondary market. As businesses hold existing equipment longer, thus lowering the supply of used equipment, and purchase used equipment in lieu of new equipment, the combined decrease in supply and increase in demand for used equipment results in higher prices.

Furthermore, the dependence of vendor lessors upon residual values forces the manufacturers to be careful in the introduction of more technologically advanced equipment, lest it outmode previous models and cause an impairment of residual values. Another economic trend supporting used equipment prices is the demand for used equipment outside the United States.

The direct consequence of used equipment holding its resale value is that lessors should be able to depend more upon residual values in structuring their leases. Since there now are fewer tax benefits that can be transferred by lessors to lessees in the form of lower lease rates, there also will be corresponding lessee pressure for lessors to take greater residual positions in order to keep lease rates lower. Greater residual reliance in lease structuring results in lower lease rates to lessees, higher profit to the lessor, or a combination of both. As a lessor offers lower lease rates to lessees, those leases also stand a better chance of qualifying for operating lease status per Financial Accounting Standards Board Statement No. 13.

Lessees increasingly are being attracted to operating leases and rental programs, especially when obsolescence avoidance is considered an important consideration or when the asset is needed for short-term or experimental use. Then, too, some captive lessors use rentals and operating leases as marketing tools to encourage lessees to try out products with short-term commitments, in the hope those same lessees will subsequently buy or convert to longer-term leases.

Of course, off balance sheet financing will remain a strong selling point for the use of operating leases. This, plus the other motive forces such as improved residual value management, shorter-term leases and rate pressures, will prompt increases in operating leases.

IMPORTANCE OF LESSOR NICHES

No longer can leasing companies allow themselves the luxury of being equipment leasing generalists in an increasingly complex industry and unpredictable economy. Therefore, lessors will find their niche, focusing on specialized opportunities and markets. For example, they will concentrate on a particular ticket size, align themselves with specific lessee industries and attempt to better understand specific industry and product economics, peculiarities and needs. They also will limit the range of equipment they lease, thus allowing themselves to become more expert in the residual management of specific types of equipment. For many, recognizing the importance of lessor niches will be the key to survival.

GREATER FOREIGN COMPETITION (DOMESTICALLY)

US leasing companies will face increasing foreign competition domestically, from captive leasing subsidiaries of foreign equipment manufacturers, foreign banks and foreign independent leasing companies. The entrance of foreign banks into leasing is natural since the same economic forces that have prompted US banks to enter leasing are now impacting these banks. Foreign banks, other than United Kingdom banks, have only recently begun to exploit leasing. The enormous size of certain of these entities, however, could lead to a significant penetration of the leasing market as they offer leasing to their existing, as well as new, customers. Some foreign banks have lower costs of funds than US lenders, which further enhances the competitive position of the foreign player.

One of the economic underpinnings influencing the entrance of foreign lessors into the US leasing marketplace relates to balance of trade surpluses with the US. Japan, for example, has such a surplus. Japan's surplus in US dollars can be used to: (1) buy US goods for consumption in Japan (not yet popular); (2) invest in the US money, bond and stock markets; (3) invest in US equipment for lease to Second and Third World countries; or (4) invest in US equipment for lease to US lessees (direct leasing competition). The latter two utilizations of trade surplus dollars increase competition in the US domestic market and, possibly, foreign leasing markets. Due to these reasons, there will be greater foreign competition domestically.

INCREASED OPPORTUNITIES FOR US COMPANIES ABROAD

Expansion of leasing into Second and Third World leasing markets will continue. Nations in the process of industrialization require capital, but have a paucity of cash for equipment acquisition. Leasing represents a feasible solution to the problem since the lessor provides the capital and the lessee pays only for use of the equipment over time. Given the many benefits of leasing, the reason why it has taken emerging nations so long to adopt leasing as a means of solving capital shortages has always been puzzling. Of course, part of the answer lies in the legal complexities involving repossession and other problems connected with collection.

Laws are being passed by many countries to encourage foreign leasing. For example, Turkey has passed a series of laws that facilitates repossession, foreign leasing and foreign investment in Turkish leasing companies. As the world grows smaller, the export of financial services will increase.

International leasing on the part of US leasing companies traditionally has been centered primarily in Western Europe. Recent economic activity in Southeast Asia, as well as in China and Arab countries, has shifted the focus of many US leasing companies who are now researching leasing potential in these areas. All these factors indicate increased opportunities for US companies abroad.

EMERGENCE OF A COMPREHENSIVE FINANCIAL THEORY OF LEASING

Although far from complete, a theory of leasing addressing questions that have puzzled both lessors and lessees for years will continue to emerge. Questions important to the lessor, such as the appropriateness of external rate of return yields, what constitutes yield, the validity of various yield assumptions and debt optimization in leveraged leases, the impact of various structuring techniques and the adequate level of return on a lessor's equity in a highly leveraged transaction, are finally being answered.

Questions important to the lessee are also being answered. As software for lease and loan negotiating and analysis becomes more available, the resolution of previously unanswered financial questions becomes even more feasible. Answers as to the appropriate discount rate to use, lease versus buy comparisons in regulated environments, dual rate discounting, the integration of factors such as net operating loss displacement into financial decisions and many other issues will contribute to this emergence of a comprehensive financial theory of leasing.

GREATER UNIFORMITY OF LAWS REGARDING LEASING

As leasing became a popular mode of equipment financing, the necessity for regulation increased. Leasing, however, was little understood by regulators in the 1950s and 1960s, which resulted in numerous and, at times, contradictory and ambiguous laws governing leasing. However, there will be a trend towards uniformity in the laws and regulations governing leasing. Unfortunately, the regulatory objective of properly defining a lease appears to be the slowest in evolving. Once all regulatory agencies and governments agree on the essential attributes of a lease, the goal of standardization will be more easily met. Legislators, regulators and judges now are informing themselves about leasing prior to legislating, regulating and adjudicating. Although by no means standard yet, there will be greater uniformity of laws regarding leasing, as the Internal Revenue Service Code, Securities and Exchange Commission regulations, Uniform Commercial Code, bankruptcy laws and state laws strive to achieve the same regulatory objectives.

INCREASED INTEREST IN CONSUMER LEASING

There will be an increase in the volume and type of consumer leasing. Over the past 20 to 30 years many consumers have been introduced to leasing through an exposure to vehicle leasing. Consumer vehicle leasing recently has gained considerable momentum, as many have opted for the lower up-front costs and monthly payments, as well as the ability that leasing provides to obtain a more expensive car. The loss of the interest tax deduction on consumer loans will also prompt more consumers to seriously consider the lease, versus the purchase, option.

Vehicle leasing statistics support the estimate that approximately 50% of all new automobiles will be leased in the next 5 to 10 years. The acceptance of leasing as a financing tool in the vehicle market is spreading to other consumer marketplaces as well. Personal computers and other types of office equipment for home use are now being leased more often than before. Consumers are able to acquire the use of various equipment sooner than they normally would have been able to through the use of leasing. This trend is expected to increase dramatically as more consumers are exposed to, and, subsequently, exhibit increased interest in, consumer leasing.

CONCLUSION

The trends of the leasing industry presented in this chapter portray a very favorable outlook for the leasing industry of the future. Over time, these trends will substantially contribute to the widespread use and acceptance of equipment leasing as a strong, viable and creative financing alternative. In addition, the fundamental benefits of leasing that have existed for over 4,000 years, such as affordability, cash management and the transfer of risk, will continue to support a very strong base from which the equipment leasing industry can grow.

Just as in the past, the creative marketing and structuring efforts of the leasing industry will make the concept of leasing even more acceptable and realistic to the acquirers of equipment in the years ahead. If history can be considered a prologue to the future, the professionals in the leasing industry will step forward to meet the ever-changing and challenging needs presented by the financial service marketplace of the future.

Part 6
APPENDICES

APPENDIX A

DEBT FUNDING ACCOUNTING ISSUES
(CHAPTER ELEVEN)

The section in the appendix on accounting issues related to debt funding consists of three documents:

- Accounting By Lease Brokers
- Emerging Issues Task Force Issue No. 84-25
- Amembal & Isom Letter to the FASB

ACCOUNTING BY LEASE BROKERS

The Accounting by Lease Brokers Issues Paper is reprinted by permission of the American Institute of Certified Public Accountants, Inc.

June 20, 1980
File 3424

ISSUES PAPER

ACCOUNTING BY LEASE BROKERS

Prepared by
The Task Force on Accounting by Lease Brokers
Accounting Standards Division
American Institute of Certified Public Accountants

TABLE OF CONTENTS

---

[1] Page numbers have been adjusted to reflect the page numbers of this Appendix.

---

[2] Appendix I and II of this document have not been included.

INTRODUCTION

1. A party, called a lease broker for purposes of this paper, serves as an intermediary between a lessor and a lessee for a fee. The fee may be a cash payment at the closing of the lease transaction, rights to share in the proceeds from the sale or release of leased assets (share of the residual value) at the end of the initial lease term, or both. A lease broker may provide various related services to lessors, lessees, and third party financers (lenders), may assume various risks related to the lease transactions, may receive several additional benefits, and may receive his compensation in various forms.

2. Lease brokers currently account for transactions in which they are involved in various ways. This paper discusses the issues surrounding the nature and characteristics of transactions of lease brokers and the accounting for such transactions.

3. Transactions in which lease brokers act as intermediaries span a spectrum. At one end, the lease broker acts purely as an intermediary, bringing together parties to leases. Or, he may participate in the lease rights and duties to a greater or lesser extent. At the other end of the spectrum, the lease broker's participation in the terms of the lease may be so great that he appears to be a lessor or lessee and not merely an intermediary, and his accounting may be guided by FASB Statement No. 13, "Accounting for Leases."

4. A lease broker may, in form, be a lessor, but since he has little or no continued involvement in the lease, he may, in substance, be a broker. Conversely, although a lease broker may in form be an intermediary, he may, in substance, be a lessor or a lessee because of the responsibilities he assumes.

5. For purposes of this paper, a lease broker transaction is one in which a lease broker acts, in substance, as an intermediary between a lessor and a lessee, and his involvement is not sufficient to qualify the transaction as one that he should account for under FASB Statement No. 13. Conditions to determine whether his involvement is sufficient are discussed in this paper.

BACKGROUND

6. The lease brokerage industry originated from the need of parties not in the leasing business to obtain the services of parties knowledgeable in leasing to assist them in arranging leasing transactions. As leasing activities increased, more lease brokers entered the industry and competition increased. Lease brokers began to offer more services and assume greater risk to accommodate lessees and lessors.

Services Provided by Lease Brokers

7. A lease broker may provide a combination of the following services:

    a. Locates assets to be leased.

    b. Locates a lessee for the assets.

    c. Locates a lessor-investor.

    d. Negotiates the terms of the lease between the lessor and lessee.

    e. Assists in obtaining IRS tax rulings for the transaction and processes other necessary documentation.

    f. Arranges for financing.

    g. Guarantees that the lessee will make the payments called for during the initial lease term.

    h. Guarantees to the lessor a specified residual value of the leased assets at the end of the initial lease term.

    i. Obtains insurance on the residual value.

    j. Guarantees that a renewal lessee will make specified payments called for during the renewal lease term.

    k. Remarkets the leased assets during the initial lease term if the lessee defaults.

    l. Remarkets the leased assets at the end of the initial lease term if the lessee does not renew.

  m. Provides administrative services to the lessor or lender, such as handling billings, collections, and property taxes.

    n. Services, inspects, and maintains the leased property.

8. In some transactions, the lease broker may assume no risks that extend beyond the beginning of the initial lease term. Alternatively, in other transactions, he may assume various risks related to future guarantees. A lease broker may also participate both as an equity investor and as intermediary in the same transaction.

9. Examples of transactions in which lease brokers participate are presented in Appendix I.

Benefits Received by Lease Brokers

10. Lease brokers may receive benefits in one or a combination of the following forms of consideration:

    a. Cash fees paid at the closing of the transaction (beginning of the initial lease term) or over the initial lease term.

    b. All or a percentage of the residual value of the leased assets, payable at the end of the initial lease term.

    c. The right to become the lessee at the end of the initial lease term at less than a fair market rental (bargain rental) and sublease the assets at the market lease rate and retain the excess.

    d. The right to become the owner of the leased asset at the end of the initial lease term at less than fair market value (bargain price).

Money-over-Money Transactions

11. Lease brokers are sometimes involved in transactions called "money-over-money," in which the lease broker purchases an asset, obtains a lessee, and sells or assigns, on a nonrecourse basis, his right to receive rentals for the leased asset to unrelated third party financers for an amount that exceeds his investment in the leased asset. For example, the lease broker purchases an asset for $100,000, leases it to a lessee, and sells or assigns on a nonrecourse basis the right to receive rentals to a financer for $105,000. The lease broker receives $5,000 in excess of his cost at the beginning of the lease term plus he may also receive the right to the asset at the end of the initial lease term.

12. In a similar form of money-over-money transactions, the lease broker may pledge his right to receive rental payments and his residual value interest in the leased asset as collateral for a nonrecourse loan from an unrelated third party while retaining title to the leased asset.

13. The cash income to the lease broker for arranging the transaction is the excess of cash at the beginning of the lease term from the sale or assignment of the rental payments over his cost of the assets leased. The lease broker may also retain title to the leased asset (and thus have a right to the residual value) and receive income tax benefits, for example, investment tax credits and depreciation expense deductions.

PRESENT PRACTICE

Recording Fee Income

14. Frequently, a lease broker performs various services, with fees paid partly in cash at the beginning of the lease term and partly in rights to share in the proceeds from the sale or release of the assets at the end of the lease term. For the service of bringing together a lessor and a lessee and arranging the lease (brokerage service), lease brokers generally record as income the total cash fee plus the present value of the rights to the estimated residual value when the brokerage service is provided (at the beginning of the initial lease term). However, a few lease brokers recognize in income only the cash fee for brokerage services when the transaction is completed (at the beginning of the lease term) and recognize their share of the residual value when they receive the cash from disposing of the residual value.

15. Practice also varies as to the recognition of total fee income if a lease broker provides services in addition to bringing together the lessor and lessee and arranging the lease. Lease brokers may recognize all the fee income, some of the fee income, or none of the fee income at the inception of the lease depending in part on whether, in addition to brokering the lease, they have also agreed to remarket (paragraph 20), provide some form of guarantee (paragraph 21), or provide other services (paragraph 22). For example, if a lease broker provides a combination of services for a single fee (cash and a residual value share), practice varies as to whether and to what extent the lease broker allocates the single fee to the various

services and recognizes the fee income when the related service is rendered ("unbundling" — also see paragraph 19).

Money-over-Money Transactions

16. Money-over-money transactions are generally accounted for as brokerage transactions, that is, the excess of the cash received from third party financers or lessees over the cost of the assets leased is recorded as fee income at the beginning of the lease term. Any residual value retained is generally discounted and also recorded as fee income at the inception of the initial lease term. However, some account for money-over-money transactions as leases, recognizing the excess cash received in income over the lease term.

17. Practice also varies as to the balance sheet presentation for money-over-money transactions. Some reflect the transaction "net" (the nonrecourse borrowing offset against the lease receivable), consistent with the concept that the transaction is a brokerage transaction. A few, while they recognize fee income at the inception of the lease reflect the transaction "broad" on the balance sheet, that is, they do not offset assets and the nonrecourse borrowing. Others reflect the transaction "broad" and recognize the fee income over the lease term.

Both Lessor and Lease Broker

18. The lease broker may not only locate outside investors to participate in a lease transaction but sometimes may also retain an equity interest in the leased asset. Practice varies in accounting for the fee the lease broker receives at the beginning of the lease term for locating the other equity participants. Frequently, lease brokers recognize the fee income at the beginning of the lease term. A few lease brokers, however, defer such fees and recognize them in income over the initial lease term.

Unbundling of Services

19. The lease broker frequently provides a combination of services for a single fee — cash at the beginning of the lease term plus a share of the leased asset's residual value at the end of the lease term. Practice varies as to whether lease brokers "unbundle" (see paragraph 15) the services and the fees associated with each service. Some lease brokers "unbundle" and some do not (see paragraphs 20, 21, 22).

Remarketing

20. As part of arranging the lease package, **the lease broker may also agree to remarket the leased asset at the end of the initial lease period. Practice varies in accounting for the income related to such services. Some lease brokers do not allocate a portion of the fee to the service of remarketing. Others do allocate a portion of the fee and recognize it at the end**

of the lease term when the remarketing service is rendered. Still others use estimates in recording their residual value share fee income that they believe implicitly allocate a portion of the fee income for recognition at the end of the lease term when the remarketing service is rendered and the residual value is realized.

Guarantees

21. In addition to arranging the lease, the lease broker may guarantee to the lessor (a) a stipulated residual value at the end of the lease term, (b) payments by the lessee during the initial period, or (c) payments by the initial lessee or another lessee during a renewal period. Practice varies in accounting for the income related to such guarantees. Some brokers do not allocate any of the fee to the guarantee service and recognize all the income on the entire transaction at the beginning of the initial lease period. Others use estimates in recording their rights to the residual value share that they believe implicitly defer a portion of the fee for recognition at the end of the lease term. Others explicitly allocate a portion of the fee income for recognition in income at a later date. Still others defer recognizing all income on the transaction until the guarantee responsibilities have been passed on to others (for example, through reinsurance) or eliminated.

Other Services

22. Practice varies as to the time at which lease brokers recognize income from other services that are in addition to arranging the lease, such as billing, obtaining insurance coverage, or administering payment of property taxes for the lessor. Such income may be recognized
    a. At the inception of the initial lease, except to the extent of the costs to be incurred in providing the additional services.
    b. At the inception, with no provision for costs to be incurred in providing the additional services, on the assumption that such costs are insignificant.
    c. Over the initial lease term, with the costs expensed when incurred.
    d. At the end of the initial lease term, with the direct costs to render the services deferred until that time.

Interest Rate to Be Used

23. If the present value of the estimated residual or other future value is recorded at the time the brokerage transaction is completed (at the beginning of the initial lease term), various rates are used in practice to discount the future values, such as the lease broker's incremental borrowing rate, the rate of the nonrecourse debt associated with the transaction, or the rate implicit in the lease.

Accretion

24. If the fees paid in the form of rights to the residual value are recorded at present value, practice varies as to whether lease brokers accrete that value to the full estimated residual value over the term of the lease. Some lease brokers accrete to full value over the lease term, while others recognize at the end of the lease term a gain or loss equal to the difference between the residual value share realized at the end of the initial lease term and the original present value of the estimated residual value.

MAJOR ISSUES

25. The major issues in accounting for transactions of lease brokers are

* **Identifying Lease Broker Transactions.** To what types and extent of involvement by a lease broker should a transaction be confined to qualify it as a lease broker transaction and thereby exempt it from FASB Statement No. 13 treatment?

* **Recognizing Fee Income at the Beginning of the Initial Lease Term.** In what circumstances should a lease broker recognize fees for a lease broker transaction as income at the beginning of the initial lease term? Should the answer differ depending on the form of the consideration, the risks and responsibilities assumed by the lease broker, the time services are rendered, or the time fees are paid to the lease broker?

* **Both Lessor and Lease Broker.** Should an intermediary be permitted or required to account for a transaction as both a lessor and a lease broker?

* **Unbundling.** If a lease broker charges one fee for a combination of services, should he "unbundle" (paragraphs 15 and 19) the services to determine the applicable income from each of the services?

* **Interest Rates to Be Used.** If fees paid over the lease term or at the end of the lease term should be recognized at the beginning of the initial lease term, what rates should be used to discount the payments?

* **Accreting Residual Value.** If fees measured by a share of the residual value of the leased asset are recognized at the time the lease is negotiated, should the lease broker accrete the present value to the full estimated residual value over the lease term?

Considerations in Identifying Lease Broker Transactions

26. Whether a transaction should be accounted for as a lease broker transaction depends on the relationships of the lease broker to the leased assets, his participation in the rights and

duties under the lease or to the parties to the lease, the services he provides, the risks he assumes, and the benefits he receives. Factors to be considered are whether

a. The lease broker has or participates in title to the lease assets.
b. He is in form the lessor for a part of the lease term.
c. He has an investment in the leased assets through use of his own funds or through his credit.
d. He receives tax benefits related to the leased assets.
e. He is a party to a related financing obligation as debtor and guarantor.
f. His obligation is with or without recourse.
g. He has assumed obligations that involve primary or market risk, for example, guarantee of a specific amount of residual value.
h. He has assumed a secondary credit risk by guaranteeing payments by the lessee under the initial lease.
i. He has agreed to remarket the assets at the end of the initial lease term.
j. He has reinsured the primary market or secondary credit risks he has assumed.

27. Some believe the guarantee responsibilities assumed by a lease broker in a transaction may be so significant that the lease broker is in substance a lessee and a sublessor and should account for the transaction under FASB Statement No. 13. Others believe the form of the transaction should generally govern and the lease broker need not follow FASB Statement No. 13 unless he is stated to be the lessee or lessor.

Money-over-Money Transactions

28. Some believe that, although, in form a lease broker in a money-over-money transaction is the lessor-owner of the assets, in substance the excess cash he receives is the same as the cash fee he receives at the beginning of the initial lease term for negotiating a lease broker transaction. They argue that since the financing is nonrecourse, the lease broker assumes no risk. Furthermore, he does not use the assets in his trade or business. The lease broker in effect retains no cash investment in the leased assets because the proceeds from the financing, borrowing, or assignment of the lease are equal to or in excess of the cost of the assets. They also argue that the lease broker locates all the parties to the transaction at the inception of the lease as in a lease broker transaction, and he could obtain the form of an intermediary by transferring the title while retaining a bargain purchase option to the leased asset at the end of the lease term. They further argue that this accounting is consistent with paragraph 20 of FASB Statement No. 13 relating to sale and assignment of leases.

29. Others argue that money-over-money transactions are similar to leveraged leases and the accounting should be analogous to that under FASB Statement No. 13, by deferring the income and recognizing it over the term of the lease. Others counter that a money-over-money transaction differs from a leveraged lease in that, in a money-over-money transac-

tion, the broker has no net cash investment in the asset while in a leveraged lease he has such as investment.

30. Still others believe the nonrecourse financing associated with a money-over-money transaction should be accounted for as a borrowing. Those holding this view believe the borrowing should be shown as a liability regardless of whether the borrowing is recourse or nonrecourse, and the borrowing should not give rise to immediate profit recognition. They argue that this position is consistent with accounting in other areas, since the accounting literature has not permitted nonrecourse debt to be shown net of the related asset and to influence profit recognition except for leveraged leases.

Time to Recognize Fee Income under Lease Broker Transactions

31. Once a transaction has been identified as a lease broker transaction, the question arises as to the timing of the recognition of the fee income. The major factors to be considered are

   a. The form of the consideration to the lease broker.
   b. The nature and extent of uncertainties related to obligations of or guarantees by the lease broker.

32. **Form of Consideration.** Some believe the form of the consideration, whether cash or the rights to a share of the residual value, should not influence the time at which the lease broker recognizes the related fee income. Others believe that if rights to a residual share are part of the fee, this part of the fee is a contingent asset, which should not be recognized until realized in cash.

33. **Uncertainties.** Obligations or guarantees assumed by the lease broker as part of arranging a lease may be grouped into the following types: (a) primary or market obligations or guarantees such as a guarantee that the asset will be released at the end of the initial lease term, a guarantee that the residual value of the asset will be a specified amount, or a primary obligation to make lease payments as lessee and (b) credit guarantees such as a secondary obligation in the form of a guarantee that the initial lessee will pay during the initial lease term.

34. Some believe any obligations or guarantees by the lease broker are merely contingent liabilities. They believe all fee income should be recognized at the beginning of the initial lease term because the fees relate primarily to the services provided in arranging the lease.

35. Others believe that if lease broker guarantees are present, the transaction should be "unbundled" (see paragraphs 15, 19, and 43). The fee attributable to the brokerage services would be recognized at the beginning of the initial lease term and the fee attributable to the various types of guarantees would be recognized either over the period of risk or at the date the risk is removed.

36. Some believe a lease broker may assume guarantee responsibilities and still account for substantially all the fee at the beginning of the initial lease term if the guarantee responsibilities are minor. Those holding that view believe that if the lease broker is not "too involved" in the transaction, a guarantee of minor responsibilities should not preclude him from recognizing fee income at the beginning of the lease term.

37. Some would make the distinction by analyzing the underlying lease. For example, if the underlying lease is a direct financing lease, the broker may recognize fee income at the inception of the initial lease even if he has assumed guarantee responsibilities. They argue that if, in the underlying lease, substantially all risk and rewards have passed to the lessee, the lease broker risk would be minor.

38. Others emphasize primary or market obligations and guarantees and believe that permitting a specified minor level (for example, a percentage) of primary or market type guarantee responsibilities and still recognizing the fee income at the beginning of the initial lease term is impracticable and arbitrary. Even a minor amount of such guarantee responsibilities in relationship to the specific transaction can be significant to the fee income from the transaction or the broker's financial position. They believe the only meaningful resolution is to preclude recording fee income at the beginning of the initial lease when primary or market risk responsibilities are retained by the broker and have not been passed on to others (for example, by reinsurance).

39. Some believe a secondary credit risk differs, in substance, from a primary or market guarantee. They argue that the lease broker should still be permitted to recognize income at the beginning of the initial lease term if his only risk is credit risk.

Both Lessor and Lease Broker

40. Some believe the lease broker may recognize the fee income he receives at the beginning of the lease term for locating all the outside equity participants to a lease transaction even though he retains an equity interest in the leased asset. They argue that if the lease broker's rights in the leased asset are the same as the other equity participants and are in proportion to his equity interest, such fees are in substance compensation for the lease broker's services.

41. Others argue that whether the lease broker is, in substance, a lessor or a lease broker depends on the percentage of equity interest he retains in the leased asset. They argue that only if the lease broker retains a minor equity interest in the lease asset should he be permitted to recognize fee income at the beginning of the lease term.

42. Still others argue that if the lease broker is an equity participant in a lease transaction, he is in fact solely a lessor and he should therefore follow the guidance in FASB Statement No. 13 in accounting for leases and recognize the fee income over the term of the lease.

Unbundling of Services

43. If the lease broker provides a combination of services and charges a single fee — cash at the beginning of the lease term plus a share of the leased asset's residual value at the end of the lease term, some believe the lease broker should "unbundle" the services and the fees associated with each service and recognize in income the fees for certain services at the time the service is rendered. They argue that unbundling is consistent with the position taken in the FASB Invitation to Comment, "Accounting for Service Transactions." They also argue that the lease broker can objectively determine the fees charged for each service based on "relative sales value."

44. Others argue that unbundling is impractical and the total fee should be recognized at the time the lease is negotiated, since that is when the lease broker has substantially performed.

Measurement of Fee Income

45. **Cash Fees.** Cash received at the closing of the lease transaction presents no measurement problem. However, if cash fees are received over the term of the lease and are to be recognized in income at times other than when received, there is general agreement that the cash fees should be recognized at their present values.

46. **Estimating Residual Values.** If the fee income is based on the residual value of the leased assets and the lease broker recognizes it other than when he receives the cash from disposing of the asset, he needs to estimate the amount of the residual value. Issues related to estimating residual values in these circumstances include those related to estimating residual values in these circumstances nclude [sic] those related to estimating residual values in accounting by lessors under FASB Statement No. 13, for example, issues involving technological and physical obsolescence. If the fee is based on a spread between the fair market rental rate and bargain rental rate, the lease broker may also need to estimate the residual value of the leased assets as a method of computing the present value of the spread to measure the income at the beginning of the lease term. Also, if the fee is the right to purchase the leased assets at the end of the lease term at a bargain price, the lease broker needs to estimate the residual value of the leased assets to compute the present value of the spread at the end of the lease term to measure the income at the beginning of the lease term.

47. **Effect of Remarketing.** Those who believe fees related to remarketing services should be unbundled believe that lease brokers should reduce the estimated "retail" residual value by an estimate of the cost to sell or release, the cost to restore, and an amount for profit. Alternatively, some lease brokers use an estimated "wholesale" residual value. A

"wholesale" value reflects the assumption of a zero to minimal remarketing effort and therefore if the lease broker remarkets the residual value, the proceeds he receives from disposing of it should cover the costs of remarketing and profit. Others, however, believe remarketing costs are minimal and should not be a consideration when measuring fee income at the beginning of the lease term.

48. **Present Values.** In addition to estimating the amount of the residual value, there is general agreement that if the amount is recognized other than at the date it is realized in cash, it should be recognized at its present value.

49. **Limitations on Residual Rights.** If the lease broker has rights to share in the residual value proceeds only if the leased asset is remarketed within a specified time, some believe the proper estimate of the value of such rights at the beginning of the lease term is zero. Others believe recording an estimate of the residual value share other than zero is appropriate in these circumstances except if the time is unreasonably short.

Interest Rate to Be Used

50. Some believe the lease broker should use a current market interest rate to compute the present value of payments received over the lease term or at the end of the lease term. They argue that the market interest rate relates to the lease broker transaction and it is sanctioned by the accounting literature in FASB Statement No. 15, "Accounting by Debtors and Creditors for Troubled Debt Restructuring," and APB Opinion No. 21, "Interest on Receivables and Payables." Others believe such rates are not objectively determinable.

51. Some believe the lease broker should use his incremental borrowing rate to compute the present value because that rate relates to the lease broker and it is objectively determinable. Others believe the lease broker's incremental borrowing rate is unrelated to the lease broker transaction.

52. Some believe the lease broker should use the interest rate implicit in the lease to compute the present value. They argue that the implicit interest rate relates to the risks inherent in the lease broker transaction and it is objectively determinable. Others argue that the rate implicit in the lease is unrelated to the lease broker.

53. Some believe the interest rate on related debt, such as on the leveraged lease nonrecourse debt, should be used to compute present values since that rate is known and it is an objectively determinable rate. Others believe those rates are related to the lessee rather than the lease broker.

54. Still others believe the lease broker's cost of capital, as defined in SOP 75-2, "Accounting Practices of Real Estate Investment Trusts," should be used to compute present values. They argue that this rate is related to the lease broker. Others argue that this rate is unrelated to the lease broker transaction.

Accretion

55. If a lease broker records the present value of his share of the estimated residual value of the leased asset as fee income at the beginning of the lease term, some believe the present value amount should be subsequently accreted to full estimated residual value over the lease term. Those who believe the lease broker should accrete argue that

   a. Since the residual value is initially recorded at present value, accretion follows.
   b. A share of the residual value may be viewed as a long-term receivable.
   c. FASB Statement No. 13 provides for accretion of residual values on sales-type and direct financing leases.

   Others believe the lease broker should not accrete the residual value over the term of the lease. They argue that

   a. A residual value in a leased asset is a long-term nonmonetary asset and such assets generally are not accreted.
   b. Even though the measure of current values for nonmonetary assets may involve discounting, the discount is generally not accreted.

   Still others believe the lease broker should accrete for some types of assets but not others, for example, high technology equipment because of the high risk associated with estimating the residual value of these assets.

OTHER ISSUES

56. The following are other issues involved in lease broker transactions:

   * How should subsequent changes in residual value estimates due to changes in the value of the leased asset be accounted for?
   * How should the recovery of the residual value by the lease broker at the end of the lease term be accounted for if it is not received in cash (for example, if recovery is by release)?
   * What special types of information should the lease broker disclose in his financial statements?

* * * * * * * *

ADVISORY CONCLUSIONS

57. The following paragraphs present the advisory conclusions of the Task Force on Accounting by Lease Brokers on the issues raised in this paper and the advisory votes on these conclusions of the Accounting Standards Executive Committee.

Considerations in Identifying Lease Broker Transactions

58. In determining whether a transaction should be accounted for as a lease broker transaction or a transaction that should be accounted for under FASB Statement No. 13, **the most important factor is the primary or market obligations and guarantees that the lease** broker assumes (see paragraph 33). In making that determination, the substance rather than the form of the transaction should govern the accounting for it. **A purported lease broker may be so involved in a transaction and assume such risks and obligations that he is in substance a lessee and a sublessor and should follow FASB Statement No. 13 even though he is not the stated lessee or lessor.** Alternatively, although he may in form be a lessor, in substance he may serve as an intermediary.

59. **The assumption of some primary or market obligations or guarantees does not necessarily lead to the conclusion that the purported lease broker should follow FASB Statement No. 13, but rather his involvement should be material relative to the transaction before he accounts for the transaction under FASB Statement No. 13.** However, **when the lease broker assumes a portion of the total risk and responsibility, for example, residual value guarantees, such relative involvement should influence when he recognizes fee income** (see paragraph 64).

(Paragraphs 58-59 - 11 For, 2 Against, 1 Abstain)

Money-over-Money Transactions

60. A lease broker should account for a money-over-money transaction as a lease broker transaction if

   a. The financing is nonrecourse to the lease broker,
   b. He receives more cash (excluding the amount he recognizes based on his residual value share) from third party financers or lessees (both on a nonrecourse basis) than he paid for the leased asset,
   c. All parties to the transactions are arranged for at the beginning of the initial lease term, and
   d. The leased asset is acquired at the same time the transaction is arranged.

61. If the transaction meets all those criteria, the lease broker should recognize in income at the beginning of the lease term the sum of the excess of cash he receives over his investment plus the present value of his residual value share. The balance sheet of the lease broker should

present only the residual value share retained. Neither the lease receivables nor the nonrecourse financing should be presented.

62. The substance of such a transaction is that the lease broker serves as intermediary for a fee, which should be recognized at the beginning of the initial lease term. The accounting should not differ if he retains the title to the leased assets and the related tax benefits.

63. If the money-over-money transaction is arranged at a later date, (for example, if the lease broker initially warehouses a direct financing or operating lease for future sale and subsequently arranges a money-over-money transaction), he should account for the transaction under FASB Statement No. 13.
(Paragraphs 60-63 - 12 For, 1 Against, 1 Abstain)

Time to Recognize Fee Income under Lease Broker Transactions

64. For income to be recognized at the beginning of the initial lease term in a lease broker transaction, the transaction should in substance meet all the following criteria:

   a. The lease broker has no investment in the assets leased through his own funds or through his credit other than as described in paragraph 69.
   b. The lessor, the lessee, and the third party financer do not have recourse to the lease broker except for credit risk as described in paragraph 67.
   c. The lease broker assumes only minor primary or market type risks and obligations (see paragraph 33) that meet both of the following conditions:

   (1) The present value of the total gross amount of payments that the lease broker may be required to make when combined with any investment by the broker in the lease (see paragraph 69) is 10% or less of the fair value (measured at the inception of the lease) of the asset subject to guarantee or obligation.
   (2) The amount of the guarantee or obligation is substantially less than the estimated future fair value (estimated at the inception of the lease) of the residual value or renewal period lease payments begin guaranteed.

65. **Thus, to recognize income at the beginning of the lease term, the broker may not, in excess of a minor amount (see paragraph 64c), (a) guarantee a residual value, (b) provide assurances of a renewal lease term and the lease payments during that period, or (c) assume primary responsibilities to make lease payments during the initial lease term.**

66. Notwithstanding the foregoing, if the cash fee received or the present value of the cash fee guaranteed to be received by the lease broker exceeds the sum of the present value of the gross amount of the lease broker's primary or market type guarantees or obligations and

any broker investment in the lease, such excess should be recognized in income at the beginning of the lease term if the other conditions in paragraph 64a and b are met.

67. A lease broker's secondary obligation to make a lessee's payments during the initial lease term (a credit risk) does not preclude recognizing income at the beginning of the lease unless the credit risk assumed cannot be evaluated (see paragraph 68d). Such an obligation, in substance, differs from a guarantee of a specified residual amount or a lease renewal guarantee which involve primary or market risks.

68. Also concerning the recognition of fee income:

   a. Lease brokers should recognize the fee income associated with the brokerage services only after all the substantive brokerage services necessary to obtain contractual rights to such fees have been performed.

   b. If a lease broker has primary or market obligations associated with the leased assets in excess of minor amounts (see paragraph 64c), the lease broker should recognize fee income only as he performs and is relieved of the obligations. Examples of this type of obligation would be a guarantee of the residual value or obligation to become the lessee after the initial noncancellable lease term.

   c. **If significant uncertainties exist in estimating fee income, a lease broker should recognize such income only after the uncertainties are eliminated and the services associated with the fee income have been rendered.** For example, **if the lease broker cannot reasonably estimate the residual value or the cost of future services to be rendered, he should defer income recognition of the related fees until the residual value or the cost of the services is known and** the services associated with the fee income **have been rendered.**

   d. If the collectibility of the lease payments subject to a secondary credit guarantee by the lease broker are not reasonably predictable (see paragraph 8a of FASB Statement No. 13), the broker should defer total fee income until the uncertainty is resolved.

   e. **A lease broker should charge initial direct costs and direct costs associated with a transaction to income at the time the related fees are recognized.**

   f. If a lease broker guarantees the initial lessee's credit, he should provide an allowance for estimated amounts to be paid under such guarantees.

Both Lessor and Lease Broker

69. If a lease broker invests (for example, as an equity participant) in a leasing transaction he has also brokered and the sum of his investment and the present value of the gross payments he may be required to make under a primary or market type obligation does not exceed a

minor amount (see paragraph 64c), such investment should not preclude him from recognizing fee income at the beginning of the initial lease term. Otherwise, the fee income should be deferred and recognized in income over the lease term.

(Paragraphs 64-69 - 12 For, 1 Against, 1 Abstain)

Unbundling of Services

70. **If the lease broker receives fees for services to be performed in the future or for guarantees, he should "unbundle" and allocate a portion of the fee for each service based on the fair value of the services.** (The task force did not consider the accounting for such services if they are not offered in combination with arranging the initial leasing transaction since it believes that the accounting is adequately covered in the accounting literature or is being addressed by the Financial Accounting Standards Board.)

(Paragraph 70 - 12 For, 1 Against, 1 Abstain)

Measurement of Fee Income

71. If the lease broker recognizes income at the beginning of the initial lease term, the fees should be measured as follows:

   a. **Cash fees received at the beginning of the lease term should be measured by the amounts received, and cash fees receivable at future dates should be discounted to the beginning of the lease term.**

   b. If the lease broker receives rights to the difference between the fair market rental rate and a zero or bargain rental rate during a renewal lease term, he should estimate the difference and recognize its present value at the beginning of the initial lease term.

   c. If the lease broker has a right to purchase the leased assets at the end of the initial lease term at a bargain amount, he should recognize the present value of the difference between the estimated residual value and the option price as fee income at the beginning of the initial lease term.

   d. **If the lease broker shares in the residual value of the leased assets, he should compute the present value of the assets' "wholesale" residual value, and if such a value is not available, he should use the assets' "retail" residual value reduced by estimated costs of disposition and profit. This approach results in fees associated with the lease broker's remarketing effort being accounted for separately.**

   e. **Fees measured by a share of the estimated residual value should be recognized at the beginning of the lease term only if the lease broker has an unconditional right to the**

residual value. The right should be for a period long enough to provide the lease broker with enough time to complete any responsibility he may have to remarket the assets. **If the lease broker's rights are conditional, the fees should be interpreted to be payment for the remarketing effort and recognized at the time of remarketing.**

f. Fees associated with other services to be rendered at other than the beginning of the lease term should be excluded from the fee income recognized at the beginning of the lease term (see paragraph 70).

g. The market interest rate described in APB Opinion No. 21 should be used for discounting fees recognized before they are received in cash.

(Paragraph 71a, f, g - 13 For, 0 Against, 1 Abstain
Paragraphs 71b - 8 For, 5 Against, 1 Abstain)

Accretion

72. **If the lease broker records the present value of his share of the estimated residual value of the leased assets at the beginning of the initial lease term, he should subsequently accrete the value over the term of the lease using the interest method.**
(Paragraph 72 - 12 For, 1 Against, 1 Abstain)

Other Issues

73. **If recorded fee income includes a share of the estimated residual value, that value should be reviewed at least annually. If the estimated residual value has declined and if the revised estimate (before discounting) is between the original estimate (before discounting) and the then current carrying amount, the lease broker should adjust the discount amortization rate prospectively so that the carrying amount of the residual will equal the revised estimate at the end of the initial lease term.** However, **if the revised estimate (before discounting) is less than the current carrying amount, the lease broker should recognize a loss currently by an amount sufficient to reduce the carrying amount to the revised estimate.**

74. **If the property is released at the end of the initial lease term, the lease broker should record income or loss on his rights to the estimated residual value in the period in which the release occurs, using the same accounting standards that apply to leases under FASB Statement No. 13.**

75. **If lease brokerage activities are significant to the reporting entity, its financial statements should disclose**

a. The method used to record lease broker fee income.

b. The gross amounts before discounting and the present (discounted) values of estimated residual values expected to be realized for each of the five fiscal years after the date of the latest balance sheet presented and in the aggregate for periods thereafter.

c. The gross amounts before discounting and the present (discounted) values of the estimated residual values broken down by the major classes of assets to which the estimated residual values relate as of the current balance sheet date.

d. The gross amounts before discounting and the present (discounted) values, as of the current balance sheet date, of any residual value guarantees relating to recorded estimated residual values obtained from unrelated guarantors of economic substance.

e. Disposition proceeds and gains or losses arising from disposition of residual value rights included in the determination of net income for each income statement presented.

f. The gross amount before discounting and the present (discounted) value of the aggregate maximum amount of primary or market obligations or guarantees assumed by the lease broker.

g. The present value of the aggregate maximum amount of any secondary credit guarantees by the lease broker.

An example of disclosures by a lease broker in accordance with this paragraph is presented in Appendix II.

(Paragraphs 73-75 - 13 For, 0 Against, 1 Abstain)

EMERGING ISSUES TASK FORCE
ISSUE NO. 84-25

Issue No. 84-25, of the Emerging Issues Task Force, is reprinted by permission of the Financial Accounting Standards Board.

Issue Number: 84-25

EMERGING ISSUES TASK FORCE

Issues Summary

Issue: Netting of non-recourse debt   Raised by: E. Jenkins
          with sales-type or direct
          financing lease receivables

Description of Transaction/Event:

A company enters into a lease, as lessor, that is accounted for as a sales-type or direct financing lease under FASB Statement 13. The company subsequently discounts the lease receivables at a bank and assigns the receivables as collateral to the bank. The proceeds received equal the present value of the lease receivables discounted at the bank's lending rate. The company signs a non-recourse note payable secured by the lease receivables and the equipment being leased. The non-recourse note may or may not contain a prepayment option (with a penalty) on the part of the lessor. Lease payments made by the lessee may be received directly by the bank or received by the company who then disburses funds to the bank. The transaction may be done on a lease-by-lease basis or involve a pool of lease receivables.

Accounting Issues:

Practice varies as to the accounting for the above transaction. Some believe the lessor has in substance sold the lease receivables and thus the lease receivables (net of unearned income) are removed from the balance sheet and a gain or loss recognized currently. Any residual value recorded, net of related unearned income, would remain as an asset. Those following this approach point to paragraph 20 of Statement 13, as amended by Statement 77. Others believe that the authoritative accounting literature does not permit netting non-recourse borrowings against an asset, except for leveraged leases. The transaction described above does not so qualify. Thus, they believe the lease receivables and debt should be shown "broad," with no immediate gain or loss recognized. See attached Arthur Andersen & Co. file memorandum for further discussion of the issue.

Authoritative Accounting Literature:

SFAS 13, paragraph 20
SFAS 77

Activity to Date (companies, SEC, FASB, etc):

We are not aware of any recent SEC or FASB activities specifically addressing this issue for sales-type and direct financing leases.

Prepared by: Edmund L. Jenkins   Date Prepared: 10/3/84
                      John E. Stewart

ARTHUR ANDERSEN & CO.

October 3, 1984

MEMORANDUM FOR THE FILES

RE: NETTING OF NON-RECOURSE DEBT WITH SALES-TYPE OR DIRECT
FINANCE LEASE RECEIVABLES

Set forth below are the arguments (pro and con) that support the two alternative accounting practices being following in practice for the transaction described in the Issues Summary.

Arguments Supporting Sales (Netting) Treatment

Those who hold the view that the transaction should be shown as a sale (and the non-recourse debt effectively netted against the lease receivables) do so for the following reasons:

1. They believe that the substance of transaction is a sale not a borrowing, which is the form of the transaction. Because the arrangement is non-recourse, the lessor transfers the risks and rewards of the receivables to the bank. The sole reason the transaction is structured as a borrowing in form is to avoid an unfavorable tax consequence - i.e., an outright sale would presumably result in current taxation of prepaid rental income (proceeds). Other than for the tax treatment and the possible pledging of the lessor's residual value, the transaction at hand is indistinguishable economically from a traditional non-recourse sale of trade receivables.

   Even though in some transactions the lessor may prepay the debt (and "recapture" the lease receivables), it is not the intent of the company to speculate in interest rate fluctuations. Most of these prepayment option have penalties attached that discourage prepayment. Further, any decision by the lessor to subsequently pay the bank in the event of lessee default (e.g., in order to avoid an adverse tax consequence or to retain the residual value of the equipment) would be a voluntary business decision made at that time and presumably would be beneficial (not detrimental) to the lessor. In any event, if sales-type or direct financing lease treatment is appropriate in the first place, lessee default should not occur on a regular basis.

   Thus, it is argued that the lessor has transferred the risk and rewards of the lease receivables to the bank, particularly in those cases when no prepayment options exist. The borrowing form is chosen for tax reasons. It is inappropriate for the financial reporting to be driven by the tax-oriented form of the transaction.

ARTHUR ANDERSEN & CO.

MEMORANDUM FOR THE FILES   –2–   October 3, 1984

RE: NETTING OF NON-RECOURSE DEBT WITH SALES-TYPE OR DIRECT
      FINANCE LEASE RECEIVABLES

2. Paragraph 20 of Statement 13, as amended by Statement 77, provides for current recognition of any profit or loss on the "sale or assignment" (emphasis added) of a lease or of property subject to a lease that was accounted for as a sales-type lease or direct financing lease except that, (a) if the sale or assignment is between related parties, the provisions of paragraphs 29 and 30 should be applied or (b) if the sale or assignment is the recourse, it should be accounted for in accordance with Statement 77. The transaction at hand is on a non-recourse basis with an independent third party. Those who support sales treatment believe that the "or assignment" language of paragraph 20 either specifically supports their position and was so intended by the FASB, or the spirit of it does.

3. They further note that Statement 77 would appear to ratify their viewpoint. Under that Statement, companies are required to report a transfer of lease receivables with recourse as a sale, assuming certain criteria are met. In the case at issue, the company is at least as well off economically as in a sale with recourse, if not better since the transaction is without the recourse.

4. The direction in which the FASB is apparently heading on collateralized mortgage obligations (CMO's) could also be argued to support sales treatment. While nothing has been issued yet, it is believed that if the CMO's meet certain criteria (e.g., they are non-recourse and little or no residual cash flows from the mortgage receivables are anticipated), the presumption for borrowing treatment would be overcome and thus sales treatment may be permitted. The transaction discussed here would appear to meet these criteria, particularly if no prepayment option exists.

5. Those who support sales (netting) treatment point out that this approach is followed by more than a few companies in the leasing business. Thus, current practice would seem to support sales treatment.

6. It is also argued that the spirit of the advisory conclusions in the AICPA's Issues Paper, "Accounting by Lease Brokers," supports sales treatment. The Issues Paper recommends treating a lease transaction involving non-recourse debt as a lease broker transaction (fee income recognized currently and the debt presented net) if specified criteria are met. While these criteria may not be met precisely, the analogies are viewed as being strong.

7. Supporters of sales treatment argue that the alternative treatment would make the resulting balance sheet treatment confusing or misleading for financial statement users. Large amounts of assets and liabilities would be reported that the company does not have an economic interest in, responsibility for, or economic exposure from.

ARTHUR ANDERSEN & CO.

MEMORANDUM FOR THE FILES   –3–   October 3, 1984

RE: NETTING OF NON-RECOURSE DEBT WITH SALES-TYPE OR DIRECT FINANCE LEASE RECEIVABLES

Arguments Supporting Borrowing Treatment

Those who support accounting for the transaction as a borrowing do so for the following reasons:

1. The authoritative accounting literature provides for netting of non-recourse debt only for leveraged leases. The transaction at hand does not so qualify (i.e., the lease transaction is a sales-type lease or the lessor accounts for investment tax credit on the flow-through method).

   Further, even if the AICPA Issues Paper on accounting by lease brokers were authoritative, many of the transactions under discussion here would not meet the specific criteria recommended for lease broker accounting since (a) the equipment to be leased or the lease receivables may be inventoried or "warehoused" prior to discounting at the bank or (b) the lessor's fair market value investment in the equipment is not fully cashed out. Those criteria were specifically and precisely developed by the AICPA to distinguish brokerage transactions and transactions that should be accounted for under Statement 13.

2. Those who believe borrowing treatment is appropriate also argue that the "or assignment" language of paragraph 20 of Statement 13 does not support netting non-recourse debt in the case at hand or treating the transaction as a sale. Their reading of that paragraph as originally stated and as amended by Statement 77 does not find any discussion of the reporting treatment of debt. They believe the dissent of Mr. Kirk to Statement 13 sheds some light on this matter:

   "Mr. Kirk also objects to the inconsistent classification of non-recourse debt required by this Statement (i.e., if the lease meets the criteria of paragraph 42, the non-recourse debt financing the lease is a valuation account and <u>not</u> a liability; if the lessor is the manufacturer of the leased asset or if the lease does not meet all the criteria of paragraph 42, the non-recourse debt <u>is</u> a liability)."

3. They additionally note that Statement 77 addressed the transfer of receivables with recourse and provides for recording the transaction as a sale if certain conditions are met. The Statement does not address non-recourse debt. Specifically, paragraph 4 of the Statement says in part that it does not address accounting and reporting of loans collateralized by receivables, for which the receivables and the loan are reported on the borrower's balance sheet.

ARTHUR ANDERSEN & CO.

MEMORANDUM FOR THE FILES   –4–   October 3, 1984

RE: NETTING OF NON-RECOURSE DEBT WITH SALES-TYPE OR DIRECT
FINANCE LEASE RECEIVABLES

Those who support borrowing accounting for non-recourse debt are very troubled with where the alternative position might lead when considered in conjunction with Statement 77 which deals with recourse transfers. Does sales treatment of non-recourse debt collateralized by receivables ultimately lead to similar treatment for <u>recourse</u> debt collateralized by receivables? This is an unsupportable and unacceptable result calling into question sales treatment for non-recourse debt.

Even if Statement 77 applied to the transaction at issue, there is also a question whether it would qualify for sales accounting in some cases because of the existence of prepayment options on the non-recourse debt. Statement 77 prescribed sales treatment when the transferor has an option to repurchase the receivables at a later date. Exercise of the prepayment option would allow the lessor to "recapture" the lease receivables from the bank.

4. As alluded to in the point above, the netting of non-recourse debt against lease receivables may have broad implications for reporting non-recourse debt generally, for example in the real estate as well as other industries. To date, the general practice has been that recourse and non-recourse debt are accorded similar financial reporting treatment - borrowing accounting.

5. Those who support borrowing treatment are also concerned with the validity of the substance over form argument made by those who support sales/net treatment. One of those concerns is whether the lessor really does have the ability and the intent to "walk away" from the non-recourse debt should the lessee default. While legally the lessor may possess this ability, whether it will actually "walk away" and leave the bank "hanging out" is another matter. For example, the lessor may desire to transact business in the future with the same bank and thus would be hesitant to leave the bank with a loss. Or, the lessor may have an informal agreement that it will not leave the bank with a loss.

A further concern is whether the lessor might be motivated (e.g., to avoid adverse tax consequences, to retain the residual value of the equipment, etc.) to pay off the nonrecourse debt and hence, possibly negate sales treatment. Also, as noted above, the lessor can "recapture" the receivables in those cases when a prepayment option exists in the debt. Thus, it would appear the lessor has retained some rewards as well as some risks in the form of an economic penalty.

6. With respect to the FASB's project on CMO's, the supporters of borrowing treatment note that (a) the project is presently limited to a proposed technical bulletin specifically on CMO's and (b) the FASB's conclusions have not been finalized or exposed for public comment.

ARTHUR ANDERSEN & CO.

MEMORANDUM FOR THE FILES   –5–   October 3, 1984

RE: NETTING OF NON-RECOURSE DEBT WITH SALES-TYPE OR DIRECT
       FINANCE LEASE RECEIVABLES

Further, at the time the FASB last discussed CMO's at a public Board meeting, it decided not to add to the Board's formal agenda a full-scale project on CMO's <u>and similar instruments</u> (presumably other non-recourse borrowing arrangement collateralized by receivables). It is also worth noting that the transaction would not qualify as extinguishment of debt under Statement 76 even if it were not "instant."

7. Those who favor borrowing accounting note that at its July 1984 meeting, the Emerging Issues Task Force addressed not monetization (Issue 84-11), a transaction that has many similarities to the transaction being discussed in this Issues Summary. More specifically, a note monetization transaction in effect is a non-recourse borrowing secured by an installment receivable and under which the receivable could be used to pay down the debt. As reported in the minutes for the meeting, a consensus of the Task Force was reached that set-off in these circumstances was not permitted by the existing authoritative literature. Several Task Force members commented that set-off could only be applied in very limited circumstances, and expressed concern about the implication of permitting the practice to expand.

<u>Our Views</u>

After considering the arguments both for and against the alternative accounting treatments, we have concluded that borrowing treatment is the more appropriate and have taken that position in responding to client inquiries.

EDMUND L. JENKINS
JOHN E. STEWART

PM

AMEMBAL & ISOM LETTER TO THE FASB

The following letter was submitted to the Financial Accounting Standards Board by Amembal & Isom. It sets forth Amembal & Isom's views and proposed treatment of nonrecourse assignments.

May 11, 1987

Mr. James J. Leisenring
Director, Research and Technical Activities
Financial Accounting Standards Board
High Ridge Park
Box 3821
Stamford, CT 06905-0821

Subject: Offsetting of nonrecourse debt against lease receivables.

Dear Mr. Leisenring:

As you are well aware, the topic of netting nonrecourse debt has been receiving considerable attention. The issue of the proper treatment is a cloudy one at best when one considers the ambiguity and, in some cases, the outright contradictory treatment of similar transactions under various statements and technical bulletins. Of course, APB Opinion 10 precludes netting in general. However, FASB Statement No. 77 permits netting (sale treatment) of recourse debt (as does Statement No. 76 in certain cases) yet a virtually identical transaction with nonrecourse debt cannot be netted. This is the same for similar transactions treated under Technical Bulletin 85-2. Such disparity has created much confusion. We have spoken to Arthur Wyatt, Ed Wallace, and Paul LaPage about our perspective concerning the offsetting of nonrecourse debt against lease receivables and they have all recommended that we summarize our position and submit it to you in written form. As way of background, our commercial education firm specialized in lease education and two of our more popular courses are on the subject of accounting for leases. We provide education and consulting services to many leasing companies and captive finance subsidiaries (GECC, GTE, A T & T, Contel, etc.) who have recently voiced concern over the unresolved, question (at least in their minds) as to whether nonrecourse debt can be offset against a lease receivable that is transferred as the sole collateral for a borrowing. To these companies the issue still remains unresolved, notwithstanding certain events such as the February 26, 1987 FASB Emerging Issues Task Force (the "EITF") meeting that expressed the SEC's disdain, etc., for such transactions.

This unresolved problem is currently on the minds of captives more than ever primarily because of the proposed statement on consolidation of all majority owned subsidiaries. If the proposal becomes an FASB Statement then captives become concerned about finding ways of obtaining off-balance sheet funding techniques to keep their parents from being burdened with consolidated subsidiary debt. They are all aware that FASB Statement No. 13 provides for off-balance sheet treatment of nonrecourse debt in the form of leveraged leasing, but most of their direct financing capital leases do not qualify as being "leveraged" simply because their terms match the MACRS depreciation recovery periods of the leased assets. When such matching occurs, the net investment in the lease will decline through the lease term without ever rising, which disqualifies it as a leveraged lease (per FASB Statement No. 13, paragraph 42d). Therefore, to create leveraged leases with nonrecourse debt they must stretch the lease term beyond the MACRS depreciation tax life until the net investment begins to go negative. While simple enough in theory, the market, unfortunately, does not always allow this to happen.

These leasing companies, therefore, are very interested in continuing to net nonrecourse debt. To this end they put forth several arguments, one being that the term of a lease in relation to tax law classlife should not be the deciding factor as to whether a lease is accounted for as leveraged, (i.e. nonrecourse debt is netted, or not). They conclude that anytime a direct financing capital lease is funded (at its inception or later) with a significant amount of nonrecourse debt, offsetting of the nonrecourse debt against the lease receivable should be allowed.

These people cite some additional arguments which would allow the right of offsetting:

1. FASB Statement No. 13, paragraph 20 states that *"Any profit or loss on the sale or assignment shall be recognized at the time of the transaction except that . . . "*, and then goes on to list the exceptions as (1) transactions between related parties and (2) those subject to recourse debt. There are those who believe that lease receivables can be removed from the balance sheet based solely on Statement No. 13, since nonrecourse borrowings were not excepted from this treatment.

2. FASB Technical Bulletin No. 86-2, paragraph 21, dealing with offsetting lease receivables with nonrecourse debt, gives the impression that such offsetting is appropriate, subject to the following caveat – *"It is a general principle of accounting that the offsetting of assets and liabilities in the balance sheet is improper except where a right of setoff exists (APBO 10, paragraph 7). Therefore, offsetting the lease receivable with nonrecourse debt is appropriate only in those circumstances in which a legal right of setoff exists."* Captives conclude that when a lease is pledged as collateral for a nonrecourse loan that no better example for the "right of setoff" exists because the asset has been irrevocably assigned to the lender who can not look at all to the lessor in the case of lessee default, and, in most cases, the lessee will pay the lender directly. We have heard some people espouse the argument that

there has been no legal right of setoff because there must be (1) two parties to the transaction, (2) the transaction must be monetary, (3) an intent of the parties to settle net, and (4) no indirect rights in the transferred lease receivable in the event of bankruptcy. Captives respond to these four attributes of "offsetting" by stating:

a. Where in the accounting literature ("GAAP") do these four attributes of "setoff" exist?

b. Why, if these were essential attributes of the right of offsetting, did FASB Statement No. 76, paragraph 3b, APBO 10, paragraph 7, and FASB Technical Bulletin 86-2, paragraph 21, not even mention these four attributes at all?

c. In most nonrecourse assignments the last three "offsetting attributes" are met anyway, including the prevention of bankruptcy rights in the assigned collateral, (depending upon the wording of the assignment). The least important attribute would be the number of parties involved in the offsetting - leveraged leasing involves three parties and does not preclude the right of setoff.

3. FASB Statement No. 76, paragraph 3b states *"A debtor shall consider debt to be extinguished for financial reporting purposes in the following circumstances: . . . b. The debtor is legally released from being the primary obligor under the debt either judicially or by the creditor and it is probable that the debtor will not be required to make future payments with respect to that debt under any guarantees . . . "* Captives argue that what is described above in fact happens in many nonrecourse debt arrangements which they view as two party transactions. First, money is lent to a borrower, and second, the borrower exchanges its interest in a lease receivable in consideration for the creditor's release of the debtor as the primary obligor. The lessee thus becomes the primary obligor and the lessor is wholly released from its debtor position, not even being considered a secondary obligor. That is basically what nonrecourse debt means to these captives.

4. The main argument cited by captives is that if FASB Statement No. 77 permits recourse sales of lease receivables to result in an offset of sale proceeds against lease receivables, where a similar transaction is without any recourse whatsoever, why should it not result in the same offsetting procedure? We are stymied by the untenable position of having recourse debt off-balance sheet and nonrecourse debt on balance sheet. Of course it can be argued that Statement 77 relates to recourse **sales** and not to recourse **pledges** of receivables, but the substance of a recourse sale is that it is a type of financing arrangement more akin to a recourse loan (pledge) than an outright sale. Or, it can be argued that a nonrecourse pledge of a lease receivable is more akin to a FASB 77 sale. Either argument results in the same conclusion: nonrecourse debt should be off-balance sheet.

Setting aside these arguments and others presented in the AICPA study on Broker Lease Accounting and Arthur Andersen's position paper on the subject, we still remain in the middle of a quagmire of our own making. We feel we can remove the ambiguity regarding the proper accounting treatment for these transactions. These are our suggestions:

1. Differentiate clearly between a **sale** of an asset and a **pledge** of an asset. Use of words like

"transfer" or "assignment" of receivables only confuses the issue since an "assignment" can be used to effectuate either a sale or pledge of receivables.

2. Restrict FASB Statement No. 77 solely to **sales** of receivables effectuated by assignment (remember the word assignment does not equate to sale - this is what started a lot of the confusion). We believe the intent of Statement No. 77 anyway was in regard to sales only and not pledges.

3. Classify all debt into one of four general groups solely as a function of the nature of the recourse nature of the transactions. Please note that we are not addressing "true" sales of lease receivable here. These transactions would continue to be netted and generate gains and losses on sale. Following are the four groups that we see debt being classified as:

a. **General Recourse** - debt provided to a debtor with general recourse to any or all of the assets of the company without specific collateralization of any particular asset. Such general recourse is available to the creditor only by obtaining a deficiency judgement against the debtor or through bankruptcy. Typical bond agreements and bank credit lines are of this nature.

   Accounting Treatment - on balance sheet liability without any right of offset

b. **Specific Recourse with Additional Rights** - debt provided to a debtor with recourse to a specific asset. However, should repossession and salvaging of the specific asset not cover the debt then the creditor can seek satisfaction by having recourse against any or all of the creditor's other assets.

   Accounting Treatment - on balance sheet liability without any right of offset.

c. **Nonrecourse Without Offset** - debt provided to a debtor where the creditor's sole recourse in the event of default would be to repossess the collateralized asset. No rights beyond repossession salvage value exist. Furthermore, no transfer of receivables has occurred; i.e., the lessee still pays the lessor his rentals even though the lease has been used as collateral for a loan. The right of offset here, though it could be exercised, exists only as an option on the debtor's part in the event of default. Such transactions would have bankruptcy ramifications, which is key here, since the right of offset is executory (not yet effectuated).

   Accounting Treatment - allow the debt to be shown as a contra account against the assigned asset so the debt still appears on the face of the balance sheet in the same fashion that an allowance for doubtful accounts is an offset against receivables. The asset, along with its associated offsetting debt, would appear as a net debit balance causing it to be classified as an asset. If a credit balance occurs, then a net liability would appear. As the lease receivable is collected and the loan repaid, the debit or credit balance would disappear over the lease term. The debtor would have to allow for any contingencies under FASB Statement No. 5 that might arise due to a bankruptcy contingency, etc. or others similar to the requirements of FASB Statement No. 77. The merits of this accounting technique are:

1) Front loading of assignment profit or loss is avoided. The difference between loan proceeds and collateralized assets flows to income over the transaction life.

2) Both the asset and related debt still appear on the balance sheet without distorting the traditional financial ratios of the firm, which should not be impacted by this unique type of funding.

3) Readers of the financial statements would have greater insight as to the operations of the company.

4) Tax benefits of lessors using this funding method would not be jeopardized. The IRS denies lessors MACRS tax benefits if the associated lease receivable and asset are "sold" to a creditor. The proposed treatment is consistent with the tax books.

d. **Nonrecourse With Offset** - debt provided to a debtor where the creditor's sole recourse in the event of default would be to repossess the collateralized asset. No rights beyond repossession salvage value exist. However, unlike "c" above, the actual transfer of the asset has occurred. For example, the creditor collects lease payments directly from the lessee. It is assumed that a defacto and de jure offset has occurred which mitigates any bankruptcy problems. This transaction is closely related to leveraged leasing where lessees frequently remit payments not to the lessor but to the nonrecourse creditor who acts as though an actual offset has occurred. We believe that the degree of offset is in fact determined by how the parties act; if the lessee pays directly to a creditor then that is good evidence of a real offset. If bankruptcy issues are limited or nonexistent, then another attribute of offsetting has occurred. In this case the lessor is still treating the asset as owned for tax purposes as opposed to a sale of the asset. In this case the debt would be considered truly nonrecourse.

Accounting Treatment - Allow the debt to be netted, as in a leveraged lease. There would not be any assignment gain or loss recognized up front but it would be, instead, spread over the life much like leveraged lease income. Adequate disclosure of the nature of the transaction would be made. The merits of this accounting technique are:

1) Recognition that a borrowing has occurred, consistent what these leasing companies are telling to the IRS. What is being purported then becomes what is reported, as front loading of assignment (gain) or loss is avoided. The difference between loan proceeds and collateralized assets flows to income over the transaction life through the lease earnings.

2) The fact that the lessor has indeed been relieved of any liability is accurately reflected through netting of the nonrecourse debt of the firm, which should not be impacted by this unique type of funding.

3) Readers of the financial statements would have greater insight as to the operations of the company.

4) Tax benefits of lessors using this funding method would still not be jeopardized. The IRS denies lessors MACRS tax benefits if the associated lease receivable and asset are "sold" to a creditor. The proposed treatment is consistent with the tax books.

A summary of the following appears below:

	Recourse Type	Balance Sheet Treatment	Income Statement Treatment
1.	**General Recourse**	On B/S as liability	None
2.	**Specific Recourse with Additional Rights**	On B/S as liability	None
3.	**Nonrecourse without offset**	On B/S as a contra account against pledged asset.	None
4.	**Nonrecourse with offset**		
	a. Assignor retains tax benefits, payments made to the creditor, minimum additional risks.	On B/S similar to leveraged lease accounting	Assignment proceeds an an integral part of the "leveraged lease" income.

We realize the AICPA study on Accounting for Lease Brokers addressed some of these issues in a different manner. Nevertheless, we feel we need some changes in this area since the pressure is increasing on the part of captives to know what alternative means of off-balance sheet financing will be available in the future. If we could clarify some of our ideas or assist in any other way do not hesitate to enlist our assistance.

Sincerely,

Terry A. Isom, CPA, MBA

Sudhir P. Amembal, CPA, MBA

Shawn D. Halladay, CPA, MBA

Enclosed is a summary of how we are currently teaching the subject of lease assignments at our seminars. The flowchart of the various assignment issues may be especially helpful.

Financial Accounting Standards Board Response

The following letter is the Financial Accounting Standards Board's response to Amembal & Isom's letter of May 11, 1987.

Financial Accounting Standards Board

HIGH RIDGE PARK, STAMFORD, CONNECTICUT 06905 | 203·329·8401

Project Manager
Research and Technical Activities

July 17, 1987

Messrs. Terry A. Isom, CPA, MBA
Sudhir P. Amembal, CPA, MBA
Shawn D. Halladay, CPA, MBA
1406 South 1100 East
Salt Lake City, Utah 84105

Dear Sirs:

Mr. Leisenring has asked me to respond to your May 11, 1987 letter
addressing the offsetting of nonrecourse debt against lease
receivables. In that letter, you suggest that offsetting is
appropriate because a right of setoff exists between the lessor and
the financial institution holding the nonrecourse debt.

As your letter indicates, the FASB staff believes that a right of
setoff exists only when the transaction is between two parties and
is monetary, and when the original intent of the parties is to
settle net. Accordingly, the FASB staff believes that offsetting
nonrecourse debt with lease receivables is <u>not</u> appropriate.

The staff of the SEC has recently released Staff Accounting
Bulletin No. 70 that also prohibits nonrecourse debt to be offset
with lease receivables and refers to the legal right of offset as
"the existence of a right between two parties, owing ascertainable
amounts to each other, to set off their respective debts by way of
mutual deduction so that in any action brought for the larger debt,
only the remainder after the deduction may be recovered."
Therefore, it would appear that offsetting nonrecourse debt with
lease receivables is no longer appropriate for public registrants.

Messrs. Terry A. Isom et al
July 17, 1987
Page Two

For your convenience, I have included a copy of Staff Accounting
Bulletin No. 70. In addition, I have enclosed the issue summary
for EITF Issue No. 87-7, "Accounting for the sale of an asset
subject to a lease and nonrecourse debt," that may address related
issues and the effect "money over money" transactions (as described
by the June 1980 AICPA Issues Paper "Accounting by Lease Brokers")
have on accounting for nonrecourse borrowings.

Thank you for your interest in the activities of the FASB and the
invitation to attend your conference. I found your conference very
informative. If you have any questions or need any additional
information, please call me.

Sincerely yours,

Ed Wallace /z

Ed Wallace
Practice Fellow

Enclosures

8102A:EW

SECURITIES AND EXCHANGE COMMISSION

17 CFR Part 211

[Release No. SAB-70]

Staff Accounting Bulletin No. 70

AGENCY: Securities and Exchange Commission

ACTION: Publication of Staff Accounting Bulletin.

SUMMARY: This staff accounting bulletin expresses the
staff's views relative to the accounting and balance sheet
presentation for non-recourse debt that is collateralized
by lease receivables and/or the related leased assets.
It also deletes certain interpretations published in
Staff Accounting Bulletin No. 52 that are no longer
relevant because of accounting standards adopted by the
Financial Accounting Standards Board.

DATE: June 5, 1987

FOR FURTHER INFORMATION CONTACT: James R. Bradow, Office
of the Chief Accountant (202/272-2130); or Howard P.
Hodges, Jr., Division of Corporation Finance (202/272-2553),
Securities and Exchange Commission, Washington, D.C. 20549.

SUPPLEMENTARY INFORMATION: The statements in Staff
Accounting Bulletins are not rules or interpretations of
the Commission nor are they published as bearing the
Commission's official approval. They represent interpretations and practices followed by the Division of Corporation

- 2 -

Finance and the Office of the Chief Accountant in administering

the disclosure requirements of the Federal securities laws.

Jonathan G. Katz
Secretary

June 5, 1987

- 3 -

Part 211 - [Amended]

Part 211 of Title 17 of the Code of Federal Regulations is amended by adding Staff Accounting Bulletin No. 70 to the table found in Subpart B.

STAFF ACCOUNTING BULLETIN NO. 70

The staff hereby adds Section R to Topic 5 and deletes Topic 5-I of the staff accounting bulletin series. Topic 5-R discusses the staff's views relative to the accounting and balance sheet presentation for non-recourse debt that is collateralized by lease receivables and/or the related leased assets. Topic 5-I relates to recognition of gains on terminations of overfunded defined benefit pension plans, the accounting for which is now addressed by FASB Statement No. 88.

TOPIC 5: MISCELLANEOUS ACCOUNTING

*   *   *   *   *

R.   Accounting for Non-recourse Debt Collateralized
     by Lease Receivables and/or Leased Assets

*   *   *   *   *

Facts: A registrant borrows on a non-recourse basis and assigns to the lender a security interest in lease receivables and/or the related leased assets.

- 4 -

Question: Can the lease receivables and non-recourse debt be removed from the balance sheet either by (a) accounting for this transaction as a sale or assignment of the lease receivables or (b) by offsetting the lease receivables and non-recourse debt?

Answer: No. The staff believes that under existing Generally Accepted Accounting Principles this type of transaction should be accounted for as a borrowing and, as such, the resultant debt should be reflected in the registrant's balance sheet. 1/ Paragraph 20 of FASB

1/   The staff also has noted certain transactions in which leasing companies borrow non-recourse by collateralizing with lease receivables and/or the related leased assets and also sell a portion of the interest in the residual value of the leased assets to third party investors. These transactions may include the sale of the assets (subject to the leasing company's non-recourse borrowing and the lender's interest in the lease receivables and related leased assets) to the investor group, with the retention by the leasing company of a portion of the residual interest in the leased assets. The staff believes transactions in which the leasing company retains a future benefit in the leased assets and is not relieved of its (non-recourse) debt obligation, do not alter the leasing company's status with respect to either the end user of the assets (lessee) or the lender under the non-recourse borrowing and should not result in the recognition of a sale of the lease receivables or the offsetting of the lease receivables and non-recourse debt.

- 5 -

Statement No. 13, as amended by FASB Statement No. 77, indicates that the "sale or assignment of a lease or of property subject to a lease accounted for as a sales-type or direct financing shall not negate the original accounting treatment accorded the lease" and that "any profit or loss on the sale or assignment shall be recognized at the time of the transaction." 2/ However, the staff understands that the FASB intended the term "assignment" as used in that Statement to represent the transfer from one party to another of a direct interest in a contractual right or property, and not a security interest in a right or property. Non-recourse borrowing arrangements that involve the assignment 3/ of a security interest in a lease and/or property subject to lease,

---

2/ Special provisions apply, however, if the sale or assignment is between related parties or with recourse.

3/ The term "sale" is generally used to refer to a contract or agreement by which property is transferred from a seller to a buyer in exchange for cash or a promise to pay a fixed price. "Assignment" is generally used to describe transfers of interests or rights. The legal determination of when a particular transaction represents a "sale" or an "assignment" is a matter of individual state law.

- 6 -

therefore, do not result in recognition "as if" a sale had occurred under the provisions of paragraph 20 of FASB Statement No. 13. 4/

Further, the accounting literature 5/ generally does not allow non-recourse debt and lease receivables and/or the related leased assets to be offset in the balance sheet. This was recently reaffirmed by the staff of the

---

4/   In addition, the staff does not believe that non-recourse borrowing arrangements (which may be structured as sales with repurchase options) involving operating leases and/or the underlying leased assets should result in the recognition of a sale of the leased assets. Therefore, registrants involved in these transactions should continue to reflect the assets under lease on their balance sheets and should also record the resultant non-recourse debt.

5/   Paragraph 7 of Accounting Principles Board (APB) Opinion No. 10 indicates that "it is a general principle of accounting that the offsetting of assets and liabilities in the balance sheet is improper except where a right of setoff exists." Topic 11-D of the staff accounting bulletin series also indicates that "even when items can be directly associated it is not appropriate to offset assets and liabilities without the benefit of an existing legal right." The concept of legal right of offset embodied in Topic 11-D refers to the existence of a right between two parties, owing ascertainable amounts to each other, to set off their respective debts by way of mutual deduction so that in any action brought for the larger debt, only the remainder after the deduction may be recovered. The debts must, therefore, be to and from the same parties acting on their own behalf. It should be noted that "right of setoff" as embodied in APB Opinion No. 10 and the concept of legal right of offset in Topic 11-D are intended to be similar in meaning.

- 7 -

FASB in Technical Bulletin No. 86-2, "Accounting for an Interest in the Residual Value of a Leased Asset." 6/

The guidance in this Bulletin should be applied in financial statements issued after the issuance of this Staff Accounting Bulletin. Such financial statements should reflect the full amount of non-recourse borrowings and lease receivables outstanding. The staff strongly encourages application of this SAB to prior balance sheets for comparability. However, it will not insist on such treatment providing full disclosure is made in the financial statements and management's discussion and analysis of the effects on prior year's financial statements (including disclosure of the amount of non-recourse borrowing not reflected in the balance sheet) of the different accounting treatment being followed.

6/   Paragraph 21 of this Technical Bulletin indicates that "offsetting the lease receivable with non-recourse debt is appropriate only in those circumstances in which a legal right of offset exists or when, at the inception of the lease, the lease meets all the characteristics of paragraph 42 of Statement 13 and is appropriately classified as a leveraged lease."

APPENDIX B

DOCUMENTS (CHAPTER NINETEEN)

The section in the appendix on documents contains the following exhibits:

- Lease Documents (Exhibits I-XI)
- Loan Documents (Exhibits XII-XXI).

Exhibit I

MASTER LEASE

THIS MASTER LEASE (the "Lease") is dated as of the 23rd day of April, 1983 by and between **Sentry Financial Corporation**, a Utah corporation ("Lessor"), having its principal office and place of business at 3450 South Highland Drive, Suite 104, Salt Lake City, Utah 84106 and **Bono & Company**, a Utah corporation ("Lessee"), having its principal office and place of business at 2732 South 2140 East, Salt Lake City, Utah 84105.

IN CONSIDERATION of the mutual agreements set forth hereinafter and the payment of rent as provided for herein, the parties agree as follows:

1. **Property Leased.** This contract is a Master Lease and the terms of each Equipment Schedule hereto are subject to any and all conditions and provisions set forth herein as may from time to time be amended. Each Equipment Schedule shall be substantially in the form annexed hereto as Exhibit A and made a part hereof, shall incorporate therein all of the terms and conditions of this Master Lease and shall contain such additional terms and conditions as Lessor and Lessee shall agree upon. Each Equipment Schedule is enforceable according to the terms and conditions contained therein. In the event of a conflict between the language of this Master Lease and any Equipment Schedule hereto, the language of the Equipment Schedule shall prevail with respect to that Equipment Schedule.

Lessor, by its acceptance hereof at its home office, agrees to lease to Lessee, and Lessee agrees to lease from Lessor, in accordance with the terms and conditions herein, the equipment and features together with all replacements, parts, repairs, additions attachments and accessories incorporated therein (collectively called the "Equipment" and individually called a "Leased Item") described in each executed Equipment Schedule which shall be made a part hereof. Lessee shall have no right, title or interest in the Equipment, except as expressly set forth in this Master Lease. Lessor shall have no obligation hereunder until the execution and delivery of an Equipment Schedule by Lessor and Lessee.

2. **Term, Rent and Termination.** The term of this Master Lease shall commence on the date set forth above and shall continue thereafter so long as any Equipment Schedule entered into pursuant to this Master Lease remains in effect.

The Initial Lease Term and the Rent payable with respect to each Leased Item shall be as set forth in and as stated in the respective Equipment Schedule(s). Lessee or Lessor may terminate any Equipment Schedule effective at the expiration of the Initial Lease Term or any renewal term thereof, by giving the other party 180 days prior written notice. If notice of termination is not given at least 180 days prior to such expiration, then the Initial Lease Term shall be automatically extended for an additional period of six months on the same terms provided for during the Initial Lease Term. No notice of termination may be revoked without prior written consent of the other party.

3. **Acceptance, Warranties, Limitation of Liability.** Lessee represents and agrees that, as of the date each Leased Item is accepted hereunder (the **"Acceptance Date"**), each Leased Item is

of a size, design, capacity and manufacture selected by Lessee and that Lessee has inspected such Leased Item, found it to be in good order, and unconditionally accepted such Leased Item, without prejudice, however, to any right or remedy Lessee may have against the manufacturer or supplier thereof. On the Acceptance Date, Lessee will execute and deliver a Certificate of Acceptance in the form attached as <u>Exhibit B</u> with respect to each Leased Item, which certificate of acceptance will be conclusive evidence of the foregoing. **Lessor shall have no liability to lessee for any claim, loss or damage caused or alleged to be caused directly, indirectly, incidently or consequentially by the equipment, by any inadequacy thereof or deficiency or defect therein, by any incident whatsoever in connection therewith, arising in strict liability, negligence or otherwise, or in any way related to or arising out of this agreement. Lessor makes no express or implied warranties or any kind, including those of merchantability, durability or fitness for a particular purpose or use with respect to the equipment and expressly disclaims the same.** Notwithstanding the foregoing, Lessee will be entitled to the benefit of any applicable manufacturer's warranties, and, to the extent assignable, such warranties are hereby assigned by Lessor for the benefit of Lessee, and Lessee shall take all reasonable action to enforce such warranties where available to Lessee.

4. **Assignment, Obligation to Pay Rent Unconditional**. Lessor may assign or sell all or a portion of its right, title and interest in and to the Equipment, this Master Lease, and/or any Equipment Schedule, and/or grant a security interest in the Equipment, any Leased Item, this Master Lease, and/or any Equipment Schedule, to one or more lenders or equity sources ("Assignees"). Lessee hereby (i) consents to such assignments and/or grants, (ii) agrees to promptly execute and deliver such further acknowledgements, agreements and other instruments as may be reasonably requested by Lessor or any Assignee to effect such assignments and/or grants, from time to time as each Equipment Schedule is executed, and (iii) agrees to comply fully with the terms of any such assignments and/or grants. In the event of an assignment, Lessor shall notify Lessee of such assignment and thereafter all references herein to Lessor shall include Assignee; provided, however, that Assignee shall not be obligated to perform the obligations of Lessor hereunder unless Assignee expressly agrees to do so in writing.

This Master Lease is a net lease and Lessee agrees that its obligation to pay all Basic Rent and other sums payable hereunder (collectively, **"Rent"**), and the rights of Lessor and Assignee in and to such Rent, are absolute and unconditional and are not subject to any abatement, reduction, setoff, defense, counterclaim or recoupment due or alleged to be due, to or by reason of, any past, present or future claims which Lessee may have against Lessor, Assignee, the manufacturer or seller of the Equipment, or against any person for any reason whatsoever.

5. **Installation, Maintenance and Repair**. Lessee shall, at its expense, be responsible for the delivery, installation, deinstallation, redelivery, maintenance and repair of the Equipment by a party acceptable to Lessor. Lessee agrees, at all times during the term of each Equipment Schedule, at its sole expense, to keep the Equipment in good repair, condition and working order, and to furnish all parts, mechanisms or devices which may be required in the course of so doing. Lessee will at all times during the term of each Equipment Schedule maintain in force a maintenance agreement covering the Equipment with the manufacturer thereof or such other party as may be acceptable to Lessor and, upon the surrender of the Equipment to Lessor,

Lessee shall provide a letter from the manufacturer(s) of the Equipment certifying that the Equipment is eligible for maintenance. Lessee shall not make any alternations, additions, or improvements to the Equipment without Lessor's prior written consent. Lessor or Assignee will have the right, but not the obligation, to inspect the Equipment during reasonable business hours.

Lessee shall permit manufacturer access to the Equipment to install "no charge" engineering changes in order to keep the Equipment at current engineering levels.

6. **Representations and Warranties**. Lessee represents and warrants for the benefit of Lessor, and if requested by Lessor will provide an opinion of counsel and other supporting documents to the effect that:

(a) Lessee is a legal entity, duly organized, validly existing and in good standing under the laws of the jurisdiction where the Equipment will be located and has adequate power to enter into and perform this Master Lease and each Equipment Schedule executed hereunder;

(b) This Master Lease and each Equipment Schedule executed hereunder have been duly authorized, executed and delivered by Lessee and together constitute a valid, legal and binding agreement of Lessee, enforceable in accordance with its terms;

(c) The entering into and performance of this Master Lease and each Equipment Schedule executed hereunder will not violate any judgment, order, law or regulation applicable to Lessee or any provision of Lessee's articles of incorporation or bylaws or result in any breach of, or constitute a default under, or result in the creation of any lien, charge, security interest or other encumbrance upon any assets of Lessee or on the Equipment pursuant to any instrument to which Lessee is a party or by which it or its assets may be bound;

(d) There are no actions, suits or proceedings pending or, to the knowledge of the Lessee, threatened, before any court, administrative agency, arbitrator or governmental body which will, if determined adversely to Lessee, materially adversely affect its ability to perform its obligations under this Master Lease, or any Equipment Schedule executed hereunder or any related agreement to which Lessee is a party;

(e) Lessee is not a tax exempt organization; and

(f) Lessee is not in any material default under any loan agreements.

7. **Risk of Loss and Damage**. (a) Lessee agrees to bear the entire risk of loss with respect to any damage, destruction, loss, theft, or governmental taking of any Leased Item, whether partial or complete and whether or not through any default or neglect of Lessee. Except as provided in this Section 7, no such event shall relieve Lessee of its obligation to pay Rent hereunder.

(b) If any Lease Item is damaged, Lessee must promptly notify Lessor and within 60 days of such damage shall, at Lessee's expense, cause such repairs to be made as are necessary to return such Leased Item to its previous condition. Lessee shall then and only then, be entitled to receive from Lessor or Assignee as the case may be, any insurance proceeds received or attributable to such damage.

(c) In the event that any Leased Item is destroyed, damaged beyond repair, lost, stolen, or taken by government action or a stated period extending beyond the term of the applicable Equipment Schedule(s) (an "Event of Loss"), Lessee must promptly notify Lessor and Assignee and pay to Lessor or Assignee, as the case may be, on the next Basic Rent payment date following the Event of Loss, an amount equal to the Casualty Value set forth in <u>Exhibit C</u> of such Leased Item in effect on the date of the Event of Loss and all Rent accrued on such item up to the date of payment. Upon payment of such amounts, Lessee's obligation to pay any further Rent will cease with respect to that Leased Item (but not with respect to any remaining Equipment) and Lessee will be entitled to receive any insurance proceeds or other recovery received by Lessor or Assignee in connection with such Event of Loss.

(d) In the event of a governmental taking of a Leased Item for an indefinite period or for a stated period which does not extend beyond the term of the applicable Equipment Schedule(s), all obligations of the Lessee with respect to such Leased Item (included payment of Rent) will continue. So long as Lessee is not in default hereunder, Lessor will pay to Lessee all sums received by Lessor by reason of such governmental taking up to the amount paid by Lessee during such period.

8. **Insurance**. Lessee, at its sole expense, shall insure the Equipment against all risks and in such amounts as Lessor reasonably requires (but not less than the Casualty Value as identified on each <u>Exhibit C</u> with respect to the corresponding Equipment Schedule) with carriers acceptable to Lessor, shall maintain a loss payable endorsement in favor of Lessor and Assignee affording them such additional protection as they reasonably require, and shall maintain liability insurance satisfactory to Lessor. Such insurance policies shall insure against, among other exposures, bodily and personal injury, property damage liabilities and other risks customarily insured against by Lessee on Equipment owned by Lessee. All such insurance policies must name Lessor, Lessee and Assignee as insureds and loss payees, and must provide that they may not be cancelled or altered without at least 30 days prior written notice to Lessor and Assignee. Upon Lessor's and Assignee's prior written consent, Lessee may act as a self-insurer in amounts acceptable to Lessor and any Assignee.

9. **Indemnity**. Lessee agrees to indemnify, hold harmless and defend, Lessor and Assignee from any and all claims, demands, actions, suits, proceedings, costs, expenses, damages and liabilities, at law or in equity, including attorneys' fees, arising out of, connected with, or resulting from, this Master Lease, any Equipment Schedule executed hereunder, or the Equipment, including, without limitation, the manufacture, selection purchase, delivery, possession, condition, use, operation or return thereof. Lessee's obligations hereunder will survive the expiration of this Master Lease with respect to acts or events occurring or alleged to have occurred prior to the return of the Equipment to Lessor at the end of the term of the applicable Equipment Schedule(s).

10. **Liens and Taxes**. Lessee will, at its sole expense, keep the Equipment free and clear of all levies, liens and encumbrances. Lessee shall not assign or otherwise encumber this Master Lease, any Equipment Schedule or any of its rights hereunder without the prior written consent of Lessor. Lessee will declare and pay when due all license fees, registration fees, assessments, charges and taxes, whether municipal, state or federal, including, but not limited to, sales, use, excise and property taxes, and penalties and interest with respect thereto, excluding, however, any taxes based on or measured solely by Lessor's net income. Lessee shall provide evidence of any payment hereunder upon request of Lessor.

11. **Lessee's Failure to Perform**. Should Lessee fail to make any payment or fail to do any act required herein, Lessor has the right, but not the obligation and without releasing Lessee

from any obligation hereunder to make or do the same, to pay, purchase, contest or compromise any encumbrance, charge or lien which, in the judgment of Lessor, appears to affect the Equipment and, in exercising any such rights, incur any liability and expend whatever amount in Lessor's absolute discretion Lessor may deem necessary therefor. All sums so incurred or expended by Lessor shall be, without demand, immediately due and payable by Lessee shall be considered Rent hereunder, and will bear interest at the lesser of 2% per month or the highest interest rate legally permissible.

12. **Equipment is Personal Property; Location of Equipment**. Lessee covenants and agrees that the Equipment is, and will at all times be and remain, personal property of Lessor or Assignee. If requested by Lessor, Lessee will obtain, prior to delivery of any Leased Item, a certificate in a form satisfactory to Lessor from all parties with an interest in the premises wherein the Equipment may be located, waiving any claim with respect to the Equipment.

Lessee will not move any Leased Item nor permit any Leased Item to be moved from the address set forth in Exhibit A without Lessor's consent, which consent will not be unreasonably withheld; **provided, however**, that in no event will any Leased Item be moved to a location outside the United States of America or to any jurisdiction within the United States of America which has not adopted the Uniform Commercial Code.

13. **Designation of Ownership**. If at any time during the term hereof Lessee is supplied with labels, plates or other markings stating that the Equipment is owned by Lessor or is subject to any interest of Assignee, Lessee agrees to affix and keep the same prominently displayed on the equipment. Lessee agrees to execute and file Uniform Commercial Code financing statements and any and all other instruments necessary to perfect Lessor's or Assignee's interest in this Master Lease, Equipment Schedule(s), the payments due hereunder or the Equipment. Lessor may file a copy of this Master Lease and appropriate Equipment Schedule(s) as a financing statement.

14. **Use**. Lessee shall use the Equipment in a careful and proper manner in conformance with manufacturer's specifications and shall comply with, and conform to, all federal, state, municipal and other laws, ordinances and regulations in any way relating to the possession, use or maintenance of the Equipment.

15. **Surrender of Equipment**. Upon the expiration or earlier termination of each Equipment Schedule with respect to any Leased Item, Lessee shall, unless Lessee has paid Lessor in cash the Casualty Value of the Equipment pursuant to Section 7, return the same to Lessor in good repair, condition and working order, ordinary wear and tear resulting from proper use thereof alone excepted, to the location to be advised by Lessor. Such deinstallation shall be done in a manner resulting in no harm or damage either to the Equipment or to any equipment to which the Equipment is attached. All costs of deinstallation, packaging, insurance and transportation of the Equipment will be borne by Lessee.

16. **Default**. The occurrence of any of the following events, among others, shall constitute an Event of Default and shall, at the option of Lessor, terminate (a) any or all Equipment Schedule(s) with respect to which such Event of Default relates and (b) Lessee's right to possession of the Equipment:

(i)   The nonpayment by Lessee of any item of Rent within 10 days of the date on which it is due.

(ii)   The failure by Lessee to perform or observe any other term, covenant or condition of this Master Lease or any Equipment Schedule, which is not cured within 10 days after notice thereof from Lessor or Assignee.

(iii)   Any affirmative act of insolvency by Lessee, or the filing by Lessee of any petition or action under any bankruptcy, reorganization, insolvency arrangement, liquidation, dissolution or moratorium law, or any other law or laws for the relief of, or relating to debtors.

(iv)   The filing of any involuntary petition against Lessee under any bankruptcy, reorganization, insolvency arrangement, liquidation, dissolution or moratorium law for the relief of or relating to debtors which is not dismissed within 60 days thereafter, or the appointment of any receiver, liquidator or trustee to take possession of any substantial portion of the properties of Lessee, unless the appointment is set aside or ceases to be in effect within 60 days from the date of said filing or appointment.

(v)   The subjection of a substantial part of Lessee's property or any Lease Item to any levy, seizure, assignment or sale for or by any creditor or governmental agency.

(vi)   Any representation or warranty made by Lessee in this Master Lease or in any Equipment Schedule or in any document furnished by Lessee to Lessor or Assignee in connection with this Master Lease or any Equipment Schedule or with respect to the acquisition or use of the Equipment shall be untrue in any material respect.

(vii)   The default by Lessee under any other lease or loan agreement.

17.   **Remedies.** Upon the happening of any Event of Default:

(i)   Lessee will, without demand, on the next Basic Rent payment date following the Event of Default, pay to Lessor, as liquidated damages and not as a penalty, an amount equal to the Casualty Value set forth in Exhibit C of such Equipment, together with any Rent then due and owing by Lessee hereunder (collectively, "Default Value"): and

(ii)   Lessor may, without notice to or demand upon Lessee:

(a)   Take possession of the Equipment and lease the same, or any portion thereof, in such manner or amount, and to such entity as Lessor, in Lessor's discretion shall elect. The proceeds of such lease will be applied by Lessor (A) first, to pay all costs and expenses, including reasonable legal fees and disbursements (in-house or otherwise) incurred by Lessor as a result of the Event of Default and the exercise of Lessor's remedies with respect thereto; (B) second, to pay Lessor an amount equal to the Default Value, to the extent not previously paid by Lessee, and (C) third, to reimburse Lessor for the Default Value to the extent previously paid by Lessee. Any surplus remaining thereafter will be retained by Lessor. To the extent Lessee has not paid Lessor the amounts specified in this Section 17, Lessee will forthwith pay such amounts to Lessor plus interest at the Late Payment Rate as defined in the applicable Equipment Schedule on such amounts, computed from the date the Default Value is payable hereunder until such amounts are paid.

(b)   Take possession of the Equipment and sell the same, or any portion thereof, at public or private sale and without demand or notice of intention to sell. The proceeds of such sale will be applied by Lessor (A) first, to pay all costs and expenses, including reasonable legal fees and disbursements (in-house or otherwise), incurred by Lessor as a result of the Event of Default and exercise of Lessor's remedies with respect thereto; (B) second, to pay Lessor an amount equal to the Default Value, to the extent not previously paid by Lessee, and (C) third, to reimburse Lessee for the Default Value to the extent previously paid by Lessee. Any surplus remaining thereafter will be retained by Lessor. To the extent Lessee has not paid Lessor the amounts specified in this Section 17, Lessee will forthwith pay such amounts to Lessor plus interest at the Late Payment Rate as defined in the applicable Equipment Schedule on such amounts, computed from the date the Default Value is payable hereunder until such amounts are paid.

(c) Take possession of the Equipment and hold and keep idle the same or any portion thereof.

The exercise of any of the foregoing remedies by Lessor will not constitute a termination of this Master Lease or any Equipment Schedule unless Lessor so notifies Lessee in writing. No remedy referred to in this Section 17 is intended to be exclusive, but each shall be cumulative and in addition to any other remedy referred to above or otherwise available to Lessor at law or in equity.

18. **Special Terms.** Any special terms set forth in one or more Exhibits, Schedules or Riders to this Master Lease as they apply to the applicable Equipment Schedule(s) will be applicable as though fully set forth herein.

19. **Miscellaneous.**

(a) **Effect of Waiver.** No delay or omission to exercise any right or remedy accruing to Lessor upon any breach or default of Lessee will impair any such right or remedy or be construed to be a waiver of any such breach or default, nor will a waiver of any single breach or default be deemed a waiver of any other breach or default theretofore or thereafter occurring. Any waiver, permit, consent or approval on the part of Lessor of any breach or default under this Master Lease, or any Equipment Schedule or of any provision or condition hereof, must be in writing specifically set forth. All remedies, either under this Master Lease, or at law or in equity or otherwise afforded to Lessor, are cumulative and not alternate.

(b) **Notices.** Any notice required or permitted to be given by the provisions hereof must be in writing and will be conclusively deemed to have been received by a party hereto on the day it is delivered to such party at the address indicated below (or at such other address as such party specifies to the other party in writing) or, if sent by registered or certified U.S. mail, on the fifth business day after the day on which mailed, addressed to such party at such address:

IF TO LESSOR: 3450 South Highland Drive
                         Suite 104
                         Salt Lake City, UT 84106
                         Attention: General Counsel

IF TO LESSEE: As set forth in Exhibit A.

(c) **Attorneys' Fees and Costs.** In the event of any action at law or suit in equity in relation to this Master Lease or any Equipment Schedule, the prevailing party will be entitled to a reasonable sum for its attorneys' fees and costs.

(d) **Applicable Law.** This Master Lease and Equipment Schedule(s) will be governed by, and construed in accordance with, the laws of the State of Utah (without giving effect to principles relating to conflicts of laws).

(e) **Security Interest.**

(i) Each executed copy of this Master Lease will be an Original. To the extent, if any, that this Master Lease constitutes chattel paper (as such term is defined in the Uniform Commercial Code as in effect in any applicable jurisdiction) no security interest in this Master Lease may be created through the transfer or possession of any counterpart other than an Original.

(ii) There shall be only one original of each Equipment Schedule to the Master Lease, and it shall be marked "Original," and all other counterparts will be duplicates. To the extent, if any, that any Equipment Schedule(s) to this Master Lease constitutes chattel paper (or as such term is defined in the Uniform Commercial Code as in effect in any applicable jurisdiction) no security interest in any Equipment Schedule(s) may be created in any document(s) other than the "Original."

(f) **Suspension of Obligations of Lessor.** The obligations of Lessor hereunder will be suspended to the extent that Lessor is hindered or prevented from complying therewith because of labor disturbances including, but not limited to, strikes and lockouts, acts of God, fires, storms, accidents, failure of the manufacturer to deliver any Leased Item, governmental regulations or interference or any cause whatsoever not within the sole and exclusive control of Lessor.

(g) **Financial Statements.** Lessee agrees promptly to furnish, or cause to be furnished, to Lessor and Assignee such audited financial or other statements for the most recent period respecting the Equipment as Lessor or Assignee may from time to time reasonably request.

(h) **Entire Agreement.** Lessor and Lessee acknowledge that there are no agreements or understandings, written or oral, between Lessor and Lessee with respect to the Equipment, other than as set forth herein and in each Equipment Schedule and that this Master Lease and each Equipment Schedule contain the entire agreement between Lessor and Lessee with respect thereto. Neither this Master Lease nor any Equipment Schedule may be altered, modified, terminated or discharged except by a writing signed by the party against whom such alteration, modification or discharge is sought.

(i) **Severability.** Any provision of this Master Lease or any Equipment Schedule prohibited by, or unlawful or unenforceable under, any applicable law or any jurisdiction shall, at the sole option of the Lessor, be ineffective as to such jurisdiction without invalidating the remaining provisions of this Master Lease; provided, however, that to the extent that the provisions of any such applicable law can be waived, they are hereby waived by Lessee.

(j) **Nonspecified Features.** If the Equipment delivered pursuant to any Equipment Schedule contains any features not specified therein, Lessee grants Lessor, at Lessor's option and Lessor's expense, the right to remove or deactivate any of such features. Such removal or deactivation shall be performed by the manufacturer or another party acceptable to Lessee upon the request of Lessor, at a time convenient to Lessee, provided that Lessee shall not unreasonably delay the removal of such features.

(k) **Quiet Enjoyment.** Provided that no Event of Default has occurred or is continuing hereunder, Lessor, Assignee or their agents or assigns shall not interfere with Lessee's right of quiet enjoyment and use of the Equipment.

(l) **Miscellaneous Equipment.** Lessor shall provide only certain standard items such as cables, manuals, kickplates and micro-fiche as required to have the Equipment accepted for a maintenance agreement. Additional items, such as extra length cables, will be provided on an "as available basis" or at Lessee's expense.

(m) **Substitution.** Lessor may, upon written notice to Lessee, provide Equipment with different serial numbers and locations than those shown on the applicable Equipment Schedule if Lessor determines that it is in the best interest of both Lessee and Lessor to do so. Any such substituted Equipment will meet or exceed specifications of Equipment specified on the applicable Equipment Schedule.

(n) **Alterations.** Lessee shall be permitted with Lessor's prior written consent and at Lessee's own expense to make alterations or improvements to the Equipment which are readily removable without causing material damage to the Equipment and do not adversely affect any manufacturer's warranties with respect to such Equipment.

(o) **Headings.** Section headings are for convenience only and shall not be construed as part of this Master Lease.

IN WITNESS WHEREOF, Lessor and Lessee have caused this Master Lease to be duly executed as of the date first above written.

LESSOR:
SENTRY FINANCIAL CORPORATION, a Utah corporation

LESSEE:
BONO & COMPANY, a Utah corporation

By:_____

By:_____

Name:_____

Name:_____

Title:_____

Title:_____

Exhibit II

EQUIPMENT SCHEDULE NO. F

under

Master Lease Agreement dated as of April 23, 1983

Equipment Schedule Date: May 19, 1987

LESSEE: **LESSOR:**

Bono & Company   Sentry Financial Corporation
2732 South 2140 East   3450 South Highland Drive
Salt Lake City, Utah 84105   Suite 104
                                     Salt Lake City, Utah 84106

Address for Notices: 2732 South 2140 East
                                 Salt Lake City, Utah 84105

Location of Equipment: 2732 South 2140 East
                                 Salt Lake City, Utah 84105

Expected Delivery Date: April 15, 1987

Equipment:

Quantity	Model Number	Unit Purchase Description	Total Purchase Price	Price	Serial Number
1	MTS8218	TAPE SUBSYSTEM	$44,800	$44,800	
2	MXF8913	IOP CHANNEL	8,000	16,000	
1	MTF8204	SWITCH CHANNEL	8,000	8,000	
1	MTF8201	2X16 TAPE	6,130	6,130	
2	MXF8913	HYPRCHANNELS	8,000	16,000	
7	MTU8208	TAPE DRIVES	21,000	147,000	
2	DCU8130	DN 8/30	80,000	160,000	
4	DCE8111	HOST CONNECTS	8,000	32,000	
2	DCP8130	ADDITIONAL CPU	27,000	54,000	
2	DCF8002	CONSOLE	795	1,590	
2	DCF8003	PRINTERS	1,195	2,390	
6	DCF8052	MLCP-16	2,700	16,200	
6	DCF8061	CIA	2,200	13,200	
6	DCF8069	V.35	450	2,700	
6	DCF8049	HDLC	3,200	19,200	
8	DCF8073	ASYN/SYNC	2,000	16,000	
		Sub-Total		$555,210	

Lessor_____   Lessee_____

Return of Equipment: To be advised by Lessor.

Basic Rent Payment Date: The first day of each month, in advance, beginning with the Rent Commencement Date.

Acceptance Date: The date, as referred to in Section 2 of Exhibit B, the installing engineers declare the Equipment ready for use.

Rent Commencement Date: May 1, 1987

Initial Lease Term: The lease term commences on the Rent Commencement Date and continues for forty-eight (48) months after the Rent Commencement Date.

Rent: (a) Interim Rent: An amount equal to 1/30th of the Basic Rent multiplied by the number of days elapsed from and including the Acceptance Date but excluding the Rent Commencement Date. If the first day of the month during the term of this Lease is not a business day, Rent shall be due on the next subsequent business day.

  (b) Basic Rent (payable on each Basic Rent Payment Date): $12,048.00
  Interest for overdue rent shall equal the lesser of 2% per month on the overdue rental balance, or the maximum amount allowable by law.

Special Terms: Rider Nos. 1 and 2 dated May 19, 1987 apply to this Equipment Schedule No. F. Lessee agrees to include applicable use tax of $753.00 with monthly rental payment, making the total monthly remittance amount $12,801.00.

Master Lease: This Equipment Schedule No. F is issued pursuant to the Master Lease Agreement identified on page 1 hereof. All of the terms and conditions of the Master Lease Agreement are hereby incorporated herein and made a part hereof as if such terms and conditions were set forth herein. By their execution and delivery of this Equipment Schedule, the parties hereby reaffirm all of the terms and conditions of the Master Lease Agreement, except to the extent, if any, modified hereby.

  IN WITNESS WHEREOF, the parties hereto have executed this Equipment Schedule No. F as of the day and year first set forth above.

LESSOR: **LESSEE:**

SENTRY FINANCIAL CORPORATION,   BONO & COMPANY, a Utah corporation
a Utah corporation

By:_____   By:_____

Name:_____   Name:_____

Title:_____   Title:_____

Exhibit III

Rider No. 1

to Equipment Schedule No. F dated May 19, 1987

under

Master Lease dated as of April 23, 1983

FAIR MARKET VALUE PURCHASE OPTION

(a) Provided that Lessee shall not at the time be in default under any of the terms or conditions of the above referenced Equipment Schedule (the "Equipment Schedule"), Lessee shall have the option (the "Purchase Option") upon not less than one hundred eighty (180) days prior written notice delivered to Lessor and to the then Assignee or Assignees, if any, of Lessor, with respect to the Equipment Schedule, to purchase all of the equipment (the "Equipment") described in the Equipment Schedule upon the expiration (the "Expiration Date") of the Initial Lease Term.

(b) The exercise price of the Purchase Option shall be the Fair Market Value of the Equipment on the Expiration Date. "Fair Market Value" shall mean and refer to the value, as reasonably determined by Lessor, which would be obtained in an arms length transaction between an informed and willing buyer-user under no compulsion to buy and an informed and willing seller under no compulsion to sell.

IN WITNESS WHEREOF, this Rider No. 1 is executed as of the 19th day of May, 1987.

LESSOR: **LESSEE:**

SENTRY FINANCIAL CORPORATION,   BONO & COMPANY, a Utah corporation
a Utah corporation

By:_____   By:_____

Name:_____   Name:_____

Title:_____   Title:_____

EXHIBIT IV

Rider No. 2

to Equipment Schedule No. F dated May 19, 1987

under

Master Lease dated as of April 23, 1983

FAIR RENTAL VALUE RENEWAL OPTION

(a) Provided that Lessee shall not at the time be in default under any of the terms or conditions of the above-referenced Equipment Schedule (the "Equipment Schedule"), Lessee shall have the option (the "Renewal Option") upon not less than one hundred eighty (180) days prior written notice delivered to Lessor and to the then Assignee or Assignees, if any, of Lessor, with respect to the Equipment Schedule, to lease all of the equipment (the "Equipment") described in the Equipment Schedule upon the expiration (the "Expiration Date") of the Initial Lease Term, for an additional term (the "Additional Term") of as little as twelve (12) months or as much as sixty (60) months, at Lessee's option.

(b) The exercise price of the Renewal Option shall be the Fair Rental Value of the Equipment on the Expiration Date for the Additional Term. "Fair Rental Value" shall mean and refer to the value, as reasonably determined by Lessor, which would be obtained in an arms length transaction for the Additional Term between an informed and willing user under no compulsion to lease and an informed and willing lessor under no compulsion to lease.

IN WITNESS WHEREOF, this Rider No. 2 is executed as of the 19th day of May, 1987.

LESSOR:

SENTRY FINANCIAL CORPORATION,

By:_____

Name:_____

Title:_____

LESSEE:

BONO & COMPANY, a Utah corporation
a Utah corporation

By:_____

Name:_____

Title:_____

EXHIBIT V

Tax Indemnification (Leveraged)
Rider No. 3

to Equipment Schedule No. F dated May 19, 1987
under
Master Lease dated as of April 23, 1983

This Tax Indemnification shall apply to all Equipment Schedules executed under the Master Lease referenced above. Where inapplicable, the Equipment Schedule shall state "ITC Lessor Rider No. 1 to the Master Lease Does Not Apply" or similar language under the Special Terms for such Equipment Schedule or on the related Certificate of Acceptance.

(a) The Master Lease and all Equipment Schedules executed pursuant thereto have been entered into on the assumption that Lessor will be entitled to the following deductions, credits, and other benefits which are provided to an owner of property, including, without limitation:

(1) the cost recovery deduction pursuant to the Accelerated Cost Recover System provided by the Code for each Lease item listed on such Equipment Schedule, based upon the recovery period of 5 year class property; and

(2) the deduction under the Code in the full amount of any interest paid or accrued by Lessor (the "Interest Deduction"), using Lessor's method of tax accounting, for any indebtedness incurred by Lessor in financing its purchase of any Leased Item listed on such Equipment Schedules.

The deductions and other benefits referred to in clauses (1) and (2) of this subparagraph (a) are hereinafter collectively referred to as the "Tax Benefits."

(b) The Master Lease and all such Equipment Schedules executed pursuant thereto have also been entered into on the basis of, among other things, the following assumptions (the "Assumptions"): (i) the federal income tax law in effect on January 1, 1987 shall apply to all aspects of the lease transactions covered by the Master Lease and all Equipment Schedules executed pursuant thereto, including, without limitation, the availability of deductions under the accelerated cost recovery system and the Interest Deduction, without respect to any application, retrospective or otherwise, of changes in the Code subsequent to January 1, 1987; (ii) at the time Lessor becomes the owner of each Lease Item listed on such Equipment Schedules, each such Leased Item will constitute "New section 38 property" within the meaning of Section 46 and 48 of the Code, and, at the time Lessor becomes the owner of each Leased Item listed on such Equipment Schedule, each Leased Item will not have been used by any person so as to preclude "the original use of such property," within the meaning of Section 48(b) and 167(c)(2) of the Code, from commencing with Lessor and such Lease Item will not have been "placed in service" by any person within the meaning of Treas. Reg. Section 1.46-3 (d) or Section 168(e)(1) of the Code; (iii) each Leased Item is an asset described in the 5 year class referred to in clause (2) of subparagraph (a) above; (iv) Lessee will not at any time during the Lease Term of such Equipment Schedule use, fail to use, or permit another to use or fail to use such Lease Item in such a way as to disqualify it as "section 38 property" within the meaning of Section 48(a) of the Code; (v) for federal income tax purposes, the transaction will be characterized as a true lease and all amounts includable in the gross income of Lessor with respect to each Leased Item and all deductions allowable to Lessor with respect to each Leased Item will be treated as derived from, or allocable to, sources within the United States, and (vi) Lessee will maintain sufficient records to verify such use, which records will be furnished to Lessor within 30 days after receipt of a request therefor.

(c) If, by reason of (1) the inaccuracy of any one or more of the Assumptions, including, but not limited to, any change in the Code, (2) the inaccuracy of any statement in the Master Lease, any Equipment Schedule, or any letter or document furnished to Lessor by or on behalf of Lessee in connection with, among other things, the financing of any Lease Item listed on such equipment Schedules or (3) the act, failure to act or omission of or by Lessee or any successor, assignee, or transferee of Lessee, Lessor shall lose, shall not have, or shall lose the right to claim or there shall be disallowed or recaptured with respect to Lessor, all or any portion of the Tax Benefits with respect to a Lease Item (such event being hereinafter referred to as a "Loss"), then at the option of Lessor, (i) the Basic Rent shall, on and after the next succeeding Rent Payment Date, after notice to Lessee by Lessor that a Loss has occurred, be increased by such amount which, in the reasonable option of Lessor, supported by documentation reasonably acceptable to Lessee, will cause Lessor's net return over the Initial Lease Term to equal the net return that would have been available if Lessor had been entitled to the utilization of all the Tax Benefits, and Lessee shall forthwith pay Lessor the amount of any penalties or interest which may be assessed by the United States or any state against Lessor as the result of the Loss, or (ii) Lessee shall pay to Lessor, in a lump sum, an amount which, after deduction of all taxes owed by Lessor as a result of such lump sum payment, will cause Lessor's net return to be equal to the net return that would have been available if Lessor had been entitled to the utilization of all Tax Benefits, plus the aforementioned penalties and interest attributable to the Loss.

For purposes of this Paragraph (c), the net return shall be computed assuming the maximum Federal, State, and local tax rates which could be applicable to Lessor and taking into consideration all relevant factors, including, but not limited to, (1) the increase in Lessor's tax liability as a result of the Loss, the increases in Basic Rent, the lump sum payments, and the payments of interest and penalties attributable to the Loss; (2) timing differences in tax years; and (3) the time value of money using a monthly discount rate equal to .008333.

(d) For purposes of this Rider, a Loss shall occur upon the earliest of (1) the happening of any event (such as an adverse change in the Code or a disposition or change in the use of any Lease Item) which may caused such Loss, (2) the payment by Lessor to the Internal Revenue

Service of the tax increase resulting from such Loss, or (3) the adjustment of the tax return of Lessor to reflect such Loss. With respect to any Leased Item, Lessor shall be responsible for, and shall not be entitled to a payment under this Rider on account of, and Loss due to any event which by the terms of such Equipment Schedule requires payment by Lessee of the Casualty Value or Termination Value (if applicable), if such Casualty Value or Termination Value is thereafter actually paid by Lessee, to the extent that such payment reimburses Lessor for amounts otherwise payable by Lessee pursuant to this Rider.

(e) All of Lessor's rights and privileges arising from the indemnities contained in this Rider will survive the expiration or other termination of such Equipment Schedule. Such indemnities are expressly made for the benefit of, and are enforceable by Lessor and its successor and assigns.

(f) In the event the Basic Rent is increased, or any other payment is made, pursuant to paragraph (c) of this Rider, the Casualty Values and the Termination Values (if applicable) contained in such Equipment Schedule will, if appropriate, be adjusted accordingly.

LESSOR:

SENTRY FINANCIAL CORPORATION, a Utah corporation

By:_____

Name:_____

Title:_____

LESSEE:

BONO & COMPANY, a Utah corporation

By:_____

Name:_____

Title:_____

EXHIBIT VI

<u>CERTIFICATE OF ACCEPTANCE</u>

EXHIBIT B

to EQUIPMENT SCHEDULE NO. F dated May 19, 1987

under

MASTER LEASE dated as of April 23, 1983 between SENTRY FINANCIAL CORPORATION, a Utah corporation, as Lessor, and Bono & Company, a Utah corporation, as Lessee.

1. Items of Equipment

Lessee hereby certifies that the items of Equipment referred to in this Exhibit B (which includes the amount of Lessor's Basis of each such item) have been delivered to the location referred to below, inspected by Lessee, found to be in good order and accepted as Leased Items under this Equipment Schedule and the Master Lease, all on the Acceptance Date referred to below, without prejudice, however, to any right or remedy Lessee may have against the manufacturer or supplier thereof.

Locations of Leased Items:

> 2732 South 2140 East
> Salt Lake City, Utah 84105

2. Acceptance Date: _____

3. Representations by Lessee

Lessee hereby represents and warrants to Lessor and Lender that on the Acceptance Date:

(1) The representations and warranties of Lessee contained in the Master Lease and Equipment Schedule No. 1 are true and correct in all material respects as though made on and as of the Acceptance Date.

(2) Lessee has satisfied or complied with all requirements set forth in the Master Lease and Equipment Schedule No. 1 on or prior to the Acceptance Date.

(3) No Event of Default under the Master Lease, or the Equipment Schedule, has occurred and is continuing on the Acceptance Date.

(4) Lessee has obtained, and there are in full force and effect, such insurance policies with respect to each Leased Item accepted pursuant hereto as are required to be obtained under the terms of the Master Lease and Equipment Schedule No. F.

4. Description of Equipment and Lessor's Basis

Quantity	Model Number	Unit Purchase Description	Total Purchase Price	Price	Serial Number
1	MTS8218	TAPE SUBSYSTEM	$44,800	$44,800	
2	MXF8913	IOP CHANNEL	8,000	16,000	
1	MTF8204	SWITCH CHANNEL	8,000	8,000	
1	MTF8201	2X16 TAPE	6,130	6,130	
2	MXF8913	HYPRCHANNELS	8,000	16,000	
7	MTU8208	TAPE DRIVES	21,000	147,000	
2	DCU8130	DN 8/30	80,000	160,000	
4	DCE8111	HOST CONNECTS	8,000	32,000	
2	DCP8130	ADDITIONAL CPU	27,000	54,000	
2	DCF8002	CONSOLE	795	1,590	
2	DCF8003	PRINTERS	1,195	2,390	
6	DCF8052	MLCP-16	2,700	16,200	
6	DCF8061	CIA	2,200	13,200	
6	DCF8069	V.35	450	2,700	
6	DCF8049	HDLC	3,200	19,200	
8	DCF8073	ASYN/SYNC	2,000	16,000	
		Sub-Total		$555,210	

LESSOR:

SENTRY FINANCIAL CORPORATION,
a Utah corporation

By:_____

Name:_____

Title:_____

LESSEE:

BONO & COMPANY, a Utah corporation

By:_____

Name:_____

Title:_____

EXHIBIT VII

CASUALTY VALUES

EXHIBIT C

to EQUIPMENT SCHEDULE NO. F dated May 19, 1987

under

MASTER LEASE dated as of April 23, 1983 between SENTRY FINANCIAL CORPORA-TION, a Utah corporation, as Lessor, and BONO & COMPANY, a Utah corporation, as Lessee.

The Casualty Value of each Leased Item is the percentage of Lessor's Basis (as set forth in each Sub-Schedule to this Master Equipment Schedule) juxtaposed with the applicable rent payment:

If the Initial Lease Term is Thirty-Six (36) months:

RENT PAYMENT NUMBER	CASUALTY VALUE	RENT PAYMENT NUMBER	CASUALTY VALUE
1	110.50%	19	65.50%
2	108.00%	20	63.00%
3	105.50%	21	60.50%
4	103.00%	22	58.00%
5	100.50%	23	55.50%
6	98.00%	24	53.00%
7	95.50%	25	50.50%
8	93.00%	26	48.00%
9	90.50%	27	45.50%
10	88.00%	28	43.00%
11	85.50%	29	40.50%
12	83.00%	30	38.00%
13	80.50%	31	35.50%
14	78.00%	32	34.00%
15	75.50%	33	33.00%
16	73.00%	34	32.00%
17	70.50%	35	31.00%
18	68.00%	36	30.00%

If the Lease Term is Forty-Eight (48) months:

RENT PAYMENT NUMBER	CASUALTY VALUE	RENT PAYMENT NUMBER	CASUALTY VALUE
1	105.69%	25	62.25%
2	103.88%	26	60.44%
3	102.07%	27	58.63%
4	100.26%	28	56.82%
5	98.45%	29	55.01%
6	96.64%	30	53.20%
7	94.83%	31	51.39%
8	93.02%	32	49.58%
9	91.21%	33	47.77%
10	89.40%	34	45.96%
11	87.59%	35	44.15%
12	85.78%	36	42.34%
13	83.97%	37	40.53%
14	82.16%	38	38.72%
15	80.35%	39	36.91%
16	78.54%	40	35.10%
17	76.73%	41	33.29%
18	74.92%	42	31.48%
19	73.11%	43	29.67%
20	71.30%	44	27.86%
21	69.49%	45	26.05%
22	67.88%	46	24.24%
23	65.87%	47	22.43%
24	64.06%	48	20.62%

Lessee_____   Lessor_____

755

EXHIBIT VIII

Accidental Insurance Company
CERTIFICATE OF INSURANCE
(FM COMPREHENSIVE PROPERTY POLICY)

This certificate is issued as a matter of information only and confers no rights upon the certificateholder. This certificate does not amend, extend or alter the coverage afforded by the policy listed below. We hereby certify that insurance coverage is now in force with our Company as outlined below.

Title Of Insured:

BONO & COMPANY

Effective: May 19, 1987	Expires: May 19, 1988	Policy No: UA 035

Description & Location Of Property Covered: (Except as otherwise specifically excluded)

Personal Property
Replacement Value
$50,000 Combined Deductible

Location No. MSU
Index No. 00920

2732 South 2140 East
Salt Lake City, Utah 84105

Coverage: All risks of physical loss or damage. Subject to the terms and conditions of our Property Damage Form 3000 policy and any endorsements attached to this policy.

This certifies insurance in force at above described location of Policy is not less than $

Effective Date of Interest:
This policy contains the following clause(s):

This is to show Evidence of Coverage only for Equipment Schedule G issued pursuant to Master Lease dated April 23, 1983

Issued to: Sentry Financial Corporation
3450 South Highland Drive
Suite 104
Salt Lake City, Utah 84106

Account No. ....

By ....
Authorized Signature

EXHIBIT IX

OFFICER'S CERTIFICATE

The undersigned, _____, of Bono & Company, a Utah corporation (the "Corporation"), hereby certifies as follows to Sentry Financial Corporation ("SFC") in connection with Equipment Schedule Nos. F & G issued pursuant to Master Lease dated April 23, 1983 between the Corporation as Lessee and SFC as Lessor.

The following persons are, and have been at all times since _____, 1987, duly qualified and acting officers or authorized agents of the Corporation, duly elected or appointed to the offices or positions set forth opposite their respective names, and are authorized to execute on behalf of the Corporation the Master Lease, Equipment Schedules with Exhibits and Riders, and all related documents.

Names	Office
_____	_____
_____	_____

IN WITNESS WHEREOF, the undersigned officer has executed this Certificate as of the _____ day of _____, 1987.

Corporate
Seal

_____

_____

Exhibit X

Bono & Company
2732 South 2140 East
Salt Lake City, Utah 84105

May 19, 1987

Sentry Financial Corporation
3450 South Highland Drive
Suite 104
Salt Lake City, Utah 84106

RE: Opinion of Counsel

Gentlemen:

Reference is made to that certain Master Lease dated as of April 23, 1987, Equipment Schedule No. F & G thereto, all subsequent Equipment Schedules issued from time to time thereto, and all riders and amendments to any of the foregoing, between Sentry Financial Corporation, as Lessor ("Lessor") and Bono & Company, a Utah corporation, as Lessee ("Lessee").

I have reviewed the foregoing Master Lease, Equipment Schedule Nos. F & G, the form of Equipment Schedule (Exhibit A), and such other documents as I have deemed necessary in the circumstances. Based on the foregoing, I am of the opinion that:

(a)   Lessee is a legal entity, duly organized, validly existing and in good standing under the laws of the jurisdiction of its organization, and has adequate power to enter into and perform the Master Lease and Equipment Schedules executed from time to time thereunder.

(b)   The Master Lease and Equipment Schedules have been duly authorized, executed and delivered by Lessee and together constitute a valid, legal and binding agreement of Lessee, enforceable in accordance with their terms, except to the extent the enforceability thereof may be limited by future proceedings or other laws of general application or principles of equity relating to or affecting the enforcement of creditors' rights.

(c)   The entering into and performance of the Master Lease and Equipment Schedules will not violate any judgment, order, law or regulation applicable to Lessee of which I have knowledge, or any provision of Lessee's articles of incorporation or bylaws or result in any breach of, or constitute a default under, or result in the creation of any lien, charge, security interest or other encumbrance upon any assets of Lessee or on the equipment pursuant to any instrument to which Lessee is a party or by which it or its assets may be bound.

(d)   I have no knowledge of any actions, suits or proceedings pending or threatened against the Lessee before any court, administrative body, arbitrator or governmental body which will, if determined adversely to the Lessee, materially adversely affect its ability to perform its obligations under the Master Lease or Equipment Schedules.

(e)   To my knowledge, all conditions under the Master Lease and Equipment Schedules have been met by Lessee. The lease is in effect, and to my knowledge, no default or breach under the Equipment Schedules has occurred or is continuing at this time.

This opinion may be relied on by any assignee of Lessor.

Very truly yours,

General Counsel

Exhibit XI

Form UCC-1

07-01-06 (Rev. 6/84)

Kelly Co. #10448

UTAH

STANDARD FORM

UNIFORM COMMERCIAL CODE - FINANCING STATEMENT - FORM UCC-1

INSTRUCTIONS:

1. PLEASE TYPE this form. Fold only along perforation for mailing.
2. Remove Secured Party and Debtor copies and send other 3 copies with interleaved carbon paper to the filing officer. Enclose filing fee. The filing fee is $2.00 for each name listed in the Debtors box with Soc. Sec. No. and/or Emp. Fed. Tax I.D. No., otherwise the fee is $10.00.
3. If the space provided for any item(s) on the form is inadequate the item(s) should be continued on additional sheets, preferably 5'' X 8'' or 8'' X 10''. Only one copy of such additional sheets need be presented to the filing officer with a set of three copies of the financing statement. Long schedules of collateral, indentures, etc., may be on any size paper that is convenient for the secured party. Indicate the number of additional sheets attached.
4. If collateral is crops or goods which are or are to become fixtures, describe generally the real estate and give name of record owner.
5. When a copy of the security agreement is used as a financing statement, it is requested that it be accompanied by a completed but unsigned set of these forms, without extra fee.
6. At the time of original filing, filing officer should return third copy as an acknowledgment. At a later time, secured party may date and sign Termination Legend and use third copy as a Termination Statement.

This **FINANCING STATEMENT** is presented to a filing officer for filing pursuant to the Uniform Commercial Code.

1. Debtor(s) (Last Name First) and address(es)

   Lessee

   Bono & Company

   2732 South 2140 East

   Salt Lake City, UT 84105

   Social Security or

   Emp. Fed. I.D. No. _____

2. Secured Party(ies) and address(es)

   Lessor

   Sentry Financial Corporation

   3450 South Highland Drive, #104

   Salt Lake City, UT 84106

For Filing Officer (Date, Time, Number, and Filing Office)

Abacus Financial

50 South Main

Salt Lake City, UT 84130

Attn: Leasing Dept.

5. Assignee(s) of Secured Party and Address(es)   [X] if so)

Microfilm No.

4. This Financing Statement covers the following types (or items) of property:

All computer and related equipment under lease to Bono & Company pursuant to Master

to Equipment Schedule No. F dated April 19, 1987 issued pursuant to Master

Lease dated April 23, 1983 between Sentry Financial Corporation as original

Lessor, and Bono & Company, as Lessee. This UCC-1 is filed pursuant to Section

9-408 of the UCC for informational purposes only. The transaction covered by this

UCC-1 is intended by the Lessor and Lessee to be a true lease.

The Secured party is _____ is not _____ a seller or _____ gross sales price $ _____

Purchase money lender of the collateral. _____ or use tax paid to the State of _____ Sales

This statement is filed without the debtor's signature to perfect a security interest in collateral. (Check

[ ] already subject to a security interest in another jurisdiction when it was brought into this state.

which is proceeds of the original collateral described above in which a security interest was perfected:

Check [X] if covered: [X] Proceeds of Collateral are also covered.   [X] Products of Collateral are also covered. No. of additional Sheets presented:

3. Maturity date (if any):

Approved by Division of Corporations and Commercial Code, Department of Business Regulations.

Bono & Company

Sentry Financial Corporation

By: _____

By: _____

Signature(s) of Debtor(s)

Signature(s) of Secured Party(ies)

STANDARD FORM - FORM UCC-1.

(1) FILING OFFICER COPY — ALPHABETICAL

Exhibit XII
$740,624.04

January 11, 1988
Salt Lake City, Utah

SECURED NOTE

THIS NOTE HAS NOT BEEN REGISTERED UNDER THE SECURITIES ACT OF 1933, AS AMENDED, AND MAY NOT BE TRANSFERRED IN VIOLATION OF SUCH ACT AND THE RULES AND REGULATIONS THEREUNDER

9.00 % Secured Note

Sentry Financial Corporation, a Utah corporation ("Debtor"), for value received, hereby promises to pay to Abacus Financial Corporation ("Payee"), or assigns, on or before April 1, 1991, as hereinafter provided, the principal sum of Seven Hundred Forty Thousand Six Hundred Twenty-Four and 04/l00 Dollars to pay interest on the unpaid principal and amount thereof from the date hereof to maturity at the rate 9.00% per annum, computed as if each year consisted of 360 days and each month consisted of 30 days. Such principal and interest shall be payable without presentation of this Note, in lawful money of the United States, at 50 South Main, Salt Lake City, Utah, in 39 consecutive payments of principal and interest (the "Installment Payments") in and at the following amounts and times: $21,919.00 on the first day of each month beginning on February 1, 1988, and continuing for thirty-eight (38) consecutive months thereafter. The amortization schedule attached hereto reflects the payment of interest and amortization of principal under this Note by the Installment Payments.

Each Installment Payment, when paid, shall be applied first to the payment of all interest accrued and unpaid on this Note and then to payment on account of principal hereof.

This Note is secured as provided in and subject to the provisions of a Security Agreement of even date herewith between Debtor and Payee and the terms used in this Note and not hereinabove defined have the meanings indicated in Article V of the Security Agreement.

This Note is subject to prepayment in the manner, to the extent, under the circumstances and at the price provided for in the Security Agreement, and not otherwise.

Debtor hereby waives presentment, demand for payment, notice of dishonor, protest, notice of protest, and any other notices or demands in connection with the enforcement of this Note.

During the continuance of an Event of Default under the Security Agreement, the principal hereof and the interest accrued and unpaid hereon may be declared due and payable forthwith as provided in the Security Agreement.

Should any of the indebtedness represented by this Note be collected in any Proceeding, or this Note be placed in the hands of attorneys for collection after default, Debtor agrees to pay, in addition to the principal and interest due and payable hereon, all costs of collecting this Note, including reasonable attorneys' fees and expenses.

No recourse shall be had for the payment of the principal of, or any interest or any other sums payable on this Note against Debtor personally or against any incorporator, shareholder, officer or director of Debtor. Payee agrees (and shall cause any assignee hereof to agree) that all such obligations are non-recourse obligations enforceable only against the Collateral. The foregoing shall not be deemed to bar or prohibit Payee from asserting a claim against Debtor in the event any material representation, covenant or warranty contained in this Note or in the Security Agreement other than the obligations of Payee set forth in the first paragraph of this note shall prove to be untrue or to have been breached.

This Note shall be governed by and construed in accordance with the laws of the state wherein the principal office of the Payee is located (without giving effect to principles relating to conflicts of laws).

IN WITNESS WHEREOF, Debtor has duly executed this Note as of the 11th day of January, 1988.

DEBTOR:

SENTRY FINANCIAL CORPORATION, a Utah corporation

BY:_____

NAME:_____

TITLE:_____

Exhibit XIII

SECURITY AGREEMENT

SECURITY AGREEMENT, dated as of January 11, 1988 ("Agreement"), between Sentry Financial Corporation, a Utah corporation ("Debtor"), as debtor, and Abacus Financial Corporation ("Secured Party").

Preliminary Statement

Pursuant to a Secured Note of even date herewith, Debtor is borrowing a sum of money from Secured Party and granting to Secured Party a security interest in the Collateral as security for the payment of all sums payable and the performance of all obligations under the Secured Note and hereunder. Debtor is entering this agreement, and Secured Party is accepting the grant made hereby, for good and valuable consideration, the receipt and sufficiency of which are hereby acknowledged. Certain terms used in this Agreement, and not defined elsewhere, are defined in Article V herein.

Granting Clauses

Debtor hereby Grants to Secured Party all of Debtor's right, title, interest, claim and demand in, to and under (a) the Equipment, (b) the Lease (other than amounts payable to Debtor pursuant to the tax and indemnification provisions of the Master Lease and the Equipment Schedules thereof), (c) After-Acquired Property, and (d) all proceeds (other than proceeds of a transfer permitted by Section 2.02 hereof) of the conversion, voluntary or involuntary, of the foregoing into cash or other liquidated claims, including, without limitation, all insurance proceeds and condemnation awards to which Debtor is or may be entitled for the benefit and security of the Note, and for the enforcement of the payment of the principal of and interest on the Note in accordance with its terms, and all other sums payable under this Agreement, or on the Note, and compliance with the provisions of this Agreement, all as herein provided, subject, however, to Permitted Encumbrances existing on the date hereof.

It is hereby covenanted, declared and agreed that the Note is to be issued and secured, and the Collateral is to be held, dealt with and disposed of by Secured Party, upon and subject to the provisions of this Agreement.

ARTICLE I

Particular Covenants of Debtor

SECTION 1.01. Warranty of Title to Equipment. Debtor hereby warrants that: (i) it owns the Equipment free and clear of all liens, charges and other encumbrances, except Permitted

Encumbrances, and that this Agreement constitutes a valid lien on the Equipment, subject only to Permitted Encumbrances, and (ii) it has and enjoys all right, title and interest in and to the Lease, free and clear of all liens, charges and other encumbrances except Permitted Encumbrances. Until payment in full of the Note and all of its other obligations secured hereby, and except as otherwise specifically permitted hereby, Debtor will warrant and defend its title in and to the Equipment and its interest in the Lease against the claims and demands of all persons and will maintain the lien created under this Agreement. Debtor has full power and lawful authority to grant the security interest in the property granted by this Agreement.

SECTION 1.02. Existence. Debtor will keep in full force and effect its existence and rights as a corporation under the laws of the jurisdiction of its incorporation and will obtain and preserve its right to do business as a corporation in each jurisdiction in which such qualification is or shall be necessary to protect the validity and enforceability of this Agreement, the Note or any Security Instrument unless Debtor is acquired, merged, or otherwise becomes a part of another corporate entity, in which case Debtor will insure that any such other corporate entity will assume for itself and undertake to perform all of Debtor's obligations, to the same extent as Debtor is obligated hereunder, under the Note, or any Security Instrument.

SECTION 1.03. Protection of Collateral. Debtor will from time to time execute and deliver all such supplements and amendments hereto and to any Security Instrument, and all such financing statements, continuation statements, instruments of further assurance and other instruments, and will take such other action, as Secured Party reasonably requests and deems necessary or advisable to (a) maintain or preserve the lien created under this Agreement or carry out more effectively the purposes hereof, (b) perfect, publish notice of, or protect the validity of any Security Instrument, or of any Grant made or to be made by this Agreement, whether or not any of the Equipment is moved from its situs as of any date, (c) enforce any Security Instrument, or (d) preserve and defend title to the Collateral and the rights of the Secured Party therein against the claims of all persons and parties.

SECTION 1.05. Negative Covenants. Debtor will not:

(a) sell, lease, transfer, exchange or otherwise dispose of any of the Collateral except in accordance with the provisions of Section 2.02 hereof;

(b) take or permit any action which would result in an Event of Default under subsection (d) or (e) of Section 4.01; or

(c) claim any credit on, or make any deduction from, the principal or interest payable on the Note by reason of the payment of any taxes levied or assessed upon any of the Collateral.

SECTION 1.06. Payment of Taxes. Debtor will pay or cause to be paid all taxes respecting the Equipment and the Lease (including franchise and gross receipts taxes) which are at any time or from time to time levied upon or assessed against it. The foregoing sentence shall not prevent

Debtor from contesting any such tax by appropriate proceedings so long as (a) such proceedings shall suspend the collection thereof, (b) no part of the Collateral would be subject to sale, forfeiture or diminution and (c) Debtor shall have furnished such security as may be required in the proceedings or reasonably requested by Secured Party. Debtor will conduct such contests in good faith and with due diligence and will, promptly after the final determination of each such contest, pay all amounts which shall be determined to be payable in respect thereof.

SECTION 1.07. Assignment of Lease. Confirmatory of its Grant of the Lease, Debtor hereby irrevocably Grants to Secured Party, subject to the provisions of this Agreement, as security for the payment of all amounts payable under or in respect of the Note and this Agreement, and as security for compliance with the provisions hereof and thereof, all of its right, title, interest, claim and demand in, to and under the Lease, and all rental payments and rental installments due thereunder (commencing with the rental payments due on February 1, 1988), damages and other moneys from time to time payable to or receivable by Debtor under the Lease other than amounts payable to Debtor pursuant to the indemnification provisions of the Master Lease and the Equipment Schedules thereof, said sums being herein called the "Money". So long as no Event of Default shall have occurred and be continuing under this Agreement, Debtor shall be entitled to exercise all of its rights under the Lease except the right to receive Moneys directly from the Lessee (which right shall be Secured Party's irrespective of whether an Event of Default shall have occurred) and except to the extent that such exercise would violate any provision of this agreement. Upon the occurrence and continuance of an Event of Default under this Agreement, Secured Party is hereby assigned the Lease and shall be entitled to exercise all of Debtor's rights under the Lease to the extent assigned hereby upon notice to Debtor as provided for herein, and Debtor shall have no further rights thereunder with respect to such rights (except to receive copies of all notices given and received thereunder) until the termination of the lien created under this Agreement as provided herein, whereupon all rights granted hereunder to Secured Party shall terminate and revert to Debtor. The obligations of Debtor, however, owing to Lessee under the Lease shall continue to be personal obligations of Debtor and shall continue to be owing to the Lessee by Debtor notwithstanding this Agreement or any Event of Default or any enforcement proceedings hereunder.

ARTICLE II

Possession, Use and Transfer

SECTION 2.01. Collection of Moneys. Secured Party shall receive and collect all Moneys and other property payable to or receivable by Secured Party pursuant to this Agreement or any Security Instrument, commencing with the rental payments due under the Lease on February 1, 1988. Secured Party shall apply the Moneys as provided in this Agreement. If any default occurs in the making of any payment or performance under any Security Instrument, Secured Party may take such action as it shall have power to take and as may be appropriate to enforce such payment or performance, including the institution and prosecution of appropriate proceedings. Any such action shall be without prejudice to any right to claim a Default or Event of Default under this Agreement and to proceed thereafter as provided in Article IV.

SECTION 2.02 <u>Transfer of Collateral</u>. Debtor may sell, transfer or assign its interest in the Collateral, or part thereof, to one or more third parties who may sell, transfer or assign their interest in the Collateral, or part thereof, either directly or indirectly, to one or more additional parties who, along with their successors, may make further sales, transfers and assignments. Any such sale, transfer or assignment shall be permitted by Secured Party if: (a) such sale, transfer or assignment is expressly subject and subordinate in all respects to the rights and interest of Secured Party, and (b) the purchaser, transferee or assignee (a "Transferee") delivers to Secured Party an agreement, in substantially the form attached hereto as <u>Exhibit A</u>, to Secured Party evidencing such subordination. Upon compliance with the foregoing, no further consent from Secured Party shall be required. No such sale, transfer or assignment shall relieve Debtor of any of its obligations hereunder.

SECTION 2.03. <u>Condemnation</u>. Debtor shall notify Secured Party of any condemnation or other eminent domain proceedings with respect to the Equipment immediately upon its obtaining knowledge thereof. Secured Party may participate in any such proceedings. Debtor shall use its best efforts to provide Secured Party with all instruments required by it to permit such participation upon obtaining actual knowledge thereof.

ARTICLE III

Application of Moneys' Prepayment

SECTION 3.01. <u>Rental Payments</u>. So long as no Event of Default shall be continuing, rental payments under the Lease received by Secured Party shall be applied to the payment of each Installment Payment then payable on the Note, and any rental payment amounts made under the Lease in excess of the Installment Payment amount then required and due under the Note shall be forthwith transferred to Debtor by means of a bank check to the order of Debtor at the address provided in Section 7.02 hereof. Secured Party's security interest in such funds shall terminate upon payment to Debtor's account. Notwithstanding the foregoing, (i) in the event any such rental payment in excess of the Installment Payment is paid to reimburse an expense incurred by Secured Party, by Debtor, or by Sentry Financial Corporation, a Utah corporation ("Sentry") (such as payment of taxes or insurance premiums), which excess expense Lessee is obligated to pay under the Lease, then such excess amount shall constitute a reimbursement only and shall be received by the party which incurred the expense as its separate property, and (ii) any such rental payment received by Secured Party in excess of the Installment Payment which was separately stated on Lessee's invoice as tax required to be paid by Lessee shall not be subject to the lien of this agreement but shall be paid to Debtor (or such other party as directed by Debtor from time to time) within (15) days of receipt by Lender, and Secured Party shall not apply those monies to principal, interest, or any costs or expenses allowed under this Agreement or the Note. If Secured Party does not remit such tax monies to Debtor (or such other party as directed by Debtor from time to time) within fifteen days, then Lender shall be liable to Debtor (or such other party as directed by Debtor from time to time) for any penalties and/or interest assessed by the taxing authority on account of such late payment.

SECTION 3.02 Insurance and Condemnation Proceeds; Casualty Value. If no Event of Default shall be continuing (a) proceeds of casualty insurance not applied by the Lessee to repair or replace the affected Equipment, (b) condemnation awards (or settlements in respect thereof) and (c) any payment of casualty values made pursuant to Section 7 of the Lease received by Secured Party shall be applied to the prepayment of the Note without any prepayment penalty or premium, and the balance, if any, shall be paid to or upon the order of Debtor.

SECTION 3.03. Prepayment in General; Partial Prepayments. The Note shall be prepaid as provided in Section 3.02 and may otherwise be prepaid by Debtor (or Debtor's transferee) in whole or in part at any time and, in the case of partial prepayments, from time to time. Each partial prepayment of the Note shall be in an amount which will cause the principal balance remaining to be paid under the Note to be equal to the amount which will be amortized in full, in equal monthly installments of principal and interest (at 9.00% per annum) due on each remaining installment due date under the Note, out of the Basic Rents remaining to be paid by Lessee under the Lease over the remaining term of the Lease after Secured Party's receipt of the moneys applied to such prepayment. In the event of any prepayment, Secured Party and Debtor shall provide one another with all documents reasonably required by the other to reflect such prepayment.

ARTICLE IV

Events of Default and Remedies

SECTION 4.01 Events of Default. Any of the following occurrences or acts shall constitute an Event of Default under this Agreement:

(a) If default shall be made in the payment of any interest or principal on the Note when and as the same shall become payable, whether at maturity or by acceleration or as part of any prepayment or otherwise, and such default shall have continued for a period of 10 days after notice has been given to Debtor by or on behalf of Secured Party; or,

(b) If there shall be default in the due observance of any provision of Section 1.05 hereof and such default shall have continued for a period of 10 days after receipt by Debtor of written notice from Secured Party; or,

(c) If there shall be a default in the due observance or performance of any other provision of this Agreement and such default shall have continued for a period of 10 days after notice thereof shall have been given to Debtor by Secured Party; or,

(d) If the validity or effectiveness of this Security Agreement, the Lease or of their assignment by Debtor to Secured Party shall be impaired, and such impairment shall continue for a period of 30 days after receipt by Debtor of written notice from Secured Party of such impairment, or if Debtor shall amend, hypothecate, subordinate, terminate or discharge any Security Instrument and as a result thereof Debtor or the Lessee shall be released from any of its covenants or obligations under any Security Instrument, in each case except to the extent that the same shall be caused by, or shall occur with the express written consent of, Secured Party; or

(e) If any lien, charge, security interest, mortgage, pledge or other encumbrance shall be created on or extend to or otherwise arise upon or burden the Collateral or any part thereof or any interest therein or the revenues, rents, issues or profits thereof, other than Permitted Encumbrances, and such lien, charge, security interest, mortgage, pledge or other encumbrance shall continue for a period of 30 days after receipt by Debtor of written notice from Secured Party thereof; or,

(f) If any representation or warranty of Debtor made in this Agreement, in a Security Instrument or in any certificate or other writing delivered pursuant hereto or thereto shall prove to be incorrect in any material respect as of the time when the same shall have been made; or,

(g) If any Event of Default of the nature specified in the Lease shall be continuing beyond the applicable grace period provided therein; or,

(h) If the person owning the Equipment (for purposes of clauses (h), (i), (j) and (k) of this Section 4.01 and clauses (c) and (e) of Section 4.02 (the "Equipment Owner")) shall file a petition for relief under Title 11 of the United States Code looking to or seeking any reorganization, arrangement, composition, readjustment, liquidation, dissolution or similar relief under any other present or future federal or state statute, law or regulation; or,

(i) If a petition or action shall be filed against the Equipment Owner looking to or seeking any reorganization, arrangement, composition, readjustment, liquidation, dissolution or similar relief with respect to it pursuant to any other present or future federal or state statute, law or regulation, and the Equipment Owner shall consent to the filing thereof, or such petition or action shall not be discharged or denied within 30 days after the filing thereof; or,

(j) If a receiver, trustee, custodian or liquidator of the Equipment Owner or of any property or assets of the Equipment Owner shall be appointed and shall not be discharged within 30 days thereafter, or if the Equipment Owner shall consent to or acquiesce in such appointment; or,

(k) If the Equipment Owner shall make an assignment for the benefit of its creditors or shall be unable to pay its debts as they become due.

SECTION 4.02. Remedies. If an Event of Default shall be continuing, Secured Party may do one or more of the following:

(a) give notice to Debtor declaring the entire unpaid principal amount of the Note, together with all accrued interest and other sums then owing under this Agreement, to be forthwith payable, and demanding that the same be paid, and thereupon all such amounts shall be forthwith payable, together with (i) all costs and expenses of collection and (ii) interest on all of the foregoing from the date of receipt of such notice to the date of payment at a rate per annum equal to the lesser of (a) twelve percent (12%) per annum or (b) the highest interest rate permitted by law, notwithstanding any contrary provision contained in this Agreement or the Note;

(b) institute Proceedings for the collection of all amounts then payable on the Note or under this Agreement, whether by acceleration or otherwise, enforce any judgment obtained and collect moneys adjudged due from the Collateral;

(c) upon reasonable notice to Debtor and the Equipment Owner (if other than Debtor), sell the Collateral or any portion thereof or rights or interest therein, free and clear of any and all interests of Debtor and the Equipment Owner in and to the Collateral, at one or more public or private sales called and conducted in any manner permitted by law (written notice ten days in advance of any sale shall be deemed commercially reasonable);

(d) institute Proceedings from time to time for the complete or partial foreclosure of this Agreement;

(e) exclude Debtor and the Equipment Owner from the Equipment and take possession of their respective interests therein, and, at the expense of the Collateral, maintain, repair, alter, add to, improve, insure, lease, operate and manage the Equipment in such manner as Secured Party shall reasonably see fit;

(f) take any other reasonable action to protect and enforce the rights and remedies of Secured Party hereunder, or under or in respect of any Security Instrument, or otherwise; and,

(g) have all the rights and remedies provided to a secured party by the Uniform Commercial Code with respect to all parts of the Collateral which are and which are deemed to be governed by the Uniform Commercial Code; provided, that, so long as the Lessee shall not be in default of any of the provisions of the Lease, Secured Party shall not disturb the Lessee's quiet and peaceful possession of the Equipment and its unrestricted right to use the Equipment for its intended purpose.

The unpaid principal amount of the Note and all accrued interest and other sums payable under this Agreement shall be forthwith payable upon a sale (a "Sale") of any portion of the Collateral pursuant to Subsection (c) or (d) above, notwithstanding any provision to the contrary contained in this Agreement of the Note. All earnings, revenues, proceeds, rents, issues, profits and income derived pursuant to Subsection (e) above (after deducting costs and expenses of operation and other proper charges), all proceeds of any sale, and all other money and property received or recovered by the Secured Party pursuant to this Section 4.02 shall become part of the Collateral.

SECTION 4.03. Sale of Collateral.

(a) The power to effect any Sale shall not be exhausted by any one or more Sales as to any portion of the Collateral remaining unsold, but shall continue unimpaired until the entire Collateral shall have been sold or all amounts payable on the Note and under this Agreement shall have been paid. Secured Party may from time to time postpone any Sale by public announcement made at the time and place of such Sale.

(b) Secured Party may bid or acquire any portion thereof, and may pay all or part of the purchase price by crediting against amounts owing on the Note or other amounts secured by this Agreement, all or part of the net proceeds of such Sale after deducting the costs, charges and expenses incurred by Secured Party in connection with such Sale. The Note need not be produced in order to complete any such Sale, or in order to cause to be credited thereon its share of such net proceeds. Secured Party may hold, lease, operate, manage or otherwise deal with any property so acquired in any manner permitted by law.

(c) Secured Party shall execute and deliver an appropriate instrument of conveyance transferring its interest in any portion of the Collateral in connection with a Sale thereof. No purchaser or transferee at such a Sale shall be bound to ascertain Secured Party's authority, inquire into the satisfaction of any condition precedent, or see to the application of any moneys.

In addition, upon the occurrence of an Event of Default, Secured Party is hereby irrevocably appointed the agent and attorney in fact of the Equipment Owner to transfer and convey its interest in any portion of the Collateral in connection with a Sale thereof, and to take all actions necessary to effect such Sale.

(d) If any Equipment is subject to the Lease at the time of any Sale, Secured Party shall not obtain actual possession of such Equipment in order to effect such Sale, but shall effect such Sale subject to the Lease without interference with the rights of the Lessee so long as Lessee shall not be in default under the Lease, including, without limitation, the right to quiet and peaceful possession of the Equipment and the unrestricted right to use the Equipment for its intended purpose.

SECTION 4.05. Distribution of Collateral. Upon enforcement of this Agreement, all Moneys constituting a part of the Collateral shall be applied from time to time by Secured Party as follows:

First: To the payment of all costs, expenses and liabilities of Secured Party (including fees and expenses of its agents and counsel) incurred or accrued in connection with any proceedings brought by Secured Party or in connection with the maintenance, Sale or other disposition of the Collateral.

<u>Second</u>: To the payment of all interest then due and payable on the Note.

<u>Third</u>: To the payment of all principal then due and payable on the Note.

<u>Fourth</u>: To the payment of all other sums secured by this Agreement.

<u>Fifth</u>: To the payment of any surplus to Debtor or any other person legally entitled thereto.

SECTION 4.06. <u>Rights Cumulative</u>. All rights and remedies from time to time conferred upon or reserved to Secured Party are cumulative, and none is intended to be exclusive of another. No delay or omission in insisting upon the strict observance or performance of any provision of this Agreement, or to exercise any right or remedy, shall be construed as a waiver or relinquishment of such provision, nor shall it impair such right or remedy. Every right and remedy may be exercised from time to time and as often as deemed expedient.

SECTION 4.07. <u>Ability to Cure</u>. If an Event of Default shall occur as defined in Section 4.01 hereof, any party, including any subsequent transferee or transferees may cure such default by remedying the deficiency responsible for the Event of Default within the time period so provided in Section 4.01.

ARTICLE V

Defined Terms

SECTION 5.01. <u>Definitions</u>. When used in this Agreement, each term defined in this Article V shall have the meaning indicated:

"After-Acquired Property" - all future extensions, improvements, betterments, alterations, repairs, renewals, substitutions, and replacements of, and all future additions and appurtenances to, and all other equipment to be physically annexed to, the Equipment except any of the foregoing which are not financed by Secured Party pursuant to this Agreement or any Security Instrument.

"Collateral" - all money, instruments, the Equipment, and other property subject or intended to be subject to the lien of this Agreement as of any particular time (including, without limitation, all property and interest granted in the granting clauses of this Agreement), and all right, title and interest of Secured Party in, to and under each Security Instrument and all money and property received by Secured Party pursuant thereto.

"Consent and Agreement" - the Consent and Agreement of Lessee addressed to and acknowledged by Secured Party, or the Notice of Assignment letter addressed by Secured Party to and acknowledged by Lessee.

"Default" - any occurrence which with notice or lapse of time would be an Event of Default.

"Equipment" - the property described in Exhibit B attached hereto.

"Event of Default" - as defined in Section 4.01.

"Grant" - to grant, bargain, sell, warrant, alien, remise, release, convey, assign, transfer, mortgage, pledge, deposit, set over, confirm and create a security interest under the Uniform Commercial Code. A grant of any instrument shall include all rights, powers and options (but none of the obligations) of the granting party thereunder, including, without limitation, the right generally to do anything which the granting party is or may be entitled to do thereunder or with respect thereto.

"Installment Payments" - as defined in the Note.

"Lease" - Equipment Schedule Nos. F & G dated April 19, 1987, incorporating Master Lease dated as of April 23, 1983, between Debtor, Sentry Financial Corporation, as original lessor, and Lessee, as lessee.

"Lessee" - Bono & Company.

"Note" - Sentry Financial Corporation's 9.00% Secured Note in the principal amount of $740,624.04.

"Permitted Encumbrances" - with respect to the Collateral: (i) any lien thereon for any governmental charge or for work or service performed or materials furnished, which lien secures amounts which are not due and payable or which are not delinquent; (ii) this Agreement, the Lease and any sublease or assignment permitted thereby; (iii) liens for taxes not yet due; (iv) liens or encumbrances which arise out of transfer as permitted in Section 2.02; and the lien of the manufacturer or other seller of the Equipment pending payment of the purchase price.

"Proceeding" - any suit in equity, action at law or other judicial or administrative proceeding in respect of the Note, this Agreement or the Collateral.

"Sale" - as defined in Section 4.02.

"Secured Party" - as defined in the introductory paragraph of this Agreement.

"Security Instrument" - the Lease, this Agreement, the Consent and Agreement and any other instrument with respect to which any right or interest in or in respect of the Collateral has been Granted to Secured Party.

ARTICLE VI

Discharge of Agreement

SECTION 6.01. Final Discharge. This Agreement and all agreements contained herein shall cease and terminate when all principal, interest and other amounts payable under or in respect of this Agreement shall have been paid in full, whether at the end of the term of the Note, by acceleration, by prepayment or otherwise.

SECTION 6.02. Delivery of Discharge. Upon the termination of this Agreement, Secured Party shall execute and deliver such instruments as Debtor shall furnish and which shall be reasonably required to satisfy and discharge the lien of this Agreement.

ARTICLE VII

Miscellaneous

SECTION 7.01. Non-Recourse Obligations. No recourse shall be had against the Debtor personally, or against any incorporator, shareholder, officer or director of Debtor under or in respect of this Agreement or the Note. It is expressly understood that all such obligations are non-recourse obligations enforceable only against the Collateral. The foregoing shall not be deemed to bar or prohibit Payee from asserting a claim against Debtor in the event any material representation, covenant or warranty contained in the Note or this Security Agreement (other than those involving the payment of none by Debtor to Secured Party) shall prove to be untrue or to have been breached.

SECTION 7.02. Notices. All notices and demands hereunder shall be in writing and shall be deemed to have been given upon receipt by Debtor or Secured Party, said notice to be accomplished by registered or certified mail, return receipt requested, postage prepaid, and addressed in each case as follows:

(a) if to Secured Party, at:

> Abacus Financial Corporation
> 50 South Main
> Salt Lake City, Utah 84130
> Attention: Leasing Department

or (b) if to Debtor at:

> Sentry Financial Corporation
> 3450 South Highland Drive
> Suite 104
> Salt Lake City, Utah 84106

Either party may change its address for notices hereunder by giving notice of such change to the other party in accordance with the provisions of this Section 7.02.

SECTION 7.03. Powers and Agencies. Whenever in this Agreement Secured Party is granted the power of attorney or is appointed the agent and attorney-in-fact with respect to any person, such grant or appointment is irrevocable and coupled with an interest. Secured Party shall have full power of substitution and delegation in respect of all such grants and appointments.

SECTION 7.04. Severability. No provision hereof, or of the Note, shall require the payment or permit the collection of interest in excess of the maximum permitted by the applicable law, any contrary provision herein or in the Note notwithstanding. Any provision hereof, or of the Note, which is prohibited or unenforceable in any jurisdiction will, as to such jurisdiction, be ineffective to the extent of such prohibition or unenforceability without invalidating the remaining provisions hereof, or of the Note, and any such prohibition or unenforceability in any jurisdiction will not invalidate or render unenforceable such provision in any other jurisdiction. To the extent permitted by law, the parties hereto waive any provision of law which renders any such provision prohibited or unenforceable in any respect.

SECTION 7.05 Binding Effect. All provisions hereof shall be binding upon and inure to the benefit of the parties hereto and the respective successors and assigns of the parties hereto.

SECTION 7.06. Amendment and Waiver. The provisions of this Agreement may not be changed orally, but only be an instrument signed by Debtor and Secured Party. No requirement of this Agreement may be waived at any time except by an instrument signed by Secured Party, nor shall any waiver be deemed a waiver of any subsequent breach or default.

SECTION 7.07 Counterpart Execution; Construction; Governing Law. The section and article headings herein are for convenience of reference only, and shall not limit or otherwise affect the meaning hereof. This Agreement may be executed in several counterparts, each of which shall constitute an original, but all of which together constitute one and the same Agreement. This Agreement shall be governed by and construed in accordance with the laws of the state wherein the principal office of Secured Party is located (without giving effect to principles relating to conflict of laws).

IN WITNESS WHEREOF, Debtor and Secured Party have caused this Agreement to be executed, all as of the day and year first above written.

SECURED PARTY:

ABACUS FINANCIAL CORPORATION,
a Utah corporation

By:_____

Print Name:_____

Title:_____

DEBTOR:

SENTRY FINANCIAL CORPORATION,
a Utah corporation

By:_____

Print Name:_____

Title:_____

Exhibit XIV

EXHIBIT A

(LETTERHEAD OF TRANSFEREE)

(Date)

To:_____

_____

_____

_____

Attention:_____

Gentlemen:

Reference is made to the Security Agreement dated as of January 11, 1988 (the "Security Agreement"), between Abacus Financial Corporation (the "Lender"), and Sentry Financial Corporation, a Utah corporation (the "Debtor"). Terms used herein and not otherwise defined shall have the meanings specified in the Security Agreement, a copy of which is attached hereto as Exhibit A.

_____(Name of Transferee) _____(the "Transferee") and Debtor have entered into a Sales Agreement, dated as of _____(the "Sales Agreement"), pursuant to which, on _____, Debtor sold the Equipment described on Exhibit B hereto (the "Equipment") to Transferee and assigned to Transferee its rights under Equipment Schedule Nos. F & G to Master Lease dated April 23, 1983 (the "Lease") between Debtor, as original lessor, and Bono & Company ("Bono & Company"), as lessee, or sold the Equipment to Transferee subject to such rights.

Pursuant to the Security Agreement, Debtor has granted to the Lender a first priority security interest in all its rights and interests in and to the Equipment and the Lease, except as otherwise provided therein, to secure Debtor's obligations to the Lender under the Security Agreement and under the Note. In order to comply with the requirements of Section 2.02 of the Security Agreement, Transferee hereby covenants and agrees with the Lender as follows:

1. Grant of Security Interest to Lender. To secure Debtor's obligations to the Lender under the Security Agreement and under the Note, Transferee hereby assumes Debtor's prospective obligations under the Note, and Security Agreement as if Transferee were the original debtor therein, and hereby grants to the Lender a security interest in the Equipment and all its right, title and interest in the Lease, such security interest having priority over any other interests of

Transferee in the Equipment and the Lease or any substitutions therefor; provided, however, that nothing contained herein shall constitute or be deemed to constitute any release of Debtor from any of its obligations arising prior to the date hereof, or a waiver by Transferee of any rights or remedies it may have against Debtor, under the Sales Agreement or otherwise; provided, further, that the exercise by Transferee of any and all such rights and remedies will not disturb the validity, priority or perfection of the security interest of the Lender in and to the Equipment and the Lease. Upon the occurrence of an event of default under the Security Agreement or the Note, the Lender shall, except as otherwise provided herein, have the same remedies hereunder with respect to the Equipment and the Lease as are provided with respect to the Collateral by the Security Agreement and by law and such remedies shall be exercisable simultaneously with those with respect to the security interest granted to the Lender by Debtor under the Security Agreement; provided, however, that as additional consideration to Lender for permitting the transfer, Transferee and Lender hereby agree that, as regards Transferee, its obligations under the Note and Security Agreement shall be recourse to the extent of $_____, which amount shall be reduced proportionately with each payment made under the Note. Upon full payment of the Note and satisfaction of Debtor's obligations thereunder and under the Security Agreement, the Lender agrees to execute and deliver to Transferee such releases, termination statements or other documents reasonably requested by Transferee as may be necessary or desirable to evidence such satisfaction.

2. Acknowledgment of Lender's Security Interest. In order to preserve and protect the security interest granted to the Lender under the Security Agreement and this Agreement, Transferee hereby (i) acknowledges the execution and delivery of the Security Agreement by Debtor, (ii) waives any objection to the enforceability thereof, (iii) recognizes the security interest granted to the Lender thereby, (iv) agrees that Transferee's ownership interest in the Equipment and its interest in the Lease shall in all respects be subject and subordinate to the security interest granted to the Lender by the Security Agreement and this Agreement, (v) to the extent deemed necessary or desirable by the Lender, agrees that it shall execute and deliver to the Lender, for the purpose of further perfecting or confirming the security interests of the Lender created by the Security Agreement and this Agreement, financing statements, and, from time to time, continuation statements, under the Uniform Commercial Code with respect to the security interest created by the Security Agreement and this Agreement.

3. Representations, Warranties and Agreements of Transferee. Transferee represents and warrants that:

(a) Transferee has, on the date hereof, the same title to the Equipment as was conveyed to it by Debtor. Transferee has not taken, or failed to take, nor will it take or omit to take, any action which would result in the imposition of a lien by, through or under Transferee on the Equipment, other than Permitted Encumbrances and the liens of the Lender pursuant to the Security Agreement and this Agreement.

(b) Transferee has filed all tax returns required to be filed by it and is not in default in the payment of any taxes levied or assessed against it or any of its assets which have or could have a material effect on Transferee's ability to perform its obligations hereunder.

(c) Transferee has full authority to enter into this Agreement and to consummate the transactions contemplated hereby. The execution and delivery of this Agreement and the performance of Transferee's obligations hereunder have been duly authorized by all necessary corporate action on the part of Transferee; and this Agreement constitutes the valid and binding agreement and obligation of Transferee, enforceable against the Transferee in accordance with its terms, except as enforceability may be limited by applicable bankruptcy, reorganization, insolvency, moratorium or similar laws relating to or affecting creditors' rights generally.

(d) Transferee's chief executive office is located at the address set forth above, and Transferee will give the Lender at least 30 days prior written notice of any change in the location of its chief executive office.

4. <u>Transfer of Equipment</u>. Transferee hereby agrees that it shall not after the date hereof transfer its interest in the Equipment unless Transferee's transferee shall have executed and delivered to Lender a letter in form and content substantially identical to this Letter.

5. <u>Miscellaneous</u>. All notices hereunder shall be in writing and shall be delivered or mailed by first class, registered or certified mail, postage prepaid, addressed to the parties at their respective addresses first set forth above, or at such other address as either party hereto shall have designated by written notice, as aforesaid, to the other. Neither this Agreement nor any provision hereof may be changed, waived, discharged or terminated orally, but only by an instrument in writing signed by the party against which the enforcement of the change, waiver, discharge, or termination is sought. The terms of this Agreement shall be binding upon and inure to the benefit of and be enforceable by the respective successors and assigns of the parties hereto. This Agreement may be executed in two or more counterparts, each of which when so executed shall be an original, but all of which shall constitute one and the same instrument.

Very truly yours,

(Name of Transferee)

By:_____

Print Name:_____

Title:_____

Agreed as of the date
first written above:

ABACUS FINANCIAL CORPORATION

By:_____

Print Name:_____

Title:_____

Exhibit XV

EXHIBIT B

Equipment

F & G   3   Honeywell   Datanet Communication System with controllers and (1) Tape Sub-System as follows:

Quantity	Model Number	Description	Unit Purchase Price	Total Purchase Price
2	DCU8130	DN 8/30	$80,000	$160,000
4	DCE8111	HOST CONNECTS	8,000	32,000
2	DCP8130	ADDITIONAL CPU	27,000	54,000
2	DCF8002	CONSOLE	795	1,590
2	DCF8003	PRINTER	1,195	2,390
20	DCF8052	MLCP-16	2,700	54,000
6	DCF8061	CIA	2,200	13,200
6	DCF8069	V.35	450	2,700
10	DCF8049	HDLC	3,200	32,000
44	DCF8073	ASYN/SYNC	2,000	88,000
2	DCE8131	LINE EXPANSION	7,500	15,000
		Sub-Total		$454,880
1	MTS8218	TAPE SUBSYSTEM	$44,800	$44,800
2	MXF8913	IOP CHANNEL	8,000	16,000
1	MTF8204	SWITCH CHANNEL	8,000	8,000
1	MTF8201	2X16 TAPE	6,130	6,130
2	MXF8913	HYPRCHANNELS	8,000	16,000
7	MTU8208	TAPE DRIVES	21,000	147,000
2	DCU8130	DN 8/30	80,000	160,000
4	DCE8111	HOST CONNECTS	8,000	32,000
2	DCP8130	ADDITIONAL CPU	27,000	54,000
2	DCF8002	CONSOLE	795	1,590
2	DCF8003	PRINTERS	1,195	2,390
6	DCF8052	MLCP-16	2,700	16,200
6	DCF8061	CIA	2,200	13,200
6	DCF8069	V.35	450	2,700
6	DCF8049	HDLC	3,200	19,200
8	DCF8073	ASYN/SYNC	2,000	16,000
		Sub-Total		$555,210

January 11, 1988

Exhibit XVI

Abacus Financial Corporation
50 South Main Street
Suite 2007
Salt Lake City, Utah 84130
Attention: Leasing Department

RE: Loan Secured by Bono & Company, Equipment Schedule Nos. F & G dated April 19,
         1987

Dear Ladies & Gentlemen:

Please wire transfer the proceeds in the amount of $740,624.04 of the loan with respect to the
above lease to:

> Last National Bank
> 310 South Main
> Salt Lake City, Utah 84111
> Attention: Vicki

For the account of:

> Honeywell Bull Corporation
> Department #1128
> Pasadena, California 91050

Very truly yours,

Jonathan M. Ruga
Chief Operating Officer

Exhibit XVII

SENTRY FINANCIAL CORPORATION'S

OFFICERS' CERTIFICATE

The undersigned, G. Stephen Browning and Jonathan M. Ruga, of Sentry Financial Corporation, a Utah corporation (the "Corporation"), hereby certify as follows to Abacus Financial Corporation ("Lender") in connection with a loan from Lender to the Corporation:

The following persons are, and have been at all times since October 1, 1987, duly qualified and acting officers or authorized agents of the Corporation, duly elected or appointed to the offices or positions set forth opposite their respective names, and are authorized to execute on behalf of the Corporation, Notes, Security Agreements and all related documents.

Names	Office
Jonathan M. Ruga	Chief Operating Officer
Mark D. Hood	President, and Chief Executive Officer
G. Stephen Browning	Executive Vice President and Controller

IN WITNESS WHEREOF, the undersigned officer has executed this Certificate as of the 11th day of January, 1988.

_____

Jonathan M. Ruga
Chief Operating Officer

_____

G. Stephen Browning
Executive Vice President and Controller

Exhibit XVIII

January 11, 1988

Abacus Financial Corporation
50 South Main
Salt Lake City, Utah 84130

Re: Computer Equipment subject to lease under Equipment Schedule Nos. F & G issued pursuant to Master Lease dated as of April 23, 1983 (the "Lease") between Bono & Company, as lessee ("Lessee") and Sentry Financial Corporation, as original lessor ("Sentry").

Ladies and Gentlemen:

I have acted as general counsel for Sentry Financial Corporation, a Utah corporation (the "Corporation"), in connection with (i) the execution and delivery by the Corporation of the Lease pursuant to which the Corporation leased to the Lessee certain computer equipment (the "Equipment"), (ii) the execution and delivery by the Corporation of a Note (the "Note") to Abacus Financial Corporation (the "Lender"), and (iii) the execution and delivery by the Corporation of a Security Agreement dated as of January 11, 1988 (the "Security Agreement") between the Corporation and the Lender (the Lease, the Note, and the Security Agreement are collectively referred to as the "Agreements").

In this connection I have examined originals or copies, certified or otherwise identified to my satisfaction, of the Articles of Incorporation of the Corporation, executed counterparts of the Agreements, and such other documents or materials as I have deemed necessary for purposes of this opinion.

A. <u>OPINION</u>

Upon the basis of the foregoing, I am of the opinion that:

1. The Corporation (i) is a corporation duly organized and validly existing under the laws of the state of its incorporation, (ii) has the power to engage in the transactions contemplated by the Purchase Agreement, and (iii) has the power and authority to enter into and perform its obligations under the Agreements.

2. The Agreements have been duly authorized, executed and delivered by the Corporation and constitute valid, legal and binding agreements, enforceable in accordance with their terms,

except as such enforcement may be limited by bankruptcy, reorganization, insolvency or other laws affecting creditors' rights generally.

3. No event is continuing which constitutes an Event of Default as defined in the Security Agreement. There is no action, suit or proceeding pending or, to my knowledge, threatened against or affecting the Corporation before or by any court, administrative agency or other governmental authority which brings into question the validity of the transactions contemplated by the Agreements or which might materially impair the ability of the Corporation to perform its obligations under the Agreements or the transactions contemplated thereby.

4. Neither the execution and delivery by the Corporation of the Agreements, nor compliance by the Corporation with the provisions of any thereof, conflicts with or results in a breach of any of the provisions of the articles of incorporation or bylaws of the Corporation, or of any applicable law, judgment, order, writ, injunction, decree, rule or regulation of any court, administrative agency or other governmental authority, or of any agreement or other instrument to which the Corporation is a party or by which it is bound, or constitutes or will constitute a default under any thereof.

5. No consent, approval or other authorization of or by any court, administrative agency or other governmental authority is required in connection with the execution, delivery or performance by the Corporation of, or the consummation by the Corporation of, the transactions contemplated by the Agreements.

6. The Corporation is not (i) a "public utility company" or a "holding company" or "affiliate" or "a subsidiary company" of such a "holding company," or an "affiliate" of such a "subsidiary company", as such terms are defined in the Public Utility Holding Company Act of 1935, as amended, or (ii) a "public utility" as defined in the Federal Power Act, as amended, or (iii) an "investment company" or an "affiliated person" thereof of an "affiliated person" of such affiliated person, as such terms are defined in the Investment Company Act of 1940, as amended, or (iv) a "carrier," as such term is defined in any provision of the Interstate Commerce Act.

B. <u>EXCEPTIONS AND COMMENTS</u>

The opinions set forth herein are predicated upon the assumptions set forth herein and are subject to the following additional qualifications, exceptions, and limitations:

1. No opinion is expressed as to whether any provisions of the Agreements referred to herein are specifically enforceable in equity, or as to the availability or enforceability of certain provisions which purport to permit the recitals in any conveyance of any Collateral (as that term is defined in the Security Agreement) to conclusively establish the truth of the matters stated therein, or which provide equitable remedies; self-help remedies; the establishment of evidentiary standards for suits or proceedings to enforce said documents; waivers by any parties; the

prohibition of the transfer or further encumbrance of properties or assets of the Corporation; or authorization of the Lender to execute or record other documents or instruments or to take any other action as attorney-in-fact for and on behalf of the Corporation.

2. The enforceability of the documents referred to herein may be limited by applicable bankruptcy, insolvency, reorganization, moratorium, and other similar laws affecting the rights of creditors generally. I express no opinion as to the priority of the lien or liens established by the recording and filing of the Security Agreement or any financing statements authorized thereby.

3. The opinions set forth herein are based on the genuineness of all signatures, the authenticity and regularity of all of the Agreements submitted to me as originals or copies of the originals, and the due authority of the officers executing the same for the Lender.

4. The opinions set forth herein are limited to the applicable statutes of the State of Utah and the applicable published decisions of the Utah Supreme Court (to the extent not affected by subsequent law), and I express no opinion as to Federal laws or the laws of any other state.

5. The opinions set forth herein are given in connection with the Agreements and the transactions contemplated therein, and neither you nor any other party shall have right to rely thereon for any other purpose.

6. The opinions set forth herein are based upon facts and circumstances contemplated by the Agreements including, but not limited to, the accuracy of the representations and warranties set forth therein.

7. This letter is not to be quoted in whole or in part or otherwise referred to in any document, nor is it to be filed with any party and/or government agency or provided to any other party without my prior written consent in each and every instance, which consent shall not be unreasonably withheld.

8. Unless otherwise indicated, the opinions set forth herein are as of the date hereof; and I disclaim any undertaking or obligation to advise you of changes which may hereafter be brought to my attention.

Very truly yours,

Jonathan M. Ruga

Exhibit XIX

December 28, 1987

Bono & Company
2732 South 2140 East
Salt Lake City, Utah 84105

Re: **Notice of Assignment of Equipment subject to Equipment Schedules F & G issued pursuant to Master Lease Agreement dated as of April 23, 1983.**

Ladies & Gentlemen:

By Master Lease Agreement dated April 23, 1983 between Sentry Financial Corporation, as lessor ("Lessor"), and Bono & Company, as lessee ("Lessee"), Lessor leased to Lessee certain electronic data processing equipment (the "Equipment") listed in Equipment Schedule Nos. F & G (the "Lease"). Lessor assigned the Lease and granted a security interest in the Equipment to Abacus Financial Corporation (the "Lender") in connection with a loan (the "Loan") from Lender to Lessor.

You are hereby requested to execute the attached Consent and Agreement, and return it to my attention at Sentry Financial Corporation.

Thank you for your cooperation in this matter, and I apologize in advance for any inconvenience this request may cause you. If you have any questions or comments, please contact me.

Sincerely,

Jonathan M. Ruga
Chief Operating Officer

Enclosure

Exhibit XX

Consent & Agreement

To: Abacus Financial Corporation
       50 South Main Street
       Salt Lake City, Utah 84130
       Attention: Leasing Department

Reference is made to Master Agreement of Lease dated as of April 23, 1983, between Sentry Financial Corporation ("Sentry"), as Lessor, and Bono & Company (the "Company"), as Lessee, and Equipment Schedule Nos. F & G thereto, dated as of April 19, 1987, between the same parties, true and correct copies of which are attached hereto as Exhibit 1. The Master Lease Agreement and the Equipment Schedule are hereinafter referred to together as the "Lease".

The Company hereby acknowledges and consents to the assignment by Sentry to Abacus Financial Corporation ("Abacus") of all right, title, interest, claim and demand, as Lessor, in, to and under the Lease, and the rental payments due thereunder (commencing with the rental payment due on January 1, 1988 and all other moneys from time to time payable to or receivable by Sentry under any of the provisions of the Lease, all such amounts being hereinafter referred to as the "Moneys"; provided, however, that such assignment does not alter the terms and conditions of the Lease or expand or modify the obligations of Sentry or the Company thereunder.

The Company agrees:

(i)   to remit and deliver all Moneys directly to Abacus Financial Corporation as follows:

> ABACUS FINANCIAL CORPORATION
> 50 South Main
> Salt Lake City, Utah 84130

> with identification of the source and application of funds, without abatement, reduction, counterclaim or offset; and

(ii)   to deliver copies of all material notices and other communications given, made or received by the Company pursuant to the Lease to Abacus, at the address shown above.

(iii)   to make no change or modification of the Lease without Abacus' consent.

The Company acknowledges to Abacus that the Lease is in full force and effect, that the Company has executed only three consecutively numbered counterparts of the Equipment Schedule, that the Company has accepted the equipment (the "Equipment") under the Lease and the Equipment has been installed at, 2732 South 2140 East, Salt Lake City, Utah 84105 that the Company has entered into no agreement with respect to the Equipment or to the Lease other than agreements of the company contained in the Lease and herein, and that as of December 31, 1987, forty (40) monthly rental payments of $12,048.00 for Equipment Schedule F and $9,871.00 for Equipment Schedule No. G will remain payable under the Lease.

Abacus hereby agrees that so long as no Event of Default (as defined in the Lease shall have occurred and be continuing, it will not disturb the Company's quiet and peaceful possession of the Equipment and its unrestricted use of the Equipment for its intended purpose under the terms of the Lease.

IN WITNESS WHEREOF, the Company has executed this Consent and Agreement as of the 31st day of December, 1987.

Bono & Company

By:_____

Name:_____

Title:_____

Exhibit XXI

Form UCC-1

07-01-06 (Rev. 6/84)

Kelly Co. #10448

STANDARD FORM

UNIFORM COMMERCIAL CODE - FINANCING STATEMENT - FORM UCC-1

UTAH

INSTRUCTIONS:

1. PLEASE TYPE this form. Fold only along perforation for mailing.
2. Remove Secured Party and Debtor copies and send other 3 copies with interleaved carbon paper to the filing officer. Enclose filing fee. The filing fee is $2.00 for each name listed in the Debtors box with Soc. Sec. No. and/or Emp. Fed. Tax I.D. No., otherwise the fee is $10.00.
3. If the space provided for any item(s) on the form is inadequate the item(s) should be continued on additional sheets, preferably 5'' X 8'' or 8'' X 10''. Only one copy of such additional sheets need be presented to the filing officer with a set of three copies of the financing statement. Long schedules of collateral, indentures, etc., may be on any size paper that is convenient for the secured party. Indicate the number of additional sheets attached.
4. If collateral is crops or goods which are or are to become fixtures, describe generally the real estate and give name of record owner.
5. When a copy of the security agreement is used as a financing statement, it is requested that it be accompanied by a completed but unsigned set of these forms, without extra fee.
6. At the time of original filing, filing officer should return third copy as an acknowledgment. At a later time, secured party may date and sign Termination Legend and use third copy as a Termination Statement.

This **FINANCING STATEMENT** is presented to a filing officer for filing pursuant to the Uniform Commercial Code.

1. Debtor(s) (Last Name First) and address(es)

Sentry Financial Corporation
3450 S. Highland Dr., #104
Salt Lake City, UT 84106

Social Security or
Emp. Fed. I.D. No. _____

2. Secured Party(ies) and address(es)

Abacus Financial Corporation
50 South Main
Salt Lake City, UT 84130
Attn: Leasing Department

For Filing Officer (Date, Time, Number, and Filing Office)

4. This Financing Statement covers the following types (or items) of property:

LEASE: Equipment Schedule No. F dated April 19, 1987 issued pursuant to Master Lease dated April 23, 1983 between Sentry Financial Corporation, as original Lessor, and Bono & Company, as Lessee.

EQUIPMENT: All computer and related equipment under lease to Bono & Company pursuant to Equipment Schedule No. F described above.

5. Assignee(s) of Secured Party and Address(es)   [X] if so)   Microfilm No.

6. Gross sales price of collateral $_____ Sales

or use tax paid to State of _____

The Secured party is _____ is not _____ a seller or Purchase money lender of the collateral.

This statement is filed without the debtor's signature to perfect a security interest in collateral. (Check [ ])

[ ] already subject to a security interest in another jurisdiction when it was brought into this state.

[ ] which is proceeds of the original collateral described above in which a security interest was perfected.

Check [X] if covered: Proceeds of Collateral are also covered.   [ ] Products of Collateral are also covered. No. of additional Sheets presented:

3. Maturity date (if any):

Sentry Financial Corporation

By: _____
Signature(s) of Debtor(s)

Approved by Division of Corporations and Commercial Code, Department of Business Regulations.

Abacus Financial Corporation

By: _____
Signature(s) of Secured Party(ies)

STANDARD FORM - FORM UCC-1.

(1) FILING OFFICER COPY — ALPHABETICAL

GLOSSARY

Accelerated Cost Recovery System (ACRS)

The tax depreciation, or cost recovery, method for Internal Revenue Service (IRS) purposes, which was introduced by the 1981 Economic Recovery Tax Act and was effective for all depreciable property placed in service after December 31, 1980 and before January 1, 1987. ACRS replaced the Asset Depreciation Range (ADR) system and was replaced itself by the Modified Accelerated Cost Recovery System (MACRS) of the 1986 Tax Reform Act.

Accelerated Depreciation

Any depreciation method that allows for greater deductions or charges in the earlier years of an asset's depreciable life, with charges becoming progressively smaller in each successive period. Examples would include the double declining balance and sum-of-the-years digits methods.

Accumulated Depreciation

A financial reporting term for a contra-asset balance sheet account that shows the total depreciation charges for an asset since acquisition.

Actuarial Interest

A constant interest charge (or return) based upon a declining principal balance.

Adjusted (or Remaining) Basis

The undepreciated amount of an asset's original basis that is used, for tax purposes, to calculate the gain or loss on disposition of an asset.

ADR System

A tax depreciation system that establishes the minimum, midpoint and maximum number of years, by asset category, over which an asset can be depreciated. The midpoint life has become synonymous with the term "ADR classlife."

Advance Payments

One or more lease payments required to be paid to the lessor at the beginning of the lease term. Lease structures commonly require one payment to be made in advance.

Alternative Minimum Tax (AMT)

A penalty tax of sorts, in which a taxpayer must pay the higher of its regular tax or AMT liability. The corporate AMT rate, although lower than the regular tax rate, is applied to a different, typically higher, taxable income than for regular taxes. The Tax Reform Act of 1986 substantially modified the AMT, which must be calculated for all taxpayers.

Annuity

A stream of even (equal) cash flows occurring at regular intervals, such as even monthly lease payments. An annuity in advance is one in which the annuity payment is due at the beginning of each period. An annuity in arrears is one in which the annuity payment is due at the end of each period.

Asset Classlife

The updated ADR midpoint life as modified by the 1986 Tax Reform Act. An asset classlife represents the IRS designated economic life of an asset, and is used as the recovery period for alternative tax depreciation computations.

Assign

To transfer or exchange future rights. In leasing, the right to receive future lease payments in a lease is usually transferred to a funding source, in return for up-front cash. The up-front cash represents the loan proceeds from the funding source, and is equal to the present value of the future lease payments discounted at the leasing company's cost of borrowing. A lease assigned by the lessor to a funding source is called an assigned lease. The assignment of leases is a very common funding technique used by leasing companies.

Bargain Purchase Option

A lease provision allowing the lessee, at its option, to purchase the leased property at the end of the lease term for a price that is sufficiently lower than the expected fair market value of the property, such that exercise of the option appears, at the inception of the lease, to be reasonably assured.

Bargain Renewal Option

A lease provision allowing the lessee, at its option, to extend the lease for an additional term in exchange for periodic rental payments that are sufficiently less than fair value rentals for the property, such that exercise of the option appears, at the inception of the lease, to be reasonably assured.

Basis

The original cost of an asset plus other capitalized acquisition costs such as installation charges and sales tax. Basis reflects the amount upon which depreciation charges are computed.

Basis Point

One one-hundredth of a percent (.01%).

Bundled Lease

A lease that includes many additional services such as maintenance, insurance and property taxes that are paid for by the lessor, the cost of which is built into the lease payments.

Call Option

Any option in a lease, such as a purchase or a renewal option, that is exercised at the discretion of the lessee, not the lessor.

Capital Lease

From a financial reporting perspective, a lease that has the characteristics of a purchase agreement, and also meets certain criteria established by Financial Accounting Standards Board Statement No. 13 (FASB 13). Such a lease is required to be shown as an asset and a related obligation on the balance sheet of the lessee.

Capitalize

To record an expenditure that may benefit future periods as an asset rather than as an expense to be charged off in the period of its occurrence.

Capitalized Cost

The amount of an asset to be shown on the balance sheet, from a financial reporting perspective. The total capitalized cost (or basis) also is the amount upon which tax benefits, such as MACRS depreciation deductions, are based and may include asset cost plus other amounts such as sales tax.

Captive Lessor

A leasing company that has been set up by a manufacturer or dealer of equipment to finance the sale or lease of its own products to end-users or lessees.

Certificate of Delivery and Acceptance

A document that is signed by the lessee to acknowledge that the equipment to be leased has been delivered and is acceptable. Many lease agreements state that the actual lease term commences once this document has been signed.

Closed-End Lease

A lease that does not contain a purchase or renewal option, thereby requiring the lessee to return the equipment to the lessor at the end of the initial lease term.

Commitment Fee

A fee required by the lessor, at the time a proposal or commitment is accepted by the lessee, to lock in a specific lease rate and/or other lease terms.

Commitment Letter

A document prepared by the lessor that sets forth its commitment, including rate and term, to provide lease financing to the lessee. This document, if utilized, precedes final documentation, and may or may not be subject to lessor credit approval.

Compensating Balances

The amount of funds that a bank requires a borrower to keep on deposit during the term of a loan. The amount of this noninterest earning deposit is typically based upon some percentage of the loan and effectively increases the borrower's interest cost.

Conditional Sales Contract

An agreement for the purchase of an asset in which the lessee is treated as the owner of the asset for federal income tax purposes (thereby being entitled to the tax benefits of ownership, such as depreciation), but does not become the legal owner of the asset until all terms and conditions of the agreement have been satisfied.

Cost of Capital

The weighted-average cost of funds that a firm secures from both debt and equity sources in order to fund its assets. The use of a firm's cost of capital is essential in making accurate capital budgeting and project investment decisions.

Cost of Debt

The costs incurred by a firm to fund the acquisition of assets through the use of borrowings. A firm's component cost of debt is used in calculating the firm's overall weighted-average cost of capital.

Cost of Equity

The return on investment required by the equity holders of a firm. Cost of equity can be calculated using any number of different theoretical approaches and must take into consideration the current and long-term yield requirements of a firm's investors. A firm's component cost of equity is used in calculating the firm's overall weighted-average cost of capital.

Debt Optimization

A method of borrowing funds in a leveraged lease where the equity participants borrow and repay the obligation in such a manner as to maximize their return on equity, maintain a constant return while offering a lower lease payment, maximize cash flow, etc., or to maximize a combination of factors.

Declining Balance Depreciation

A type of accelerated depreciation in which a constant percentage of an asset's declining remaining basis is depreciated each year. The constant percentage amount is often calculated at 125%, 150% or 200% (double declining balance) of the straight-line percentage over the same recovery period.

Depreciation

A means for a firm to recover the cost of a purchased asset, over time, through periodic deductions or offsets to income. Depreciation is used in both a financial reporting and tax context, and is considered a tax benefit because the depreciation deductions cause a reduction in taxable income, thereby lowering a firm's tax liability.

Direct Financing Lease

A lessor capital lease (per FASB 13) that does not give rise to manufacturer's or dealer's profit (or loss) to the lessor.

Discount Rate

A certain interest rate that is used to bring a series of future cash flows to their present value in order to state them in current, or today's, dollars. Use of a discount rate removes the time value of money from future cash flows.

Discounted Lease

A lease in which the lease payments are assigned to a funding source in exchange for up-front cash to the lessor.

Dry Lease

A net lease. This term is traditionally used in aircraft and marine leasing to describe a lease agreement that provides financing only and, therefore, requires the lessee to separately procure personnel, fuel and provisions necessary to operate the craft.

Early Termination

Occurs when the lessee returns the leased equipment to the lessor prior to the end of the lease term, as permitted by the original lease contract or subsequent agreement. At times, this may result in a penalty to the lessee.

Economic Recovery Tax Act of 1981 (ERTA '81)
The federal tax act that introduced ACRS, among other provisions.

End-of-Term Options
Options stated in the lease agreement that give the lessee flexibility in its treatment of the leased equipment at the end of the lease term. Common end-of-term options include purchasing the equipment, renewing the lease or returning the equipment to the lessor.

Equipment Schedule
A document, incorporated by reference into the lease agreement, that describes in detail the equipment being leased. The schedule may state the lease term, commencement date, repayment schedule and location of the equipment.

Equipment Specifications
A specific description of a piece of equipment that is to be acquired, including, but not limited to, equipment make, model, configuration and capacity requirements.

Equity Investor
An entity that provides equity funding in a leveraged lease transaction and thereby becomes the owner and ultimate lessor of the leased equipment.

Executory Costs
Recurring costs in a lease, such as insurance, maintenance and taxes for the leased property, whether paid by the lessor or the lessee. Executory costs also include amounts paid by the lessee in consideration for a third-party residual guarantee, as well as any profits realized by the lessor on any executory costs paid by the lessor and passed on to the lessee.

External Rate of Return (ERR)
A method of yield calculation. ERR is a modified internal rate of return (IRR) that allows for the incorporation of specific reinvestment, borrowing and sinking fund assumptions.

Fair Market Value
The value of a piece of equipment if the equipment were to be sold in a transaction determined at arm's length, between a willing buyer and a willing seller, for equivalent property and under similar terms and conditions.

FASB 13
Financial Accounting Standards Board Statement No. 13, 'Accounting for Leases.' FASB 13, along with its various amendments and interpretations, specifies the proper classification, accounting and reporting of leases by lessors and lessees.

Finance Lease
An expression oftentimes used in the industry to refer to a capital lease or a nontax lease. It is also a type of tax-oriented lease that was introduced by the Tax Equity and Fiscal Responsibility Act of 1982, to be effective in 1984, but later repealed by the Tax Reform Act of 1986.

Financial Accounting Standards Board (FASB)
The rule-making body that establishes financial reporting guidelines.

Financial Institution Lessor
A type of independent leasing company that is owned by, or a part of, a financial institution, such as a commercial bank, thrift institution, insurance company, industrial loan company or credit union.

Financing Statement

A notice of a security interest filed under the Uniform Commercial Code (UCC).

Full-payout Lease

A lease in which the lessor recovers, through the lease payments, all costs incurred in the lease plus an acceptable rate of return, without any reliance upon the leased equipment's future residual value.

Full-service Lease

A lease that includes many additional services such as maintenance, insurance and property taxes that are paid for by the lessor, the cost of which is built into the lease payments.

Funding Source

An entity that provides any part of the funds used to pay for the cost of the leased equipment. Funds can come from either an equity funding source, such as the ultimate lessor in a lease transaction, or a debt funding source, such as a bank or other lending institution.

Guaranteed Residual Value

A situation in which the lessee or an unrelated third party (e.g., equipment manufacturer, insurance company) guarantees to the lessor that the leased equipment will be worth a certain fixed amount at the end of the lease term. The guarantor agrees to reimburse the lessor for any deficiency realized if the leased equipment is subsequently salvaged at an amount below the guaranteed residual value.

Guideline Lease

A tax lease that meets or follows the IRS guidelines, as established by Revenue Ruling 75-21, for a leveraged lease.

Half-Year Convention

A tax depreciation convention that assumes all equipment is purchased or sold at the midpoint of a taxpayer's tax year. The half-year convention allows an equipment owner to claim a half-year of depreciation deductions in the year of acquisition, as well as in the year of disposition, regardless of the actual date within the year that the equipment was placed in service, or disposed of.

Implicit Rate

The discount rate that, when applied to the minimum lease payments (excluding executory costs) together with any unguaranteed residual, causes the aggregate present value at the inception of the lease to be equal to the fair market value (reduced by any lessor retained Investment Tax Credits) of the leased property.

Independent Lessor

A type of leasing company that is independent of any one manufacturer, and, as such, purchases equipment from various unrelated manufacturers. The equipment is then leased to the end-user or lessee. This type of lessor is also referred to as a third-party lessor.

Initial Direct Costs

Costs incurred by the lessor that are directly associated with negotiating and consummating a lease. These costs include, but are not necessarily limited to, commissions, legal fees, costs of credit investigations, the cost of preparing and processing documents for new leases acquired and so forth.

Interim Rent

A charge for the use of a piece of equipment from its in-service date, or delivery date, until the date on which the base term of the lease commences. The daily interim rent charge is typically equal to the daily equivalent of the base rental payment. The use of interim rent allows the lessor to have one common base term commencement date for a lease agreement having multiple deliveries of equipment.

Internal Rate of Return (IRR)

The unique discount rate that equates the present value of a series of cash inflows (i.e., lease payments, purchase option) to the present value of the cash outflows (equipment or investment cost). IRR is the most common method used to compute yields.

Investment Tax Credit (ITC)

A credit that a taxpayer is permitted to claim on the federal tax return (a direct offset to tax liability) as a result of ownership of qualified equipment. ITC was generally repealed by the Tax Reform Act of 1986, for all equipment placed in service after 1985.

Lease Acquisition

The process whereby a leasing company purchases or acquires a lease from a lease originator, such as a lease broker or leasing company.

Lease Agreement

The contractual agreement between the lessor and the lessee that sets forth all the terms and conditions of the lease.

Lease Broker

An entity that provides one or more services in the lease transaction, but that does not retain the lease transaction for its own portfolio. Such services could include finding the lessee, working with the equipment manufacturer, securing debt financing for the lessor to use in purchasing the equipment and locating the ultimate lessor or equity participant in the lease transaction. The lease broker is also referred to as a packager.

Lease Origination

The process of uncovering (through a sales force), developing and consummating lease transactions. Steps in the process could include, but are not limited to, prospecting for new lease business, pricing potential transactions, performing credit reviews and completing the necessary documentation.

Leveraged Lease

A specific form of lease involving at least three parties: a lessor, lessee and funding source. The lessor borrows a significant portion of the equipment cost on a nonrecourse basis by assigning the future lease payment stream to the lender in return for up-front funds (the borrowing). The lessor puts up a minimal amount of its own equity funds (the difference between the equipment cost and the present value of the assigned lease payments) and is generally entitled to the full tax benefits of equipment ownership.

MACRS Classlife

The specific tax cost recovery (depreciation) period for a class of assets as defined by MACRS. Asset classlives (ADR midpoint lives) are used to determine an asset's MACRS classlife and, hence, its recovery period.

Maintenance Contract

An agreement whereby the lessee contracts with another party to maintain and repair the leased property during the lease term, in exchange for a payment or stream of payments.

Master Lease

A lease line of credit that allows a lessee to obtain additional leased equipment under the same basic lease terms and conditions as originally agreed to, without having to renegotiate and execute a new lease contract with the lessor. The actual lease rate for a specific piece of equipment will generally be set upon equipment delivery to the lessee.

Match Funded Debt

Debt incurred by the lessor to fund a specific piece of leased equipment, the terms and repayment of which are structured to correspond to the repayment of the lease obligation by the lessee.

Midquarter Convention

A depreciation convention (replacing half-year convention for certain taxpayers in certain years) that assumes all equipment is placed in service halfway through the quarter in which it was actually placed in service. Allowable acquisition and disposition year depreciation deductions are pro rated based upon the midquarter date of the quarter in which the asset was placed in service.

Minimum Lease Payments

From the lessee perspective, all payments that are required to be made, may be required to be made or, in all probability, will be made to the lessor per the lease agreement. Minimum lease payments for the lessee include, but are not limited to, the lease payments (excluding executory costs) during the noncancellable lease term, bargain purchase options, any put purchase options, the amount of any lessee residual guarantees and nonrenewal penalties that are insufficiently severe to cause renewal. Minimum lease payments for the lessor include all payments to be received from the lessee, as described above, as well as the amount of any residual guarantees by unrelated third-party guarantors.

Modified Accelerated Cost Recovery System (MACRS)

The current tax depreciation system as introduced by the Tax Reform Act of 1986, generally effective for all equipment placed in service after December 31, 1986.

Money-Over-Money Lease

A nontax lease. This type of lease is a conditional sales contract in the guise of a lease, in which the lessee is, or will become, the owner of the leased equipment by the end of the lease term, and, therefore, is entitled to the tax benefits of ownership.

Multiple Investment Sinking Fund (MISF)

Method of income allocation used to report earnings on a leveraged lease. This method is similar to the internal rate of return (IRR) method of yield calculation except that it assumes a zero earnings rate during periods of disinvestment (a sinking fund rate equal to 0).

Municipal Lease

A conditional sales contract disguised in the form of a lease available only to municipalities, in which the interest earnings are tax-exempt to the lessor.

Net Lease

A lease in which all costs in connection with the use of the equipment, such as maintenance, insurance and property taxes, are paid for separately by the lessee and are not included in the lease rental paid to the lessor.

Net Present Value

The total discounted value of all cash inflows and outflows from a project or investment.

Nonrecourse

A type of borrowing in which the borrower (a lessor in the process of funding a lease transaction) is not at-risk for the borrowed funds. The lender expects repayment from the lessee and/or the value of the leased equipment; hence, the lender's credit decision will be based upon the creditworthiness of the lessee, as well as the expected value of the leased equipment.

Nontax Lease

A type of lease in which the lessee is, or will become, the owner of the leased equipment, and, therefore, is entitled to all the risks and benefits (including tax benefits) of equipment ownership.

Off Balance Sheet Financing

Any form of financing, such as an operating lease, that, for financial reporting purposes, is not required to be reported on a firm's balance sheet.

Open-End Lease

A lease in which the lessee guarantees the amount of the future residual value to be realized by the lessor at the end of the lease. If the equipment is sold for less than the guaranteed value, the lessee must pay the amount of any deficiency to the lessor. This lease is referred to as open-end because the lessee does not know its actual cost until the equipment is sold at the end of the lease term.

Operating Budget

A budget that lists the amount of noncapital goods and services a firm is authorized by management to expend during the operating period.

Operating Lease

From a financial reporting perspective, a lease that has the characteristics of a usage agreement and also meets certain criteria established by the FASB. Such a lease is not required to be shown on the balance sheet of the lessee. The term is also used to refer to leases in which the lessor has taken a significant residual position in the lease pricing and, therefore, must salvage the equipment for a certain value at the end of the lease term in order to earn its rate of return.

Payments in Advance

A payment stream in which each lease payment is due at the beginning of each period during the lease.

Payments in Arrears

A payment stream in which each lease payment is due at the end of each period during the lease.

Payoff

Occurs when the lessee purchases the leased asset from the lessor prior to the end of the lease term.

Placed in Service

Delivered and available for use, although the equipment may still be subject to final installation and/or assembly.

Point

One percent, or one percentage point (1.00%). A point also represents 100 basis points.

Pooled Funds

A funding technique used by lessors in which several forms of borrowing are pooled, or grouped, for use in funding leases and are not specifically tied to the purchase of one piece of leased equipment.

Present Value

The discounted value of a payment or stream of payments to be received in the future, taking into consideration a specific interest or discount rate. Present value represents a series of future cash flows expressed in today's dollars.

Pricing

Arriving at the periodic rental amount to charge a lessee. A lessor must factor many variables into its pricing, which may include lease term, lessor targeted yield, security deposits, residual value and tax benefits.

Purchase Option

An option in the lease agreement that allows the lessee to purchase the leased equipment at the end of the lease term for either a fixed amount or at the future fair market value of the leased equipment.

Put Option

An option in a lease (e.g., for equipment purchase or lease renewal) in which the exercise of the option is at the lessor's, not the lessee's, discretion.

Recourse

A type of borrowing in which the borrower (a lessor funding a lease) is fully at-risk to the lender for repayment of the obligation. The recourse borrower (lessor) is required to make payments to the lender whether or not the lessee fulfills its obligation under the lease agreement.

Refundable Security Deposit

An amount paid by the lessee to the lessor as security for fulfillment of all obligations outlined in the lease agreement that is subsequently refunded to the lessee once all obligations have been satisfied. Security deposits are typically returned at the end of the lease term but, according to mutual agreement, can be refunded at any point during the lease.

Remarketing

The process of selling or leasing the leased equipment to another party upon termination of the original lease term. The lessor can remarket the equipment or contract with another party, such as the manufacturer, to remarket the equipment in exchange for a remarketing fee.

Renewal Option

An option in the lease agreement that allows the lessee to extend the lease term for an additional period of time beyond the expiration of the initial lease term, in exchange for lease renewal payments.

Residual Value

The value, either actual or expected, of leased equipment at the end, or termination, of the lease.

Retained Transaction

A lease transaction or investment kept for one's own portfolio; a retained transaction is not sold to another lessor or investor.

Return on Assets (ROA)

A common measure of profitability based upon the amount of assets invested; ROA is equal to the ratio of either: (1) net income to total assets or (2) net income available to common stockholders to total assets.

Return on Equity (ROE)

A measure of profitability related to the amount of invested equity; ROE is equal to the ratio of either: (1) net income to owners' equity or (2) net income available to common stockholders to common equity.

Rule of 78

An accelerated method of allocating periodic earnings in a lease (or a loan) based upon the sum-of-the-years method.

Running Rate

The rate of return to the lessor, or cost to the lessee, in a lease based solely upon the initial equipment cost and the periodic lease payments, without any reliance on residual value, tax benefit, deposits or fees. This rate is referred to also as the street or stream rate.

Sale-Leaseback

A transaction that involves the sale of equipment to a leasing company and a subsequent lease of the same equipment back to the original owner, who continues to use the equipment.

Sales-Type Lease

A capital lease from the lessor's perspective (per FASB 13) that gives rise to manufacturer's or dealer's profit to the lessor.

Salvage Value

The expected or realized value from selling a piece of equipment.

Single Investor Lease

A lease in which the lessor is fully at-risk for all funds (both equity and pooled funds) used to purchase the leased equipment.

Sinking Fund

A reserve set aside for the future payment of taxes (generally applicable only in leveraged leases), or for the purpose of payment of any liability anticipated to become due at a future date.

Sinking Fund Rate

The earnings rate allocated to a sinking fund.

Skipped-Payment Lease

A lease that contains a payment stream requiring the lessee to make payments only during certain periods of the year.

Step-Payment Lease

A lease that contains a payment stream requiring the lessee to make payments that either increase (step-up) or decrease (step-down) in amount over the term of the lease.

Stipulated Loss Value Table

A schedule included in the lease agreement, generally used for purposes of minimum insurance coverage, that sets forth the agreed-upon value of the leased equipment at various points throughout the lease term. This value establishes the liability of the lessee to the lessor in the event the leased equipment is lost or becomes unusable due to casualty loss during the lease term.

Straight-line Depreciation

A method of depreciation (for financial reporting and tax purposes) where the owner of the equipment claims an equal amount of depreciation in each year of the equipment's recovery period.

Structuring

Pulling together the many components of a lease to arrive at a single lease transaction. Structuring includes, but is not limited to, lease pricing, end-of-term options, documentation issues, indemnification clauses, funding and residual valuations.

Subchapter S Corporation

A firm legally organized as a corporation but taxed as a partnership.

Takeout

A flexible lease option in which the lessor replaces existing leased equipment with either different equipment or newer equipment of the same make.

Tax Equity and Fiscal Responsibility Act of 1982 (TEFRA '82)

Tax law enacted in 1982 that, among other things, modified the Accelerated Cost Recovery System (ACRS) and Investment Tax Credit (ITC) rules, as well as introduced the finance lease (which has since been repealed.)

Tax Lease

A generic term for a lease in which the lessor takes on the risks of ownership (as determined by various IRS pronouncements) and, as the owner, is entitled to the benefits of ownership, including tax benefits.

Tax Reform Act of 1984 (TRA '84)

Tax law enacted in 1984 that included changes to the general effective date for finance leases (renamed transitional finance leases), defined limited use property, set forth the luxury automobile rules and placed restrictions on equipment leases to tax-exempt users.

Tax Reform Act of 1986 (TRA '86)

Recent tax law that effected a major overhaul of the US tax system by lowering tax rates, modifying the Accelerated Cost Recovery System (now MACRS), repealing the Investment Tax Credit (ITC) and repealing the transitional finance lease.

Tax-Exempt User Lease

A type of tax lease available to tax-exempt or nonprofit entities, in which the lessor receives only limited tax benefits.

Terminal Rental Adjustment Clause (TRAC)

A lessee guaranteed residual value for vehicle leases (automobiles, trucks or trailers), the inclusion of which will not, in and of itself, disqualify the tax lease status of a tax-oriented vehicle lease.

Third-Party Lessor

An independent leasing company, or lessor, that writes leases involving three parties: (1) the unrelated manufacturer, (2) the independent lessor and (3) the lessee.

Ticket Size

Refers to the cost of equipment being leased. The leasing market place is roughly segmented into the small, middle and large ticket markets.

True Lease

Another term for a tax lease where, for IRS purposes, the lessor qualifies for the tax benefits of ownership and the lessee is allowed to claim the entire amount of the lease rental as a tax deduction.

Two-Party Lessor

A captive leasing company, or lessor, that writes leases involving two parties: (1) the consolidated parent and captive leasing subsidiary and (2) the lessee or end-user of the equipment.

UCC Financing Statement

A document, under the UCC, filed with the county (and sometimes the Secretary of State) to provide public notice of a security interest in personal property.

Unguaranteed Residual Value

The portion of residual value for which the lessor is at-risk. The lessor takes on the risk that the equipment may or may not be worth this expected value at the end of the lease term.

Upgrade

An option that allows the lessee to add equipment to an existing piece of leased equipment in order to increase its capacity or improve its efficiency.

Vendor Leasing

Lease financing offered to an equipment end-user in conjunction with the sale of equipment. Vendor leases can be provided by the equipment vendor (manufacturer or dealer) or a third-party leasing company with a close working relationship with the equipment vendor.

Wet Lease

A lease in which the lessor provides bundled services, such as the payment of property taxes, insurance, maintenance costs, fuel or provisions, and may even provide persons to operate the leased equipment. This type of lease is typically referred to in aircraft leasing and marine charters.

Yield

The rate of return to the lessor in a lease investment.

INDEX